The Buyer, Seller & Broker's Guide to Creative Home Finance

The Buyer, Seller & Broker's Guide to Creative Home Finance

Norman G. Miller
Associate Professor of Real Estate
University of Cincinnati

Paul R. Goebel
The Stribling Company
and Adjunct Professor of Finance
Texas Tech University

Prentice-Hall, Inc., Englewood Cliffs, New Jersey 07632

Library of Congress Cataloging in Publication Data

Miller, Norman G.
The buyer, seller & broker's guide to creative home finance.

1. House buying. 2. House selling. 3. Dwellings—Finance. 4. Housing—Finance. 5. Mortgages. 6. Real estate business. I. Goebel, Paul R. II. Title. III. Title: Buyer, seller, and broker's guide to creative home finance.
HD1390.5.M54 1983 332.7'22 83-9520
ISBN 0-13-109421-1
ISBN 0-13-109413-0 (pbk.)

Editorial/production supervision
and interior design: Margaret Rizzi
Cover design: Ray Lundgren
Cover art: Charles Pelletreau
Manufacturing buyer: Ed O'Dougherty

Printed in the United States of America

10 9 8 7 6 5 4 3 2 1

ISBN 0-13-109421-1

ISBN 0-13-109413-0 {PBK}

Prentice-Hall International, Inc., *London*
Prentice-Hall of Australia Pty. Limited, *Sydney*
Editora Prentice-Hall do Brasil, Ltda., *Rio de Janeiro*
Prentice-Hall Canada Inc., *Toronto*
Prentice-Hall of India Private Limited, *New Delhi*
Prentice-Hall of Japan, Inc., *Tokyo*
Prentice-Hall of Southeast Asia Pte. Ltd., *Singapore*
Whitehall Books Limited, *Wellington, New Zealand*

To Marcy
and Katherine

chapter **8**

How to Use Financial Tables 134

Tables

List of Exhibits

Preface

Life during the "old" days of fixed rate mortgages seems relatively simple compared with the complexity of today's financing alternatives for real estate. The buyers and sellers of today must sift through myriad financing alternatives and new mortgage instruments, for example, the "equalizer," "flex," "flip," "graduated payment variable rate capped plan," and many others. It is not surprising that most buyers and sellers do not understand all these new options when the lenders, as well, are still figuring them out. As if the new mortgage alternatives were not enough to baffle most consumers, buyers and sellers are also presented with a host of "creative financing" alternatives by lenders, real estate brokers, and builders. Buyers are sometimes given the impression that all creative financing is oriented toward saving them money and making homes more affordable. In fact, all creative financing goes both ways, affecting both sellers and buyers.

The primary intention of this book is to provide an in-depth review of all the options, plans, and risks inherent in today's real estate financing techniques for both buyers and sellers. Special emphasis is given to the latest mortgage instrument variations and to the "creative" financing techniques, where sellers often act as lenders.

Chapter 1 reviews the home buying process and finding the "perfect" home. Chapter 2 reviews sources of money for financing a home. Chapter

3 answers the question: "What determines the cost of money?" Chapter 4 reviews the process of applying for and getting approval on a mortgage loan. Chapter 5 reviews the numerous mortgage plans and variations available today and determines which one is best for a particular individual as well as discusses when to refinance an existing home. Chapter 6 is entirely devoted to seller-assisted financing, including negotiating tips, federal taxation, and risk considerations. Chapter 7 deals with closing the sale, settlement costs, and the closing process. Finally, Chapter 8 explains the use of the financial tables for finding payments, loan balances, the APR (annual percentage rate cost of borrowing), as well as the FHA graduated payment plans.

Throughout the book, actual forms used in real estate transactions for buying, applying for loans, and closing the sale are included and incorporated in illustrative examples. This book is a follow-up to the *Handbook of Mortgage Mathematics and Financial Tables,* also written by Goebel and Miller (Prentice-Hall, 1981), and is intended as another primary reference book.

Acknowledgments and great appreciation are extended to Steve Strickland for programming assistance and to Pat Burns for typing and editing. All errors and omissions are, of course, the sole responsibility of the authors.

Norman G. Miller
University of Cincinnati

Paul R. Goebel
The Stribling Company
and Texas Tech University

The Buyer, Seller & Broker's Guide to Creative Home Finance

chapter 1

The Home Buying Process

Shelter is among the most basic of all human needs. People must satisfy the need for shelter from the elements and from hostile animals, both human and otherwise, before worrying about tax shelters, formal dining rooms, and crabgrass. Fortunately, housing in the United States has not only provided shelter but it has also been an excellent investment, both in terms of tax shelter and a hedge against inflation. Housing will continue to provide shelter and to serve as an investment vehicle, although in some areas, the rate of appreciation may not be as great as it was in the 1970s. Still, given the subsidy provided to homeownership through the tax laws, housing remains a wise investment, yielding benefits in terms of enjoyment and shelter, both from the elements and from the government's tax arm. This book will guide you through the process of buying a home, covered in this chapter, as well as the financing process, covered in depth throughout the remainder of the book.

SHOULD YOU BUY OR RENT A HOME?

In most cases, at least superficially, it is cheaper to rent an apartment or house than it is to purchase a home. Since rent levels are usually less than mortgage payments, and the landlord is usually responsible for property maintenance, renting appears to be very attractive. But when all factors are considered, purchasing a home may turn out not only to be cheaper but may provide an investment medium as well. In addition to the financial aspects of the buy versus rent decision, which will be discussed next, there are other considerations that need to be incorporated.

Two very important factors to consider in the purchase decision are mobility and liquidity. If a person or family is relatively mobile, then purchasing a home may not be a wise decision due to the time and transaction costs involved in selling. In that respect, housing is considered illiquid. Another consideration that must be mentioned is the pride associated with homeownership. Many people regard owning their own home as an inalienable right, which of course will affect the rent versus buy decision even if the economics of homeownership may not be particularly attractive.

One of the primary attractions of buying a home is the fact that historically housing has been a high-yielding investment. Many homeowners in the past have earned a very high rate of return through homeownership, a return attributed to the fact that housing prices have kept pace with, and have often exceeded, the general increases in prices in the economy. Another reason for this historically high return on housing has been the result of financial leverage. Most homeowners finance their purchase, placing only a small amount of equity, between 10 and 30 percent, down. When prices increase faster than the cost of the debt, the homeowner's return is magnified. The mortgaged amount is usually fixed (historically), which means that all (or most) of the increase in value goes to the owner's equity position.

Another primary attraction to homeownership that renting does not provide is the tax advantage. Since taxation is too complex a subject to deal with in depth here, it is sufficient to say that owning a home provides a good tax shelter. This stems from the fact that certain items connected with homeownership are tax deductible, specifically mortgage interest payments and property taxes. By deducting these items, taxable income is lowered, thus lowering the tax obligation. In that way, the federal government subsidizes, in effect, a sizable portion of the monthly mortgage payment. And by incorporating this tax deductibility, many homeowners find that their net-after-tax cost of owning is actually less than what it would be if they rented. How much of a subsidy the tax deductibility provides will differ by the borrower's marginal tax rate and by future tax laws affecting rates.

Probably the most important consideration in the rent versus buy decision is whether you can currently afford the home you desire. Owning a home can be very expensive, requiring among other things enough capital for a down payment and closing costs; monthly payments to principal, interest, hazard insurance, and property taxes; monthly repair and replacement of items; and utility charges (electricity, gas, water, sewer, garbage collection, etc.). While the impact of some of these items is reduced by the tax deductibility just discussed, the owner must still be able to handle the *before-tax cash outlay*. Potential homeowners must therefore consider exactly how much home their assets and income will purchase. To aid in that part of the decision process, Chapter 4 discusses the affordability issue and provides a worksheet to help in the affordability calculations.

ADVANTAGES ARISING AFTER PURCHASING A HOME

Several factors that influence the home purchase decision arise after the purchase. One of these can be termed the "home cycle." It is claimed that there is currently an affordability problem that prohibits people from buying houses in today's market. The persons most affected by this affordability problem are the first-time buyers. Those already owning have been accumulating an equity base in their homes, a forced savings, if you will, stemming from the reduction of loan principal, albeit slight in the early years of the loan, and the inflationary increase in value. This equity base allows previous homeowners to sell their existing homes and use that equity as a down payment on a larger home. As long as housing values continue to increase, this cycle will persist, enabling owners to continue to upgrade their housing over time.

Another aspect that makes homeownership appealing is again related to taxation. Tax laws effective after 1981 provide a one-time exclusion to capital gains on the sale of a taxpayer's principal residence to individuals who are 55 years of age or older. The maximum exclusion is currently $125,000. To qualify for this exclusion, the individual must have owned and used the property as his or her principal residence for three or more years out of the five-year period preceding the sale.

In addition, tax laws effective after 1981 permit deferring of capital gains taxes due upon sale of a residence if a new or existing residence is purchased within two years of sale of the old residence. This deferral, when combined with the one-time exclusion, means that a homeowner could continue to invest in housing over a period of time, continually trading up with no immediate tax liability. The homeowner could then take the exclusion and in effect negate up to $125,000 of capital gains tax liability due, all of which conceivably could be attributed to deferred capital gains taxes. This factor further magnifies the investment aspect of homeownership since not only does the tax law in effect subsidize the annual payments to housing, but it also allows substantial, if not complete, exclusion of a capital gains tax liability. In addition, the tax laws encourage sustained homeownership once a person has passed beyond the rent or buy decision and has entered the home cycle.

SELECTING THE TYPE OF HOUSE

One of the more difficult tasks in this consumption-oriented society is distinguishing between wants and needs. A "want" for one person might be an absolute "need" for another. Do you really need that extra bedroom, bath, or an office, or are they wants that could be done without? Each person must analyze his or her own wants and needs carefully before making any purchase decision, and especially before signing any contract or spending any money.

Among the factors that should be considered in determining the appropriate size and type of housing are family type and size, life-style, and career and earnings, both current and future. One of the interesting aspects of living today is the multiplicity of housing options available. A host of different types and styles of housing are available in most markets. Basically, the various types of residential housing are the following:

Single-Family Detached Housing

Most people are familiar with the single-family detached house. Most persons regard owning a house, unattached to any other houses and surrounded by its own yard on all sides, as the American dream. This type of housing is perceived to afford the most privacy. However, when lot sizes are small, this may not be the case. During the years following World War II, land on the urban fringes was cheap, transportation costs were declining, and cities made large investments in expanding services, thus giving birth to urban sprawl. Recent years, however, have been characterized by rapidly increasing land and energy costs, as well as environmental concerns, which are now impacting the viability of owning the detached single-family home as we know it. After years of growth, Americans are now turning to more intense land usage through such design aspects as single-family attached housing and rehabilitation of previously less desirable urban developments.

Single-Family Attached Housing

Single-family attached houses generally share with other units one or more common walls. Townhouses, plexes, patios, and some zero-lot-line homes are all examples of attached housing.

A *townhouse* has one or more walls in common with another unit. Each unit has its own front and back entrance and may or may not have front- and backyards. Townhouses may be one or more stories high (two stories are very common) and may front either a common area or a street. A townhouse typically includes ownership of the individual living unit as well as the land on which the unit sits.

A *plex* may contain two or more units, each with its own entrance, and thus shares some of the characteristics of the townhouse or single-family detached house. A structure built for two families is called a duplex, for three families a triplex, for four families a quadraplex or fourplex, and so on. In many areas, plexes have been geared toward the rental market and, thus, have fallen into disfavor by homeowners. However, there is a growing trend toward owner-occupancy in plexes, either by the owner occupying one unit and renting the rest or by all the units being owned separately.

Similar to a single-family detached home is the *patio* or *zero-lot-line house*. It differs in that construction is typically U-shaped or L-shaped and extends from lot line to lot line, thus using the entire lot. The outdoor living areas are enclosed by the house in a patio home or by the house and walls in a zero-lot-line home. Often, the exterior wall of the house on the bordering lot is used for enclosure in the zero-lot-line home. This particular type of housing offers a great deal of privacy, with maximum utilization of the lots, which are usually much smaller than typical single-family detached lots.

Multifamily housing may be divided into three broad areas: garden apartments, midrise apartments, and high-rise apartments. It should be noted that the term "apartment" is being used rather loosely. Any of these apartment types may be owned or rented, depending on the developer. "Apartment" is used here merely to describe a type of building.

Garden apartments are usually two or three stories high, typically without elevators, and are located in suburban areas. The term "garden" can refer to an enclosed open space, but it usually denotes narrow strips of lawn or ground cover buffering a parking lot or street. Well-designed garden apartments take on the amenities of single-family housing and can accomplish a relatively low-density land usage while preserving open space.

Midrise and *high-rise apartments* are similar, although differing in height and number of elevators. A midrise is typically from four to eight stories high with one or more elevators, depending on the number of units in the development. A high-rise apartment is generally anything over eight stories and having two or more elevators. While midrise and high-rise buildings vary in shape and design, they are distinguished from garden apartments in their construction. Where garden apartments are generally wood frame with brick veneer or masonry walls, buildings above six stories are fireproofed and are of steel frame or concrete construction. Most high-rise apartments have been rental units until recent years, when condominium ownership has expanded rapidly both through new construction as well as the conversion of apartment units. This type of ownership, along with several others, is explained next.

TYPE OF OWNERSHIP

Fee Simple Ownership

The most common form of ownership, whether it is for attached or detached housing, is on a fee simple basis. In this form of ownership, the owner has an interest in the land, usually limited only by governmental powers as when a fee simple absolute ownership exists, that allows unlimited use (subject to government restriction) and ability to transfer. This complete ownership interest constitutes the maximum ownership rights possible. Other forms of fee simple ownership place some additional limitations on the owner's right to use the land, typically in terms of the ability to transfer the ownership. The fee simple absolute ownership is typically associated with single-family detached housing, where the resident owns the land and buildings on the property as well as the rights associated with the property. These rights give the owner the ability to do whatever is desired with the property, subject to restrictions such as zoning, building codes, deeds and easements.

Condominiums

A variation of fee simple ownership is the condominium. In a condominium, the owner holds a fee simple title to the particular unit occupied and shares ownership in the common areas of the development, such as the land, parking lot, hallways, and pool, with the other condominium owners. Condominiums, which have become very popular in the past decade, are usually associated with attached or midrise or high-rise projects. Condos have increased in popularity because that form of ownership still provides some of the amenities of single-family ownership, especially the tax advantages, while offering a more affordable alternative to the home buyer than the generally larger detached housing units.

Cooperatives

A concept similar to the condominium in that it is typically associated with midrise or high-rise multifamily dwellings is the cooperative. A cooperative consists of shareholders in a typically nonprofit corporation that owns the building. The shareholder, in effect, has the rights of a tenant with the corporation being the landlord. A key distinction between a cooperative and a condominium is that a cooperative shareholder owns personal property rather than real property as in a condominium. When cooperative shareholders buy or sell their interests, they buy from or sell to the cooperative under controlled market conditions, unlike the condominium owner who buys or sells in the open market. In some ways, this may lower the risk of marketability to the cooperative owner relative to a condominium form of ownership, but it also lessens the potential returns from open market sales.

Timesharing

A variation of ownership revolving around the condominium that has become popular in the past few years is known commonly as timesharing. Under timesharing a number of buyers invest in a single dwelling, typically a condominium, where each buyer gets exclusive use of the dwelling for a specified time period each year. This ownership interest is much like the traditional condominium ownership in that the interest can be sold, leased, or willed. Timesharing thus is a convenient way for people to "own" a second home.

By owning a condominium via timesharing, you get the tax advantage of homeownership such as depreciation allowances and deduction of maintenance, albeit on a prorated basis, and you enjoy the use of a vacation home without the hassle of dealing with tenants. The disadvantage of timesharing, however, is that many of the recent programs have been fraught with deceit, high-pressure sales, and ultimately failure. So caution is advised when investigating this ownership option.

FINDING THE PERFECT HOME

After deciding on the type and style of home, the actual search for the house that best fits your wants and needs begins. At this point a crucial question is, "Should I use a real estate agent?" At the outset, it would appear that by not using an agent, it might be possible to save some money on your home purchase. Agents are typically paid on a commission basis, with the seller usually paying the commission. If the agent could be bypassed, a savings to the seller would result, which in theory could be passed on to the buyer. Commissions are negotiable by law, but a fairly common residential real estate commission at present is 6 or 7 percent, which when multiplied by the current average selling price of approximately $70,000 yields a commission of $4,200 or $4,900, respectively.

Volumes could be written on the subject of whether real estate agents actually deserve such a substantial commission. The pertinent question here is whether you can benefit from using an agent. As a buyer, it is usually to your advantage to use a real estate agent, especially if you are not experienced in the home buying process. Agents typically have access to a large number of listings, particularly if they are members of the local multiple listing service (MLS). An MLS is a nonprofit organization set up to provide a pool of listings to which all member firms contribute and from which all draw. This, in effect, substantially increases the houses that an agent is able to show the prospective buyer and reduces search time.

Using an agent also allows the buyer to see the subject property without having the owner present. This makes it easy for the buyer to make an honest evaluation of decorations, floor plans, materials, and so on without worrying about offending the homeowner. Real estate agents also are familiar with amenities and price ranges that buyers desire. By using an agent, you can usually save considerable time and effort in the research process, since the agent can aid in narrowing down the possible choices. Toward this end, the qualification stage, at which time the agent assesses the buyer's wants and needs in terms of house type, size, location, and price, is extremely important. But probably the most important reason for using a real estate agent is the assistance he or she can give in guiding the buyer through the process of negotiating and closing the sale.

Finding the "perfect home" requires first an idea of the market value of the type of home desired. The buyer should request some market analysis from the sales agent. This should include a list of similar properties that have sold recently. Pertinent information includes (1) selling price; (2) size in square feet; (3) number of bedrooms, baths, garages; (4) lot size; and (5) property taxes. While other information may be desirable, an accounting of these items is generally available from public or MLS records. A comparison of the property you are considering purchasing with similar property nearby on a price per square foot basis may help you to find the market value range. Naturally, a buyer wishes to pay the lowest price per square foot. This simple objective comparison method is also used by appraisers at lending institutions. If an agent cannot collect such information for you, it may be appropriate to either find a new agent or consider hiring an independent appraiser on a fee basis to collect this market information.

NEGOTIATING THE SALE

Once the buyer has decided on the ideal property, the negotiations begin. These negotiations are usually carried out through purchase offer or sales contracts, with the sales agents or attorneys involved acting as intermediaries. If no agents or attorneys are involved, the negotiation process is typically verbal, with the final purchase agreement specified in the sales contract.

The Listing Contract

When a seller gives an agent the authority to sell his or her property, it is normally expressed in a written document called a *listing agreement.* This agreement describes the property, what rights are being offered for sale, sales price, amount of commission, type of listing, and time of possession. Since the listing agreement is a contract, it needs to have all the elements of a contract to be valid. Two of the most important elements of the listing agreement to the buyer, aside from the purchase price, are the types of financing the seller is offering (assumption, owner carrying a second loan, FHA-VA, etc.) and what property is included in the sale. Listing agreements vary by state, but most agreements a buyer will encounter will be standardized forms if the seller is using an agent. If the buyer accepts all conditions of the listing agreement, a sales contract is drawn up; when the buyer agrees to the specified terms and conditions, it is called an *acceptance.*

If the buyer does not agree to the original offer of the seller, it is possible to make a *counteroffer* to the seller, such as by the buyer agreeing to all original terms except offering to pay, say, $2,000 less than the listed price. If the seller accepts the counteroffer, a sales contract is then drawn up stating the new terms and is signed by both parties. It is not unusual to have several offers and counteroffers made before the final terms and conditions are agreed upon.

The Sales Contract

The sales contract, executed between the buyer and the seller, is the most important aspect of the home buying process. This contract specifies all the terms and conditions of the sale, and it is there that the buyer obtains the most protection in terms of legal recourse. Sales contracts can be as simple or complex as desired, although most states have standard contracts approved for use by legal and real estate groups. A sample of a standard contract used in Texas is presented in Exhibit 1-1.

The contract in Exhibit 1-1 is an FHA-insured loan resale contract; that is, the buyer is attempting to purchase a preowned home using Federal Housing Administration-insured financing. There are several elements of this sales contract that need to be discussed.

First, the buyer needs to be especially concerned with item 2, Property. This section specifies the property included in the contract. If additional personal property is to be included, such as kitchen appliances,

EXHIBIT 1-1. FHA-Insured Loan Resale Contract

REALTOR®

LUBBOCK BOARD OF REALTORS

FHA INSURED LOAN — RESIDENTIAL EARNEST MONEY CONTRACT (RESALE)

PROMULGATED BY TEXAS REAL ESTATE COMMISSION

1. PARTIES: ______________________________ (Seller) agrees to sell and convey to ______________________________ (Buyer) and Buyer agrees to buy from Seller the following property situated in ______________ County, Texas, known as ______________________________ (Address).

2. PROPERTY: Lot ______________, Block __________, ______________ Addition, City of ______________, or as described on attached exhibit, together with the following fixtures, if any: curtain rods, drapery rods, venetian blinds, window shades, screens and shutters, awnings, wall-to-wall carpeting, mirrors fixed in place, attic fans, permanently installed heating and air conditioning units and equipment, lighting and plumbing fixtures, TV antennas, mail boxes, water softeners, shrubbery and all other property owned by Seller and attached to the above described real property. All property sold by this contract is called "Property".

3. CONTRACT SALES PRICE:
   A. Cash down payment payable at closing .... $__________
   B. Amount of Note (the Note) described in 4-A below .... $__________
   C. Sales Price payable to Seller on Loan funding after closing (Sum of A plus B) .... $__________

4. FINANCING CONDITIONS:
   A. This contract is subject to approval for Buyer of a Section ______________ FHA Insured Loan (the Loan) of not less than the amount of the Note, amortizable monthly for not less than ________ years, with interest at maximum rate allowable at time of Loan funding. Buyer shall apply for the Loan within ________ days from the effective date of this contract and shall make every reasonable effort to obtain approval of the Loan. If the Loan has not been approved by the Closing Date, this contract shall terminate and Earnest Money shall be refunded to Buyer without delay.
   B. As required by HUD-FHA regulation, if FHA valuation is unknown, "It is expressly agreed that, notwithstanding any other provisions of this contract, the Purchaser (Buyer) shall not be obligated to complete the purchase of the Property described herein or to incur any penalty by forfeiture of Earnest Money deposits or otherwise unless the Seller has delivered to the Purchaser (Buyer) a written statement issued by the Federal Housing Commissioner setting forth the appraised value of the Property (excluding closing costs) of not less than $ ________, which statement the Seller hereby agrees to deliver to the Purchaser (Buyer) promptly after such appraised value statement is made available to the Seller. The Purchaser (Buyer) shall, however, have the privilege and option of proceeding with the consummation of this contract without regard to the amount of the appraised valuation made by the Federal Housing Commissioner. <u>The appraised valuation is arrived at to determine the maximum mortgage the Department of Housing and Urban Development will insure. HUD does not warrant the value or the condition of the property. The purchaser should satisfy himself/herself that the price and the condition of the property are acceptable.</u>"

5. EARNEST MONEY: $__________ is herewith tendered and is to be deposited as Earnest Money with ______________________________, as Escrow Agent, upon execution of the contract by both parties. Additional Earnest Money, if any, shall be deposited with the Escrow Agent on or before ______________, 19 ____, in the amount of $__________.

6. TITLE: Seller at Seller's expense shall furnish either:
   ☐ A. Owner's Policy of Title Insurance (the Title Policy) issued by ______________________________ in the amount of the Sales Price and dated at or after closing: OR
   ☐ B. Complete Abstract of Title (the Abstract) certified by ______________________________ to current date.
   NOTICE TO BUYER: AS REQUIRED BY LAW, Broker advises that YOU should have the Abstract covering the Property examined by an attorney of YOUR selection, or YOU should be furnished with or obtain a Title Policy.

7. PROPERTY CONDITION (Check "A" or "B"):
   ☐ A. Buyer accepts the Property in its present condition, subject only to FHA required repairs and ______________________________.
   ☐ B. Buyer requires inspections and repairs required by the Property Condition Addendum (the Addendum) and those required by FHA.
   Upon Seller's receipt of the Loan approval and inspection reports Seller shall commence and complete prior to closing all required repairs at Seller's expense.
   All inspections, reports and repairs required of Seller by this contract and the Addendum shall not exceed $__________. If Seller fails to complete such requirements, Buyer may do so and Seller shall be liable up to the amount specified and the same paid from the proceeds of the sale. If such expenditures exceed the stated amount and Seller refuses to pay such excess, Buyer may pay the additional cost or accept the Property with the limited repairs and this sale shall be closed as scheduled, or Buyer may terminate this contract and the Earnest Money shall be refunded to Buyer. Broker and sales associates have no responsibility or liability for repair or replacement of any of the Property.

8. BROKER'S FEE: ______________________________ Listing Broker (____%) and ______________________________ Co-Broker (____%), as Real Estate Broker (the Broker), has negotiated this sale and Seller agrees to pay Broker in ______________ County, Texas, on consummation of this sale or on Seller's default (unless otherwise provided herein) a total cash fee of ______________ of the total Sales Price, which Escrow Agent may pay from the sale proceeds.

9. CLOSING: The closing of the sale (the Closing Date) shall be on or before ______________, 19 ____, or within 7 days after objections to title have been cured, whichever date is later; however, if necessary to complete Loan requirements, the Closing Date shall be extended daily up to 15 days.

10. POSSESSION: The possession of the Property shall be delivered to Buyer on ______________ in its present or required improved condition, ordinary wear and tear excepted. Any possession by Buyer prior to or by Seller after Closing Date shall establish a landlord-tenant at sufferance relationship between the parties.

11. SPECIAL PROVISIONS:

№ 27

(Insert terms and conditions of a factual nature applicable to this sale, e.g., prior purchase or sale of other property, lessee's surrender of possession, and the like.)

1 Mr 79 TREC No. 5-0

EXHIBIT 1-1. (Cont.)

12. SALES EXPENSES TO BE PAID IN CASH AT OR PRIOR TO CLOSING:
    A. Loan appraisal fee (FHA application fee) shall be paid by ______.
    B. Seller's Expenses:
       (1) Seller's Loan discount points not exceeding ______.
       (2) FHA required repairs and any other inspections, reports and repairs required of Seller herein, and in the Addendum.
       (3) Expenses incident to Loan (e.g., preparation of Loan documents, survey, recording fees, copies of restrictions and easements, amortization schedule, Mortgagee's Title Policy, Loan origination fee, credit reports, photographs).
       (4) Releases of existing loans, including prepayment penalties and recordation; tax statements; preparation of Deed; escrow fee; and other expenses stipulated to be paid by Seller under other provisions of this contract.
    C. Buyer's Expenses: All prepaid items required by applicable HUD-FHA or other regulations (e.g., required premiums for flood and hazard insurance; required reserve deposits for FHA and other insurance, ad valorem taxes and special assessments); interest on the Note from date of disbursement to one month prior to date of first monthly payment; expenses stipulated to be paid by Buyer under other provisions of this contract.
    D If any sales expenses exceed the maximum amount herein stipulated to be paid by either party, either party may terminate this Contract unless other party agrees to pay such excess. In no event shall Buyer pay charges and fees other than those expressly permitted by FHA regulation.
13. PRORATIONS: Insurance (at Buyer's option), taxes, and any rents and maintenance fees shall be prorated to the Closing Date.
14. TITLE APPROVAL: If Abstract is furnished, Seller shall deliver same to Buyer within 20 days from the effective date hereof. Buyer shall have 20 days from date of receipt of Abstract to deliver a copy of the title opinion to Seller, stating any objections to title, and only objections so stated shall be considered. If Title Policy is furnished, the Title Policy shall guarantee Buyer's title to be good and indefeasible subject only to (i) restrictive covenants affecting the Property (ii) any discrepancies, conflicts or shortages in area or boundary lines or any encroachments, or any overlapping of improvements (iii) all taxes for the current and subsequent years (iv) any existing building and zoning ordinances (v) rights of parties in possession (vi) any liens created as security for the sale consideration and (vii) any reservations or exceptions contained in the Deed. In either instance, if title objections are disclosed, Seller shall have 30 days to cure the same. Exceptions permitted in the Deed and zoning ordinances shall not be valid objections to title. Seller shall furnish at Seller's expense tax statements showing no delinquent taxes and a General Warranty Deed conveying title subject only to liens securing debt created as part of the consideration, taxes for the current year, usual restrictive covenants and utility easements common to the platted subdivision of which the Property is a part and any other reservations or exceptions acceptable to Buyer. The Note shall be secured by Vendor's and Deed of Trust liens. In case of dispute as to the form of Deed, such shall be upon a form prepared by the State Bar of Texas.
15. CASUALTY LOSS: If any part of Property is damaged or destroyed by fire or other casualty loss, Seller shall restore the same to its previous condition as soon as reasonably possible, but in any event by Closing Date; and if Seller is unable to do so without fault, this contract shall terminate and Earnest Money shall be refunded with no Broker's fee due.
16. DEFAULT: If Buyer fails to comply herewith, Seller may either enforce specific performance or terminate this contract and receive the Earnest Money as liquidated damages, one-half of which (but not exceeding the herein recited Broker's fee) shall be paid by Seller to Broker in full payment for Broker's services. If Seller is unable without fault to deliver Abstract or Title Policy or to make any non-casualty repairs required herein within the time herein specified, Buyer may either terminate this contract and receive the Earnest Money as the sole remedy, and no Broker's fee shall be earned, or extend the time up to 30 days. If Seller fails to comply herewith for any other reason, Buyer may (i) terminate this contract and receive the Earnest Money, thereby releasing Seller from this contract (ii) enforce specific performance hereof or (iii) seek such other relief as may be provided by law. If completion of sale is prevented by Buyer's default, and Seller elects to enforce specific performance, the Broker's fee is payable only if and when Seller collects damages for such default by suit, compromise, settlement or otherwise, and after first deducting the expenses of collection, and then only in an amount equal to one-half of that portion collected, but not exceeding the amount of Broker's fee.
17. ATTORNEY'S FEES: Any signatory to this contract who is the prevailing party in any legal proceeding against any other signatory brought under or with relation to this contract or transaction shall be additionally entitled to recover court costs and reasonable attorney fees from the non-prevailing party.
18. ESCROW: Earnest Money is deposited with Escrow Agent with the understanding that Escrow Agent (i) does not assume or have any liability for performance or nonperformance of any party (ii) has the right to require the receipt, release and authorization in writing of all parties before paying the deposit to any party and (iii) is not liable for interest or other charge on the funds held. If any party unreasonably fails to agree in writing to an appropriate release of Earnest Money, then such party shall be liable to the other parties to the extent provided in paragraph 17. At closing, Earnest Money shall be applied to any cash down payment required, next to Buyer's closing costs and any excess refunded to Buyer. Before Buyer shall be entitled to refund of Earnest Money, any actual and FHA allowable expenses incurred or paid on Buyer's behalf shall be deducted therefrom and paid to the creditors entitled thereto.
19. REPRESENTATIONS: Seller represents that there will be no Title I liens, unrecorded liens or Uniform Commercial Code liens against any of the Property on Closing Date. If any representation above is untrue this contract may be terminated by Buyer and the Earnest Money shall be refunded without delay. Representations shall survive closing.
20. AGREEMENT OF PARTIES: This contract contains the entire agreement of the parties and cannot be changed except by their written consent.
21. CONSULT YOUR ATTORNEY: This is intended to be a legally binding contract. READ IT CAREFULLY. If you do not understand the effect of any part, consult your attorney BEFORE signing. The Broker cannot give you legal advice — only factual and business details concerning land and improvements. Attorneys to represent parties may be designated below, and, so employment may be accepted, Broker shall promptly deliver a copy of this contract to such attorneys.

Seller's Atty: ______ Buyer's Atty: ______

EXECUTED in multiple originals effective the ____ day of ______, 19 ____. **(BROKER FILL IN THE DATE LAST PARTY SIGNS).**

______ Listing Broker License No.	______ Seller
By ______	______ Seller
______ Co-Broker License No.	______ Seller's Address Tel.
By ______	______ Buyer
Receipt of $______ Earnest Money is acknowledged in the form of ______.	______ Buyer
______ ______ Escrow Agent Date	______ Buyer's Address Tel.
By ______	

The form of this contract has been approved by the Texas Real Estate Commission and the State Bar of Texas. Such approval relates to this contract form only. No representation is made as to the legal validity or adequacy of any provision in any specific transaction. It is not suitable for complex transactions. Extensive riders or additions are not to be used. (8-78) TREC No. 5-0

Nº 27

draperies, or carpets, or if any listed property is to be excluded, an addendum to the contract is needed. Do not assume that the property to be included in the sale can be determined at the closing or when actual possession occurs! The sales contract dictates what is included, so it needs to be very clear to prevent any problems down the road. Generally, anything that is permanently attached is considered to be a "fixture"; however, it never hurts to make sure that the sellers do not plan to take down the ceiling fan and replace it with another light fixture on their way out. The same may be said for draperies, fireplace equipment, garage door openers, special shower heads, fuel oil, wall-to-wall carpeting, and so forth.

The second section of utmost importance to the buyer is in item 4, Financing Conditions. This section not only specifies the financing arrangement being applied for, but it also allows for an appraised value less than the contract price to terminate the contract without penalty. In addition, this section includes the disclaimer that the Department of Housing and Urban Development (HUD) does not warrant the value or the condition of the property. HUD expects the purchaser to examine the property to ensure that the price and the condition are acceptable. This again emphasizes the fact that the buyer receives protection through a well-written contract and that the buyer, if not competent in these areas, should put a contingency in the contract that allows for an appraisal and inspection. For specific tips on negotiating financing contingencies, see Chapter 6.

Finally, item 12, Sales Expenses to Be Paid at Closing, is important in that it defines what closing costs are to be paid, and by whom. While closings and the costs involved are covered in depth in Chapter 7, it is important to note that these costs should be clearly specified in the contract. In the FHA contract, the seller is required to pay certain costs, including loan discount points, that are often a substantial portion of the total costs. In conventional contracts where the costs are not specified by law, it is important to decide who will bear what costs and have them fully specified in the contract.

Actual possession of the property should also be specified in the sales contract. Possession may be given before, at the time of, or after the closing. While possession prior to closing is unusual, at times it cannot be avoided. In that case, specific articles need to be developed to protect both parties. The buyer is usually required to pay an agreed-upon amount of rent and must agree to accept the property as is except for any repairs required by the Property Condition Addendum. In most cases, possession is given at closing. However, should the sellers want to remain after closing, then an agreed-upon rent, specified in the contract, should be paid to the buyers.

Other clauses a buyer might want to have placed in the contract are that (1) the seller agrees to provide good title, free and clear of all encumbrances except those specifically agreed to; (2) the buyer can obtain a refund of the earnest money deposit (the cash deposit usually given to the seller's broker which is generally applied to the purchase price upon closing) and cancellation of the sale if a satisfactory first mortgage loan, as specified in the contract, is unable to be secured by the buyer; and (3) an agreement that specifies how property taxes, insurance policy premiums, sewer and water charges, utility bills, and so on are to be divided between buyer and seller as of the date of closing.

ARRANGING THE FINANCING

After signing a contract to purchase a house, the next step is securing the financing to enable the purchase to be completed. Many people assume that all lenders are alike and that there is no need, or benefit, to shop around for financing. This is far from the truth. Loan terms and closing costs do vary, often substantially, among lenders. The choice of a lender, and the variety of options available through many lenders, has made the financing process the most complicated, and important, step in the home buying process in today's economic climate. The majority of this book is devoted to guiding buyers and sellers through the maze of financing alternatives in an effort to uncomplicate the decision-making process.

In the past few years the financing of the great American dream has undergone dramatic changes. Before the money crunch of the late 1970s and early 1980s, there were three basic types of home mortgages: conventional, FHA, and VA. The main attraction of these loans was that they typically had one fixed rate of interest and level payments for the entire term of the loan. (One notable exception is in the State of California, which pioneered the use of a variety of mortgage instruments beginning in the 1970s by state chartered lenders.) Conventional wisdom had it that the home buyer took on as much mortgage as was humanly possible. The first few years might be tight, but after several years, increases in income would catch up so that payments would become more and more manageable.

Combined with the traditional mortgage forms, there currently exists a smorgasbord of "creative" mortgage instruments available to today's home buyer. The new mortgage instruments have one factor in common—the amount of the monthly payment does not remain constant over the life of the loan. This requires new thinking when taking the plunge into homeownership. Increases or decreases in the monthly payment must be considered in respect to anticipated increases or decreases in monthly income. While lenders are allowing higher debt ratios than they have in the past, buyers must realize that using a creative mortgage may make payments difficult not only over the early years but over the total life of the loan as well.

CLOSING THE SALE

After selecting a lender and applying for and being approved on a loan, the final step in the process is the closing. Actually, there are two closings involved: the title closing and the loan closing. Typically, both closings occur at the same time and place. At the closing, legal documents are signed that pass title of the property to the buyer, obligate the buyer to repayment of the mortgage loan, and pledge the property as collateral for the loan.

Also at the closing, the final financial settlements among all parties involved occur. The buyer pays all amounts due, typically in one check; the seller receives the proceeds of the sale, after deducting the appropriate amounts for closing costs, unpaid mortgages, and brokers fees; and the ancillary parties, such as attorneys and closing agents, are compensated. Chapter 7 covers the closing process, including a discussion of closing costs, in depth.

A HOME BUYING CASE

To help in understanding the process and paperwork involved in the home buying arena, an example is presented that will be followed throughout the book. While this example is for a specific type of transaction, a Veterans Administration-guaranteed loan, the format used will be similar for most purchase transactions.

Mr. Floyd Moyer has decided to utilize his veterans' entitlements to purchase an existing home located at 3725 51st Street in Lubbock, Texas. He has placed $750 down as a deposit on the property, which has a sales price of $59,500. Mr. Moyer is applying for a 16.5 percent, 30-year, $58,000 VA loan.

Both Mr. and Mrs. Moyer are currently employed. Mr. Moyer has been with his present employer, Acme Printing Company, for 10 years and makes $8.50 minimum per hour, plus incentives and bonus. Mr. Moyer's normal gross paycheck is $1,572.50 per month. Mr. Moyer is 46 years old.

Mrs. Moyer is 44 years old and works for Speedy Delivery Service, earning a base pay of $1,042.50 per month. She has been with the firm for a year and a half, and her employer feels that she will be a career employee.

The Moyers currently reside at 3202 Avenue Q, Lubbock, which they own. The mortgage on this single-family dwelling has a remaining balance of $25,916.00. Their intention is to move into the new home and retain the present one as a rental property. They feel that they will be able to rent or lease the Avenue Q property for $300 per month. The present mortgage payment is $225 per month, plus a monthly property tax and insurance payment of $72, for a total of $297 per month.

The VA-guaranteed loan contract for the case described is presented in Exhibit 1-2. The Moyers worked with a real estate agent, Johnny Agent, in finding the house they intend to purchase. Prior to executing the contract of sale, the Moyers had the house inspected by a local contractor, for which they paid $150. The contractor specified that the house was in good condition, except for the water heater, which needed replacing. The Moyers used this information in the negotiation process, and the sellers, Joseph P. and Thelma Q. Seller, agreed to include a new water heater with the sales price at $59,500. Possession of the house is to transfer at closing, and a brokers commission of 6 percent has been agreed upon by the seller and the agents.

EXHIBIT 1-2. VA-Guaranteed Loan Resale Contract

REALTOR®

LUBBOCK BOARD OF REALTORS

VA GUARANTEED LOAN — RESIDENTIAL EARNEST MONEY CONTRACT (RESALE)

PROMULGATED BY TEXAS REAL ESTATE COMMISSION

1. PARTIES: Joseph P. and Thelma Q. Seller (Seller) agrees to sell and convey to Floyd A. and Elizabeth R. Moyer (Buyer) and Buyer agrees to buy from Seller the following property situated in Lubbock County, Texas, known as 3725 51st Street, Lubbock, Texas (Address).

2. PROPERTY: Lot 279, Block 14, of Midway Gardens Addition, City of Lubbock, or as described on attached exhibit, together with the following fixtures, if any: curtain rods, drapery rods, venetian blinds, window shades, screens and shutters, awnings, wall-to-wall carpeting, mirrors fixed in place, attic fans, permanently installed heating and air conditioning units and equipment, lighting and plumbing fixtures, TV antennas, mail boxes, water softeners, shrubbery and all other property owned by Seller and attached to the above described real property. All property sold by this contract is called "Property".

3. CONTRACT SALES PRICE:
   A. Cash down payment payable at closing . . . . . $ 1,500
   B. Note described in 4 below (the Note) in the amount of $58,000
   C. Sales Price payable to Seller on Loan funding after closing (Sum of A and B) $59,500

4. FINANCING CONDITIONS: This contract is subject to approval for Buyer of a VA loan (the Loan) of not less than the amount of the Note, amortizable monthly for not less than 30 years, with interest at maximum rate allowable at time of Loan funding. Buyer shall apply for the Loan within 30 days from the effective date of this contract and shall make every reasonable effort to obtain approval. If the Loan has not been approved by the Closing Date, this contract shall terminate and the Earnest Money shall be refunded to Buyer without delay. VA NOTICE TO BUYER: "It is expressly agreed that, notwithstanding any other provisions of this contract, the Buyer shall not incur any penalty by forfeiture of earnest money or otherwise or be obligated to complete the purchase of the Property described herein, if the contract purchase price or cost exceeds the reasonable value of the Property established by the Veterans Administration. The Buyer shall, however, have the privilege and option of proceeding with the consummation of this contract without regard to the amount of the reasonable value established by the Veterans Administration." Buyer agrees that should Buyer elect to complete the purchase at an amount in excess of the reasonable value established by VA, Buyer shall pay such excess amount in cash from a source which Buyer agrees to disclose to the VA and which Buyer represents will not be from borrowed funds except as approved by VA. If VA reasonable value of the Property is less than the Sales Price (3C above), Seller may reduce the Sales Price to an amount equal to the VA reasonable value and both parties agree to close the sale at such lower Sales Price with appropriate adjustments to 3A and 3B above.

5. EARNEST MONEY: $ 750 is herewith tendered and is to be deposited as Earnest Money with Johnny Agent and Associates, as Escrow Agent, upon execution of the contract by both parties. Additional Earnest Money, if any, shall be deposited with the Escrow Agent on or before na, 19 ____, in the amount of $ na.

6. TITLE: Seller at Seller's expense shall furnish either:
   XX A. Owner's Policy of Title Insurance (the Title Policy) issued by West Lubbock Title Company in the amount of the Sales Price and dated at or after closing: OR
   ☐ B. Complete Abstract of Title (the Abstract) certified by ________ to current date.
   NOTICE TO BUYER: AS REQUIRED BY LAW, Broker advises that YOU should have the Abstract covering the Property examined by an attorney of YOUR selection, or YOU should be furnished with or obtain a Title Policy.

7. PROPERTY CONDITION (Check "A" or "B"):
   XX A. Buyer accepts the Property in its present condition, subject only to VA required repairs and replacement of hot water heater by seller.
   ☐ B. Buyer requires inspections and repairs required by the Property Condition Addendum (the Addendum) and those required by VA. Upon Seller's receipt of the Loan approval and inspection reports Seller shall commence and complete prior to closing all required repairs at Seller's expense.

   All inspections, reports and repairs required of Seller by this contract and the Addendum shall not exceed $ 500. If Seller fails to complete such requirements, Buyer may do so and Seller shall be liable up to the amount specified and the same paid from the proceeds of the sale. If such expenditures exceed the stated amount and Seller refuses to pay such excess, Buyer may pay the additional cost or accept the Property with the limited repairs and this sale shall be closed as scheduled, or Buyer may terminate this contract and the Earnest Money shall be refunded to Buyer. Broker and sales associates have no responsibility or liability for repair or replacement of any of the Property.

8. BROKER'S FEE: $3,570 (6%) Peter Lister Listing Broker (50 %) and Johnny Agent ________ Co-Broker (50 %), as Real Estate Broker (the Broker), has negotiated this sale and Seller agrees to pay Broker in Lubbock County, Texas, on consummation of this sale or on Seller's default (unless otherwise provided herein) a total cash fee of ________ of the total Sales Price, which Escrow Agent may pay from the sale proceeds.

9. CLOSING: The closing of the sale (the Closing Date) shall be on or before March 30, 19 83, or within 7 days after objections to title have been cured, whichever date is later; however, if necessary to complete Loan requirements, the Closing Date shall be extended daily up to 15 days.

10. POSSESSION: The possession of the Property shall be delivered to Buyer XX at closing in its present or required improved condition, ordinary wear and tear excepted. Any possession by Buyer prior to or by Seller after Closing Date shall establish a landlord-tenant at sufferance relationship between the parties.

11. SPECIAL PROVISIONS:

(Insert terms and conditions of a factual nature applicable to this sale, e.g., prior purchase or sale of other property, lessee's surrender of possession, and the like.)

Nº 27

1 Mr 79 TREC No. 3-0

EXHIBIT 1-2. (Cont.)

12. SALES EXPENSES TO BE PAID IN CASH AT OR PRIOR TO CLOSING:
   A. Loan appraisal fees shall be paid by buyer.
   B. Seller's Expenses:
      (1) Seller's Loan discount points not exceeding five(5) points.
      (2) VA required repairs and any other inspections, reports and repairs required of Seller herein, and in the Addendum.
      (3) Releases of existing loans, including prepayment penalties and recordation: escrow fee; tax statements; preparation of Deed, Note and Deed of Trust; expenses VA prohibits Buyer to pay, (e.g., copies of restrictions, photos, excess cost of survey of Property); other expenses stipulated to be paid by Seller under other provisions of this contract.
   C. Buyer's Expenses: Expenses incident to Loan (e.g., credit reports; recording fees; Mortgagee's Title Policy; Loan origination fee; that portion of survey cost Buyer can pay by VA regulation; Loan related inspection fees; premiums for 1 year's hazard insurance and any flood insurance; required reserve deposits for insurance premiums, ad valorem taxes and special assessments; interest from date of disbursement to 1 month prior to date of first monthly payment on the Note); premiums on non-required insurance; expenses stipulated to be paid by Buyer under other provisions of this contract.
   D. If any sales expenses exceed the maximum amount herein stipulated to be paid by either party, either party may terminate this contract unless the other party agrees to pay such excess. In no event shall Buyer pay charges and fees other than those expressly permitted by VA Regulations.

13. PRORATIONS: Insurance (at Buyer's option), taxes and any rents and maintenance fees shall be prorated to the Closing Date.

14. TITLE APPROVAL: If Abstract is furnished, Seller shall deliver same to Buyer within 20 days from the effective date hereof. Buyer shall have 20 days from date of receipt of Abstract to deliver a copy of the title opinion to Seller, stating any objections to title, and only objections so stated shall be considered. If Title Policy is furnished, the Title Policy shall guarantee Buyer's title to be good and indefeasible subject only to (i) restrictive covenants affecting the Property (ii) any discrepancies, conflicts or shortages in area or boundary lines or any encroachments, or any overlapping of improvements (iii) all taxes for the current and subsequent years (iv) any existing building and zoning ordinances (v) rights of parties in possession (vi) any liens created as security for the sale consideration and (vii) any reservations or exceptions contained in the Deed. In either instance, if title objections are disclosed, Seller shall have 30 days to cure the same. Exceptions permitted in the Deed and zoning ordinances shall not be valid objections to title. Seller shall furnish at Seller's expense tax statements showing no delinquent taxes and a General Warranty Deed conveying title subject only to liens securing debt created as part of the consideration, taxes for the current year, usual restrictive covenants and utility easements common to the platted subdivision of which the Property is a part and any other reservations or exceptions acceptable to Buyer. The Note shall be secured by Vendor's and Deed of Trust liens. In case of dispute as to the form of Deed, such shall be upon a form prepared by the State Bar of Texas.

15. CASUALTY LOSS: If any part of Property is damaged or destroyed by fire or other casualty loss, Seller shall restore the same to its previous condition as soon as reasonably possible, but in any event by Closing Date; and if Seller is unable to do so without fault, this contract shall terminate and Earnest Money shall be refunded with no Broker's fee due.

16. DEFAULT: If Buyer fails to comply herewith, Seller may either enforce specific performance or terminate this contract and receive the Earnest Money as liquidated damages, one-half of which (but not exceeding the herein recited Broker's fee) shall be paid by Seller to Broker in full payment for Broker's services. If Seller is unable without fault to deliver Abstract or Title Policy or to make any non-casualty repairs required herein within the time herein specified, Buyer may either terminate this contract and receive the Earnest Money as the sole remedy, and no Broker's fee shall be earned, or extend the time up to 30 days. If Seller fails to comply herewith for any other reason, Buyer may (i) terminate this contract and receive the Earnest Money, thereby releasing Seller from this contract (ii) enforce specific performance hereof or (iii) seek such other relief as may be provided by law. If completion of sale is prevented by Buyer's default, and Seller elects to enforce specific performance, the Broker's fee is payable only if and when Seller collects damages for such default by suit, compromise, settlement or otherwise, and after first deducting the expenses of collection, and then only in an amount equal to one-half of that portion collected, but not exceeding the amount of Broker's fee.

17. ATTORNEY'S FEES: Any signatory to this contract who is the prevailing party in any legal proceeding against any other signatory brought under or with relation to this contract or transaction shall be additionally entitled to recover court costs and reasonable attorney fees from the non-prevailing party.

ESCROW: Earnest Money is deposited with Escrow Agent with the understanding that Escrow Agent (i) does not assume or have any liability for performance or nonperformance of any party (ii) has the right to require the receipt, release and authorization in writing of all parties before paying the deposit to any party and (iii) is not liable for interest or other charge on the funds held. If any party unreasonably fails to agree in writing to an appropriate release of Earnest Money, then such party shall be liable to the other parties to the extent provided in paragraph 17. At closing, Earnest Money shall be applied to any cash down payment required, next to Buyer's closing costs and any excess refunded to Buyer. Before Buyer shall be entitled to refund of Earnest Money, any actual and VA allowable expenses incurred or paid on Buyer's behalf shall be deducted therefrom and paid to the creditors entitled thereto.

19. REPRESENTATIONS: Seller represents that there will be no Title I liens, unrecorded liens or Uniform Commercial Code liens against any of the Property on Closing Date. If any representation above is untrue this contract may be terminated by Buyer and the Earnest Money shall be refunded without delay. Representations shall survive closing.

20. AGREEMENT OF PARTIES: This contract contains the entire agreement of the parties and cannot be changed except by their written consent.

21. **CONSULT YOUR ATTORNEY: This is intended to be a legally binding contract. READ IT CAREFULLY. If you do not understand the effect of any part, consult your attorney BEFORE signing. The Broker cannot give you legal advice — only factual and business details concerning land and improvements. Attorneys to represent parties may be designated below, and, so employment may be accepted, Broker shall promptly deliver a copy of this contract to such attorneys.**

Seller's Atty: Herman Hound   Buyer's Atty: Edward Ralph

EXECUTED in multiple originals effective the 28 day of January, 19 83 **(BROKER FILL IN THE DATE LAST PARTY SIGNS).**

Listing Broker ___ License No.	Seller
By ___	Seller
Co-Broker ___ License No.	3725 51st St. Lubbock, Tx Seller's Address ___ Tel.
By ___	Buyer
Receipt of $ 750 Earnest Money is acknowledged in the form of Cash	Buyer
Escrow Agent ___ Date 1/28/83	3202 Ave Q. Lubbock, Tx Buyer's Address ___ Tel.
By ___	

The form of this contract has been approved by the Texas Real Estate Commission and the State Bar of Texas. Such approval relates to this contract form only. No representation is made as to the legal validity or adequacy of any provision in any specific transaction. It is not suitable for complex transactions. Extensive riders or additions are not to be used. (8-78) TREC No. 3-0.   № 27

chapter 2

Sources of Money for Financing a Home

If you decide to buy a home, will you need to borrow money? Where will the money come from? What factors in the economy affect your ability to get a mortgage loan? These are some of the questions addressed in this chapter.

SAVINGS: THE KEY SOURCE OF MORTGAGE MONEY

Disposable income is the amount of income left after paying taxes. Two things can be done with that disposable income: spend it or save it. To "save it" means to "invest it" in some asset you expect to convert back to cash for spending sometime in the future. Historically, Americans have saved 5 to 7 percent of their disposable incomes. This compares with savings of over 13 percent in Canada and West Germany and over 20 percent in Japan. The rate of savings is important in that capital accumulation for borrowing is totally dependent on new savings and retained business earnings. In other words, in a year when you buy an asset, for example, a home or a car, and you borrow money to complete the purchase, it is likely that your spending in that year will exceed your total disposable income. Everyone cannot simultaneously spend more than they earn. To the extent that some people spend over their current incomes, others currently or historically spend less than they earned. The difference, *their savings,* facilitates your spending and purchase of a new home. Thus, incentives in our economy to save are quite important to all of us. As you will see, without savings, the necessary funds that enable the purchase of that new house or automobile would not be available.

WHERE DO WE PUT OUR SAVINGS?

The major recipients of our unspent income—savings—are the major financial institutions. These include commercial banks, savings and loan associations, mutual savings banks, and life insurance companies. The major financial institutions provide guaranteed returns on the investment derived from their investment income. Table 2-1 shows the level of savings and time deposits in the major financial institutions as of November 1982. As can be seen from the breakdown of deposit information, commercial banks have the largest dollar amount of deposits, accounting for 56 percent of the total deposits. Savings and loan associations are the next largest depository for savings and time deposits, with 32 percent of the total deposits as of November 1982. In addition to the major financial institutions, our savings could be invested directly for us by financial intermediaries such as the investment companies of Merrill Lynch, Payne Webber, E. F. Hutton, and so on.

TABLE 2-1. Savings and Time Deposits of Major Institutions[1]

Institution	1982 Total Deposits[2] (millions of dollars)	Percentage of Total
Commercial banks	$1,013,100	56%
Savings and loan associations	548,439	32
Mutual savings banks	151,304	8
Credit unions	79,799	4
Total deposits	$1,792,642	100%

[1]Source: *Federal Reserve Bulletin* (Washington, D.C.: Board of Governors of the Federal Reserve System, February 1983).

[2]End of November 1982.

WHY DO WE NEED THE FINANCIAL INSTITUTIONS?

Traditionally, financial institutions have provided four essential functions. First, they pool small sums of money together into large sums, giving more investment opportunities for such funds. Second, they take short-term commitments, such as those on passbook accounts, where upon demand all the money will be returned to the depositor, and they convert this to a long-term commitment, such as a 30-year mortgage loan. Third, they provide expertise in the management of investments. Fourth, they provide a safe place for people's savings. If these functions are not *needed* by a saver because he or she has enough skill to manage his or her own investments, or enough money so that pooling of funds is not an advantage, or enough liquidity and safety, then the saver would likely invest through a financial intermediary (investment company or broker). The size and future viability of the major financial institutions rests on their ability to perform functions that we cannot easily perform on our own or through other financial intermediaries. A safe place to keep liquid funds easily accessible, such as checking accounts, will likely remain a major function needed by most of us.

WHAT DETERMINES IF SAVINGS GO INTO THE MORTGAGE MARKET?

There are no guarantees that our savings will be channeled into any particular type of investment. All dollar bills look alike and none is marked "this one goes into stocks," "this one goes into bonds," "this one goes into mortgages." The markets compete for all our dollars on the basis of yield. Whichever type of investment yields the greatest return at any given risk level will succeed in attracting the dollar. The exception to the market-determined allocation of savings dollars occurs when government regulation requires an institution to invest in mortgages. Such regulation has constrained the savings and loan associations to place the dominant share of their funds in mortgage loans.

With a mortgage market nearing $2 billion, savings and loan associations still provide the largest share of all outstanding mortgage loans. They are the most critical source of conventional single-family home financing. However, their ability to attract new savings has been severely hampered in the late 1970s and early 1980s by regulations on what they can pay depositors for their money. These regulations are known as Regulation Q. To maintain liquidity and circumvent regulations on yields payable on passbook accounts and certificates of deposits, savings and loan associations began issuing money market certificates in 1978. Unfortunately, the extensive use of money market certificates has greatly increased the cost of funds for the savings and loans.

In 1960 nearly 100 percent of all savings known as "time deposits" in all savings and loan associations were in passbook accounts. By 1975 less than 50 percent of all time deposits were from passbook accounts, and over 50 percent were from certificates of deposit. In 1982 less than 20 percent of all time deposits were from passbook accounts and over 35 percent were from money market certificates. In 1981, the average cost of funds for savings and loan associations surpassed their average portfolio yield, creating losses for over half of all savings and loans. The result was a rash of mergers through 1981 and 1982 of the strong with the weak, along with a re-evaluation of this historically important source of mortgage money and the regulations imposed on the major financial institutions. A reorganization of the industry has been proposed that would take the low-yielding mortgages out of ailing savings and loan associations, thus strengthening them. But it is unlikely that this type of proposal will come about unless the financial condition of the industry deteriorates even further.

WHY DOES THE MORTGAGE AND HOUSING MARKET MOVE IN CYCLES?

Why does the mortgage and housing market seem to always be in a "boom" or a "bust"? Regulations of the major financial institutions, along with the federal government's historically unconstrained budget, creating inflation and high interest rates, are the major causes of the boom or bust housing cycles. When the federal government spends more than it collects in taxes, the difference, known as a "budget deficit," must come from borrowed dollars. When Uncle Sam enters the market competing for borrowed funds, money is drawn away from the competing private sector, borrowing for their own business needs. To facilitate their borrowing and not directly drain off capital for private business needs, the federal government is inclined to increase the money supply. This is called "monetarization of the debt." When the money supply increases faster than our productivity (real economic growth), the result is "too much money chasing the same level of goods as before," otherwise called inflation. Inflation induces lenders to charge higher interest rates. If inflation is expected to be greatest in the short run but eventually decline (an optimistic view), then short-term interest rates will increase more than long-term rates. Short-term rates are evidenced on investments such as Treasury bills, known as *money market instruments,* or by the "prime rate," the short-term borrowing rate of good credit borrowers. Long-term rates are evidenced by capital market instruments such as Treasury and private bonds and home mortgages.

With inflation and high yields available on short-term investments, savings are attracted to the money market and are taken out of the major financial institutions. This phenomenon is known as "financial disintermediation." This is what happened in 1973-1974 and 1979-1982, when savings were withdrawn from major financial institutions and were placed into higher-yielding money market investments. Regulation Q limited the ability of the financial institutions to compete effectively for savings. At the same time that the lenders were losing savings, when interest rates were relatively high, the rate at which existing borrowers were paying off their old mortgages declined. This is because people postponed selling or paying off "low-cost," below-market, fixed rate loans. Thus, the problem for lenders is compounded: no new net savings and a decline in the rate of borrowers paying off existing mortgages. The result is a "bust" market, with little or no mortgage money available and that which is available is at a very high interest rate.

Boom markets occur when the situation is reversed. While money is tight, as in 1973-1974 or 1979-1982, households are still growing and demanding housing. But much of this demand is pent up and shut off by the lack of mortgage funds or high cost. So when rates do come down and savings flows increase, and old mortgages are paid off, much of the pent-up demand is released. The result is a surging housing market and often surging home prices as well.

WHERE DO I GO TO GET A PARTICULAR TYPE OF MORTGAGE LOAN?

While the four major institutions, savings and loan associations, commercial banks, life insurance companies, and mutual savings banks, are the major source of mortgage funds, a number of other sources exist as well. Table 2-2 lists the categories of lenders with the amount and percentage of mortgage debt outstanding, by type of loan. Savings and loan associations are the primary source of conventional single-family and multifamily mortgage loans. Savings and loans are also the largest mortgage lender, with 29 percent of the total mortgage debt outstanding. The specialty of savings and loan associations are the conventional single-family residential loans, made in the individual association's local market.

TABLE 2-2. Mortgage Debt Outstanding by Type of Holder, 1982[1, 2] (in millions of dollars)

Institution	1 to 4 Family (percent)	Multifamily (percent)	Commercial (percent)	Farm (percent)	Total (percent)
Savings and loan associations	$ 400,563	$ 36,177	$ 47,557	—	$ 484,297
	(36)	(25)	(16)		(29)
Commercial banks	177,122	15,841	100,269	$ 8,510	301,742
	(16)	(11)	(34)	(8)	(18)
Life insurance companies	16,975	19,107	92,322	12,900	141,304
	(2)	(13)	(31)	(12)	(9)
Mutual savings banks	63,708	14,946	15,200	28	93,882
	(6)	(10)	(5)	(0)	(6)
Federal and related agencies	76,276	10,426	150	47,811	134,663
	(7)	(7)	(0)	(45)	(8)
Mortgage pools or trusts	198,122	16,553	7,306	8,956	230,937
	(18)	(11)	(2)	(8)	(13)
Individual and others[3]	187,325	31,352	31,905	28,918	279,500
	(17)	(22)	(11)	(27)	(17)
Total[4]	$1,120,091	$144,402	$294,709	$107,123	$1,666,325

[1]Source: *Federal Reserve Bulletin* (Washington, D.C.: Board of Governors of the Federal Reserve System, February 1983).

[2]Fourth quarter 1982.

[3]Mortgage companies, real estate investment trusts, state and local credit agencies, retirement funds, pension funds, credit unions.

[4]May not total to 100 percent due to rounding.

Commercial banks are the second largest source of single-family mortgage loans, with 16 percent of the total. While the commercial banks are by far the largest depository of savings, they account for only 18 percent of the total mortgage debt outstanding. This situation stems from the fact that commercial banks are primarily short-term lenders, which limits their interest in real estate loans except for construction lending, which is short term and one of their specialties.

Life insurance companies are an important factor in multimillion-dollar mortgages, such as those on commercial properties. As Table 2-2 illustrates, life insurance companies account for 34 percent of commercial loans and 13 percent of multifamily loans. Life insurance companies rely not on deposits for their investment funds but rather on insurance premium reserves. So while they have not been affected by the disintermediation problems as much as the other financial institutions have, the life insurance companies' total mortgage investments have been decreasing over the past several years. This is due largely to recent estate tax law changes that have decreased the need for large amounts of insurance as well as population age group changes, subsequently decreasing the insurance companies' premium reserves and revenues. Life insurance companies make mortgage loans directly, as well as rely on mortgage brokers and bankers to act as intermediaries to bring the borrower and lender together.

The mutual savings banks, which are located in the northeastern United States, are also a major factor in the multifamily mortgage market. These institutions place a large portion of their assets in single-family mortgages, most of which are Housing and Urban Development-, Federal Housing Administration (FHA)-, or Veterans Administration (VA)-backed mortgages. Their portion of the total multifamily market amounts to 10 percent, making the mutual savings banks a large factor in that market as well. These institutions are also active in the secondary mortgage market, where they buy FHA- and VA-backed mortgages originated in other areas of the country from government and quasi-government agencies.

The federal and related agencies are known primarily for their participation in the secondary market, where basically they stand ready either to buy or to sell pools of mortgages, as the market need dictates. One major exception to this is the Federal Land Bank and the Farmers Home Administration, which along with individual seller financing, account for the majority of farmland financing. In the single-family sector, government and quasi-government agencies such as the Government National Mortgage Association and the Federal National Mortgage Association are the largest holders of FHA and VA mortgages.

The largest originator of FHA and VA mortgages are the mortgage bankers, included in the Individual and Others category of Table 2-2. Mortgage companies operate by bringing borrowers and lenders, such as life insurance companies and pension funds, together for a fee. The mortgage companies then typically earn a fee for collecting the mortgage payment on the loan from the borrower and passing it on to the lender. The reason then that the total mortgage amount held by the Other category of lender is relatively small is that mortgage companies typically do not hold the originated mortgages, but instead pass them on to the ultimate lender. When mortgage companies do originate mortgages for their own accounts, they typically sell these in the secondary market, to provide money to originate additional mortgages.

Individuals have, in recent years, become a very important source of mortgage financing, both for first and second mortgages. Historically, individual sellers have "carried paper" on a sales transaction, providing second mortgage financing to a qualified buyer. With recent high interest rates, buyers are relying on sellers not only to provide second financing but also to provide creative financing vehicles as well. Mortgage arrangements such as installment land contracts, contracts for deed, wraparound loans, and purchase money mortgages are becoming not only fairly common but are often necessary to facilitate the sales transaction. As long as interest rates remain high, seller financing will continue to be a major component of the total mortgage debt outstanding.

WHAT IS "CREATIVE FINANCING" AND WHAT ARE THE "CREATIVE SOURCES" OF MORTGAGE MONEY?

"Creative financing" is a misleading expression. The term "creative" was appropriate at one time, when certain types of financial arrangements were unusual, perhaps creative, and exceptions to the typical deals. But, today, "creative financing" is used so commonly that it is really just modern finance. In fact, over 50 percent of all residential sales during 1981 involved what we have generally referred to as creative financing. Thus, creative financing really refers to any type of nontraditional financing where a second mortgage, seller financing, lease with purchase options, or any type of arrangement where more than a single conventional mortgage loan from a major financial institution is involved.

Of the nontraditional sources of mortgage money, the largest one is the equity that many sellers have in their homes. Americans today are said to be "house rich." Take, for example, a family that purchased a home in 1970 for $50,000, with $10,000 down and a $40,000 mortgage. By 1982, in many parts of the country, the house would be worth at least $150,000 and the mortgage balance would be somewhere under $30,000. That means the family actually has $120,000 of equity sitting in the home. When it comes time to sell, these sellers will not immediately need all their equity. If a lender comes up with $120,000 and the buyer needs another $20,000 loan to close the deal, the seller can easily provide it and still walk away with $100,000 on the sale of the house after paying off the existing loan. Such financing is certainly not without risk, as will be discussed further in Chapter 6. But the example does illustrate how home price inflation and huge reserves of home equity are being converted into a major new source of mortgage money.

Other sources of creative financing include (1) second mortgages provided by commercial banks or other financial institutions and (2) contractual relationships that allow a purchaser to control and possess a home and postpone or finalize the total financing and transfer of title until a later date. Leases, with purchase options, temporary land contracts or purchase money mortgages, and deferred payments are all examples of creative financing. These are also discussed along with the advantages and disadvantages of each in Chapter 6.

The objectives of creative financing, as well as many of the new types of mortgage instruments, are discussed in Chapter 5. These objectives are generally twofold. One is to lower the initial cash outlay required, especially for the first-time home buyer. The second is to lower the early year or even future mortgage payments, sometimes avoiding current "high" interest rates in hopes of financing later at lower, more "affordable" rates. If either of these objectives is achieved, then indeed creative finance does make homes more affordable. However, to the extent that creative financing is relied on, such techniques serve to maintain home price inflation, continuing part of the problem they are designed to help overcome.

chapter 3

What Determines the Cost of Money?

In this chapter we discuss the factors that influence the cost of borrowing money. Some of the myths about inflation and borrowing cost are also explored. Examine the following questions and check off (at least in your mind) what you think is the appropriate answer to each.

1. America is in a housing crisis today because mortgage costs are so high.
________True ________False

2. Buying is always cheaper than renting.
________True ________False

3. Anytime inflation occurs, borrowers are better off and lenders worse off.
________True ________False

4. The use of mortgage debt will always increase your return on investment in the purchase of investment real estate.
________True ________False

5. Inflation always makes the purchase of homes more difficult.
________True ________False

6. Oil price increases are the biggest cause of inflation.
________True ________False

If you answered any of these questions true, shame on you. There may be a few circumstances in which the relationships stated are true, but in general all the statements are myths. It is hoped that, by the end of this book, you will understand why.

SHORT-TERM AND LONG-TERM MARKETS

As was introduced in Chapter 2, short-term investments are those that mature quickly, such as in 1 year or less. Short-term investments are relatively liquid and can be converted to cash or money very easily, hence the term "money market instruments." The most common example of a money market instrument is the government Treasury bill, or "T bill." T bills usually mature in 3 or 6 months, but longer maturities are available. Beyond 1 year, most T bills are referred to as "notes," of up to around 5-year maturities. These are intermediate-term investments. Longer-term investments such as bonds and mortgages may have maturities of 10, 20, and 30 years or longer and are said to be instruments of the capital market.

Money market investments compete with capital market investments; however, their yields do not necessarily have to be similar to be competitive. In general, the longer the term of the investment commitment, the greater the required yield. This is because of the lower liquidity of longer-term investments and also the *interest rate risk* associated with longer-term investments. Interest rate risk is similar to the concept of "opportunity cost." Opportunities in the market may have to be forgone because of a long-term investment commitment. The extra return required on longer-term investments resulting from the possibility of forgone opportunities is called a *liquidity premium*. Real estate, in general, requires a liquidity premium over most other more liquid investments.

Interest rate risk broadly includes all factors affecting interest rates, including inflation. Long-term commitments are more price volatile (risky) than are short-term investments with a given change in yield, independent of the cause of the yield change. The risk associated with price movements, created by yields that may change, is interest rate risk.

The relationship between yield and the time of commitment (maturity or term) required to receive those yields is called the *term structure*. Typically because of the liquidity premium and interest rate risks, the term structure slopes upward, as shown in Exhibit 3-1.

On occasion the short-term yields might exceed the long-term yields. This is known as an *inverted term structure curve* and is associated with the phenomenon known as financial disintermediation, discussed in Chapter

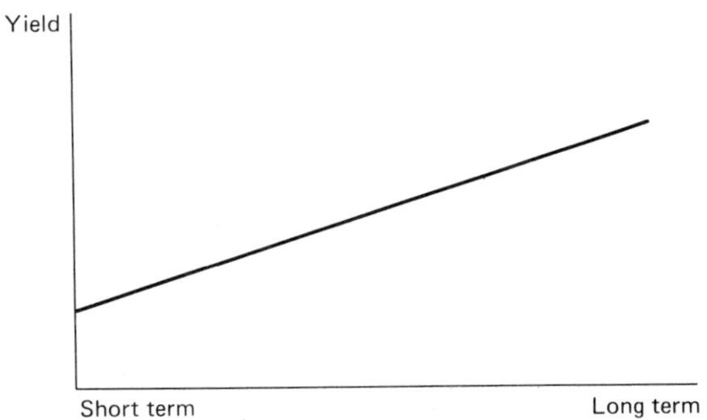

EXHIBIT 3-1. Typical Term Structure

2. This is likely to occur when inflation is expected to be higher in the short run than in the long run, as will be discussed in the next section.

INFLATION AND INTEREST RATES

The interest rates or yields we see in the market are called *nominal yields*. Nominal yields are the actual yields paid or received. Nominal yields are composed of two parts: the "real" interest rate and the inflation component. The inflation component, known in finance as the *Fisher effect*, is the amount of yield required over some investment period to hold expected purchasing power constant.

A friend wants to borrow $1,000 from you for exactly one year. In determining the amount of interest to charge for the loan, if you decide to make the loan, you must consider two things. First, what is the probability of getting the $1,000 back, the true risk of the loan? This risk requires a real return. Second, how much money will be required in one year to buy what $1,000 buys today? This is the inflation component of the loan. Together, both components, the real return plus the expected inflation component, make up the actual nominal rate you will charge your friend.

Historically, real returns have been estimated at only 2 to 4 percent: 1 to 3 percent for the short-term yields and 3 to 4 percent for long-term yields. The real returns have a term structure, the same as nominal rates, except that there should be much less variation. If the expected inflation rate is zero, then the nominal term structure and real interest rate term structure would be the same. If the expected inflation rate is constant over time, then the nominal term structure is parallel to the real rate term structure and will slope upward, as shown in Exhibit 3-2.

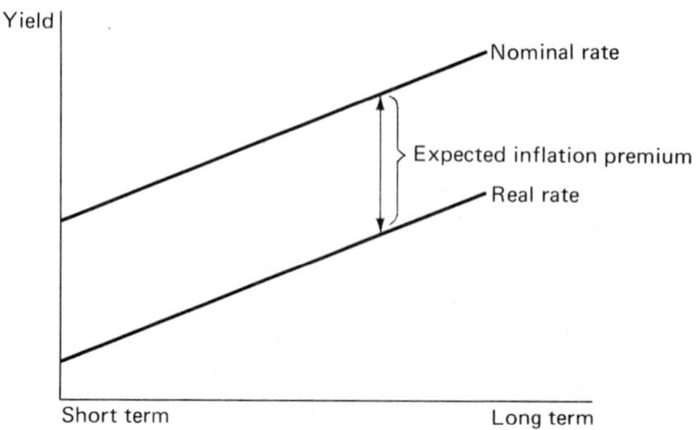

EXHIBIT 3-2. Constant Expected Inflation

If the expected inflation is higher in the short term than the long term or expected to decline, then the nominal rates may be a flat term structure curve or even be sloped downward, as shown in Exhibit 3-3.

Exhibit 3-3 is the type of term structure that existed through much of 1980 and 1981, where short-term rates exceeded long-term rates. This was due to the inflationary expectations and "uncertainty" that existed due to "Reaganomics." It was uncertain as to whether President Reagan's economic program would work to balance the budget and increase the productivity of the nation through supply-side economics. The uncertainty that resulted from the new programs, coupled with a tight money supply, caused the charging of a large premium, pushing short-term rates higher than long-term rates. In that situation, the large nominal rate was composed of a real rate, an inflationary premium, as well as an uncertainty premium, producing the inverted term structure.

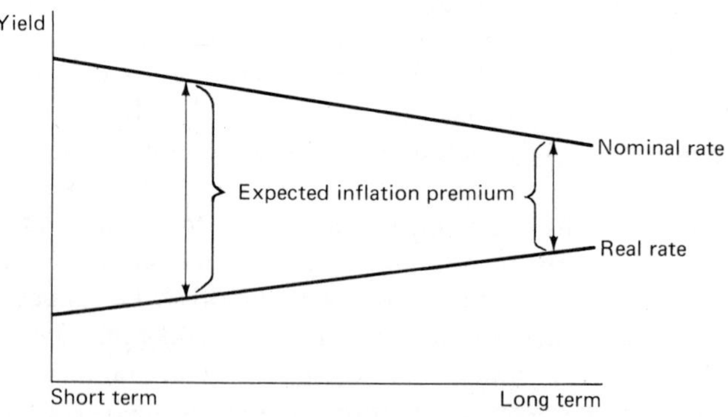

EXHIBIT 3-3. Decreasing Expected Inflation

DOES THE PRIME RATE REALLY MATTER?

When the announcer on the nightly news states that "the prime rate hit an all-time high today" or "the prime rate went up a record 2 percent today," does it really matter to the home buyer? Should the home buyer shudder in desperation?

The prime rate does matter, but not as much as other rates. The prime rate is that short-term rate charged the best credit borrowers, typically large stable corporations or businesses. The prime rate affects construction costs and new home prices. But the vast majority of buyers purchase existing homes, the prices of which are not as directly affected by the prime rate as new homes.

The most important rates for home buyers are the mortgage rates of the capital markets, competing most directly with other long-term investments. Just because short-term rates rise by 1 percent does not mean that long-term rates will rise by 1 percent. On what do long-term rates depend most? If you thought inflationary expectations, you would be right. If long-term inflationary expectations do not rise as much as short-term inflationary expectations, then the long-term rates need not move as much as short-term rates. This is not to say that mortgage rates are independent of short-term rates, just that they are not correlated 100 percent with one another. Historically, long-term rates are much more stable than short-term rates. So there is no need to panic when the prime rate goes up, but it is a warning signal, and eventually long-term rates may edge up if the basic causes of the short-term rate rise are not changed.

THE LENDER'S PERSPECTIVE ON MORTGAGE RATES

Throughout the preceding section, the role of expectations was emphasized in the formation of nominal interest rates. That same relationship must be further emphasized and explored in reviewing the lender's perspective on mortgage rates. In particular, the question is, "How does a lender determine what interest rate to charge?"

Until around 1981, the predominant mortgage instrument had been a *fixed rate mortgage* (FRM) for a fairly long term of commitment, usually 25 or 30 years. This was both because of regulation of the federally chartered financial institutions, which until 1978 did not allow the use of variable rate instruments, and because of a preference for the rather simple, by today's standards, fixed rate mortgage. With this in mind, lenders had to determine what interest rate to charge, a rate that they may have had to live with for some 25 or 30 years, even though most mortgages are historically paid off in 7 to 12 years.

In determining the nominal interest rate to charge, the lenders had to consider the future cost of money, a cost directly affected by inflation as are all interest rates. With a past inflation rate of only 5 to 7 percent, many lenders in the late 1960s and 1970s set their fixed mortgage rates at only 6.5 to 9.5 percent. In the late 1970s, many fixed rate mortgages were still available for 9 percent. Many of those mortgages are still in the portfolios of financial institutions.

But what happened to inflation? It kept going up throughout the late 1970s and into the 1980s. Often the inflation rate during that period exceeded 10 percent, forcing up the cost of money for many financial institutions, as was discussed briefly in Chapter 2. Many homeowners and investment property owners benefited from inflation, and these benefits were further compounded by the use of below-market, fixed rate loans borrowed in earlier years. The lenders, however, had *underpredicted the expected inflation rate* throughout the 1960s and 1970s, creating many of the problems faced by savings and loan associations in the early 1980s. Their losses, however, were the gains for many real estate owners.

Take a simple example in which the lender expects an inflation rate of 9 to 10 percent and charges 12 percent on a fixed rate basis for a $100,000 mortgage on a property purchased for $125,000. Now, assume that the actual annual inflation rate turns out to be 15 percent. What is the effect on the lender and borrower?

The property will go up in value due to inflationary increases. Assume that the property gains 15 percent in value, which is $18,750 in the first year. The $100,000 mortgage loan will cost in interest, very roughly, about $12,000 in the first year. On the $100,000 of borrowed money, the property value went up 15 percent or $15,000, which is $3,000 more than the cost of the money: $3,000 more return than expected by the property owner in the first year alone. The $3,000 additional return on the $25,000 equity amounts to 12 percent per year, all at the lender's expense.

If the lender knew that 15 percent inflation was going to occur, he would have charged *at least* 15 percent in interest for the use of his money. No one then would have been subsidized by the failure of the lender to predict correctly future inflation rates and interest costs. It is hoped that this discussion will help the reader to understand the more conservative approaches that lenders are taking today in their lending practices and the seemingly sky-high rates we have seen in the early 1980s. Lenders are trying to ensure that they will not be hurt in the future, as they have been in the past, by getting locked into below-market interest rate mortgages.

Understanding the effect of underpredicting inflation rates on mortgage rates and property values should also help the reader to understand why so many real estate investors did so well during the 1970s. The danger, of course, is that some investors will confuse luck with intelligence and assume that inflation will *always* be underpredicted by lenders.

The truth is that *inflation does not* benefit borrowers (debtors) at the expense of lenders (creditors); *only unexpected inflation* benefits debtors at the expense of creditors. If the lenders knew for certain what inflation rates would be, they would include that prediction in their decision as to where to set mortgage rates. The morals of this story are that "lenders are smarter than they used to be," and "history need not always repeat itself."

HOW DOES THE LENDER DETERMINE WHAT INTEREST RATE TO CHARGE?

While lenders must consider future expected inflation and the future cost of money, they must, of course, consider their current cost of money. Once the current cost of money is determined, the lender adds administrative costs to cover mortgage servicing (collecting the payments, paying miscellaneous costs in connection with the paperwork) and a reasonable profit.

AN EXAMPLE

Second Federal Savings and Loan is currently paying yields of 6.59 percent on its passbook accounts, 9.86 percent on its certificates of deposit, and 14.12 percent on its money market certificates. Passbook accounts constitute 20 percent of the net increase in its funds this year, 38 percent of the new net funds are certificates of deposit, and 42 percent are from money market certificates. Multiplying the cost times the proportional weighting of new net funds results in

Average effective cost × proportion = weighted cost

or

$$
\begin{aligned}
.0659 \times .20 &= .01318 \\
.0986 \times .38 &= .037468 \\
.1412 \times .42 &= \underline{.059304} \\
\text{Total weighted cost} &= .109952 \text{ or} \\
&= 10.9952\%
\end{aligned}
$$

Next, Second Federal must add administrative costs and a reasonable profit. This typically requires an additional 1.5 percent or so, more or less depending on competitive conditions. Adding 1.5 to 10.9952 equals 12.4952 percent. Rounding off implies that the lender must achieve a minimum of a 12.5 percent yield based on current costs. If future inflation is expected to increase, and therefore money costs as well will increase, the lender must charge above 12.5 percent to average his required profit margin. Further considerations are based on the type of mortgage being considered, as discussed in Chapter 5. Mortgages with adjustable interest rates create less concern over future expected costs than do fixed rate mortgages.

CONTRACT RATES, "POINTS," AND THE TRUE COST OF MONEY

Now that you understand that nominal rates are the actual interest rates we see or hear occurring in the marketplace, it is time to add a few more concepts and definitions.

When a lender tells you that the current mortgage rates are 14.25 percent for an 80 percent loan-to-value mortgage, does that mean you are really paying 14.25 percent or could the cost be something other than 14.25 percent? The answer is that if you are not paying *any points* then the "true" cost of the money is 14.25 percent. But, if points are involved, then the true cost of borrowing, known as *the effective yield,* is actually greater than 14.25 percent. First, some definitions:

Contract rate The interest rate quoted that will be used to determine the actual mortgage payments based on the full original mortgage value.

Loan-to-value ratio The ratio of the mortgage loan (in dollars) over the *lower* of the purchase price or the appraisal value of the property. Typical loan-to-value ratios are 75, 80, 90, and sometimes 95 percent. The higher the loan-to-value ratio, the riskier the loan from the lender's perspective. Furthermore, lenders are restricted by regulation as to the percentage of assets they can put into the high loan to value mortgages.

Points One "point" is 1 percent of the original mortgage loan, so for a $50,000 loan, 1 point would be $500. Points are used to raise the effective yield on mortgage loans. They are in addition to the typical closing costs, such as credit check, appraisal, title search, and so forth that are also paid. Points and closing costs are paid at the time of closing, when the mortgage loan is actually made. Closing costs and points are discussed further in Chapter 7.

Effective yield Every point charged raises the effective yield to the lender. The effective yield is the actual return on the money actually lent out, with the effects of the contract rate and the charged points combined.

Annual percentage rate The annual percentage rate is the effective yield of the mortgage loan assuming no early prepayment. It is widely known as the APR and must be disclosed under Regulation Z to borrowers in a truth-in-lending statement.

HOW DO POINTS AFFECT THE APR?

Every point charged reduces the net dollar outlay by the lender. When a lender charges 3 points, the lender is making a net cash outlay of the original mortgage loan less 3 percent times the original mortgage, or a net of 97 percent of the original mortgage. However, the payments are based on the contract rate and the full value of the original mortgage loan; therefore, the actual yield will be greater than the stated contract rate.

Here are a few examples for 30-year mortgages:

If the Contract Rate Is	And the Points Charged Are	Then the APR Is
9.50%	3.0	9.855%
12.25	1.0	12.387
15.00	5.0	15.829
15.50	2.0	15.831
15.75	.5	15.833

Did you notice anything peculiar about the APRs for the mortgages in the 15 percent range? Yes, they were almost identical, all within .004 percentage points of each other. The last example was intended to show not only the effect of points on the APR but also the trade-off between the contract rate and the points charged. A 15.5 percent contract rate mortgage with 2.0 points would actually have a lower effective cost, APR, than would a 15.0 percent contract rate with 5.5 points to close. The conclusion is that one cannot select a mortgage, even of the same type, based on contract rates alone. One must consider the trade-offs.

Keep in mind that (1) points for personal residences are no longer deductible in the year incurred for tax purposes but must be prorated over the life of the loan; (2) points also mean more cash outlay at the time of closing and even though the APR may be lower, the current cash outlay is an important consideration; and (3) even though points are typically paid by buyers on conventional mortgages, and must be paid by sellers in the case of FHA or VA mortgages, they are an item that can be negotiated separately between buyer and seller where the seller could agree to pay the buyer's points and/or closing costs.

POINTS AND RULES OF THUMB ON YIELD EFFECTS

While rules of thumb are not perfect for all decisions, they sometimes can provide helpful information. An old rule of thumb that has almost become a dogma of mortgage finance is that 1 discount point is equal to one-eighth of one percentage point in interest yield, or that 8 points charged would increase the yield by 1 percent. This rule of thumb tends to be fairly accurate over old interest rate ranges, with certain amortization terms, but it is fairly inaccurate today and tends to underestimate true APRs in the higher interest rate ranges. For those persons who prefer to use simple rules of thumb, however, rather than higher math, Table 3-1 provides some new rules of thumb. Points and closing costs are discussed further in Chapter 7.

TABLE 3-1. New Discount Point Rules of Thumb

	APPROXIMATE POINT CHARGES THAT WILL RAISE THE APR BY ONE-EIGHTH OF 1 PERCENT	
Contract Interest Rate Range (in percent)	25-Year Term	30-Year Term
7.0 to 7.99	1.05	1.15
8.0 to 8.99	1.00	1.10
9.0 to 9.99	.95	1.00
10.0 to 10.99	.90	.98
11.0 to 11.99	.85	.95
12.0 to 12.99	.80	.90
13.0 to 13.99	.78	.85
14.0 to 14.99	.75	.80
15.0 to 15.99	.70	.75
16.0 plus	.68	.71

To use Table 3-1, you simply find the approximate point charge corresponding to the contract rate of the loan. This point charge, when divided into the number of points actually charged, will provide the actual increase in yield if multiplied by one-eighth of a percent. As an example, assume you have a 15 percent contract rate loan with 3 points being charged by the lender. What is the actual yield being realized by the lender?

To find the solution, go to Table 3-1 to see what approximate point charge corresponds to the 15 percent contract rate. On a 30-year loan, this is .75. Dividing the number of points charged by .75 yields 3.00/.75 = 4.00. This means that the actual yield would be 15 percent plus 4(1/8) or 15.5 percent.

chapter 4

Getting Approval on a Mortgage Loan

This chapter concerns both the buyer's perspective on "what is an affordable home purchase" and the lender's perspective on "what is an acceptable mortgage and financing arrangement." Putting these two perspectives together gives us an insight into whether or not a particular mortgage loan would be approved.

WHAT CAN I AFFORD?

There are two primary issues in the question of affordability: one is the amount of cash required at the time of closing; the second is the amount of cash required per month to carry the property. The amount of cash required for purchase depends on the size of the down payment, typically 20 or 25 percent of the purchase price with conventional financing, and also the closing costs, such as points, incurred by the buyer. (See Chapter 7 for further discussion on closing costs.) The amount of cash required to carry the property is a function of all the direct costs of ownership. These include the mortgage payment as well as property taxes, property hazard insurance, maintenance and repair, and utilities. While property taxes may not be a significant factor in most parts of the country, they can be very significant in others in affecting affordability. Insurance as well as utilities may be significant factors on some properties. As an example, wood homes are generally more expensive to insure than are all-brick homes. Utilities for all-electric homes, unless unusually well insulated, will typically run more than they will in natural gas- and oil-heated homes. These generalizations have at least been true historically. Needless to say, one must consider all these factors as well as financing and price in determining which property to buy and what to pay.

With respect to the cash down payment on a home and the financing needed, there is an obvious trade-off. The larger the down payment, the less you will have to finance on any given priced home, and the more "affordable" the carrying costs will be. Many home buyers between 1980 and 1982 placed large down payments on their homes for exactly that purpose, to lower otherwise difficult mortgage payments. The luxury of large down payments, however, is primarily a benefit of previous homeownership.

Inflation, the demon of high interest rates, may be working against the average first-time home buyer who finds both prices and terms hard to handle. But inflation has actually aided many existing homeowners who are considering another home. For example, the average price of an existing home in April 1975, according to the National Association of Realtors Department of Economics and Research, was $34,900. That same home could have been sold on average for $65,300 in April 1981, an increase in value of $30,400. If we subtract 7 percent for selling expenses, that still leaves a net increase of $25,829. Add that to a typical 20 percent down payment on the first home, plus a small amount of equity buildup for mortgage principal repaid, and the owner has a total of around $33,000 to use as a down payment on another home. The $33,000 would provide a substantial percentage down payment even if the owner moved up to an $80,000 or $90,000 home. Thus, inflation has created an American public that is "house rich," and much of the stored-up equity is being used to reduce mortgage payments on the next purchase. For this reason, old rules of thumb with respect to price and income, such as buying a home that would cost no more than 2½ times your income, are not always valid today.

Other rules of thumb, however, are still valid to a substantial degree, not just because they actually determine "affordability" but because lenders use them to determine whether or not a particular mortgage loan should be approved. Two of these rules of thumb are (1) the mortgage payments should require no more than 25 percent of your gross monthly income and (2) all monthly housing costs including mortgage payments, property taxes, and property insurance should not exceed one-third of your gross monthly income. With the use of mortgage insurance, many lenders will bend the 25 percent rule up to a maximum of 30 percent if the borrower's income is expected to increase and if the borrower seems to be a good credit risk.

CONVERTING RULES OF THUMB TO PRICE

Let's use the maximum 25 percent rule of thumb and see how to convert this to a maximum "affordable" price. As an example, assume a typical American family with an average annual income of $30,000 and $25,000 of cash available for a home purchase. With interest rates at 14.25 percent, a 30-year mortgage requires monthly payments of $1.205 for every $100 borrowed or .01205 for every dollar. To solve for the mortgage that this family's income could support, we first divide $30,000 by 12 to get the monthly gross income of $2,500. Then $2,500 times 25 percent is $625 per month which could be spent on mortgage payments. Dividing $625 by .01205 will tell us how large a mortgage this family's income will support. The result is $51,867. If typical closing costs are 3 percent, then $51,807

WORKSHEET 4-1. How Much Home Can I Afford?

1.	Total annual income	________
2.	Divided by 12 equals monthly income	________
3.	Monthly income, from (2), times .25 equals affordable monthly mortgage payment	________
4.	Current mortgage rate (estimate from lender)	________
5.	Current term to maturity (estimate from lender)	________
6.	Monthly payment per $100 from Loan Amortization Table, using (4) and (5), in Chapter 8	________
7.	Payment, from (6), divided by 100 equals loan payment per dollar	________
8.	Amount of mortgage affordable is monthly payment, from (3), divided by payment per dollar, from (7)	________
9.	Closing costs (estimate from lender)	________
10.	Available down payment, minus closing costs, from (9)	________
11.	Amount of home affordable is the sum of (8) and (10)	________

× .03 equals $1,556 required for closing. Thus, from the $25,000 available must be deducted $1,556 for closing costs, leaving $23,444. The conclusion is that the family could buy a home for a maximum of $23,444 plus $51,867 or $75,311 in total, which you could round off to $75,000.

If this same family had $50,000 in cash to put down toward a home, the maximum affordable price would increase to around $100,000, with no new income required. If this family had only $10,000 to put down, then the affordable price would have to be lowered by some $15,000 to $60,000. And with the down payment being under 20 percent, the lender might require private mortgage insurance, which would increase closing costs.

Ultimately, the question of "affordability" is really a personal one. It depends on how much of your budget you wish to allocate to homeownership versus spending on autos, vacations, college education for children, or other items of importance to you. No one can generate rules of thumb appropriate for all persons in all situations. As an aid in determining how much house you can afford, Worksheet 4-1 has been included.

MORTGAGE INTEREST RATES AND AFFORDABILITY

Certainly price is of concern in determining affordability, but it is only one of the important factors. In recent years, interest rates have had a very significant effect on the mortgage component of total price that a buyer could pay. To illustrate the effect of various mortgage interest rates, assume that a family has $20,000 to put toward a home purchase, plus enough cash to cover closing costs and $24,000 in annual income. Using 25 percent of their income means that $500 per month could be used to make mortgage payments. Table 4-1 indicates the value of the mortgage and total purchase price that they could afford at various interest rates.

Table 4-1 illustrates the dramatic decline in what a buyer can afford with a given level of income as interest rates increase, or how much more a buyer can pay if interest rates decrease. This does not imply that as interest rates increase home prices will decrease, as shown in the table. Some sellers will lower their prices; others will simply take their homes off the market or postpone selling. To the extent that home prices do not decrease as much as necessary to offset higher interest rates, buyers must buy homes that are not up to their previous aspirations.

In Table 4-2 the same calculations are made as in Table 4-1, the only difference being that the mortgage was extended to 30 years from 25 years.

TABLE 4-1. Mortgage Interest Rates and Equivalent Prices with $500 Monthly Payments and a 25-Year Term

Interest Rate	Mortgage Value	Equivalent Affordable Price
7.0%	$70,721	$90,721
8.0	65,531	85,531
9.0	59,595	79,595
10.0	55,006	75,006
11.0	51,020	71,020
12.0	47,483	67,483
13.0	44,326	64,326
14.0	41,528	61,528
15.0	39,032	59,032
16.0	36,792	56,792
17.0	34,770	54,770

Comparing the values in Table 4-2 to 4-1 will reveal the positive effect on value of an increase in the term of a mortgage. As an example, with interest rates at 14 percent and a 25-year term, the $500-per-month payments could purchase a $61,528 house, with a $20,000 down payment. The same income and down payment could purchase a $62,194 house with a 14 percent mortgage and 30-year term to maturity. Most homeowners do not own their homes for 25 or 30 years, so the extra years of payments are not as important as the effect of the term on the size of the payments. For any given mortgage amount, extending the term will decrease the size of the monthly payment. For any given amount of in-

TABLE 4-2. Mortgage Interest Rates and Equivalent Prices with $500 Monthly Payments and a 30-Year Term

Interest Rate	Mortgage Value	Equivalent Affordable Price
7.0%	$75,154	$95,154
8.0	68,120	88,120
9.0	62,141	82,141
10.0	56,948	76,948
11.0	52,503	72,503
12.0	48,591	68,591
13.0	45,200	65,200
14.0	42,194	62,194
15.0	39,543	59,543
16.0	37,175	57,175
17.0	35,071	55,071

come that can be allocated toward mortgage payments, extending the term will allow the income to support a slightly larger mortgage.

Most current mortgage loans are made at the maximum limit of allowable repayment terms. Unless such limits are increased, higher interest rates will simply mean higher payments or lower-valued purchases.

Higher interest rates and higher energy costs combined with higher land and construction costs mean that future generations may have to live in slightly smaller, more energy-efficient homes than did the generations of the 1960s and 1970s.

MORTGAGE RISK ANALYSIS, OR WHAT DETERMINES IF I DO GET APPROVAL ON A MORTGAGE?

In the last chapter, we discussed the mortgage lender's perspective on the cost of money. In this chapter, we explore further the area of risk analysis. Besides charging an interest rate that will provide a margin above cost, the lender is also concerned with the overall risk of the mortgage investment. To the lender, the mortgage is just an investment, and *risk* and *return* are the two most important factors in all investment decisions.

The overall risk of a mortgage investment is composed of two questions: "What is the probability of repayment (or default)?" and "What is the probability of a loss after foreclosure given that default has occurred?" The first question is by far the more important consideration because lenders are not benefited by the foreclosure process and they wish to avoid the second question if possible.

How does a lender evaluate the probability of default? While many lenders may tell you that they can judge the risk of default on a mortgage application with their "experience" and lending policies based on "experience," the real answer is *through statistics* and "statistical experiences." Through the examination of circumstances behind "bad" mortgage loans, where default has occurred, formal policies are developed within the lending institutions. These policies are typically statistical relationships between the size of mortgage payments and income or wealth or between the size of other significant homeownership costs or other current debts and income or wealth or any other relationship that the lender has found relates to the probability of default on a mortgage loan. An example of such a policy is that the mortgage payment should not exceed 25 percent of total monthly income. There are also exceptions to such policies. One common exception to the 25 percent income rule occurs when private mortgage insurance is purchased by the borrower, which helps to protect the lender from losses. The lender then may accept up to 30 percent of income being used for the current mortgage payments.

Formal policies, aimed at determining the probability of default for most mortgage lenders, commonly include the following:

1. Total monthly mortgage payments should not exceed 25 percent of gross monthly income.
2. Total monthly mortgage payments plus property taxes and property insurance should not exceed 30, and in some cases 35, percent of gross monthly income. In some cases, lenders desire to keep all monthly ownership expenses, including utilities and an estimate for maintenance and repair, at no more than 35 percent of gross monthly income.
3. Total monthly payments for the items in (2) plus installment debt for auto loans or other credit should not exceed 50 percent of gross monthly income.

Informal policies may include certain standards for income stability, employment history, past credit history and rating, minimum net worth (total assets less total debts), and other considerations deemed important by the lender as long as they do not discriminate by race, creed, color, origin, or geographical area (known as "redlining").

A formal guideline or policy is also administered with respect to the value of the property and the size of the mortgage loan. While lenders will consider different loan-to-value ratios, such as 75, 80, 90, or 95 percent as typical ratios, the "value" is based on the lower of the appraised value or purchase price. The higher the loan-to-value ratio, the riskier is the loan, based on the probability of a loss given that foreclosure is necessary.

In general, lenders look at five areas in determining whether or not to make a mortgage loan:

1. *Income* of the borrower (and co-borrower, if any)
2. *Employment history:* stability or upward moves
3. *Financial condition:* assets, liabilities, life insurance
4. *Credit:* past credit record, current credit lines and rating
5. *Collateral:* the value of the property behind the mortgage loan

A sixth area not part of the formal review is *character,* the general attitude of the borrower, willingness to repay, plans, and ambitions.

Collecting the information used to determine whether a borrower should be approved or not is the responsibility of a loan officer. While there is no "required" form or format that a lender must use for a conventional loan, a typical standardized form often utilized is that of the Federal Home Loan Mortgage Corporation. This form is presented in Exhibit 4-1. The

EXHIBIT 4-1. Residential Loan Application

RESIDENTIAL LOAN APPLICATION **The Lubbock National Bank, P. O. Box 421, Lubbock, Texas 79408**

MORTGAGE APPLIED FOR	☐ Conventional ☐ FHA ☐ VA ☐ ____	Amount $	Interest Rate %	No. of Months	Monthly Payment Principal & Interest $	Escrow/Impounds (to be collected monthly) ☐ Taxes ☐ Hazard Ins. ☐ Mtg. Ins. ☐ ____

Prepayment Option

SUBJECT PROPERTY

Property Street Address	City	County	State	Zip	No. Units

Legal Description (Attach description if necessary) | Year Built

Purpose of Loan: ☐ Purchase ☐ Construction-Permanent ☐ Construction ☐ Refinance ☐ Other (Explain)

Complete this line if Construction-Permanent or Construction Loan	Lot Value Data Year Acquired ____	Original Cost $	Present Value (a) $	Cost of Imps. (b) $	Total (a + b) $	ENTER TOTAL AS PURCHASE PRICE IN DETAILS OF PURCHASE.

Complete this line if a Refinance Loan | Purpose of Refinance | Describe Improvements [ ] made [ ] to be made

Year Acquired	Original Cost	Amt. Existing Liens		
	$	$		Cost: $

Title Will Be Held In What Name(s) | Manner In Which Title Will Be Held

Source of Down Payment and Settlement Charges

This application is designed to be completed by the borrower(s) with the lender's assistance. The Co-Borrower Section and all other Co-Borrower questions must be completed and the appropriate box(es) checked if ☐ another person will be jointly obligated with the Borrower on the loan, or ☐ the Borrower is relying on income from alimony, child support or separate maintenance or on the income or assets of another person as a basis for repayment of the loan, or ☐ the Borrower is married and resides, or the property is located, in a community property state.

BORROWER	CO-BORROWER
Name / Age / School Yrs ____	Name / Age / School Yrs ____
Present Address No. Years ____ ☐ Own ☐ Rent	Present Address No. Years ____ ☐ Own ☐ Rent
Street	Street
City/State/Zip	City/State/Zip
Former address if less than 2 years at present address	Former address if less than 2 years at present address
Street	Street
City/State/Zip	City/State/Zip
Years at former address ☐ Own ☐ Rent	Years at former address ☐ Own ☐ Rent
Marital Status ☐ Married ☐ Separated ☐ Unmarried (incl. single, divorced, widowed) — DEPENDENTS OTHER THAN LISTED BY CO-BORROWER: NO. / AGES	Marital Status ☐ Married ☐ Separated ☐ Unmarried (incl. single, divorced, widowed) — DEPENDENTS OTHER THAN LISTED BY BORROWER: NO. / AGES
Name and Address of Employer / Years employed in this line of work or profession? ____ years / Years on this job ____ / ☐ Self Employed*	Name and Address of Employer / Years employed in this line of work or profession? ____ years / Years on this job ____ / ☐ Self Employed*
Position/Title / Type of Business	Position/Title / Type of Business
Social Security Number*** / Home Phone / Business Phone	Social Security Number*** / Home Phone / Business Phone

GROSS MONTHLY INCOME

Item	Borrower	Co-Borrower	Total
Base Empl. Income	$	$	$
Overtime			
Bonuses			
Commissions			
Dividends/Interest			
Net Rental Income			
Other† (Before completing, see notice under Describe Other Income below.)			
Total	$	$	$

MONTHLY HOUSING EXPENSE**

	PRESENT	PROPOSED
Rent	$	
First Mortgage (P&I)		$
Other Financing (P&I)		
Hazard Insurance		
Real Estate Taxes		
Mortgage Insurance		
Homeowner Assn. Dues		
Other:		
Total Monthly Pmt	$	$
Utilities		
Total	$	$

DETAILS OF PURCHASE

Do Not Complete If Refinance

a. Purchase Price	$
b. Total Closing Costs (Est.)	
c. Prepaid Escrows (Est.)	
d. Total (a + b + c)	$
e. Amount This Mortgage	( )
f. Other Financing	( )
g. Other Equity	( )
h. Amount of Cash Deposit	( )
i. Closing Costs Paid by Seller	( )
j. Cash Reqd. For Closing (Est.)	$

DESCRIBE OTHER INCOME

B—Borrower C—Co-Borrower	NOTICE: † Alimony, child support, or separate maintenance income need not be revealed if the Borrower or Co-Borrower does not choose to have it considered as a basis for repaying this loan.	Monthly Amount
		$

IF EMPLOYED IN CURRENT POSITION FOR LESS THAN TWO YEARS COMPLETE THE FOLLOWING

B/C	Previous Employer/School	City/State	Type of Business	Position/Title	Dates From/To	Monthly Income
						$

THESE QUESTIONS APPLY TO BOTH BORROWER AND CO-BORROWER

If a "yes" answer is given to a question in this column, explain on an attached sheet.	Borrower Yes or No	Co-Borrower Yes or No	If applicable, explain Other Financing or Other Equity (provide addendum if more space is needed).
Have you any outstanding judgments? In the last 7 years, have you been declared bankrupt?			
Have you had property foreclosed upon or given title or deed in lieu thereof?			
Are you a co-maker or endorser on a note?			
Are you a party in a law suit?			
Are you obligated to pay alimony, child support, or separate maintenance?			
Is any part of the down payment borrowed?			

*FHLMC/FNMA require business credit report, signed Federal Income Tax returns for last two years, and, if available, audited Profit and Loss Statements plus balance sheet for same period.

**All Present Monthly Housing Expenses of Borrower and Co-Borrower should be listed on a combined basis.

***Neither FHLMC nor FNMA requires this information.

FHLMC 65 Rev. 8/78

EXHIBIT 4-1. (Cont.)

This Statement and any applicable supporting schedules may be completed jointly by both married and unmarried co-borrowers if their assets and liabilities are sufficiently joined so that the Statement can be meaningfully and fairly presented on a combined basis; otherwise separate Statements and Schedules are required (FHLMC 65A/FNMA 1003A). If the co-borrower section was completed about a spouse, this statement and supporting schedules must be completed about that spouse also. ☐ Completed Jointly ☐ Not Completed Jointly

STATEMENT OF ASSETS AND LIABILITIES

ASSETS | **LIABILITIES AND PLEDGED ASSETS**

Indicate by (*) those liabilities or pledged assets which will be satisfied upon sale of real estate owned or upon refinancing of subject property

Description	Cash or Market Value	Creditors' Name, Address and Account Number	Acct. Name If Not Borrower's	Mo. Pmt. and Mos. left to pay	Unpaid Balance
Cash Deposit Toward Purchase Held By	$	Installment Debts (include "revolving" charge accts)		$ Pmt./Mos.	$
				/	
Checking and Savings Accounts (Show Names of Institutions/Acct. Nos.)				/	
				/	
				/	
Stocks and Bonds (No./Description)				/	
				/	
Life Insurance Net Cash Value Face Amount ($)				/	
SUBTOTAL LIQUID ASSETS	$	Other Debts Including Stock Pledges		/	
Real Estate Owned (Enter Market Value from Schedule of Real Estate Owned)		Real Estate Loans		X	
Vested Interest in Retirement Fund					
Net Worth of Business Owned (ATTACH FINANCIAL STATEMENT)					
Automobiles (Make and Year)		Automobile Loans		/	
Furniture and Personal Property		Alimony, Child Support and Separate Maintenance Payments Owed To		/	X
Other Assets (Itemize)		TOTAL MONTHLY PAYMENTS		$	X
TOTAL ASSETS	A $	NET WORTH (A minus B) $		TOTAL LIABILITIES	B $

SCHEDULE OF REAL ESTATE OWNED (If Additional Properties Owned Attach Separate Schedule)

Address of Property (Indicate S if Sold, PS if Pending Sale or R if Rental being held for income)	⇩	Type of Property	Present Market Value	Amount of Mortgages & Liens	Gross Rental Income	Mortgage Payments	Taxes, Ins. Maintenance and Misc.	Net Rental Income
			$	$	$	$	$	$
		TOTALS →	$	$	$	$	$	$

LIST PREVIOUS CREDIT REFERENCES

⇩ B–Borrower C–Co-Borrower	Creditor's Name and Address	Account Number	Purpose	Highest Balance	Date Paid
				$	

List any additional names under which credit has previously been received ______

AGREEMENT: The undersigned applies for the loan indicated in this application to be secured by a first mortgage or deed of trust on the property described herein, and represents that the property will not be used for any illegal or restricted purpose, and that all statements made in this application are true and are made for the purpose of obtaining the loan. Verification may be obtained from any source named in this application. The original or a copy of this application will be retained by the lender, even if the loan is not granted. The undersigned ☐ intend or ☐ do not intend to occupy the property as their primary residence.

I/we fully understand that it is a federal crime punishable by fine or imprisonment, or both, to knowingly make any false statements concerning any of the above facts as applicable under the provisions of Title 18, United States Code, Section 1014.

______ Borrower's Signature Date ______ ______ Co-Borrower's Signature Date ______

INFORMATION FOR GOVERNMENT MONITORING PURPOSES

The following information is requested by the Federal Government if this loan is related to a dwelling, in order to monitor the lender's compliance with equal credit opportunity and fair housing laws. You are not required to furnish this information, but are encouraged to do so. The law provides that a lender may neither discriminate on the basis of this information, nor on whether you choose to furnish it. However, if you choose not to furnish it, under Federal regulations this lender is required to note race and sex on the basis of visual observation or surname. If you do not wish to furnish the above information, please initial below.

BORROWER: I do not wish to furnish this information (initials) ______
RACE/NATIONAL ORIGIN ☐ American Indian, Alaskan Native ☐ Asian, Pacific Islander ☐ Black ☐ Hispanic ☐ White ☐ Other (specify) ______
SEX: ☐ Female ☐ Male

CO-BORROWER: I do not wish to furnish this information (initials) ______
RACE/NATIONAL ORIGIN ☐ American Indian, Alaskan Native ☐ Asian, Pacific Islander ☐ Black ☐ Hispanic ☐ White ☐ Other (specify) ______
SEX ☐ Female ☐ Male

FOR LENDER'S USE ONLY

(FNMA REQUIREMENT ONLY) This application was taken by ☐ face to face interview ☐ by mail ☐ by telephone

______ (Interviewer) ______ Name of Employer of Interviewer

FHLMC 65 Rev. 8/78 **REVERSE** FNMA 1003 Rev. 8/78

Federal Housing Administration and Veterans Administration both require their own loan applications and procedures to be used for that type of loan, which are discussed further in Chapter 5.

Much of the information provided on the residential loan application must be verified by the loan officer. This verification process can be done by letter as well as by standard forms. As an example, the loan officer may request a letter from your employer about your employment contract and may send a "verification of deposit" form to your bank to check on information you gave about a checking account or a savings account. The important point to remember here is that honesty is the best policy on all initial loan forms because of the verification process used to check out the numbers. Large discrepancies in the numbers do not leave a good impression.

In addition to the formal process of collecting information on forms, the loan officer will require a copy of the purchase contract and will initiate a credit check and an appraisal, all of which you must pay for through a loan application fee. The process and cost of getting a loan approved and closed are covered in Chapter 7.

When all the information is collected and placed in a file, it goes to the loan committee, a group of several members of the lending institution charged with the formal responsibility of all final decisions on mortgage loans.

A final point to remember is that the faster the information necessary to process your loan application is collected, the faster a decision will be made. Therefore, it is a good idea when applying for a loan to come prepared with accurate records on credit cards, bank accounts, loans, assets, and life insurance as well as names, addresses, and telephone numbers where information can be verified.

LOAN APPLICATION EXAMPLE

At this point, the Moyers, whose sales contract was presented in Chapter 1, are ready to apply for a mortgage loan. They have chosen as a lender, after calling all savings and loan associations and mortgage bankers in town, The Lubbock National Bank (LNB). This lender had the best combination of interest rate, discount points, and closing costs of all lenders called. The completed VA application form used by LNB for the Moyers' loan is presented in Exhibit 4-2.

Most items on this form are self-explanatory. Note that the lender, and ultimately the VA, requires a host of information concerning the ability of the borrower to repay the loan. Needed information is how the title will be vested, monthly expenses of the new home, and all other monthly

EXHIBIT 4-2. VA Application for Home Loan Guaranty

VETERANS ADMINISTRATION
APPLICATION FOR HOME LOAN GUARANTY

1. VA LOAN NUMBER:
2. LENDER'S LOAN NO.: LNB 20382

3. NAME AND PRESENT ADDRESS OF VETERAN (Include ZIP Code)
Floyd A. Moyer
3202 Avenue Q, Lubbock, Texas 79413

4. NAME AND ADDRESS OF LENDER (Include No., street or rural route, city, P.O., State and ZIP Code)
Lubbock National Bank
916 Main Street
Lubbock, Texas 79408

5A. VETERAN: If you do not wish to complete Items 5B or 5C, please initial here — INITIALS
5B. RACE/NATIONAL ORIGIN: ☐ AMERICAN INDIAN ALASKAN NATIVE ☐ ASIAN, PACIFIC ISLANDER ☐ BLACK ☐ HISPANIC ☐ WHITE ☐ OTHER (Specify)
5C. SEX: ☐ FEMALE ☐ MALE

6A. SPOUSE OR OTHER CO-BORROWER: If you do not wish to complete Items 6B or 6C, please initial here — INITIALS
6B. RACE/NATIONAL ORIGIN: ☐ AMERICAN INDIAN ALASKAN NATIVE ☐ ASIAN, PACIFIC ISLANDER ☐ BLACK ☐ HISPANIC ☐ WHITE ☐ OTHER (Specify)
6C. SEX: ☐ FEMALE ☐ MALE

7. PROPERTY ADDRESS INCLUDING NAME OF SUBDIVISION, LOT AND BLOCK NO., AND ZIP CODE
3725 51st Street
Lubbock, Texas 79414
Lot 279, Block 14 of Midway Gardens Addition

8A. LOAN AMOUNT	8B. INTEREST RATE	8C. PROPOSED MATURITY
$ 58,000	16.5 %	30 YRS. 0 MOS.
DISCOUNT: (Only if veteran to pay under 38 U.S.C. 1803 (c) (3) (C) or (D))	8D. PERCENT 0 %	8E. AMOUNT $ 0

The undersigned veteran and lender hereby apply to the Administrator of Veterans' Affairs for Guaranty of the loan described here under Section 1810, Chapter 37, Title 38, United States Code to the full extent permitted by the veteran's available entitlement and severally agree that the Regulations promulgated pursuant to Chapter 37, and in effect on the date of the loan shall govern the rights, duties, and liabilities of the parties.

SECTION I-PURPOSE, AMOUNT, TERMS OF AND SECURITY FOR PROPOSED LOAN

9. PURPOSE OF LOAN-TO: [X] PURCHASE EXISTING HOME PREVIOUSLY OCCUPIED ☐ CONSTRUCT A HOME-PROCEEDS TO BE PAID OUT DURING CONSTRUCTION ☐ PURCHASE EXISTING HOME NOT PREVIOUSLY OCCUPIED ☐ PURCHASE NEW CONDOMINIUM UNIT ☐ PURCHASE EXISTING CONDOMINIUM UNIT

10. TITLE WILL BE VESTED IN: ☐ VETERAN [X] VETERAN AND SPOUSE ☐ OTHER (Specify)
11. LIEN: [X] 1ST MORTGAGE ☐ OTHER (Specify)
12. ESTATE WILL BE: [X] FEE SIMPLE ☐ LEASEHOLD (Show expiration date)
13. IS THERE A MANDATORY HOMEOWNERS ASSOCIATION? ☐ YES [X] NO (If "YES", complete Item 14F)

14. ESTIMATED TAXES, INSURANCE AND ASSESSMENTS		15. ESTIMATED MONTHLY PAYMENT	
A. ANNUAL TAXES	$ 817.92	A. PRINCIPAL AND INTEREST	$ 803.39
B. AMOUNT OF HAZARD INSURANCE ON SECURITY	50,000.00	B. TAXES AND INSURANCE DEPOSITS	110.66
C. ANNUAL HAZARD INSURANCE PREMIUMS	510.00	C. OTHER	
D. ANNUAL SPECIAL ASSESSMENT PAYMENT	-		
E. UNPAID SPECIAL ASSESSMENT BALANCE	-		
F. ANNUAL MAINTENANCE ASSESSMENT	-	D. TOTAL	$ 914.05

SECTION II-PERSONAL AND FINANCIAL STATUS OF VETERAN

16. PLEASE CHECK THE APPROPRIATE BOX(ES). IF ONE OR MORE ARE CHECKED, ITEMS 18B, 21, 22 AND 23 MUST INCLUDE INFORMATION CONCERNING THE VETERAN'S SPOUSE (OR FORMER SPOUSE IF BOX "D" IS CHECKED). IF NO BOXES ARE CHECKED, NO INFORMATION CONCERNING THE SPOUSE NEED BE FURNISHED.

[X] A. THE SPOUSE WILL BE JOINTLY OBLIGATED WITH THE VETERAN ON THE LOAN
[X] B. THE VETERAN IS RELYING ON THE SPOUSE'S INCOME AS A BASIS FOR REPAYMENT OF THE LOAN
[X] C. THE VETERAN IS MARRIED AND THE PROPERTY TO SECURE THE LOAN IS LOCATED IN A COMMUNITY PROPERTY STATE
☐ D. THE VETERAN IS RELYING ON ALIMONY, CHILD SUPPORT, OR SEPARATE MAINTENANCE PAYMENTS FROM A SPOUSE OR FORMER SPOUSE AS A BASIS FOR REPAYMENT OF THE LOAN

17A. MARITAL STATUS OF VETERAN	17B. MARITAL STATUS OF CO-BORROWER OTHER THAN VETERAN'S SPOUSE	17C. MONTHLY CHILD SUPPORT OBLIGATION	17D. MONTHLY ALIMONY OBLIGATION	18A. AGE OF VETERAN	18B. AGE OF SPOUSE	18C. AGE(S) OF DEPENDENT(S)
[X] MARRIED ☐ UNMARRIED ☐ SEPARATED	☐ MARRIED ☐ UNMARRIED ☐ SEPARATED	$ 0	$ 0	46	44	

19. NAME AND ADDRESS OF NEAREST LIVING RELATIVE (Include telephone number, if available): Herbert W. Moyer, Route 3, Idalou, Texas
20A. MONTHLY PAYMENT ON RENTED PREMISES VETERAN NOW OCCUPIES: $ na
20B. UTILITIES INCLUDED? ☐ YES ☐ NO

21. ASSETS		22. LIABILITIES (Itemize all debts) NAME OF CREDITOR	MO. PAYMENT	BALANCE
A. CASH (Including deposit on purchase)	$ 2,019			
B. SAVINGS BONDS-OTHER SECURITIES	-	Real Estate, 3202 Ave Q, Lub.	$ 297	$ 25,916
C. REAL ESTATE OWNED	40,000	(thru 2nd Nat. Bank of Lub.		
D. AUTO 1978 Cadillac	3,500	includes taxes and insur.)		
E. FURNITURE AND HOUSEHOLD GOODS	15,000	J.C. Penny	35	405
F. OTHER (Use separate sheet, if necessary)	12,000	MasterCard	20	200
Money Market Fund G. TOTAL	$ 72,519	JOB-RELATED EXPENSE (Specify) TOTAL	$ 352	$ 26,521

23. INCOME AND OCCUPATIONAL STATUS ITEM	VETERAN		SPOUSE		24. ESTIMATED TOTAL COST ITEM	AMOUNT
A. OCCUPATION	Printer		Distribution Clerk		A. PURCHASE EXISTING HOME	$ 59,500
					B. ALTERATIONS, IMPROVEMENTS, REPAIRS	-
					C. CONSTRUCTION	-
B. NAME OF EMPLOYER	Acme Printing Co. Lubbock, Texas		Speedy Delivery Lubbock, Texas		D. LAND (If acquired separately)	-
					E. PURCHASE OF CONDOMINIUM UNIT	-
					F. PREPAID ITEMS	1,323.65
C. NUMBER OF YEARS EMPLOYED	10 years		1 1/2 years		G. ESTIMATED CLOSING COST	925.00
					H. DISCOUNT (Only if veteran permitted to pay)	-
D. GROSS PAY	MONTHLY $ 1,572.50	HOURLY $ 8.50	MONTHLY $ 1,042	HOURLY $ 6.50	I. TOTAL COST (Add Items 24A through 24H)	61,748.65
					J. LESS CASH FROM VETERAN	750.00
E. OTHER INCOME (Disclosure of child support, alimony and separate maintenance income is optional)	Rental of existing $ home at $300/month		$		K. LESS OTHER CREDITS to be paid	2,998.65
					L. AMOUNT OF LOAN	$ 58,000

NOTE - IF LAND ACQUIRED BY SEPARATE TRANSACTION, COMPLETE ITEMS 25A AND 25B.
25A. DATE ACQUIRED: na
25B. UNPAID BALANCE: $ na

READ CERTIFICATIONS ON REVERSE CAREFULLY

VA FORM JUN 1977 **26-1802a** SUPERSEDES VA FORM 26-1802a, DEC 1975, WHICH WILL NOT BE USED. VA 2

EXHIBIT 4-2. (Cont.)

SECTION III – LENDER'S CERTIFICATIONS *(Must be signed by lender)*

The undersigned lender makes the following certifications to induce the Veterans Administration to issue a certificate of commitment to guarantee the subject loan:

26A. The information furnished in Section I is true, accurate and complete.

26B. The information contained in Section II was obtained directly from the veteran by a full-time employee of the undersigned lender or its duly authorized agent and is true to the best of the lender's knowledge and belief.

26C. The credit report submitted on the subject veteran (and spouse, if any) was ordered by the undersigned lender or its duly authorized agent directly from the credit bureau which prepared the report and was received directly from said credit bureau.

26D. The verification of employment and verification of deposits were requested and received by the lender or its duly authorized agent without passing through the hands of any third persons and are true to the best of the lender's knowledge and belief.

26E. This application was signed by the veteran after Sections I, II and IV were completed.

26F. This proposed loan to the named veteran meets the income and credit requirements of the governing law in the judgment of the undersigned.

26G. The names and functions of any duly authorized agents who developed on behalf of the lender any of the information or supporting credit data submitted are as follows:

	NAME	ADDRESS	FUNCTION (e.g., obtained information in Sec. II; ordered credit report, verification of employment, verification of deposits, etc.)
(1)			
(2)			
(3)			

☐ *(Check box if all information and supporting credit data were obtained directly by the lender.)*

26H. The undersigned lender understands and agrees that it is responsible for the acts of agents identified in Item 26G as to the functions with which they are identified.

26I. The proposed loan conforms otherwise with the applicable provisions of Title 38, U.S. Code, and of the regulations concerning guaranty or insurance of loans to veterans.

27. DATE	28. NAME OF LENDER	29. TELEPHONE NO. *(Include area code)*	30. SIGNATURE AND TITLE OF OFFICER OF LENDER

PRIVACY ACT INFORMATION: No loan may be approved unless a complete application form is received (38 U.S.C. 1810). Failure to provide the information will deprive VA of data needed in reaching decisions which could affect you. Any disclosure of information outside VA will only be made as permitted by law.

SECTION IV – VETERAN'S CERTIFICATIONS *(Must be signed by veteran)*

31. As a GI home loan borrower you will be legally obligated to make the mortgage payments called for by your mortgage loan contract. The fact that you dispose of your property after the loan has been made WILL NOT RELIEVE YOU OF LIABILITY FOR MAKING THESE PAYMENTS.

Some GI home buyers have the mistaken impression that if they sell their homes when they move to another locality, or dispose of it for any other reason, they are no longer liable for the mortgage payments and that liability for these payments is solely that of the new owners. Even though the new owner may agree in writing to assume liability for your mortgage payments, this assumption agreement will not relieve you from liability to the holder of the note which you signed when you obtained the loan to buy the property. Also, unless you are able to sell the property to a credit-worthy obligor who is acceptable to the VA and who will assume the payment of your obligation to the lender and the Veterans Administration, you will not be relieved from liability to repay any guaranty claim which the VA may be required to pay your lender on account of default in your loan payments. The amount of any such claim payment will be a debt owed by you to the Federal Government. This debt will be the object of established collection procedures.

Payment of the loan in full ordinarily is the way in which continuing liability on a mortgage note is ended. Therefore, if you expect to move from the area in which you are now considering the purchase of a home and should you be unable to sell such home with the purchaser obtaining new financing to pay off your loan you should understand that you may continue to be liable to the holder of your mortgage and to the Veterans Administration.

I, THE UNDERSIGNED VETERAN, CERTIFY THAT:

a. I have read and understand the foregoing concerning my liability on the loan.

b. I now actually occupy the above-described property as my home or intend to move into and occupy said property as my home within a reasonable period of time.

c. I have been informed that $ is the reasonable value of the property as determined by the VA.

IF THE CONTRACT PRICE OR COST EXCEEDS THE VA REASONABLE VALUE, COMPLETE EITHER ITEM d. OR e., WHICHEVER IS APPLICABLE.

d. ☐ I was aware of this valuation when I signed my contract and I have paid or will pay in cash from my own resources at or prior to loan closing a sum equal to the difference between the contract purchase price or cost and the VA reasonable value. I do not and will not have outstanding after loan closing any unpaid contractual obligation on account of such cash payment.

e. ☐ I was not aware of this valuation when I signed my contract but have elected to complete the transaction at the contract purchase price or cost. I have paid or will pay in cash from my own resources at or prior to loan closing a sum equal to the difference between the contract purchase price or cost and the VA reasonable value. I do not and will not have outstanding after loan closing any unpaid contractual obligation on account of such cash payment.

f. Neither I, nor anyone authorized to act for me, will refuse to sell or rent, after the making of a bona fide offer, or refuse to negotiate for the sale or rental of, or otherwise make unavailable or deny the dwelling or property covered by this loan to any person because of race, color, religion, sex or national origin. I recognize that any restrictive covenant on this property relating to race, color, religion, sex or national origin is illegal and void and civil action for preventive relief may be brought by the Attorney General of the United States in any appropriate U.S. District Court against any person responsible for the violation of the applicable law.

g. The foregoing information contained in these certifications and in Section II of this application is true and complete to the best of my knowledge and belief.

READ CERTIFICATIONS CAREFULLY – DO NOT SIGN UNLESS APPLICATION IS FULLY COMPLETED

32. DATE	33. SIGNATURE OF VETERAN *(Before signing, review accuracy of application and certifications.)*

FEDERAL STATUTES PROVIDE SEVERE PENALTIES FOR ANY FRAUD, INTENTIONAL MISREPRESENTATION, OR CRIMINAL CONNIVANCE OR CONSPIRACY PURPOSED TO INFLUENCE THE ISSUANCE OF ANY GUARANTY OR INSURANCE BY THE ADMINISTRATOR.

obligations, monthly income, employment information, assets and liabilities, and total cost of purchasing the new house.

It might be interesting to see how the Moyers' expenses compare with their anticipated income, as given in Chapter 1. Table 4-3 provides the suggested rules of thumb as well as the Moyers' expected expense-to-income ratios with and without the rental income. As can be seen, the Moyers' ratios are higher than the suggested ratios from their monthly mortgage payment and total monthly house payment, but their total monthly debt is within acceptable limits. At this point, the lender would probably look at other factors, such as stability of employment and credit history, before making a decision.

TABLE 4-3. Expense-To-Income Ratios[1] For The Moyers' Anticipated VA Purchase

Category	Suggested Rule-of-Thumb Ratios	Ratios Without Rental Income	Ratios With Rental Income
1. Mortgage payment	25%	31%	27%
2. Property taxes and insurance plus (1)	30	35	31
3. Installment debt plus (2)	50	48	43

[1]Ratios are as a percentage of gross income.

It might also be mentioned in this example that the VA does not use the traditional rules of thumb in making a loan accept/reject decision, but has a specific format for determining affordability. This format involves finding effective gross income of the borrowers and then subtracting federal withholding taxes, social security, retirement payments, all mortgage principal and interest, taxes, insurance payments, a shelter maintenance expense based on the square footage of the house, and any debts of over seven months' duration. To this is added any additional income, such as social security or disability payments. The VA then requires that the amount left for food, recreation, and so on be greater than a given dollar amount. For a veteran with a spouse and no other dependents, that amount might be somewhere in the range of $400. If the remaining amount is over the minimum required, the loan would be approved. Since the exact format and dollar limits are not made public by the VA, the formal VA procedure cannot be applied in this example.

In checking the Moyers' stability of employment and other related factors, a process of verification is used. First, the lender will want to verify employment, which is done through a letter of employment verification. Exhibit 4-3 provides the completed employment verification request forms for the Moyers.

The lender will also want to verify the assets and liabilities listed by the Moyers. This is done through a request for verification of deposit, a credit bureau report, and a letter verifying the existing loan on owned real estate. The completed forms for the Moyers are given as Exhibits 4-4, 4-5, and 4-6, respectively.

Finally, the lender and the VA will want to ensure that the collateral is sufficient to support the loan. This is done through an appraisal of the property on which the borrower has put a sales contract. Exhibit 4-7 is a completed VA Request for Determination of Reasonable Value for the property the Moyers are attempting to purchase. The actual appraisal that has been returned to the lender by the VA appraiser is given in Exhibit 4-8. As can be seen from the appraisal, the market value of the property is the same as the contract price, which confirms to the lender that the property is sufficient collateral for the requested loan. Given all the facts and figures involved in this case, the lender and the VA have approved the Moyers for the requested VA loan. The VA Certificate of Commitment is presented in Exhibit 4-9. The next step in this process is the loan closing paperwork, including a Loan Cost Disclosure Statement as required by Federal Reserve Regulation Z. The closing paperwork for the Moyers is presented in Chapter 7.

EXHIBIT 4-3. VA/FHA Request for Verification of Employment

FHA FORM NO. 2004-G Rev. 5/75
VA FORM NO. 26-8497 Rev. 5/75

Form Approved
OMB No. 63R-1062

VETERANS ADMINISTRATION
and
U. S. DEPARTMENT OF HOUSING AND URBAN DEVELOPMENT
FEDERAL HOUSING ADMINISTRATION

REQUEST FOR VERIFICATION OF EMPLOYMENT

INSTRUCTIONS: Lender – Complete Items 1 through 6. Have applicant complete Items 7 and 8. Forward the completed form directly to the employer named in Item 1.
Employer – Complete Items 9A through 15 and return form directly to lender named in Item 2.

PART I REQUEST

1. TO: (Name and Address of Employer):	2. FROM: (Name and Address of Lender):
Acme Printing Company 638 4th Street Lubbock, Texas 79413	Lubbock National Bank 916 Main Street Lubbock, Texas 69408

3. Signature of Lender:	4. Title of Lender:	5. Date:	6. HUD-FHA or VA Number:
	Assistant Vice-Pres. Real Estate Division	Feb. 7, 1983	

I certify that this verification has been sent directly to the employer and has not passed through the hands of the applicant or any other interested party.

I have applied for a mortgage loan and stated that I am employed by you. My signature below authorizes verification of this information.

7. Name and Address of Applicant:	8. Employee's Identification Number: 123-45-6789
Floyd A. Moyer 3202 Avenue Q Lubbock, Texas 79413	[signature] Floyd A. Moyer Signature of applicant

PART II VERIFICATION

9A. Is applicant now employed by you? ☒ Yes ☐ No	10A. Position or Job Title: Master Printer	11. TO BE COMPLETED BY MILITARY PERSONNEL ONLY	
9B. Present Base Pay is $ 8.50 This amount is paid: ☐ Annually ☒ Hourly ☐ Monthly ☐ Other (Specify) ☐ Weekly	10B. Length of Applicant's employment: 10 years, 3 months	Pay Grade:	
9C. EARNINGS LAST 12 MONTHS		Base Pay	$
Amount $ 18,870	10C. Probability of continued employment: Excellent	Rations	$
Basic Earnings $ 1,572.50/month		Flight or Hazard	$
Normal Hours worked per Week: 40	10D. Date Applicant left:	Clothing	$
Overtime Earnings $ ☐ Regular ☐ Temporary	10E. Reason for leaving:	Quarters	$
Other Income $ ☐ Regular ☐ Temporary		Pro-Pay	$
		Overseas or Combat	$

12. REMARKS:

Floyd Moyer has been a very hard and capable worker. He has a job with Acme Printing for as long as he wants it.

13. Signature of Employer:	14. Title of Employer:	15. Date:
George Parsons	General Manager	February 22, 1983

Previous Edition Obsolete

RETURN DIRECTLY TO LENDER

U.S. GOVERNMENT PRINTING OFFICE 1979 — 671-005/1189

EXHIBIT 4-3. (Cont.)

FHA FORM NO. 2004-G Rev. 5/75
VA FORM NO. 26-8497 Rev. 5/75

Form Approved
OMB No. 63R-1062

VETERANS ADMINISTRATION
and
U. S. DEPARTMENT OF HOUSING AND URBAN DEVELOPMENT
FEDERAL HOUSING ADMINISTRATION

REQUEST FOR VERIFICATION OF EMPLOYMENT

INSTRUCTIONS: Lender – Complete Items 1 through 6. Have applicant complete Items 7 and 8. Forward the completed form directly to the employer named in Item 1.
Employer – Complete Items 9A through 15 and return form directly to lender named in Item 2.

PART I REQUEST

1. TO: (Name and Address of Employer):	2. FROM: (Name and Address of Lender):
Speedy Delivery Company 5210 38th Drive Lubbock, Texas 79407	Lubbock National Bank 916 Main Street Lubbock, Texas 79408

3. Signature of Lender:	4. Title of Lender:	5. Date:	6. HUD-FHA or VA Number:
	Assist. Vice-Presid. Real Estate Division	Feb. 7, 1983	

I certify that this verification has been sent directly to the employer and has not passed through the hands of the applicant or any other interested party.

I have applied for a mortgage loan and stated that I am employed by you. My signature below authorizes verification of this information.

7. Name and Address of Applicant:	8. Employee's Identification Number: 231-54-9876
Elizabeth R. Moyer 3202 Avenue Q LUbbock, Texas 79413	[signature] Signature of applicant

PART II VERIFICATION

9A. Is applicant now employed by you?	10A. Position or Job Title:	11. TO BE COMPLETED BY MILITARY PERSONNEL ONLY	
[X] Yes [ ] No	Counter Clerk	Pay Grade:	
9B. Present Base Pay is $ 6.50 This amount is paid: [ ] Annually [X] Hourly [ ] Monthly [ ] Other (Specify) [ ] Weekly	10B. Length of Applicant's employment: 1 year 7 months	Base Pay	$
		Rations	$
9C. EARNINGS LAST 12 MONTHS	10C. Probability of continued employment: Very Good	Flight or Hazard	$
Amount $ 12,500		Clothing	$
Basic Earnings $ 1,042/month			
Normal Hours worked per Week: 40	10D. Date Applicant left:	Quarters	$
Overtime Earnings $ [ ] Regular [ ] Temporary	10E. Reason for leaving:	Pro-Pay	$
Other Income $ [ ] Regular [ ] Temporary		Overseas or Combat	$

12. REMARKS:

Ms. Moyer has been a very good employee. She has learned the position quickly, and is very good at meeting the public. Her employment is expected to continue as long as business remains good.

13. Signature of Employer:	14. Title of Employer:	15. Date:
[signature]	Owner	February 19, 1983

Previous Edition Obsolete

RETURN DIRECTLY TO LENDER

U.S. GOVERNMENT PRINTING OFFICE [illegible]

EXHIBIT 4-4. VA/FHA Request for Verification of Deposit

FHA FORM NO. 2004-F Rev. 12/75
VA FORM NO. 26-8497a Rev. 12/75

Form Approved
OMB No. 63R-1062

VETERANS ADMINISTRATION
AND
U. S. DEPARTMENT OF HOUSING AND URBAN DEVELOPMENT
FEDERAL HOUSING ADMINISTRATION

REQUEST FOR VERIFICATION OF DEPOSIT

INSTRUCTIONS: LENDER - Complete Items 1 through 7. Have applicant complete Items 8 and 9. Forward directly to bank or depository named in Item 1.
BANK or DEPOSITORY - Please complete Items 10 through 13. Return directly to lender named in Item 2.

PART I — REQUEST

1. TO: (Name and Address of Bank or other Depository)

Second National Bank
1414 Avenue w
Lubbock, Texas 79408

2. FROM: (Name and Address of Lender)

Lubbock National Bank
916 Main Street
Lubbock, Texas 79408

3. *I certify that this verification has been sent directly to the bank or other depository and has not passed through the hands of the applicant or any other interested party.*

Signature of Lender

4. Title: Assistant Vice-President
Real Estate Division

5. Date: February 7, 1983

6. FHA or VA Number:

7. STATEMENT OF APPLICANT:

7A. Name and Address of Applicant:

Floyd A. Moyer
3202 Avenue Q
Lubbock, Texas 79413

7B. TYPE OF ACCOUNT	BALANCE	ACCOUNT NUMBER
Checking	$ 600.00	2NBC34289
Savings	$ 669.00	2NBS4569
Certificate of Deposit	$	

7C. TYPE OF LOAN	BALANCE	ACCOUNT NUMBER
Secured	$	
Unsecured	$	

8. I have applied for a mortgage loan and stated that I maintain account(s) with the bank or other depository named in Item 1. My signature below authorizes that bank or other depository to furnish the lender named in Item 2 the information set forth in Part II. Your response is solely a matter of courtesy for which no responsibility is attached to your institution or any of your officers.

Signature of Applicant

9. Date:

PART II — VERIFICATION

10A. Does Applicant have any outstanding loans? XX YES ☐ NO (If YES, enter total in Item 10B.)

10B. TYPE OF LOAN	MONTHLY PAYMENT	PRESENT BALANCE
Secured	$ 225.00	$ 25,916
Unsecured	$	$

10C. Payment experience:
XX Favorable
☐ Unfavorable (If Unfavorable, explain in Remarks.)

CURRENT STATUS OF ACCOUNTS:

	Checking	Savings	Cert. of Deposit
11A. Is account less than two months old? (If YES, give date account was opened in Item 11B)	☐ YES ☒ NO	☐ YES ☒ NO	☐ YES ☐ NO
11B. Date the account was opened.	Jan., 1973	Jan., 1973	
11C. Present Balance.	$ 542.98	$ 669.00	$
11D. Is account other than individual, e.g., Joint or Trust? (If YES, explain in Remarks)	☒ YES ☐ NO	☒ YES ☐ NO	☐ YES ☐ NO
11E. Is account satisfactory?	XX YES ☐ NO		

12. REMARKS:

Joint checking and savings, held as Tenants in Common

The above information is provided in response to your request.

13A. Signature of Official of Bank or other Depository:

13B. Title: Vice-President
Customer Service

13C. Date: February 15, 1983

THIS INFORMATION IS FOR THE SOLE PURPOSE OF ASSISTING THE APPLICANT IN OBTAINING A MORTGAGE LOAN.

RETURN DIRECTLY TO LENDER

U.S. GOVERNMENT PRINTING OFFICE 1979 – 671-005

EXHIBIT 4-4. (Cont.)

FHA FORM NO. 2004-F Rev. 12/75
VA FORM NO. 26-8497a Rev. 12/75

Form Approved
OMB No. 63R-1062

VETERANS ADMINISTRATION
AND
U. S. DEPARTMENT OF HOUSING AND URBAN DEVELOPMENT
FEDERAL HOUSING ADMINISTRATION

REQUEST FOR VERIFICATION OF DEPOSIT

INSTRUCTIONS: LENDER – Complete Items 1 through 7. Have applicant complete Items 8 and 9. Forward directly to bank or depository named in Item 1.
BANK or DEPOSITORY – Please complete Items 10 through 13. Return directly to lender named in Item 2.

PART I — REQUEST

1. TO: (Name and Address of Bank or other Depository)	2. FROM: (Name and Address of Lender)
Providential Prudential Funds, Inc. 2010 Main Street Lubbock, Texas 79408	Lubbock National Bank 916 Main Street Lubbock, Texas 79408

3. I certify that this verification has been sent directly to the bank or other depository and has not passed through the hands of the applicant or any other interested party.	4. Title:	5. Date:
Signature of Lender	Assistant Vice-President Real Estate Division	February 7, 1983 6. FHA or VA Number:

7. STATEMENT OF APPLICANT:

7A. Name and Address of Applicant:

Floyd A. Moyer
3202 Avenue Q
Lubbock, Texas 79413

7B. TYPE OF ACCOUNT	BALANCE	ACCOUNT NUMBER
Checking	$	
Savings	$	
Certificate of Deposit	$ 12,000	23443

7C. TYPE OF LOAN	BALANCE	ACCOUNT NUMBER
Secured	$	
Unsecured	$	

8. I have applied for a mortgage loan and stated that I maintain account(s) with the bank or other depository named in Item 1. My signature below authorizes that bank or other depository to furnish the lender named in Item 2 the information set forth in Part II. Your response is solely a matter of courtesy for which no responsibility is attached to your institution or any of your officers.

Signature of Applicant

9. Date:

PART II — VERIFICATION

10A. Does Applicant have any outstanding loans?
☐ YES ☒ NO (If YES, enter total in Item 10B.)

10B. TYPE OF LOAN	MONTHLY PAYMENT	PRESENT BALANCE
Secured	$	$
Unsecured	$	$

10C. Payment experience:
☐ Favorable
☐ Unfavorable (If Unfavorable, explain in Remarks.)

CURRENT STATUS OF ACCOUNTS:

	Checking	Savings	Cert. of Deposit
11A. Is account less than two months old? (If YES, give date account was opened in Item 11B)	☐ YES ☐ NO	☐ YES ☐ NO	☐ YES ☒ NO
11B. Date the account was opened.			June 1978
11C. Present Balance.	$	$	$12,347.98
11D. Is account other than individual, e.g., Joint or Trust? (If YES, explain in Remarks)	☐ YES ☐ NO	☐ YES ☐ NO	☒ YES ☐ NO
11E. Is account satisfactory?	☐ YES ☐ NO		

12. REMARKS:

Joint account with spouse, Elizabeth R., held as Tenants in Common

The above information is provided in response to your request.

13A. Signature of Official of Bank or other Depository:	13B. Title:	13C. Date:
	Account Executive	February 18, 1983

THIS INFORMATION IS FOR THE SOLE PURPOSE OF ASSISTING THE APPLICANT IN OBTAINING A MORTGAGE LOAN.

RETURN DIRECTLY TO LENDER

U.S. GOVERNMENT PRINTING OFFICE: 1979 — 671-005/1188

EXHIBIT 4-5. Credit Bureau Reports, Inc.

CREDIT BUREAU REPORTS, INC.

Name	- Floyd A. Moyer	Case Number	- CBR14389
Street Address	- 3202 Avenue Q	Date on Order	- February 12, 1983
City and State	- Lubbock, Texas	Date Report Mailed	- February 15, 1983

1a.	Do name and address agree with information shown on request for report? If not, explain below.	1a.	yes
b.	Date of birth.	b.	June 12, 1936 wife - Dec. 6, 1938
2a.	Marital status - number of dependents including self.	2a.	married 2 dependents
b.	Length of time married.	b.	1967
c.	Any separation or divorce?	c.	none found
3a.	Name of present employer(s).	3a.	Acme Printing Lubbock, TX
b.	Position held - length of present employment.	b.	Printer - 10 years
c.	Has employment status changed within the past two years?	c.	no
4a.	If spouse is presently employed, give name of employer.	4a.	Speedy Delivery Lubbock, TX
b.	Position held - length of present employment.	b.	Dist. clerk - 1 1/2 years
c.	Approximate income.	c.	unknown

Kind of Business	Date Account Opened	Date of Last Sale	Highest Credit	Amount Owing	Manner of Payment
1/83 - Lubbock Trade:	File since 3/73 - Info. verified 1/83				
JC Penny	8/75	11/82	$650	$370	Inst.-$35
MasterCard	6/76	9/82	$980	$208	Rev. -$20

Subject is employed by Acme Printing Co. Lubbock as printer for over 10 years. Subject served in the U.S. Army from 1956 to 1958 - honorable discharge. Wife is employed by Speedy Printing Company, Lubbock as clerk for over 1 year.

Address History: 3202 Avenue Q, Lubbock since 1974, buying $225 month.
Item of record: neither subject or spouse previously married. Record of payment satisfactory.

end of record

verified by [signature]

date Feb 14, 1983

EXHIBIT 4-6. Verification of an Existing Loan

THE LUBBOCK NATIONAL BANK

LUBBOCK, TEXAS

Re: Name Floyd A. Moyer
Property Address 3202 Avenue Q., Lubbock

Loan No. 2NB 44398

Gentlemen:

This letter is a request for verification on the captioned individual and property.

We shall appreciate your cooperation in giving us the information listed below, and we assure you that the data will be used in strict confidence by The Lubbock National Bank.

Sincerely,

Signature of authorization

1.	Date of mortgage	January 12, 1973
2.	Original loan amount	$29,250
3.	Present loan balance	$25,916
4.	Type of loan	Conventional
5.	FHA/VA Case #	na
6.	Monthly principal & interest	$225.00
7.	Monthly taxes	$37.00
8.	Monthly hazard insurance	$35.00
9.	Monthly mortgage insurance	na
10.	Total Monthly Payment	$297
11.	Was he original mortgagor?	yes
12.	Paying record	good, 1 late payment in 1975

Signature of Lender — Vice-President, Collections (Title) — January 29, 1983 (Date)

ML-FL-19 916 MAIN STREET BOX 421 79408 806 762-8800

EXHIBIT 4-7. VA Request for Determination of Reasonable Value

VA REQUEST FOR DETERMINATION OF REASONABLE VALUE (Real Estate)
HUD APPLICATION FOR PROPERTY APPRAISAL AND COMMITMENT

HUD Section of Act | 1. CASE NUMBER

2. PROPERTY ADDRESS *(Include ZIP Code and county)*
3725 51st Street
Lubbock, Texas 79414
Lubbock County

3. LEGAL DESCRIPTION
Lot 279, Block 14 of
Midway Gardens Addition

4. TITLE LIMITATIONS AND RESTRICTIVE COVENANTS
Utility Easement, south 5' of property.
1. ☐ CONDOMINIUM 2. ☐ PLANNED UNIT DEVELOPMENT

5. NAME AND ADDRESS OF FIRM OR PERSON MAKING REQUEST/APPLICATION *(Include ZIP Code)*
Lubbock National Bank
916 Main Street
Lubbock, Texas 79408

6. LOT DIMENSIONS:
60' x 120'
1. ☐ IRREGULAR: 7,200 SQ/FT 2. ☐ ACRES:

7. UTILITIES (✓)	ELEC.	GAS	WATER	SAN. SEWER
1. PUBLIC	XX	XX	XX	XX
2. COMMUNITY				
3. INDIVIDUAL				

8. EQUIP.: 1. [X] RANGE/OVEN 2. ☐ REFRIG. 3. [X] DISHWASHER 4. ☐ CLOTHES WASHER 5. ☐ DRYER 6. [XX] GARBAGE DISP. 7. [X] VENT FAN 8. [X] W/W CARPET 9. ☐

9. BUILDING STATUS: 1. ☐ PROPOSED 2. ☐ SUBSTANTIAL REHABILITATION 3. ☐ UNDER CONSTR. 4. [X] EXISTING

10. BUILDING TYPE: 1. [X] DETACHED 2. ☐ SEMI-DETACHED 3. ☐ ROW 4. ☐ APT. UNIT

11. FACTORY FABRICATED? 1. ☐ YES 2. [XX] NO

12. NUMBER OF UNITS: 1

13A. STREET ACCESS: 1. ☐ PRIVATE 2. [X] PUBLIC

13B. STREET MAINT.: 1. ☐ PRIVATE 2. [XX] PUBLIC

14A. CONSTRUCTION WARRANTY INCLUDED? 1. ☐ YES 2. [X] NO *(If "Yes" complete Items 14B and C also.)*

14B. NAME OF WARRANTY PROGRAM: na

14C. EXPIRATION DATE *(Month, day, year)*: na

15. CONSTR. COMPLETED *(Mo., yr.)*: June, 1966

16. NAME OF OWNER: Joseph P. Seller

17. PROPERTY: [X] OCCUPIED BY OWNER ☐ NEVER OCCUPIED ☐ VACANT ☐ OCCUPIED BY TENANT *(Complete Item 18 also)*

18. RENT *(If applic.)*: $ /MONTH

19. NAME OF OCCUPANT: Joseph P. Seller

20. TELEPHONE NO.: 555-1212

21. NAME OF BROKER: Johnny Agent

22. TELEPHONE NO.: 555-1234

23. DATE AND TIME AVAILABLE FOR INSPECTION: by appt. w/owner ☐ AM ☐ PM

24. KEYS AT *(Address)*: contact owner

25. ORIGINATOR'S IDENT. NO.: 1234-5678

26. SPONSOR'S IDENT. NO.:

27. INSTITUTION'S CASE NO.: LNB 20382

28. PURCHASER'S NAME AND ADDRESS *(Complete mailing address. Include ZIP code.)*
Floyd A. Moyer
3202 Avenue Q
Lubbock, Texas 79413

EQUAL OPPORTUNITY IN HOUSING

NOTE – Federal laws and regulations prohibit discrimination because of race, color, religion, sex, or national origin in the sale or rental of residential property. Numerous State statutes and local ordinances also prohibit such discrimination. In addition, section 805 of the Civil Rights Act of 1968 prohibits discriminatory practices in connection with the financing of housing.

If HUD/VA finds there is noncompliance with any antidiscrimination laws or regulations, it may discontinue business with the violator.

29. NEW OR PROPOSED CONSTRUCTION – *Complete Items 29A through 29G for new or proposed construction cases only.*

A. COMPLIANCE INSPECTIONS WILL BE OR WERE MADE BY: ☐ FHA ☐ VA ☐ NONE MADE

B. PLANS *(check one)*: ☐ FIRST SUBMISSION ☐ REPEAT CASE *(If checked complete Item 29C.)*

C. PLANS SUBMITTED PREVIOUSLY UNDER CASE NO.:

D. NAME AND ADDRESS OF BUILDER | E. TELEPHONE NO. | F. NAME AND ADDRESS OF WARRANTOR | G. TELEPHONE NO.

30. COMMENTS ON SPECIAL ASSESSMENTS OR HOMEOWNERS ASSOCIATION CHARGES: None

31. ANNUAL REAL ESTATE TAXES: $ 817.92

32. MINERAL RIGHTS RESERVED? ☐ YES *(Explain)* [X] NO

33. LEASEHOLD CASES *(Complete if applicable)*
LEASE IS: ☐ 99 YEARS ☐ RENEWABLE ☐ HUD/VA APPROVED
EXPIRES *(Date)*:
ANNUAL GROUND RENT: $

34. SALE PRICE OF PROPERTY: $ 59,500

35. REFINANCING – AMOUNT OF PROPOSED LOAN: $ 58,000

36. PROPOSED SALE CONTRACT ATTACHED: [XX] YES ☐ NO

37. CONTRACT NUMBER PREVIOUSLY APPROVED BY VA THAT WILL BE USED:

CERTIFICATIONS FOR SUBMISSIONS TO HUD

In submitting this application for a conditional commitment for mortgage insurance, it is agreed and understood by the parties involved in the transaction, that if, at the time of application for a Firm Commitment, the identity of the seller has changed, the application for a Firm Commitment will be rejected and the application for a Conditional Commitment will be reprocessed upon request by the mortgagee.

It is further agreed and understood that in submitting the request for a Firm Commitment for mortgage insurance, the seller, the purchaser and the broker involved in the transaction shall each certify that the terms of the contract for purchase are true to his or her best knowledge and belief, and that any other agreement entered into by any of these parties in connection with this transaction is attached to the sales agreement.

BUILDER/SELLER'S AGREEMENT: **All Houses:** The undersigned agrees to deliver to the purchaser HUD's statement of appraised value. **Proposed Construction:** The undersigned agrees, upon sale or conveyance of title within one year from date of initial occupancy, to deliver to the purchaser Form HUD-92544, warranting that the house is constructed in substantial conformity with the plans and specifications on which HUD based its value and to furnish HUD a conformed copy with the purchaser's receipt thereon that the original warranty was delivered to him/her. **All Houses:** In consideration of the issuance of the commitment requested by this application, I (we) hereby agree that any deposit or down payment made in connection with the purchase of the property described above, whether received by the undersigned, or an agent of the undersigned, shall upon receipt be deposited in escrow or in trust or in a special account which is not subject to the claims of my creditors and where it will be maintained until it has been disbursed for the benefit of the purchaser or otherwise disposed of in accordance with the terms of the contract of sale.

Signature of: ☐ Mortgagee ☐ Builder ☐ Seller ☐ Other X ______ Date ______ 19__

MORTGAGEE'S CERTIFICATE: The undersigned mortgagee certifies that to the best of his/her knowledge, all statements made in this application and the supporting documents are true, correct and complete.

Signature and Title of Mortgage Officer: X [signature] Date Jan 29 1983

CERTIFICATIONS FOR SUBMISSIONS TO VA

1. On receipt of "Certificate of Reasonable Value" or advice from the Veterans Administration that a "Certificate of Reasonable Value" will not be issued, we agree to forward to the appraiser the approved fee which we are holding for this purpose.
2. CERTIFICATION REQUIRED ON CONSTRUCTION UNDER FHA SUPERVISION *(Strike out inappropriate phrases in parentheses)*

I hereby certify that plans and specifications and related exhibits, including acceptable FHA Change Orders, if any, supplied to VA in this case, are identical to those (submitted to) (to be submitted to) (approved by) FHA, and that FHA inspections (have been) (will be) made pursuant to FHA approval for mortgage insurance on the basis of proposed construction under Sec. ______

38. SIGNATURE OF PERSON AUTHORIZING THIS REQUEST: [signature]

39. TITLE:

40. DATE: Feb 3, 1983

41. DATE OF ASSIGNMENT: Feb 4, 1983

42. NAME OF APPRAISER: James Appraiser

WARNING: Section 1010 of Title 18, U.S.C. provides: "Whoever for the purpose of . . . influencing such Administration . . . makes, passes, utters or publishes any statement knowing the same to be false . . . shall be fined not more than $5,000 or imprisoned not more than two years or both."

VA FORM 26-1805, AUG 1980
HUD FORM 92800-1

SUPERSEDES VA FORM 26-1805, AUG 1977, AND HUD 92800, JUL 1979, WHICH WILL NOT BE USED.

VA/HUD FILE COPY 1

EXHIBIT 4-8. Residential Appraisal Report

RESIDENTIAL APPRAISAL REPORT

HUD Section of Act | 1. CASE NUMBER

2. PROPERTY ADDRESS *(Include ZIP Code and county)*
3725 51st Street
Lubbock, Texas 79414
Lubbock County

3. LEGAL DESCRIPTION
Lot 279, Block 14 of
Midway Gardens Addition

4. TITLE LIMITATIONS AND RESTRICTIVE COVENANTS
Utility Easement, south 5' of property.

1. ☐ CONDOMINIUM 2. ☐ PLANNED UNIT DEVELOPMENT

5. NAME AND ADDRESS OF FIRM OR PERSON MAKING REQUEST/APPLICATION *(Include ZIP Code)*
Lubbock National Bank
916 Main Street
Lubbock, Texas 79408

6. LOT DIMENSIONS: 60' x 120'
1. ☐ IRREGULAR: 7,200 SQ/FT 2. ☐ ACRES:

7. UTILITIES (√)	ELEC.	GAS	WATER	SAN. SEWER
1. PUBLIC	XX	XX	XX	XX
2. COMMUNITY				
3. INDIVIDUAL				

8. EQUIP. 1. [XX] RANGE/OVEN 2. ☐ REFRIG. 3. [X] DISHWASHER 4. ☐ CLOTHES WASHER 5. ☐ DRYER 6. [XX] GARBAGE DISP. 7. [X] VENT FAN 8. [X] W/W CARPET 9. ☐

9. BUILDING STATUS 1. ☐ PROPOSED 2. ☐ SUBSTANTIAL REHABILITATION 3. ☐ UNDER CONSTR. 4. [X] EXISTING

10. BUILDING TYPE 1. [X] DETACHED 2. ☐ SEMI-DETACHED 3. ☐ ROW 4. ☐ APT. UNIT

11. FACTORY FABRICATED? 1. ☐ YES 2. [XX] NO

12. NUMBER OF UNITS 1

13A. STREET ACCESS 1. [X] PRIVATE 2. [X] PUBLIC

13B. STREET MAINT. 1. [X] PRIVATE 2. [XX] PUBLIC

14. STRUCTURE 1. [XX] FRAME 2. ☐ MASONRY 3. ☐ CONCRETE

15. DESCRIPTION *(Complete only one Item)* 7. ☐ SPLIT FOYER 8. ☐ BI-LEVEL 9. ☐ SPLIT LEVEL OTHER *(Enter No. of Stories)* 1

16. UNDERGROUND WIRE? 1. ☐ YES 2. [X] NO

17. CONSTR. WARRANTY INCLUDED? 1. ☐ YES 2. [X] NO

18. NEIGHBORHOOD DATA

A. CHECK ONE: 1. ☐ URBAN 2. [XX] SUBURBAN 3. ☐ RURAL

B. PRESENT LAND USE: Residential

C. ANTICIPATED LAND USE: Residential

D. BUILT-UP 98% E. OWNED 75% F. RENTED 23% G. VACANT 2%

H. TYPICAL RENT $375-425 /MO.

I. TYP. BLDG. AGE 15-20 YEAR(S)

J. PRICE RANGE $45,000-$75,000

20. OFFSITE IMPROVEMENTS 1. [XX] CURB 2. [XX] SIDEWALK 3. [X] GUTTER 4. ☐ STORM SEWER

21. STREET SURFACE paved

22A. FEDERAL FLOOD HAZARD MAP ISSUED? 1. ☐ YES 2. [XX] NO

22B. PROPERTY IN SPECIAL FLOOD HAZARD AREA? 1. ☐ YES 2. [XX] NO

23. EVIDENCE OF: 1. ☐ DRY ROT 2. ☐ TERMITES 3. ☐ SETTLEMENT 4. ☐ DAMPNESS 5. [X] NO EVIDENCE

24. UNIT RATING (Check (√))	GOOD	AVG.	POOR
A. GENERAL CONDITION		X	
B. ROOM SIZES AND LAYOUT		X	
C. ADEQUACY OF CLOSETS/STORAGE		X	
D. KITCHEN CABINETS/WORKSPACE		X	

25. ESTIMATED REMAINING LIFE 40 YEAR(S) 1. ☐ ECONOMIC 2. [X] PHYSICAL

19. BUILDING DATA

ITEM	DESCRIPTION	COND. (Observed)
FOUNDATION	slab	good
ROOF	asphalt	good
EXT. WALLS	brick	good
INT. WALLS	sheetrock	good
FLOORS	concrete	good
HTG. SYSTEM	GFA	fair
PLUMBING	copper	good
INSULATION	R19/R11 batt	adeq.
ELEC. (Amps)	120/220	adeq.

1. 0 % BSMT. 2. [XX] SLAB 3. ☐ CRAWL SP.
1. [X] CENT. AIR COND. 2. ☐ WALL AIR COND. NO. OF UNITS:
1. [X] FIREPLACE 2. ☐ REC. ROOM 3. ☐

26. MARKET DATA ANALYSIS

ITEM	SUBJECT PROPERTY	COMPARABLE NO. 1		COMPARABLE NO. 2		COMPARABLE NO. 3	
ADDRESS		3978 52nd Street Lubbock		2788 Oxblood Dr. Lubbock		3466 Rutledge Lubbock	
PROXIMITY TO SUBJ.		1/4 mile		1/2 mile		1/4 mile	
DATA SOURCE		app. recap		app. recap		app. recap	
TYPE OF FINANCING AND SALE PRICE		FHA	$62,500	FHA	$59,000	assump.	$63,000
ITEM	DESCRIPTION	DESCRIPTION	(+)(-) ADJ.	DESCRIPTION	(+)(-) ADJ.	DESCRIPTION	(+)(-) ADJ.
ROOM COUNT (ROOMS / BDRMS / BATH) / TOTAL LIVING AREA (Square feet)	7 / 3 / 2 / 1,830	7 / 3 / 1.5 / 1910	$-800	7 / 3 / 2 / 1810	$+200	8 / 4 / 2 / 1950	$-1200
DATE OF SALE	January, 1983	December 1982	+250	January, 1983	-	November 1982	+500
LOCATION	Midway Gardens	same	-	same	-	same	-
SITE/VIEW	inside lot	corner lot	-500	no landscaping	+500	good landscap.	-1000
DESIGN AND APPEAL	average	average	-	average	-	average	-
CONSTR. QUALITY	average	good	-1500	average	-	average	-
AGE/CONDITION	15 years/good	12/good	-3000	16/fair	+1500	15/good	-
BSMT./BSMT FIN. RMS.	none	none	-	none	-	none	-
FUNCTIONAL UTILITY	adequate	inadequate	+1000	adequate	-	adequate	-
AIR CONDITIONING	central elec.	central	-	evaporative	+1000	central	-
ENERGY EFFIC. ITEMS	R-19/R-11	R-19/R-11	-	R-19/R-11	-	R-26/R-13	-1000
STORAGE	adequate	adequate	-	adequate	-	poor	+500
PARKING FACILITIES	adequate	adequate	-	adequate	-	adequate	-
COMMON ELEMENTS AND MONTHLY ASSESSMENT	none	none		none		none	
OTHER (e.g. Fireplace, kitchen equipment, remodeling, etc.)		needs painting	+1500	all new carpet	-2000	loan assumption	-2000
TOTAL NET ADJUSTMENT		ENTER (+) OR (-) -	$3,050	ENTER (+) OR (-) +	$1,200	ENTER (+) OR (-) -	$4,200
INDICATED VALUE			$59,450		$60,200		$58,800

RECONCILIATION

27A. INDICATED VALUE BY MARKET DATA APPROACH ► $59,500

27B. INDICATED VALUE BY INCOME APPROACH *(If applicable)* ECON. MRKT. RENT TIMES GROSS RENT MULTIPL. $425 /MO. x 120 ► $51,000

27C. IND. VAL. BY COST APPROACH *(If appl.) (Attach calculations.)* ► $56,050

28. ESTIMATED LAND VALUE $6,000

29. LEASE DATA *(Complete if applic.)* A. ANNUAL GROUND RENT $ CAP. AT % = $ B. VAL. OF LEASED FEE $ na C. VAL. OF LEASEHOLD EST. $ na

30. DOES PROP. CONFORM TO APPLICABLE MINIMUM PROPERTY REQUIREMENTS? 1. [X] YES 2. ☐ NO *(If "No," explain in Item 32.)*

31. APPRAISAL IS MADE: 1. [X] AS IS 2. ☐ SUBJECT TO COMPLETION PER PLANS/SPECS. 3. ☐ SUBJECT TO REPAIRS, ALTERATIONS, ETC.

32. ADDITIONAL COMMENTS *(Include repairs necessary to make property conform to applicable MPR's. Attach separate sheet if necessary.)*
Income approach not considered valid measure of market value for this property. Most emphasis placed on market approach.

33. FINAL RECONCILIATION/ESTIMATED VALUE $59,500

NOTE: No determination of reasonable value may be made unless a completed appraisal report is received (38 U.S.C. 1810 (VA ONLY)).
I CERTIFY that (a) I have carefully viewed the property described in this report, INSIDE AND OUTSIDE, so far as it has been completed; that (b) it is the same property that is identified by description in my appraisal assignment; that (c) I HAVE NOT RECEIVED, HAVE NO AGREEMENT TO RECEIVE, NOR WILL I ACCEPT FROM ANY PARTY ANY GRATUITY OR PAYMENT OTHER THAN MY APPRAISAL FEE FOR MAKING THIS APPRAISAL (HUD/VA ONLY); that (d) I have no interest, present or prospective, in the applicant, seller, property, or mortgage; that (e) in arriving at the estimated value I have not been influenced in any manner whatsoever by the race, color, religion, national origin, or sex of any person residing in the property or in the neighborhood wherein it is located. I understand that, if I am a fee appraiser, violation of this certification can result in my removal from the fee appraiser's roster.

34A. SIGNATURE OF APPRAISER *(Enter I.D. No. for HUD cases only)* | 34B. DATE Jan 29 1983 | OFFICE USE ONLY *(Reviewer's I.D. No. – HUD cases only)*

VA FORM 26-1803, AUG 1980
HUD 92800-3 FmHA 1922-8

VA/HUD/FmHA FILE COPY 5

EXHIBIT 4-9. VA Certificate of Commitment

VETERANS ADMINISTRATION **CERTIFICATE OF COMMITMENT**	1. VA LOAN NUMBER LH	2. LENDER'S LOAN NO. LNB 20382

3. NAME AND PRESENT ADDRESS OF VETERAN *(Include ZIP Code)*

Floyd A. Moyer
3202 Avenue Q, Lubbock, Texas 79413

4. ISSUED TO: *(Name and address of lender)*

Lubbock National Bank
916 Main Street
Lubbock, Texas 79408

5. PROPERTY ADDRESS INCLUDING NAME OF SUBDIVISION, LOT AND BLOCK NO., AND ZIP CODE	6A. LOAN AMOUNT	6B. INTEREST RATE	6C. PROPOSED MATURITY
3725 51st Street Lubbock, Texas 79414 Lot 279, Block 14 of Midway Gardens Addition	$ 58,000	16.5 %	30 YRS. 0 MOS.
	DISCOUNT ▶	6D. PERCENT 0 %	6E. AMOUNT $ 0

FOR VA USE ONLY

(NOTE: To be completed by VA and returned to Lender.)

PERCENT OF GUARANTY %

☒ CERTIFICATION OF ACTIVE DUTY STATUS AS OF DATE OF NOTE REQUIRED.

THE TERMS OF THIS COMMITMENT ARE ON THE REVERSE

Administrator of Veterans Affairs

By: Clyde Olsen
(AUTHORIZED AGENT)

Waco, Texas
(ISSUING OFFICE)

March 10, 1983
(DATE)

TERMS OF COMMITMENT

The documents submitted in connection with the loan described on the face of this certificate have been examined and the loan has been determined to be eligible under Chapter 37, Title 38, U.S.C., and the regulations effective thereunder.

Upon receipt of a duly executed "Certificate of Loan Disbursement"* showing full compliance with the applicable regulations, the Administrator will issue: A Loan Guaranty Certificate as indicated on the face of this Certificate; subject to any adjustment necessary under Section 36:4303(g) of the Regulations upon ascertainment of the exact principal amount of the loan, or upon submission of the loan disbursement report under Section 36:4305 thereof.

In the case of a joint loan as defined in Section 36:4307 of the Regulations the portion of such loan eligible for guaranty shall be as provided therein. This Certificate of Commitment will expire and will be invalid 6 months from the date hereof, unless the loan described herein is closed prior to such expiration date. The expiration date is not applicable if this Certificate relates to a loan which was heretofore closed and so reported to VA.

*If the loan described on the face of this Certificate is made by the lending institution named herein this certificate need not be returned to the VA. Otherwise this certificate or a copy of the agreement assigning this certificate must accompany the Certificate of Loan Disbursement.

chapter 5

Mortgage Types: Traditional and New Instruments, or How To Get "Fixed," "Graduated," "Wrapped," and "Rammed" All in One Easy Lesson

The old days of fixed rate mortgages where the only questions were "Where should I get a mortgage loan?" and "What interest rates will I have to pay?" are long gone. Not only must mortgage buyers shop around to compare interest rates, points, and closing costs, but they must also make that comparison for myriad types of mortgage instruments.

This chapter lays out the choices of modern home finance, first concentrating on a few of the legal aspects and clauses common to all mortgages and then exploring the different financial arrangements within each of the many mortgage types available today.

First, a warning: don't be fooled by "brand" names. In reviewing this chapter, you may or may not see a mortgage type you have heard of in the past, such as the "Wachovia plan," or the "equalizer," or one of many others. This is because mortgage types have become just like over-the-counter drugs; each lender tries to come up with its own name and acts as if it has derived the all-time-unique formula best for all concerned. As with drugs, however, mortgage types have common *generic* foundations. There are only so many financial variations possible: payments will stay the same or go up or down, the balance owed will go up or down, the term will increase or decrease, the payments may be subsidized or not, but the way in which we combine these possibilities gives rise to a variety of names. At the end of this chapter, you will be well enough versed to see through the brand names and to understand the generically different mortgage choices available to you today.

LEGAL ASPECTS OF THE MORTGAGE CONTRACT

What Is a Mortgage?

A *mortgage* is any form of instrument whereby a lien is created upon real estate or whereby title to real estate is reserved or conveyed as security for the payment of a money debt. A *lien* is a legal claim on the property that allows the lien holder to satisfy the debt through foreclosure and sale of the property if necessary.

All mortgages are basically composed of two parts, the *mortgage deed* or *deed of trust*[1] and the *promissory note*. The mortgage deed describes the real estate to be used as collateral against the repayment of the note. The promissory note is a personal promise to repay the note, and even in the absence of any security real estate, the borrower would still have an obligation to repay the note. The note spells out the financial terms of repayment as well as the rights and interest of the lender and borrower. A deed of trust is similar to a mortgage deed except that the borrower creates a trust and conveys the title of the property to a trustee who holds it as security for the benefit of the lender. The deed of trust is used in Alabama, Arkansas, California, Colorado, the District of Columbia, Delaware, Illinois, Mississippi, Missouri, Nevada, New Mexico, Tennessee, Texas, Utah, Virginia, and West Virginia.

There are two general approaches used in most states to establish the legal relationship between a borrower and a lender. One is called *title theory*, wherein title is held by, or rests with, the mortgagee (lender). The other is called *lien theory*, wherein the mortgagor (borrower) retains title and the mortgagee merely has a lien against the property. Lien theory is more modern in origin and the most common approach in most states, although many states have a hybrid approach encompassing both theories in part.

---

[1]In Georgia, a "security deed" is used; this instrument basically secures payment of the debt, grants power of attorney to sell the property upon default (avoiding court delays), and cancels the deed upon payment of the debt.

The basic difference between lien and title theory states lies in the process of foreclosure and the rights of the borrower and lender during this process. In all states, a foreclosure process must be initiated by the lender upon default of the borrower to recoup the balance of the note owed. But in title theory states, the right of possession and control of the property during the foreclosure process belongs to the lender, who is the title holder. In a lien theory state, the borrower would have the right to remain in possession of the property until the foreclosure process is completed. One must keep in mind that while lenders may have eviction power, they need not exercise it, and many lenders are patient in exercising their full rights.

What Is a Default?

Mortgage default is the failure to fulfill the mortgage contract. The most common failure is not making the mortgage payments. Mortgage default could also result from not paying property taxes or allowing other liens to form against the property specifically prohibited by the mortgage.

Defaults are much more common than foreclosures. One must keep in mind that a lender is generally not interested in owning or foreclosing on property. Lenders will try to work out a plan with borrowers that will avoid foreclosure if possible. The best policy is to be open and honest with a lender and tell in advance if you have a problem and need some help to work it out. Most lenders will try very hard to work out temporary arrangements, such as interest-only mortgage payments or adding a few payments onto the mortgage balance, if they perceive your problem as temporary and if you have been honest with them.

What Is Foreclosure?

Foreclosure is the process of collecting on a mortgage where the mortgagor has defaulted and there appears to be no other remedy than to sell the property. Technically, foreclosure is an elimination of the mortgagor's equity of redemption. *Equity of redemption* is the right of the mortgagor to redeem his or her property upon meeting all obligations. The equity of redemption ceases at the time a property is sold, but up until then, a mortgagor could pay all back interest and legal and other expenses expended by the lender in the process of foreclosure and again be on good terms with respect to the mortgage note. In a few states, there is a similar right, which extends beyond the point of sale, called *statutory redemption*. In such states, the new purchaser only has a tentative title while the foreclosed upon mortgagor tries to redeem himself or herself.

If a property is foreclosed upon and the proceeds from the sale are not enough to cover all monies owed the mortgagee, a *deficiency judgment* can be obtained by the mortgagee against the mortgagor so that the balance owed can still be collected, even at a later date.

Important Clauses in Most Mortgages

Independent of the particular type of mortgage, most mortgages contain similar types of clauses, some of which are negotiable, some of which are not. They include the following:

1. *Covenants* are required from the borrower to keep the property in good repair, to insure it against loss (fire), to pay property taxes, and not to remove or damage any of the property in such a way as to negatively affect value.
2. An *acceleration clause* specifies that if the mortgagor fails to comply with the covenants or is otherwise in default, then the entire debt balance becomes due and collectible through the foreclosure process. This clause may also apply where there are provisions against assumption, lease or sale. In such a case, the acceleration clause is referred to as a *due-on-sale* clause or a "nonassumption clause." Lenders today, in their attempts to prevent assumptions of mortgages that may be at below-market rates or may be otherwise assumed by a nonqualified borrower, are taking great care to insert "nonassumption," "due-on-sale," and "due-on-lease" clauses into current mortgage instruments.
3. The *defeasance clause* voids the mortgage upon repayment of the entire debt and is sometimes called a "release of mortgage" clause.
4. The *prepayment clause*, or prepayment privilege, generally describes the acceptable arrangements or conditions for early repayment of a substantial portion (or the entire balance) of the mortgage principal owed. Prepayment penalties, when they exist, are usually a small percentage of the mortgage balance, perhaps as little as 1 percent, and are often eliminated as the mortgage ages. Generally, most lenders have low or no prepayment penalties if the property is sold, but a small prepayment penalty in the case of refinancing on the part of the mortgagor.

The primary reason for such penalties is to try and prevent a sudden flood of mortgage refinancing caused by declining interest rates.

5. The *subordination clause* asserts a lower lien position for a mortgage that may otherwise assert a higher or first lien position. For example, if a seller acted as a lender and took part of the price of the sold property in the form of a mortgage, such a mortgage would normally have a first lien on the property. Most financial institutions, however, require first liens on the mortgage loans they hold. If the buyer were to arrange a new first mortgage, the new lender would insist on a subordination clause in the existing mortgages, forcing the seller to release his or her first lien position to the lender. Such a clause is especially common today with the large proportion of seller-financed transactions in combination with traditional mortgage instruments.
6. The *estoppel clause* states that upon request of the mortgagee, the mortgagor will furnish a written statement, or "estoppel certificate," that will duly acknowledge the amount due on the mortgage and whether any offsets or defenses exist against the mortgage debt. This clause allows the mortgagee to sell the mortgage to another investor without concern over the actual amount owed.

First and Second Mortgages

First mortgage simply means a first lien; second mortgage means a second lien. Second mortgages are also sometimes called "junior mortgages"; when provided by sellers, second mortgages are generally referred to as "purchase money mortgages," in the case of the seller passing the title to the buyer. In the event of foreclosure, the proceeds of the sale would be allocated first to the first lien holders, then to second lien holders, and so forth. A special type of second mortgage is called the "wraparound," which includes the first mortgage in its note. The "wraparound" is discussed further later in this chapter.

FHA, VA, and Conventional Mortgages

There are three basic types of mortgages: FHA, VA, and conventional. Within each of these there are many variations, especially among conventional mortgages. The FHA (Federal Housing Administration) is under the jurisdiction of HUD (Department of Housing and Urban Development). The FHA was set up to encourage homeownership primarily through the reduction of the up-front cash required by home buyers and, in some cases, by the reduction of payments in the early years (see "FHA Graduated Payment Mortgage Plans," discussed later). The VA (Veterans Administration) was set up to enable veterans to purchase housing with low or no down payments. In general, the term *conventional* simply means that the mortgage is neither of the FHA nor the VA type. Note that, for the most part, VA and FHA loans are not made with funds from any government agency but are merely insured in the case of FHA or guaranteed in the case of VA by the respective government agencies, with the actual funds provided by private financial institutions.

Much of the money actually lent for FHA and VA loans comes from mutual savings banks as well as from the other major financial institutions, but much of it is lent out through local mortgage banking companies.

To qualify for a VA mortgage, one must be an honorably discharged veteran with a minimum number of active service days (181 days for recent vets) or a spouse of a veteran who died in active service. (Complete eligibility requirements are available at a VA office or local mortgage banking company.) A qualified borrower may finance up to 100 percent of the purchase price (or appraised value, if lower). In addition, on both FHA and VA loans, sellers are required to pay points, further reducing the up-front cash requirement of buyers. The VA and FHA inspect a property to be sure that it meets their standards of construction quality and repair. Upon approval, the VA guarantees up to $27,500 or 60 percent of the loan, whichever is less, if a foreclosure is necessary, to the mortgagee. This dramatically lowers the risk of most mortgage loans for the lender. Note that the current guarantee of $27,500 periodically is increased with rising home prices, and you should check with a lender or the VA to find out current limits. Qualifying for an FHA or VA loan would require similar standards as for a private lender with respect to the borrower's ability to meet mortgage payments, although the specific requirements the borrower must meet are set by the FHA and VA.

Unlike the VA program, which is a free benefit available only to veterans, the FHA program of insurance is available to the general public. The monthly FHA insurance premium is one-half of 1 percent of the mortgage balance and is similar in effect to the borrower adding .5 percent interest onto the contract rate of the loan. The current down payment required on an FHA loan is 3 percent of the first $25,000 of purchase price or appraised value and 5 percent of the next $25,000 and above. The maximum FHA-*insured* loan amount is currently $70,000 in most areas but it can be expected to be increased with home prices in the future. A few examples of the down payment required in an FHA loan are the following:

1. A buyer purchases a home for $50,000. The FHA down payment will be

   $$\begin{aligned} .03\ (\$25{,}000) &= \$\ \ 750 \text{ plus} \\ .05\ (\$25{,}000) &= \underline{\ 1{,}250\ } \\ &= \$2{,}000 \text{ total down payment} \end{aligned}$$

   thus the loan-to-value ratio is $48,000 over $50,000 or 96 percent, with only 4 percent required as a down payment.

2. A buyer purchases a home for $70,000. The FHA down payment will be

   $$\begin{aligned} .03\ (\$25{,}000) &= \$\ \ 750 \text{ plus} \\ .05\ (\$42{,}500) &= \ 2{,}125 \text{ plus} \\ \$70{,}000 - \$67{,}500 &= \underline{\ 2{,}500\ } \\ \text{(maximum)} \quad &= \$5{,}375 \text{ total down payment} \end{aligned}$$

   or a loan-to-value ratio of ($70,000 minus $5,375)/$70,000, or just over a 92 percent loan-to-value ratio. You can see that the higher the purchase price, the greater the down payment required as a percentage of the purchase price.

Unlike conventional mortgages, the contract rates on FHA and VA loans are set by regulation rather than by the market, by the secretary of HUD for FHA loans, and by the VA for VA loans. These regulated contract rates are often below the market rates of conventional loans. Just because FHA or VA loans may be at a below-market contract rate does not mean the lender is willing to subsidize the borrowers of such loans. Rather, points, as discussed in Chapter 3, are usually charged to boost the effective yields on FHA and VA loans to the equivalent of the conventional yields. Thus, FHA and VA loans generally have higher point charges paid at closing than do conventional loans. Since these points are paid by the sellers, and the sellers like the lenders do not want to subsidize anyone, they generally insist on a higher price in the case of an FHA or VA sale to offset the expected cost of the points. This does not mean that all benefits are lost to the buyer, because at least the majority of the points-increased price are financed and not required in cash at the closing.

The major advantage of FHA or VA financing is the high loan-to-value mortgage. The major disadvantage is that both FHA and VA paperwork slow down the closing process and generally require greater patience on the part of both the buyer and seller.

Private Mortgage Insurance

FHA and VA mortgages are government-sponsored programs that assist buyers wishing to purchase a home with lower than typical down payments. But VA loan guarantees are limited to veterans and FHA-insured loans are limited in value so that they do not significantly benefit the upper price range of home buyers, of, say, $75,000 and up. Furthermore, both the FHA and VA are typical government bureaucracies and thus require patience and a willingness to deal with more red tape than is involved with the private sector alone. Because of these factors and because lenders want to find other ways in which to lower their risk exposure on high loan-to-value mortgages, the private mortgage insurance market has developed.

In 1957, the Mortgage Guaranty Insurance Corporation (MGIC) began its operations to provide private mortgage insurance to lenders. MGIC is the largest and best known of the private mortgage insurance firms, but today there are several others, including American Mortgage Insurance Company; Continental Mortgage Insurance, Inc.; United Guaranty Corporation (UGC); Foremost Guaranty Corporation; Investor Mortgage Insurance Company; Liberty Mortgage Insurance Corporation; PMI Mortgage Insurance Company; Republic Mortgage Insurance Company; Ticor Mortgage Insurance Company; as well as new ones being created over time.

Whenever the loan-to-value ratio of a mortgage exceeds 80 percent, most lenders require private mortgage insurance on conventional mortgages. In addition, the lenders are allowed to require property taxes and property insurance be paid monthly into an escrow account by the borrower, in order to have greater control over these areas of risk exposure. This is called a *budget mortgage*, and it is common on FHA and VA loans as well as on conventionals.

As with the FHA, private mortgage insurance companies charge a premium for their insurance function. Typical charges to the borrower may be 2½ percent of the mortgage as a one-time premium at closing or 1 percent at closing and ¼ percent thereafter on the mortgage balance. For such charges, the insurance company would cover up to 20 percent of the mortgage balance if a deficiency arose after foreclosure, protecting the lender from all but the most severe cases of default and property value declines. However, it should be noted that competition has arisen among the private mortgage insurance companies, and numerous variations on the premium charges and coverage are now available. Both lenders and borrowers would be wise to check around for competitive alternatives.

As a further note on private mortgage insurance, lenders only require such coverage when loan-to-value ratios exceed 80 percent. In an area where much price appreciation has occurred quickly, borrowers paying the premiums for private mortgage insurance may be wise to go to their lender and request an appraisal one or two years after purchase. Most lenders will charge for the new appraisal, but such costs will be much less than the continued premium on private mortgage insurance. Lenders will often be surprised when a borrower insists on a new appraisal to eliminate private mortgage insurance, but after getting over their initial shock at meeting an educated consumer, most will readily consent.

SOME VARIATIONS OF CONVENTIONAL MORTGAGES BASED ON COLLATERAL OR SIZE OF LOAN

Before delving into all the new financial arrangements included in the current mortgage alternatives, some old alternatives must be reviewed. These variations of conventional mortgages apply only to the collateral or size of the loan. They are the following:

The *blanket mortgage* is a mortgage that covers more than one parcel of property. It is often used by builders to cover construction loans, but it may also be used as a way of financing 100 percent of a new purchase using two or more properties as collateral, one having substantial equity relative to the value. This form of mortgage is often used in financing subdivisions.

The *package mortgage* includes certain items of personal property such as appliances, carpeting, and so forth to be included as collateral and supporting value for the mortgage loan.

The *open-end mortgage* is developed by establishing a credit limit up to which the mortgagor can borrow. Initially the mortgagor need not borrow the full amount, but may later increase the loan up to the maximum without changing the terms of the note. This form of mortgage is common in construction loans.

FIXED RATE MORTGAGES (FRMs)

Fixed rate mortgages have been around as long as most people can remember. As their name implies the interest rate charged is fixed for the full term of the mortgage. This term is usually 25 or 30 years, although some states may differ, such as Georgia, where 29 years is the typical maximum term allowed. The total monthly payments to principal and interest are level and fixed in total over the term of the loan. Since the interest owed is always based on the current mortgage balance, the interest portion of the payment is by far the greatest in the early years. In the later years, when the mortgage balance is much lower but the mortgage payments are the same as before, much of the payment applies to principal reduction of the balance owed. The result is a very slow reduction of the mortgage balance but a lower level of payments than would be possible if a borrower wished to pay off a fixed amount of principal each period.

To illustrate the mortgage balance payoff of the FRM, Exhibit 5-1 graphically presents the percentage of mortgage balance remaining at the end of each year of a 30-year, 12 percent mortgage. As can be seen, a very small percentage of the mortgage is paid off in the early years of the loan, due to the fact that most of the initial mortgage payments are primarily to interest. Only in the later years does the bulk of the payment go to principal reduction, resulting in a rapid decrease in the percentage of mortgage balance remaining after about the fifteenth year. This will be covered in depth in Chapter 8.

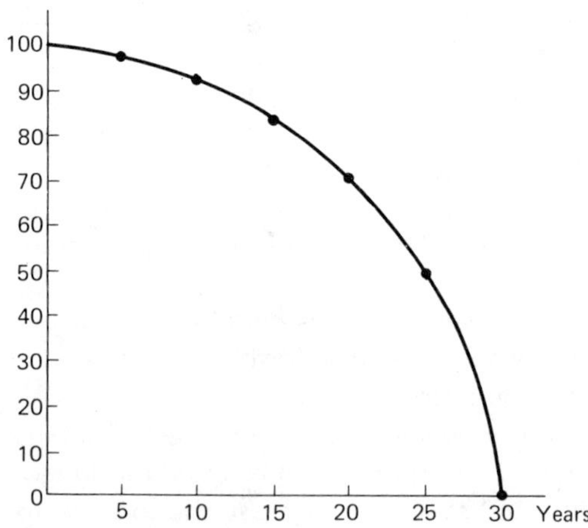

EXHIBIT 5-1. Percent of Mortgage Balance Remaining for 30-Year Term, 12 Percent Loan

AN EXAMPLE

Suppose that a borrower had $36,000 of gross annual income, or $3,000 monthly, and wished to borrow $72,000 for a 30-year term at the prevailing interest rate of 12 percent. With level payments, the monthly payment would be $740.60, just under 25 percent of the borrower's income (just enough to qualify). However, even after 10 years of payments, the borrower still owes $67,260.96 or 93.418 percent of the original balance. This may not appeal to many borrowers, but look at the alternative.

Suppose that the borrower wished to knock off the $72,000 more quickly and evenly at $72,000/360 months or $200 per month, plus interest. In this case, the total payments of principal and interest would decline each month as the mortgage balance declined. In the first month, the interest would be $72,000 times 1/12 of 12 percent or $720. Add to the $720 in interest $200 in principal repayment for a total of $920 the first month. In this situation, the mortgage balance would decline much more rapidly, in fact 33 percent versus 6.6 percent in the first 10 years, but the problem is the $920 monthly payment. The $920 is over 30 percent of the borrower's total monthly income, and the loan would probably not be approved. Thus, level-payment mortgages reduce the balance owed very slowly at first, but they enable us to purchase larger, more expensive homes than possible with most alternative plans. (The calculation of mortgage payments and the mortgage balance remaining are covered in detail in Chapter 8.)

Fixed rate mortgages require the lender to project the future cost of money for a long period of time. The typical mortgage life is 7 to 12 years; many, however, go 20 or even 30 years. Because of the difficulty of such long-term projections, lenders today are quite conservative on the rate charged on fixed rate mortgages, and often the FRM interest rate will exceed that of many alternative instruments from which the borrower may choose. Fixed rate mortgages are also more likely to have prepayment penalties than are many of the alternative variable rate instruments discussed next.

Some financial analysts have indicated their belief that the fixed rate mortgage would not survive as a viable alternative since variable rate mortgages are now available. However, two surveys conducted in 1982, one by Mortgage Guaranty Insurance Corporation of 500 lenders and another by American Mortgage Insurance Company of 400 savings and loan associations, show that the FRM is indeed alive and well. The MGIC survey results indicated that the most likely lenders of the FRM will be mortgage bankers. This is a result of the greater ease of FRM resale to secondary mortgage market buyers.

In general, in the future, borrowers will see most lenders offering several alternative instruments, including many variable rate mortgage variations, discussed next.

INTEREST VARIABLE MORTGAGES

Most lenders today have forsaken their reliance on the old fixed mortgages in favor of those instruments with less interest rate risk. There are a number of variations on the "interest variable mortgages" or "adjustable rate mortgages" or "variable rate mortgages," all of which are acceptable generic descriptions for these fairly modern instruments. Variable rate mortgages (VRMs) have been used extensively in California in the 1970s but only since 1980 have they become popular elsewhere.

As their name implies, the contract rate of interest varies and may go up or down at specific time intervals as spelled out in the mortgage note. The key to whether the contract rate moves up or down is an index to which the rate is tied. Typically, this index is tied to a government agency, such as the Federal Home Loan Bank Board's index of average mortgage yields or cost of funds. But some VRMs are tied to other indexes, some external, some internal determined based on the market cost of funds or yields. The key to an acceptable index from the federal regulator's point of view is that *the index cannot be manipulated in any way* by the lending institution but is primarily affected by market conditions. VRM borrowers should be careful that they know what the index is at the time the mortgage loan is closed and how it may change, so that they can follow later adjustments.

Prior to 1981, the VRMs were restricted as to the minimum acceptable interval for payment adjustments, such as no more than once or twice a year. Another "old" regulation limited such adjustments to no more than one-half of 1 percent annually, with a total minimum or maximum interest rate limit of plus or minus 5 percent. *Today, all those regulations are gone,* and the way in which VRMs are being set up is much more flexible and negotiable.

Currently, there is no limit as to the minimum time interval acceptable for mortgage payment adjustments, and even monthly changes are permissible. Note that lenders must give a borrower notice between 30 and 45 days in advance of any interest adjustments. There is no limit on the minimum or maximum interest rate change from one interval to another or in total for the life of the mortgage. That is not to say all VRMs are set up on such a flexible basis. Most lenders select a combination of adjustments that are currently acceptable to consumers. Thus, the market will restrain some of the lenders' options. In addition, administrative costs may preclude lenders from using indexes that are too short term, for example, Treasury bills, requiring rapid interest rate changes and much administrative paperwork.

As a result of interest rate changes, borrowers often have two or three options, such as to increase (decrease) their mortgage payments, increase (decrease) the remaining term of the mortgage, or in some cases increase (decrease) the balance of the mortgage owed.

How Does the Indexed Interest Adjustment Work?

Assume that an individual borrows on a variable rate mortgage of $80,000 at 12.5 percent for 25 years (300 months), so that the initial monthly payments are $872.28. Also assume initially that the appropriate index is at 12.00 percent but one year later moves to 12.24 percent. The new interest rate on the mortgage is

$$\text{New variable rate} = \frac{\text{index (end of period)}}{\text{index (beginning of period)}} \begin{array}{c}\text{(initial interest rate}\\ \text{on mortgage)}\end{array}$$

$$= \frac{12.24}{12.00}(12.5\%) = 12.75\%$$

The new interest rate will be 12.75 percent, up one-fourth of a percentage point from 12.5 percent beginning in period 2. Assuming that the borrower decides to increase the size of the payments to offset the higher interest rate, the new payments will be based on the current balance of $79,504.80 for the remaining term of 288 months at 12.75 percent interest or $887.00, an increase of $14.72 monthly.

If the borrower decided to increase the term of the mortgage and hold payments nearly constant, and was given such an option, the remaining term would have to be increased from 288 months to 327 months, an increase of 39 months. This shows one of the problems that lenders have in extending the term of the mortgage to accommodate interest rate changes. In this case, a slight change of only one-fourth of a percentage point, which would have required only a 2 percent increase in the size of the monthly payment, required a term increase of 39 months, or over 13.5 percent of the existing term, to accommodate the borrower's desire to hold payments constant. For extreme interest rate increases, terms would be infinity with the entire mortgage payment only going toward interest. In the previous case, if the interest rate were increased beyond 13 percent, payments would have to be increased to ever pay off the mortgage. For this reason, most options on extending mortgage terms are constrained to 40 years[2] (480 months) even though initial loan terms are constrained to 30 years (360 months).

Since there are many specific types of variable rate mortgages, a few of the more common VRMs are discussed next.

Renegotiated Rate Mortgages (RRMs)

Renegotiated rate mortgages were a very popular form of VRM during 1980 and 1981. Most RRMs were set up to have interest rates and payments adjusted every three or five years, with maximum changes of plus or minus one-half of 1 percent per year, ½ percent maximum for the three-year case and a 2½ percent maximum for the five-year case. The term "renegotiated" is somewhat misleading in that, as with all VRMs, the interest rate adjustment is based on an index and is not really "renegotiated." In the United States, lenders *must roll over* the RRMs, unlike the case in some other countries, at the new indexes and cannot refuse to maintain the loan. In addition, there is no prepayment penalty on RRMs at the first renewal period or at any interval of renewal thereafter. Thus, borrowers do not have to accept the new interest rate if better refinancing opportunities exist. The major advantage to borrowers of the RRMs are the more stable pattern of mortgage payments. Sometimes RRMs are referred to as "rollover" mortgages.

Adjustable Rate Mortgages (ARMs)

The adjustable rate mortgage is just another name for a VRM. Typically, the adjustment period on such named mortgages has been once per year, but there are no such federal restrictions tied to the name "adjustable rate mortgages."

There are several other forms of variable rate mortgages possible, but most are combinations with generically different instruments such as the variable balance mortgage types and the graduated payment plans. Such combinations will be explored after the basic concepts of each generically different instrument are discussed.

---

[2]By regulation, federally chartered savings and loan associations may not extend the term of a VRM beyond 40 years, although commerical banks may.

VARIABLE BALANCE MORTGAGES (VBMs)

Variable balance mortgages are similar to variable rate mortgages except that, instead of varying the payment or term in response to an interest rate change, the balance owed is varied. That is, the rate at which the mortgage balance is being reduced will increase if interest rates go down and the payment is held stable because more of the payment may then be allocated to the principal. If interest rates go up and more of the payment is needed for interest, the balance will not be reduced as quickly, and the balance could possibly even increase in the case of the interest owed exceeding the actual payment.

A major advantage to the borrower of such an arrangement is the ability to keep payments stable. Also, over the life of the average mortgage, the principal balance may increase and/or decrease at various rates, yet come out the same in the end where the balance would have been no different than under alternative instruments and the borrower need not react to all the changes during the term of the mortgage. One disadvantage is that at the end of the mortgage term there may still be a positive mortgage balance requiring the borrower to sell or refinance the property.

To give an example of a variable balance mortgage, assume a \$100,000 mortgage at 12.0 percent with a 30-year term, requiring initial payments of \$1,028.61 monthly. Now suppose after one month the index to which the interest rate is attached moves up, requiring a new interest rate of 12.25 percent. How is the balance affected?

First, the interest portion of the first month's payment is \$1,000 calculated as follows:

$$\left(\frac{12.0\%}{12 \text{ months}}\right) (\$100{,}000) = \$1{,}000 \text{ interest}$$

and the principal portion is

$$\text{Total payment} - \text{interest} = \text{principal repaid}$$

or

$$\$1{,}028.61 - \$1{,}000 = \$28.61$$

The mortgage balance remaining after month 1 is

$$\$100{,}000 - \$28.61 = \$99{,}971.39$$

In the second month, the new annual interest rate is 12.25 percent, requiring a monthly interest charge of

(New monthly interest rate)(mortgage balance remaining) = interest owed,

or

$$\left(\frac{12.25\%}{12\text{ months}}\right)\ (\$99{,}971.39) = \$1{,}020.54$$

But, because we are now using a variable balance mortgage and are holding payments constant, the principal reduction rate will be changed as follows:

$$\text{Total payment} - \text{interest} = \text{principal repaid}$$

or

$$\$1{,}028.61 - \$1{,}020.54 = \$8.07$$

and the balance in the third month will be

$$\$99{,}971.39 - \$8.07 = \$99{,}963.32$$

As you can see, variable balance mortgages might require a lot of calculations, but with the extensive use of computers today by lending institutions, this is not much of a problem. Variable balance mortgages are becoming quite popular, because they still allow the lender to maintain market yields and allow the borrower to keep payments stable. Most of the nonfixed rate mortgages in the future will have some of the variable balance features contained as options for the borrower. Next is a discussion of some specific types and names for variable balance mortgages.

Split Rate Mortgages (SRMs)

The split rate mortgage is a mortgage that combines the stability of a renegotiated rate mortgage with the interest variability of a VRM by adjusting the mortgage balance as shown in the last illustration. The difference is that payments may also be adjusted, as well as the balance, but payment adjustments are held to longer intervals, such as three or five years.

Variable Rate Mortgage with Capped Payments (Wachovia Plan)

The capped payment VRM, or the Wachovia Plan, is not a new concept, but because of some pioneering work on its use by a particular bank, the plan is sometimes referred to by the namesake of the bank, hence, the Wachovia Plan.

The capped payment VRM works in the following way. The interest rate is varied with an index, as are all VRMs, at certain intervals (monthly, quarterly, semiannually, etc.). Then the payments are also adjusted up or down as other VRMs are as a result of the interest rate change. However, an upper limit on the potential increase per interval is predetermined in the mortgage note. In this sense, the upper limit the mortgage payments may reach is "capped," limiting extremely high payment movements. For example, suppose that a borrower begins with a $100,000 mortgage at 13.5 percent for a 30-year term. Initial monthly payments would be $1,145.41. Assuming annual interval adjustments, one year later the index to which the contract rate is tied requires an interest increase to 15.5 percent. Unless the payments were capped, this would mean new monthly payments of $1,303.27 based on the existing balance of $99,739 with a 29-year remaining term. But if the payments were capped at a maximum of 10 percent increase per year, then the maximum new payment would be $1,259.95 for the second year. Since the interest due during the second year is based on 15.5 percent, the interest required would actually exceed the payment. In the first month of the second year,

$$
\begin{aligned}
\text{Interest due} &= \left(\frac{\text{new interest rate}}{\text{12 months}}\right) \text{(mortgage balance)} \\
&= \left(\frac{15.5\%}{12}\right) (\$99{,}739) \\
&= \$1{,}288.29
\end{aligned}
$$

The payment of $1,259.95 leaves a deficit of $28.34 that would be added onto the balance, with similar additions for each following month during the year, including interest on the increased balance as well.

The previous example is rather extreme in that the interest rate adjustment was a full 2 percent, but it is certainly not impossible. Most interest rate adjustments of 1 or 1½ percent would have been within the limit of the capped mortgage payments. The major advantage to the borrowers under such an arrangement is simply protection from payment increases that may exceed the borrowers' capacity to pay. Limiting maximum payment increases would give even greater protection from erratic payment changes, but also allows for the possibility of an increasing mortgage balance under extreme circumstances.

Price Level Adjusted Mortgages (PLAMs)

Historically, the price level adjusted mortgage, common in Brazil and other South American countries, has required the borrower to enter into a loan that frees the lender from all inflationary consequences involving the interest rate. The mortgage payments are based on a contract rate that does not change over the term of the loan. The mortgage balance, however, does change based on an index traditionally tied to a cost-of-living inflation index such as the consumers price index (CPI). Today, a PLAM could be set up with the balance adjusted by any other acceptable index.

AN EXAMPLE

Assume that a borrower agrees to an 8 percent, 30-year term mortgage in the amount of $50,000 with initial monthly payments of $366.88. After one year, assume that the mortgage balance is adjusted up to 10 percent because the CPI had moved up 10 percent. The balance at the end of one year would be $49,582.50 with zero inflation, but now it will be $49,582.50 (1.10) or $54,540.75 at the start of the second year. The new mortgage payments based on 8 percent with a 29-year term and $54,540.75 will be $403.57. With a PLAM approach, the lender is guaranteed against inflation losses and will earn a real return of approximately the initial contract rate. Therefore, initial contract rates should be very low, in the range of 2 to 4 percent, for PLAM-type mortgages. As of 1982, PLAMs have not been used extensively in the United States. They are only likely to become popular if inflation becomes extremely high and erratic, even more so than that seen in 1980 through 1982.

GRADUATED PAYMENT MORTGAGES (GPMs)

To facilitate borrowers who aspire to homeownership, but cannot afford the current mortgage payments that match their desires, a beneficial variation of mortgage payment patterns is possible. Most GPM plans are designed for younger borrowers with expectations of increasing income. A graduated payment mortgage begins with some base mortgage payment that increases over time, even if interest rates do not change. In some cases, the initial payments may actually be lower than the interest due, thus increasing the mortgage balance owed in the early years by adding on the unpaid interest. GPMs may also be combined with variable rate mortgages and/or variable balance mortgages. Some of these variations are discussed after the common types of GPM plans are explored.

The "Generic" Graduated Payment Mortgage

Any mortgage payment plan with increasing mortgage payments incorporated into the payment pattern is generically, or by definition, a graduated payment mortgage. The variations of most GPM plans are a result of how often and over what intervals payment increases are scheduled as well as the method of handling the unpaid interest. Two general methods of handling unpaid interest are either to add it to the mortgage balance or to supplement the early-year mortgage payments with other funds. The key to all GPMs is that a growth rate is built into the pattern of payments. Often the growth rate period is limited to the early life, say, 5 to 10 years, of the total mortgage term, so that payments do eventually level out.

Early-Year Interest-Only Graduated Payment Mortgage

The simplest variation of a GPM is one in which the borrower pays interest *only* for the first year or two of the mortgage term. This variation keeps the mortgage balance constant (unless combined with a variable interest or balance plan) for the first few years and minimizes the potential size of the mortgage payment without an increasing balance or the use of supplemental funds. Such mortgages may be referred to as "step-up plans" or "interest-only mortgages."

AN EXAMPLE

Assume that an $80,000 mortgage at 10.5 percent for a 30-year term, paid monthly, is set up as a 2-year interest-only loan. The interest due each month for the first 2 years would be

$$\text{Interest payments} = \left(\frac{\text{annual interest rate}}{12 \text{ months}}\right) (\text{mortgage loan})$$

$$\$700.00 = \left(\frac{10.5\%}{12}\right) (\$80{,}000)$$

Each month for 2 years the interest only payment would be $700.00. Then after 2 years, the payments would be based on a 28-year term, $80,000 loan, at 10.5 percent (or some other rate if indexed). Thus, in the third year, the monthly payments would be $739.60. As can be seen, payment of interest only in the early years of a mortgage is only slightly less than total mortgage payments and may not have a significant impact on all borrowers. Therefore, most graduated mortgage plans involve more steeply increasing payment plans.

FHA Graduated Payment Mortgage Plans

As of this writing, there are five major graduated payment plans endorsed by the Federal Housing Administration where FHA insurance is available. The five plans are as follows:

Plan I Five years of increasing payments at 2½ percent each year, then level payments.

Plan II Five years of increasing payments at 5 percent each year, then level payments.

Plan III Five years of increasing payments at 7½ percent each year, then level payments.

Plan IV Ten years of increasing payments at 2 percent each year, then level payments.

Plan V Ten years of increasing payments at 3 percent each year, then level payments.

Each of these mortgage plans allows the early-year mortgage payments to be less than the interest due. Therefore, mortgage balances will actually increase in the early years. As payments increase and overtake the interest due, balances peak out and then start to decline. In each of the plans described, balances tend to peak out at around four to five years for plans I, II, and III and seven or eight years for plans IV and V. To determine the actual mortgage payments with the FHA GPM plans, see Chapter 8 and the tables included later in this book.

The following is an example of how the unpaid interest due is handled. Assume that a borrower arranges a $56,000 FHA GPM loan at 11½ percent interest for a 30-year term and chooses plan I. The first-year payments, including the ½ percent insurance premium, would be $530.95. In the second year, payments would increase to $543.77. In the first month of the first year, the interest owed is

$$\left(\frac{11.5\%}{12}\right) (\$56{,}000) = \$536.67$$

Since the payment is $530.95, there is a deficit in interest unpaid of $5.72, which means that in the second month, the mortgage balance remaining is $56,005.72. The interest due for the second month will be

$$\left(\frac{11.5\%}{12}\right)\ (\$56{,}005.72)\ =\ \$536.72$$

and the interest unpaid will be $536.72 − $530.85 or $5.77, which is added onto the balance in the third month. This process is repeated until in later years the payments become larger than the interest due and the balance begins to decline.

While GPM plans may help to facilitate borrowers to push up the price limits of what they can pay for a home, there is also the burden and risk of an increasing mortgage balance. If the price of the home does not increase as fast as the mortgage balance in the early years, sellers could face the possibility of having less cash equity in their home than when they bought it.

While lenders today can negotiate and design similar GPM plans on a non-FHA-insured basis, most lenders have opted for more conservative arrangements by using supplement account funds to prevent planned mortgage balance increases. Some of these plans are discussed next.

Graduated Mortgage Payment Plans Using Supplemental Account Funds (FLIP), (PAL), (Equalizer), (Action)

There are numerous brand names for the GPM plans that use supplemental account funds to "self-subsidize" mortgage payments in the early years. Some of the common names are PAL for "pledged account loan," FLIP for "flexible loan insurance program," and "Equalizer," and "Action," among others, all of which merely adds to the confusion consumers face today when trying to decipher their alternative mortgage options.

The name FLIP derives from the FLIP Mortgage Company, which is not a lender but a corporation that offers a computer package and program to lenders to calculate the information necessary for such GPM plans.

All these plans have one element in common. They avoid the problem of negative amortization (an increasing mortgage balance) by setting up a separate account of funds that will be used to supplement the borrower's mortgage payments in the early years. With this type of GPM, part of the borrower's down payment goes into an interest-bearing savings account that is pledged to be used to supplement the mortgage payments. This pledged account also serves as additional cash collateral for the lender. Each month during the early years of the mortgage, the lender draws predetermined amounts from the pledged account and adds them to the payments provided directly from the borrower. Together, the total is sufficient to amortize the mortgage as in a level payment plan. Eventually, the pledged account is reduced to zero, and the entire mortgage payment, now at a higher level, is paid directly by the borrower.

AN EXAMPLE

Assume that a borrower can arrange a fixed rate mortgage at 13 percent for a 30-year term. For a $100,000 mortgage, the payments are $1,106.70 monthly. Assume that the borrower has $50,000 of cash that could be put toward a home purchase and that the borrower puts a contract on a home for $143,000. The lender estimates closing costs of $3,000, so the borrower will need $46,000 of cash to close. However, the borrower prefers a lower monthly mortgage payment, at least in the early years, and the lender does not mind bringing the loan-to-value ratio up to 80 percent or so. So a GPM, subsidized by an escrow or pledged account, is set up as follows: $10,000 of the down payment ($46,000) is placed in an escrow account yielding 5½ percent annually to be used to subsidize the monthly payments for three years. Simultaneously, the mortgage loan is brought up to $110,000, requiring new monthly payments of $1,216.82 on a level basis.

Using the $10,000 escrow account for monthly supplements over three years results in $301.96 per month if the account is to be totally depleted over three years. Thus, for three years the borrower's direct cash payments will be $1,216.82 − $301.96 = $914.86, which is $191.34 less than if the escrow account arrangement were not used.

Note that, even though $914.86 is the monthly payment from the borrowers, the borrowers may still deduct the entire interest part of the $1,216.82 since it is their funds being used to supplement the payments. For the first month, for example, the interest portion would be $1,191.67. As a result of the tax deduction of interest, the annual net cash outlay for this type of mortgage is reduced even further.

Note also that while $301.96 was a constant reduction over the three-year term with one major increase in direct payments planned for the fourth year on, the same escrow account could be used up incrementally with larger subsidies in the beginning, say, $400 or so, and smaller subsidies later on, such as $200 or so. In this manner, the direct payment increases may be made more gradually.

Lenders are being attracted to such escrow account arrangements for several reasons. One is that the escrow account provides a relatively cheap source of funds and provides additional collateral. Another is that such mortgages often are attractive to borrowers who may then be willing to pay slightly higher interest rates than for other alternative payment plans.

Obviously, not all borrowers are suited for such mortgages. The escrow account arrangement means that the borrower must have substantial equity and often this means a second or third time home buyer. In addition, the borrowers must generally expect substantial increases in their future incomes.

Growing Equity Mortgages

One other type of graduated payment mortgage being used in the marketplace involves payment increases over time, with the increase in payments going toward principal reduction. This type of mortgage is commonly referred to as a growing equity mortgage (GEM), or rapid payoff loan, or equity building loan.

The effect of this type of loan is to reduce the principal over time with gradual increase in the monthly payments. The increase is set in advance, ranging from 2 to 5 percent per year, for an agreed-upon number of years. By increasing the monthly payment to principal, the loan is paid off in a shorter period of time, in some cases less than one-half of the full-term amortization.

AN EXAMPLE

Assume that you receive a $40,000 growing equity loan at 13.375 percent interest, with a 30-year amortization. Monthly payments to principal and interest will increase by 3.5 percent per year for years 2 through 10. What would the monthly payments be over the life of the loan, and how long would it take to completely pay off this 30-year loan by applying the increase in monthly payments to principal reduction?

The monthly payment in the first year would be calculated as in a traditional fixed rate mortgage. This payment would be $454.23. The payment in the second year would be $454.23(1.035) or $470.13. The monthly payment in each of years 3 through 10 would be found in a similar manner, by simply increasing the previous year's monthly payment by 3.5 percent. The monthly payment would level off at $619.07 in year 10 until the loan is completely paid off.

Since the increase in monthly payment goes to decreasing the principal amount still owed, the loan will be paid off prior to the 30-year maturity. In addition, the portion of the normal monthly payment going to principal reduction will also increase after the first year, since a smaller principal amount remains on which the interest portion of the payment is calculated. Without illustrating the calculations, it is sufficient to state that the loan in this example would be completely paid off in about 14 years, instead of the 30-year amortization originally assumed.

The advantage of this type of mortgage is readily apparent. It is possible to pay off the loan completely in a relatively short period of time, thus saving substantial interest payments in the process. In the example, approximately $100,000 in interest would be saved. The drawback to this arrangement is, of course, that the borrower must have the ability to meet the monthly payments as they increase over time. But if this arrangement can be afforded, it does bear looking into.

MORE COMBINATIONS OF MORTGAGE TYPES, OR WHICH ONE IS BEST FOR YOU?

Now that the basic types of mortgages have been defined, just imagine how confusing all this could get if you worked out all the possible combinations of variable rate, variable balance, and graduated payment mortgages. Certain combinations will appeal to some lenders and some borrowers more than to others.

Variable rate mortgages combined with variable balance provisions enable borrowers to prevent extreme increases in their current mortgage payments and still allow lenders to maintain market-level yields. Similarly, graduated payment mortgages could be indexed and interest rate adjustments made periodically. Thus, the planned pattern of increase in the mortgage payments would be further adjusted by an indexed interest rate change. Such mortgages could also have built in limits or "caps" on the potential size of payment changes with further adjustments made in the mortgage balance.

Why deal with such a confusing number of variations? The borrowers of today and tomorrow will not find as many lenders willing to make long commitments at fixed rates. Interest indexing will be a common feature of many mortgages. The only question may be how often the interest rate may change, not if it will change. At the same time, borrowers cannot change their earnings level as fast as the interest rates may change, and to ensure some stability of mortgage payments, the variable balance feature must be built in. While graduated payment plans are not for everyone, those with expected increases in future incomes, and higher home aspirations than current income allows, will find the GPM plans the only viable choice. Those borrowers without much cash to put down will have to consider negative amortization types, where the mortgage balances increase before they decrease, such as the FHA-GPM. Those borrowers with substantial cash or equity from previous homes may find the pledged account GPM their optimal choice.

The conclusion is that no one mortgage alternative is best for everyone. One must consider current and future income expectations, expectations of current versus future home prices, willingness to accept potential interest rate or payment changes, and also the expected period of homeownership. In addition, once two or three types of mortgages are determined to be acceptable arrangements, borrowers must consider the current interest rate and points on each alternative.

Lenders do not just develop three or four types of mortgages and then set a common interest rate that will be used for all. Mortgages that allow for more frequent interest rate adjustments are less risky for lenders than those with fixed rates for longer intervals. Higher loan-to-value mortgages are riskier than lower loan-to-value mortgages. Additionally, consumer resistance to, or demand for, certain types of mortgage instruments will affect the "pricing" (terms of interest rates and points) on each mortgage type.

As an example of how mortgage "pricing" by lenders could affect your decision, consider a fixed rate mortgage at 14.0 percent versus a 3-year interval renegotiated rate mortgage with an initial interest rate of 13.0 percent, both for 30 years and both with identical closing costs. If you are a very conservative person expecting to stay in the purchased property for a long time, and/or if you expect interest rates to go up substantially, then the fixed rate mortgage would be best for you. If you do not expect interest rates to go up and/or you do not expect to own the property for a very long time then the renegotiated rate mortgage would be best for you.

Consider living in the purchased property for six years. If interest rates went up to 15 percent in three years, and you ended up paying 13 percent for three years and 15 percent for three years, or an average of 14 percent with the RRM, which mortgage would have been better? The RRM may still have been better because the higher 15 percent rate payments were postponed three years when they may be more affordable than 14 percent was in the beginning years. So your expectations of future interest rates and future income cannot be separated from your choice of which mortgage is preferred.

Also note that adjustable rate indexed mortgages need not always be priced so that initial interest rates are lower than for fixed rate mortgages. If interest rates are expected to decline in the future, fixed rate loans would be set lower than the initial rate on adjustable or variable rate mortgages. In this way, the lender is building an expected average return on various mortgage types that may initially differ but average out to be similar in the long run, adjusted slightly for risk differences.

OTHER TYPES OF SPECIALIZED MORTGAGE INSTRUMENTS

Under special circumstances, some specialized types of mortgage instruments might be appropriate, other than those previously discussed. These include the shared appreciation mortgage, reverse annuity mortgage, balloon note mortgage, wraparound mortgage, and buy down mortgage. Each of these with their particular application to real estate finance is discussed next.

Shared Appreciation Mortgages (SAMs)

The shared appreciation mortgage is a significant departure from the lender's traditional role of being interested in only a return of his or her loan along with the required yield. With a SAM arrangement, the lender actually shares in the future appreciation of the property. The percentage of future appreciation is agreed upon when the loan is initially underwritten and is called a "contingent interest." For federally chartered lenders, SAM loans can be set up so that the lender receives as much as 40 percent of the net appreciation on the property at some future point in time, up to 10 years from the time the loan is made. If the borrower sells the property before the agreed-upon time limit, the contingent interest would have to be paid at that time. In exchange for a share of appreciation, the lender reduces the interest rate used in the determination of current mortgage payments. Note that the amortization term can still be 30 years, even though the balance is due in 10 years or at the time of sale, whichever comes first. If the borrower does not wish to sell the home when the contingent interest is due, the expected "net appreciated value" can be determined by a professional appraisal and the contingent interest paid directly to the lender from the borrower at that time.

Net appreciated value of the property is determined by subtracting from the market value (selling price or appraisal) of the property (1) the original cost to the borrower, (2) the cost of any legitimate capital improvements made to the property by the borrower, (3) the cost of any appraisals needed to determine market value, and (4) any direct selling costs such as commissions, cost of title insurance, inspection fees, legal fees, and payments to clear title of prior liens.

There are several obvious problems with SAMs. One is that the lender now has a greater interest in your home and what you do to it, how you modify it, and how you live in it, since these actions typically affect value. The lender will want protection from activities that could negatively affect value. Some problems can be prevented by very clear and extensive legal documents spelling out the rights, interests, and responsibilities of the lender/borrower in a SAM arrangement, but all problems and conflicts cannot be predicted.

From the lender's point of view, the uncertainty of the contingent interest return requires that the total expected return via a SAM arrangement versus other noncontingent interest mortgages must be greater. The higher risk position of the lender requires a higher expected return.

SAM arrangements make a lot of sense for investment or commercial property, but there are severe doubts about their future viability as a method of personal residential financing from the traditional financial institutions.

There are several name variations of SAM plans, one being the *equity participation mortgage* (EPM), another being *shared equity participation* (SEP). If the problem or possibility of a forced sale as a result of the borrower's not being able to come up with the contingent interest (by refinancing or otherwise) can be overcome, then SAM plans may begin to be a viable residential mortgage instrument for some savings and loans or banks.

During 1982, a substantial increase began in the usage of equity participation real estate financing. However, such equity participation has generally been of more interest to investors and investment firms than to traditional lenders. Dubbed the "partnership mortgage" when third-party investors are involved, the plan pairs cash-short home buyers with investors. The third-party investor typically provides the down payment portion of the home purchase price, or a substantial share of the initial equity, in exchange for a substantial chunk of the appreciated value of the property down the road. Real estate brokerage firms such as ERA are getting involved in developing such financing arrangements. Another group in Houston refers to its financing plans as SAVE (Shared Appreciation Venture Equity). Thus, while SAMs have not been of much interest to highly regulated traditional mortgage lenders, a variation on their concept through direct cash "equity" loans has been of interest to venture capital firms and real estate brokerage firms seeking attractive yields and/or increased sales.

Reverse Annuity Mortgages (RAMs)

The reverse annuity mortgage is more of a retirement annuity than it is a traditional mortgage. The RAM allows a homeowner to draw upon the equity in his or her home as a source of income. RAMs have been generally designed to assist elderly homeowners with significant home equities in their retirement plans. There are several variations of RAMs, with two of the more common plans discussed here.

1. "Mortgage" annuity payments are made directly from the lender to the borrower with each payment increasing the balance of the debt owed, along with compounded interest on the balance. This is the purest form of the "reverse annuity" where payments go from the lender to the borrower. The payments are usually made for a fixed term or the life of the borrower, whichever ends first.

AN EXAMPLE

Assuming that the borrower had sufficient home equity value, the lender arranges to pay $434.71 per month for 10 years at a 12 percent interest rate charge built in. At the end of 10 years, the borrower will owe $100,000, which must be paid through refinancing or the sale of the property. The primary risk for the borrower is that he or she may be forced to sell the house, although for elderly borrowers that may be consistent with their financial plans. Current regulations require the lender to renegotiate the loan with the homeowner, should he or she still be alive, at the end of the loan term. If the borrower should die (the last living borrower in the case of a jointly financed RAM), the proceeds of the estate would be used to pay the mortgage balance owed.

2. A fixed debt interest-only loan is paid from the lender to the borrower and is used to purchase a straight-life annuity or straight plus variable life annuity combination. This is similar to borrowing an interest-only mortgage and then using the proceeds to purchase a retirement annuity. Retirement annuities are purchased from life insurance companies. The straight portion of the annuity must be sufficient to cover the interest expense on the mortgage note. The difference above the interest is paid on a net basis to the borrower. Such annuities can be purchased on a fixed term basis or for life. Fixed term plans have similar risks as the previously discussed plan, where the borrower may be forced to sell the property or refinance if he or she has sufficient income to qualify.

To avoid the possibility of a forced sale, many borrowers, as well as lenders, will desire a term life insurance policy in the event of death of the borrower. The insurance proceeds would be used to pay off the mortgage balance with the lender established as a beneficiary.

Balloon Notes

Balloon notes are loans that are designed for temporary or interim financing, usually before permanent financing is used. Payments may be interest only or based on a very long amortization term where most of the payment is interest and a small part is principal repayment. However, the balance is due or "callable" before the full amortization term. The balance owed is paid in one large "balloon" payment. Terms of balloon notes are usually short, from one to five years. Refinancing, permanent financing, or the sale of the property are typical methods of deriving the balloon payment.

Developers have historically been users of balloon notes. The interest rate is usually close to other short-term rates, such as prime rate plus 1 or 2 percent, if the money is used for construction purposes. A commitment on permanent financings, called a "take-out" commitment, is often a prerequisite before lenders will make balloon notes. Developers sometimes refer to intermediate-term balloon notes of, say, 5 to 10 years as "bullets."

Balloon notes may also be second mortgages, such as the financing provided "temporarily" by a seller at the time the property is sold. This type of arrangement is discussed further in Chapter 6.

Wraparound Mortgages

In some cases, it may not be desirable to pay off an existing mortgage, as when there are high prepayment penalties or "low" interest rates on an existing mortgage. However, new funds may be desired by the borrower for a variety of reasons. At current prices, an assumable existing mortgage may require more cash than a purchaser has. Additional financing may be necessary to consummate a purchase. An existing owner may wish to raise new funds but not wish to pay off an existing "low"-rate mortgage. If the value of the property is sufficient and the credit of the borrower is satisfactory, a "wraparound" mortgage could be set up.

A wraparound mortgage, sometimes called a "blended" mortgage, is a second mortgage with a note that includes the first mortgage balance. The note encompasses, or "wraps around," the existing mortgage, keeping the first mortgage intact but arranging for payments sufficient to amortize the first mortgage and the new funds (second mortgage). The lender will then "service" the wraparound by passing the appropriate payments through to the first mortgage lender. In this way, the new lender has better control over its lien position.

AN EXAMPLE

Assume that you had purchased a house 10 years ago for $35,000, taking out a $30,000, 8 percent, 30-year FRM at the time. The monthly payments to service this loan are $220.13. The house has increased in value over the 10-year period so that it is now worth $65,000, with the mortgage balance remaining on the first mortgage being $26,317.41.

You have found a buyer for the house at $65,000, but with interest rates currently at 17 percent, and with only $5,000 available for a down payment, the buyer cannot qualify for a new first mortgage. To facilitate closing the sale, you as the seller provide a wraparound loan of $60,000, keeping the original first mortgage intact, actually providing only $60,000 minus $26,317.41, or $33,682.59, in new funds. You are willing to charge the buyer only 12 percent interest, with a 20-year term, which is substantially below the market rate of interest.

The buyer's payments on the $60,000, 20-year, 12 percent wraparound loan are $660.65 per month, which is $194.76 per month less than the payments on a $60,000, 17 percent, 30-year first mortgage would be. The buyer benefits by the wraparound arrangement and is now able to afford the house. But how do you as the seller fare in this transaction?

You would collect the $660.65 monthly payment from the buyer, but would have to pass $220.13 of that on to the existing first mortgage holder. That leaves a monthly payment of $660.65 minus $220.13, or $440.52 as debt service on the $33,682.59 actually lent by you to the buyer. Calculating the yield on the $440.52 payment over the 20-year term results in an annual interest rate earned by you, the seller, of almost 15 percent. The interest rate earned is greater than the contract rate of 12 percent because you are earning 12 percent on the new funds, as well as 4 percent on the existing funds due to the difference in the 12 percent contract rate and the 8 percent first mortgage rate.

Wraparound mortgage required yields are similar to second mortgage rates because the second lien position of the lender requires greater returns than on a first mortgage position of lower risk. However, many lenders may not be willing to make a straight second mortgage loan where the borrowers pay separately to the first and second mortgage lenders. Thus, a wraparound mortgage may be the only method by which a borrower is able to arrange additional financing. The question may not be one of cost but merely one of getting the loan.

Buy Down Mortgage Arrangements

Beginning in late 1981, "buy down" mortgage arrangements became a common variation on the "high" rate of interest on fixed rate mortgages. Buy down arrangements are another name for the paying of points to increase a lender's effective yield. The buy down points may be paid by the seller, builder-seller, or buyer. Typical point payments may run from 1 to 4 points for a competitive-yielding mortgage. When several points are paid, the lender may decrease the mortgage contract rate of interest and still achieve the desired yield. Thus, when more than the typical number of points are paid, the interest rate is reduced or "bought down."

In 1981, when mortgage interest rates hit 17 percent and higher, and sellers were having trouble selling their homes, one alternative to lowering their prices was to use part of the sale proceeds to pay part or all of the points for the buyer. In this way, the buyer trades off a home price for lower current payments. Thus, the seller or buyer may "buy down" mortgage rates. When the seller uses a buy down arrangement, the cost of the buy down is usually passed through to, and indirectly paid by, the buyer through a higher selling price. Mortgage payments will be reduced by the effect of the lower interest rate, but increased by the effect of the higher price. As long as the net effect is to reduce payments, especially in the early years, the deal may be attractive to some purchasers.

Buyers may also decide to buy down mortgage rates using cash otherwise planned for the down payment. Again, as long as the effect of the lower interest rates is greater than the effect of the larger mortgage, the current size of the payments will be reduced.

AN EXAMPLE

A buyer facing 17 percent mortgage rates has $75,000 cash that may be put toward the purchase of a $150,000 home. Assume that 2 points and 17 percent interest for a 30-year term are current competitive terms. If the buyer puts $50,000 down and paid 2 points, or $2,000 for a $100,000 mortgage, the monthly payments at 17 percent would be $1,425.67.

The lender desires an effective yield of at least 17.40 percent, which it expects to receive with 2 points and 17 percent interest on a 30-year term, with an average mortgage life of 9 years. That is, the lender expects the mortgages loaned out will on average be paid off in 9 years because of borrowers selling their homes and moving. The APR, annual percentage rate, in this case would be 17.358 percent based on a borrower paying the mortgage off over the full 30-year term. But, if the borrower pays off the loan early, as expected, the lender's yield will exceed 17.358 percent.

The borrower could, as discussed, buy the rate down. If the borrower were willing to pay 23 points (21 more than with the first alternative), the lender would charge 13 percent on the full mortgage loan, lowering the payments to $1,106.20, a reduction of $319.47 per month. However, the cost of the mortgage payment reduction is $21,000 (21 percent of

$100,000). The $21,000 obviously could be invested elsewhere if it were not used to buy down the mortgage. One must also consider that the interest portion of the mortgage payments is deductible for tax purposes. Therefore, if a before-tax interest rate is lowered from 17 percent to 13 percent, the after-tax savings may only be 4 percent times the marginal tax rate of the borrower. For someone in the 50 percent tax bracket, the savings after taxes is only 2 percent. The principal advantage of a borrower paid buy down is simply the more comfortable position of lower fixed monthly payment commitments.

Seller-paid buy downs may be more attractive because the money used by the seller to pay the buy down comes from the purchase price and thus may be financed, and the cost spread out, over the mortgage term. Seller buy downs, which can be expected to proliferate in the coming years, typically reduce the interest rate for only one to five years. An example of a seller-paid buy down is given in the next chapter. Builders, as sellers, frequently arrange for precommitted below-market rate loans. These are also buy downs and the costs are passed on to buyers in the form of higher selling prices. This will also be discussed further in the next chapter.

WHEN TO REFINANCE?

Many disgruntled home buyers in the last few years accepted what they felt were unusually high mortgage rates with the expectation that such rates were only temporary. Only time will tell for sure how temporary such rates

TABLE 5-1. Monthly Mortgage Payments for Each $10,000 of Loan

	ORIGINAL TERM OF MORTGAGE		
Interest Rate	30 Years	20 Years	10 Years
10%	$ 87.80	$ 96.50	$132.20
11	95.20	103.20	137.80
12	102.90	110.10	143.50
13	110.60	117.20	149.30
14	118.50	124.40	155.30
15	130.50	131.70	161.30
16	134.50	139.10	167.50
17	142.60	146.70	173.80

TABLE 5-2. Mortgage Balance Remaining for an Original $10,000 Loan with a 30-Year Original Term

	AGE OF LOAN	
Interest Rate	10 Years	20 Years
10%	$9,093.80	$6,640.70
11	9,226.30	6,913.40
12	9,341.80	7,169.50
13	9,442.00	7,408.70
14	9,528.40	7,631.20
15	9,602.50	7,837.40
16	9,665.80	8,027.80
17	9,719.60	8,203.10

were. But one thing is certain: if new mortgage rates are lower than are those on existing mortgages, it may be desirable to refinance. The only real protection lenders have from refinancing away their existing mortgage loans is a substantial prepayment penalty. Even if prepayment penalties are large, refinancing may be attractive if the interest rate decrease is sufficiently large.

There are two major costs of refinancing: prepayment penalties on the old loan and closing costs and points required for the new loan. All these costs together can be referred to as the "transaction costs" of refinancing. The question then is how much must rates decline to make it worth paying off the old mortgage for a new one?

Tables 5-1 of mortgage payments and 5-2 of mortgage balance remaining have been set up to illustrate the following problem. Tables provided in Chapter 8 may be used for many other combinations of problems.

AN EXAMPLE

Assume that a buyer originally borrows $100,000 at 17 percent for 30 years. The monthly payments will be $142.60 for each $10,000 of loan, or 10 × $142.60 = $1,426.00 monthly. After 10 years, the balance owed will be $97,196.00 (from Table 5-2, 10 × $9,719.60). If the rates fell to 16 percent, the borrower could refinance for 20 years and lower the monthly payments to $1,352.00. If the rates fell instead to 15 percent, the mortgage could be refinanced for 20 years and the monthly payments lowered to $1,280.07 and so on for lower rates. But how far down do rates have to fall before it is worth refinancing? That depends on what the refinancing costs are. Assume that total refinancing costs (new closing costs, points, and any prepayment penalties) are 3 percent of the mortgage balance.

The cost of refinancing would then be .03 × $97,196.00 or $2,915.88. The benefits of refinancing are lower payments by $74.00 per month if rates drop 1 percent and $145.93 per month if rates drop 2 percent. The $2,915.88 could be part of the refinancing and the mortgage balance increased by that amount or paid in cash. Assume the latter in this case. Then the decision is whether the lower mortgage payments are worth the cost. To solve the problem, we need to know the current opportunity cost of the borrower, that is, what alternative investment opportunities exist, and then discount the decrease in mortgage payments to find a present value at that rate. In this case, assume that the opportunity cost is the same as the new mortgage rate.

Discounting $74 per month for 20 years at 16 percent results in a $5,318.94 present value, which exceeds the cost of refinancing. In fact, a total cost of up to 5 points could be paid and it would still be worth refinancing in this case. If rates came down 2 percent or more, the case for refinancing is even stronger. If the term of the loan were extended, that would further lower the new mortgage payments.

To derive the present value of $5,318.94 requires a present value of annuity factor.[3] The present value of annuity factor for 16 percent, 20 years is 71.8775.[4] Then 71.8775 × $74 equals the present value of $5,318.94, which is used to make the refinancing decision.

It is difficult to come up with general rules, but the decision to refinance will often be worthwhile if there is a sufficient number of years left to pay, say, 15 or more, and interest rates are reduced at least one full percentage point.

---

[3]Present value of annuity factors can be found in Paul R. Goebel and Norman G. Miller, *Handbook of Mortgage Mathematics and Financial Tables* (Englewood Cliffs, N.J.: Prentice-Hall, 1981).

[4]Ibid., p. 93.

chapter 6

Seller-Assisted Financing

According to the National Association of Realtors, over half the existing property sales during 1981 involved the seller in the financing process of the buyer. There are several ways in which sellers become involved in the financing process, and many of these are reviewed in this chapter; however, most of the seller involvement in financing is a result of one single objective, *to sell the property!* Many sellers, at first, resist even the notion of participating in the financing of their property. But when the need to sell is strong enough, or when the sellers-as-buyers are also able to arrange seller participatory financing, many relent. This is not to imply that seller financing is bad. It is just something that the American public had not been used to prior to the 1980s.

Seller financing is often referred to as "creative financing," as if it were unusual. But seller financing is not unusual today, and there are advantages and disadvantages for those considering it.

In the most common form of seller financing, the seller lends the buyer part of the purchase price, typically at below market interest rates for a short period of time, such as two to four years. The buyer may arrange a first mortgage and the seller financing will constitute a second mortgage, or if the first mortgage is assumable, then it will be taken over by the buyer. In many cases, the existing mortgage is not assumable so the seller keeps making payments and retains liability as he or she collects the total mortgage payments from the buyer. These situations are all discussed in depth later in this chapter.

The major problem with seller-financed sales in the late 1970s and early 1980s is that many were set up in *anticipation of lower interest rates.* Everyone thought "as soon as rates come down, I'll refinance," but of course if you bought in the late 1970s at rates of from 10 to 13 percent and waited for rates to come down, the wait may have been longer than allowed in the seller-financed contract. The result was, and may still be for many in the future, that buyers simply could not qualify for, nor afford, the higher interest rate payments required upon refinancing. When sellers will not extend the term of their "temporary" financing, the result is often foreclosure. The major pitfall of seller financing then is banking on an optimistic economic future, which may or may not occur.

YOU NAME THE PRICE AND I'LL NAME THE TERMS, OR YOU NAME THE TERMS AND I'LL NAME THE PRICE

The impact of changes in mortgage interest rates on the value of income properties has always been apparent, but in recent years dramatic home price fluctuations have also become common as a result of changing interest rates. In many cities, nominal home prices have actually come down in the early 1980s as a result of high interest rates.

In today's home market, where the same property might sell in 15 different ways at several different interest rates, one cannot consider price alone in determining how well the buyer and seller come out in the deal. There are obviously trade-offs involved. To the extent that sellers are willing to finance at below-market rates, they will possibly sell at above-market prices. There are also tax consequences of the trade-offs between interest rates and price in the seller-financed deal. Interest income is taxable at ordinary income tax rates, whereas appreciation profits contained in price are taxed at capital gains tax rates. From the seller's viewpoint, it is best to choose the lowest acceptable interest rate for a given size mortgage payment and achieve the highest possible price. Note that the "lowest acceptable interest rate" is constrained by the Internal Revenue Service, currently at 9 percent, and if rates below that are used, an imputed interest rate of 10 percent (or whatever the current minimum is) will be assumed. From the buyer's viewpoint, maximizing the interest rate, a tax-deductible item, and minimizing price are usually preferable. Thus, the price and terms of all seller-financed deals are ultimately a result of negotiation: "You name the price and I'll name the terms, or you name the terms and I'll name the price."

TABLE 6-1. Mortgage Loan Value with Mortgage Payments Held Constant at $1,250

30-YEAR TERM ASSUMED		
Interest Rate	Mortgage Loan Supported[1]	Maximum Purchase Price[2]
8%	$170,300	$195,300
9	155,279	170,279
10	142,369	167,369
11	131,303	156,303
12	121,477	146,477
13	113,020	138,020
14	105,485	130,485
15	98,892	123,892
16	92,937	117,937
17	87,658	112,658
18	82,946	107,946

[1]Rounded to nearest dollar, determined by dividing $1,250 by a "mortgage constant" (see Chapter 3 and Chapter 8 discussion).

[2]Sum of mortgage loan supported and $25,000 available down payment.

The Buyer's Viewpoint

If a buyer has a certain amount of cash that he or she is willing to put toward a house and a certain level of income, the various "values" that the buyer can afford can be determined. As an example, assume that a buyer has $25,000 for a down payment plus enough cash to cover closing costs and a monthly income of $5,000 of which the buyer is willing to use $1,250 to support mortgage payments. At various interest rates, it can be determined what the $1,250 will support in terms of mortgage loans, as shown in Table 6-1.

From a review of Table 6-1, the potential effects of interest rates on "affordable" prices are obvious. As interest rates decline, home prices are bid up, negating much of the benefits of the lower interest rates. If interest rates dropped from 16 to 14 percent, a buyer could "afford" to pay $12,548, or 10.6 percent, more for an identical home using the assumed income from the previous example.

One cannot look at the size of mortgage payments as the only determinant of price. The mortgage balance must also be reckoned with at the time of sale. Therefore, if a buyer expected to sell a home in less than the full term of the mortgage, he or she should consider that the mortgage balance must be paid out of the future price at which the property is expected to sell. Consider a buyer who pays $167,369, while market interest rates are at 18 percent, based on the maximum affordable price in Table 6-1 with the seller taking back a 30-year first mortgage at 10 percent. If the buyer then wishes to sell the property five years later or if the buyer is required to refinance based on the original purchase contract, the buyer will still owe $137,491. Assuming that the property is worth only $160,000 at the time of sale with current interest rates at 16 percent, the buyer will net $22,509, *less* selling costs, which at 6 percent brings the net amount down to $14,259, or a loss of almost $11,000 from the original investment, not to mention the inflationary loss. If the buyer had financed the property instead at 18 percent and had paid $107,946, the mortgage balance in five years would have been $82,380 and the buyer would walk away from a sale at $160,000 with over $68,000, even after the 6 percent selling cost. Hence, it is important to consider the effect of financing at lower rates on the mortgage payment size but not by ignoring the greater mortgage balance, which must eventually be repaid.

The conclusions are that (1) the shorter the period of expected homeownership in the prospective home, the *more* important are mortgage balance considerations (a lower mortgage balance) and the *less* valuable are financing concessions (lower interest rates) from the seller (the same is true for refinancing agreements, where the buyer should maximize the minimum term before refinancing is required); (2) the buyer should try and purchase the property as close to the market value given current interest rate financing as possible; and (3) the higher the income tax rate bracket, the less costly the higher interest rates and the more valuable the price concessions. So contrary to popular opinion, it may be to your benefit to purchase the home at a high interest rate, but at a *lower* relative price, if your expected holding period is relatively short.

The Seller's Viewpoint

Not all sellers can consider providing financing for part of the purchase of their property. They must be able to forgo a substantial portion of equity for some length of time. But it may be a way of selling their property during a tight mortgage market or achieving a slightly higher price during periods of high interest rates. The basic problem for sellers is that they face the same risks as any other lender. There is always the possibility of the borrower defaulting on the mortgage payments, and *foreclosure* may or may not recoup all their money.

In general, the seller will be better off negotiating for the lowest interest rate and the highest price that the buyer is willing to accept because of the tax consequences of interest income and capital gains. Also, in general, it will be best for the seller to negotiate the shortest period of time before refinancing is required with the recognition that one may force a foreclosure if market rates are not low enough for the buyer to qualify. For this reason, an alternative to a predetermined time period within which the buyer must refinance is to build in a clause that requires refinancing within a specified number of days (say, 60 or 90 days) of interest rates dropping below a certain point, such as, "This property is to be refinanced within 60 days of prevailing mortgage interest rates dropping to 14.0 percent or below." One might also build in a maximum time limit for refinancing even if rates do not decline.

One final consideration of the seller is the effect of below-market interest rates on *selling costs.* The primary selling cost, brokerage fees, tend to be a substantial percentage of the sales price, in some areas as high as 7 percent. Thus, if below-market financing created a sale price some $20,000 or $30,000 higher than with market rates, the brokerage costs could run *$1,400* or *$2,100* more than with traditional financing. One might argue that the higher price makes it worth paying the 7 percent on the difference. This may be true if the broker is the one who created the terms of the deal. If not, a seller might want to negotiate for a lower commission rate on the "inflated" portion of the selling price based on a discounted mortgage value table or some other agreed-upon formula.

Another consideration in negotiating brokerage costs is that while much of the price is received in the future because of financing, the brokerage costs are based on the full price and are due at the time of the sale. Thus, if a seller consummates a sale at $150,000 and finances $120,000 of the sale, he or she will owe $10,500 based on a 7 percent commission, which is 35 percent of the equity currently being received. For this reason, if a broker is strongly encouraging seller financing, the seller might also attempt to negotiate a postponement of part of the brokerage commission, possibly until the property is refinanced or paid off. This type of arrangement would definitely strengthen the interest of the broker in working out a deal where the actual cash is received as soon as possible, instead of just an I.O.U., and also making sure that the buyer is qualified to handle the financing arranged.

There is a possibility that a seller can finance the sale of his or her home and then "cash out" at a later date. This is discussed next.

THE FANNIE MAE HOME SELLER LOAN PROGRAM

"Fannie Mae" is the term used to refer to the Federal National Mortgage Association, a secondary mortgage market agency that *buys* mortgages from the initial lenders. Under the Fannie Mae home seller loan program, homeowners who finance the sale of their homes by taking back *first* mortgages from buyers will be able to use the services of professional mortgage lenders and *convert the loans to cash.*

Fannie Mae would create a market where such mortgages could be sold, provided that they met certain criteria. In particular, the loans must be made on Fannie Mae standard documents. The property must meet certain appraisal standards. The borrower must meet certain credit and financial condition standards, and the mortgage must be serviced by an approved lender. Such mortgages could be converted to cash by selling them to Fannie Mae, at *current market yields.* That is, if the interest rate is below market, Fannie Mae would purchase the mortgage at a discount from its face value (mortgage balance). The primary advantage for the seller is the conversion of the mortgage to cash. The buyer would be unaffected by the sale of the mortgage.

AN EXAMPLE

A homeowner sells his home at $130,000 and takes back a first mortgage for $100,000 for 30 years at 12.5 percent interest. The homeowner arranges for a lender to service the mortgage for a charge of one-half of 1 percent, resulting in a net yield of 12.0 percent. If Fannie Mae desired at the time a yield of 14.5 percent and assumed a 12-year prepayment, it would be willing to purchase the mortgage at a *discount* of 13.855 percent. Then $100,000 (.13855) = $13,855, and Fannie Mae would pay cash of $100,000 − $13,855 for a net of $86,145.[1]

If the seller "cashed out," he or she would end up receiving the original down payment of $30,000 plus $86,145 for a total of $116,145. Again, we see the effect of financing on value. Note, however, that the seller would also expect to pay a fee to the servicing lender for processing paperwork and "selling" the loan to Fannie Mae.

There is a similar seller-financed plan being instituted by the Mortgage Guarantee Insurance Corporation (MGIC). This plan stems from the fact that most sellers do not know how to underwrite or service a loan, yet some sort of seller financing is being used in a great many sales in today's market. In the MGIC plan, a seller would deal with a local approved lender, who would assist with the underwriting and then service the loan for the seller. The lender would charge a servicing fee and, in some cases, an underwriting fee as well. MGIC would provide mortgage insurance on the loan, also charging a fee, that would cover the seller in the event of default. More information on this program is available from any MGIC-connected lender.

COMBINING SELLER-ASSISTED FINANCING WITH TRADITIONAL FINANCING

There are several ways in which a seller can assist in the financing of his or her property upon sale, other than being the first mortgage lender. A seller could take back a second mortgage as part of the purchase price. Another arrangement without any direct lending involved is the seller buy down discussed briefly in the last chapter. Both these possibilities are discussed next.

Seller-Provided Second Mortgage

There are several financial arrangements that a seller might consider that are all variations of second mortgages. The primary purpose of a seller-provided second mortgage is usually to enable the purchaser to finance a greater total proportion of the purchase price. A secondary purpose may be to reduce early-year payments with below-market interest rates. In either case, the seller will generally have to accept a "subordination clause" in the second mortgage that explicitly states that the mortgage is in the second lien position behind the primary first mortgage lender. The seller will also generally wish to require refinancing or limit the term of the second mortgage to as short a period as possible. There are several financial arrangements that a seller might consider; all are variations of second mortgages.

Three common variations are the balloon note, the level amortization mortgage, and the wraparound mortgage. In the balloon note, the seller usually collects interest only and limits the time in which the note is paid off or refinanced. By keeping the payments at interest only, the seller is minimizing the required payments. The interest rate can also be set below market, down to, say, 9 percent, maximizing the value of the second mortgage. In this way the seller is really postponing part of the purchase price for the buyer and mimimizing current carrying costs. At the end of the loan term, such as three to five years, the principal on the second mortgage is repaid in full, or "ballooned."

In the level amortization mortgage, the seller will usually find it advisable to use a fairly long amortization term for the second mortgage, such

---

[1]Discount table values used for this calculation were taken from Paul R. Goebel and Norman G. Miller, *Handbook for Mortgage Mathematics and Financial Tables* (Englewood Cliffs, N.J.: Prentice-Hall, 1981).

as 10, 15, or even 20 years, but simultaneously require refinancing based on a maximum time limit, or an interest decrease in the market, or a combination of both. The longer the amortization period, the more this arrangement is like a balloon note, since the note is usually paid off before the full term.

In a wraparound mortgage arrangement, the seller collects the payments due on the first and second mortgage and passes through the share due the first mortgage lender, as illustrated in the previous chapter. This approach results in better control of the second mortgage holder's lien position and can be combined with any of the approaches discussed.

Assumable Mortgages

Another variation of seller-assisted financing that may also be combined with a seller-provided second mortgage is to have the new buyer *assume* the existing mortgage on the property. This is extremely common with FHA and VA mortgages as well as some conventional mortgages that do not contain language preventing assumption. The principal benefit of assuming an existing mortgage is the ability to retain below-market interest rate financing. This benefits the buyer by keeping payments lower than if financed at higher current market rates and helps the seller who is able to sell at a higher price than if the mortgage were not assumable. Many mortgages may allow assumption, but at a slightly higher interest rate, and generally lenders charge a fee of one or more points to the new borrower, along with collecting financial and credit information about the new borrower. There is also the possibility that a mortgage may be "assumable" only in the sense that some new person is allowed to make the payments, but the seller retains all the previous liabilities in the event the buyer defaults on the payments. The question of whether a mortgage can be assumed or not is based primarily on the interpretation of clauses known as "due-on-sale" clauses.

Due-on-sale clauses preserve for the lender the right to accelerate a loan, that is, require immediate payment of the mortgage balance, when the borrower sells the property. Similar protection for the lender can be built in with "due-on-lease" clauses that prevent an owner from leasing his or her property without the written consent of the lender or paying off the loan. "Due-on-encumbrance" clauses prevent a second mortgage without lender approval. Such clauses have been in mortgages for years, but only in recent years have lenders tried to strengthen the language of due-on-sale or due-on-lease clauses and tried to force prepayment of old mortgage loans when property is sold, leased, or otherwise used as collateral. Lenders argue that without such clauses they may be forced to accept uncreditworthy purchasers or tenants and be placed in a higher risk position than anticipated with the original borrower.

Many borrowers in recent years have attempted to sell conventionally mortgaged property only to find out about the due-on-sale clause. This clause allows a lender the right to accelerate the loan, in effect requiring the mortgage to be completely paid off when the property sells. Many lenders have suffered and are still bearing losses on old fixed rate mortgages that are exceeded by the lender's cost of funds. Lenders have argued that they did not approve a loan to other than the original borrower and may be forced to accept higher than justified risk for modest or below-market returns. These arguments have been supported by the U.S. Supreme Court, which upheld the right of savings and loan associations to exercise due-on-sale clauses, pre-empting some state laws that had restricted lenders from exercising this right (such as California). Therefore, we should anticipate fewer "assumable" conventional mortgages in the future, and when such mortgages are assumable, it will likely be at market adjusted rates of interest. Sellers should also be wary of passing on an old mortgage to a new purchaser when the seller must retain liability for the old mortgage payments.

Seller-Paid Buy Downs

Buy down arrangements, as introduced in Chapter 5, are methods of lowering mortgage interest costs by paying the lender a fee, similar to points, which maintains their desired yield. Buy down arrangements combined with precommitted financing have long been used by builders. Sellers may also buy down the interest rate for buyers for part or all of the mortgage term. Each of these is discussed in turn.

1. Builder Buy Downs and Commitment Fees

Builders have long arranged financing for major subdivisions of single-family homes or condominiums. The procedure is quite simple. The builder pays a "commitment fee" to the lender in exchange for a minimum commitment of a specified number of dollars in mortgage loans for qualified buyers of properties within the development. Not only do lenders commit the funds, but they usually do it at a guaranteed interest rate. The lower this guaranteed rate and the longer the commitment term, the higher the commitment fee. Typical commitment terms may be six months, one year, or even longer under stable economic conditions. These commitments require the lender to forecast future interest rates. In some cases in the past, lenders have been sorry that they committed so much money at what turned out to be below-market rates, this to the benefit of both buyers and builders. Today, lenders are more conservative on long-term arrangements that force them to predict the future. However, they will allow builders to "buy down" the rates so that the mortgage loans appear to be at below-market rates.

AN EXAMPLE

Assume that the current mortgage rates are 16 percent, with 2 points to close, for 30-year terms for a 3-year interval adjustable rate mortgage. A builder of several homes in the $115,000 to $125,000 price range arranges for precommitted financing of $100,000 on each of several homes in a subdivision at 12 percent for a six-month commitment term. For the lenders to receive their required 16 percent plus 2 points yield they must determine how much in *points* or *commitment fees* to charge the builder. Assuming an average 12-year prepayment term, the lender must charge enough to make up for the difference in the mortgage payments:

$$\text{Mortgage payment at } 16\% - \text{Mortgage payment at } 12\% = \text{Mortgage payment reduction}$$

or

$$\$1{,}345.00 - \$1{,}202.90 = \$142.10$$

Thus, buyers of these homes will be paying $1,202.90 monthly instead of $1,345, a reduction of $142.10. Furthermore, using the 25 percent of income rule of thumb, the builder has reduced the gross income required to be able to buy one of his homes by a significant amount: $142.10 × 12 × 4 = $6,820.80 annually less the effect of the slightly higher price charged by the builder to cover the points or fees. The lender wants to receive a fee equal to the present value of the $142.10 forgone for 12 years at 16 percent. Using a present value of annuity factor[2] of 63.86409 × 142.10 results in a present value of $9,075.09. Thus, the lender will charge the builder approximately 9 points, or $9,000, to commit financing at 12 percent while the market rate is at 16 percent. Further, if the builder wished to pay the normal 2 points charge with 16 percent loans, the lender would commit the loans at 12 percent, no points to close, and charge the builder approximately 11 points or $11,000 for each $100,000 mortgage loan.

---

[2]Ibid.

It should be obvious that the builder cannot arbitrarily pay $11,000 out of his profit or he may soon be out of business. But, if a home that normally would sell for around $115,000 to $120,000 is priced at $125,000 to $130,000, the builder can incorporate these fees into the building cost. While the proces may appear to be a bit high at first, think what the builder can do in the advertisement of these homes: *12 percent financing, NO POINTS* in large headlines above his home ads.

The conclusions are that "there is no free lunch," to use an old cliche, but that does not mean that purchasing into a development with precommitted financing is not worth it. Paying a slightly higher price may be an acceptable trade-off given the fact that *monthly mortgage payments will be lower.* If a purchaser has no plans to move for many years, such below-market-rate loans are even more attractive. Note that it does not matter that the mortgage is adjustable or fixed or any other type of instrument. It will always remain at below-market rates by the same differential as when it was committed, unless provisions to move it toward market rates are built in.

Such precommitted financing arrangements are quite common on condominiums and large-scale home developments today and will continue to be so in the future.

2. Seller Buy Down Examples

Unlike builder buy down arrangements, seller buy downs tend to be arrangements for lower mortgage interest rates during the early part of the mortgage term, such as from one to five years. That is, the seller pays a "buy down" fee (or points) that is sufficient to have the lender reduce the current rate of interest charged the buyer for just the first few years of the loan. The effect is to reduce the early-year mortgage payments for the purchaser, much like a one-step graduated payment mortgage, but then the payments would increase to the higher market rate for the remainder of the loan.

AN EXAMPLE

Using numbers similar to those in the previous builder full-term buy down, assume that the seller accepts a contract where he or she must buy the rate down from 16 percent to 12 percent on a $100,000 mortgage for 3 years of the full 30-year term. The 16 percent mortgage payments would be $1,345, but for the first 3 years, the purchaser would pay $1,202.90 as if it were a 12 percent mortgage; then in the fourth and remaining years on, the monthly payments would be $1,345. The lender is forgoing $142.10 monthly for 3 years. The present value of $142.10 for 36 months at 16 percent (based on a present value of annuity factor of 28.44381) is $4,041.87. thus, the seller would pay approximately 4 points at closing to subsidize the payments for the buyer.

If the buyer and seller agreed on a five-year buy down, where the payments stayed at $1,202.90 for five years, the lender would charge a fee of $5,843, or nearly 6 points, at closing.

Why would the seller be willing to pay buy down fees? The answer is quite simple: it might be the only way in which a particular buyer is able to afford to buy the house, or it might be a method of selling the property quicker or at a higher net price to the seller during an otherwise tight market. Also, such financing charges are an immediate tax deduction for the seller, whereas buyers must prorate such point charges over the term of the mortgage.

Again, there is no free lunch for buyers. If a seller has to pay points to subsidize one buyer, the seller will not be willing arbitrarily to deduct this from what he or she feels the property is worth. Just as with FHA and VA financing, sellers will want to net out the same, whether they or the buyers pay points. Thus, the seller will add part or all of the cost of such points onto the minimum acceptable price. At the same time, such arrangements allow a buyer to finance most of the cost of such points added into price, and the home may be more affordable in terms of the early-year monthly payments than at current market rates.

For those buyers and sellers who understand the financial trade-off of price and terms, buy downs are an excellent consideration to counter temporarily the effects of relatively "high" interest rates. It should be noted that any number of buy down combinations can be created, with either the seller or the buyer paying for the buy down. However, from a tax viewpoint, it is better for the seller to pay the buy down and increase the price of the property. In the previous example, if the seller paid for a five-year buy down from 16 to 12 percent, it would cost the seller, before taxes, $5,843. After taxes, the cost would be less by the seller's tax bracket times the $5,843. If the seller were in the 50 percent tax bracket, the after-tax cost would be $2,921.50. If instead the seller had lowered the price of the home by $5,843, he or she would have saved only capital gains taxes, $1,168.60. The after-tax cost of lowering the price would be $4,674.40, or $1,752.90 more than if the seller held firm on the price and purchased the buy down arrangement. Furthermore, if the seller were going to continue to buy another home of equal or greater price or is 55 years of age or older, the seller would not have incurred any capital gains taxes at all. (This will be discussed further under installment sales.)

Another very popular arrangement is a graduated buy down, where from the previous example, the interest rate might be 12 percent in the first year, 13 percent in the second year, and so on, leveling off at 16 percent in the fifth and subsequent years. An example of this type of arrangement is presented in Chapter 8.

LAND CONTRACTS AND INSTALLMENT SALES

Most of the previous discussions of seller financing have assumed that the seller passes title to the buyer at the time of the sale. When a seller provides mortgage money while passing title, the mortgage is known as a "purchase money mortgage." There may be situations, however, in which it is difficult or not advisable to pass a clear title to the buyer. Seller-financing arrangements in which the seller *keeps the title* until some agreed-upon point in the future, but still provides financing to the buyer, are known as *land contracts*. Today such sales are referred to as "contract sales" or "contracts for deeds."

Holding the title involves a little less risk for the seller in the event of a default. That is not to say that foreclosure is not necessary, but it is certainly much easier to foreclose and the "buyer" can be evicted more quickly from the property. On the other hand, holding the title means that the seller, as "owner" of the property, is still liable for property taxes and assessments on the property and any other liens that are created.

Sometimes contract sales are used as a method of trying to retain a below-market mortgage. The seller may take back a note for the entire mortgage, but keep the first mortgage intact, passing through the necessary portion of the mortgage payments. Again, the sellers must realize that they retain liability if the mortgage payments are not made. Further, the due-on-sale clause may prevent a seller from utilizing such arrangements, and if the lender finds out that a contract sale has occurred, he or she will probably call in the loan. Contract sales may be excellent short-term legal arrangements for seller-financed sales.

Installment sales are regarded as a tax interpretation of the seller's profits when seller financing is involved rather than as a method of finance. The current tax laws are such that you may report a real property sale on the "installment method" automatically, regardless of how much is received in the year of sale or the number of years over which the payments are made. Under the "installment method," the profit on the property is equal to the difference between the purchase price and the selling price less all selling costs and capital improvements (not maintenance and repair, but major additions or remodeling). Then the percentage profit of the total selling price is calculated and is applied to the payments received by the seller in determining taxable income in each year as the payments are received. In addition, the Internal Revenue Service insists on a minimum imputed interest (currently 10 percent) on the balance owed be treated as interest income. The general advantage of the installment sale method is that it allows "profits" to be realized as they are received through the payments rather than all at the time of sale. That is, an installment sale postpones the payment of a tax on the sale of property to a later date.

Installment sales are, of course, not necessary if a seller purchases another personal residence (new or used) of equal or greater value within 24 months of the first sale. Then the seller can defer all taxes on capital gains (profits from the sale). Further, if the seller is 55 years of age or older, there is a once-in-a-lifetime exclusion of $125,000 (currently) of all profits on the sale of a personal residence, with certain restrictions. The $125,000 amount will probably be increased in the coming years.

As a final comment on tax considerations, the laws are so complex that it is advisable to consult with an accountant or tax attorney to find out about the specific tax implications of any unusual real estate transactions.

LEASE WITH PURCHASE OPTIONS

Sometimes, no matter how creative you are, you just cannot work out an acceptable arrangement to both buyer and seller with the title passing to the buyer. Financing a property and passing title has risk for the seller. In the event of default, the seller must foreclose on the buyer, which is a general headache and an expense. However, if the seller does not need the current equity out of the property, leasing may be a viable alternative. At the time the lease is negotiated, an acceptable purchase price is also predetermined and a closing date set when the option must be exercised. For the buyer, this arrangement allows possession and control of the home and more time to find permanent financing. The longer the term of the lease, the higher the seller will want the price to be and the more difficult for the buyer and seller will be the prediction of future market conditions. Leases can be set up for any length of time as short as six months, or less, if desirable. The longer the term of the lease, the larger the nonrefundable "security deposit" and consideration on the purchase contract the seller will need. An advantage of leasing the property for longer periods of time, one year or more, is that the property may be depreciated, by the owner, as with any other investment property. As a final caveat to both buyers and sellers, lease with purchase options, or any other type of longer-term agreement between a buyer and seller, is difficult at best in terms of spelling out precise, clear, nondisputable arrangements between buyer and seller. An attorney should definitely be involved in preparing such agreements.

NEGOTIATING TIPS AND RISK CONSIDERATIONS

The American public is used to paying the sticker or list price on most retail items such as food, clothing, and other frequent purchases. But when it comes to buying a home, we have "the great American bargaining process" in which both buyers and sellers expect to offer, counteroffer, modify, and generally bicker over a number of details. People take pride in "driving a hard bargain." Have you ever met a buyer who did not feel, or at least imply, that he or she "got a real deal" on his or her house? Have you ever met a seller who admitted not receiving at least a "fair price" for his or her home?

After reading this book, you should understand that the financial terms are at least *as important as price* in the negotiation process. In addition, the following are some general bargaining tips.

The Value of a Property Has Nothing to Do with the Asking Price

That is not to say the asking price is not fair, or that true market value may not equal or even exceed asking price, but the value of the property should be determined *independent of the asking price.* This independent analysis should be based on the general market conditions and the selling prices of very similar properties. If such information is not readily available, buyers should consider hiring an appraiser for an opinion of value before determining an offering price.

Once the value of the property is assessed, buyers should not hesitate to use it as a guide in determining initial bids, even if that means bidding way under or very close to the asking price. The fact that a property is listed at $175,000 should not keep you from bidding $135,000 if you feel that it is worth no more than $140,000 or so. It is amazing how many times buyers feel that they "got a deal" based solely on the criteria that the seller made a large price concession. On the other hand, if you feel that a property listed at $135,000 is really worth $140,000 (but perhaps just came on the market) do not hesitate to bid close to or even at $135,000. Paying the asking price does not mean that you are getting ripped off.

From the seller's point of view, sellers should also consider hiring an appraiser or at least demand a thorough, well-documented market analysis from their broker before determining listing price. Once a seller has a good idea of the true current market value for his or her home, there are two general strategies that may be adopted. One is to *price close to true value* to maximize the number of potential purchasers. If a price is too high, some potential buyers (and brokers) may not even bother with it. This strategy will minimize selling time. The other strategy is to *overprice significantly* and plan on accepting a substantial price concession, if necessary. This strategy is aimed at maximizing selling price, possibly at the expense of more time on the market, and is based on the hope that buyers will not analyze asking price, as suggested in this book, but rather will be biased to their bid price based on your listing price. Which strategy is best for you depends on which of your needs is stronger, a quicker sale or a higher price. *In no way can any broker guarantee both these objectives to you,* "highest price and quickest sale," because they are theoretically inconsistent with each other. Only "luck" can bring about both simultaneously, so that is not to say do not go for both, just do not expect both.

Past Price Trends Do Not Matter

Past market trends do not tell you what a property is worth today. That is, just because the market prices in your area have been going up at, say, 20 percent a year for the last five years does not mean they will go up *this* year at the same 20 percent. Only *current market conditions* with special consideration for the current financing costs and terms, and current social-economic trends in the market, are relevant. Similarly, a house that sold six months ago with financing at 3 percent under current market rates does not give an accurate picture of what it would have sold for at current market rates. Comparisons thus should be made with caution by seeking out differences in the conditions that could affect price.

Don't Bicker over Nickels and Dimes

There are two major problems often encountered by brokers as they deal with sellers and buyers, but in a word it is "stubbornness." One of the problem areas is bickering over *what is included in the sale.* The other is often bickering over *price* when the buyer and seller are close, but neither is willing to compromise. The best advice is to be *willing to compromise.* Five hundred dollars on a $125,000 home or a washer and dryer may be insignificant points in relation to the size of the entire transaction and what it means to your future.

With respect to what is included in the sale, any item that is *questionable* should be spelled out clearly to all potential buyers by the seller or his or her broker upon first inspection. This does not mean that you should go through the house pointing out what is *not* included. But it does mean a written statement should be provided to the buyer spelling out which items will stay and which the seller would like to take. This is the only way of avoiding disputes over items that are legally referred to as "fixtures." Fixtures are items that were once personal property but because of their unique adaptation or permanent attachment are now part of the property and legally remain. Such items include attached light fixtures, wall-to-wall carpeting, custom-made window shades, and so forth. Questionable items include television antennas, curtain rods, curtains, fireplace equipment, refrigerators of a certain size built into the cabinets, and oil in the oil heating tanks. If you are not sure what comes with a property, the best thing is to spell it out specifically in the purchase contract. Then if there is disagreement, it will be straightened out before the deal is closed instead of in court after the sale.

With respect to price concessions, do not let a few hundred dollars stop you from buying or selling your home. Paying $500 more on a home that will require an $80,000 mortgage at 12 percent means about $5 more per month, not enough to make you start looking for another home. The same logic applies to sellers: do not lose a potential buyer this month because of an offer a few hundred dollars short. It may require an extra month or two to sell the home if you lose this buyer, and that may mean another thousand dollars in mortgage payments, property taxes, property insurance, and the general headache of always cleaning and showing your home.

Last, for both buyers and sellers, do not make "final offers" unless you really mean it. That is one of the quickest ways of totally breaking down the negotiating process of a reasonable settlement for all parties.

Dealing with Contingencies

Several types of contingencies are included in most offers to buy a home, such as contingencies based on financing, negative termite reports, certain inspections of questionable problems such as plumbing and electrical, and contingencies based on the sale of another property or some other event.

As a general rule, sellers and buyers should try to make the contingencies reasonable. A financing contingency clause that states "this offer contingent upon securing a 90 percent loan-to-value mortgage at no more than 13 percent interest for a 30-year term" may be unreasonable if prevailing rates for 80 percent loan-to-value mortgages are at rates above 13 percent. Such a contingency clause, if accepted by the seller, merely ties up the property and is an easy out for a buyer. From the seller's point of view, financing contingencies should be based on reasonable efforts and prevailing mortgage terms as much as possible.

From the buyer's point of view, financing contingencies should be as specific as possible in setting worst possible conditions for the purchase offer, especially during times of erratic financing. As an example, "this offer is contingent upon financing with 20 percent down or less, at an interest rate not to exceed an annual percentage rate of 15.5 percent." If the prevailing mortgage rates are 14.5 to 15.5 percent with a few points to close, this clause may not be unreasonable. But it does protect the buyer from sudden interest rate increases that may make a home just beyond the affordable region, and it does consider the effect or cost of points as well as the contract rate on the mortgage by stating an upper limit on the APR rather than just the contract rate.

Contingency clauses based on the sale of another home, most likely the one in which the buyer now resides, should be handled by sellers with great caution. From the buyer's point of view, making an offer based on the sale of his or her own home is a great low-risk proposition if accepted. From the seller's point of view, it is only an opportunity to tie up one buyer in a contract. The seller should consider accepting such a contract only if he or she has an out. As an example, the seller can counteroffer, "this offer accepted except that the seller retains the right to continue to market the property, and if a new qualified buyer is found, the first (name of) buyer has the right to close the sale within (10, 15, 30, or so) days or forgo all interest in the property." Such a clause, known as a "right of first refusal," does not force you to depend on the first buyer's property selling and allows you to continue to find new buyers; however, it gives the buyer a first right of refusal to follow through on the contract. Again, from the buyer's perspective, the buyer should try and negotiate as long a delay as possible built into the first right of refusal if another buyer is found.

As a general rule for the seller, the greater the risk position accepted, the larger the deposit on the contract should be. Most contingencies allow for a refund of the entire deposit if contingencies cannot be eliminated. But, if the risk position of the seller is large, such as accepting a contingency clause dependent on the sale of the buyer's house within a time period of, say, six months, then the seller should insist that part or all of the deposit is nonrefundable and is retained by the seller (and/or broker depending on the listing agreement).

Dealing with Closing Dates and Time of Possession

From the seller's point of view, the sooner the closing date the better, because it means getting the money. From the buyer's point of view, the closing date should be as close to the actual time of possession and desired move-in date as possible. If you cannot move in for three months, then it would be ideal to have the closing date in three months. Some sellers may accept lengthy closing dates if there is a large enough and partially nonrefundable deposit, in the event that the buyer does not follow through for some reason, legitimate or not. On the other hand, in some cases the seller may not wish to give up possession because he or she has no place to move to. In such a case, it is still best for the seller to have an early closing date but to postpone the time of possession until sometime after the closing. Usually, time of possession is within a day or so of the closing, but there is no reason why it cannot be longer if both parties agree. A seller might try and postpone it 10 or 20 days or so as part of the deal. If a buyer refuses, an alternative is to offer to rent it for the time of possession after closing with a maximum time built in. Such rental can be prepaid and deducted at the closing so all financial transactions are recorded and completed at the closing. Reasonable rental rates should relate to the actual cost of owning the home for the new buyer such as mortgage payments, property taxes, and property insurance prorated for the period of rental. Sometimes because of tax considerations (tax savings to the buyer from interest payments and property tax deductions), a reasonable rental figure can be arrived at which may be slightly less than actual before-tax cash costs.

When in Doubt, Use an Attorney

Obviously there are many considerations in negotiating and purchasing or selling the largest single investment in most persons' lifetimes. The best advice for buyer or seller is that when there are doubts or situations that are atypical and unclear, get some expert advice. Expert advice generally comes from engaging an attorney who specializes in real estate law and/or contracts. "Experienced" friends who are on their third or fourth home should not be relied upon nor should most real estate brokers when the deal is especially complex. In fact, in most situations, brokers will be the first to recommend an attorney.

chapter 7

Closing the Sale

Prior to closing the house sale, the buyer and seller would have completed an agreement on the purchase price and terms, as specified in a sales contract. This contract legally binds the buyer and seller to all the specified terms and conditions of the written document. A well-written contract thus provides the maximum protection for both against problems arising before and after the closing.

Once a purchase or sale contract is completed, the normal process involves the buyer applying for financing and arranging property insurance to become effective by the date of the closing. The seller, and/or the seller's broker, works to eliminate any contingencies placed in the contract by the buyer, such as those requiring inspections or specific actions (e.g., repairs). Upon *loan commitment* for financing and the elimination of all other contingencies, the closing can occur. It is advisable that a buyer shop around for financing, by phone at first, at several different lending institutions. It is not unusual today to see a number of different financing alternatives with a range of over 1 percent in the interest rate lenders charge on mortgages. However, each lender will charge a loan *application fee* to cover the evaluation process, and this is not refundable in the event that the buyer decides to accept another loan commitment. Typical loan commitments are for 60 days, but they can be longer or shorter depending on current economic conditions as well as on the policies of the financial institution. Some lenders will extend the term of the commitment for an additional commitment fee.

The closing process generally involves the actual transfer of title from the seller to the buyer. In some cases, only possession and control are given from the seller to the buyer and the title is passed at a later date (e.g., land contract sales). This chapter reviews the closing process, using the Moyer family case begun in Chapters 1 and 4.

THE CLOSING PROCESS

The closing process is a complicated procedure in which the buyer signs numerous papers and documents filled with fine print. One of these documents is a deed from the seller to the buyer that actually passes title. Most of the other documents establish the relationship of the buyer with the lending institution and reveal the true costs behind the loan. The entire process is generally orchestrated and directed by a *closing officer*, sometimes known as a *settlement agent*. The closing officer may be an employee of the lending institution, an attorney who works for the lending institution, or a title company agent if title insurance is being purchased. In rare cases a real estate broker will conduct the closing. Parties typically present at the closing are the buyer, seller, their respective sales agents and attorneys, if involved, and a closing officer or settlement agent.

The settlement agent typically handles both the title and the loan closing. It is the settlement agent's responsibility to make sure that all required documents have been correctly prepared and are properly executed and recorded. The settlement agent also calculates the cost, fees, and prorations connected with the real estate transaction for both the buyer and the seller. This is done through a *settlement* or *closing* statement, an example of which is included in the Moyer closing case later in this chapter. The settlement statement summarizes all the fees and expenses that must be paid by both the buyer and seller. In that respect, both the buyer and seller pay or receive all funds due at the closing to complete the transaction, in a single check.

The final phase of the closing process is to sign and transfer all documents. This basically involves the seller transferring title to the buyer, and the buyer signing a promissory note guaranteeing repayment of the loan to the lender and pledging the purchased property as collateral to be sold in the event of default on the loan. The settlement agent or closing officer then has the necessary documents legally recorded, and the final settlement statement, title, and mortgages, or copies thereof, are sent to the appropriate parties.

LENDER GOOD FAITH ESTIMATES

When a loan application is submitted, the lender must provide, under the terms of the Real Estate Settlement Procedures Act (RESPA), a good faith estimate of what settlement service charges will likely be incurred. This estimate is based upon the lender's experience in the local market and may be stated as either a dollar amount or a range for each charge. While lenders are not required to provide a good faith estimate of reserve deposits for property tax and hazard insurance premiums, they typically can give the borrower a good idea of what these costs will be as well. From the good faith estimates the lender provides, the borrower can get a very close approximation of the amount needed for closing. In addition, the borrower would be able to use the good faith estimates to compare total costs and loan packages between lenders. RESPA also requires the lender to provide the borrower a booklet discussing settlement costs at the time of the loan application.

It should be emphasized that the lender only provides an estimate of what closing costs will be. If fees change or if the date of settlement changes, thus changing the escrow and prorations, then the estimates may not reflect the actual costs charged. But the lender, again required under RESPA, must provide the actual itemized fees and charges one business day before the settlement. This still allows the borrower time before the settlement to clarify any charges or conceivably change lenders if it is felt that the actual charges are unreasonable or are calculated erroneously.

CLOSING COSTS

A number of costs must be paid at closing, including commissions, loan fees, prepaid items, and reserve deposits. This section discusses most of the major costs. Keep in mind that in some instances, who pays what costs is negotiable between the buyer and the seller, whereas in other instances, such as government-backed loans, the responsibility for closing costs is dictated by the agency involved. The division of the negotiable closing costs should be clearly specified in the sales contract. There are several major types of closing costs. Each of these is discussed in turn; however, note that when talking to a lending institution, lenders often lump most of the major closing costs together in giving verbal estimates and quote these in terms of dollars and "points," a percentage of the mortgage loan. As an example, a lender might say, "closing costs run four and one-half points plus $500.00," where the $500.00 is actually a loan origination fee and two and a half of the four and one-half points are discount points, and the remainder is for items connected with processing the loan.

Loan Origination Fees and Discount Points

A loan origination fee is virtually always charged by the lender in connection with the loan. The origination fee is usually paid by the borrower and theoretically goes toward covering the lender's overhead costs. While this fee will vary among lenders and localities, it is usually expressed as a percentage of the loan and typically amounts to no more than 1 percent of the loan amount.

Discount points are another fee usually charged by the lender in connection with the loan. One discount point is equal to 1 percent of the loan amount. The effect of charging points is to raise the yield to the lender. The lender receives the points at closing, thus reducing the amount actually lent while the lender is paid back the full contract loan amount. Who pays the points is negotiable, although under an FHA or a VA loan, the borrower is prohibited from paying any loan discount, thus forcing the seller to make this settlement. While the intention of this restriction is admirable, sellers often raise their selling prices to compensate, at least in part, for this often large fee. This shifting of the points to the buyer is not necessarily bad, however, in that the buyer is still able to finance most of the costs of these points. The primary benefit to the buyer, then, is the lower down payment possible with FHA and VA financing. Another benefit is that, in the past, FHA/VA loans have been assumable, and to the extent such mortgages are at below-market rates, sellers are able to receive a higher price for their homes upon sale.

Both origination fees and "points" must be included along with the contract rate in the lender's calculation of the annual percentage rate (APR), which is the true cost of money to the buyer, assuming full-term repayment.

If the buyer does not originate a new loan but instead assumes the payments on the loan held by the seller, then an assumption fee rather than an origination fee is charged. The assumption fee is typically less than an origination fee, which often makes it advantageous to assume an existing loan even if the interest rate on the existing loan escalates to a market rate of interest. As in the origination fee, usually the buyer is charged the assumption fee.

Items Related to Processing the Loan

In making the decision to accept or reject the loan applicant, the lender must analyze the borrower's ability to repay and the value of the collateral behind the loan. To analyze the borrower's ability to pay, the lender requires documentation on the borrower's income, assets, liabilities, and a credit report. Information on each of these is collected with various letters and verification forms. A credit report is obtained from a credit bureau from the region where you either currently or formerly reside, or from both. This report includes information on your income and some personal data. Under the Fair Credit Reporting Act, you are not entitled to inspect or receive an exact copy of the report, although you are entitled to a summary of the report. If your loan application has been denied because of your credit report, you have a right to inspect the summary free of charge. If the report is inaccurate, it can be challenged and corrected. The credit report fee, which again varies by location and agency, is usually paid by the borrower. Knowing what the lender needs to complete the investigation of the borrower can be helpful. The borrower can speed up the entire review process by assembling accurate information, account numbers from loans, bank documents, and so forth and accurate addresses of references and employers and providing this to the loan officer in charge of collecting this information at the time of the loan application.

The property appraisal fee, which can vary substantially from transaction to transaction, covers the statement of property value for the lender. The appraisal is ordered by the lender and can be done by an independent fee appraiser, an in-house appraiser of the lender, or an appraiser of a government agency backing the loan. The appraiser inspects the property and neighborhood and provides the lender with an estimate of the most probable selling price. The appraisal fee may be paid by either the buyer or seller, but the buyer usually is responsible for this fee. If either the buyer or seller had an appraisal done for their own use in negotiating the sales contract, then they typically would pay that fee external to the closing. As many as three appraisals may be done on a property, one for the buyer, the seller, and the lender.

The lender often requires a property survey to determine the exact location of the house and lot lines. This is done to ensure that there are no encroachments, boundary disputes, or legal code violations that might cloud the title. Since this survey is for the buyer's protection, the buyer typically pays for the survey.

Lenders, or the government agencies backing the loan, also often require a pest inspection. This inspection determines whether there is termite or other pest infestation of the house. In many states pest inspections are mandatory (e.g., in Georgia). The pest inspection fee is again negotiable between the borrower and seller, with responsibility for payment usually dictated by local custom.

Other fees payable in connection with the loan are new construction inspection fees, private mortgage insurance application fees, and occasionally document preparation or loan amortization schedule fees. These again are often negotiable between the buyer and seller and vary between lenders and localities.

Charges Associated with the Title

Title charges refer to any expense related to transferring the property deed. Title closings and practices vary widely from area to area, and your particular settlement may or may not include the charges discussed here. Your settlement agent is able to tell you exactly what procedure is followed in your locale, which in turn allows an accurate estimate of charges involved.

Of utmost concern to the lender is the quality of the title; that is, is it good against defects? To ascertain the quality of title, lenders rely on a title search. A title searcher researches the public records of the county clerk for any defects in the title of the seller. The title searcher also checks the civil court for liens filed by repairmen who may have worked on the property but not been paid, called "mechanics' liens." Additionally, the tax assessor's office will be checked to see if there are any unpaid property tax liens.

An abstract of title is a compilation of all legal, publicly recorded documents pertinent to the subject property ownership. Any person can compile an abstract, although this is typically done by attorneys, abstractors, or title company employees. Having an abstract of title performed does not necessarily protect the borrower or lender from title problems that might arise after the sale.

As a result, lenders in some areas of the country require a legal interpretation of the abstract. This amounts to nothing more than an abstract with a statement from an attorney attached, called a certificate of opinion or abstract opinion, which provides a legal interpretation of the validity of the title. Yet this still does not offer the maximum protection to the borrower and the lender in case a defect arises.

Thus, many lenders require title insurance to be provided at the closing. Title insurance protects the lender against loss if a defect in title surfaces after the house is purchased. This insurance is usually furnished by a title insurance company or by attorneys providing bar-related title insurance as part of their services in furnishing the certificate of title opinion. When a lender requires a title insurance policy, it is provided by the seller and in effect gives evidence that the seller's title is good. But it is important to note that the lender's policy only protects the lender in event of a problem arising after the sale. The borrower may also want to get an owner's title policy for self-protection. If an owner's policy is purchased at the same time the lender's policy is purchased, it is typically available at a relatively low cost.

In some states, title insurance rates are fixed and thus will not vary among insurers. In other states, rates are negotiable, which means it may be advantageous to compare rates, services, and coverage offered by different insurers. It is also possible in some states to get a lower "reissue rate" if you are buying a house that was recently transferred and you simply have the previous owner's title policy updated. This reissue rate also applies to a property survey, where it might be possible to have a recent property survey updated at a lower cost rather than undertake a new survey.

The fees for the abstract, certificate of opinion, or title insurance vary by location and by what the lender requires. In those areas where a lender only requires an abstract of title to verify that the title is good, the borrower should still consider title insurance to protect against the possibility of past defects surfacing. Examples of such defects would be unpaid tax, mechanics' or mortgage liens, leases, easements, and so on that would limit the use or enjoyment of the property.

Other fees connected with the title transfer are a settlement fee, paid to the settlement agent for handling the closing; document preparation fees for such things as preparation of the mortgage, deeds, and notes; and notary fees for having a licensed person authenticate the execution of the documents by the involved parties. Occasionally, an attorney's fee is also charged for title services, although this is usually included in the cost of the title abstract or title insurance.

Generally, there are transfer fees charged by the county (or city) in connection with the actual transferring and public recording of the deeds, both from the seller to the buyer and of the mortgage or security deed, as well as the recording of any other legal document connected with the transaction. Payment of such fees is negotiable between the buyer and seller, although the buyer usually pays for the recording fees of the mortgage and deed. The recording fees are minimal, usually under $10.00 in most areas. Typical transfer fees run one-tenth of 1 percent of the purchase price (e.g., a transfer fee of $150 would be required on the purchase of a $150,000 home).

The old system of transfer fees was to use transfer stamps that a person would buy and "post" on the actual deed. Some buyers would overpurchase stamps to mislead those who reviewed the public records for appraisal research. Today, the stamp posting practice has all but been eliminated; however, a buyer is still allowed to pay excessive transfer fees, if they desire, in some areas.

Items Required by the Lender to Be Paid in Advance

The lender may require certain items to be paid in advance of the closing. These items are called *prepaids* and include such things as interest, hazard insurance premiums, and mortgage insurance premiums.

As will be discussed further in Chapter 8, a mortgage payment is based on an *ordinary annuity,* which requires payments to be made at the end of the month. This means that when you make your September 1 mortgage payment, for example, you are actually paying for August. When your loan closes, the first payment is typically due between one and two months later. Since that first payment covers the previous month's charges, there are often several days between the closing and the period the first payment covers that are unpaid. To collect the interest on these days, the lender charges prepaid interest on a daily rate, based on the amount borrowed and the contract interest rate, at the closing.

AN EXAMPLE

Your settlement takes place on June 19, and your first regular monthly payment is due on August 1 to cover the month of July. At the settlement, the lender will collect prepaid interest for the period from June 19 to July 1. If you borrowed $60,000 at 15 percent, the prepaid interest would be $60,000 (.15/360) = $25 per day × 12 = $300.00.

Lenders require borrowers to keep their property insured against fire, vandalism, natural hazards, and so on, to maintain the value of the collateral. This coverage typically takes the form of a homeowner's policy. Lenders require evidence of this coverage at the closing, typically by having the borrower provide the first year's hazard insurance premium. The borrower is free to obtain this insurance from an agent or company independently. RESPA prohibits lenders from requiring borrowers to purchase hazard insurance from companies with which they are affiliated or from which they receive referral kickbacks.

When a prospective buyer applies for a high loan-to-value conventional loan, the lender may require private mortgage insurance to be secured by the borrower. This helps to protect the lender from loss in the event of default and foreclosure on the mortgage. The lender often requires the first mortgage insurance premium to be paid on the day of settlement. Since this insurance reduces the lender's risk, the borrower is able to get approved on a larger loan than otherwise, thus justifying the mortgage insurance expense.

Since 1978 private mortgage insurance has been issued on a greater volume of mortgages than both the FHA and VA combined. A big factor in this growth has been that private mortgage insurers can process an application in a day or two, compared with weeks or sometimes even months for FHA processing. Private mortgage insurance, unlike FHA insurance, is coinsurance with the insurer assuming the top portion of the risk, typically 20 to 25 percent of the loan balance, and the lender assuming the remainder.

In the early 1970s, one firm, the Mortgage Guarantee Insurance Company (MGIC), dominated the private mortgage insurance market. Today a number of companies offer different types of coverage and differing rates. The following is a list of some of the major private mortgage insurance companies:

1. American Mortgage Insurance Company
2. Continental Mortgage Insurance Company
3. Foremost Guaranty Insurance Corporation
4. Home Guaranty Insurance Corporation
5. Investors Mortgage Insurance Company
6. Liberty Mortgage Insurance Corporation
7. Mortgage Guarantee Insurance Corporation
8. PMI Mortgage Insurance Company
9. Republic Mortgage Insurance Corporation
10. Secura Insurance Company
11. Ticor Mortgage Insurance Company
12. Tiger Investors Mortgage Insurance Company
13. United Guaranty Corporation.

In comparing private mortgage insurance rates for a 20 percent coverage policy on an 86 to 90 percent loan-to-value mortgage, one of the companies listed quoted 1 percent of the original mortgage at closing and .25 percent on the balance thereafter. Another insurer quoted .5 percent of the original mortgage at closing and .25 percent on the balance thereafter. The conclusion that borrowers should encourage competitive private mortgage insurance selection with their lenders is obvious.

Reserves Deposited with the Lender

A reserve account, also referred to as an escrow or impound account, is established by the lender to set aside funds for future payment of such items as hazard insurance and real estate taxes. As explained in Chapter 5 under the budget mortgage, lenders typically require a prorated portion of the annual taxes and insurance to be included by the borrower in the monthly payment. These reserve accounts typically require an initial amount to be paid at closing to establish the account, although RESPA places limitations on the amount of funds that may be required by a lender.

In addition to the first year's hazard insurance premium at the settlement, lenders typically require a portion of the second year's premium to be paid at closing, such as 2 month's worth. The effect of requiring the additional hazard insurance premium to open the escrow account is to have the borrower pay 14 months of hazard insurance at closing.

The lender also typically requires a portion of city and county taxes to be paid into a reserve account at closing. Since the seller has incurred a responsibility for the taxes during the year up to the settlement date, the seller will be assessed his or her portion at closing as a credit to the buyer. In a budget mortgage, the first payment that the borrower makes usually will not cover all the taxes the buyer will owe at the end of the current year. As a result, the lender requires part of the future tax liability to be paid at closing and held in an escrow account, so that at the end of the year, sufficient funds exist in the reserve account to pay the property taxes owed.

Occasionally, the lender will require part of the annual mortgage insurance premium placed into escrow for later payment. Also, annual assessments for such things as homeowner association dues or special improvements may be required by lenders to be prorated and part of the annual amount due placed into an escrow account. These items, however, are negotiable between the borrower and the lender.

Brokerage Commissions

The salesperson's or broker's commission is typically paid at the closing and is indicated on the settlement statement. This commission is negotiated between the broker and the seller and varies from region to region. Although buyers may have their own real estate agents, such agents are typically compensated by receiving a cooperative split or portion of the seller's brokerage commission.

CLOSING THE MOYER EXAMPLE

Good Faith Estimate

To illustrate a settlement, including all the typical costs and forms involved, we conclude the Moyers' example from Chapters 1 and 4 by following them through their closing. Prior to the closing, the lender is required under RESPA to provide the Moyers with a good faith estimate of closing costs they will incur. This has been done by The Lubbock National Bank in Exhibit 7-1.

As can be seen, the lender specifies the general information concerning the loan at the top of the form, such as the loan type and amount applied for, anticipated loan terms, and address of property. Part A of the form lists the estimated closing costs anticipated. These total $925.00, which is listed on the form and also transferred to the application for home loan guaranty, which is presented as Exhibit 4-2. This estimate is thus incorporated in the lender's loan accept/reject decision as it applies to the borrower's ability to be able to afford the purchase.

The estimated prepaid items are listed in part B of the form. Notice that the lender is requiring the first year's hazard insurance to be paid in advance, as well as the first 2 months of the second year's hazard insurance to be paid at closing, to be put into an escrow account. The lender is also requiring 2½ months of property taxes to be paid at closing, which will cover the borrower's tax liability up to the first mortgage payment. The amount of prepaid interest, which is 21 days' worth, is required to compensate the lender for the use of its money from the estimated day of closing until the first payment interest coverage is received. The total of the estimated prepaids is $1,323.65, which is also listed on the form and Exhibit 4-2.

Part C of Exhibit 7-1 specifies the down payment required from the borrower. In the Moyers' case, this amount is $1,500.00, which is the difference between the sales price of $59,500.00 and the requested loan amount of $58,000.00. This down payment includes the earnest money of $750.00, which the Moyers have already paid. The total estimated move in cost for the Moyers then is the sum of the closing costs, prepaid items, and the downpayment, which amounts to $3,748.65. After subtracting the $750 earnest money already paid, this leaves $2,998.65 estimated to be paid by the Moyers at closing. This amount is also reflected on the application for home loan guaranty in Exhibit 4-2.

The monthly payment section of the estimated settlement charges form indicates that the lender is requiring a budget mortgage. This means

EXHIBIT 7-1. Closing Costs Estimate

THE LUBBOCK NATIONAL BANK
REAL ESTATE DIVISION
762-8800

ADDRESS 3725 51st Street INTEREST RATE 16.5% SALES PRICE $59,500

TYPE LOAN VA TERM 30 years LOAN AMOUNT $58,000

(A) CLOSING COSTS

	Item		Amount	Line
1.	Loan Origination Fee	1.	$580.00	(801)
2.	Appraisal Fee	2.	85.00	(803)
3.	Credit Report	3.	50.00	(804)
4.	Lender's Inspection Fee	4.	-	(805)
5.	Loan Submission Fee	5.	-	(809)
6.	Loan Commitment Fee	6.	-	(808)
7.	Photographs	7.	-	(810)
8.	Amortization Schedule	8.	-	(811)
9.	Document Preparation	9.	-	(1105)
10.	Attorney's Fee	10.	75.00	(1107)
11.	Mortgagee's Title Policy	11.	-	(1108)
12.	Tax Certificates	12.	-	(1204)
13.	Recording Fees	13.	15.00	(1201)
14.	Survey	14.	85.00	(1301)
15.	Pest Inspection	15.	-	(1302)
16.	Mortgagor's title policy	16.	35.00	(1303)
17.		17.		(1304)
		TOTAL (A)	$925.00	

(B) PREPAID ITEMS

	Item		Amount	Line
1.	Hazard Insurance 14 months @ $42.50 per month	1.	$595.00	(901)
2.	PMI Initial Premium - % of loan amount	2.	-	(902)
3.	Tax Proration 2.5 months @ $68.16 per month	3.	170.40	(1001)
4.	MIP or PMI Deposit - months @ - per month	4.	-	(1002)
5.	Prepaid Interest 21 days @ $26.58 per day	5.	558.25	(1003)
6.		6.		(1006)
7.		7.		(1007)
		TOTAL (B)	$1,323.65	

TOTAL SETTLEMENT CHARGES (A&B) $2,248.65

(C) DOWN PAYMENT TOTAL (C) $1,500.00

TOTAL MOVE-IN COST (Total of items A,B,&C) $3,748.65

MONTHLY PAYMENT

16.5% for 30 years

Principal & Interest	$803.39
Taxes	68.16
Hazard Insurance	42.50
FHA (MIP) or Private Mortgage Insurance	
TOTAL	$914.05

These figures are estimates only and may not cover all items you will be required to pay at closing. You may wish to check with your title company prior to closing.

I hereby acknowledge that at time of loan application, I have received (1) A GOOD FAITH ESTIMATE OF SETTLEMENT CHARGE and (2) A copy of the Special Information Booklet that has been prepared by the Department of Housing and Urban Development.

Date Jan 29, 1983 Applicant [signature]
[signature]

ML-FL 56 (REV. 8-79)

EXHIBIT 7-1. (Cont.)

NOTICE TO APPLICANTS

This is notice to you as required by the Right to Financial Privacy Act of 1978 that (the Veterans Administration or Department of Housing and Urban Development, whichever is appropriate) has a right of access to financial records held by financial institutions in connection with the consideration or administration of assistance to you. Financial records involving your transactions will be available to (VA or HUD) without further notice or authorization but will not be disclosed or released to another Government agency or Department without your consent except as required or permitted by law.

Date: ____________________ Borrower: ____

Borrower: ____

COMMITMENT TO BORROWER

Subject to approval of this Application, the undersigned commits to loan to you the amount of your application under the terms and conditions set out herein, this commitment being in effect for a period of sixty (60) days from date. Should the FHA/VA rate of interest change, by acceptance hereof, you agree to close the loan at the highest prevailing FHA/VA rate of interest, and should the undersigned determine, in its sole opinion, that the loan would be illegal, then it may withdraw this commitment.

Upon filing of this Application, the undersigned is setting aside the funds for your possible use.

Date: ____________________ Borrower: ____

Borrower: ____

EXHIBIT 7-2. HUD Settlement Statement

A. U.S. DEPARTMENT OF HOUSING AND URBAN DEVELOPMENT
SETTLEMENT STATEMENT

Form Approved OMB No. 63—R1501

B. TYPE OF LOAN:
1. ☐ FHA 2. ☐ FMHA 3. ☐ CONV. UNINS.
4. ☒ VA 5. ☐ CONV. INS.
6. FILE NUMBER
7. LOAN NUMBER LNB 20382
8. MORTGAGE INS. CASE NO.

C. NOTE: This form is furnished to give you a statement of actual settlement costs. Amounts paid to and by the settlement agent are shown. Items marked "(p.o.c.)" were paid outside the closing; they are shown here for informational purposes and are not included in the totals.

D. BORROWER NAME AND ADDRESS	Floyd A. Moyer ET UX Elizabeth R. Moyer 3202 Avenue Q, Lubbock, Texas
E. SELLER NAME AND ADDRESS	Joseph P. Seller ET UX Thelma Q. Seller 3725 51st Street, Lubbock, Texas
F. LENDER NAME AND ADDRESS	Lubbock National Bank 916 Main, Lubbock, Texas
G. PROPERTY LOCATION	Lot 279, Block 14 of Midway Gardens Addition to the City of Lubbock, Lubbock County, Texas
H. SETTLEMENT AGENT PLACE OF SETTLEMENT	West Lubbock Title Company Lubbock, Texas
I. DATE OF SETTLEMENT: March 11, 1983	DATE OF LOAN COMMITMENT: March 10, 1983

J. SUMMARY OF BORROWER'S TRANSACTION		K. SUMMARY OF SELLER'S TRANSACTION	
100. GROSS AMOUNT DUE FROM BORROWER:		400. GROSS AMOUNT DUE TO SELLER:	
101. Contract sales price	$59,500.00	401. Contract sales price	$59,500.00
102. Personal property	-0-	402. Personal property	-0-
103. Settlement charges to borrower (line 1400)	2,419.05	403.	
104.		404.	
105.		405.	
Adjustments for items paid by seller in advance		Adjustments for items paid by seller in advance	
106. City/town taxes to	-0-	406. City/town taxes to	-0-
107. County taxes to	-0-	407. County taxes to	-0-
108. Assessments to	-0-	408. Assessments to	-0-
109. to		409. to	
110.		410.	
111.		411.	
112.		412.	
120. GROSS AMOUNT DUE FROM BORROWER	61,919.05	420. GROSS AMOUNT DUE TO SELLER	59,500.00
200. AMOUNTS PAID BY OR IN BEHALF OF BORROWER:		500. REDUCTIONS IN AMOUNTS DUE TO SELLER:	
201. Deposits or earnest money	750.00	501. Excess deposits (see instructions)	-0-
202. Principal amount of new loan(s)	58,000.00	502. Settlement charges to seller (line 1400)	7,063.00
203. Existing loan(s) taken subject to	-0-	503. Existing loan(s) taken subject to	-0-
204.		504. Payoff of first mortgage loan	32,873.00
205.		505. Payoff of second mortgage loan	-0-
206.		506.	
207.		507.	
208.		508.	
209.		509.	
Credit to borrower for items unpaid by seller		Credit to borrower for items unpaid by seller	
210. City/town taxes @ 1.64/day to 3/11/83	119.72	510. City/town taxes @ 1.64/day to 3/11/83	119.72
211. County taxes @ .63/day to 3/11/83	45.99	511. County taxes @ .63/day to 3/11/83	45.99
212. Assessments to		512. Assessments to	
213. (credit 73 days)		513. (lose 73 days)	
214.		514.	
215.		515.	
216.		516.	
217.		517.	
218.		518.	
219.		519.	
220. TOTAL PAID BY/FOR BORROWER	58,915.71	520. TOTAL REDUCTION AMOUNT DUE SELLER	40,101.71
300. CASH AT SETTLEMENT FROM/TO BORROWER:		600. CASH AT SETTLEMENT TO/FROM SELLER:	
301. Gross amount due from borrower (line 120)	61,919.05	601. Gross amount due to seller (line 420)	59,500
302. Less amounts paid by/for borrower (line 220)	(58,915.71)	602. Less reductions in amount due seller (line 520)	(40,101.71)
303. CASH (☒ FROM) (☐ TO) BORROWER	$3,003.34	603. CASH (☒ TO) (☐ FROM) SELLER	$19,398.29

that the monthly housing payment that the Moyers will make inc only the principal and interest of $803.39 but also a prorated taxe of $68.16 and hazard insurance of $42.50, for a total pay $914.05.

Settlement Statement

At the time of settlement, the settlement agent will prepare a sett statement outlining the exact costs to be paid by both the buyer a seller. A standardized settlement form used by many lenders is that U.S. Department of Housing and Urban Development. The sett statement for the Moyers is presented in Exhibit 7-2. Sections B thr of this statement provide background information such as type of borrower, seller, lender, property location, settlement agent, and ment location and date.

Section J of the settlement statement is the summary of the rower's transaction. Most of the items listed are self-explanatory. Lin is the settlement charges from line 1400 on page 2 of the settlement ment, which will be explained shortly. Two other items that need panded discussion are lines 210 and 211. These items are the city county taxes owed from January 1, 1983 to March 11, 1983, the da closing. These taxes are owed by the seller, so the Moyers get a credi 73 days of taxes, which amounts to $165.71.

The total amount paid for or by the Moyers amounts to $58,915 which when subtracted from the amount due of $61,919.05 lea $3,003.34 to be paid at closing by the Moyers. It is interesting to comp this actual amount owed with the estimated amount due from the lend good faith estimate. That amount, from Exhibit 4-2, is $2,998.65, or a ference of $4.69. It is not unusual to see the lender's good faith estim relatively close to the actual closing costs required.

Section K of the settlement statement is the summary of the selle transaction. These items are again self-explanatory, with the possible e ception of items 502, 504, 510, and 511. Item 502 is the charge from li 1400 on page 2 of the settlement statement, which will also be explaine shortly. Item 504 is the amount that the seller still owes on the mortgag taken out at the time the seller purchased the property. This amount is ob tained by the settlement agent from the seller's lender to determine how much must be deducted from the purchase price received by the seller to repay the outstanding loan. Items 510 and 511 are the city and county

EXHIBIT 7-2. (Cont.)

PAGE 2 OF
Form Approved OMB No. 63-R1501

L. SETTLEMENT CHARGES	PAID FROM BORROWER'S FUNDS AT SETTLEMENT	PAID FROM SELLER'S FUNDS AT SETTLEMENT
700. Sales/Broker's commission based on price $ 59,500 @ 6.0 %		
Division of Commission (line 700) as follows:		
701. $ 1,785 to Johnny Agent, Johnny Agent and Associates		
702. $ 1,785 to Peter Lister, Johnny Agent and Associates		
703. Commission paid at settlement		$3,570.00
704.		
800. ITEMS PAYABLE IN CONNECTION WITH LOAN		
801. Loan origination fee 1 %	$580.00	
802. Loan discount 5 %		2,900.00
803. Appraisal fee to	85.00	
804. Credit report to	50.00	
805. Lender's inspection fee		
806. Mortgage insurance application fee to		
807. Assumption fee/Refinancing fee		
808. Amortization Schedule		2.00
809.		
810.		
811.		
900. ITEMS REQUIRED BY LENDER TO BE PAID IN ADVANCE		
901. Interest from 3/11/83 to 3/31/83 @ 26.58 /day	558.25	
902. Mortgage insurance premium for mo. to		
903. Hazard insurance premium for 1 yrs. to Lubbock Insurance Corp.	510.00	
904. yrs. to		
905.		
1000. RESERVES DEPOSITS WITH LENDER		
1001. Hazard insurance 2 /mo. @ $42.50 /mo.	85.00	
1002. Mortgage insurance /mo. @ /mo.		
1003. City property taxes 5 /mo. @ $49.26 /mo.	246.30	
1004. County property taxes 5 /mo. @ $18.90 /mo.	94.50	
1005. Annual assessments /mo. @ /mo.		
1006. Flood insurance /mo. @ /mo.		
1007. Sanitary tax /mo. @ /mo.		
1008. /mo. @ /mo.		
1100. TITLE CHARGES		
1101. Settlement or closing fee to		
1102. Abstract or title search to		
1103. Title examination to		
1104. Title insurance binder to		
1105. Document preparation to		
1106. Notary fees to		
1107. Attorney's fees to Herman Hound, Edward Ralph	75.00	75.00
(includes above items numbers; 1105)		
1108. Title insurance to West Lubbock Title Company		
(includes above items numbers; 1101,1102,1103,1104)		
1109. Lender's coverage $ 58,000		438.00
1110. Owner's coverage $ 59,500	35.00	
1111. Escrow fee		30.00
1112.		
1113.		
1200. GOVERNMENT RECORDING AND TRANSFER CHARGES		
1201. Recording fees: Deed $ 6.00 Mortgage $ 9.00 Releases $5.00	15.00	5.00
1202. City/County tax/stamps: Deed $ Mortgage $		
1203. State tax/stamps: Deed $ Mortgage $		
1204. Tax certificates		8.00
1205.		
1300. ADDITIONAL SETTLEMENT CHARGES		
1301. Survey to Plains Surveyors, Inc., Lubbock, Texas	85.00	
1302. Pest inspection to Bomb Em Bug Service, Lubbock, Texas		35.00
1303.		
1304.		
1305.		
1400. TOTAL SETTLEMENT CHARGES (enter on lines 103, Section J and 502, Section K)	$2,419.05	$7,063.00

SELLER'S AND/OR PURCHASER'S STATEMENT

Seller's and Purchaser's signature hereon acknowledges his/their approval of tax prorations, and signifies their understanding that prorations were based on figures for preceding year, or estimates for current year, and in event of any change for current year, all necessary adjustments must be made between Seller and Purchaser direct; likewise any DEFICIT in delinquent taxes will be reimbursed to Title Company by the Seller.

We approve the foregoing settlement statement, in its entirety, authorize payments in accordance therewith and acknowledge receipt of a copy thereof.

Signature ______________________ ______________________

Seller Purchaser

____

Escrow Officer

taxes for which the seller is responsible and that are deducted from the sales proceeds. After paying off the existing loan, the settlement charges, and the property tax liability, the net amount to the seller from the sale is $19,398.29, as specified on line 603.

Page 2 of the settlement statement contains section L, which itemizes the settlement charges paid by both the buyer and the seller. The first part of this section details the breakdown of the commission to be paid. The commission in the Moyers' case, negotiated to be 6 percent of the selling price, is split between the selling and listing agents and is paid entirely by the seller.

The loan fees are a 1 percent origination fee paid by the Moyers, 5 discount points paid by the seller, an appraisal and credit report fee paid by the Moyers, and a loan amortization schedule, which in this transaction is paid by the seller. The prepaid items for which the Moyers are responsible are, as previously discussed, interest to cover the amount owed to the lender from the closing date to the first payment and the first year's hazard insurance premium of $510.00.

Since this is a budget mortgage, the Moyers are required by the lender to pay at closing the first 2 months of the second year's hazard insurance premium. This amounts to $85.00 and is deposited by the lender into an escrow account. The lender is also requiring the first 5 months of city and county property taxes to be paid at closing into the escrow account. But since the Moyers get a credit for 73 days of taxes owed by the seller, the net effect is that the Moyers only pay for about 2½ months at the closing.

In this transaction the lender is requiring that title insurance be furnished. This policy, costing $438.00 and paid for by the seller, assures the lender that title is good, and if problems arise, the lender is protected. The title insurance policy fee covers the closing fee, title search, and title examination; thus, no charges are incurred for these items. Since the Moyers are not protected under the lender's policy, they have purchased coverage of their own in the form of a mortgagor's policy, which cost them $35.00. Both the Moyers and the seller had their own lawyers examine all documents pertaining to the transaction, so each is responsible for that cost.

The other settlement charges in this transaction are deed, mortgage, and release recording fees, split by the seller and the Moyers. A survey is required by the lender, which is paid by the Moyers. A pest inspection is also required, which is paid for out of the seller's proceeds. The settlement charges for the buyer and seller are totaled on line 1400 and are transferred to lines 103 and 502, respectively.

Disclosure Statement

The last form required in this case is the loan cost disclosure statement. Lenders must furnish this information to borrowers as required by Federal Reserve Regulation Z. The loan cost disclosure statement for the Moyers is presented in Exhibit 7-3. Most of the information on this form has been detailed in the previous exhibits. One exception is the annual percentage rate. The APR is calculated to be 17.77 percent, which incorporates the contract interest rate of 16.50 percent, the prepaid finance charges, and the discount points. As discussed in Chapter 3, the APR is the rate of interest the lender actually earns on the loan, assuming no prepayment. Although the lender contracts to lend $58,000 and will be paid back that amount by the Moyers, less money is actually lent since points and fees are required to be paid by the buyer and seller to the lender at closing.

One final item of interest on the loan cost disclosure statement con-concerns late payments by the Moyers. The lender, as noted in item 11 of Exhibit 7-3, requires a late charge in the amount of 4 percent of the monthly installment if not received within 15 days after the installment is due. While the borrower is technically in default for being late with an installment payment, most lenders will accept a late payment, charging a penalty.

After explaining the settlement to all parties involved, the settlement agent then has all the appropriate documents signed, collects the money due from the Moyers, and arranges payment to the seller. The Moyers legally take possession of the subject property after the closing and have their deed, settlement papers, and all other pertinent documents mailed to them after they are recorded.

CLOSING STATEMENT SUMMARY

Upon the actual transfer of title from seller to buyer, adjustments, deductions, and credits related to the transfer are shown on a closing statement or statement of settlement. The adjustments relate to the cash balances required by the buyer or due to the seller.

Generally, from the total purchase price received, the seller must deduct (1) the remaining mortgage balance, if any, plus a fee for cancellation; (2) the total brokerage commission(s); (3) transfer fees, generally at one-tenth of 1 percent of the purchase price; (4) prorated property taxes to date of closing and miscellaneous items that may appear (such as termite

EXHIBIT 7-3. Loan Cost Disclosure Statement

LUBBOCK NATIONAL BANK
916 MAIN
LUBBOCK, TEXAS 79408

LOAN COST DISCLOSURE STATEMENT
as required by Federal Reserve Regulation "Z"
Real Property Transaction Secured By First Lien on a Dwelling

Date March 11, 1983

1. The **AMOUNT OF THE LOAN** in this transaction is $ 58,000

2. The **FINANCE CHARGE** on this transaction will begin to accrue on March 11, 1983

3. The **ANNUAL PERCENTAGE RATE** on this transaction is 17.77 %. The interest component of the Finance Charge will be computed at the annual contractual rate of 16.50 % on the outstanding balance of the loan from time to time.

4. The **PREPAID FINANCE CHARGE** includes:

Loan Origination Fee	$ 580.00
Assumption Fee	$ -
Interest From Date of Settlement Until Amortized Interest Begins	$ 558.25
Initial Mortgage/F.H.A. Insurance Premium	$ -
	$
	$
	$

4a. Total **PREPAID FINANCE CHARGE** $1,138.25

5. The **AMOUNT FINANCED** in this transaction (Subtract 4a from Amount of Loan) $56,861.75

6. Itemized Charges Excludable from **FINANCE CHARGE**:

	6a. Paid By Cash	6b. Paid From Loan Proceeds
Title Examination/Insurance	$35.00	$
Appraisal Fee	$85.00	$
Credit Report Fee	$50.00	$
Survey	$85.00	$
Initial Hazard Insurance Premium	$510.00	$
Insurance Reserve/Escrow	$85.00	$
Tax Reserve/Escrow	$136.32	$
Recording Fees	$15.00	$
Attorney Fee	$75.00	$
	$	$
	$	$

Total Itemized Charges **Paid From Loan Proceeds (6b)** and included in the **Amount Financed** $ 0

7. **NET PROCEEDS** (Subtract Total 6b from Line 5) $56,861.75

COMPLETE THIS SECTION IF MORTGAGE GUARANTY INSURANCE PREMIUMS ARE INVOLVED -OR- IF THIS IS OTHER THAN A PURCHASE TRANSACTION

8. The **FINANCE CHARGE** on this transaction totals $________ This amount includes:

Total Prepaid Finance Charge (from 4a)	$
Total Interest to be Earned over life of Loan	$
Private or F.H.A. Mortgage Insurance collected after the outset of the transaction	$
	$

TOTAL OF PAYMENTS on this transaction **(Amount Financed (5) plus total FINANCE CHARGE (8)** will be) .. $________

9. Payments of principal and Finance Charge exclusive of mortgage insurance premiums on this transaction shall number 360 with the first payment due on the 1st day of May, 1983 , ________ and all subsequent payments due on the 1st day of every month thereafter. Such payments shall be in the amount of $ 803.39

COMPLETE THIS SECTION ONLY WHEN MORTGAGE GUARANTY INSURANCE PREMIUMS ARE INVOLVED

In addition, the first ________ payments will include additional amounts for mortgage insurance premiums. These additional amounts will range from $________ in the first payment due ________, ________ to $________ in the payment due ________, which is the last payment on which mortgage insurance premiums are due. Thereafter, all monthly payments, if any, will be $________

10. This institution's security interest in this transaction is a FIRST LIEN on property located at 3725 51st Street, Lubbock, Texas also specifically described in the documents furnished for this loan. The documents executed in connection with this transaction stand as security for future advances, the terms for which are discribed in the documents. Such documents also cover the following after-acquired property, if any.

11. Late payment formula: Borrower shall pay to the Note holder a late charge of four percent of any monthly installment not received by the Note holder within fifteen days after the installment is due.

12. Prepayment formula:
XX FHA-VA PREPAYMENT PENALTY; NONE.
☐ CONVENTIONAL PREPAYMENT PENALTY; NONE.

13. Miscellaneous disclosures:

14. **PROPERTY INSURANCE:** Hazard insurance, if written in connection with this loan, may be obtained by borrower through any person of his choice, provided, however, the creditor reserves the right to refuse, for reasonable cause, to accept an insurer offered by the borrower.

I hereby acknowledge receipt of the disclosures made in this notice.

LUBBOCK NATIONAL BANK
Lender

Authorized Signature — Date 1/29/83

Borrower — Date 1/29/83
Borrower — Date 1/29/83

LNB 23

inspection); (5) legal fees and preparation of deed; (6) "points" if the financing is VA or FHA; (7) rental income proration if the property is an investment type; and (8) miscellaneous items. Whatever is left after making these deductions is the net amount due to the seller. Note that some closing costs items are negotiable between the buyer and seller, depending on the purchase contract. Also, some items may be billed directly to the seller or buyer, such as a termite inspection or legal fees, and they will never appear on a closing statement.

Typically to the purchase price the buyer must add (1) closing "points" on the mortgage, if conventional; (2) mortgage and deed recording fees, which vary with the length of the instruments, but typically are nominal for both; (3) interest on the mortgage from the closing date to the end of the month so as to begin regular, level amortization payments on the first of the following month; (4) legal fees, abstract opinion, or title insurance, unless paid by seller or billed direct; (5) transfer fees, unless paid by the seller; and (6) other prepaid items. Deductions from the cash required by the buyer are (1) the new mortgage, (2) the same tax proration that was deducted from what the seller would receive, and (3) miscellaneous items such as rental income credit.

The financial institution lending the new mortgage handles all the payments that are due as shown on the closing statement. Thus, the buyer and seller need to only write or receive a single check.

A final note concerning this example is that all costs shown are used for illustrative purposes only. While these costs are realistic, procedures and costs will vary substantially among lenders and areas. You can get a good idea of the procedures and approximate costs in your area by contacting a local broker or lender.

chapter 8

How to Use Financial Tables

This chapter presents and discusses financial tables. Included are (1) the methodology of calculating a mortgage payment for a traditional fixed rate mortgage, fully amortized with level payments over the contract term; (2) calculation of the mortgage balance remaining; (3) calculation of the annual percentage rate; and (4) calculation of a graduated payment mortgage under the FHA plans. The methodology of using these types of tables is covered in depth, and comprehensive tables covering the typical terms in today's financial climate are presented.

FIXED RATE MORTGAGE

As discussed in Chapter 5, the FRM has historically been the predominant form of mortgage instrument. And while it is currently being replaced by adjustable and renegotiable rate mortgages, most "creative" mortgages still share the features and calculation procedures of the FRM in the initial years. So regardless of whether the loan you are contemplating is an FRM or any of the more creative types, the methodology presented here will still apply in helping you to calculate a mortgage payment. Only the FRM, however, will have the same payment over the life of the loan. Since indications are that the FRM will regain its popularity if and when interest rates become more stable, it is important to understand this payment structure.

How Do I Calculate a Monthly Payment?

Most mortgages are amortized, or paid off, on a monthly basis. This payment takes the form of an "ordinary annuity," which simply means that the payments are made at the end of the month. So when you make your August 1 payment, for example, you are actually paying for the month of July. The method used to calculate a payment for any given interest rate, loan amount, and term to maturity is quite simple, being a mathematical relationship that solves for the "annuity" to the lender to provide a return "on" the investment equal to the interest rate, as well as a return "of" the loaned capital over the life of the loan.[1]

Several methods can be used to find the mortgage payment for a given set of loan terms. Probably the easiest is to call a lender or broker in your local market and ask for the current mortgage types, terms, and payments. While this is recommended to find the current conditions, most lenders do not enjoy being bothered by "what ifs" (e.g., finding the mortgage payments if interest rates changed, or if the term were changed, or if the mortgage amount were increased or decreased). So calling a local lender will probably give you the general information you need to start with. It may not help you determine the optimal terms and payments for your particular situation, both because the lender may not know your unique circumstances and because all lenders do not deal in all the alternative mortgage instruments available today.

Once you have determined the typical mortgage terms, one method that could be used to find a mortgage payment is with a hand-held calculator. There are several calculators on the market that will perform this task very quickly. In most of these calculators, the known variables—monthly interest rate, monthly term to maturity, and the mortgage amount—are entered, and the unknown variable—the monthly payment—is calculated. While these calculators are very convenient, they range greatly in price, generally require a knowledge of several methodologies, and are usually only justified if they are used on a regular basis.

---

[1]For a mathematical explanation of this relationship, see Paul R. Goebel and Norman G. Miller, *Handbook of Mortgage Mathematics and Financial Tables* (Englewood Cliffs, N.J.: Prentice-Hall, 1981).

A third method of finding a monthly mortgage payment is to use a table that contains all the necessary calculations. Mortgage payment tables are available from lenders, finance companies, and so on and are widely used in the industry. Since this method is very easy to use, a number of tables for various interest rates, loan amounts, and term to maturities have been developed and are included in this book. In the next few pages, you will learn how to use these tables in a number of different ways to help you find a payment, or how much mortgage you can afford, for any given set of mortgage terms.

1. Fixed Rate Mortgage Payments

Finding an FRM payment is the easiest, and most common, example since once the initial payment is found, it remains the same for the life of the loan.

AN EXAMPLE

Assume that you are buying a home for $50,000 and have found a lender who will make an 80 percent loan-to-value mortgage at 15 percent, with a 30-year term to maturity. To find the payment, you first need to know the loan amount. That is, simply, $50,000(.80) = $40,000. Now to find the monthly payment to amortize that loan, you would look in the 15 percent table under the $40,000 row and 30-year column. From the 15 Percent Monthly Payment Table, which follows this chapter, the monthly payment is $505.78. This means that you would pay $505.78 at the end of every month for the next 30 years, or 360 months, to pay back completely the $40,000 you borrowed as well as to provide the lender with a 15 percent return on its investment.

Let us assume that the lender decided that you were a very good risk and agreed to lend you 85 percent of the value of the property instead of only 80 percent. Now what would the payment be? First, calculate the loan amount as before, which is $50,000(.85) = $42,500. To find the payment, go again to the 15 Percent Monthly Payment Table, but notice that there is no $42,500 row. You can still use the table, but now you must add the $40,000, $2,000, and the $500 payments together to get your total monthly payment. The solution is

$40,000 monthly payment	=	$505.78
$2,000 monthly payment	=	25.29
$500 monthly payment	=	6.32
Total monthly payment	=	$537.39

For the larger loan of $42,500, the monthly payment increases to $537.39.

The monthly payment tables included here allow the calculation of any mortgage payment above $50, in $50 increments, and for terms of 10 through 35 years, in 5-year increments. The interest rates that the tables cover range from 10.0 to 21.75 percent, in ¼ percent increments. The tables are additive only in respect to the loan amount for a given interest rate and term. It is not possible to combine the interest rate or term to maturity features to derive a combination not already included in the tables. The tables use monthly compounding, which is common for residential loans.

Not only do the tables allow the calculation of a specific mortgage payment, but as the previous example illustrates, they permit a "sensitivity analysis" to determine how the mortgage payment would change given a change in any of the variables. Along these lines, it is also possible to find out how much mortgage, or what interest rate, or what term to maturity you can afford for a given level of income.

ANOTHER EXAMPLE

Your gross monthly income is $1,660, which, according to the 25 percent housing payment to gross income rule of thumb, will allow a mortgage payment of $1,660(.25), or $415. If the current FRM interest rates are 13.75 percent, with a 25-year term, what is the most you can afford to borrow?

The answer to this type of question can again be found by using the monthly payment tables, but in a slightly different manner. You still go to the appropriate table, in this case 13.75 percent, and look under the 25-year term column. But you now must look up the maximum payment that can be afforded and follow that row across to the corresponding loan amount. The payment closest to the $415 maximum is $414.64, which corresponds to a $35,000 loan amount. This means that with the present income level of $1,660 per month, a 13.75 percent interest rate, and 25-year term, a loan of $35,000 would be the most that could be carried.

2. Adjustable Rate Mortgage Types and Buy Downs

The monthly payment tables can also be used with the adjustable rate mortgages, such as any of the renegotiable rate or variable balance mortgages. An exception is the graduated payment mortgage, which is covered separately later in this chapter. The initial mortgage payments for the adjustable rate mortgages would be calculated in the same manner as an FRM, but would change if the interest rates changed. After the change, a new mortgage payment could be calculated based on the remaining loan amount, the remaining term, and the new interest rates. An example of this type of arrangement requires the ability to calculate the mortgage balance remaining when the interest rate changes, and so will be deferred until later in this chapter.

Another form of creative financing, very popular in the current market, that can be handled with this mortgage payment calculation methodology is the buy down mortgage. To calculate the monthly payment in each year of the loan, you simply need to know what the rate of interest in each of the early years will be bought down to.

AN EXAMPLE

Assume that you are buying a $75,000 house, with a $60,000 loan. Current interest rates are 16.0 percent, with a 30-year term. You anticipate that interest rates will drop in the future, and while you cannot qualify for the loan at 16 percent, you could qualify if the interest rate were 13 percent in the first year. You arrange for the seller to buy down your mortgage to 13 percent in the first year, 14 percent in the second, 15 percent in the third, and leveling off at 16 percent for the fourth and successive years. What will your payments be in each of these periods, and what is the cost of this buy down arrangement?

Calculation of the monthly payments in each year is straightforward. The first-year payments would be found from the 13 Percent Monthly Payment Table, under the 30-year column and $60,000 row. This payment is $663.72. The payment for the second year would be taken from the 14 Percent Monthly Payment Table, also under the 30-year column and $60,000 row, and would be $710.93. The monthly payments in each of the following years would be found in a similar manner:

Year of Payments	Percentage Interest Rate	Monthly Borrower Payments	Monthly Buy Down Payments	Total Monthly Payment Received by Lender
1	13%	$663.72	$143.13	$806.85
2	14	710.93	95.92	806.85
3	15	758.67	48.18	806.85
4-30	16	806.85	—	806.85

The payment for the 16 percent, 30-year, $60,000 loan would be $806.85. Since this is the loan actually made, the lender will collect $806.85 each month, although you as the borrower pay a lower amount in each of the first three years as a result of the buy down. The total amount of the buy down is $143.13(12) + $95.92(12) + $48.18(12) = $3,446.76. Dividing the buy down amount by the $60,000 loan indicates that slightly less than 6 points would be paid by the seller for the buy down arrangement at the closing. The lender would thus lend $60,000, but collect $3,446.76 from the seller, for a net amount loaned to you of $56,553.24, although you are still obligated to repay $60,000.

The advantage of this arrangement to the buyer is that a lower income is required to qualify at the 13 percent rate in this first year. Once the loan is obtained, the buyer could refinance if rates were to fall. The disadvantage of the buy down is that if rates do not fall, the buyer has to make payments at the higher rate each year, which might not be affordable in the later years, possibly resulting in a default and foreclosure.

What Is Included in the Monthly Payment?

The monthly payment, calculated in the previous section, is made at the end of the period and includes payment to principal and interest only. Most borrowers are surprised if they find that the total monthly payment required by a lender exceeds the payment derived from the appropriate mortgage table. The difference is attributed to what is referred to as a "budget mortgage," which includes items beyond principal and interest.

Most lenders require the borrower to keep hazard insurance on the subject property and pay the property taxes each year. Payments for these items are typically due at the end of the year and are generally a large family expense, varying by location and type of property and coverage. One way in which a lender can ensure that the borrower has enough money to pay for these big-ticket items when they come due is to have the borrower pay a portion of the total each month. This is set up on a prorated basis by the lender so that the borrower would pay one-twelfth of the taxes and one-twelfth of the hazard insurance each month. The total pro-rata amount is added to the principal and interest payment, so the total payment is then composed of principal, interest, property taxes, and insurance. This is called a budget mortgage, because the lender is forcing the borrower to budget money each month to pay the taxes and insurance when they come due.

The taxes and insurance portion of the payment is placed by the lender into a typically noninterest-bearing escrow account. When the tax or insurance payment notice is received, the lender generally pays the bill with the escrow funds, thus making sure the mortgaged property is protected and remains free of tax liens. While this arrangement relieves the borrower of any responsibility concerning separately budgeting and paying for these items, it also forces the borrower to set aside a substantial amount of money, usually earning no, or very low, interest on it.

AN EXAMPLE

Assume that you are buying a $90,000 house with a $75,000 mortgage at 14 percent interest, with a 30-year term. The annual taxes on the property are $1,800, and the hazard insurance policy has been quoted to be $900 for the first year. The lender requires that hazard insurance and property taxes be paid monthly into an escrow account. What would your total monthly budget mortgage payment be in the first year?

Since this problem is solved as before, you first need to calculate the monthly principal and interest payment, but then you must also prorate the taxes and insurance over the first year and add them to the principal and interest payment. To find the monthly principal and interest payment, go to the 14 Percent Monthly Payment Table, under the 30-year column and $75,000 row. The payment is $888.66. Since total taxes and insurance are $1,800 plus $900, which sum to $2,700 in the first year, the monthly prorated amount would be $2,700(1/12) = $225. The total monthly payment to the lender would thus be $888.66 plus $225.00, which equals $1,113.66. If the amount due for taxes or insurance changes in subsequent years, the total monthly payment to the lender would change over time, although the principal and interest portion would remain at $888.66.

Unfortunately, some lenders will not allow a borrower, regardless of how well qualified, to handle this budgeting process individually. Depending on the loan-to-value ratio, the size of the escrow funds involved, and your relationship with the lender, it may be to your advantage to negotiate for a nonbudget mortgage. You would then have the responsibility of saving for the tax and insurance payments due at the end of the year, but you would also have the use of the prorated money in the interim.

CALCULATING THE REMAINING MORTGAGE BALANCE

Americans are very mobile. Statistics indicate that a family moves on the average of once every five years. Because of this mobility and changing market conditions, most borrowers will not pay their mortgage loan off over the full contract term, but will prepay in some shorter period. With certain mortgage instruments, such as renegotiable or balloon mortgages, this prepayment may be required. It is often necessary then to be able to calculate how much of a mortgage remains to be paid at any given point in time. This section details a procedure that can be used in finding the mortgage balance remaining and analyzes the composition of the total monthly FRM payment.

How Much of My Payment Goes Toward Actually Paying Off the Loan?

As discussed in Chapter 5, part of the monthly payment of most mortgage types goes to payment of interest, and the remainder goes to reducing the principal owed. In the early years of this type of loan, most of the monthly payment goes to interest, with very little going to principal.

AN EXAMPLE

You have a $40,000 mortgage with a 15 percent interest rate and 30-year term. The monthly payment to principal and interest, as calculated from the monthly payment table, is $505.78. What portion of this payment goes to principal and what portion goes to interest in the first month?

Finding the interest portion is the easiest way to proceed here, since the monthly interest rate, .15/12 is known. Multiplying the loan amount by the monthly interest rate, $40,000(.15/12), gives an interest portion of $500 for the first month. Since the total monthly payment is $505.78, the portion going to principal is $505.78 – $500.00 = $5.78. Calculation of the portion of the payment going to principal and interest in the second and subsequent months is summarized as follows:

Month	Monthly Payment	Beginning Mortgage Balance	×	Monthly Interest .Factor	=	Portion to Interest	Portion to Principal	Ending Mortgage Balance
1	$505.78	$40,000.00	×	(.15/12)	=	$500.00	$ 5.78	$39,994.22
2	505.78	39,994.22	×	(.15/12)	=	499.93	5.85	39,988.37
3	505.78	39,988.37	×	(.15/12)	=	499.85	5.93	39,982.44
.	.	.	.	.	.	.	.	.
.	.	.	.	.	.	.	.	.
.	.	.	.	.	.	.	.	.
359	505.78	992.90	×	(.15/12)	=	12.41	493.37	499.53
360	505.78	499.53	×	(.15/12)	=	6.25	499.53	0.00

While a complete amortization schedule could be constructed in this manner, it would be very tedious indeed. Several points can be made from this illustration. The first is that the bulk of the payment in the early years of the loan goes to payment of interest, with very little going to principal amortization. In the later years of the loan, the payment composition is reversed so that most of the payment goes to principal reduction, with only a small portion going to interest. The reason for this is that as the mortgage balance remaining gets smaller, less interest is required to service the loan. Unfortunately, as was shown in Chapter 5, it is not until after about the fifteenth year that the principal portion becomes dominant.

The main objective of this illustration is determining the ending mortgage balance. While this can be derived for any given month with some manipulation, it is the remaining mortgage balance that needs to be known when the property is sold and the mortgage paid off.

How Do I Find the Mortgage Balance Remaining?

As in the derivation of the FRM monthly payment table from the previous section, a simple mathematical process exists by which the mortgage balance remaining can be calculated. A table has been included following this section that performs that process and thus provides mortgage balance remaining amounts for interest rates ranging from 9.00 to 20.75 percent, in .25 percent increments. The initial mortgage terms to maturities covered range from 10 to 35 years, in 5-year increments, and the mortgage balance remaining percentages are listed for the year end of every year of the initial term to maturity.

Since the values presented in the mortgage balance remaining tables are listed as a percentage of the initial mortgage, to get the dollar amount of mortgage remaining, the listed percentage must be multiplied by the initial mortgage amount.

AN EXAMPLE

Ten years ago you borrowed $30,000 at 9.5 percent interest on a 30-year loan. You are now selling your home. What is the mortgage balance remaining to be paid off?

To find the mortgage balance remaining, go to the 9.5 Percent Mortgage Balance Remaining Table. Looking under the 30-year original term column, and the 10-year age of loan row, you will find the percentage of the loan remaining to be paid as .90208. Multiplying this percentage by the initial loan amount, $30,000(.90208), equals $27,062.40. This means that after paying on the loan for 10 years, $27,062.40 is the amount that is still owed the lender and must be paid off at the time of sale.

How Can the Mortgage Balance Remaining Table Be Used with Adjustable Rate Mortgages?

In some of the adjustable rate instruments, such as the variable or renegotiable rate mortgage, it is necessary to know the mortgage balance remaining to be able to calculate a new payment at the time of interest rate change. The mortgage balance tables can be used to facilitate the new payment calculation.

AN EXAMPLE

Assume that you have financed a home purchase under a municipal bond program where the initial interest rate was 11 percent, with a 30-year amortization, but with a 5-year call provision. This provision means that at the end of the fifth year, the loan has to be renegotiated at the prevailing interest rate. If you had borrowed $60,000, what is your initial payment, what will remain to be paid after 5 years, and what will your new payments be if rates are expected to be 14.5 percent?

The monthly mortgage payments can be calculated for the original loan by going to the 11 Percent Monthly Payment Table and looking under the 30-year column and $60,000 row. The payment is found to be $571.40, which is the amount that would be due each month for the first 5 years of the loan.

At the end of the 5 years, the mortgage balance remaining is found by going to the mortgage balance remaining table under 11 percent. Looking under the 30-year column and 5-year row, the percentage remaining is .97165. To find the dollar amount remaining to be paid, you must multiply the initial loan amount by the appropriate percentage, or $60,000(.97165) = $58,299.00, which can be rounded to $58,300.00.

The new payment is found by looking under the 14.5 Percent Monthly Payment Table. Since $58,300 is not directly in the table, it will have to be built. Getting the appropriate monthly payment factors from the 25-year column, which is the term remaining under the original agreement, yields

$55,000 monthly payment	=	$683.19
$3,000 monthly payment	=	37.27
$300 monthly payment	=	3.73
Total monthly payment	=	$724.19

The monthly payment for the remaining 25 years under the original municipal bond program loan agreement would be $724.19.

CALCULATING THE ANNUAL PERCENTAGE RATE

Often the interest rate actually earned by the lender is different from the contract rate of interest charged. This results from additional charges being made by the lender at the loan inception, which raises the yield to the lender. Typical charges made are discount points, discussed in Chapter 3, origination fees, financing charges, and prepaid items. The lender is required by the Real Estate Settlement Procedures Act (RESPA) to report the actual yield earned, which is the annual percentage rate. Since the APR is usually different from the contract interest rate, it is necessary to understand how the APR is calculated.

Contract Rates versus the True Cost of Money

In Chapter 3, it was stated that the "contract rate" of interest was the rate commonly quoted by a lender, but when any other charges, such as discount points, were made, the "effective yield" was actually higher. This results from the fact that the lender commits to a certain loan amount, but when funds are received from the buyer or seller at closing, the actual net amount advanced by the lender is less than the amount that will be paid back by the borrower. This results in an increase in the lender's yield. In Chapter 3, some rules of thumb were given to help determine what the APR would be if points were paid at the loan closing, but it may be desirable to calculate the actual APR for a given set of mortgage loan terms.

One method of solving for the APR is to use a financial calculator, but even if you can justify the cost, finding the APR is a little more difficult than just getting a mortgage payment or mortgage balance remaining. The process requires first solving for the mortgage payment at the loan amount, term to maturity, and contract rate and then subtracting the points or finance charges received by the lender from the loan amount and finally having the calculator solve for the new interest rate at the lower loan amount. An easier method is to use an APR table into which all the manipulating has been built. Such a table is included here for contract interest rates ranging from 8.000 to 22.875 percent, in .125 percent increments, for .5 to 12 points charged at closing, in .5-point increments, and for 10-, 20-, and 30-year terms to maturities. To use the tables, the total charges paid at the closing should be divided by the contract loan amount to get the points charged. The APR can then be found by looking under the appropriate term to maturity table, number of points charged column, and contract interest row. The resulting number in the body of the table is the APR. Note that the points in the column headings refer to total points paid at closing, including discount points, prepaid items, and loan origination fees, where 1 point is again equal to 1 percent of the loan amount.

AN EXAMPLE

Assume that you are purchasing a house for $75,000, with an 11.5 percent, 30-year, $61,000 loan. The lender requires you to pay an origination fee of 1 percent, or $610, plus prepaid interest of $300. The lender also requires 3 discount points, which you as the purchaser are also paying. What is the APR on this loan?

To find the APR, you need to calculate the total points charged by the lender. The total charges are $610 + $300 + $61,000(.03), or $1,830, which equals $2,740. The points then are found by dividing $2,740 by $61,000 to get approximately 4.5 points. Looking under the 30-Year Annual Percentage Rate Table under the 4.5 points charged column and 11.5 percent contract rate row yields an APR of 12.1083 percent. The lender commits to a $61,000 loan at 11.5 percent interest, on which the payments are calculated, but since only $61,000 less $2,740 equals $58,260 is advanced, the lender's yield is actually 12.1083 percent. The 12.1083 would be reported as the APR by the lender on the RESPA truth-in-lending form.

Using the APR to Shop for Loans

Annual percentage rate tables can also be used to compare different mortgage and point combinations offered by different lenders. Since lenders often charge different costs at closing, as well as different interest rates and discount point amounts, it would pay to compare the various alternatives offered by different lenders.

AN EXAMPLE

You are contemplating purchasing a home for $130,000, with a $115,000, 30-year loan. After calling several lenders, you have received several combinations of interest rates and discount points, but all other closing costs and prepaid items are basically the same. The different combinations are

Lender	Contract Interest Rate	Discount Points
1	14.000%	4
2	14.375	1
3	13.750	6
4	14.250	2
5	14.000	3

What is the effective interest rate of each, and what is your best loan combination?

To find the APR of each, look under the 30-Year Annual Percentage Rate Table for each combination. For lender 1, the 4 points column and 14 percent interest rate row would correspond to an APR of .146216. For lender 2, the APR would be found under the 1 point column and the 14.375 percent contract interest rate row. The appropriate APR for lender 2 is .145292. Looking up the APRs for the rest of the lender quoted combinations results in

Lender	Contract Interest Rate	Discount Points (in percent)	APR
1	14.000%	4	14.6216%
2	14.375	1	14.5292
3	13.750	6	14.6874
4	14.250	2	14.5593
5	14.000	3	14.4618

As can be seen, the best combination of contract interest rate and discount points would be from lender 5 since that provides the lowest cost to you, all other things being equal. If the other costs are also varied by lender, these differences could be incorporated in the analysis. It might be noted that the APRs listed in the preceding table would only be true APRs if they included all costs required by Regulation Z incorporated in calculating an APR.

The APR must be quoted for all mortgages, assuming payment over the full term. Although most mortgages are paid off before the full term, which would substantially increase the yield to the lender, the APR does not incorporate an assumed prepayment. The greater the number of points paid, the higher is the true effective yield (cost) when a mortgage is prepaid. And while the FRM is the easiest instrument to associate with the APR tables, the adjustable rate mortgages would also be able to utilize the APR tables, although the same selection criteria would not apply if, for example, different adjustable rate mortgages were tied to different indexes where one index was more favorable than another.

GRADUATED PAYMENT MORTGAGE PAYMENTS

As was discussed in Chapter 5, any mortgage plan with increasing mortgage payments incorporated into the payment pattern is, by definition, a graduated payment mortgage. The key feature of a GPM is that the payments start out relatively low and then increase at a given percentage, typically from 2 to 5 percent per year, over a set period of time, typically from 5 to 10 years. The payments eventually level out at an amount higher than the FRM payments would have been for the same term and interest rate, but since the GPM payments are lower in the early years of the loan, the GPM reduces the affordability problem and aids a home buyer with expected increasing income.

There are a number of GPM plans being used, although the most common is the FHA-insured program discussed in Chapter 5. In arriving at the monthly payments for the different FHA plans, a mathematical relationship is again solved for in each year. This relationship is very complex, so much so that nonprogrammable financial calculators are not able to solve for the different payments directly. The only way of arriving at the payments for a given plan then is to resort to a table that includes the necessary calculations.

A number of graduated payment tables have been generated and included in this book. The tables included are for the FHA GPM plans I through V and are all for a term of 30 years. The interest rate ranges are from 12.0 to 20.5 percent, in .5 percent increments. The graduations and lengths of graduation for each plan are

Plan	Percentage of Graduation per Year	Years of Graduation
I	2.5%	5
II	5.0	5
III	7.5	5
IV	2.0	10
V	3.0	10

The tables include the monthly payments to principal and interest for any given year under each plan. Since these are insured plans, the FHA also adds an insurance premium to each payment. The tables do not include the insurance portion because (1) that would limit the tables to an FHA program only, where some lenders are using the FHA format, although not using the FHA-insured program per se, and (2) the insurance premiums are subject to frequent change, where incorporating the current premiums would immediately date the tables. The actual monthly premium for a typical FHA GPM would be relatively small, approximately one-twelfth of one-half of 1 percent of the mortgage balance.

The tables included are used just like the FRM tables, where you simply find the appropriate table, given the plan desired and the interest rate quoted and then find the monthly payment appropriate for each year.

AN EXAMPLE

Assume that you are purchasing a home for $65,000, with a 90 percent loan-to-value ratio, 14.5 percent FHA GPM. The term is for 30 years, with a 5 percent graduation for 5 years, which makes this plan II. What are your monthly payments to principal and interest for each year of the loan?

To solve this problem, you first need the mortgage amount, which is $65,000(.90) = $58,500. To get the monthly payments, proceed to the 14.5 Percent, FHA Graduated Payment Plan II Table. Finding that table, we note that there is no direct amount for $58,500 listed, which means that we will have to build the payment, as previously demonstrated. The appropriate monthly payment numbers for each year of the loan are found as

Loan Amount	Year 1	Year 2	Year 3	Year 4	Year 5	Years 6-30
$55,000	$571.15	$599.71	$629.69	$661.18	$694.24	$728.95
3,000	31.15	32.71	34.35	36.06	37.87	39.76
500	5.19	5.45	5.72	6.01	6.31	6.63
$58,500	$607.49	$637.87	$669.76	$703.25	$738.42	$775.34

The monthly payment to principal and interest for the first year is $607.49, the payment for each month in the second year is $637.87, the third year's monthly payment is $669.76, the fourth year's is $703.25, the fifth year's is $738.42, and the monthly payment for years 6 to 30 levels out at $775.34.

The GPM tables can also be used to compare the monthly payments of various GPM plans with other types of mortgages. For instance, it might be of interest to see what the monthly payment would be for the five GPM plans as compared with an FRM.

ANOTHER EXAMPLE

You are considering purchasing an $80,000 home with a $75,000, 30-year mortgage. You have several alternatives, where you can either get a GPM or an FRM. What would the monthly payments to principal and interest be under each type, assuming a 16 percent interest rate?

To answer this question, the monthly payment for each GPM plan must be obtained from the appropriate 16 percent table, under the corresponding year column. The monthly payment for the FRM would come from the monthly payment table previously presented. The various monthly payments for the corresponding years would be

Year	GPM I	GPM II	GPM III	GPM IV	GPM V	FRM
1	$ 931.63	$ 860.34	$ 794.39	$ 918.85	$ 875.94	$1,008.57
2	954.92	903.35	853.96	937.22	902.22	1,008.57
3	978.79	948.52	918.01	955.97	929.29	1,008.57
4	1,003.26	995.95	986.86	975.09	957.17	1,008.57
5	1,028.35	1,045.75	1,060.88	994.59	985.88	1,008.57
6	1,054.05	1,098.03	1,140.44	1,014.48	1,015.46	1,008.57
7	1,054.05	1,098.03	1,140.44	1,034.77	1,045.92	1,008.57
8	1,054.05	1,098.03	1,140.44	1,055.47	1,077.30	1,008.57
9	1,054.05	1,098.03	1,140.44	1,076.58	1,109.62	1,008.57
10	1,054.05	1,098.03	1,140.44	1,098.11	1,142.91	1,008.57
11-30	1,054.05	1,098.03	1,140.44	1,120.07	1,177.19	1,008.57

Which type of mortgage is best? That of course depends on your current and expected income. If your income is low, but is expected to increase in the near future, a plan that offers lower payments in the early years would probably be optimal. The initial payments in GPM plan III are the lowest, beginning at $794.39 in year 1. But under plan III, the payments level off at $1,140.44 in years 6 to 30, which is an amount greater than all other plans except plan V. If you expect your current income to remain relatively stable, plan IV might be the best, since the level of graduation is relatively small and is spread over a longer period of time. And if your income is expected to remain constant, or decline, the FRM may be the best option, assuming that you can afford the higher initial payments.

There will always be considerations other than income involved in the decision-making process. One of the most important considerations is the length of holding period. Since most homeowners do not pay off their loans over the full loan term, but instead prepay, a plan that provides the lowest payment in the early years may be optimal. But a word of caution, one of the features of most GPM plans is that the initial payments are not large enough to cover all the interest owed. This means that in the early years you are not reducing the outstanding loan amount but, instead, are borrowing more money. So when you go to sell and prepay your GPM, you might end up having to pay off a larger mortgage balance than you initially borrowed.

Usually, if a GPM and an FRM are originated at the same interest rate and with the same costs, the effective yield, or APR, will be the same. So while the GPM is suitable in many situations, and does make the initial home purchase more affordable, it needs to be studied carefully by the borrower, considering the size of the monthly payments each year relative to income, along with the mortgage balance and future property value trends.

Tables

TABLE I.	Fixed Rate Mortgage Tables, 10 to 35 Years in 5-Year Increments, 10.0% to 21.75% Interest by Increments of .25%
TABLE II.	Mortgage Balance Remaining Tables, 10- to 35-Year Term in 5-Year Increments, 9.0% to 20.75% Interest by Increments of .25%
TABLE III.	Annual Percentage Rate Tables, 8.0% to 22.75% Contract Interest by Increments of .125% with .5 to 12 Points by Increments of .5
TABLE IV.	Graduated Payment Mortgage Tables, FHA Plans I to V with a 30-Year Term at 12.0% to 20.5% Interest by Increments of .5%

TABLE I-1. Fixed Rate Mortgage at 10.00%

MONTHLY PAYMENT
NECESSARY TO AMORTIZE A LOAN 10.00%

AMOUNT \ TERM	10 YEARS	15 YEARS	20 YEARS	25 YEARS	30 YEARS	35 YEARS
50	0.66	0.54	0.48	0.45	0.44	0.43
100	1.32	1.07	0.97	0.91	0.88	0.86
200	2.64	2.15	1.93	1.82	1.76	1.72
300	3.96	3.22	2.90	2.73	2.63	2.58
400	5.29	4.30	3.86	3.63	3.51	3.44
500	6.61	5.37	4.83	4.54	4.39	4.30
600	7.93	6.45	5.79	5.45	5.27	5.16
700	9.25	7.52	6.76	6.36	6.14	6.02
800	10.57	8.60	7.72	7.27	7.02	6.88
900	11.89	9.67	8.69	8.18	7.90	7.74
1,000	13.22	10.75	9.65	9.09	8.78	8.60
2,000	26.43	21.49	19.30	18.17	17.55	17.19
3,000	39.65	32.24	28.95	27.26	26.33	25.79
4,000	52.86	42.99	38.60	36.35	35.10	34.39
5,000	66.08	53.73	48.25	45.44	43.88	42.98
6,000	79.29	64.48	57.90	54.52	52.65	51.58
7,000	92.51	75.23	67.55	63.61	61.43	60.18
8,000	105.73	85.97	77.20	72.70	70.21	68.77
9,000	118.94	96.72	86.85	81.78	78.98	77.37
10,000	132.16	107.46	96.50	90.87	87.76	85.97
15,000	198.24	161.20	144.76	136.31	131.64	128.95
20,000	264.31	214.93	193.01	181.74	175.52	171.94
25,000	330.39	268.66	241.26	227.18	219.40	214.92
30,000	396.47	322.39	289.51	272.62	263.27	257.90
35,000	462.55	376.13	337.77	318.05	307.15	300.89
40,000	528.63	429.86	386.02	363.49	351.03	343.87
45,000	594.71	483.59	434.27	408.92	394.91	386.86
50,000	660.79	537.32	482.52	454.36	438.79	429.84
55,000	726.87	591.05	530.78	499.79	482.67	472.82
60,000	792.94	644.79	579.03	545.23	526.55	515.81
65,000	859.02	698.52	627.28	590.67	570.43	558.79
70,000	925.10	752.25	675.53	636.10	614.31	601.78
75,000	991.18	805.98	723.79	681.54	658.19	644.76
80,000	1,057.26	859.72	772.04	726.97	702.07	687.74
85,000	1,123.34	913.45	820.29	772.41	745.95	730.73
90,000	1,189.42	967.18	868.54	817.85	789.82	773.71
95,000	1,255.49	1,020.91	916.80	863.28	833.70	816.70
100,000	1,321.57	1,074.64	965.05	908.72	877.58	859.68
110,000	1,453.73	1,182.11	1,061.55	999.59	965.34	945.65
120,000	1,585.89	1,289.57	1,158.06	1,090.46	1,053.10	1,031.62
130,000	1,718.05	1,397.04	1,254.56	1,181.33	1,140.86	1,117.58
140,000	1,850.20	1,504.50	1,351.07	1,272.20	1,228.62	1,203.55
150,000	1,982.36	1,611.97	1,447.57	1,363.08	1,316.37	1,289.52
160,000	2,114.52	1,719.43	1,544.08	1,453.95	1,404.13	1,375.49
170,000	2,246.67	1,826.90	1,640.58	1,544.82	1,491.89	1,461.46
180,000	2,378.83	1,934.36	1,737.09	1,635.69	1,579.65	1,547.42
190,000	2,510.99	2,041.83	1,833.59	1,726.56	1,667.41	1,633.39
200,000	2,643.15	2,149.29	1,930.10	1,817.44	1,755.17	1,719.36

TABLE I-2. Fixed Rate Mortgage at 10.25%

MONTHLY PAYMENT
NECESSARY TO AMORTIZE A LOAN — 10.25%

TERM / AMOUNT	10 YEARS	15 YEARS	20 YEARS	25 YEARS	30 YEARS	35 YEARS
50	0.67	0.55	0.49	0.46	0.45	0.44
100	1.34	1.09	0.98	0.93	0.90	0.88
200	2.67	2.18	1.96	1.85	1.79	1.76
300	4.01	3.27	2.95	2.78	2.69	2.64
400	5.34	4.36	3.93	3.71	3.58	3.52
500	6.68	5.45	4.91	4.63	4.48	4.39
600	8.01	6.54	5.89	5.56	5.38	5.27
700	9.35	7.63	6.87	6.48	6.27	6.15
800	10.68	8.72	7.85	7.41	7.17	7.03
900	12.02	9.81	8.84	8.34	8.07	7.91
1,000	13.35	10.90	9.82	9.26	8.96	8.79
2,000	26.71	21.80	19.63	18.53	17.92	17.58
3,000	40.06	32.70	29.45	27.79	26.88	26.37
4,000	53.42	43.60	39.27	37.06	35.84	35.15
5,000	66.77	54.50	49.08	46.32	44.81	43.94
6,000	80.13	65.40	58.90	55.58	53.77	52.73
7,000	93.48	76.30	68.72	64.85	62.73	61.52
8,000	106.84	87.20	78.53	74.11	71.69	70.31
9,000	120.19	98.10	88.35	83.38	80.65	79.10
10,000	133.55	109.00	98.17	92.64	89.61	87.89
15,000	200.32	163.50	147.25	138.96	134.42	131.83
20,000	267.10	218.00	196.34	185.28	179.22	175.77
25,000	333.87	272.50	245.42	231.60	224.03	219.72
30,000	400.64	327.00	294.50	277.92	268.83	263.66
35,000	467.42	381.50	343.59	324.24	313.64	307.60
40,000	534.19	436.00	392.67	370.56	358.45	351.55
45,000	600.97	490.50	441.76	416.88	403.25	395.49
50,000	667.74	545.00	490.84	463.20	448.06	439.43
55,000	734.51	599.50	539.92	509.52	492.86	483.38
60,000	801.29	654.00	589.01	555.84	537.67	527.32
65,000	868.06	708.50	638.09	602.16	582.48	571.26
70,000	934.84	763.00	687.18	648.48	627.28	615.21
75,000	1,001.61	817.50	736.26	694.80	672.09	659.15
80,000	1,068.39	872.00	785.34	741.13	716.89	703.09
85,000	1,135.16	926.50	834.43	787.45	761.70	747.04
90,000	1,201.93	981.01	883.51	833.77	806.50	790.98
95,000	1,268.71	1,035.51	932.59	880.09	851.31	834.92
100,000	1,335.48	1,090.01	981.68	926.41	896.12	878.87
110,000	1,469.03	1,199.01	1,079.85	1,019.05	985.73	966.75
120,000	1,602.58	1,308.01	1,178.01	1,111.69	1,075.34	1,054.64
130,000	1,736.13	1,417.01	1,276.18	1,204.33	1,164.95	1,142.53
140,000	1,869.67	1,526.01	1,374.35	1,296.97	1,254.56	1,230.41
150,000	2,003.22	1,635.01	1,472.52	1,389.61	1,344.18	1,318.30
160,000	2,136.77	1,744.01	1,570.69	1,402.25	1,433.79	1,406.19
170,000	2,270.32	1,853.01	1,668.85	1,574.89	1,523.40	1,494.07
180,000	2,403.87	1,962.01	1,767.02	1,667.53	1,613.01	1,581.96
190,000	2,537.42	2,071.01	1,865.19	1,760.17	1,702.62	1,669.85
200,000	2,670.96	2,180.01	1,963.36	1,852.81	1,792.23	1,757.73

TABLE I-3. Fixed Rate Mortgage at 10.50%

MONTHLY PAYMENT
NECESSARY TO AMORTIZE A LOAN 10.50%

AMOUNT / TERM	10 YEARS	15 YEARS	20 YEARS	25 YEARS	30 YEARS	35 YEARS
50	0.67	0.55	0.50	0.47	0.46	0.45
100	1.35	1.11	1.00	0.94	0.91	0.90
200	2.70	2.21	2.00	1.89	1.83	1.80
300	4.05	3.32	3.00	2.83	2.74	2.69
400	5.40	4.42	3.99	3.78	3.66	3.59
500	6.75	5.53	4.99	4.72	4.57	4.49
600	8.10	6.63	5.99	5.67	5.49	5.39
700	9.45	7.74	6.99	6.61	6.40	6.29
800	10.80	8.84	7.99	7.55	7.32	7.19
900	12.14	9.95	8.99	8.50	8.23	8.08
1,000	13.49	11.05	9.98	9.44	9.15	8.98
2,000	26.99	22.11	19.97	18.88	18.29	17.96
3,000	40.48	33.16	29.95	28.33	27.44	26.94
4,000	53.98	44.22	39.94	37.77	36.59	35.93
5,000	67.47	55.27	49.92	47.21	45.74	44.91
6,000	80.96	66.33	59.90	56.65	54.88	53.89
7,000	94.46	77.38	69.89	66.09	64.03	62.87
8,000	107.95	88.43	79.87	75.54	73.18	71.85
9,000	121.45	99.49	89.86	84.98	82.33	80.83
10,000	134.94	110.54	99.84	94.42	91.47	89.81
15,000	202.41	165.81	149.76	141.63	137.21	134.72
20,000	269.88	221.08	199.68	188.84	182.95	179.63
25,000	337.35	276.36	249.60	236.05	228.69	224.53
30,000	404.82	331.63	299.52	283.26	274.42	269.44
35,000	472.29	386.90	349.44	330.47	320.16	314.35
40,000	539.76	442.17	399.36	377.68	365.90	359.26
45,000	607.23	497.44	449.28	424.89	411.64	404.16
50,000	674.70	552.71	499.20	472.10	457.37	449.07
55,000	742.17	607.98	549.12	519.31	503.11	493.98
60,000	809.64	663.25	599.04	566.52	548.85	538.88
65,000	877.10	718.53	648.96	613.72	594.58	583.79
70,000	944.57	773.80	698.88	660.93	640.32	628.70
75,000	1,012.04	829.07	748.80	708.14	686.06	673.60
80,000	1,079.51	884.34	798.72	755.35	731.80	718.51
85,000	1,146.98	939.61	848.64	802.56	777.53	763.42
90,000	1,214.45	994.88	898.56	849.77	823.27	808.32
95,000	1,281.92	1,050.15	948.48	896.98	869.01	853.23
100,000	1,349.39	1,105.42	998.40	944.19	914.75	898.14
110,000	1,484.33	1,215.97	1,098.24	1,038.61	1,006.22	987.95
120,000	1,619.27	1,326.51	1,198.07	1,133.03	1,097.69	1,077.77
130,000	1,754.21	1,437.05	1,297.91	1,227.45	1,189.17	1,167.58
140,000	1,889.15	1,547.59	1,397.75	1,321.87	1,280.64	1,257.39
150,000	2,024.09	1,658.14	1,497.59	1,416.29	1,372.12	1,347.21
160,000	2,159.03	1,768.68	1,597.43	1,510.71	1,463.59	1,437.02
170,000	2,293.97	1,879.22	1,697.27	1,605.13	1,555.07	1,526.84
180,000	2,428.91	1,989.76	1,797.11	1,699.55	1,646.54	1,616.65
190,000	2,563.84	2,100.31	1,896.95	1,793.96	1,738.02	1,706.46
200,000	2,698.78	2,210.85	1,996.79	1,888.38	1,829.49	1,796.28

TABLE I-4. Fixed Rate Mortgage at 10.75%

MONTHLY PAYMENT
NECESSARY TO AMORTIZE A LOAN — 10.75%

AMOUNT \ TERM	10 YEARS	15 YEARS	20 YEARS	25 YEARS	30 YEARS	35 YEARS
50	0.68	0.56	0.51	0.48	0.47	0.46
100	1.36	1.12	1.02	0.96	0.93	0.92
200	2.73	2.24	2.03	1.92	1.87	1.84
300	4.09	3.36	3.05	2.89	2.80	2.75
400	5.45	4.48	4.06	3.85	3.73	3.67
500	6.82	5.60	5.08	4.81	4.67	4.59
600	8.18	6.73	6.09	5.77	5.60	5.51
700	9.54	7.85	7.11	6.73	6.53	6.42
800	10.91	8.97	8.12	7.70	7.47	7.34
900	12.27	10.09	9.14	8.66	8.40	8.26
1,000	13.63	11.21	10.15	9.62	9.33	9.18
2,000	27.27	22.42	20.31	19.24	18.67	18.35
3,000	40.90	33.63	30.46	28.86	28.00	27.53
4,000	54.54	44.84	40.61	38.48	37.34	36.70
5,000	68.17	56.05	50.76	48.11	46.67	45.88
6,000	81.81	67.26	60.92	57.73	56.01	55.05
7,000	95.44	78.47	71.07	67.35	65.34	64.23
8,000	109.08	89.68	81.22	76.97	74.68	73.40
9,000	122.71	100.89	91.37	86.59	84.01	82.58
10,000	136.35	112.10	101.53	96.21	93.35	91.75
15,000	204.52	168.15	152.29	144.32	140.02	137.63
20,000	272.69	224.20	203.05	192.42	186.70	183.50
25,000	340.86	280.25	253.81	240.53	233.37	229.38
30,000	409.04	336.30	304.58	288.63	280.05	275.25
35,000	477.21	392.35	355.34	336.74	326.72	321.13
40,000	545.38	448.40	406.10	384.84	373.40	367.00
45,000	613.56	504.45	456.86	432.95	420.07	412.88
50,000	681.73	560.49	507.63	481.05	466.75	458.75
55,000	749.90	616.54	558.39	529.16	513.42	504.63
60,000	818.07	672.59	609.15	577.27	560.10	550.51
65,000	886.25	728.64	659.92	625.37	606.77	596.38
70,000	954.42	784.69	710.68	673.48	653.44	642.26
75,000	1,022.59	840.74	761.44	721.58	700.12	688.13
80,000	1,090.76	896.79	812.20	769.69	746.79	734.01
85,000	1,158.94	952.84	862.97	817.79	793.47	779.88
90,000	1,227.11	1,008.89	913.73	865.90	840.14	825.76
95,000	1,295.28	1,064.94	964.49	914.00	886.82	871.63
100,000	1,363.46	1,120.99	1,015.26	962.11	933.49	917.51
110,000	1,499.80	1,233.09	1,116.78	1,058.32	1,026.84	1,009.26
120,000	1,636.15	1,345.19	1,218.31	1,154.53	1,120.19	1,101.01
130,000	1,772.49	1,457.29	1,319.83	1,250.74	1,213.54	1,192.76
140,000	1,908.84	1,569.39	1,421.36	1,346.95	1,306.89	1,284.51
150,000	2,045.18	1,681.48	1,522.83	1,443.16	1,400.24	1,376.26
160,000	2,181.53	1,793.58	1,624.41	1,539.38	1,493.59	1,468.02
170,000	2,317.88	1,905.68	1,725.93	1,635.59	1,586.94	1,559.77
180,000	2,454.22	2,017.78	1,827.46	1,731.80	1,680.29	1,651.52
190,000	2,590.57	2,129.88	1,928.98	1,828.01	1,773.64	1,743.27
200,000	2,726.91	2,241.98	2,030.51	1,924.22	1,866.98	1,835.02

TABLE I-5. **Fixed Rate Mortgage at 11.00%**

MONTHLY PAYMENT NECESSARY TO AMORTIZE A LOAN 11.00%

TERM / AMOUNT	10 YEARS	15 YEARS	20 YEARS	25 YEARS	30 YEARS	35 YEARS
50	0.69	0.57	0.52	0.49	0.48	0.47
100	1.38	1.14	1.03	0.98	0.95	0.94
200	2.76	2.27	2.06	1.96	1.90	1.87
300	4.13	3.41	3.10	2.94	2.86	2.81
400	5.51	4.55	4.13	3.92	3.81	3.75
500	6.89	5.68	5.16	4.90	4.76	4.68
600	8.27	6.82	6.19	5.88	5.71	5.62
700	9.64	7.96	7.23	6.86	6.67	6.56
800	11.02	9.09	8.26	7.84	7.62	7.50
900	12.40	10.23	9.29	8.82	8.57	8.43
1,000	13.78	11.37	10.32	9.80	9.52	9.37
2,000	27.55	22.73	20.64	19.60	19.05	18.74
3,000	41.33	34.10	30.97	29.40	28.57	28.11
4,000	55.10	45.47	41.29	39.21	38.09	37.48
5,000	68.88	56.83	51.61	49.01	47.62	46.85
6,000	82.66	68.20	61.93	58.81	57.14	56.22
7,000	96.43	79.57	72.26	68.61	66.66	65.59
8,000	110.21	90.93	82.58	78.41	76.19	74.96
9,000	123.98	102.30	92.90	88.21	85.71	84.33
10,000	137.76	113.67	103.22	98.01	95.23	93.70
15,000	206.64	170.50	154.83	147.02	142.85	140.55
20,000	275.52	227.33	206.44	196.03	190.47	187.39
25,000	344.40	284.16	258.06	245.03	238.08	234.24
30,000	413.28	341.00	309.67	294.04	285.70	281.09
35,000	482.16	397.83	361.28	343.05	333.32	327.94
40,000	551.04	454.66	412.89	392.05	380.94	374.79
45,000	619.92	511.49	464.50	441.06	428.55	421.64
50,000	688.80	568.33	516.11	490.07	476.17	468.48
55,000	757.68	625.16	567.72	539.07	523.79	515.33
60,000	826.56	681.99	619.33	588.08	571.40	562.18
65,000	895.44	738.82	670.95	637.09	619.02	609.03
70,000	964.32	795.66	722.56	686.10	666.64	655.88
75,000	1,033.20	852.49	774.17	735.10	714.25	702.73
80,000	1,102.08	909.32	825.78	784.11	761.87	749.57
85,000	1,170.96	966.16	877.39	833.12	809.49	796.42
90,000	1,239.84	1,022.99	929.00	882.12	857.10	843.27
95,000	1,308.72	1,079.82	980.61	931.13	904.72	890.12
100,000	1,377.60	1,136.65	1,032.22	980.14	952.34	936.97
110,000	1,515.36	1,250.32	1,135.45	1,078.15	1,047.57	1,030.66
120,000	1,653.12	1,363.98	1,238.67	1,176.16	1,142.81	1,124.36
130,000	1,790.88	1,477.65	1,341.89	1,274.18	1,238.04	1,218.06
140,000	1,928.63	1,591.31	1,445.11	1,372.19	1,333.27	1,311.75
150,000	2,066.39	1,704.98	1,548.34	1,470.20	1,428.51	1,405.45
160,000	2,204.15	1,818.65	1,651.56	1,568.22	1,523.74	1,499.15
170,000	2,341.91	1,932.31	1,754.78	1,666.23	1,618.98	1,592.84
180,000	2,479.67	2,045.98	1,858.00	1,764.24	1,714.21	1,686.54
190,000	2,617.43	2,159.64	1,961.23	1,862.26	1,809.44	1,780.24
200,000	2,755.19	2,273.31	2,064.45	1,960.27	1,904.68	1,873.93

TABLE I-6. Fixed Rate Mortgage at 11.25%

MONTHLY PAYMENT
NECESSARY TO AMORTIZE A LOAN 11.25%

TERM / AMOUNT	10 YEARS	15 YEARS	20 YEARS	25 YEARS	30 YEARS	35 YEARS
50	0.70	0.58	0.52	0.50	0.49	0.48
100	1.39	1.15	1.05	1.00	0.97	0.96
200	2.78	2.30	2.10	2.00	1.94	1.91
300	4.18	3.46	3.15	2.99	2.91	2.87
400	5.57	4.61	4.20	3.99	3.89	3.83
500	6.96	5.76	5.25	4.99	4.86	4.78
600	8.35	6.91	6.30	5.99	5.83	5.74
700	9.74	8.07	7.34	6.99	6.80	6.70
800	11.13	9.22	8.39	7.99	7.77	7.65
900	12.53	10.37	9.44	8.98	8.74	8.61
1,000	13.92	11.52	10.49	9.98	9.71	9.56
2,000	27.83	23.05	20.99	19.96	19.43	19.13
3,000	41.75	34.57	31.48	29.95	29.14	28.69
4,000	55.67	46.09	41.97	39.93	38.85	38.26
5,000	69.59	57.62	52.46	49.91	48.56	47.82
6,000	83.50	69.14	62.96	59.89	58.28	57.39
7,000	97.42	80.67	73.45	69.88	67.99	66.95
8,000	111.34	92.19	83.94	79.86	77.70	76.52
9,000	125.26	103.71	94.43	89.84	87.41	86.08
10,000	139.17	115.24	104.93	99.82	97.13	95.65
15,000	208.76	172.86	157.39	149.74	145.69	143.47
20,000	278.35	230.47	209.85	199.65	194.25	191.30
25,000	347.93	288.09	262.32	249.56	242.82	239.12
30,000	417.52	345.71	314.78	299.47	291.38	286.95
35,000	487.11	403.33	367.25	349.39	339.94	334.77
40,000	556.69	460.95	419.71	399.30	388.51	382.60
45,000	626.28	518.57	472.17	449.21	437.07	430.42
50,000	695.87	576.19	524.64	499.12	485.63	478.25
55,000	765.45	633.80	577.10	549.04	534.20	526.07
60,000	835.04	691.42	629.56	598.95	582.76	573.90
65,000	904.63	749.04	682.03	648.86	631.32	621.72
70,000	974.21	806.66	734.49	698.77	679.89	669.55
75,000	1,043.80	864.28	786.95	748.69	728.45	717.37
80,000	1,113.39	921.90	839.42	798.60	777.01	765.20
85,000	1,182.97	979.51	891.88	848.51	825.58	813.02
90,000	1,252.56	1,037.13	944.34	898.42	874.14	860.85
95,000	1,322.15	1,094.75	996.81	948.34	922.70	908.67
100,000	1,391.73	1,152.37	1,049.27	998.25	971.27	956.50
110,000	1,530.91	1,267.61	1,154.20	1,098.07	1,068.39	1,052.15
120,000	1,670.08	1,382.84	1,259.13	1,197.90	1,165.52	1,147.80
130,000	1,809.25	1,498.08	1,364.05	1,297.72	1,262.65	1,243.45
140,000	1,948.43	1,613.32	1,468.98	1,397.55	1,359.77	1,339.10
150,000	2,087.60	1,728.56	1,573.91	1,497.37	1,456.90	1,434.75
160,000	2,226.77	1,843.79	1,678.83	1,597.20	1,554.03	1,530.40
170,000	2,365.95	1,959.03	1,783.76	1,697.02	1,651.16	1,626.05
180,000	2,505.12	2,074.27	1,888.69	1,796.85	1,748.28	1,721.70
190,000	2,644.29	2,189.50	1,993.62	1,896.67	1,845.41	1,817.35
200,000	2,783.47	2,304.74	2,098.54	1,996.50	1,942.54	1,913.00

TABLE I-7. Fixed Rate Mortgage at 11.50%

MONTHLY PAYMENT
NECESSARY TO AMORTIZE A LOAN 11.50%

AMOUNT \ TERM	10 YEARS	15 YEARS	20 YEARS	25 YEARS	30 YEARS	35 YEARS
50	0.70	0.58	0.53	0.51	0.50	0.49
100	1.41	1.17	1.07	1.02	0.99	0.98
200	2.81	2.34	2.13	2.03	1.98	1.95
300	4.22	3.50	3.20	3.05	2.97	2.93
400	5.62	4.67	4.27	4.07	3.96	3.90
500	7.03	5.84	5.33	5.08	4.95	4.88
600	8.44	7.01	6.40	6.10	5.94	5.86
700	9.84	8.18	7.47	7.12	6.93	6.83
800	11.25	9.35	8.53	8.13	7.92	7.81
900	12.65	10.51	9.60	9.15	8.91	8.79
1,000	14.06	11.68	10.66	10.16	9.90	9.76
2,000	28.12	23.36	21.33	20.33	19.81	19.52
3,000	42.18	35.05	31.99	30.49	29.71	29.28
4,000	56.24	46.73	42.66	40.66	39.61	39.04
5,000	70.30	58.41	53.32	50.82	49.52	48.81
6,000	84.36	70.09	63.99	60.99	59.42	58.57
7,000	98.42	81.78	74.65	71.15	69.32	68.33
8,000	112.48	93.46	85.32	81.32	79.22	78.09
9,000	126.54	105.14	95.98	91.48	89.13	87.85
10,000	140.60	116.82	106.65	101.65	99.03	97.61
15,000	210.91	175.24	159.97	152.47	148.55	146.42
20,000	281.21	233.65	213.29	203.30	198.06	195.22
25,000	351.51	292.06	266.62	254.12	247.58	244.03
30,000	421.81	350.47	319.94	304.95	297.09	292.83
35,000	492.12	408.89	373.26	355.77	346.61	341.64
40,000	562.42	467.30	426.59	406.60	396.12	390.45
45,000	632.72	525.71	479.91	457.42	445.64	439.25
50,000	703.02	584.12	533.23	508.24	495.15	488.06
55,000	773.33	642.53	586.55	559.07	544.67	536.86
60,000	843.63	700.95	639.88	609.89	594.18	585.67
65,000	913.93	759.36	693.20	660.72	643.70	634.48
70,000	984.23	817.77	746.52	711.54	693.21	683.28
75,000	1,054.54	876.18	799.85	762.37	742.73	732.09
80,000	1,124.84	934.60	853.17	813.19	792.24	780.89
85,000	1,195.14	993.01	906.49	864.02	841.76	829.70
90,000	1,265.44	1,051.42	959.82	914.84	891.27	878.50
95,000	1,335.75	1,109.83	1,013.14	965.67	940.79	927.31
100,000	1,406.05	1,168.24	1,066.46	1,016.49	990.30	976.12
110,000	1,546.65	1,285.07	1,173.11	1,118.14	1,089.34	1,073.73
120,000	1,687.26	1,401.89	1,279.76	1,219.79	1,188.37	1,171.34
130,000	1,827.86	1,518.72	1,386.40	1,321.44	1,287.40	1,268.95
140,000	1,968.47	1,635.54	1,493.05	1,423.09	1,386.43	1,366.56
150,000	2,109.07	1,752.37	1,599.70	1,524.74	1,485.46	1,464.17
160,000	2,249.68	1,869.19	1,706.34	1,626.38	1,584.49	1,561.79
170,000	2,390.28	1,986.02	1,812.99	1,728.03	1,683.52	1,659.40
180,000	2,530.89	2,102.84	1,919.63	1,829.68	1,782.55	1,757.01
190,000	2,671.49	2,219.66	2,026.28	1,931.33	1,881.58	1,854.62
200,000	2,812.09	2,336.49	2,132.93	2,032.98	1,980.61	1,952.23

TABLE I-8. Fixed Rate Mortgage at 11.75%

MONTHLY PAYMENT
NECESSARY TO AMORTIZE A LOAN — 11.75%

AMOUNT \ TERM	10 YEARS	15 YEARS	20 YEARS	25 YEARS	30 YEARS	35 YEARS
50	0.71	0.59	0.54	0.52	0.50	0.50
100	1.42	1.18	1.08	1.03	1.01	1.00
200	2.84	2.37	2.17	2.07	2.02	1.99
300	4.26	3.55	3.25	3.10	3.03	2.99
400	5.68	4.74	4.33	4.14	4.04	3.98
500	7.10	5.92	5.42	5.17	5.05	4.98
600	8.52	7.10	6.50	6.21	6.06	5.97
700	9.94	8.29	7.59	7.24	7.07	6.97
800	11.36	9.47	8.67	8.28	8.08	7.97
900	12.78	10.66	9.75	9.31	9.08	8.96
1,000	14.20	11.84	10.84	10.35	10.09	9.96
2,000	28.41	23.68	21.67	20.70	20.19	19.92
3,000	42.61	35.52	32.51	31.04	30.28	29.87
4,000	56.81	47.37	43.35	41.39	40.38	39.83
5,000	71.02	59.21	54.19	51.74	50.47	49.79
6,000	85.22	71.05	65.02	62.09	60.56	59.75
7,000	99.42	82.89	75.86	72.44	70.66	69.71
8,000	113.63	94.73	86.70	82.78	80.75	79.66
9,000	127.83	106.57	97.54	93.13	90.85	89.62
10,000	142.03	118.42	108.37	103.48	100.94	99.58
15,000	213.05	177.62	162.56	155.22	151.41	149.37
20,000	284.07	236.83	216.74	206.96	201.88	199.16
25,000	355.09	296.04	270.93	258.70	252.35	248.95
30,000	426.10	355.25	325.12	310.44	302.82	298.74
35,000	497.12	414.46	379.30	362.18	353.30	348.53
40,000	568.14	473.66	433.49	413.92	403.77	398.32
45,000	639.15	532.87	487.68	465.66	454.24	448.11
50,000	710.17	592.08	541.86	517.40	504.71	497.90
55,000	781.19	651.29	596.05	569.14	555.18	547.69
60,000	852.21	710.50	650.23	620.89	605.65	597.48
65,000	923.22	769.70	704.42	672.63	656.12	647.27
70,000	994.24	828.91	758.61	724.37	706.59	697.06
75,000	1,065.26	888.12	812.79	776.11	757.06	746.85
80,000	1,136.27	947.33	866.98	827.85	807.53	796.64
85,000	1,207.29	1,006.53	921.17	879.59	858.00	846.43
90,000	1,278.31	1,065.74	975.35	931.33	908.47	896.22
95,000	1,349.33	1,124.95	1,029.54	983.07	958.95	946.01
100,000	1,420.34	1,184.16	1,083.72	1,034.81	1,009.42	995.80
110,000	1,562.38	1,302.57	1,192.10	1,138.29	1,110.36	1,095.38
120,000	1,704.41	1,420.99	1,300.47	1,241.77	1,211.30	1,194.96
130,000	1,846.45	1,539.41	1,408.84	1,345.25	1,312.24	1,294.54
140,000	1,988.48	1,657.82	1,517.21	1,448.73	1,413.18	1,394.12
150,000	2,130.51	1,776.24	1,625.59	1,552.21	1,514.12	1,493.70
160,000	2,272.55	1,894.65	1,733.96	1,655.69	1,615.07	1,593.28
170,000	2,414.58	2,013.07	1,842.33	1,759.17	1,716.01	1,692.86
180,000	2,556.62	2,131.49	1,950.70	1,862.66	1,816.95	1,792.44
190,000	2,698.65	2,249.90	2,059.08	1,966.14	1,917.89	1,892.02
200,000	2,840.69	2,368.32	2,167.45	2,069.62	2,018.83	1,991.60

TABLE I-9. Fixed Rate Mortgage at 12.00%

MONTHLY PAYMENT
NECESSARY TO AMORTIZE A LOAN 12.00%

AMOUNT \ TERM	10 YEARS	15 YEARS	20 YEARS	25 YEARS	30 YEARS	35 YEARS
50	0.72	0.60	0.55	0.53	0.51	0.51
100	1.43	1.20	1.10	1.05	1.03	1.02
200	2.87	2.40	2.20	2.11	2.06	2.03
300	4.30	3.60	3.30	3.16	3.09	3.05
400	5.74	4.80	4.40	4.21	4.11	4.06
500	7.17	6.00	5.51	5.27	5.14	5.08
600	8.61	7.20	6.61	6.32	6.17	6.09
700	10.04	8.40	7.71	7.37	7.20	7.11
800	11.48	9.60	8.81	8.43	8.23	8.12
900	12.91	10.80	9.91	9.48	9.26	9.14
1,000	14.35	12.00	11.01	10.53	10.29	10.16
2,000	28.70	24.00	22.02	21.06	20.57	20.31
3,000	43.04	36.01	33.03	31.60	30.86	30.47
4,000	57.39	48.01	44.04	42.13	41.15	40.62
5,000	71.74	60.01	55.06	52.66	51.43	50.78
6,000	86.09	72.01	66.07	63.19	61.72	60.93
7,000	100.44	84.02	77.08	73.73	72.00	71.09
8,000	114.78	96.02	88.09	84.26	82.29	81.24
9,000	129.13	108.02	99.10	94.79	92.58	91.40
10,000	143.48	120.02	110.11	105.32	102.86	101.56
15,000	215.22	180.03	165.17	157.99	154.29	152.33
20,000	286.96	240.04	220.22	210.65	205.73	203.11
25,000	358.70	300.06	275.28	263.31	257.16	253.89
30,000	430.44	360.07	330.34	315.97	308.59	304.67
35,000	502.18	420.08	385.39	368.64	360.02	355.45
40,000	573.92	480.09	440.45	421.30	411.45	406.22
45,000	645.66	540.10	495.50	473.96	462.88	457.00
50,000	717.40	600.11	550.56	526.62	514.31	507.78
55,000	789.14	660.12	605.62	579.28	565.74	558.56
60,000	860.88	720.13	660.67	631.95	617.18	609.33
65,000	932.63	780.15	715.73	684.61	668.61	660.11
70,000	1,004.37	840.16	770.78	737.27	720.04	710.89
75,000	1,076.11	900.17	825.84	789.93	771.47	761.67
80,000	1,147.85	960.18	880.90	842.60	822.90	812.45
85,000	1,219.59	1,020.19	935.95	895.26	874.33	863.22
90,000	1,291.33	1,080.20	991.01	947.92	925.76	914.00
95,000	1,363.07	1,140.21	1,046.06	1,000.58	977.19	964.78
100,000	1,434.81	1,200.22	1,101.12	1,053.25	1,028.63	1,015.56
110,000	1,578.29	1,320.25	1,211.23	1,158.57	1,131.49	1,117.11
120,000	1,721.77	1,440.27	1,321.34	1,263.89	1,234.35	1,218.67
130,000	1,865.25	1,560.29	1,431.46	1,369.22	1,337.21	1,320.22
140,000	2,008.73	1,680.31	1,541.57	1,474.54	1,440.08	1,421.78
150,000	2,152.21	1,800.34	1,651.68	1,579.87	1,542.94	1,523.34
160,000	2,295.69	1,920.36	1,761.79	1,685.19	1,645.80	1,624.89
170,000	2,439.17	2,040.38	1,871.91	1,790.52	1,748.66	1,726.45
180,000	2,582.65	2,160.40	1,982.02	1,895.84	1,851.53	1,828.00
190,000	2,726.14	2,280.43	2,092.13	2,001.17	1,954.39	1,929.56
200,000	2,869.62	2,400.45	2,202.24	2,106.49	2,057.25	2,031.12

TABLE I-10. Fixed Rate Mortgage at 12.25%

MONTHLY PAYMENT
NECESSARY TO AMORTIZE A LOAN 12.25%

TERM / AMOUNT	10 YEARS	15 YEARS	20 YEARS	25 YEARS	30 YEARS	35 YEARS
50	0.72	0.61	0.56	0.54	0.52	0.52
100	1.45	1.22	1.12	1.07	1.05	1.04
200	2.90	2.43	2.24	2.14	2.10	2.07
300	4.35	3.65	3.36	3.22	3.14	3.11
400	5.80	4.87	4.47	4.29	4.19	4.14
500	7.25	6.08	5.59	5.36	5.24	5.18
600	8.70	7.30	6.71	6.43	6.29	6.21
700	10.14	8.51	7.83	7.50	7.34	7.25
800	11.59	9.73	8.95	8.57	8.38	8.28
900	13.04	10.95	10.07	9.65	9.43	9.32
1,000	14.49	12.16	11.19	10.72	10.48	10.35
2,000	28.98	24.33	22.37	21.44	20.96	20.71
3,000	43.48	36.49	33.56	32.15	31.44	31.06
4,000	57.97	48.65	44.74	42.87	41.92	41.41
5,000	72.46	60.82	55.93	53.59	52.40	51.77
6,000	86.95	72.98	67.11	64.31	62.87	62.12
7,000	101.45	85.14	78.30	75.02	73.35	72.48
8,000	115.94	97.31	89.49	85.74	83.83	82.83
9,000	130.43	109.47	100.67	96.46	94.31	93.18
10,000	144.92	121.63	111.86	107.18	104.79	103.54
15,000	217.39	182.45	167.79	160.76	157.19	155.31
20,000	289.85	243.26	223.72	214.35	209.58	207.07
25,000	362.31	304.08	279.64	267.94	261.98	258.84
30,000	434.77	364.90	335.57	321.53	314.37	310.61
35,000	507.23	425.71	391.50	375.11	366.77	362.38
40,000	579.69	486.53	447.43	428.70	419.16	414.15
45,000	652.16	547.34	503.36	482.29	471.56	465.92
50,000	724.62	608.16	559.29	535.88	523.95	517.69
55,000	797.08	668.98	615.22	589.46	576.35	569.46
60,000	869.54	729.79	671.15	643.05	628.74	621.22
65,000	942.00	790.61	727.08	696.64	681.14	672.99
70,000	1,014.46	851.42	783.00	750.23	733.53	724.76
75,000	1,086.93	912.24	838.93	803.81	785.93	776.53
80,000	1,159.39	973.06	894.86	857.40	838.32	828.30
85,000	1,231.85	1,033.87	950.79	910.99	890.72	880.07
90,000	1,304.31	1,094.69	1,006.72	964.58	943.11	931.84
95,000	1,376.77	1,155.50	1,062.65	1,018.16	995.51	983.60
100,000	1,449.24	1,216.32	1,118.58	1,071.75	1,047.90	1,035.37
110,000	1,594.16	1,337.95	1,230.43	1,178.93	1,152.69	1,138.91
120,000	1,739.08	1,459.58	1,342.29	1,286.10	1,257.48	1,242.45
130,000	1,884.01	1,581.22	1,454.15	1,393.28	1,362.27	1,345.99
140,000	2,028.93	1,702.85	1,566.01	1,500.45	1,467.06	1,449.52
150,000	2,173.85	1,824.48	1,677.87	1,607.63	1,571.85	1,553.06
160,000	2,318.78	1,946.11	1,789.72	1,714.80	1,676.64	1,656.60
170,000	2,463.70	2,067.74	1,901.58	1,821.98	1,781.43	1,760.14
180,000	2,608.62	2,189.38	2,013.44	1,929.15	1,886.22	1,863.67
190,000	2,753.55	2,311.01	2,125.30	2,036.33	1,991.01	1,967.21
200,000	2,898.47	2,432.64	2,237.15	2,143.50	2,095.80	2,070.75

TABLE I-11. Fixed Rate Mortgage at 12.50%

MONTHLY PAYMENT
NECESSARY TO AMORTIZE A LOAN 12.50%

TERM / AMCUNT	10 YEARS	15 YEARS	20 YEARS	25 YEARS	30 YEARS	35 YEARS
50	0.73	0.62	0.57	0.55	0.53	0.53
100	1.46	1.23	1.14	1.09	1.07	1.06
200	2.93	2.47	2.27	2.18	2.13	2.11
300	4.39	3.70	3.41	3.27	3.20	3.17
400	5.86	4.93	4.54	4.36	4.27	4.22
500	7.32	6.16	5.68	5.45	5.34	5.28
600	8.78	7.40	6.82	6.54	6.40	6.33
700	10.25	8.63	7.95	7.63	7.47	7.39
800	11.71	9.86	9.09	8.72	8.54	8.44
900	13.17	11.09	10.23	9.81	9.61	9.50
1,000	14.64	12.33	11.36	10.90	10.67	10.55
2,000	29.28	24.65	22.72	21.81	21.35	21.11
3,000	43.92	36.98	34.09	32.71	32.02	31.66
4,000	58.55	49.30	45.45	43.61	42.69	42.21
5,000	73.19	61.63	56.81	54.52	53.36	52.76
6,000	87.83	73.95	68.17	65.42	64.04	63.32
7,000	102.47	86.28	79.53	76.33	74.71	73.87
8,000	117.11	98.61	90.89	87.23	85.38	84.42
9,000	131.75	110.93	102.26	98.13	96.05	94.97
10,000	146.39	123.26	113.62	109.04	106.73	105.53
15,000	219.58	184.89	170.43	163.56	160.09	158.29
20,000	292.77	246.51	227.23	218.07	213.45	211.05
25,000	365.96	308.14	284.04	272.59	266.82	263.82
30,000	439.16	369.77	340.85	327.11	320.18	316.58
35,000	512.35	431.40	397.66	381.63	373.54	369.34
40,000	585.54	493.03	454.47	436.15	426.91	422.10
45,000	658.73	554.66	511.28	490.67	480.27	474.87
50,000	731.93	616.29	568.09	545.19	533.63	527.63
55,000	805.12	677.91	624.89	599.71	587.00	580.39
60,000	878.31	739.54	681.70	654.22	640.36	633.16
65,000	951.50	801.17	738.51	708.74	693.72	685.92
70,000	1,024.70	862.80	795.32	763.26	747.09	738.68
75,000	1,097.89	924.43	852.13	817.78	800.45	791.45
80,000	1,171.08	986.06	908.94	872.30	853.82	844.21
85,000	1,244.27	1,047.69	965.75	926.82	907.18	896.97
90,000	1,317.47	1,109.32	1,022.55	981.34	960.54	949.73
95,000	1,390.66	1,170.94	1,079.36	1,035.85	1,013.91	1,002.50
100,000	1,463.85	1,232.57	1,136.17	1,090.37	1,067.27	1,055.26
110,000	1,610.24	1,355.83	1,249.79	1,199.41	1,174.00	1,160.79
120,000	1,756.62	1,479.09	1,363.41	1,308.45	1,280.72	1,266.31
130,000	1,903.01	1,602.34	1,477.02	1,417.48	1,387.45	1,371.84
140,000	2,049.39	1,725.60	1,590.64	1,526.52	1,494.18	1,477.37
150,000	2,195.78	1,848.86	1,704.26	1,635.56	1,600.90	1,582.89
160,000	2,342.16	1,972.12	1,817.87	1,744.60	1,707.63	1,688.42
170,000	2,488.55	2,095.37	1,931.49	1,853.63	1,814.36	1,793.94
180,000	2,634.93	2,218.63	2,045.11	1,962.67	1,921.08	1,899.47
190,000	2,781.32	2,341.89	2,158.72	2,071.71	2,027.81	2,005.00
200,000	2,927.70	2,465.15	2,272.34	2,180.75	2,134.54	2,110.52

TABLE I-12. Fixed Rate Mortgage at 12.75%

MONTHLY PAYMENT
NECESSARY TO AMORTIZE A LOAN — 12.75%

TERM / AMOUNT	10 YEARS	15 YEARS	20 YEARS	25 YEARS	30 YEARS	35 YEARS
50	0.74	0.62	0.58	0.55	0.54	0.54
100	1.48	1.25	1.15	1.11	1.09	1.08
200	2.96	2.50	2.31	2.22	2.17	2.15
300	4.44	3.75	3.46	3.33	3.26	3.23
400	5.91	5.00	4.62	4.44	4.35	4.30
500	7.39	6.24	5.77	5.55	5.43	5.38
600	8.87	7.49	6.92	6.65	6.52	6.45
700	10.35	8.74	8.08	7.76	7.61	7.53
800	11.83	9.99	9.23	8.87	8.69	8.60
900	13.31	11.24	10.38	9.98	9.78	9.68
1,000	14.78	12.49	11.54	11.09	10.87	10.75
2,000	29.57	24.98	23.08	22.18	21.73	21.50
3,000	44.35	37.47	34.61	33.27	32.60	32.26
4,000	59.14	49.95	46.15	44.36	43.47	43.01
5,000	73.92	62.44	57.69	55.45	54.33	53.76
6,000	88.71	74.93	69.23	66.54	65.20	64.51
7,000	103.49	87.42	80.77	77.63	76.07	75.26
8,000	118.27	99.91	92.31	88.72	86.94	86.02
9,000	133.06	112.40	103.84	99.82	97.80	96.77
10,000	147.84	124.89	115.38	110.91	108.67	107.52
15,000	221.76	187.33	173.07	166.36	163.00	161.28
20,000	295.69	249.77	230.76	221.81	217.34	215.04
25,000	369.61	312.21	288.46	277.26	271.67	268.80
30,000	443.53	374.66	346.15	332.72	326.01	322.56
35,000	517.45	437.10	403.84	388.17	380.34	376.32
40,000	591.37	499.54	461.53	443.62	434.68	430.08
45,000	665.29	561.98	519.22	499.08	489.01	483.84
50,000	739.22	624.43	576.91	554.53	543.35	537.60
55,000	813.14	686.87	634.60	609.98	597.68	591.36
60,000	887.06	749.31	692.29	665.44	652.02	645.12
65,000	960.98	811.76	749.98	720.89	706.35	698.88
70,000	1,034.90	874.20	807.68	776.34	760.69	752.64
75,000	1,108.82	936.64	865.37	831.79	815.02	806.40
80,000	1,182.74	999.08	923.06	887.25	869.36	860.16
85,000	1,256.67	1,061.53	980.75	942.70	923.69	913.92
90,000	1,330.59	1,123.97	1,038.44	998.15	978.03	967.68
95,000	1,404.51	1,186.41	1,096.13	1,053.61	1,032.36	1,021.44
100,000	1,478.43	1,248.86	1,153.82	1,109.06	1,086.70	1,075.20
110,000	1,626.27	1,373.74	1,269.20	1,219.96	1,195.37	1,182.72
120,000	1,774.12	1,498.63	1,384.59	1,330.87	1,304.04	1,290.24
130,000	1,921.96	1,623.51	1,499.97	1,441.78	1,412.71	1,397.76
140,000	2,069.80	1,748.40	1,615.35	1,552.68	1,521.38	1,505.28
150,000	2,217.65	1,873.28	1,730.73	1,663.59	1,630.05	1,612.80
160,000	2,365.49	1,998.17	1,846.12	1,774.49	1,738.72	1,720.32
170,000	2,513.33	2,123.05	1,961.50	1,885.40	1,847.38	1,827.84
180,000	2,661.18	2,247.94	2,076.88	1,996.31	1,956.05	1,935.36
190,000	2,809.02	2,372.83	2,192.26	2,107.21	2,064.72	2,042.88
200,000	2,956.86	2,497.71	2,307.65	2,218.12	2,173.39	2,150.40

TABLE I-13. **Fixed Rate Mortgage at 13.00%**

MONTHLY PAYMENT
NECESSARY TO AMORTIZE A LOAN 13.00%

TERM / AMOUNT	10 YEARS	15 YEARS	20 YEARS	25 YEARS	30 YEARS	35 YEARS
50	0.75	0.63	0.59	0.56	0.55	0.55
100	1.49	1.27	1.17	1.13	1.11	1.10
200	2.99	2.53	2.34	2.26	2.21	2.19
300	4.48	3.80	3.51	3.38	3.32	3.29
400	5.97	5.06	4.69	4.51	4.42	4.38
500	7.47	6.33	5.86	5.64	5.53	5.48
600	8.96	7.59	7.03	6.77	6.64	6.57
700	10.45	8.86	8.20	7.89	7.74	7.67
800	11.95	10.12	9.37	9.02	8.85	8.76
900	13.44	11.39	10.54	10.15	9.96	9.86
1,000	14.93	12.65	11.72	11.28	11.06	10.95
2,000	29.86	25.31	23.43	22.56	22.12	21.90
3,000	44.79	37.96	35.15	33.84	33.19	32.86
4,000	59.73	50.61	46.86	45.11	44.25	43.81
5,000	74.66	63.26	58.58	56.39	55.31	54.76
6,000	89.59	75.92	70.30	67.67	66.37	65.71
7,000	104.52	88.57	82.01	78.95	77.43	76.66
8,000	119.45	101.22	93.73	90.23	88.50	87.62
9,000	134.38	113.87	105.44	101.51	99.56	98.57
10,000	149.32	126.53	117.16	112.78	110.62	109.52
15,000	223.97	189.79	175.74	169.18	165.93	164.28
20,000	298.63	253.05	234.32	225.57	221.24	219.04
25,000	373.29	316.32	292.90	281.96	276.55	273.80
30,000	447.95	379.58	351.48	338.35	331.86	328.56
35,000	522.61	442.85	410.06	394.75	387.17	383.32
40,000	597.27	506.11	468.64	451.14	442.48	438.08
45,000	671.92	569.37	527.22	507.53	497.79	492.84
50,000	746.58	632.64	585.80	563.92	553.10	547.60
55,000	821.24	695.90	644.38	620.32	608.41	602.36
60,000	895.90	759.16	702.96	676.71	663.72	657.12
65,000	970.56	822.43	761.54	733.10	719.03	711.88
70,000	1,045.21	885.69	820.12	789.49	774.34	766.64
75,000	1,119.87	948.96	878.70	845.88	829.65	821.40
80,000	1,194.53	1,012.22	937.28	902.28	884.96	876.16
85,000	1,269.19	1,075.48	995.86	958.67	940.28	930.92
90,000	1,343.85	1,138.75	1,054.43	1,015.06	995.59	985.68
95,000	1,418.50	1,202.01	1,113.01	1,071.45	1,050.90	1,040.44
100,000	1,493.16	1,265.27	1,171.59	1,127.85	1,106.21	1,095.20
110,000	1,642.48	1,391.80	1,288.75	1,240.63	1,216.83	1,204.72
120,000	1,791.80	1,518.33	1,405.91	1,353.42	1,327.45	1,314.24
130,000	1,941.11	1,644.86	1,523.07	1,466.20	1,438.07	1,423.76
140,000	2,090.43	1,771.38	1,640.23	1,578.99	1,548.69	1,533.28
150,000	2,239.74	1,897.91	1,757.39	1,691.77	1,659.31	1,642.80
160,000	2,389.06	2,024.44	1,874.55	1,804.55	1,769.93	1,752.31
170,000	2,538.38	2,150.97	1,991.71	1,917.34	1,880.55	1,861.83
180,000	2,687.69	2,277.49	2,108.87	2,030.12	1,991.17	1,971.35
190,000	2,837.01	2,404.02	2,226.03	2,142.91	2,101.79	2,080.87
200,000	2,986.33	2,530.55	2,343.19	2,255.69	2,212.41	2,190.39

TABLE I 14. Fixed Rate Mortgage at 13.25%

MONTHLY PAYMENT
NECESSARY TO AMORTIZE A LOAN 13.25%

TERM / AMOUNT	10 YEARS	15 YEARS	20 YEARS	25 YEARS	30 YEARS	35 YEARS
50	0.75	0.64	0.59	0.57	0.56	0.56
100	1.51	1.28	1.19	1.15	1.13	1.12
200	3.02	2.56	2.38	2.29	2.25	2.23
300	4.52	3.85	3.57	3.44	3.38	3.35
400	6.03	5.13	4.76	4.59	4.50	4.46
500	7.54	6.41	5.95	5.73	5.63	5.58
600	9.05	7.69	7.14	6.88	6.75	6.69
700	10.56	8.97	8.33	8.03	7.88	7.81
800	12.06	10.25	9.52	9.17	9.01	8.92
900	13.57	11.54	10.71	10.32	10.13	10.04
1,000	15.08	12.82	11.89	11.47	11.26	11.15
2,000	30.16	25.64	23.79	22.93	22.52	22.30
3,000	45.24	38.45	35.68	34.40	33.77	33.46
4,000	60.32	51.27	47.58	45.87	45.03	44.61
5,000	75.40	64.09	59.47	57.34	56.29	55.76
6,000	90.48	76.91	71.37	68.80	67.55	66.91
7,000	105.56	89.72	83.26	80.27	78.80	78.07
8,000	120.63	102.54	95.16	91.74	90.06	89.22
9,000	135.71	115.36	107.05	103.20	101.32	100.37
10,000	150.79	128.18	118.94	114.67	112.58	111.52
15,000	226.19	192.26	178.42	172.01	168.87	167.29
20,000	301.59	256.35	237.89	229.34	225.16	223.05
25,000	376.98	320.44	297.36	286.68	281.44	278.81
30,000	452.38	384.53	356.83	344.01	337.73	334.57
35,000	527.78	448.62	416.31	401.35	394.02	390.34
40,000	603.17	512.70	475.78	458.68	450.31	446.10
45,000	678.57	576.79	535.25	516.02	506.60	501.86
50,000	753.97	640.88	594.72	573.35	562.89	557.62
55,000	829.36	704.97	654.19	630.69	619.18	613.38
60,000	904.76	769.06	713.67	688.03	675.47	669.15
65,000	980.16	833.14	773.14	745.36	731.76	724.91
70,000	1,055.55	897.23	832.61	802.70	788.04	780.67
75,000	1,130.95	961.32	892.08	860.03	844.33	836.43
80,000	1,206.35	1,025.41	951.56	917.37	900.62	892.20
85,000	1,281.74	1,089.50	1,011.03	974.70	956.91	947.96
90,000	1,357.14	1,153.58	1,070.50	1,032.04	1,013.20	1,003.72
95,000	1,432.54	1,217.67	1,129.97	1,089.37	1,069.49	1,059.48
100,000	1,507.93	1,281.76	1,189.44	1,146.71	1,125.78	1,115.24
110,000	1,658.73	1,409.94	1,308.39	1,261.38	1,238.36	1,226.77
120,000	1,809.52	1,538.11	1,427.33	1,376.05	1,350.93	1,338.29
130,000	1,960.31	1,666.29	1,546.28	1,490.72	1,463.51	1,449.82
140,000	2,111.11	1,794.46	1,665.22	1,605.39	1,576.09	1,561.34
150,000	2,261.90	1,922.64	1,784.17	1,720.06	1,688.67	1,672.87
160,000	2,412.69	2,050.82	1,903.11	1,834.73	1,801.25	1,784.39
170,000	2,563.48	2,178.99	2,022.06	1,949.40	1,913.82	1,895.92
180,000	2,714.28	2,307.17	2,141.00	2,064.08	2,026.40	2,007.44
190,000	2,865.07	2,435.34	2,259.95	2,178.75	2,138.98	2,118.97
200,000	3,015.86	2,563.52	2,378.89	2,293.42	2,251.56	2,230.49

TABLE I-15. Fixed Rate Mortgage at 13.50%

MONTHLY PAYMENT
NECESSARY TO AMORTIZE A LOAN 13.50%

TERM / AMOUNT	10 YEARS	15 YEARS	20 YEARS	25 YEARS	30 YEARS	35 YEARS
50	0.76	0.65	0.60	0.58	0.57	0.57
100	1.52	1.30	1.21	1.17	1.15	1.14
200	3.05	2.60	2.41	2.33	2.29	2.27
300	4.57	3.90	3.62	3.50	3.44	3.41
400	6.09	5.19	4.83	4.66	4.58	4.54
500	7.61	6.49	6.04	5.83	5.73	5.68
600	9.14	7.79	7.24	6.99	6.87	6.81
700	10.66	9.09	8.45	8.16	8.02	7.95
800	12.18	10.39	9.66	9.33	9.16	9.08
900	13.71	11.69	10.87	10.49	10.31	10.22
1,000	15.23	12.98	12.07	11.66	11.45	11.35
2,000	30.46	25.97	24.15	23.31	22.91	22.71
3,000	45.68	38.95	36.22	34.97	34.36	34.06
4,000	60.91	51.93	48.30	46.63	45.82	45.41
5,000	76.14	64.92	60.37	58.28	57.27	56.77
6,000	91.37	77.90	72.44	69.94	68.73	68.12
7,000	106.60	90.88	84.52	81.60	80.18	79.47
8,000	121.82	103.87	96.59	93.25	91.63	90.83
9,000	137.05	116.85	108.67	104.91	103.09	102.18
10,000	152.28	129.84	120.74	116.57	114.54	113.53
15,000	228.42	194.75	181.11	174.85	171.81	170.30
20,000	304.56	259.67	241.48	233.13	229.08	227.07
25,000	380.70	324.59	301.85	291.41	286.35	283.84
30,000	456.84	389.51	362.22	349.70	343.63	340.60
35,000	532.98	454.42	422.59	407.98	400.90	397.37
40,000	609.12	519.34	482.96	466.26	458.17	454.14
45,000	685.27	584.26	543.33	524.55	515.44	510.91
50,000	761.41	649.18	603.70	582.83	572.71	567.67
55,000	837.55	714.10	664.07	641.11	629.98	624.44
60,000	913.69	779.01	724.44	699.39	687.25	681.21
65,000	989.83	843.93	784.81	757.68	744.52	737.97
70,000	1,065.97	908.85	845.18	815.96	801.79	794.74
75,000	1,142.11	973.77	905.55	874.24	859.06	851.51
80,000	1,218.25	1,038.69	965.92	932.53	916.34	908.28
85,000	1,294.39	1,103.60	1,026.29	990.81	973.61	965.04
90,000	1,370.53	1,168.52	1,086.66	1,049.09	1,030.88	1,021.81
95,000	1,446.67	1,233.44	1,147.03	1,107.38	1,088.15	1,078.58
100,000	1,522.81	1,298.36	1,207.40	1,165.66	1,145.42	1,135.34
110,000	1,675.09	1,428.19	1,328.14	1,282.22	1,259.96	1,248.88
120,000	1,827.37	1,558.03	1,448.88	1,398.79	1,374.50	1,362.41
130,000	1,979.66	1,687.86	1,569.62	1,515.36	1,489.05	1,475.95
140,000	2,131.94	1,817.70	1,690.36	1,631.92	1,603.59	1,589.48
150,000	2,284.22	1,947.54	1,811.10	1,748.49	1,718.13	1,703.02
160,000	2,436.50	2,077.37	1,931.84	1,865.05	1,832.67	1,816.55
170,000	2,588.78	2,207.21	2,052.57	1,981.62	1,947.21	1,930.09
180,000	2,741.06	2,337.04	2,173.31	2,098.18	2,061.76	2,043.62
190,000	2,893.34	2,466.88	2,294.05	2,214.75	2,176.30	2,157.16
200,000	3,045.62	2,596.71	2,414.79	2,331.32	2,290.84	2,270.69

TABLE I-16. Fixed Rate Mortgage at 13.75%

MONTHLY PAYMENT
NECESSARY TO AMORTIZE A LOAN 13.75%

TERM AMOUNT	10 YEARS	15 YEARS	20 YEARS	25 YEARS	30 YEARS	35 YEARS
50	0.77	0.66	0.61	0.59	0.58	0.58
100	1.54	1.32	1.23	1.18	1.17	1.16
200	3.08	2.63	2.45	2.37	2.33	2.31
300	4.61	3.95	3.68	3.55	3.50	3.47
400	6.15	5.26	4.90	4.74	4.66	4.62
500	7.69	6.58	6.13	5.92	5.83	5.78
600	9.23	7.89	7.35	7.11	6.99	6.93
700	10.76	9.21	8.58	8.29	8.16	8.09
800	12.30	10.52	9.80	9.48	9.32	9.24
900	13.84	11.84	11.03	10.66	10.49	10.40
1,000	15.38	13.15	12.25	11.85	11.65	11.55
2,000	30.76	26.30	24.51	23.69	23.30	23.11
3,000	46.13	39.45	36.76	35.54	34.95	34.66
4,000	61.51	52.60	49.02	47.39	46.60	46.22
5,000	76.89	65.75	61.27	59.23	58.26	57.77
6,000	92.27	78.90	73.53	71.08	69.91	69.33
7,000	107.64	92.05	85.78	82.93	81.56	80.88
8,000	123.02	105.20	98.03	94.77	93.21	92.44
9,000	138.40	118.35	110.29	106.62	104.86	103.99
10,000	153.78	131.50	122.54	118.47	116.51	115.55
15,000	230.66	197.26	183.82	177.70	174.77	173.32
20,000	307.55	263.01	245.09	236.94	233.02	231.10
25,000	384.44	328.76	306.36	296.17	291.28	288.87
30,000	461.33	394.51	367.63	355.40	349.54	346.65
35,000	538.22	460.26	428.90	414.64	407.79	404.42
40,000	615.10	526.01	490.17	473.87	466.05	462.20
45,000	691.99	591.77	551.45	533.11	524.30	519.97
50,000	768.88	657.52	612.72	592.34	582.56	577.75
55,000	845.77	723.27	673.99	651.58	640.82	635.52
60,000	922.65	789.02	735.26	710.81	699.07	693.29
65,000	999.54	854.77	796.53	770.04	757.33	751.07
70,000	1,076.43	920.53	857.80	829.28	815.59	808.84
75,000	1,153.32	986.28	919.08	888.51	873.84	866.62
80,000	1,230.21	1,052.03	980.35	947.75	932.10	924.39
85,000	1,307.09	1,117.78	1,041.62	1,006.98	990.35	982.17
90,000	1,383.98	1,183.53	1,102.89	1,066.21	1,048.61	1,039.94
95,000	1,460.87	1,249.28	1,164.16	1,125.45	1,106.87	1,097.72
100,000	1,537.76	1,315.04	1,225.43	1,184.68	1,165.12	1,155.49
110,000	1,691.53	1,446.54	1,347.98	1,303.15	1,281.63	1,271.04
120,000	1,845.31	1,578.04	1,470.52	1,421.62	1,398.15	1,386.59
130,000	1,999.08	1,709.55	1,593.06	1,540.09	1,514.66	1,502.14
140,000	2,152.86	1,841.05	1,715.61	1,658.56	1,631.17	1,617.69
150,000	2,306.64	1,972.56	1,838.15	1,777.02	1,747.68	1,733.24
160,000	2,460.41	2,104.06	1,960.69	1,895.49	1,864.20	1,848.78
170,000	2,614.19	2,235.56	2,083.24	2,013.96	1,980.71	1,964.33
180,000	2,767.96	2,367.07	2,205.78	2,132.43	2,097.22	2,079.88
190,000	2,921.74	2,498.57	2,328.32	2,250.90	2,213.73	2,195.43
200,000	3,075.52	2,630.07	2,450.87	2,369.37	2,330.24	2,310.98

TABLE I-17. Fixed Rate Mortgage at 14.00%

MONTHLY PAYMENT
NECESSARY TO AMORTIZE A LOAN 14.00%

TERM / AMOUNT	10 YEARS	15 YEARS	20 YEARS	25 YEARS	30 YEARS	35 YEARS
50	0.78	0.67	0.62	0.60	0.59	0.59
100	1.55	1.33	1.24	1.20	1.18	1.18
200	3.11	2.66	2.49	2.41	2.37	2.35
300	4.66	4.00	3.73	3.61	3.55	3.53
400	6.21	5.33	4.97	4.82	4.74	4.70
500	7.76	6.66	6.22	6.02	5.92	5.88
600	9.32	7.99	7.46	7.22	7.11	7.05
700	10.87	9.32	8.70	8.43	8.29	8.23
800	12.42	10.65	9.95	9.63	9.48	9.41
900	13.97	11.99	11.19	10.83	10.66	10.58
1,000	15.53	13.32	12.44	12.04	11.85	11.76
2,000	31.05	26.64	24.87	24.08	23.70	23.51
3,000	46.58	39.95	37.31	36.11	35.55	35.27
4,000	62.11	53.27	49.74	48.15	47.40	47.03
5,000	77.64	66.59	62.18	60.19	59.24	58.78
6,000	93.16	79.91	74.61	72.23	71.09	70.54
7,000	108.69	93.22	87.05	84.26	82.94	82.30
8,000	124.22	106.54	99.48	96.30	94.79	94.05
9,000	139.74	119.86	111.92	108.34	106.64	105.81
10,000	155.27	133.18	124.35	120.38	118.49	117.57
15,000	232.91	199.77	186.53	180.57	177.73	176.35
20,000	310.54	266.35	248.71	240.75	236.98	235.14
25,000	388.18	332.94	310.88	300.94	296.22	293.92
30,000	465.82	399.53	373.06	361.13	355.46	352.70
35,000	543.45	466.12	435.24	421.32	414.71	411.49
40,000	621.09	532.71	497.42	481.51	473.95	470.27
45,000	698.72	599.30	559.59	541.70	533.19	529.05
50,000	776.36	665.89	621.77	601.89	592.44	587.84
55,000	854.00	732.47	683.95	662.07	651.68	646.62
60,000	931.63	799.06	746.12	722.26	710.93	705.41
65,000	1,009.27	865.65	808.30	782.45	770.17	764.19
70,000	1,086.90	932.24	870.48	842.64	829.41	822.97
75,000	1,164.54	998.83	932.65	902.83	888.66	881.76
80,000	1,242.18	1,065.42	994.83	963.02	947.90	940.54
85,000	1,319.81	1,132.01	1,057.01	1,023.21	1,007.15	999.32
90,000	1,397.45	1,198.59	1,119.18	1,083.39	1,066.39	1,058.11
95,000	1,475.08	1,265.18	1,181.36	1,143.58	1,125.63	1,116.89
100,000	1,552.72	1,331.77	1,243.54	1,203.77	1,184.88	1,175.68
110,000	1,707.99	1,464.95	1,367.89	1,324.15	1,303.36	1,293.24
120,000	1,863.26	1,598.13	1,492.25	1,444.52	1,421.85	1,410.81
130,000	2,018.53	1,731.30	1,616.60	1,564.90	1,540.34	1,528.38
140,000	2,173.81	1,864.48	1,740.95	1,685.28	1,658.83	1,645.95
150,000	2,329.08	1,997.66	1,865.31	1,805.66	1,777.32	1,763.51
160,000	2,484.35	2,130.83	1,989.66	1,926.03	1,895.80	1,881.08
170,000	2,639.62	2,264.01	2,114.01	2,046.41	2,014.29	1,998.65
180,000	2,794.89	2,397.19	2,238.37	2,166.79	2,132.78	2,116.22
190,000	2,950.17	2,530.37	2,362.72	2,287.16	2,251.27	2,233.78
200,000	3,105.44	2,663.54	2,487.08	2,407.54	2,369.75	2,351.35

TABLE I-18. Fixed Rate Mortgage at 14.25%

MONTHLY PAYMENT
NECESSARY TO AMORTIZE A LOAN 14.25%

AMOUNT \ TERM	10 YEARS	15 YEARS	20 YEARS	25 YEARS	30 YEARS	35 YEARS
50	0.78	0.67	0.63	0.61	0.60	0.60
100	1.57	1.35	1.26	1.22	1.20	1.20
200	3.14	2.70	2.52	2.45	2.41	2.39
300	4.70	4.05	3.79	3.67	3.61	3.59
400	6.27	5.39	5.05	4.89	4.82	4.78
500	7.84	6.74	6.31	6.11	6.02	5.98
600	9.41	8.09	7.57	7.34	7.23	7.18
700	10.97	9.44	8.83	8.56	8.43	8.37
800	12.54	10.79	10.09	9.78	9.64	9.57
900	14.11	12.14	11.36	11.01	10.84	10.76
1,000	15.68	13.49	12.62	12.23	12.05	11.96
2,000	31.36	26.97	25.23	24.46	24.09	23.92
3,000	47.03	40.46	37.85	36.69	36.14	35.88
4,000	62.71	53.94	50.47	48.92	48.19	47.84
5,000	78.39	67.43	63.09	61.15	60.23	59.80
6,000	94.07	80.92	75.70	73.38	72.28	71.75
7,000	109.75	94.40	88.32	85.61	84.33	83.71
8,000	125.42	107.89	100.94	97.84	96.38	95.67
9,000	141.10	121.38	113.56	110.06	108.42	107.63
10,000	156.78	134.86	126.17	122.29	120.47	119.59
15,000	235.17	202.29	189.26	183.44	180.70	179.39
20,000	313.56	269.72	252.35	244.59	240.94	239.18
25,000	391.95	337.16	315.44	305.74	301.17	298.98
30,000	470.34	404.59	378.52	366.88	361.41	358.77
35,000	548.73	472.02	441.61	428.03	421.64	418.57
40,000	627.12	539.45	504.70	489.18	481.88	478.36
45,000	705.51	606.88	567.78	550.32	542.11	538.16
50,000	783.91	674.31	630.87	611.47	602.35	597.95
55,000	862.30	741.74	693.96	672.62	662.58	657.75
60,000	940.69	809.17	757.05	733.76	722.82	717.54
65,000	1,019.08	876.60	820.13	794.91	783.05	777.34
70,000	1,097.47	944.04	883.22	856.06	843.29	837.13
75,000	1,175.86	1,011.47	946.31	917.21	903.52	896.93
80,000	1,254.25	1,078.90	1,009.39	978.35	963.76	956.73
85,000	1,332.64	1,146.33	1,072.48	1,039.50	1,023.99	1,016.52
90,000	1,411.03	1,213.76	1,135.57	1,100.65	1,084.23	1,076.32
95,000	1,489.42	1,281.19	1,198.66	1,161.79	1,144.46	1,136.11
100,000	1,567.81	1,348.62	1,261.74	1,222.94	1,204.70	1,195.91
110,000	1,724.59	1,483.49	1,387.92	1,345.24	1,325.16	1,315.50
120,000	1,881.37	1,618.35	1,514.09	1,467.53	1,445.63	1,435.09
130,000	2,038.15	1,753.21	1,640.27	1,589.82	1,566.10	1,554.68
140,000	2,194.94	1,888.07	1,766.44	1,712.12	1,686.57	1,674.27
150,000	2,351.72	2,022.93	1,892.62	1,834.41	1,807.04	1,793.86
160,000	2,508.50	2,157.80	2,018.79	1,956.71	1,927.51	1,913.45
170,000	2,665.28	2,292.66	2,144.96	2,079.00	2,047.98	2,033.04
180,000	2,822.06	2,427.52	2,271.14	2,201.29	2,168.45	2,152.63
190,000	2,978.84	2,562.38	2,397.31	2,323.59	2,288.92	2,272.22
200,000	3,135.62	2,697.25	2,523.49	2,445.88	2,409.39	2,391.81

TABLE I-19. Fixed Rate Mortgage at 14.50%

MONTHLY PAYMENT
NECESSARY TO AMORTIZE A LOAN 14.50%

TERM AMOUNT	10 YEARS	15 YEARS	20 YEARS	25 YEARS	30 YEARS	35 YEARS
50	0.79	0.68	0.64	0.62	0.61	0.61
100	1.58	1.37	1.28	1.24	1.22	1.22
200	3.17	2.73	2.56	2.48	2.45	2.43
300	4.75	4.10	3.84	3.73	3.67	3.65
400	6.33	5.46	5.12	4.97	4.90	4.86
500	7.91	6.83	6.40	6.21	6.12	6.08
600	9.50	8.19	7.68	7.45	7.35	7.30
700	11.08	9.56	8.96	8.70	8.57	8.51
800	12.66	10.92	10.24	9.94	9.80	9.73
900	14.25	12.29	11.52	11.18	11.02	10.95
1,000	15.83	13.66	12.80	12.42	12.25	12.16
2,000	31.66	27.31	25.60	24.84	24.49	24.32
3,000	47.49	40.97	38.40	37.27	36.74	36.49
4,000	63.32	54.62	51.20	49.69	48.98	48.65
5,000	79.15	68.28	64.00	62.11	61.23	60.81
6,000	94.97	81.93	76.80	74.53	73.47	72.97
7,000	110.80	95.59	89.60	86.95	85.72	85.13
8,000	126.63	109.24	102.40	99.37	97.96	97.29
9,000	142.46	122.90	115.20	111.80	110.21	109.46
10,000	158.29	136.55	128.00	124.22	122.46	121.62
15,000	237.44	204.83	192.00	186.33	183.68	182.43
20,000	316.58	273.10	256.00	248.43	244.91	243.23
25,000	395.73	341.38	320.00	310.54	306.14	304.04
30,000	474.87	409.66	384.00	372.65	367.37	364.85
35,000	554.02	477.93	448.00	434.76	428.60	425.66
40,000	633.16	546.21	512.00	496.87	489.82	486.47
45,000	712.31	614.48	576.00	558.98	551.05	547.28
50,000	791.45	682.76	640.00	621.08	612.28	608.09
55,000	870.60	751.04	704.00	683.19	673.51	668.89
60,000	949.74	819.31	768.01	745.30	734.74	729.70
65,000	1,028.89	887.59	832.01	807.41	795.96	790.51
70,000	1,108.03	955.86	896.01	869.52	857.19	851.32
75,000	1,187.18	1,024.14	960.01	931.63	918.42	912.13
80,000	1,266.32	1,092.42	1,024.01	993.74	979.65	972.94
85,000	1,345.47	1,160.69	1,088.01	1,055.84	1,040.88	1,033.75
90,000	1,424.61	1,228.97	1,152.01	1,117.95	1,102.10	1,094.55
95,000	1,503.76	1,297.24	1,216.01	1,180.06	1,163.33	1,155.36
100,000	1,582.90	1,365.52	1,280.01	1,242.17	1,224.56	1,216.17
110,000	1,741.19	1,502.07	1,408.01	1,366.39	1,347.01	1,337.79
120,000	1,899.48	1,638.62	1,536.01	1,490.60	1,469.47	1,459.41
130,000	2,057.78	1,775.18	1,664.01	1,614.82	1,591.93	1,581.02
140,000	2,216.07	1,911.73	1,792.01	1,739.04	1,714.38	1,702.64
150,000	2,374.36	2,048.28	1,920.01	1,863.25	1,836.84	1,824.26
160,000	2,532.65	2,184.83	2,048.01	1,987.47	1,959.29	1,945.88
170,000	2,690.94	2,321.38	2,176.01	2,111.69	2,081.75	2,067.49
180,000	2,849.23	2,457.94	2,304.02	2,235.90	2,204.21	2,189.11
190,000	3,007.52	2,594.49	2,432.02	2,360.12	2,326.66	2,310.73
200,000	3,165.81	2,731.04	2,560.02	2,484.34	2,449.12	2,432.34

TABLE I-20. Fixed Rate Mortgage at 14.75%

MONTHLY PAYMENT
NECESSARY TO AMORTIZE A LOAN 14.75%

TERM / AMOUNT	10 YEARS	15 YEARS	20 YEARS	25 YEARS	30 YEARS	35 YEARS
50	0.80	0.69	0.65	0.63	0.62	0.62
100	1.60	1.38	1.30	1.26	1.24	1.24
200	3.20	2.77	2.60	2.52	2.49	2.47
300	4.79	4.15	3.90	3.78	3.73	3.71
400	6.39	5.53	5.19	5.05	4.98	4.95
500	7.99	6.91	6.49	6.31	6.22	6.18
600	9.59	8.30	7.79	7.57	7.47	7.42
700	11.19	9.68	9.09	8.83	8.71	8.66
800	12.79	11.06	10.39	10.09	9.96	9.89
900	14.38	12.44	11.69	11.35	11.20	11.13
1,000	15.98	13.83	12.98	12.61	12.44	12.36
2,000	31.96	27.65	25.97	25.23	24.89	24.73
3,000	47.94	41.48	38.95	37.84	37.33	37.09
4,000	63.93	55.30	51.93	50.46	49.78	49.46
5,000	79.91	69.13	64.92	63.07	62.22	61.82
6,000	95.89	82.95	77.90	75.69	74.67	74.19
7,000	111.87	96.78	90.89	88.30	87.11	86.55
8,000	127.85	110.60	103.87	100.92	99.56	98.92
9,000	143.83	124.43	116.85	113.53	112.00	111.28
10,000	159.81	138.25	129.84	126.15	124.45	123.65
15,000	239.72	207.38	194.76	189.22	186.67	185.47
20,000	319.63	276.51	259.67	252.29	248.90	247.30
25,000	399.53	345.63	324.59	315.37	311.12	309.12
30,000	479.44	414.76	389.51	378.44	373.34	370.94
35,000	559.35	483.89	454.43	441.52	435.57	432.77
40,000	639.25	553.01	519.35	504.59	497.79	494.59
45,000	719.16	622.14	584.27	567.66	560.02	556.41
50,000	799.07	691.27	649.19	630.74	622.24	618.24
55,000	878.97	760.39	714.11	693.81	684.46	680.06
60,000	958.88	829.52	779.02	756.88	746.69	741.89
65,000	1,038.79	898.65	843.94	819.96	808.91	803.71
70,000	1,118.69	967.78	908.86	883.03	871.14	865.53
75,000	1,198.60	1,036.90	973.78	946.11	933.36	927.36
80,000	1,278.51	1,106.03	1,038.70	1,009.18	995.58	989.18
85,000	1,358.41	1,175.16	1,103.62	1,072.25	1,057.81	1,051.01
90,000	1,438.32	1,244.28	1,168.54	1,135.33	1,120.03	1,112.83
95,000	1,518.23	1,313.41	1,233.45	1,198.40	1,182.26	1,174.65
100,000	1,598.13	1,382.54	1,298.37	1,261.47	1,244.48	1,236.48
110,000	1,757.95	1,520.79	1,428.21	1,387.62	1,368.93	1,360.13
120,000	1,917.76	1,659.04	1,558.05	1,513.77	1,493.38	1,483.77
130,000	2,077.57	1,797.30	1,687.89	1,639.92	1,617.82	1,607.42
140,000	2,237.39	1,935.55	1,817.72	1,766.06	1,742.27	1,731.07
150,000	2,397.20	2,073.80	1,947.56	1,892.21	1,866.72	1,854.72
160,000	2,557.02	2,212.06	2,077.40	2,018.36	1,991.17	1,978.36
170,000	2,716.83	2,350.31	2,207.23	2,144.51	2,115.62	2,102.01
180,000	2,876.64	2,488.56	2,337.07	2,270.65	2,240.07	2,225.66
190,000	3,036.46	2,626.82	2,466.91	2,396.80	2,364.51	2,349.31
200,000	3,196.27	2,765.07	2,596.75	2,522.95	2,488.96	2,472.95

TABLE I-21. Fixed Rate Mortgage at 15.00%

MONTHLY PAYMENT
NECESSARY TO AMORTIZE A LOAN 15.00%

TERM / AMOUNT	10 YEARS	15 YEARS	20 YEARS	25 YEARS	30 YEARS	35 YEARS
50	0.81	0.70	0.66	0.64	0.63	0.63
100	1.61	1.40	1.32	1.28	1.26	1.26
200	3.23	2.80	2.63	2.56	2.53	2.51
300	4.84	4.20	3.95	3.84	3.79	3.77
400	6.45	5.60	5.27	5.12	5.06	5.03
500	8.07	7.00	6.58	6.40	6.32	6.28
600	9.68	8.40	7.90	7.69	7.59	7.54
700	11.29	9.80	9.22	8.97	8.85	8.80
800	12.91	11.20	10.53	10.25	10.12	10.05
900	14.52	12.60	11.85	11.53	11.38	11.31
1,000	16.13	14.00	13.17	12.81	12.64	12.57
2,000	32.27	27.99	26.34	25.62	25.29	25.14
3,000	48.40	41.99	39.50	38.43	37.93	37.70
4,000	64.54	55.98	52.67	51.23	50.58	50.27
5,000	80.67	69.98	65.84	64.04	63.22	62.84
6,000	96.80	83.98	79.01	76.85	75.87	75.41
7,000	112.94	97.97	92.18	89.66	88.51	87.98
8,000	129.07	111.97	105.34	102.47	101.16	100.55
9,000	145.21	125.96	118.51	115.28	113.80	113.11
10,000	161.34	139.96	131.68	128.08	126.44	125.68
15,000	242.01	209.94	197.52	192.13	189.67	188.52
20,000	322.68	279.92	263.36	256.17	252.89	251.36
25,000	403.35	349.90	329.20	320.21	316.11	314.20
30,000	484.02	419.88	395.04	384.25	379.33	377.04
35,000	564.69	489.86	460.88	448.29	442.56	439.89
40,000	645.36	559.84	526.72	512.33	505.78	502.73
45,000	726.03	629.82	592.56	576.38	569.00	565.57
50,000	806.70	699.80	658.40	640.42	632.22	628.41
55,000	887.36	769.78	724.24	704.46	695.45	691.25
60,000	968.03	839.77	790.08	768.50	758.67	754.09
65,000	1,048.70	909.75	855.92	832.54	821.89	816.93
70,000	1,129.37	979.73	921.76	896.59	885.11	879.77
75,000	1,210.04	1,049.71	987.60	960.63	948.34	942.61
80,000	1,290.71	1,119.69	1,053.44	1,024.67	1,011.56	1,005.45
85,000	1,371.38	1,189.67	1,119.28	1,088.71	1,074.78	1,068.29
90,000	1,452.05	1,259.65	1,185.12	1,152.75	1,138.00	1,131.13
95,000	1,532.72	1,329.63	1,250.96	1,216.80	1,201.22	1,193.97
100,000	1,613.39	1,399.61	1,316.80	1,280.84	1,264.45	1,256.81
110,000	1,774.73	1,539.57	1,448.48	1,408.92	1,390.89	1,382.50
120,000	1,936.07	1,679.53	1,580.16	1,537.00	1,517.34	1,508.18
130,000	2,097.41	1,819.49	1,711.84	1,665.09	1,643.78	1,633.86
140,000	2,258.75	1,959.45	1,843.52	1,793.17	1,770.23	1,759.54
150,000	2,420.09	2,099.41	1,975.20	1,921.26	1,896.67	1,885.22
160,000	2,581.43	2,239.37	2,106.88	2,049.34	2,023.12	2,010.90
170,000	2,742.76	2,379.34	2,238.56	2,177.42	2,149.56	2,136.59
180,000	2,904.10	2,519.30	2,370.24	2,305.51	2,276.01	2,262.27
190,000	3,065.44	2,659.26	2,501.92	2,433.59	2,402.45	2,387.95
200,000	3,226.78	2,799.22	2,633.60	2,561.67	2,528.89	2,513.63

TABLE I-22. Fixed Rate Mortgage at 15.25%

MONTHLY PAYMENT
NECESSARY TO AMORTIZE A LOAN 15.25%

AMOUNT / TERM	10 YEARS	15 YEARS	20 YEARS	25 YEARS	30 YEARS	35 YEARS
50	0.81	0.71	0.67	0.65	0.64	0.64
100	1.63	1.42	1.34	1.30	1.28	1.28
200	3.26	2.83	2.67	2.60	2.57	2.55
300	4.89	4.25	4.01	3.90	3.85	3.83
400	6.52	5.67	5.34	5.20	5.14	5.11
500	8.14	7.08	6.68	6.50	6.42	6.39
600	9.77	8.50	8.01	7.80	7.71	7.66
700	11.40	9.92	9.35	9.10	8.99	8.94
800	13.03	11.33	10.68	10.40	10.28	10.22
900	14.66	12.75	12.02	11.70	11.56	11.49
1,000	16.29	14.17	13.35	13.00	12.84	12.77
2,000	32.58	28.34	26.71	26.01	25.69	25.54
3,000	48.86	42.50	40.06	39.01	38.53	38.32
4,000	65.15	56.67	53.41	52.01	51.38	51.09
5,000	81.44	70.84	66.77	65.01	64.22	63.86
6,000	97.73	85.01	80.12	78.02	77.07	76.63
7,000	114.01	99.17	93.47	91.02	89.91	89.40
8,000	130.30	113.34	106.83	104.02	102.76	102.17
9,000	146.59	127.51	120.18	117.02	115.60	114.95
10,000	162.88	141.68	133.53	130.03	128.45	127.72
15,000	244.31	212.52	200.30	195.04	192.67	191.58
20,000	325.75	283.36	267.06	260.05	256.89	255.44
25,000	407.19	354.20	333.83	325.07	321.12	319.30
30,000	488.63	425.03	400.59	390.08	385.34	383.16
35,000	570.06	495.87	467.36	455.09	449.56	447.02
40,000	651.50	566.71	534.13	520.11	513.79	510.87
45,000	732.94	637.55	600.89	585.12	578.01	574.73
50,000	814.38	708.39	667.66	650.13	642.23	638.59
55,000	895.81	779.23	734.42	715.15	706.45	702.45
60,000	977.25	850.07	801.19	780.16	770.68	766.31
65,000	1,058.69	920.91	867.95	845.17	834.90	830.17
70,000	1,140.13	991.75	934.72	910.19	899.12	894.03
75,000	1,221.56	1,062.59	1,001.49	975.20	963.35	957.89
80,000	1,303.00	1,133.42	1,068.25	1,040.21	1,027.57	1,021.75
85,000	1,384.44	1,204.26	1,135.02	1,105.23	1,091.79	1,085.61
90,000	1,465.88	1,275.10	1,201.78	1,170.24	1,156.02	1,149.47
95,000	1,547.31	1,345.94	1,268.55	1,235.25	1,220.24	1,213.33
100,000	1,628.75	1,416.78	1,335.32	1,300.27	1,284.46	1,277.19
110,000	1,791.63	1,558.46	1,468.85	1,430.29	1,412.91	1,404.90
120,000	1,954.50	1,700.14	1,602.38	1,560.32	1,541.36	1,532.62
130,000	2,117.38	1,841.81	1,735.91	1,690.35	1,669.80	1,660.34
140,000	2,280.25	1,983.49	1,869.44	1,820.37	1,798.25	1,788.06
150,000	2,443.13	2,125.17	2,002.97	1,950.40	1,926.69	1,915.78
160,000	2,606.00	2,266.85	2,136.50	2,080.43	2,055.14	2,043.50
170,000	2,768.88	2,408.53	2,270.04	2,210.45	2,183.59	2,171.22
180,000	2,931.75	2,550.20	2,403.57	2,340.48	2,312.03	2,298.94
190,000	3,094.63	2,691.88	2,537.10	2,470.51	2,440.48	2,426.65
200,000	3,257.50	2,833.56	2,670.63	2,600.53	2,568.93	2,554.37

TABLE I-23. Fixed Rate Mortgage at 15.50%

MONTHLY PAYMENT
NECESSARY TO AMORTIZE A LOAN 15.50%

TERM AMOUNT	10 YEARS	15 YEARS	20 YEARS	25 YEARS	30 YEARS	35 YEARS
50	0.82	0.72	0.68	0.66	0.65	0.65
100	1.64	1.43	1.35	1.32	1.30	1.30
200	3.29	2.87	2.71	2.64	2.61	2.60
300	4.93	4.30	4.06	3.96	3.91	3.89
400	6.58	5.74	5.42	5.28	5.22	5.19
500	8.22	7.17	6.77	6.60	6.52	6.49
600	9.86	8.60	8.12	7.92	7.83	7.79
700	11.51	10.04	9.48	9.24	9.13	9.08
800	13.15	11.47	10.83	10.56	10.44	10.38
900	14.80	12.91	12.19	11.88	11.74	11.68
1,000	16.44	14.34	13.54	13.20	13.05	12.98
2,000	32.88	28.68	27.08	26.40	26.09	25.95
3,000	49.32	43.02	40.62	39.59	39.14	38.93
4,000	65.77	57.36	54.16	52.79	52.18	51.90
5,000	82.21	71.70	67.69	65.99	65.23	64.88
6,000	98.65	86.04	81.23	79.19	78.27	77.86
7,000	115.09	100.38	94.77	92.38	91.32	90.83
8,000	131.53	114.72	108.31	105.58	104.36	103.81
9,000	147.97	129.06	121.85	118.78	117.41	116.78
10,000	164.41	143.40	135.39	131.98	130.45	129.76
15,000	246.62	215.10	203.08	197.96	195.68	194.64
20,000	328.83	286.80	270.78	263.95	260.90	259.52
25,000	411.04	358.50	338.47	329.94	326.13	324.40
30,000	493.24	430.20	406.17	395.93	391.36	389.28
35,000	575.45	501.90	473.86	461.91	456.58	454.16
40,000	657.66	573.60	541.56	527.90	521.81	519.03
45,000	739.87	645.31	609.25	593.89	587.03	583.91
50,000	822.07	717.01	676.95	659.88	652.26	648.79
55,000	904.28	788.71	744.64	725.86	717.49	713.67
60,000	986.49	860.41	812.34	791.85	782.71	778.55
65,000	1,068.70	932.11	880.03	857.84	847.94	843.43
70,000	1,150.90	1,003.81	947.72	923.83	913.16	908.31
75,000	1,233.11	1,075.51	1,015.42	989.81	978.39	973.19
80,000	1,315.32	1,147.21	1,083.11	1,055.80	1,043.62	1,038.07
85,000	1,397.52	1,218.91	1,150.81	1,121.79	1,108.84	1,102.95
90,000	1,479.73	1,290.61	1,218.50	1,187.78	1,174.07	1,167.83
95,000	1,561.94	1,362.31	1,286.20	1,253.76	1,239.29	1,232.71
100,000	1,644.15	1,434.01	1,353.89	1,319.75	1,304.52	1,297.59
110,000	1,808.56	1,577.41	1,489.28	1,451.73	1,434.97	1,427.34
120,000	1,972.98	1,720.81	1,624.67	1,583.70	1,565.42	1,557.10
130,000	2,137.39	1,864.22	1,760.06	1,715.68	1,695.88	1,686.86
140,000	2,301.81	2,007.62	1,895.45	1,847.65	1,826.33	1,816.62
150,000	2,466.22	2,151.02	2,030.84	1,979.63	1,956.78	1,946.38
160,000	2,630.64	2,294.42	2,166.23	2,111.60	2,087.23	2,076.14
170,000	2,795.05	2,437.82	2,301.62	2,243.58	2,217.68	2,205.90
180,000	2,959.46	2,581.22	2,437.01	2,375.55	2,348.14	2,335.65
190,000	3,123.88	2,724.62	2,572.40	2,507.53	2,478.59	2,465.41
200,000	3,288.29	2,868.02	2,707.78	2,639.50	2,609.04	2,595.17

TABLE I-24. Fixed Rate Mortgage at 15.75%

MONTHLY PAYMENT
NECESSARY TO AMORTIZE A LOAN 15.75%

TERM / AMOUNT	10 YEARS	15 YEARS	20 YEARS	25 YEARS	30 YEARS	35 YEARS
50	0.83	0.73	0.69	0.67	0.66	0.66
100	1.66	1.45	1.37	1.34	1.32	1.32
200	3.32	2.90	2.75	2.68	2.65	2.64
300	4.98	4.35	4.12	4.02	3.97	3.95
400	6.64	5.81	5.49	5.36	5.30	5.27
500	8.30	7.26	6.86	6.70	6.62	6.59
600	9.96	8.71	8.24	8.04	7.95	7.91
700	11.62	10.16	9.61	9.38	9.27	9.23
800	13.28	11.61	10.98	10.71	10.60	10.54
900	14.94	13.06	12.35	12.05	11.92	11.86
1,000	16.60	14.51	13.73	13.39	13.25	13.18
2,000	33.19	29.03	27.45	26.79	26.49	26.36
3,000	49.79	43.54	41.18	40.18	39.74	39.54
4,000	66.39	58.05	54.90	53.57	52.98	52.72
5,000	82.98	72.57	68.63	66.96	66.23	65.90
6,000	99.58	87.08	82.35	80.36	79.48	79.08
7,000	116.18	101.59	96.08	93.75	92.72	92.26
8,000	132.77	116.11	109.80	107.14	105.97	105.44
9,000	149.37	130.62	123.53	120.54	119.22	118.62
10,000	165.96	145.13	137.26	133.93	132.46	131.80
15,000	248.95	217.70	205.88	200.89	198.69	197.70
20,000	331.93	290.27	274.51	267.86	264.92	263.60
25,000	414.91	362.83	343.14	334.82	331.16	329.50
30,000	497.89	435.40	411.76	401.79	397.39	395.40
35,000	580.88	507.97	480.39	468.75	463.62	461.31
40,000	663.86	580.54	549.02	535.72	529.85	527.21
45,000	746.84	653.10	617.65	602.68	596.08	593.11
50,000	829.82	725.67	686.27	669.65	662.31	659.01
55,000	912.80	798.24	754.90	736.61	728.54	724.91
60,000	995.79	870.80	823.53	803.58	794.77	790.81
65,000	1,078.77	943.37	892.16	870.54	861.00	856.71
70,000	1,161.75	1,015.94	960.78	937.51	927.24	922.61
75,000	1,244.73	1,088.50	1,029.41	1,004.47	993.47	988.51
80,000	1,327.71	1,161.07	1,098.04	1,071.44	1,059.70	1,054.41
85,000	1,410.70	1,233.64	1,166.67	1,138.40	1,125.93	1,120.31
90,000	1,493.68	1,306.20	1,235.29	1,205.37	1,192.16	1,186.21
95,000	1,576.66	1,378.77	1,303.92	1,272.33	1,258.39	1,252.11
100,000	1,659.64	1,451.34	1,372.55	1,339.30	1,324.62	1,318.02
110,000	1,825.61	1,596.47	1,509.80	1,473.23	1,457.08	1,449.82
120,000	1,991.57	1,741.61	1,647.06	1,607.16	1,589.55	1,581.62
130,000	2,157.54	1,886.74	1,784.31	1,741.09	1,722.01	1,713.42
140,000	2,323.50	2,031.87	1,921.57	1,875.02	1,854.47	1,845.22
150,000	2,489.47	2,177.01	2,058.82	2,008.95	1,986.93	1,977.02
160,000	2,655.43	2,322.14	2,196.08	2,142.88	2,119.39	2,108.83
170,000	2,821.39	2,467.28	2,333.33	2,276.81	2,251.86	2,240.63
180,000	2,987.36	2,612.41	2,470.59	2,410.74	2,384.32	2,372.43
190,000	3,153.32	2,757.54	2,607.84	2,544.67	2,516.78	2,504.23
200,000	3,319.29	2,902.68	2,745.10	2,678.60	2,649.24	2,636.03

TABLE I-25. Fixed Rate Mortgage at 16.00%

MONTHLY PAYMENT
NECESSARY TO AMORTIZE A LOAN 16.00%

TERM AMOUNT	10 YEARS	15 YEARS	20 YEARS	25 YEARS	30 YEARS	35 YEARS
50	0.84	0.73	0.70	0.68	0.67	0.67
100	1.68	1.47	1.39	1.36	1.34	1.34
200	3.35	2.94	2.78	2.72	2.69	2.68
300	5.03	4.41	4.17	4.08	4.03	4.02
400	6.70	5.87	5.57	5.44	5.38	5.35
500	8.38	7.34	6.96	6.79	6.72	6.69
600	10.05	8.81	8.35	8.15	8.07	8.03
700	11.73	10.28	9.74	9.51	9.41	9.37
800	13.40	11.75	11.13	10.87	10.76	10.71
900	15.08	13.22	12.52	12.23	12.10	12.05
1,000	16.75	14.69	13.91	13.59	13.45	13.38
2,000	33.50	29.37	27.83	27.18	26.90	26.77
3,000	50.25	44.06	41.74	40.77	40.34	40.15
4,000	67.01	58.75	55.65	54.36	53.79	53.54
5,000	83.76	73.44	69.56	67.94	67.24	66.92
6,000	100.51	88.12	83.48	81.53	80.69	80.31
7,000	117.26	102.81	97.39	95.12	94.13	93.69
8,000	134.01	117.50	111.30	108.71	107.58	107.08
9,000	150.76	132.18	125.21	122.30	121.03	120.46
10,000	167.52	146.87	139.13	135.89	134.48	133.85
15,000	251.27	220.31	208.69	203.83	201.71	200.77
20,000	335.03	293.74	278.25	271.78	268.95	267.69
25,000	418.79	367.18	347.82	339.72	336.19	334.62
30,000	502.55	440.61	417.38	407.67	403.43	401.54
35,000	586.30	514.05	486.94	475.61	470.67	468.46
40,000	670.06	587.48	556.50	543.56	537.90	535.39
45,000	753.82	660.92	626.07	611.50	605.14	602.31
50,000	837.58	734.36	695.63	679.45	672.38	669.23
55,000	921.33	807.79	765.19	747.39	739.62	736.16
60,000	1,005.09	881.23	834.76	815.33	806.85	803.08
65,000	1,088.85	954.66	904.32	883.28	874.09	870.01
70,000	1,172.61	1,028.10	973.88	951.22	941.33	936.93
75,000	1,256.36	1,101.53	1,043.45	1,019.17	1,008.57	1,003.85
80,000	1,340.12	1,174.97	1,113.01	1,087.11	1,075.81	1,070.78
85,000	1,423.88	1,248.40	1,182.57	1,155.06	1,143.04	1,137.70
90,000	1,507.64	1,321.84	1,252.13	1,223.00	1,210.28	1,204.62
95,000	1,591.39	1,395.28	1,321.70	1,290.95	1,277.52	1,271.55
100,000	1,675.15	1,468.71	1,391.26	1,358.89	1,344.76	1,338.47
110,000	1,842.67	1,615.58	1,530.39	1,494.78	1,479.23	1,472.32
120,000	2,010.18	1,762.45	1,669.51	1,630.67	1,613.71	1,606.16
130,000	2,177.70	1,909.32	1,808.64	1,766.56	1,748.19	1,740.01
140,000	2,345.21	2,056.20	1,947.77	1,902.45	1,882.66	1,873.86
150,000	2,512.73	2,203.07	2,086.89	2,038.34	2,017.14	2,007.70
160,000	2,680.24	2,349.94	2,226.02	2,174.23	2,151.61	2,141.55
170,000	2,847.76	2,496.81	2,365.14	2,310.11	2,286.09	2,275.40
180,000	3,015.27	2,643.68	2,504.27	2,446.00	2,420.56	2,409.25
190,000	3,182.79	2,790.55	2,643.40	2,581.89	2,555.04	2,543.09
200,000	3,350.30	2,937.42	2,782.52	2,717.78	2,689.52	2,676.94

TABLE I-26. Fixed Rate Mortgage at 16.25%

MONTHLY PAYMENT
NECESSARY TO AMORTIZE A LOAN 16.25%

TERM / AMOUNT	10 YEARS	15 YEARS	20 YEARS	25 YEARS	30 YEARS	35 YEARS
50	0.85	0.74	0.71	0.69	0.68	0.68
100	1.69	1.49	1.41	1.38	1.36	1.36
200	3.38	2.97	2.82	2.76	2.73	2.72
300	5.07	4.46	4.23	4.14	4.09	4.08
400	6.76	5.94	5.64	5.51	5.46	5.44
500	8.45	7.43	7.05	6.89	6.82	6.79
600	10.14	8.92	8.46	8.27	8.19	8.15
700	11.84	10.40	9.87	9.65	9.55	9.51
800	13.53	11.89	11.28	11.03	10.92	10.87
900	15.22	13.38	12.69	12.41	12.28	12.23
1,000	16.91	14.86	14.10	13.79	13.65	13.59
2,000	33.82	29.72	28.20	27.57	27.30	27.18
3,000	50.72	44.59	42.30	41.36	40.95	40.77
4,000	67.63	59.45	56.40	55.14	54.60	54.36
5,000	84.54	74.31	70.50	68.93	68.25	67.95
6,000	101.45	89.17	84.60	82.71	81.90	81.54
7,000	118.35	104.03	98.70	96.50	95.55	95.13
8,000	135.26	118.90	112.80	110.28	109.19	108.72
9,000	152.17	133.76	126.90	124.07	122.84	122.31
10,000	169.08	148.62	141.01	137.85	136.49	135.90
15,000	253.62	222.93	211.51	206.78	204.74	203.84
20,000	338.16	297.24	282.01	275.71	272.99	271.79
25,000	422.70	371.55	352.51	344.64	341.23	339.74
30,000	507.23	445.86	423.02	413.56	409.48	407.69
35,000	591.77	520.17	493.52	482.49	477.73	475.63
40,000	676.31	594.48	564.02	551.42	545.97	543.58
45,000	760.85	668.78	634.52	620.35	614.22	611.53
50,000	845.39	743.09	705.03	689.27	682.47	679.48
55,000	929.93	817.40	775.53	758.20	750.72	747.42
60,000	1,014.47	891.71	846.03	827.13	818.96	815.37
65,000	1,099.01	966.02	916.54	896.06	887.21	883.32
70,000	1,183.55	1,040.33	987.04	964.98	955.46	951.27
75,000	1,268.09	1,114.64	1,057.54	1,033.91	1,023.70	1,019.21
80,000	1,352.63	1,188.95	1,128.04	1,102.84	1,091.95	1,087.16
85,000	1,437.17	1,263.26	1,198.55	1,171.76	1,160.20	1,155.11
90,000	1,521.70	1,337.57	1,269.05	1,240.69	1,228.44	1,223.06
95,000	1,606.24	1,411.88	1,339.55	1,309.62	1,296.69	1,291.00
100,000	1,690.78	1,486.19	1,410.06	1,378.55	1,364.94	1,358.95
110,000	1,859.86	1,634.81	1,551.06	1,516.40	1,501.43	1,494.85
120,000	2,028.94	1,783.43	1,692.07	1,654.26	1,637.92	1,630.74
130,000	2,198.02	1,932.04	1,833.07	1,792.11	1,774.42	1,766.64
140,000	2,367.10	2,080.66	1,974.08	1,929.97	1,910.91	1,902.53
150,000	2,536.17	2,229.28	2,115.08	2,067.82	2,047.41	2,038.43
160,000	2,705.25	2,377.90	2,256.09	2,205.67	2,183.90	2,174.32
170,000	2,874.33	2,526.52	2,397.09	2,343.53	2,320.39	2,310.22
180,000	3,043.41	2,675.14	2,538.10	2,481.38	2,456.89	2,446.11
190,000	3,212.49	2,823.76	2,679.11	2,619.24	2,593.38	2,582.01
200,000	3,381.57	2,972.38	2,820.11	2,757.09	2,729.87	2,717.90

TABLE I-27. Fixed Rate Mortgage at 16.50%

MONTHLY PAYMENT
NECESSARY TO AMORTIZE A LOAN 16.50%

TERM AMOUNT	10 YEARS	15 YEARS	20 YEARS	25 YEARS	30 YEARS	35 YEARS
50	0.85	0.75	0.71	0.70	0.69	0.69
100	1.71	1.50	1.43	1.40	1.39	1.38
200	3.41	3.01	2.86	2.80	2.77	2.76
300	5.12	4.51	4.29	4.19	4.16	4.14
400	6.83	6.01	5.72	5.59	5.54	5.52
500	8.53	7.52	7.14	6.99	6.93	6.90
600	10.24	9.02	8.57	8.39	8.31	8.28
700	11.95	10.53	10.00	9.79	9.70	9.66
800	13.65	12.03	11.43	11.19	11.08	11.04
900	15.36	13.53	12.86	12.58	12.47	12.42
1,000	17.06	15.04	14.29	13.98	13.85	13.79
2,000	34.13	30.07	28.58	27.97	27.70	27.59
3,000	51.19	45.11	42.87	41.95	41.55	41.38
4,000	68.26	60.15	57.16	55.93	55.41	55.18
5,000	85.32	75.19	71.45	69.91	69.26	68.97
6,000	102.39	90.22	85.74	83.90	83.11	82.77
7,000	119.45	105.26	100.02	97.88	96.96	96.56
8,000	136.52	120.30	114.31	111.86	110.81	110.36
9,000	153.58	135.34	128.60	125.84	124.66	124.15
10,000	170.65	150.37	142.89	139.83	138.52	137.95
15,000	255.97	225.56	214.34	209.74	207.77	206.92
20,000	341.30	300.75	285.78	279.65	277.03	275.89
25,000	426.62	375.94	357.23	349.56	346.29	344.86
30,000	511.95	451.12	428.68	419.48	415.55	413.84
35,000	597.27	526.31	500.12	489.39	484.80	482.81
40,000	682.59	601.50	571.57	559.30	554.06	551.78
45,000	767.92	676.68	643.01	629.21	623.32	620.75
50,000	853.24	751.87	714.46	699.13	692.58	689.73
55,000	938.57	827.06	785.90	769.04	761.83	758.70
60,000	1,023.89	902.24	857.35	838.95	831.09	827.67
65,000	1,109.22	977.43	928.80	908.86	900.35	896.65
70,000	1,194.54	1,052.62	1,000.24	978.78	969.61	965.62
75,000	1,279.86	1,127.81	1,071.69	1,048.69	1,038.86	1,034.59
80,000	1,365.19	1,202.99	1,143.13	1,118.60	1,108.12	1,103.56
85,000	1,450.51	1,278.18	1,214.58	1,188.51	1,177.38	1,172.54
90,000	1,535.84	1,353.37	1,286.03	1,258.43	1,246.64	1,241.51
95,000	1,621.16	1,428.55	1,357.47	1,328.34	1,315.89	1,310.48
100,000	1,706.49	1,503.74	1,428.92	1,398.25	1,385.15	1,379.46
110,000	1,877.13	1,654.11	1,571.81	1,538.08	1,523.67	1,517.40
120,000	2,047.78	1,804.49	1,714.70	1,677.90	1,662.18	1,655.35
130,000	2,218.43	1,954.86	1,857.59	1,817.73	1,800.70	1,793.29
140,000	2,389.08	2,105.24	2,000.48	1,957.55	1,939.21	1,931.24
150,000	2,559.73	2,255.61	2,143.38	2,097.38	2,077.73	2,069.18
160,000	2,730.38	2,405.98	2,286.27	2,237.20	2,216.24	2,207.13
170,000	2,901.03	2,556.36	2,429.16	2,377.03	2,354.76	2,345.07
180,000	3,071.67	2,706.73	2,572.05	2,516.86	2,493.27	2,483.02
190,000	3,242.32	2,857.11	2,714.94	2,656.68	2,631.79	2,620.97
200,000	3,412.97	3,007.48	2,857.83	2,796.51	2,770.30	2,758.91

TABLE I-28. Fixed Rate Mortgage at 16.75%

MONTHLY PAYMENT
NECESSARY TO AMORTIZE A LOAN 16.75%

TERM / AMOUNT	10 YEARS	15 YEARS	20 YEARS	25 YEARS	30 YEARS	35 YEARS
50	0.86	0.76	0.72	0.71	0.70	0.70
100	1.72	1.52	1.45	1.42	1.41	1.40
200	3.44	3.04	2.90	2.84	2.81	2.80
300	5.17	4.56	4.34	4.25	4.22	4.20
400	6.89	6.09	5.79	5.67	5.62	5.60
500	8.61	7.61	7.24	7.09	7.03	7.00
600	10.33	9.13	8.69	8.51	8.43	8.40
700	12.06	10.65	10.13	9.93	9.84	9.80
800	13.78	12.17	11.58	11.34	11.24	11.20
900	15.50	13.69	13.03	12.76	12.65	12.60
1,000	17.22	15.21	14.48	14.18	14.05	14.00
2,000	34.44	30.43	28.96	28.36	28.11	28.00
3,000	51.67	45.64	43.43	42.54	42.16	42.00
4,000	68.89	60.85	57.91	56.72	56.22	56.00
5,000	86.11	76.07	72.39	70.90	70.27	70.00
6,000	103.33	91.28	86.87	85.08	84.32	84.00
7,000	120.55	106.49	101.35	99.26	98.38	98.00
8,000	137.78	121.71	115.83	113.44	112.43	112.00
9,000	155.00	136.92	130.30	127.62	126.49	126.00
10,000	172.22	152.13	144.78	141.80	140.54	140.00
15,000	258.33	228.20	217.17	212.70	210.81	210.00
20,000	344.44	304.27	289.57	283.60	281.08	280.00
25,000	430.55	380.33	361.96	354.50	351.35	350.00
30,000	516.66	456.40	434.35	425.40	421.62	419.99
35,000	602.77	532.47	506.74	496.30	491.89	489.99
40,000	688.88	608.53	579.13	567.20	562.16	559.99
45,000	774.99	684.60	651.52	638.10	632.43	629.99
50,000	861.10	760.67	723.91	709.00	702.70	699.99
55,000	947.21	836.74	796.30	779.90	772.97	769.99
60,000	1,033.32	912.80	868.70	850.80	843.24	839.99
65,000	1,119.43	988.87	941.09	921.70	913.51	909.99
70,000	1,205.54	1,064.94	1,013.48	992.60	983.78	979.99
75,000	1,291.65	1,141.00	1,085.87	1,063.50	1,054.05	1,049.99
80,000	1,377.76	1,217.07	1,158.26	1,134.40	1,124.32	1,119.98
85,000	1,463.87	1,293.14	1,230.65	1,205.30	1,194.59	1,189.98
90,000	1,549.98	1,369.20	1,303.04	1,276.20	1,264.86	1,259.98
95,000	1,636.09	1,445.27	1,375.44	1,347.10	1,335.13	1,329.98
100,000	1,722.20	1,521.34	1,447.83	1,418.00	1,405.40	1,399.98
110,000	1,894.42	1,673.47	1,592.61	1,559.80	1,545.94	1,539.98
120,000	2,066.64	1,825.60	1,737.39	1,701.60	1,686.48	1,679.98
130,000	2,238.86	1,977.74	1,882.18	1,843.40	1,827.02	1,819.97
140,000	2,411.08	2,129.87	2,026.96	1,985.20	1,967.56	1,959.97
150,000	2,583.30	2,282.00	2,171.74	2,127.00	2,108.10	2,099.97
160,000	2,755.52	2,434.14	2,316.52	2,268.80	2,248.64	2,239.97
170,000	2,927.74	2,586.27	2,461.31	2,410.60	2,389.17	2,379.97
180,000	3,099.96	2,738.41	2,606.09	2,552.40	2,529.71	2,519.96
190,000	3,272.18	2,890.54	2,750.87	2,694.20	2,670.25	2,659.96
200,000	3,444.40	3,042.67	2,895.65	2,836.00	2,810.79	2,799.96

TABLE I-29. Fixed Rate Mortgage at 17.00%

MONTHLY PAYMENT
NECESSARY TO AMORTIZE A LOAN 17.00%

TERM / AMOUNT	10 YEARS	15 YEARS	20 YEARS	25 YEARS	30 YEARS	35 YEARS
50	0.87	0.77	0.73	0.72	0.71	0.71
100	1.74	1.54	1.47	1.44	1.43	1.42
200	3.48	3.08	2.93	2.88	2.85	2.84
300	5.21	4.62	4.40	4.31	4.28	4.26
400	6.95	6.16	5.87	5.75	5.70	5.68
500	8.69	7.70	7.33	7.19	7.13	7.10
600	10.43	9.23	8.80	8.63	8.55	8.52
700	12.17	10.77	10.27	10.06	9.98	9.94
800	13.90	12.31	11.73	11.50	11.41	11.36
900	15.64	13.85	13.20	12.94	12.83	12.78
1,000	17.38	15.39	14.67	14.38	14.26	14.21
2,000	34.76	30.78	29.34	28.76	28.51	28.41
3,000	52.14	46.17	44.00	43.13	42.77	42.62
4,000	69.52	61.56	58.67	57.51	57.03	56.82
5,000	86.90	76.95	73.34	71.89	71.28	71.03
6,000	104.28	92.34	88.01	86.27	85.54	85.23
7,000	121.66	107.73	102.68	100.65	99.80	99.44
8,000	139.04	123.12	117.35	115.02	114.05	113.64
9,000	156.42	138.51	132.01	129.40	128.31	127.85
10,000	173.80	153.90	146.68	143.78	142.57	142.05
15,000	260.70	230.85	220.02	215.67	213.85	213.08
20,000	347.61	307.81	293.36	287.56	285.14	284.11
25,000	434.51	384.76	366.70	359.45	356.42	355.13
30,000	521.41	461.71	440.04	431.34	427.70	426.16
35,000	608.31	538.66	513.39	503.23	498.99	497.18
40,000	695.21	615.61	586.73	575.12	570.27	568.21
45,000	782.11	692.56	660.07	647.01	641.56	639.24
50,000	869.02	769.52	733.41	718.90	712.84	710.26
55,000	955.92	846.47	806.75	790.79	784.12	781.29
60,000	1,042.82	923.42	880.09	862.68	855.41	852.32
65,000	1,129.72	1,000.37	953.43	934.57	926.69	923.34
70,000	1,216.62	1,077.32	1,026.77	1,006.46	997.97	994.37
75,000	1,303.52	1,154.27	1,100.11	1,078.35	1,069.26	1,065.40
80,000	1,390.43	1,231.23	1,173.45	1,150.24	1,140.54	1,136.42
85,000	1,477.33	1,308.18	1,246.79	1,222.13	1,211.83	1,207.45
90,000	1,564.23	1,385.13	1,320.13	1,294.02	1,283.11	1,278.47
95,000	1,651.13	1,462.08	1,393.47	1,365.91	1,354.39	1,349.50
100,000	1,738.03	1,539.03	1,466.81	1,437.80	1,425.68	1,420.53
110,000	1,911.84	1,692.94	1,613.50	1,581.58	1,568.25	1,562.58
120,000	2,085.64	1,846.84	1,760.18	1,725.36	1,710.81	1,704.63
130,000	2,259.44	2,000.74	1,906.86	1,869.14	1,853.38	1,846.69
140,000	2,433.25	2,154.65	2,053.54	2,012.93	1,995.95	1,988.74
150,000	2,607.05	2,308.55	2,200.22	2,156.71	2,138.52	2,130.79
160,000	2,780.85	2,462.45	2,346.90	2,300.49	2,281.09	2,272.84
170,000	2,954.66	2,616.36	2,493.59	2,444.27	2,423.65	2,414.90
180,000	3,128.46	2,770.26	2,640.27	2,588.05	2,566.22	2,556.95
190,000	3,302.26	2,924.16	2,786.95	2,731.83	2,708.79	2,699.00
200,000	3,476.07	3,078.07	2,933.63	2,875.61	2,851.36	2,841.05

TABLE I-30. Fixed Rate Mortgage at 17.25%

MONTHLY PAYMENT
NECESSARY TO AMORTIZE A LOAN — 17.25%

TERM AMOUNT	10 YEARS	15 YEARS	20 YEARS	25 YEARS	30 YEARS	35 YEARS
50	0.88	0.78	0.74	0.73	0.72	0.72
100	1.75	1.56	1.49	1.46	1.45	1.44
200	3.51	3.11	2.97	2.92	2.89	2.88
300	5.26	4.67	4.46	4.37	4.34	4.32
400	7.02	6.23	5.94	5.83	5.78	5.76
500	8.77	7.78	7.43	7.29	7.23	7.21
600	10.52	9.34	8.92	8.75	8.68	8.65
700	12.28	10.90	10.40	10.20	10.12	10.09
800	14.03	12.45	11.89	11.66	11.57	11.53
900	15.78	14.01	13.37	13.12	13.01	12.97
1,000	17.54	15.57	14.86	14.58	14.46	14.41
2,000	35.08	31.14	29.72	29.15	28.92	28.82
3,000	52.62	46.70	44.58	43.73	43.38	43.23
4,000	70.16	62.27	59.43	58.31	57.84	57.64
5,000	87.69	77.84	74.29	72.88	72.30	72.05
6,000	105.23	93.41	89.15	87.46	86.76	86.47
7,000	122.77	108.97	104.01	102.04	101.22	100.88
8,000	140.31	124.54	118.87	116.61	115.68	115.29
9,000	157.85	140.11	133.73	131.19	130.14	129.70
10,000	175.39	155.68	148.58	145.76	144.60	144.11
15,000	263.08	233.52	222.88	218.65	216.90	216.16
20,000	350.78	311.35	297.17	291.53	289.20	288.22
25,000	438.47	389.19	371.46	364.41	361.50	360.27
30,000	526.16	467.03	445.75	437.29	433.80	432.33
35,000	613.86	544.87	520.05	510.18	506.10	504.38
40,000	701.55	622.71	594.34	583.06	578.39	576.44
45,000	789.25	700.55	668.63	655.94	650.69	648.49
50,000	876.94	778.39	742.92	728.82	722.99	720.55
55,000	964.63	856.22	817.22	801.70	795.29	792.60
60,000	1,052.33	934.06	891.51	874.59	867.59	864.66
65,000	1,140.02	1,011.90	965.80	947.47	939.89	936.71
70,000	1,227.72	1,089.74	1,040.09	1,020.35	1,012.19	1,008.76
75,000	1,315.41	1,167.58	1,114.39	1,093.23	1,084.49	1,080.82
80,000	1,403.10	1,245.42	1,188.68	1,166.12	1,156.79	1,152.87
85,000	1,490.80	1,323.26	1,262.97	1,239.00	1,229.09	1,224.93
90,000	1,578.49	1,401.09	1,337.26	1,311.88	1,301.39	1,296.98
95,000	1,666.19	1,478.93	1,411.56	1,384.76	1,373.69	1,369.04
100,000	1,753.88	1,556.77	1,485.85	1,457.64	1,445.99	1,441.09
110,000	1,929.27	1,712.45	1,634.43	1,603.41	1,590.59	1,585.20
120,000	2,104.66	1,868.13	1,783.02	1,749.17	1,735.18	1,729.31
130,000	2,280.04	2,023.80	1,931.60	1,894.94	1,879.78	1,873.42
140,000	2,455.43	2,179.48	2,080.19	2,040.70	2,024.38	2,017.53
150,000	2,630.82	2,335.16	2,228.77	2,186.47	2,168.98	2,161.64
160,000	2,806.21	2,490.83	2,377.36	2,332.23	2,313.58	2,305.75
170,000	2,981.60	2,646.51	2,525.94	2,478.00	2,458.18	2,449.86
180,000	3,156.98	2,802.19	2,674.53	2,623.76	2,602.78	2,593.97
190,000	3,332.37	2,957.87	2,823.11	2,769.52	2,747.38	2,738.07
200,000	3,507.76	3,113.54	2,971.70	2,915.29	2,891.97	2,882.18

TABLE I-31. Fixed Rate Mortgage at 17.50%

MONTHLY PAYMENT
NECESSARY TO AMORTIZE A LOAN 17.50%

AMOUNT \ TERM	10 YEARS	15 YEARS	20 YEARS	25 YEARS	30 YEARS	35 YEARS
50	0.88	0.79	0.75	0.74	0.73	0.73
100	1.77	1.57	1.50	1.48	1.47	1.46
200	3.54	3.15	3.01	2.96	2.93	2.92
300	5.31	4.72	4.51	4.43	4.40	4.39
400	7.08	6.30	6.02	5.91	5.87	5.85
500	8.85	7.87	7.52	7.39	7.33	7.31
600	10.62	9.45	9.03	8.87	8.80	8.77
700	12.39	11.02	10.53	10.34	10.26	10.23
800	14.16	12.60	12.04	11.82	11.73	11.69
900	15.93	14.17	13.54	13.30	13.20	13.16
1,000	17.70	15.75	15.05	14.78	14.66	14.62
2,000	35.40	31.49	30.10	29.55	29.33	29.23
3,000	53.10	47.24	45.15	44.33	43.99	43.85
4,000	70.79	62.98	60.20	59.10	58.65	58.47
5,000	88.49	78.73	75.25	73.88	73.32	73.08
6,000	106.19	94.48	90.30	88.65	87.98	87.70
7,000	123.89	110.22	105.35	103.43	102.64	102.32
8,000	141.59	125.97	120.40	118.20	117.31	116.93
9,000	159.29	141.71	135.45	132.98	131.97	131.55
10,000	176.99	157.46	150.50	147.75	146.63	146.17
15,000	265.48	236.19	225.74	221.63	219.95	219.25
20,000	353.97	314.92	300.99	295.51	293.27	292.34
25,000	442.46	393.65	376.24	369.38	366.58	365.42
30,000	530.96	472.38	451.49	443.26	439.90	438.50
35,000	619.45	551.11	526.74	517.14	513.21	511.59
40,000	707.94	629.84	601.98	591.01	586.53	584.67
45,000	796.43	708.57	677.23	664.89	659.85	657.75
50,000	884.93	787.31	752.48	738.77	733.16	730.84
55,000	973.42	866.04	827.73	812.65	806.48	803.92
60,000	1,061.91	944.77	902.97	886.52	879.80	877.01
65,000	1,150.41	1,023.50	978.22	960.40	953.11	950.09
70,000	1,238.90	1,102.23	1,053.47	1,034.28	1,026.43	1,023.17
75,000	1,327.39	1,180.96	1,128.72	1,108.15	1,099.75	1,096.26
80,000	1,415.88	1,259.69	1,203.97	1,182.03	1,173.06	1,169.34
85,000	1,504.38	1,338.42	1,279.21	1,255.91	1,246.38	1,242.43
90,000	1,592.87	1,417.15	1,354.46	1,329.78	1,319.70	1,315.51
95,000	1,681.36	1,495.88	1,429.71	1,403.66	1,393.01	1,388.59
100,000	1,769.85	1,574.61	1,504.96	1,477.54	1,466.33	1,461.68
110,000	1,946.84	1,732.07	1,655.45	1,625.29	1,612.96	1,607.84
120,000	2,123.82	1,889.53	1,805.95	1,773.05	1,759.59	1,754.01
130,000	2,300.81	2,046.99	1,956.45	1,920.80	1,906.23	1,900.18
140,000	2,477.80	2,204.46	2,106.94	2,068.55	2,052.86	2,046.35
150,000	2,654.78	2,361.92	2,257.44	2,216.31	2,199.49	2,192.52
160,000	2,831.77	2,519.38	2,407.93	2,364.06	2,346.13	2,338.68
170,000	3,008.75	2,676.84	2,558.43	2,511.81	2,492.76	2,484.85
180,000	3,185.74	2,834.30	2,708.92	2,659.57	2,639.39	2,631.02
190,000	3,362.72	2,991.76	2,859.42	2,807.32	2,786.02	2,777.19
200,000	3,539.71	3,149.22	3,009.92	2,955.08	2,932.66	2,923.35

TABLE I-32. Fixed Rate Mortgage at 17.75%

MONTHLY PAYMENT
NECESSARY TO AMORTIZE A LOAN 17.75%

TERM / AMOUNT	10 YEARS	15 YEARS	20 YEARS	25 YEARS	30 YEARS	35 YEARS
50	0.89	0.80	0.76	0.75	0.74	0.74
100	1.79	1.59	1.52	1.50	1.49	1.48
200	3.57	3.18	3.05	2.99	2.97	2.96
300	5.36	4.78	4.57	4.49	4.46	4.45
400	7.14	6.37	6.10	5.99	5.95	5.93
500	8.93	7.96	7.62	7.49	7.43	7.41
600	10.71	9.55	9.14	8.98	8.92	8.89
700	12.50	11.15	10.67	10.48	10.41	10.38
800	14.29	12.74	12.19	11.98	11.89	11.86
900	16.07	14.33	13.72	13.48	13.38	13.34
1,000	17.86	15.92	15.24	14.97	14.87	14.82
2,000	35.72	31.85	30.48	29.95	29.73	29.65
3,000	53.57	47.77	45.72	44.92	44.60	44.47
4,000	71.43	63.70	60.96	59.90	59.47	59.29
5,000	89.29	79.62	76.21	74.87	74.33	74.11
6,000	107.15	95.55	91.45	89.85	89.20	88.94
7,000	125.01	111.47	106.69	104.82	104.07	103.76
8,000	142.87	127.40	121.93	119.80	118.94	118.58
9,000	160.72	143.32	137.17	134.77	133.80	133.40
10,000	178.58	159.25	152.41	149.75	148.67	148.23
15,000	267.87	238.87	228.62	224.62	223.00	222.34
20,000	357.16	318.50	304.82	299.49	297.34	296.46
25,000	446.45	398.12	381.03	374.37	371.67	370.57
30,000	535.74	477.74	457.23	449.24	446.01	444.68
35,000	625.03	557.37	533.44	524.11	520.34	518.80
40,000	714.32	636.99	609.64	598.98	594.68	592.91
45,000	803.62	716.61	685.85	673.86	669.01	667.02
50,000	892.91	796.24	762.05	748.73	743.35	741.14
55,000	982.20	875.86	838.26	823.60	817.68	815.25
60,000	1,071.49	955.49	914.46	898.48	892.02	889.37
65,000	1,160.78	1,035.11	990.67	973.35	966.35	963.48
70,000	1,250.07	1,114.73	1,066.87	1,048.22	1,040.69	1,037.59
75,000	1,339.36	1,194.36	1,143.08	1,123.10	1,115.02	1,111.71
80,000	1,428.65	1,273.98	1,219.28	1,197.97	1,189.35	1,185.82
85,000	1,517.94	1,353.61	1,295.49	1,272.84	1,263.69	1,259.93
90,000	1,607.23	1,433.23	1,371.69	1,347.72	1,338.02	1,334.05
95,000	1,696.52	1,512.85	1,447.90	1,422.59	1,412.36	1,408.16
100,000	1,785.81	1,592.48	1,524.10	1,497.46	1,486.69	1,482.28
110,000	1,964.39	1,751.73	1,676.51	1,647.21	1,635.36	1,630.50
120,000	2,142.98	1,910.97	1,828.93	1,796.95	1,784.03	1,778.73
130,000	2,321.56	2,070.22	1,981.34	1,946.70	1,932.70	1,926.96
140,000	2,500.14	2,229.47	2,133.75	2,096.45	2,081.37	2,075.19
150,000	2,678.72	2,388.72	2,286.16	2,246.19	2,230.04	2,223.41
160,000	2,857.30	2,547.96	2,438.57	2,395.94	2,378.71	2,371.64
170,000	3,035.88	2,707.21	2,590.98	2,545.69	2,527.38	2,519.87
180,000	3,214.46	2,866.46	2,743.39	2,695.43	2,676.05	2,668.10
190,000	3,393.04	3,025.71	2,895.80	2,845.18	2,824.72	2,816.32
200,000	3,571.63	3,184.96	3,048.21	2,994.92	2,973.39	2,964.55

TABLE I-33. Fixed Rate Mortgage at 18.00%

MONTHLY PAYMENT
NECESSARY TO AMORTIZE A LOAN 18.00%

TERM / AMOUNT	10 YEARS	15 YEARS	20 YEARS	25 YEARS	30 YEARS	35 YEARS
50	0.90	0.81	0.77	0.76	0.75	0.75
100	1.80	1.61	1.54	1.52	1.51	1.50
200	3.60	3.22	3.09	3.03	3.01	3.01
300	5.41	4.83	4.63	4.55	4.52	4.51
400	7.21	6.44	6.17	6.07	6.03	6.01
500	9.01	8.05	7.72	7.59	7.54	7.51
600	10.81	9.66	9.26	9.10	9.04	9.02
700	12.61	11.27	10.80	10.62	10.55	10.52
800	14.42	12.88	12.35	12.14	12.06	12.02
900	16.22	14.49	13.89	13.66	13.56	13.53
1,000	18.02	16.10	15.43	15.17	15.07	15.03
2,000	36.04	32.21	30.87	30.35	30.14	30.06
3,000	54.06	48.31	46.30	45.52	45.21	45.09
4,000	72.08	64.42	61.73	60.70	60.28	60.12
5,000	90.10	80.52	77.17	75.87	75.35	75.14
6,000	108.11	96.63	92.60	91.05	90.43	90.17
7,000	126.13	112.73	108.03	106.22	105.50	105.20
8,000	144.15	128.84	123.47	121.39	120.57	120.23
9,000	162.17	144.94	138.90	136.57	135.64	135.26
10,000	180.19	161.04	154.33	151.74	150.71	150.29
15,000	270.29	241.57	231.50	227.62	226.06	225.43
20,000	360.38	322.09	308.66	303.49	301.42	300.58
25,000	450.48	402.61	385.83	379.36	376.77	375.72
30,000	540.57	483.13	463.00	455.23	452.13	450.87
35,000	630.67	563.66	540.16	531.10	527.48	526.01
40,000	720.76	644.18	617.33	606.97	602.83	601.16
45,000	810.86	724.70	694.50	682.85	678.19	676.30
50,000	900.95	805.22	771.66	758.72	753.54	751.45
55,000	991.05	885.75	848.83	834.59	828.90	826.59
60,000	1,081.15	966.27	925.99	910.46	904.25	901.74
65,000	1,171.24	1,046.79	1,003.16	986.33	979.61	976.88
70,000	1,261.34	1,127.31	1,080.33	1,062.21	1,054.96	1,052.03
75,000	1,351.43	1,207.84	1,157.49	1,138.08	1,130.32	1,127.17
80,000	1,441.53	1,288.36	1,234.66	1,213.95	1,205.67	1,202.31
85,000	1,531.62	1,368.88	1,311.83	1,289.82	1,281.02	1,277.46
90,000	1,621.72	1,449.40	1,388.99	1,365.69	1,356.38	1,352.60
95,000	1,711.81	1,529.93	1,466.16	1,441.56	1,431.73	1,427.75
100,000	1,801.91	1,610.45	1,543.32	1,517.44	1,507.09	1,502.89
110,000	1,982.10	1,771.49	1,697.66	1,669.18	1,657.80	1,653.18
120,000	2,162.29	1,932.54	1,851.99	1,820.92	1,808.51	1,803.47
130,000	2,342.48	2,093.58	2,006.32	1,972.67	1,959.21	1,953.76
140,000	2,522.67	2,254.63	2,160.65	2,124.41	2,109.92	2,104.05
150,000	2,702.86	2,415.67	2,314.99	2,276.15	2,260.63	2,254.34
160,000	2,883.05	2,576.72	2,469.32	2,427.90	2,411.34	2,404.63
170,000	3,063.25	2,737.76	2,623.65	2,579.64	2,562.05	2,554.92
180,000	3,243.44	2,898.81	2,777.98	2,731.39	2,712.76	2,705.21
190,000	3,423.63	3,059.85	2,932.32	2,883.13	2,863.47	2,855.50
200,000	3,603.82	3,220.90	3,086.65	3,034.87	3,014.18	3,005.79

TABLE I-34. Fixed Rate Mortgage at 18.25%

MONTHLY PAYMENT
NECESSARY TO AMORTIZE A LOAN 18.25%

TERM / AMOUNT	10 YEARS	15 YEARS	20 YEARS	25 YEARS	30 YEARS	35 YEARS
50	0.91	0.81	0.78	0.77	0.76	0.76
100	1.82	1.63	1.56	1.54	1.53	1.52
200	3.64	3.26	3.13	3.07	3.06	3.05
300	5.45	4.89	4.69	4.61	4.58	4.57
400	7.27	6.51	6.25	6.15	6.11	6.09
500	9.09	8.14	7.81	7.69	7.64	7.62
600	10.91	9.77	9.38	9.22	9.17	9.14
700	12.73	11.40	10.94	10.76	10.69	10.66
800	14.54	13.03	12.50	12.30	12.22	12.19
900	16.36	14.66	14.06	13.84	13.75	13.71
1,000	18.18	16.28	15.63	15.37	15.28	15.24
2,000	36.36	32.57	31.25	30.75	30.55	30.47
3,000	54.54	48.85	46.88	46.12	45.83	45.71
4,000	72.72	65.14	62.50	61.50	61.10	60.94
5,000	90.90	81.42	78.13	76.87	76.38	76.18
6,000	109.08	97.71	93.76	92.25	91.65	91.41
7,000	127.26	113.99	109.38	107.62	106.93	106.65
8,000	145.44	130.28	125.01	123.00	122.20	121.88
9,000	163.62	146.56	140.63	138.37	137.48	137.12
10,000	181.80	162.85	156.26	153.74	152.75	152.35
15,000	272.70	244.27	234.39	230.62	229.13	228.53
20,000	363.60	325.69	312.52	307.49	305.50	304.70
25,000	454.50	407.11	390.65	384.36	381.88	380.88
30,000	545.40	488.54	468.77	461.23	458.25	457.06
35,000	636.30	569.96	546.90	538.10	534.63	533.23
40,000	727.20	651.38	625.03	614.98	611.00	609.41
45,000	818.10	732.80	703.16	691.85	687.38	685.58
50,000	909.00	814.23	781.29	768.72	763.75	761.76
55,000	999.90	895.65	859.42	845.59	840.13	837.94
60,000	1,090.80	977.07	937.55	922.46	916.50	914.11
65,000	1,181.70	1,058.49	1,015.68	999.34	992.88	990.29
70,000	1,272.60	1,139.92	1,093.81	1,076.21	1,069.25	1,066.47
75,000	1,363.50	1,221.34	1,171.94	1,153.08	1,145.63	1,142.64
80,000	1,454.40	1,302.76	1,250.07	1,229.95	1,222.00	1,218.82
85,000	1,545.30	1,384.18	1,328.20	1,306.82	1,298.38	1,294.99
90,000	1,636.20	1,465.61	1,406.32	1,383.70	1,374.75	1,371.17
95,000	1,727.10	1,547.03	1,484.45	1,460.57	1,451.13	1,447.35
100,000	1,818.00	1,628.45	1,562.58	1,537.44	1,527.50	1,523.52
110,000	1,999.80	1,791.30	1,718.84	1,691.18	1,680.25	1,675.87
120,000	2,181.60	1,954.14	1,875.10	1,844.93	1,833.00	1,828.23
130,000	2,363.40	2,116.99	2,031.36	1,998.67	1,985.75	1,980.58
140,000	2,545.20	2,279.83	2,187.62	2,152.42	2,138.51	2,132.93
150,000	2,727.00	2,442.68	2,343.88	2,306.16	2,291.26	2,285.28
160,000	2,908.80	2,605.52	2,500.13	2,459.91	2,444.01	2,437.64
170,000	3,090.60	2,768.37	2,656.39	2,613.65	2,596.76	2,589.99
180,000	3,272.40	2,931.21	2,812.65	2,767.39	2,749.51	2,742.34
190,000	3,454.21	3,094.06	2,968.91	2,921.14	2,902.26	2,894.69
200,000	3,636.01	3,256.90	3,125.17	3,074.88	3,055.01	3,047.05

TABLE I-35. Fixed Rate Mortgage at 18.50%

MONTHLY PAYMENT
NECESSARY TO AMORTIZE A LOAN 18.50%

AMOUNT \ TERM	10 YEARS	15 YEARS	20 YEARS	25 YEARS	30 YEARS	35 YEARS
50	0.92	0.82	0.79	0.78	0.77	0.77
100	1.83	1.65	1.58	1.56	1.55	1.54
200	3.67	3.29	3.16	3.11	3.10	3.09
300	5.50	4.94	4.75	4.67	4.64	4.63
400	7.34	6.59	6.33	6.23	6.19	6.18
500	9.17	8.23	7.91	7.79	7.74	7.72
600	11.01	9.88	9.49	9.34	9.29	9.27
700	12.84	11.53	11.07	10.90	10.84	10.81
800	14.67	13.17	12.66	12.46	12.38	12.35
900	16.51	14.82	14.24	14.02	13.93	13.90
1,000	18.34	16.47	15.82	15.57	15.48	15.44
2,000	36.68	32.93	31.64	31.15	30.96	30.88
3,000	55.03	49.40	47.46	46.72	46.44	46.33
4,000	73.37	65.86	63.28	62.30	61.92	61.77
5,000	91.71	82.33	79.10	77.87	77.40	77.21
6,000	110.05	98.79	94.91	93.45	92.88	92.65
7,000	128.39	115.26	110.73	109.02	108.36	108.09
8,000	146.74	131.72	126.55	124.60	123.84	123.53
9,000	165.08	148.19	142.37	140.17	139.32	138.98
10,000	183.42	164.65	158.19	155.75	154.79	154.42
15,000	275.13	246.98	237.29	233.62	232.19	231.63
20,000	366.84	329.31	316.38	311.50	309.59	308.83
25,000	458.55	411.63	395.48	389.37	386.99	386.04
30,000	550.26	493.96	474.57	467.25	464.38	463.25
35,000	641.97	576.29	553.67	545.12	541.78	540.46
40,000	733.68	658.61	632.76	622.99	619.18	617.67
45,000	825.39	740.94	711.86	700.87	696.58	694.88
50,000	917.10	823.27	790.95	778.74	773.97	772.08
55,000	1,008.81	905.60	870.05	856.62	851.37	849.29
60,000	1,100.52	987.92	949.14	934.49	928.77	926.50
65,000	1,192.23	1,070.25	1,028.24	1,012.37	1,006.16	1,003.71
70,000	1,283.94	1,152.58	1,107.33	1,090.24	1,083.56	1,080.92
75,000	1,375.65	1,234.90	1,186.43	1,168.11	1,160.96	1,158.13
80,000	1,467.36	1,317.23	1,265.52	1,245.99	1,238.36	1,235.33
85,000	1,559.07	1,399.56	1,344.62	1,323.86	1,315.75	1,312.54
90,000	1,650.78	1,481.88	1,423.71	1,401.74	1,393.15	1,389.75
95,000	1,742.49	1,564.21	1,502.81	1,479.61	1,470.55	1,466.96
100,000	1,834.20	1,646.54	1,581.90	1,557.49	1,547.95	1,544.17
110,000	2,017.61	1,811.19	1,740.09	1,713.24	1,702.74	1,698.58
120,000	2,201.03	1,975.84	1,898.28	1,868.98	1,857.53	1,853.00
130,000	2,384.45	2,140.50	2,056.47	2,024.73	2,012.33	2,007.42
140,000	2,567.87	2,305.15	2,214.66	2,180.48	2,167.12	2,161.83
150,000	2,751.29	2,469.81	2,372.85	2,336.23	2,321.92	2,316.25
160,000	2,934.71	2,634.46	2,531.04	2,491.98	2,476.71	2,470.67
170,000	3,118.13	2,799.11	2,689.24	2,647.73	2,631.51	2,625.09
180,000	3,301.55	2,963.77	2,847.43	2,803.48	2,786.30	2,779.50
190,000	3,484.97	3,128.42	3,005.62	2,959.22	2,941.10	2,933.92
200,000	3,668.39	3,293.07	3,163.81	3,114.97	3,095.89	3,088.34

TABLE I-36. Fixed Rate Mortgage at 18.75%

MONTHLY PAYMENT
NECESSARY TO AMORTIZE A LOAN 18.75%

AMOUNT \ TERM	10 YEARS	15 YEARS	20 YEARS	25 YEARS	30 YEARS	35 YEARS
50	0.93	0.83	0.80	0.79	0.78	0.78
100	1.85	1.66	1.60	1.58	1.57	1.56
200	3.70	3.33	3.20	3.16	3.14	3.13
300	5.55	4.99	4.80	4.73	4.71	4.69
400	7.40	6.66	6.41	6.31	6.27	6.26
500	9.25	8.32	8.01	7.89	7.84	7.82
600	11.10	9.99	9.61	9.47	9.41	9.39
700	12.95	11.65	11.21	11.04	10.98	10.95
800	14.80	13.32	12.81	12.62	12.55	12.52
900	16.65	14.98	14.41	14.20	14.12	14.08
1,000	18.50	16.65	16.01	15.78	15.68	15.65
2,000	37.01	33.29	32.03	31.55	31.37	31.30
3,000	55.51	49.94	48.04	47.33	47.05	46.94
4,000	74.02	66.59	64.05	63.10	62.74	62.59
5,000	92.52	83.23	80.06	78.88	78.42	78.24
6,000	111.03	99.88	96.08	94.65	94.10	93.89
7,000	129.53	116.53	112.09	110.43	109.79	109.54
8,000	148.03	133.17	128.10	126.21	125.47	125.19
9,000	166.54	149.82	144.11	141.98	141.16	140.83
10,000	185.04	166.47	160.13	157.76	156.84	156.48
15,000	277.56	249.70	240.19	236.63	235.26	234.72
20,000	370.08	332.93	320.25	315.51	313.68	312.96
25,000	462.60	416.17	400.32	394.39	392.10	391.21
30,000	555.13	499.40	480.38	473.27	470.52	469.45
35,000	647.65	582.63	560.44	552.15	548.94	547.69
40,000	740.17	665.87	640.51	631.03	627.36	625.93
45,000	832.69	749.10	720.57	709.90	705.78	704.17
50,000	925.21	832.34	800.63	788.78	784.20	782.41
55,000	1,017.73	915.57	880.70	867.66	862.62	860.65
60,000	1,110.25	998.80	960.76	946.54	941.04	938.90
65,000	1,202.77	1,082.04	1,040.82	1,025.42	1,019.47	1,017.14
70,000	1,295.29	1,165.27	1,120.89	1,104.30	1,097.89	1,095.38
75,000	1,387.81	1,248.50	1,200.95	1,183.17	1,176.31	1,173.62
80,000	1,480.33	1,331.74	1,281.01	1,262.05	1,254.73	1,251.86
85,000	1,572.85	1,414.97	1,361.08	1,340.93	1,333.15	1,330.10
90,000	1,665.38	1,498.20	1,441.14	1,419.81	1,411.57	1,408.34
95,000	1,757.90	1,581.44	1,521.20	1,498.69	1,489.99	1,486.58
100,000	1,850.42	1,664.67	1,601.27	1,577.57	1,568.41	1,564.83
110,000	2,035.46	1,831.14	1,761.39	1,735.32	1,725.25	1,721.31
120,000	2,220.50	1,997.60	1,921.52	1,893.08	1,882.09	1,877.79
130,000	2,405.54	2,164.07	2,081.65	2,050.83	2,038.93	2,034.27
140,000	2,590.58	2,330.54	2,241.77	2,208.59	2,195.77	2,190.76
150,000	2,775.63	2,497.01	2,401.90	2,366.35	2,352.61	2,347.24
160,000	2,960.67	2,663.47	2,562.03	2,524.10	2,509.45	2,503.72
170,000	3,145.71	2,829.94	2,722.15	2,681.86	2,666.29	2,660.20
180,000	3,330.75	2,996.41	2,882.28	2,839.62	2,823.13	2,816.69
190,000	3,515.79	3,162.87	3,042.41	2,997.37	2,979.97	2,973.17
200,000	3,700.83	3,329.34	3,202.53	3,155.13	3,136.82	3,129.65

TABLE I-37. Fixed Rate Mortgage at 19.00%

MONTHLY PAYMENT
NECESSARY TO AMORTIZE A LOAN 19.00%

AMOUNT / TERM	10 YEARS	15 YEARS	20 YEARS	25 YEARS	30 YEARS	35 YEARS
50	0.93	0.84	0.81	0.80	0.79	0.79
100	1.87	1.68	1.62	1.60	1.59	1.59
200	3.73	3.37	3.24	3.20	3.18	3.17
300	5.60	5.05	4.86	4.79	4.77	4.76
400	7.47	6.73	6.48	6.39	6.36	6.34
500	9.33	8.41	8.10	7.99	7.94	7.93
600	11.20	10.10	9.72	9.59	9.53	9.51
700	13.07	11.78	11.34	11.18	11.12	11.10
800	14.93	13.46	12.97	12.78	12.71	12.68
900	16.80	15.15	14.59	14.38	14.30	14.27
1,000	18.67	16.83	16.21	15.98	15.89	15.85
2,000	37.34	33.66	32.41	31.95	31.78	31.71
3,000	56.00	50.49	48.62	47.93	47.67	47.56
4,000	74.67	67.32	64.83	63.91	63.56	63.42
5,000	93.34	84.14	81.03	79.88	79.44	79.27
6,000	112.01	100.97	97.24	95.86	95.33	95.13
7,000	130.67	117.80	113.45	111.84	111.22	110.98
8,000	149.34	134.63	129.66	127.81	127.11	126.84
9,000	168.01	151.46	145.86	143.79	143.00	142.69
10,000	186.68	168.29	162.07	159.77	158.89	158.55
15,000	280.01	252.43	243.10	239.65	238.33	237.82
20,000	373.35	336.58	324.14	319.54	317.78	317.10
25,000	466.69	420.72	405.17	399.42	397.22	396.37
30,000	560.03	504.87	486.21	479.30	476.67	475.65
35,000	653.37	589.01	567.24	559.19	556.11	554.92
40,000	746.70	673.16	648.28	639.07	635.56	634.20
45,000	840.04	757.30	729.31	718.96	715.00	713.47
50,000	933.38	841.45	810.35	798.84	794.45	792.75
55,000	1,026.72	925.59	891.38	878.73	873.89	872.02
60,000	1,120.06	1,009.74	972.42	958.61	953.34	951.30
65,000	1,213.40	1,093.88	1,053.45	1,038.49	1,032.78	1,030.57
70,000	1,306.73	1,178.03	1,134.49	1,118.38	1,112.23	1,109.85
75,000	1,400.07	1,262.17	1,215.52	1,198.26	1,191.67	1,189.12
80,000	1,493.41	1,346.32	1,296.55	1,278.15	1,271.12	1,268.40
85,000	1,586.75	1,430.46	1,377.59	1,358.03	1,350.56	1,347.67
90,000	1,680.09	1,514.60	1,458.62	1,437.92	1,430.00	1,426.95
95,000	1,773.42	1,598.75	1,539.66	1,517.80	1,509.45	1,506.22
100,000	1,866.76	1,682.89	1,620.69	1,597.68	1,588.89	1,585.50
110,000	2,053.44	1,851.18	1,782.76	1,757.45	1,747.78	1,744.04
120,000	2,240.11	2,019.47	1,944.83	1,917.22	1,906.67	1,902.59
130,000	2,426.79	2,187.76	2,106.90	2,076.99	2,065.56	2,061.14
140,000	2,613.47	2,356.05	2,268.97	2,236.76	2,224.45	2,219.69
150,000	2,800.14	2,524.34	2,431.04	2,396.53	2,383.34	2,378.24
160,000	2,986.82	2,692.63	2,593.11	2,556.29	2,542.23	2,536.79
170,000	3,173.49	2,860.92	2,755.18	2,716.06	2,701.12	2,695.34
180,000	3,360.17	3,029.21	2,917.25	2,875.83	2,860.01	2,853.89
190,000	3,546.85	3,197.50	3,079.32	3,035.60	3,018.90	3,012.44
200,000	3,733.52	3,365.79	3,241.39	3,195.37	3,177.79	3,170.99

TABLE I-38. Fixed Rate Mortgage at 19.25%

MONTHLY PAYMENT
NECESSARY TO AMORTIZE A LOAN 19.25%

TERM / AMOUNT	10 YEARS	15 YEARS	20 YEARS	25 YEARS	30 YEARS	35 YEARS
50	0.94	0.85	0.82	0.81	0.80	0.80
100	1.88	1.70	1.64	1.62	1.61	1.61
200	3.77	3.40	3.28	3.24	3.22	3.21
300	5.65	5.10	4.92	4.85	4.83	4.82
400	7.53	6.80	6.56	6.47	6.44	6.42
500	9.42	8.51	8.20	8.09	8.05	8.03
600	11.30	10.21	9.84	9.71	9.66	9.64
700	13.18	11.91	11.48	11.32	11.27	11.24
800	15.07	13.61	13.12	12.94	12.88	12.85
900	16.95	15.31	14.76	14.56	14.48	14.46
1,000	18.83	17.01	16.40	16.18	16.09	16.06
2,000	37.66	34.02	32.80	32.36	32.19	32.12
3,000	56.49	51.04	49.20	48.53	48.28	48.19
4,000	75.33	68.05	65.61	64.71	64.38	64.25
5,000	94.16	85.06	82.01	80.89	80.47	80.31
6,000	112.99	102.07	98.41	97.07	96.56	96.37
7,000	131.82	119.08	114.81	113.25	112.66	112.43
8,000	150.65	136.09	131.21	129.43	128.75	128.49
9,000	169.48	153.11	147.61	145.60	144.85	144.56
10,000	188.31	170.12	164.02	161.78	160.94	160.62
15,000	282.47	255.18	246.02	242.67	241.41	240.93
20,000	376.63	340.23	328.03	323.57	321.88	321.24
25,000	470.79	425.29	410.04	404.46	402.35	401.54
30,000	564.94	510.35	492.05	485.35	482.82	481.85
35,000	659.10	595.41	574.06	566.24	563.29	562.16
40,000	753.26	680.47	656.07	647.13	643.76	642.47
45,000	847.42	765.53	738.07	728.02	724.23	722.78
50,000	941.57	850.58	820.08	808.92	804.70	803.09
55,000	1,035.73	935.64	902.09	889.81	885.17	883.40
60,000	1,129.89	1,020.70	984.10	970.70	965.64	963.71
65,000	1,224.05	1,105.76	1,066.11	1,051.59	1,046.11	1,044.01
70,000	1,318.20	1,190.82	1,148.11	1,132.48	1,126.58	1,124.32
75,000	1,412.36	1,275.88	1,230.12	1,213.37	1,207.05	1,204.63
80,000	1,506.52	1,360.94	1,312.13	1,294.27	1,287.52	1,284.94
85,000	1,600.68	1,445.99	1,394.14	1,375.16	1,367.99	1,365.25
90,000	1,694.83	1,531.05	1,476.15	1,456.05	1,448.46	1,445.56
95,000	1,788.99	1,616.11	1,558.16	1,536.94	1,528.93	1,525.87
100,000	1,883.15	1,701.17	1,640.16	1,617.83	1,609.40	1,606.18
110,000	2,071.46	1,871.29	1,804.18	1,779.62	1,770.34	1,766.79
120,000	2,259.78	2,041.40	1,968.20	1,941.40	1,931.28	1,927.41
130,000	2,448.09	2,211.52	2,132.21	2,103.18	2,092.22	2,088.03
140,000	2,636.41	2,381.64	2,296.23	2,264.97	2,253.16	2,248.65
150,000	2,824.72	2,551.75	2,460.25	2,426.75	2,414.10	2,409.27
160,000	3,013.04	2,721.87	2,624.26	2,588.53	2,575.04	2,569.88
170,000	3,201.35	2,891.99	2,788.28	2,750.32	2,735.98	2,730.50
180,000	3,389.67	3,062.10	2,952.29	2,912.10	2,896.92	2,891.12
190,000	3,577.98	3,232.22	3,116.31	3,073.88	3,057.86	3,051.74
200,000	3,766.30	3,402.34	3,280.33	3,235.67	3,218.80	3,212.35

TABLE I-39. Fixed Rate Mortgage at 19.50%

MONTHLY PAYMENT
NECESSARY TO AMORTIZE A LOAN 19.50%

TERM / AMOUNT	10 YEARS	15 YEARS	20 YEARS	25 YEARS	30 YEARS	35 YEARS
50	0.95	0.86	0.83	0.82	0.81	0.81
100	1.90	1.72	1.66	1.64	1.63	1.63
200	3.80	3.44	3.32	3.28	3.26	3.25
300	5.70	5.16	4.98	4.91	4.89	4.88
400	7.60	6.88	6.64	6.55	6.52	6.51
500	9.50	8.60	8.30	8.19	8.15	8.13
600	11.40	10.32	9.96	9.83	9.78	9.76
700	13.30	12.04	11.62	11.47	11.41	11.39
800	15.20	13.76	13.28	13.10	13.04	13.01
900	17.10	15.48	14.94	14.74	14.67	14.64
1,000	19.00	17.19	16.60	16.38	16.30	16.27
2,000	37.99	34.39	33.19	32.76	32.60	32.54
3,000	56.99	51.58	49.79	49.14	48.90	48.81
4,000	75.98	68.78	66.39	65.52	65.20	65.07
5,000	94.98	85.97	82.98	81.90	81.50	81.34
6,000	113.97	103.17	99.58	98.28	97.80	97.61
7,000	132.97	120.36	116.18	114.66	114.09	113.88
8,000	151.96	137.56	132.77	131.04	130.39	130.15
9,000	170.96	154.75	149.37	147.42	146.69	146.42
10,000	189.96	171.95	165.97	163.80	162.99	162.69
15,000	284.93	257.92	248.95	245.70	244.49	244.03
20,000	379.91	343.90	331.93	327.60	325.98	325.37
25,000	474.89	429.87	414.92	409.50	407.48	406.72
30,000	569.87	515.85	497.90	491.40	488.98	488.06
35,000	664.85	601.82	580.89	573.30	570.47	569.40
40,000	759.82	687.79	663.87	655.20	651.97	650.75
45,000	854.80	773.77	746.85	737.10	733.46	732.09
50,000	949.78	859.74	829.84	819.00	814.96	813.43
55,000	1,044.76	945.72	912.82	900.91	896.46	894.78
60,000	1,139.74	1,031.69	995.80	982.81	977.95	976.12
65,000	1,234.71	1,117.67	1,078.79	1,064.71	1,059.45	1,057.46
70,000	1,329.69	1,203.64	1,161.77	1,146.61	1,140.95	1,138.81
75,000	1,424.67	1,289.62	1,244.75	1,228.51	1,222.44	1,220.15
80,000	1,519.65	1,375.59	1,327.74	1,310.41	1,303.94	1,301.49
85,000	1,614.63	1,461.56	1,410.72	1,392.31	1,385.43	1,382.84
90,000	1,709.60	1,547.54	1,493.71	1,474.21	1,466.93	1,464.18
95,000	1,804.58	1,633.51	1,576.69	1,556.11	1,548.43	1,545.52
100,000	1,899.56	1,719.49	1,659.67	1,638.01	1,629.92	1,626.87
110,000	2,089.52	1,891.44	1,825.64	1,801.81	1,792.91	1,789.55
120,000	2,279.47	2,063.38	1,991.61	1,965.61	1,955.91	1,952.24
130,000	2,469.43	2,235.33	2,157.57	2,129.41	2,118.90	2,114.93
140,000	2,659.38	2,407.28	2,323.54	2,293.21	2,281.89	2,277.61
150,000	2,849.34	2,579.23	2,489.51	2,457.02	2,444.88	2,440.30
160,000	3,039.29	2,751.18	2,655.48	2,620.82	2,607.87	2,602.99
170,000	3,229.25	2,923.13	2,821.44	2,784.62	2,770.87	2,765.68
180,000	3,419.21	3,095.08	2,987.41	2,948.42	2,933.86	2,928.36
190,000	3,609.16	3,267.03	3,153.38	3,112.22	3,096.85	3,091.05
200,000	3,799.12	3,438.97	3,319.35	3,276.02	3,259.84	3,253.74

TABLE I-40. Fixed Rate Mortgage at 19.75%

MONTHLY PAYMENT
NECESSARY TO AMORTIZE A LOAN — 19.75%

AMOUNT \ TERM	10 YEARS	15 YEARS	20 YEARS	25 YEARS	30 YEARS	35 YEARS
50	0.96	0.87	0.84	0.83	0.83	0.82
100	1.92	1.74	1.68	1.66	1.65	1.65
200	3.83	3.48	3.36	3.32	3.30	3.30
300	5.75	5.21	5.04	4.97	4.95	4.94
400	7.66	6.95	6.72	6.63	6.60	6.59
500	9.58	8.69	8.40	8.29	8.25	8.24
600	11.50	10.43	10.08	9.95	9.90	9.89
700	13.41	12.17	11.75	11.61	11.55	11.53
800	15.33	13.90	13.43	13.27	13.20	13.18
900	17.24	15.64	15.11	14.92	14.85	14.83
1,000	19.16	17.38	16.79	16.58	16.50	16.48
2,000	38.32	34.76	33.58	33.16	33.01	32.95
3,000	57.48	52.14	50.38	49.75	49.51	49.43
4,000	76.64	69.51	67.17	66.33	66.02	65.90
5,000	95.80	86.89	83.96	82.91	82.52	82.38
6,000	114.96	104.27	100.75	99.49	99.03	98.85
7,000	134.12	121.65	117.55	116.08	115.53	115.33
8,000	153.28	139.03	134.34	132.66	132.04	131.81
9,000	172.44	156.41	151.13	149.24	148.54	148.28
10,000	191.61	173.79	167.92	165.82	165.05	164.76
15,000	287.41	260.68	251.88	248.73	247.57	247.14
20,000	383.21	347.57	335.85	331.64	330.09	329.51
25,000	479.01	434.47	419.81	414.55	412.62	411.89
30,000	574.81	521.36	503.77	497.47	495.14	494.27
35,000	670.62	608.26	587.73	580.38	577.66	576.65
40,000	766.42	695.15	671.69	663.29	660.19	659.03
45,000	862.22	782.04	755.65	746.20	742.71	741.41
50,000	958.03	868.94	839.62	829.11	825.23	823.78
55,000	1,053.83	955.83	923.58	912.02	907.75	906.16
60,000	1,149.63	1,042.72	1,007.54	994.93	990.28	988.54
65,000	1,245.43	1,129.62	1,091.50	1,077.84	1,072.80	1,070.92
70,000	1,341.24	1,216.51	1,175.46	1,160.75	1,155.32	1,153.30
75,000	1,437.04	1,303.41	1,259.42	1,243.66	1,237.85	1,235.68
80,000	1,532.84	1,390.30	1,343.38	1,326.57	1,320.37	1,318.05
85,000	1,628.64	1,477.19	1,427.35	1,409.49	1,402.89	1,400.43
90,000	1,724.45	1,564.09	1,511.31	1,492.40	1,485.42	1,482.81
95,000	1,820.25	1,650.98	1,595.27	1,575.31	1,567.94	1,565.19
100,000	1,916.05	1,737.87	1,679.23	1,658.22	1,650.46	1,647.57
110,000	2,107.66	1,911.66	1,847.15	1,824.04	1,815.51	1,812.33
120,000	2,299.26	2,085.45	2,015.08	1,989.86	1,980.56	1,977.08
130,000	2,490.87	2,259.24	2,183.00	2,155.68	2,145.60	2,141.84
140,000	2,682.47	2,433.02	2,350.92	2,321.51	2,310.65	2,306.60
150,000	2,874.08	2,606.81	2,518.85	2,487.33	2,475.69	2,471.35
160,000	3,065.68	2,780.60	2,686.77	2,653.15	2,640.74	2,636.11
170,000	3,257.29	2,954.39	2,854.69	2,818.97	2,805.79	2,800.87
180,000	3,448.89	3,128.17	3,022.62	2,984.79	2,970.83	2,965.62
190,000	3,640.50	3,301.96	3,190.54	3,150.61	3,135.88	3,130.38
200,000	3,832.10	3,475.75	3,358.46	3,316.44	3,300.93	3,295.14

TABLE I-41. Fixed Rate Mortgage at 20.00%

MONTHLY PAYMENT
NECESSARY TO AMORTIZE A LOAN 20.00%

TERM / AMOUNT	10 YEARS	15 YEARS	20 YEARS	25 YEARS	30 YEARS	35 YEARS
50	0.97	0.88	0.85	0.84	0.84	0.83
100	1.93	1.76	1.70	1.68	1.67	1.67
200	3.87	3.51	3.40	3.36	3.34	3.34
300	5.80	5.27	5.10	5.04	5.01	5.00
400	7.73	7.03	6.80	6.71	6.68	6.67
500	9.66	8.78	8.49	8.39	8.36	8.34
600	11.60	10.54	10.19	10.07	10.03	10.01
700	13.53	12.29	11.89	11.75	11.70	11.68
800	15.46	14.05	13.59	13.43	13.37	13.35
900	17.39	15.81	15.29	15.11	15.04	15.01
1,000	19.33	17.56	16.99	16.78	16.71	16.68
2,000	38.65	35.13	33.98	33.57	33.42	33.37
3,000	57.98	52.69	50.96	50.35	50.13	50.05
4,000	77.30	70.25	67.95	67.14	66.84	66.73
5,000	96.63	87.82	84.94	83.92	83.55	83.41
6,000	115.95	105.38	101.93	100.71	100.26	100.10
7,000	135.28	122.94	118.92	117.49	116.97	116.78
8,000	154.61	140.50	135.91	134.28	133.68	133.46
9,000	173.93	158.07	152.89	151.06	150.39	150.15
10,000	193.26	175.63	169.88	167.85	167.10	166.83
15,000	289.89	263.45	254.82	251.77	250.65	250.24
20,000	386.52	351.26	339.77	335.69	334.20	333.66
25,000	483.14	439.08	424.71	419.61	417.75	417.07
30,000	579.77	526.89	509.65	503.54	501.31	500.48
35,000	676.40	614.71	594.59	587.46	584.86	583.90
40,000	773.03	702.52	679.53	671.38	668.41	667.31
45,000	869.66	790.34	764.47	755.30	751.96	750.73
50,000	966.29	878.15	849.41	839.23	835.51	834.14
55,000	1,062.92	965.97	934.36	923.15	919.06	917.55
60,000	1,159.55	1,053.78	1,019.30	1,007.07	1,002.61	1,000.97
65,000	1,256.18	1,141.60	1,104.24	1,090.99	1,086.16	1,084.38
70,000	1,352.80	1,229.41	1,189.18	1,174.92	1,169.71	1,167.80
75,000	1,449.43	1,317.23	1,274.12	1,258.84	1,253.26	1,251.21
80,000	1,546.06	1,405.04	1,359.06	1,342.76	1,336.82	1,334.62
85,000	1,642.69	1,492.86	1,444.00	1,426.69	1,420.37	1,418.04
90,000	1,739.32	1,580.68	1,528.95	1,510.61	1,503.92	1,501.45
95,000	1,835.95	1,668.49	1,613.89	1,594.53	1,587.47	1,584.86
100,000	1,932.58	1,756.31	1,698.83	1,678.45	1,671.02	1,668.28
110,000	2,125.84	1,931.94	1,868.71	1,846.30	1,838.12	1,835.11
120,000	2,319.09	2,107.57	2,038.59	2,014.14	2,005.22	2,001.93
130,000	2,512.35	2,283.20	2,208.48	2,181.99	2,172.32	2,168.76
140,000	2,705.61	2,458.83	2,378.36	2,349.84	2,339.43	2,335.59
150,000	2,898.87	2,634.46	2,548.24	2,517.68	2,506.53	2,502.42
160,000	3,092.13	2,810.09	2,718.13	2,685.53	2,673.63	2,669.25
170,000	3,285.38	2,985.72	2,888.01	2,853.37	2,840.73	2,836.07
180,000	3,478.64	3,161.35	3,057.89	3,021.22	3,007.83	3,002.90
190,000	3,671.90	3,336.98	3,227.78	3,189.06	3,174.94	3,169.73
200,000	3,865.16	3,512.61	3,397.66	3,356.91	3,342.04	3,336.56

TABLE I-42. Fixed Rate Mortgage at 20.25%

MONTHLY PAYMENT
NECESSARY TO AMORTIZE A LOAN 20.25%

TERM / AMOUNT	10 YEARS	15 YEARS	20 YEARS	25 YEARS	30 YEARS	35 YEARS
50	0.97	0.89	0.86	0.85	0.85	0.84
100	1.95	1.77	1.72	1.70	1.69	1.69
200	3.90	3.55	3.44	3.40	3.38	3.38
300	5.85	5.32	5.16	5.10	5.07	5.07
400	7.80	7.10	6.87	6.79	6.77	6.76
500	9.75	8.87	8.59	8.49	8.46	8.44
600	11.70	10.65	10.31	10.19	10.15	10.13
700	13.64	12.42	12.03	11.89	11.84	11.82
800	15.59	14.20	13.75	13.59	13.53	13.51
900	17.54	15.97	15.47	15.29	15.22	15.20
1,000	19.49	17.75	17.18	16.99	16.92	16.89
2,000	38.98	35.50	34.37	33.97	33.83	33.78
3,000	58.48	53.24	51.55	50.96	50.75	50.67
4,000	77.97	70.99	68.74	67.95	67.66	67.56
5,000	97.46	88.74	85.92	84.94	84.58	84.45
6,000	116.95	106.49	103.11	101.92	101.50	101.34
7,000	136.44	124.24	120.29	118.91	118.41	118.23
8,000	155.94	141.99	137.48	135.90	135.33	135.12
9,000	175.43	159.73	154.66	152.88	152.24	152.01
10,000	194.92	177.48	171.85	169.87	169.16	168.90
15,000	292.38	266.22	257.77	254.81	253.74	253.35
20,000	389.84	354.96	343.70	339.74	338.32	337.80
25,000	487.30	443.70	429.62	424.68	422.90	422.25
30,000	584.76	532.44	515.54	509.62	507.48	506.70
35,000	682.22	621.18	601.47	594.55	592.06	591.15
40,000	779.68	709.93	687.39	679.49	676.64	675.60
45,000	877.14	798.67	773.31	764.42	761.22	760.05
50,000	974.60	887.41	859.24	849.36	845.80	844.50
55,000	1,072.06	976.15	945.16	934.30	930.38	928.95
60,000	1,169.52	1,064.89	1,031.09	1,019.23	1,014.96	1,013.40
65,000	1,266.98	1,153.63	1,117.01	1,104.17	1,099.54	1,097.85
70,000	1,364.44	1,242.37	1,202.93	1,189.10	1,184.12	1,182.30
75,000	1,461.90	1,331.11	1,288.86	1,274.04	1,268.70	1,266.75
80,000	1,559.36	1,419.85	1,374.78	1,358.98	1,353.27	1,351.20
85,000	1,656.82	1,508.59	1,460.71	1,443.91	1,437.85	1,435.65
90,000	1,754.28	1,597.33	1,546.63	1,528.85	1,522.43	1,520.10
95,000	1,851.74	1,686.07	1,632.55	1,613.78	1,607.01	1,604.55
100,000	1,949.20	1,774.81	1,718.48	1,698.72	1,691.59	1,689.00
110,000	2,144.12	1,952.29	1,890.33	1,868.59	1,860.75	1,857.90
120,000	2,339.04	2,129.78	2,062.17	2,038.46	2,029.91	2,026.80
130,000	2,533.96	2,307.26	2,234.02	2,208.34	2,199.07	2,195.70
140,000	2,728.88	2,484.74	2,405.87	2,378.21	2,368.23	2,364.60
150,000	2,923.80	2,662.22	2,577.72	2,548.08	2,537.39	2,533.50
160,000	3,118.73	2,839.70	2,749.56	2,717.95	2,706.55	2,702.40
170,000	3,313.65	3,017.18	2,921.41	2,887.82	2,875.71	2,871.30
180,000	3,508.57	3,194.66	3,093.26	3,057.70	3,044.87	3,040.20
190,000	3,703.49	3,372.15	3,265.11	3,227.57	3,214.03	3,209.09
200,000	3,898.41	3,549.63	3,436.95	3,397.44	3,383.19	3,377.99

TABLE I-43. Fixed Rate Mortgage at 20.50%

MONTHLY PAYMENT
NECESSARY TO AMORTIZE A LOAN 20.50%

TERM / AMOUNT	10 YEARS	15 YEARS	20 YEARS	25 YEARS	30 YEARS	35 YEARS
50	0.98	0.90	0.87	0.86	0.86	0.85
100	1.97	1.79	1.74	1.72	1.71	1.71
200	3.93	3.59	3.48	3.44	3.42	3.42
300	5.90	5.38	5.21	5.16	5.14	5.13
400	7.86	7.17	6.95	6.88	6.85	6.84
500	9.83	8.97	8.69	8.60	8.56	8.55
600	11.79	10.76	10.43	10.31	10.27	10.26
700	13.76	12.55	12.17	12.03	11.99	11.97
800	15.73	14.35	13.91	13.75	13.70	13.68
900	17.69	16.14	15.64	15.47	15.41	15.39
1,000	19.66	17.93	17.38	17.19	17.12	17.10
2,000	39.32	35.87	34.76	34.38	34.24	34.19
3,000	58.97	53.80	52.14	51.57	51.37	51.29
4,000	78.63	71.73	69.53	68.76	68.49	68.39
5,000	98.29	89.67	86.91	85.95	85.61	85.49
6,000	117.95	107.60	104.29	103.14	102.73	102.58
7,000	137.61	125.53	121.67	120.33	119.85	119.68
8,000	157.27	143.47	139.05	137.52	136.97	136.78
9,000	176.92	161.40	156.43	154.71	154.10	153.88
10,000	196.58	179.34	173.82	171.90	171.22	170.97
15,000	294.87	269.00	260.72	257.85	256.83	256.46
20,000	393.17	358.67	347.63	343.80	342.44	341.94
25,000	491.46	448.34	434.54	429.75	428.05	427.43
30,000	589.75	538.00	521.45	515.70	513.65	512.92
35,000	688.04	627.67	608.35	601.65	599.26	598.40
40,000	786.33	717.34	695.26	687.60	684.87	683.89
45,000	884.62	807.01	782.17	773.55	770.48	769.38
50,000	982.92	896.68	869.08	859.50	856.09	854.86
55,000	1,081.21	986.34	955.99	945.45	941.70	940.35
60,000	1,179.50	1,076.01	1,042.89	1,031.40	1,027.31	1,025.83
65,000	1,277.79	1,165.68	1,129.80	1,117.35	1,112.92	1,111.32
70,000	1,376.08	1,255.34	1,216.71	1,203.31	1,198.53	1,196.81
75,000	1,474.37	1,345.01	1,303.62	1,289.26	1,284.14	1,282.29
80,000	1,572.66	1,434.68	1,390.52	1,375.21	1,369.74	1,367.78
85,000	1,670.96	1,524.35	1,477.43	1,461.16	1,455.35	1,453.27
90,000	1,769.25	1,614.02	1,564.34	1,547.11	1,540.96	1,538.75
95,000	1,867.54	1,703.68	1,651.25	1,633.06	1,626.57	1,624.24
100,000	1,965.83	1,793.35	1,738.16	1,719.01	1,712.18	1,709.72
110,000	2,162.41	1,972.69	1,911.97	1,890.91	1,883.40	1,880.70
120,000	2,359.00	2,152.02	2,085.79	2,062.81	2,054.62	2,051.67
130,000	2,555.58	2,331.36	2,259.60	2,234.71	2,225.84	2,222.64
140,000	2,752.16	2,510.69	2,433.42	2,406.61	2,397.05	2,393.61
150,000	2,948.75	2,690.03	2,607.23	2,578.51	2,568.27	2,564.59
160,000	3,145.33	2,869.36	2,781.05	2,750.41	2,739.49	2,735.56
170,000	3,341.91	3,048.70	2,954.86	2,922.31	2,910.71	2,906.53
180,000	3,538.50	3,228.03	3,128.68	3,094.21	3,081.93	3,077.50
190,000	3,735.08	3,407.37	3,302.50	3,266.11	3,253.14	3,248.48
200,000	3,931.66	3,586.70	3,476.31	3,438.02	3,424.36	3,419.45

TABLE I-44. Fixed Rate Mortgage at 20.75%

MONTHLY PAYMENT
NECESSARY TO AMORTIZE A LOAN 20.75%

TERM / AMOUNT	10 YEARS	15 YEARS	20 YEARS	25 YEARS	30 YEARS	35 YEARS
50	0.99	0.91	0.88	0.87	0.87	0.87
100	1.98	1.81	1.76	1.74	1.73	1.73
200	3.97	3.62	3.52	3.48	3.47	3.46
300	5.95	5.44	5.27	5.22	5.20	5.19
400	7.93	7.25	7.03	6.96	6.93	6.92
500	9.91	9.06	8.79	8.70	8.66	8.65
600	11.90	10.87	10.55	10.44	10.40	10.38
700	13.88	12.68	12.31	12.18	12.13	12.11
800	15.86	14.50	14.06	13.91	13.86	13.84
900	17.84	16.31	15.82	15.65	15.60	15.57
1,000	19.83	18.12	17.58	17.39	17.33	17.30
2,000	39.65	36.24	35.16	34.79	34.66	34.61
3,000	59.48	54.36	52.74	52.18	51.98	51.91
4,000	79.30	72.48	70.32	69.57	69.31	69.22
5,000	99.13	90.60	87.89	86.97	86.64	86.52
6,000	118.95	108.72	105.47	104.36	103.97	103.83
7,000	138.78	126.84	123.05	121.75	121.29	121.13
8,000	158.61	144.96	140.63	139.15	138.62	138.44
9,000	178.43	163.08	158.21	156.54	155.95	155.74
10,000	198.26	181.20	175.79	173.93	173.28	173.05
15,000	297.39	271.80	263.68	260.90	259.92	259.57
20,000	396.52	362.39	351.58	347.86	346.56	346.09
25,000	495.64	452.99	439.47	434.83	433.20	432.61
30,000	594.77	543.59	527.37	521.80	519.84	519.14
35,000	693.90	634.19	615.26	608.76	606.47	605.66
40,000	793.03	724.79	703.15	695.73	693.11	692.18
45,000	892.16	815.39	791.05	782.70	779.75	778.71
50,000	991.29	905.98	878.94	869.66	866.39	865.23
55,000	1,090.42	996.58	966.84	956.63	953.03	951.75
60,000	1,189.55	1,087.18	1,054.73	1,043.60	1,039.67	1,038.27
65,000	1,288.68	1,177.78	1,142.63	1,130.56	1,126.31	1,124.80
70,000	1,387.80	1,268.38	1,230.52	1,217.53	1,212.95	1,211.32
75,000	1,486.93	1,358.98	1,318.41	1,304.49	1,299.59	1,297.84
80,000	1,586.06	1,449.58	1,406.31	1,391.46	1,386.23	1,384.37
85,000	1,685.19	1,540.17	1,494.20	1,478.43	1,472.87	1,470.89
90,000	1,784.32	1,630.77	1,582.10	1,565.39	1,559.51	1,557.41
95,000	1,883.45	1,721.37	1,669.99	1,652.36	1,646.15	1,643.94
100,000	1,982.58	1,811.97	1,757.89	1,739.33	1,732.78	1,730.46
110,000	2,180.84	1,993.17	1,933.67	1,913.26	1,906.06	1,903.50
120,000	2,379.09	2,174.36	2,109.46	2,087.19	2,079.34	2,076.55
130,000	2,577.35	2,355.56	2,285.25	2,261.12	2,252.62	2,249.60
140,000	2,775.61	2,536.76	2,461.04	2,435.06	2,425.90	2,422.64
150,000	2,973.87	2,717.95	2,636.83	2,608.99	2,599.18	2,595.69
160,000	3,172.13	2,899.15	2,812.62	2,782.92	2,772.46	2,768.73
170,000	3,370.38	3,080.35	2,988.41	2,956.85	2,945.73	2,941.78
180,000	3,568.64	3,261.54	3,164.20	3,130.79	3,119.01	3,114.82
190,000	3,766.90	3,442.74	3,339.98	3,304.72	3,292.29	3,287.87
200,000	3,965.16	3,623.94	3,515.77	3,478.65	3,465.57	3,460.92

TABLE I-45. Fixed Rate Mortgage at 21.00%

MONTHLY PAYMENT
NECESSARY TO AMORTIZE A LOAN 21.00%

AMOUNT \ TERM	10 YEARS	15 YEARS	20 YEARS	25 YEARS	30 YEARS	35 YEARS
50	1.00	0.92	0.89	0.88	0.88	0.88
100	2.00	1.83	1.78	1.76	1.75	1.75
200	4.00	3.66	3.56	3.52	3.51	3.50
300	6.00	5.49	5.33	5.28	5.26	5.25
400	8.00	7.32	7.11	7.04	7.01	7.00
500	10.00	9.15	8.89	8.80	8.77	8.76
600	12.00	10.98	10.67	10.56	10.52	10.51
700	14.00	12.81	12.44	12.32	12.27	12.26
800	15.99	14.64	14.22	14.08	14.03	14.01
900	17.99	16.48	16.00	15.84	15.78	15.76
1,000	19.99	18.31	17.78	17.60	17.53	17.51
2,000	39.99	36.61	35.55	35.19	35.07	35.02
3,000	59.98	54.92	53.33	52.79	52.60	52.54
4,000	79.97	73.22	71.11	70.39	70.14	70.05
5,000	99.97	91.53	88.88	87.98	87.67	87.56
6,000	119.96	109.84	106.66	105.58	105.20	105.07
7,000	139.95	128.14	124.44	123.18	122.74	122.58
8,000	159.95	146.45	142.21	140.77	140.27	140.10
9,000	179.94	164.76	159.99	158.37	157.81	157.61
10,000	199.93	183.06	177.76	175.97	175.34	175.12
15,000	299.90	274.59	266.65	263.95	263.01	262.68
20,000	399.86	366.12	355.53	351.93	350.68	350.24
25,000	499.83	457.65	444.41	439.92	438.35	437.80
30,000	599.80	549.18	533.29	527.90	526.02	525.36
35,000	699.76	640.72	622.18	615.88	613.69	612.92
40,000	799.73	732.25	711.06	703.87	701.36	700.48
45,000	899.70	823.78	799.94	791.85	789.03	788.04
50,000	999.66	915.31	888.82	879.83	876.70	875.60
55,000	1,099.63	1,006.84	977.70	967.81	964.37	963.16
60,000	1,199.59	1,098.37	1,066.59	1,055.80	1,052.04	1,050.72
65,000	1,299.56	1,189.90	1,155.47	1,143.78	1,139.71	1,138.28
70,000	1,399.53	1,281.43	1,244.35	1,231.76	1,227.38	1,225.84
75,000	1,499.49	1,372.96	1,333.23	1,319.75	1,315.05	1,313.40
80,000	1,599.46	1,464.49	1,422.12	1,407.73	1,402.72	1,400.96
85,000	1,699.43	1,556.02	1,511.00	1,495.71	1,490.39	1,488.52
90,000	1,799.39	1,647.55	1,599.88	1,583.70	1,578.06	1,576.08
95,000	1,899.36	1,739.08	1,688.76	1,671.68	1,665.73	1,663.64
100,000	1,999.32	1,830.62	1,777.64	1,759.66	1,753.40	1,751.20
110,000	2,199.26	2,013.68	1,955.41	1,935.63	1,928.74	1,926.32
120,000	2,399.19	2,196.74	2,133.17	2,111.60	2,104.08	2,101.44
130,000	2,599.12	2,379.80	2,310.94	2,287.56	2,279.42	2,276.56
140,000	2,799.05	2,562.86	2,488.70	2,463.53	2,454.76	2,451.68
150,000	2,998.99	2,745.92	2,666.47	2,639.50	2,630.10	2,626.80
160,000	3,198.92	2,928.99	2,844.23	2,815.46	2,805.44	2,801.92
170,000	3,398.85	3,112.05	3,022.00	2,991.43	2,980.78	2,977.04
180,000	3,598.78	3,295.11	3,199.76	3,167.39	3,156.12	3,152.16
190,000	3,798.72	3,478.17	3,377.52	3,343.36	3,331.46	3,327.28
200,000	3,998.65	3,661.23	3,555.29	3,519.33	3,506.80	3,502.40

TABLE I-46. Fixed Rate Mortgage at 21.25%

MONTHLY PAYMENT
NECESSARY TO AMORTIZE A LOAN — 21.25%

TERM / AMOUNT	10 YEARS	15 YEARS	20 YEARS	25 YEARS	30 YEARS	35 YEARS
50	1.01	0.92	0.90	0.89	0.89	0.89
100	2.02	1.85	1.80	1.78	1.77	1.77
200	4.03	3.70	3.59	3.56	3.55	3.54
300	6.05	5.55	5.39	5.34	5.32	5.32
400	8.06	7.40	7.19	7.12	7.10	7.09
500	10.08	9.25	8.99	8.90	8.87	8.86
600	12.10	11.10	10.78	10.68	10.64	10.63
700	14.11	12.95	12.58	12.46	12.42	12.40
800	16.13	14.79	14.38	14.24	14.19	14.18
900	18.15	16.64	16.18	16.02	15.97	15.95
1,000	20.16	18.49	17.97	17.80	17.74	17.72
2,000	40.32	36.99	35.95	35.60	35.48	35.44
3,000	60.49	55.48	53.92	53.40	53.22	53.16
4,000	80.65	73.97	71.90	71.20	70.96	70.88
5,000	100.81	92.47	89.87	89.00	88.70	88.60
6,000	120.97	110.96	107.85	106.80	106.44	106.32
7,000	141.13	129.45	125.82	124.60	124.18	124.04
8,000	161.29	147.95	143.80	142.40	141.92	141.76
9,000	181.46	166.44	161.77	160.20	159.66	159.48
10,000	201.62	184.93	179.75	178.00	177.40	177.19
15,000	302.43	277.40	269.62	267.00	266.10	265.79
20,000	403.24	369.87	359.49	356.01	354.81	354.39
25,000	504.05	462.33	449.36	445.01	443.51	442.99
30,000	604.85	554.80	539.23	534.01	532.21	531.58
35,000	705.66	647.27	629.11	623.01	620.91	620.18
40,000	806.47	739.74	718.98	712.01	709.61	708.78
45,000	907.28	832.20	808.85	801.01	798.31	797.38
50,000	1,008.09	924.67	898.73	890.01	887.01	885.97
55,000	1,108.90	1,017.14	988.60	979.02	975.72	974.57
60,000	1,209.71	1,109.60	1,078.47	1,068.02	1,064.42	1,063.17
65,000	1,310.52	1,202.07	1,168.34	1,157.02	1,153.12	1,151.77
70,000	1,411.33	1,294.54	1,258.22	1,246.02	1,241.82	1,240.36
75,000	1,512.14	1,387.00	1,348.09	1,335.02	1,330.52	1,328.96
80,000	1,612.95	1,479.47	1,437.96	1,424.02	1,419.22	1,417.56
85,000	1,713.75	1,571.94	1,527.83	1,513.02	1,507.93	1,506.15
90,000	1,814.56	1,664.40	1,617.71	1,602.03	1,596.63	1,594.75
95,000	1,915.37	1,756.87	1,707.58	1,691.03	1,685.33	1,683.35
100,000	2,016.18	1,849.34	1,797.45	1,780.03	1,774.03	1,771.95
110,000	2,217.80	2,034.27	1,977.20	1,958.03	1,951.43	1,949.14
120,000	2,419.42	2,219.21	2,156.94	2,136.03	2,128.84	2,126.34
130,000	2,621.04	2,404.14	2,336.69	2,314.04	2,306.24	2,303.53
140,000	2,822.65	2,589.07	2,516.43	2,492.04	2,483.64	2,480.73
150,000	3,024.27	2,774.01	2,696.18	2,670.04	2,661.04	2,657.92
160,000	3,225.89	2,958.94	2,875.92	2,848.05	2,838.45	2,835.11
170,000	3,427.51	3,143.87	3,055.67	3,026.05	3,015.85	3,012.31
180,000	3,629.13	3,328.81	3,235.41	3,204.05	3,193.25	3,189.50
190,000	3,830.74	3,513.74	3,415.16	3,382.05	3,370.66	3,366.70
200,000	4,032.36	3,698.68	3,594.90	3,560.06	3,548.06	3,543.89

TABLE I-47. Fixed Rate Mortgage at 21.50%

MONTHLY PAYMENT
NECESSARY TO AMORTIZE A LOAN 21.50%

TERM AMOUNT	10 YEARS	15 YEARS	20 YEARS	25 YEARS	30 YEARS	35 YEARS
50	1.02	0.93	0.91	0.90	0.90	0.90
100	2.03	1.87	1.82	1.80	1.79	1.79
200	4.07	3.74	3.63	3.60	3.59	3.59
300	6.10	5.60	5.45	5.40	5.38	5.38
400	8.13	7.47	7.27	7.20	7.18	7.17
500	10.17	9.34	9.09	9.00	8.97	8.96
600	12.20	11.21	10.90	10.80	10.77	10.76
700	14.23	13.08	12.72	12.60	12.56	12.55
800	16.26	14.94	14.54	14.40	14.36	14.34
900	18.30	16.81	16.36	16.20	16.15	16.13
1,000	20.33	18.68	18.17	18.00	17.95	17.93
2,000	40.66	37.36	36.35	36.01	35.89	35.85
3,000	60.99	56.04	54.52	54.01	53.84	53.78
4,000	81.32	74.72	72.69	72.02	71.79	71.71
5,000	101.65	93.41	90.86	90.02	89.73	89.64
6,000	121.98	112.09	109.04	108.02	107.68	107.56
7,000	142.32	130.77	127.21	126.03	125.63	125.49
8,000	162.65	149.45	145.38	144.03	143.57	143.42
9,000	182.98	168.13	163.56	162.04	161.52	161.34
10,000	203.31	186.81	181.73	180.04	179.47	179.27
15,000	304.96	280.22	272.59	270.06	269.20	268.91
20,000	406.62	373.62	363.46	360.08	358.93	358.54
25,000	508.27	467.03	454.32	450.10	448.67	448.18
30,000	609.92	560.43	545.19	540.12	538.40	537.81
35,000	711.58	653.84	636.05	630.14	628.13	627.45
40,000	813.23	747.24	726.92	720.17	717.87	717.08
45,000	914.89	840.65	817.78	810.19	807.60	806.72
50,000	1,016.54	934.05	908.64	900.21	897.34	896.35
55,000	1,118.19	1,027.46	999.51	990.23	987.07	985.99
60,000	1,219.85	1,120.86	1,090.37	1,080.25	1,076.80	1,075.62
65,000	1,321.50	1,214.27	1,181.24	1,170.27	1,166.54	1,165.26
70,000	1,423.16	1,307.67	1,272.10	1,260.29	1,256.27	1,254.89
75,000	1,524.81	1,401.08	1,362.97	1,350.31	1,346.00	1,344.53
80,000	1,626.46	1,494.48	1,453.83	1,440.33	1,435.74	1,434.16
85,000	1,728.12	1,587.89	1,544.70	1,530.35	1,525.47	1,523.80
90,000	1,829.77	1,681.29	1,635.56	1,620.37	1,615.20	1,613.43
95,000	1,931.43	1,774.70	1,726.43	1,710.39	1,704.94	1,703.07
100,000	2,033.08	1,868.10	1,817.29	1,800.41	1,794.67	1,792.70
110,000	2,236.39	2,054.91	1,999.02	1,980.46	1,974.14	1,971.97
120,000	2,439.69	2,241.72	2,180.75	2,160.50	2,153.61	2,151.24
130,000	2,643.00	2,428.54	2,362.48	2,340.54	2,333.07	2,330.51
140,000	2,846.31	2,615.35	2,544.21	2,520.58	2,512.54	2,509.78
150,000	3,049.62	2,802.16	2,725.93	2,700.62	2,692.01	2,689.05
160,000	3,252.93	2,988.97	2,907.66	2,880.66	2,871.47	2,868.32
170,000	3,456.23	3,175.78	3,089.39	3,060.70	3,050.94	3,047.59
180,000	3,659.54	3,362.59	3,271.12	3,240.75	3,230.41	3,226.86
190,000	3,862.85	3,549.40	3,452.85	3,420.79	3,409.88	3,406.13
200,000	4,066.16	3,736.21	3,634.58	3,600.83	3,589.34	3,585.40

TABLE I-48. Fixed Rate Mortgage at 21.75%

MONTHLY PAYMENT
NECESSARY TO AMORTIZE A LOAN 21.75%

TERM / AMOUNT	10 YEARS	15 YEARS	20 YEARS	25 YEARS	30 YEARS	35 YEARS
50	1.03	0.94	0.92	0.91	0.91	0.91
100	2.05	1.89	1.84	1.82	1.82	1.81
200	4.10	3.77	3.67	3.64	3.63	3.63
300	6.15	5.66	5.51	5.46	5.45	5.44
400	8.20	7.55	7.35	7.28	7.26	7.25
500	10.25	9.43	9.19	9.10	9.08	9.07
600	12.30	11.32	11.02	10.92	10.89	10.88
700	14.35	13.21	12.86	12.75	12.71	12.69
800	16.40	15.10	14.70	14.57	14.52	14.51
900	18.45	16.98	16.53	16.39	16.34	16.32
1,000	20.50	18.87	18.37	18.21	18.15	18.13
2,000	41.00	37.74	36.74	36.42	36.31	36.27
3,000	61.50	56.61	55.11	54.62	54.46	54.40
4,000	82.00	75.48	73.49	72.83	72.61	72.54
5,000	102.50	94.35	91.86	91.04	90.77	90.67
6,000	123.00	113.21	110.23	109.25	108.92	108.81
7,000	143.50	132.08	128.60	127.46	127.07	126.94
8,000	164.00	150.95	146.97	145.67	145.23	145.08
9,000	184.50	169.82	165.34	163.87	163.38	163.21
10,000	205.00	188.69	183.72	182.08	181.53	181.35
15,000	307.50	283.04	275.57	273.12	272.30	272.02
20,000	410.00	377.38	367.43	364.16	363.06	362.69
25,000	512.50	471.73	459.29	455.20	453.83	453.36
30,000	615.00	566.07	551.15	546.25	544.60	544.04
35,000	717.50	660.42	643.01	637.29	635.36	634.71
40,000	820.00	754.76	734.86	728.33	726.13	725.38
45,000	922.50	849.11	826.72	819.37	816.90	816.06
50,000	1,025.00	943.45	918.58	910.41	907.66	906.73
55,000	1,127.50	1,037.80	1,010.44	1,001.45	998.43	997.40
60,000	1,230.00	1,132.14	1,102.30	1,092.49	1,089.19	1,088.08
65,000	1,332.50	1,226.49	1,194.15	1,183.53	1,179.96	1,178.75
70,000	1,435.00	1,320.84	1,286.01	1,274.57	1,270.73	1,269.42
75,000	1,537.50	1,415.18	1,377.87	1,365.61	1,361.49	1,360.09
80,000	1,640.00	1,509.53	1,469.73	1,456.65	1,452.26	1,450.77
85,000	1,742.50	1,603.87	1,561.58	1,547.70	1,543.02	1,541.44
90,000	1,845.00	1,698.22	1,653.44	1,638.74	1,633.79	1,632.11
95,000	1,947.50	1,792.56	1,745.30	1,729.78	1,724.56	1,722.79
100,000	2,050.00	1,886.91	1,837.16	1,820.82	1,815.32	1,813.46
110,000	2,255.00	2,075.60	2,020.87	2,002.90	1,996.85	1,994.81
120,000	2,460.00	2,264.29	2,204.59	2,184.98	2,178.39	2,176.15
130,000	2,665.00	2,452.98	2,388.31	2,367.06	2,359.92	2,357.50
140,000	2,870.01	2,641.67	2,572.02	2,549.15	2,541.45	2,538.84
150,000	3,075.01	2,830.36	2,755.74	2,731.23	2,722.98	2,720.19
160,000	3,280.01	3,019.05	2,939.45	2,913.31	2,904.52	2,901.54
170,000	3,485.01	3,207.74	3,123.17	3,095.39	3,086.05	3,082.88
180,000	3,690.01	3,396.43	3,306.89	3,277.47	3,267.58	3,264.23
190,000	3,895.01	3,585.13	3,490.60	3,459.56	3,449.11	3,445.57
200,000	4,100.00	3,773.82	3,674.32	3,641.64	3,630.64	3,626.92

TABLE II-1. Mortgage Balance Remaining for 9.00%

	PERCENTAGE OF MORTGAGE BALANCE REMAINING FOR 9.00%					
ORIGINAL TERM / AGE OF LOAN	10 YEARS	15 YEARS	20 YEARS	25 YEARS	30 YEARS	35 YEARS
1	.93537	.96695	.98127	.98884	.99317	.99575
2	.86467	.93079	.96079	.97664	.98570	.99110
3	.78734	.89125	.93838	.96329	.97752	.98601
4	.70276	.84799	.91388	.94869	.96858	.98045
5	.61024	.80068	.88707	.93272	.95880	.97436
6	.50904	.74893	.85775	.91526	.94810	.96770
7	.39835	.69232	.82568	.89615	.93640	.96042
8	.27728	.63041	.79060	.87525	.92361	.95246
9	.14485	.56268	.75223	.85239	.90961	.94375
10		.48861	.71026	.82739	.89430	.93422
11		.40758	.66435	.80004	.87755	.92380
12		.31895	.61414	.77013	.85923	.91240
13		.22201	.55922	.73741	.83919	.89993
14		.11598	.49914	.70162	.81728	.88629
15			.43343	.66248	.79330	.87137
16			.36155	.61966	.76708	.85505
17			.28294	.57282	.73840	.83720
18			.19694	.52159	.70703	.81768
19			.10288	.46556	.67272	.79632
20				.40427	.63518	.77297
21				.33723	.59413	.74742
22				.26390	.54922	.71947
23				.18369	.50010	.68890
24				.09596	.44638	.65547
25					.38761	.61890
26					.32334	.57890
27					.25303	.53514
28					.17613	.48728
29					.09201	.43493
30						.37768
31						.31505
32						.24654
33						.17161
34						.08965
35						

TABLE II-2. Mortgage Balance Remaining for 9.25%

PERCENTAGE OF
MORTGAGE BALANCE REMAINING FOR 9.25%

AGE OF LOAN \ ORIGINAL TERM	10 YEARS	15 YEARS	20 YEARS	25 YEARS	30 YEARS	35 YEARS
1	.93620	.96765	.98184	.98929	.99351	.99600
2	.86624	.93217	.96192	.97754	.98639	.99162
3	.78953	.89327	.94009	.96466	.97858	.98682
4	.70542	.85062	.91614	.95054	.97003	.98155
5	.61319	.80385	.88989	.93505	.96064	.97577
6	.51205	.75257	.86110	.91807	.95035	.96944
7	.40115	.69633	.82953	.89945	.93907	.96249
8	.27955	.63467	.79492	.87903	.92669	.95488
9	.14621	.56705	.75696	.85664	.91313	.94652
10		.49291	.71534	.83209	.89825	.93737
11		.41161	.66970	.80517	.88193	.92733
12		.32247	.61966	.77565	.86405	.91632
13		.22472	.56478	.74329	.84443	.90424
14		.11753	.50461	.70779	.82292	.89100
15			.43864	.66888	.79934	.87649
16			.36629	.62620	.77348	.86057
17			.28696	.57941	.74512	.84311
18			.19997	.52810	.71403	.82397
19			.10459	.47184	.67994	.80299
20				.41015	.64255	.77998
21				.34250	.60156	.75474
22				.26832	.55661	.72707
23				.18698	.50732	.69673
24				.09780	.45327	.66346
25					.39400	.62698
26					.32902	.58698
27					.25776	.54312
28					.17963	.49502
29					.09395	.44229
30						.38446
31						.32105
32						.25152
33						.17527
34						.09167
35						

TABLE II-3. Mortgage Balance Remaining for 9.50%

PERCENTAGE OF
MORTGAGE BALANCE REMAINING FOR 9.50%

ORIGINAL TERM / AGE OF LOAN	10 YEARS	15 YEARS	20 YEARS	25 YEARS	30 YEARS	35 YEARS
1	.93703	.96834	.98239	.98972	.99383	.99625
2	.86781	.93353	.96303	.97841	.98706	.99212
3	.79171	.89527	.94176	.96599	.97960	.98758
4	.70807	.85322	.91837	.95233	.97141	.98260
5	.61612	.80699	.89265	.93731	.96241	.97712
6	.51505	.75617	.86439	.92081	.95251	.97109
7	.40395	.70031	.83332	.90266	.94163	.96447
8	.28182	.63890	.79917	.88272	.92967	.95719
9	.14757	.57140	.76163	.86079	.91653	.94918
10		.49721	.72036	.83669	.90208	.94039
11		.41564	.67500	.81020	.88619	.93071
12		.32598	.62513	.78108	.86873	.92008
13		.22743	.57032	.74907	.84954	.90840
14		.11909	.51007	.71388	.82844	.89555
15			.44383	.67520	.80524	.88143
16			.37103	.63268	.77975	.86591
17			.29099	.58595	.75172	.84885
18			.20301	.53457	.72091	.83009
19			.10631	.47809	.68705	.80948
20				.41601	.64982	.78681
21				.34777	.60890	.76190
22				.27275	.56392	.73452
23				.19029	.51447	.70442
24				.09964	.46012	.67133
25					.40037	.63495
26					.33469	.59497
27					.26250	.55101
28					.18313	.50270
29					.09590	.44959
30						.39121
31						.32703
32						.25649
33						.17894
34						.09370
35						

TABLE II-4. Mortgage Balance Remaining for 9.75%

PERCENTAGE OF
MORTGAGE BALANCE REMAINING FOR 9.75%

AGE OF LOAN / ORIGINAL TERM	10 YEARS	15 YEARS	20 YEARS	25 YEARS	30 YEARS	35 YEARS
1	.93785	.96902	.98293	.99013	.99414	.99647
2	.86936	.93487	.96412	.97925	.98769	.99259
3	.79388	.89725	.94339	.96727	.98058	.98831
4	.71071	.85579	.92054	.95406	.97274	.98359
5	.61905	.81009	.89537	.93951	.96411	.97839
6	.51805	.75974	.86762	.92347	.95459	.97266
7	.40675	.70426	.83705	.90579	.94411	.96635
8	.28410	.64312	.80336	.88632	.93255	.95939
9	.14894	.57574	.76624	.86485	.91982	.95173
10		.50149	.72533	.84120	.90579	.94328
11		.41967	.68025	.81514	.89032	.93397
12		.32951	.63057	.78642	.87328	.92371
13		.23015	.57583	.75477	.85451	.91240
14		.12066	.51550	.71989	.83381	.89994
15			.44902	.68145	.81101	.88621
16			.37576	.63910	.78588	.87109
17			.29503	.59242	.75819	.85441
18			.20607	.54099	.72768	.83604
19			.10803	.48431	.69405	.81580
20				.42186	.65700	.79349
21				.35303	.61616	.76890
22				.27718	.57116	.74181
23				.19360	.52158	.71195
24				.10150	.46693	.67905
25					.40671	.64280
26					.34036	.60285
27					.26723	.55882
28					.18665	.51030
29					.09785	.45684
30						.39793
31						.33300
32						.26146
33						.18262
34						.09574
35						

TABLE II-5. Mortgage Balance Remaining for 10.00%

PERCENTAGE OF
MORTGAGE BALANCE REMAINING FOR 10.00%

AGE OF LOAN / ORIGINAL TERM	10 YEARS	15 YEARS	20 YEARS	25 YEARS	30 YEARS	35 YEARS
1	.93866	.96968	.98345	.99053	.99444	.99669
2	.87089	.93619	.96517	.98007	.98830	.99303
3	.79603	.89919	.94498	.96851	.98152	.98900
4	.71333	.85832	.92267	.95574	.97402	.98453
5	.62197	.81317	.89802	.94164	.96574	.97960
6	.52105	.76329	.87080	.92606	.95660	.97416
7	.40955	.70818	.84072	.90884	.94649	.96814
8	.28638	.64731	.80750	.88983	.93533	.96150
9	.15031	.58006	.77079	.86882	.92300	.95416
10		.50577	.73024	.84561	.90938	.94605
11		.42370	.68545	.81998	.89433	.93709
12		.33303	.63596	.79166	.87771	.92719
13		.23288	.58130	.76037	.85934	.91625
14		.12223	.52091	.72581	.83906	.90418
15			.45419	.68762	.81665	.89083
16			.38049	.64544	.79189	.87609
17			.29907	.59885	.76454	.85981
18			.20913	.54737	.73432	.84182
19			.10977	.49050	.70094	.82194
20				.42768	.66407	.79999
21				.35828	.62333	.77574
22				.28162	.57833	.74894
23				.19692	.52862	.71934
24				.10336	.47370	.68665
25					.41303	.65052
26					.34601	.61062
27					.27197	.56654
28					.19018	.51784
29					.09982	.46404
30						.40461
31						.33895
32						.26642
33						.18630
34						.09778
35						

TABLE II-6. Mortgage Balance Remaining for 10.25%

PERCENTAGE OF
MORTGAGE BALANCE REMAINING FOR 10.25%

AGE OF LOAN / ORIGINAL TERM	10 YEARS	15 YEARS	20 YEARS	25 YEARS	30 YEARS	35 YEARS
1	.93946	.97034	.98396	.99092	.99472	.99689
2	.87242	.93749	.96620	.98085	.98888	.99345
3	.79817	.90111	.94653	.96971	.98241	.98965
4	.71594	.86082	.92475	.95737	.97525	.98543
5	.62488	.81620	.90063	.94371	.96731	.98075
6	.52404	.76679	.87392	.92857	.95852	.97558
7	.41235	.71207	.84433	.91181	.94879	.96985
8	.28867	.65147	.81157	.89325	.93801	.96351
9	.15169	.58436	.77528	.87270	.92608	.95648
10		.51003	.73510	.84993	.91286	.94870
11		.42772	.69060	.82472	.89822	.94008
12		.33656	.64131	.79680	.88201	.93053
13		.23561	.58673	.76588	.86405	.91996
14		.12381	.52629	.73164	.84417	.90825
15			.45935	.69372	.82215	.89529
16			.38522	.65172	.79776	.88093
17			.30312	.60521	.77075	.86503
18			.21220	.55370	.74085	.84742
19			.11151	.49666	.70772	.82792
20				.43349	.67104	.80633
21				.36353	.63042	.78241
22				.28606	.58543	.75592
23				.20025	.53560	.72659
24				.10523	.48043	.69410
25					.41932	.65813
26					.35165	.61828
27					.27671	.57416
28					.19371	.52530
29					.10179	.47118
30						.41125
31						.34488
32						.27138
33						.18998
34						.09983
35						

TABLE II-7. Mortgage Balance Remaining for 10.50%

AGE OF LOAN \ ORIGINAL TERM	10 YEARS	15 YEARS	20 YEARS	25 YEARS	30 YEARS	35 YEARS
	PERCENTAGE OF MORTGAGE BALANCE REMAINING FOR 10.50%					
1	.94026	.97098	.98446	.99129	.99499	.99709
2	.87393	.93877	.96721	.98161	.98944	.99385
3	.80029	.90300	.94806	.97087	.98327	.99026
4	.71854	.86329	.92679	.95895	.97642	.98627
5	.62778	.81921	.90319	.94571	.96882	.98185
6	.52702	.77027	.87698	.93102	.96038	.97693
7	.41515	.71593	.84788	.91470	.95100	.97148
8	.29096	.65561	.81558	.89659	.94060	.96542
9	.15308	.58864	.77971	.87648	.92905	.95870
10		.51428	.73990	.85415	.91622	.95123
11		.43174	.69569	.82937	.90199	.94294
12		.34010	.64662	.80185	.88618	.93374
13		.23836	.59214	.77130	.86863	.92352
14		.12540	.53165	.73739	.84915	.91218
15			.46449	.69973	.82752	.89959
16			.38994	.65793	.80351	.88561
17			.30717	.61152	.77685	.87009
18			.21528	.55999	.74725	.85286
19			.11326	.50279	.71439	.83373
20				.43928	.67791	.81250
21				.36877	.63741	.78892
22				.29050	.59245	.76275
23				.20359	.54253	.73369
24				.10711	.48711	.70142
25					.42558	.66560
26					.35727	.62584
27					.28144	.58169
28					.19724	.53268
29					.10377	.47827
30						.41786
31						.35079
32						.27633
33						.19366
34						.10189
35						

TABLE II-8. Mortgage Balance Remaining for 10.75%

PERCENTAGE OF
MORTGAGE BALANCE REMAINING FOR 10.75%

AGE OF LOAN \ ORIGINAL TERM	10 YEARS	15 YEARS	20 YEARS	25 YEARS	30 YEARS	35 YEARS
1	.94104	.97161	.98495	.99165	.99525	.99727
2	.87543	.94002	.96819	.98235	.98997	.99423
3	.80240	.90486	.94954	.97200	.98409	.99084
4	.72113	.86573	.92879	.96048	.97754	.98708
5	.63067	.82218	.90569	.94766	.97026	.98288
6	.53000	.77371	.87998	.93339	.96215	.97822
7	.41795	.71976	.85137	.91752	.95313	.97302
8	.29325	.65972	.81952	.89984	.94309	.96724
9	.15447	.59290	.78408	.88017	.93192	.96081
10		.51853	.74464	.85828	.91948	.95365
11		.43575	.70074	.83392	.90564	.94569
12		.34363	.65188	.80681	.89023	.93682
13		.24111	.59750	.77663	.87308	.92695
14		.12700	.53698	.74304	.85400	.91596
15			.46962	.70566	.83276	.90374
16			.39466	.66406	.80912	.89013
17			.31122	.61776	.78281	.87499
18			.21837	.56623	.75353	.85814
19			.11502	.50887	.72095	.83938
20				.44504	.68468	.81851
21				.37400	.64431	.79527
22				.29494	.59939	.76941
23				.20694	.54939	.74064
24				.10900	.49374	.70861
25					.43181	.67296
26					.36288	.63328
27					.28616	.58913
28					.20078	.53998
29					.10576	.48529
30						.42442
31						.35667
32						.28127
33						.19735
34						.10395
35						

TABLE II-9. Mortgage Balance Remaining for 11.00%

	PERCENTAGE OF MORTGAGE BALANCE REMAINING FOR 11.00%					
ORIGINAL TERM / AGE OF LOAN	10 YEARS	15 YEARS	20 YEARS	25 YEARS	30 YEARS	35 YEARS
1	.94182	.97224	.98542	.99199	.99550	.99744
2	.87692	.94126	.96915	.98305	.99048	.99458
3	.80450	.90670	.95099	.97308	.98487	.99139
4	.72370	.86814	.93074	.96196	.97862	.98783
5	.63355	.82512	.90814	.94955	.97165	.98386
6	.53297	.77711	.88293	.93570	.96386	.97944
7	.42076	.72356	.85480	.92025	.95518	.97450
8	.29555	.66381	.82341	.90301	.94549	.96898
9	.15586	.59714	.78839	.88378	.93468	.96283
10		.52276	.74932	.86232	.92263	.95597
11		.43977	.70573	.83838	.90917	.94831
12		.34717	.65709	.81167	.89416	.93977
13		.24386	.60283	.78187	.87741	.93024
14		.12860	.54228	.74862	.85872	.91960
15			.47473	.71152	.83787	.90774
16			.39937	.67012	.81461	.89450
17			.31528	.62394	.78866	.87973
18			.22146	.57241	.75970	.86325
19			.11679	.51493	.72739	.84487
20				.45078	.69134	.82435
21				.37922	.65112	.80147
22				.29937	.60625	.77593
23				.21029	.55618	.74744
24				.11090	.50033	.71565
25					.43800	.68019
26					.36847	.64062
27					.29089	.59647
28					.20433	.54721
29					.10775	.49225
30						.43094
31						.36252
32						.28619
33						.20103
34						.10601
35						

TABLE II-10. Mortgage Balance Remaining for 11.25%

PERCENTAGE OF MORTGAGE BALANCE REMAINING FOR 11.25%

AGE OF LOAN \ ORIGINAL TERM	10 YEARS	15 YEARS	20 YEARS	25 YEARS	30 YEARS	35 YEARS
1	.94260	.97285	.98588	.99232	.99573	.99760
2	.87839	.94248	.97008	.98374	.99096	.99491
3	.80658	.90851	.95241	.97413	.98562	.99191
4	.72626	.87051	.93265	.96339	.97965	.98855
5	.63642	.82802	.91054	.95138	.97297	.98480
6	.53594	.78049	.88582	.93794	.96551	.98059
7	.42356	.72733	.85816	.92291	.95715	.97589
8	.29785	.66786	.82723	.90610	.94781	.97064
9	.15726	.60136	.79264	.88730	.93736	.96476
10		.52697	.75394	.86627	.92567	.95818
11		.44377	.71067	.84275	.91259	.95083
12		.35071	.66226	.81644	.89797	.94260
13		.24663	.60812	.78701	.88161	.93340
14		.13021	.54756	.75410	.86332	.92310
15			.47983	.71729	.84286	.91159
16			.40407	.67611	.81997	.89872
17			.31934	.63006	.79437	.88432
18			.22456	.57855	.76574	.86821
19			.11856	.52094	.73372	.85019
20				.45650	.69790	.83004
21				.38442	.65784	.80750
22				.30381	.61303	.78229
23				.21365	.56291	.75410
24				.11280	.50686	.72256
25					.44416	.68729
26					.37404	.64784
27					.29560	.60371
28					.20787	.55436
29					.10975	.49915
30						.43741
31						.36835
32						.29111
33						.20471
34						.10808
35						

TABLE II-11. Mortgage Balance Remaining for 11.50%

PERCENTAGE OF MORTGAGE BALANCE REMAINING FOR 11.50%

AGE OF LOAN \ ORIGINAL TERM	10 YEARS	15 YEARS	20 YEARS	25 YEARS	30 YEARS	35 YEARS
1	.94336	.97345	.98632	.99264	.99596	.99775
2	.87986	.94367	.97099	.98440	.99142	.99523
3	.80865	.91029	.95379	.97515	.98634	.99240
4	.72881	.87286	.93451	.96478	.98064	.98923
5	.63929	.83089	.91289	.95315	.97425	.98568
6	.53891	.78383	.88865	.94011	.96708	.98169
7	.42636	.73106	.86147	.92550	.95904	.97722
8	.30016	.67190	.83099	.90911	.95003	.97221
9	.15866	.60556	.79682	.89073	.93993	.96659
10		.53117	.75851	.87012	.92860	.96029
11		.44777	.71555	.84702	.91590	.95323
12		.35425	.66738	.82111	.90166	.94531
13		.24940	.61337	.79206	.88569	.93643
14		.13183	.55281	.75949	.86779	.92647
15			.48490	.72297	.84771	.91530
16			.40877	.68203	.82520	.90278
17			.32340	.63611	.79997	.88875
18			.22767	.58463	.77167	.87301
19			.12034	.52691	.73993	.85536
20				.46219	.70436	.83557
21				.38962	.66446	.81339
22				.30825	.61973	.78851
23				.21701	.56958	.76061
24				.11471	.51334	.72934
25					.45028	.69427
26					.37958	.65494
27					.30031	.61085
28					.21142	.56142
29					.11175	.50599
30						.44383
31						.37415
32						.29601
33						.20839
34						.11015
35						

TABLE II-12. Mortgage Balance Remaining for 11.75%

PERCENTAGE OF MORTGAGE BALANCE REMAINING FOR 11.75%

AGE OF LOAN \ ORIGINAL TERM	10 YEARS	15 YEARS	20 YEARS	25 YEARS	30 YEARS	35 YEARS
1	.94412	.97404	.98676	.99295	.99617	.99789
2	.88131	.94485	.97187	.98503	.99186	.99553
3	.81070	.91205	.95514	.97613	.98702	.99286
4	.73134	.87517	.93633	.96612	.98158	.98987
5	.64213	.83372	.91519	.95487	.97547	.98651
6	.54186	.78713	.89143	.94222	.96859	.98273
7	.42916	.73476	.86472	.92801	.96086	.97848
8	.30247	.67590	.83470	.91203	.95218	.97371
9	.16007	.60973	.80095	.89407	.94242	.96834
10		.53536	.76302	.87389	.93144	.96231
11		.45176	.72038	.85120	.91911	.95553
12		.35780	.67245	.82569	.90524	.94790
13		.25217	.61858	.79703	.88966	.93933
14		.13345	.55802	.76480	.87214	.92970
15			.48996	.72858	.85245	.91888
16			.41345	.68787	.83031	.90671
17			.32745	.64210	.80544	.89303
18			.23079	.59066	.77747	.87766
19			.12213	.53284	.74604	.86037
20				.46785	.71070	.84095
21				.39479	.67099	.81911
22				.31267	.62635	.79457
23				.22037	.57617	.76698
24				.11662	.51977	.73597
25					.45637	.70112
26					.38511	.66194
27					.30500	.61790
28					.21497	.56840
29					.11376	.51276
30						.45021
31						.37991
32						.30089
33						.21207
34						.11223
35						

TABLE II-13. Mortgage Balance Remaining for 12.00%

PERCENTAGE OF MORTGAGE BALANCE REMAINING FOR 12.00%

AGE OF LOAN / ORIGINAL TERM	10 YEARS	15 YEARS	20 YEARS	25 YEARS	30 YEARS	35 YEARS
1	.94487	.97461	.98718	.99325	.99637	.99803
2	.88274	.94601	.97273	.98564	.99228	.99581
3	.81274	.91377	.95646	.97707	.98767	.99330
4	.73386	.87745	.93811	.96741	.98248	.99048
5	.64497	.83652	.91744	.95653	.97663	.98730
6	.54482	.79040	.89415	.94427	.97004	.98372
7	.43196	.73844	.86791	.93045	.96261	.97968
8	.30478	.67988	.83834	.91488	.95424	.97513
9	.16148	.61389	.80501	.89733	.94481	.97001
10		.53954	.76746	.87756	.93418	.96423
11		.45575	.72515	.85529	.92220	.95772
12		.36134	.67747	.83018	.90871	.95039
13		.25496	.62375	.80189	.89350	.94212
14		.13508	.56321	.77002	.87637	.93281
15			.49499	.73410	.85706	.92232
16			.41813	.69363	.83530	.91049
17			.33151	.64802	.81078	.89717
18			.23391	.59664	.78316	.88215
19			.12393	.53873	.75203	.86524
20				.47348	.71695	.84617
21				.39995	.67742	.82469
22				.31710	.63288	.80049
23				.22374	.58269	.77321
24				.11854	.52614	.74248
25					.46241	.70784
26					.39060	.66882
27					.30969	.62484
28					.21851	.57529
29					.11577	.51946
30						.45654
31						.38564
32						.30576
33						.21574
34						.11430
35						

TABLE II-14. Mortgage Balance Remaining for 12.25%

PERCENTAGE OF MORTGAGE BALANCE REMAINING FOR 12.25%

AGE OF LOAN \ ORIGINAL TERM	10 YEARS	15 YEARS	20 YEARS	25 YEARS	30 YEARS	35 YEARS
1	.94561	.97518	.98759	.99354	.99656	.99815
2	.88417	.94715	.97357	.98623	.99268	.99607
3	.81477	.91548	.95774	.97799	.98830	.99371
4	.73636	.87970	.93985	.96867	.98334	.99105
5	.64780	.83929	.91965	.95814	.97775	.98805
6	.54776	.79364	.89682	.94625	.97143	.98465
7	.43475	.74207	.87104	.93282	.96429	.98082
8	.30710	.68382	.84191	.91765	.95622	.97648
9	.16289	.61802	.80901	.90051	.94711	.97159
10		.54369	.77185	.88115	.93682	.96606
11		.45973	.72987	.85928	.92520	.95982
12		.36488	.68245	.83458	.91207	.95276
13		.25774	.62888	.80667	.89723	.94479
14		.13672	.56836	.77515	.88047	.93579
15			.50001	.73954	.86155	.92562
16			.42279	.69932	.84016	.91414
17			.33556	.65388	.81601	.90116
18			.23703	.60255	.78872	.88651
19			.12573	.54457	.75790	.86995
20				.47908	.72309	.85125
21				.40509	.68376	.83012
22				.32152	.63933	.80626
23				.22711	.58915	.77930
24				.12047	.53246	.74884
25					.46842	.71444
26					.39608	.67558
27					.31436	.63169
28					.22206	.58210
29					.11779	.52609
30						.46282
31						.39134
32						.31061
33						.21940
34						.11638
35						

TABLE II-15. Mortgage Balance Remaining for 12.50%

PERCENTAGE OF MORTGAGE BALANCE REMAINING FOR 12.50%

AGE OF LOAN \ ORIGINAL TERM	10 YEARS	15 YEARS	20 YEARS	25 YEARS	30 YEARS	35 YEARS
1	.94634	.97574	.98799	.99381	.99675	.99827
2	.88558	.94826	.97439	.98680	.99306	.99632
3	.81677	.91715	.95899	.97887	.98889	.99410
4	.73886	.88192	.94155	.96988	.98417	.99159
5	.65062	.84202	.92180	.95970	.97882	.98875
6	.55070	.79684	.89944	.94817	.97276	.98554
7	.43755	.74568	.87411	.93512	.96590	.98189
8	.30942	.68774	.84543	.92034	.95813	.97777
9	.16431	.62213	.81296	.90361	.94933	.97310
10		.54784	.77618	.88465	.93937	.96781
11		.46370	.73453	.86319	.92809	.96182
12		.36843	.68737	.83888	.91531	.95504
13		.26054	.63396	.81136	.90085	.94735
14		.13836	.57348	.78019	.88447	.93866
15			.50500	.74490	.86591	.92881
16			.42744	.70493	.84491	.91765
17			.33962	.65967	.82112	.90502
18			.24016	.60841	.79417	.89072
19			.12754	.55037	.76367	.87452
20				.48465	.72912	.85617
21				.41022	.69000	.83540
22				.32593	.64570	.81188
23				.23048	.59553	.78524
24				.12240	.53871	.75508
25					.47438	.72092
26					.40153	.68224
27					.31903	.63843
28					.22560	.58883
29					.11981	.53266
30						.46904
31						.39701
32						.31544
33						.22306
34						.11846
35						

TABLE II-16. Mortgage Balance Remaining for 12.75%

PERCENTAGE OF
MORTGAGE BALANCE REMAINING FOR 12.75%

AGE OF LOAN / ORIGINAL TERM	10 YEARS	15 YEARS	20 YEARS	25 YEARS	30 YEARS	35 YEARS
1	.94707	.97629	.98838	.99408	.99692	.99838
2	.88698	.94936	.97519	.98735	.99343	.99655
3	.81877	.91880	.96021	.97971	.98946	.99447
4	.74133	.88411	.94321	.97105	.98495	.99210
5	.65343	.84472	.92391	.96121	.97984	.98942
6	.55363	.80001	.90200	.95004	.97403	.98637
7	.44034	.74925	.87713	.93736	.96744	.98292
8	.31174	.69163	.84889	.92296	.95996	.97899
9	.16574	.62622	.81684	.90662	.95147	.97453
10		.55196	.78045	.88807	.94183	.96947
11		.46767	.73914	.86701	.93088	.96373
12		.37197	.69224	.84310	.91846	.95721
13		.26333	.63901	.81596	.90435	.94981
14		.14000	.57857	.78515	.88834	.94140
15			.50997	.75017	.87016	.93186
16			.43208	.71046	.84953	.92104
17			.34367	.66539	.82610	.90874
18			.24329	.61422	.79951	.89479
19			.12935	.55613	.76932	.87894
20				.49018	.73505	.86096
21				.41532	.69614	.84054
22				.33033	.65197	.81736
23				.23386	.60184	.79105
24				.12433	.54492	.76118
25					.48030	.72727
26					.40695	.68878
27					.32367	.64508
28					.22914	.59547
29					.12183	.53915
30						.47522
31						.40264
32						.32025
33						.22672
34						.12054
35						

TABLE II-17. Mortgage Balance Remaining for 13.00%

PERCENTAGE OF
MORTGAGE BALANCE REMAINING FOR 13.00%

ORIGINAL TERM / AGE OF LOAN	10 YEARS	15 YEARS	20 YEARS	25 YEARS	30 YEARS	35 YEARS
1	.94779	.97682	.98876	.99433	.99709	.99849
2	.88837	.95045	.97596	.98788	.99377	.99677
3	.82075	.92043	.96140	.98053	.99000	.99481
4	.74380	.88627	.94483	.97218	.98570	.99258
5	.65622	.84739	.92597	.96267	.98082	.99005
6	.55656	.80315	.90451	.95184	.97526	.98717
7	.44314	.75280	.88008	.93952	.96893	.98388
8	.31406	.69550	.85229	.92551	.96172	.98015
9	.16717	.63029	.82065	.90955	.95353	.97590
10		.55608	.78466	.89140	.94420	.97106
11		.47162	.74369	.87074	.93358	.96555
12		.37551	.69707	.84723	.92150	.95929
13		.26613	.64401	.82047	.90775	.95215
14		.14166	.58363	.79002	.89211	.94404
15			.51491	.75536	.87430	.93480
16			.43671	.71592	.85403	.92429
17			.34771	.67104	.83097	.91233
18			.24643	.61996	.80473	.89872
19			.13117	.56184	.77486	.88323
20				.49568	.74087	.86560
21				.42040	.70219	.84554
22				.33473	.65817	.82270
23				.23723	.60807	.79672
24				.12627	.55106	.76715
25					.48618	.73350
26					.41234	.69520
27					.32831	.65162
28					.23268	.60202
29					.12385	.54558
30						.48134
31						.40824
32						.32504
33						.23036
34						.12262
35						

TABLE II-18. Mortgage Balance Remaining for 13.25%

PERCENTAGE OF
MORTGAGE BALANCE REMAINING FOR 13.25%

AGE OF LOAN \ ORIGINAL TERM	10 YEARS	15 YEARS	20 YEARS	25 YEARS	30 YEARS	35 YEARS
1	.94850	.97735	.98912	.99457	.99724	.99859
2	.88975	.95151	.97672	.98838	.99410	.99698
3	.82272	.92203	.96256	.98132	.99051	.99514
4	.74625	.88839	.94641	.97327	.98642	.99304
5	.65901	.85002	.92798	.96407	.98175	.99065
6	.55948	.80624	.90696	.95359	.97642	.98791
7	.44593	.75630	.88298	.94163	.97035	.98480
8	.31639	.69933	.85562	.92798	.96341	.98125
9	.16860	.63433	.82441	.91241	.95550	.97719
10		.56017	.78881	.89465	.94648	.97257
11		.47557	.74818	.87438	.93619	.96729
12		.37905	.70184	.85126	.92444	.96127
13		.26894	.64896	.82489	.91104	.95440
14		.14332	.58864	.79480	.89576	.94657
15			.51983	.76047	.87832	.93763
16			.44132	.72130	.85842	.92743
17			.35175	.67662	.83573	.91579
18			.24957	.62565	.80983	.90252
19			.13299	.56750	.78029	.88738
20				.50115	.74659	.87010
21				.42546	.70814	.85039
22				.33912	.66428	.82791
23				.24060	.61423	.80226
24				.12822	.55714	.77299
25					.49201	.73960
26					.41770	.70152
27					.33293	.65806
28					.23621	.60849
29					.12588	.55193
30						.48740
31						.41379
32						.32981
33						.23400
34						.12470
35						

TABLE II-19. Mortgage Balance Remaining for 13.50%

PERCENTAGE OF MORTGAGE BALANCE REMAINING FOR 13.50%

AGE OF LOAN \ ORIGINAL TERM	10 YEARS	15 YEARS	20 YEARS	25 YEARS	30 YEARS	35 YEARS
1	.94920	.97787	.98948	.99481	.99739	.99868
2	.89111	.95255	.97745	.98887	.99441	.99717
3	.82467	.92360	.96369	.98208	.99100	.99544
4	.74868	.89049	.94795	.97432	.98710	.99347
5	.66178	.85262	.92995	.96544	.98264	.99121
6	.56239	.80931	.90937	.95528	.97754	.98862
7	.44872	.75978	.88583	.94367	.97171	.98567
8	.31872	.70313	.85890	.93038	.96504	.98229
9	.17004	.63834	.82811	.91519	.95741	.97842
10		.56424	.79289	.89781	.94868	.97400
11		.47950	.75262	.87794	.93870	.96895
12		.38259	.70656	.85521	.92729	.96316
13		.27175	.65388	.82922	.91423	.95655
14		.14498	.59363	.79949	.89930	.94899
15			.52472	.76549	.88223	.94034
16			.44592	.72661	.86270	.93045
17			.35579	.68214	.84037	.91913
18			.25271	.63128	.81482	.90619
19			.13482	.57311	.78561	.89139
20				.50659	.75220	.87447
21				.43050	.71399	.85511
22				.34349	.67030	.83298
23				.24398	.62032	.80766
24				.13016	.56316	.77870
25					.49779	.74559
26					.42303	.70772
27					.33753	.66440
28					.23974	.61486
29					.12790	.55821
30						.49342
31						.41931
32						.33456
33						.23763
34						.12678
35						

TABLE II-20. Mortgage Balance Remaining for 13.75%

PERCENTAGE OF MORTGAGE BALANCE REMAINING FOR 13.75%

AGE OF LOAN / ORIGINAL TERM	10 YEARS	15 YEARS	20 YEARS	25 YEARS	30 YEARS	35 YEARS
1	.94990	.97837	.98983	.99503	.99753	.99877
2	.89246	.95358	.97816	.98934	.99471	.99735
3	.82661	.92515	.96479	.98282	.99147	.99573
4	.75110	.89255	.94946	.97533	.98775	.99387
5	.66454	.85518	.93188	.96675	.98349	.99174
6	.56529	.81234	.91172	.95692	.97861	.98929
7	.45151	.76322	.88861	.94564	.97301	.98649
8	.32105	.70690	.86212	.93271	.96659	.98328
9	.17148	.64233	.83175	.91789	.95923	.97959
10		.56830	.79692	.90090	.95080	.97537
11		.48343	.75700	.88141	.94112	.97053
12		.38612	.71122	.85907	.93003	.96497
13		.27456	.65874	.83346	.91732	.95861
14		.14665	.59857	.80410	.90274	.95131
15			.52959	.77043	.88603	.94294
16			.45050	.73183	.86686	.93335
17			.35982	.68758	.84489	.92235
18			.25585	.63684	.81970	.90974
19			.13666	.57867	.79082	.89528
20				.51198	.75771	.87870
21				.43552	.71975	.85970
22				.34785	.67623	.83791
23				.24735	.62633	.81293
24				.13211	.56912	.78429
25					.50353	.75145
26					.42833	.71381
27					.34211	.67064
28					.24326	.62116
29					.12993	.56442
30						.49937
31						.42479
32						.33929
33						.24125
34						.12886
35						

TABLE II-21. Mortgage Balance Remaining for 14.00%

PERCENTAGE OF
MORTGAGE BALANCE REMAINING FOR 14.00%

AGE OF LOAN \ ORIGINAL TERM	10 YEARS	15 YEARS	20 YEARS	25 YEARS	30 YEARS	35 YEARS
1	.95059	.97887	.99016	.99525	.99767	.99885
2	.89380	.95458	.97885	.98979	.99499	.99752
3	.82853	.92667	.96586	.98352	.99191	.99600
4	.75351	.89459	.95092	.97631	.98837	.99425
5	.66729	.85771	.93376	.96803	.98431	.99224
6	.56819	.81533	.91402	.95850	.97963	.98992
7	.45429	.76662	.89135	.94756	.97426	.98727
8	.32338	.71064	.86528	.93498	.96809	.98421
9	.17293	.64630	.83533	.92052	.96099	.98070
10		.57234	.80089	.90390	.95284	.97667
11		.48734	.76132	.88480	.94346	.97203
12		.38965	.71584	.86285	.93269	.96670
13		.27737	.66356	.83762	.92031	.96057
14		.14832	.60348	.80862	.90607	.95353
15			.53443	.77529	.88972	.94544
16			.45506	.73698	.87092	.93614
17			.36384	.69295	.84931	.92545
18			.25900	.64235	.82447	.91316
19			.13850	.58419	.79593	.89904
20				.51734	.76312	.88281
21				.44051	.72542	.86415
22				.35221	.68208	.84271
23				.25072	.63227	.81807
24				.13407	.57502	.78975
25					.50922	.75720
26					.43360	.71978
27					.34668	.67678
28					.24678	.62736
29					.13196	.57056
30						.50527
31						.43023
32						.34399
33						.24487
34						.13094
35						

TABLE II-22. Mortgage Balance Remaining for 14.25%

PERCENTAGE OF
MORTGAGE BALANCE REMAINING FOR 14.25%

AGE OF LOAN \ ORIGINAL TERM	10 YEARS	15 YEARS	20 YEARS	25 YEARS	30 YEARS	35 YEARS
1	.95127	.97936	.99049	.99546	.99780	.99892
2	.89513	.95557	.97953	.99023	.99526	.99768
3	.83044	.92817	.96690	.98420	.99234	.99625
4	.75590	.89659	.95235	.97726	.98897	.99461
5	.67003	.86021	.93559	.96926	.98508	.99271
6	.57108	.81829	.91628	.96004	.98061	.99052
7	.45708	.77000	.89402	.94941	.97546	.98800
8	.32572	.71435	.86838	.93717	.96952	.98510
9	.17438	.65024	.83884	.92307	.96268	.98175
10		.57636	.80481	.90683	.95480	.97790
11		.49125	.76559	.88811	.94572	.97346
12		.39318	.72040	.86654	.93525	.96835
13		.28019	.66834	.84169	.92320	.96245
14		.15000	.60836	.81305	.90931	.95566
15			.53924	.78006	.89330	.94784
16			.45961	.74205	.87486	.93882
17			.36786	.69825	.85361	.92843
18			.26214	.64779	.82913	.91646
19			.14034	.58965	.80093	.90268
20				.52266	.76843	.88679
21				.44548	.73098	.86848
22				.35655	.68784	.84739
23				.25408	.63813	.82309
24				.13602	.58086	.79509
25					.51487	.76282
26					.43883	.72565
27					.35123	.68282
28					.25029	.63348
29					.13400	.57662
30						.51111
31						.43563
32						.34867
33						.24847
34						.13302
35						

TABLE II-23. Mortgage Balance Remaining for 14.50%

PERCENTAGE OF
MORTGAGE BALANCE REMAINING FOR 14.50%

AGE OF LOAN \ ORIGINAL TERM	10 YEARS	15 YEARS	20 YEARS	25 YEARS	30 YEARS	35 YEARS
1	.95195	.97983	.99081	.99566	.99792	.99899
2	.89644	.95654	.98018	.99065	.99551	.99783
3	.83233	.92964	.96792	.98486	.99274	.99649
4	.75828	.89857	.95375	.97817	.98953	.99494
5	.67275	.86268	.93738	.97044	.98583	.99315
6	.57396	.82122	.91848	.96152	.98155	.99109
7	.45986	.77334	.89665	.95121	.97660	.98870
8	.32806	.71803	.87143	.93931	.97090	.98594
9	.17583	.65415	.84230	.92556	.96430	.98275
10		.58037	.80866	.90968	.95669	.97907
11		.49514	.76980	.89133	.94789	.97483
12		.39671	.72491	.87014	.93773	.96992
13		.28301	.67307	.84567	.92599	.96425
14		.15168	.61319	.81740	.91244	.95770
15			.54403	.78475	.89678	.95013
16			.46414	.74704	.87870	.94140
17			.37187	.70349	.85781	.93131
18			.26529	.65318	.83368	.91965
19			.14219	.59506	.80582	.90619
20				.52794	.77363	.89064
21				.45042	.73645	.87268
22				.36087	.69351	.85194
23				.25745	.64392	.82798
24				.13798	.58663	.80030
25					.52046	.76833
26					.44403	.73141
27					.35576	.68877
28					.25380	.63951
29					.13603	.58261
30						.51690
31						.44099
32						.35332
33						.25206
34						.13510
35						

TABLE II-24. Mortgage Balance Remaining for 14.75%

PERCENTAGE OF
MORTGAGE BALANCE REMAINING FOR 14.75%

AGE OF LOAN \ ORIGINAL TERM	10 YEARS	15 YEARS	20 YEARS	25 YEARS	30 YEARS	35 YEARS
1	.95261	.98030	.99111	.99585	.99803	.99906
2	.89774	.95750	.98082	.99105	.99576	.99797
3	.83421	.93109	.96891	.98548	.99312	.99672
4	.76064	.90051	.95511	.97904	.99007	.99526
5	.67546	.86511	.93913	.97159	.98653	.99357
6	.57683	.82411	.92064	.96295	.98244	.99162
7	.46263	.77664	.89922	.95295	.97770	.98935
8	.33040	.72168	.87442	.94138	.97221	.98674
9	.17729	.65804	.84570	.92797	.96586	.98370
10		.58435	.81245	.91245	.95850	.98019
11		.49902	.77395	.89448	.94998	.97612
12		.40023	.72937	.87367	.94012	.97141
13		.28583	.67775	.84957	.92870	.96596
14		.15337	.61799	.82167	.91547	.95965
15			.54878	.78937	.90016	.95234
16			.46865	.75196	.88243	.94388
17			.37587	.70865	.86190	.93407
18			.26843	.65850	.83813	.92273
19			.14404	.60043	.81061	.90959
20				.53319	.77873	.89437
21				.45533	.74183	.87676
22				.36519	.69910	.85636
23				.26081	.64963	.83274
24				.13994	.59234	.80539
25					.52601	.77373
26					.44920	.73706
27					.36027	.69461
28					.25729	.64545
29					.13806	.58853
30						.52263
31						.44631
32						.35795
33						.25564
34						.13717
35						

TABLE II-25. Mortgage Balance Remaining for 15.00%

PERCENTAGE OF
MORTGAGE BALANCE REMAINING FOR 15.00%

AGE OF LOAN / ORIGINAL TERM	10 YEARS	15 YEARS	20 YEARS	25 YEARS	30 YEARS	35 YEARS
1	.95327	.98076	.99141	.99604	.99814	.99912
2	.89903	.95843	.98144	.99143	.99599	.99811
3	.83607	.93251	.96987	.98609	.99348	.99693
4	.76299	.90243	.95643	.97989	.99058	.99556
5	.67816	.86750	.94084	.97269	.98721	.99397
6	.57970	.82697	.92274	.96434	.98329	.99212
7	.46541	.77991	.90173	.95464	.97875	.98998
8	.33274	.72530	.87735	.94338	.97347	.98749
9	.17875	.66190	.84904	.93032	.96735	.98460
10		.58831	.81618	.91515	.96025	.98125
11		.50289	.77804	.89754	.95200	.97736
12		.40374	.73378	.87711	.94243	.97284
13		.28865	.68239	.85339	.93131	.96760
14		.15506	.62274	.82585	.91841	.96152
15			.55351	.79390	.90344	.95445
16			.47314	.75680	.88606	.94625
17			.37986	.71374	.86589	.93674
18			.27158	.66375	.84247	.92569
19			.14589	.60574	.81529	.91287
20				.53839	.78374	.89799
21				.46022	.74712	.88071
22				.36948	.70461	.86066
23				.26416	.65526	.83739
24				.14191	.59799	.81037
25					.53150	.77901
26					.45433	.74261
27					.36476	.70035
28					.26078	.65131
29					.14009	.59438
30						.52830
31						.45159
32						.36256
33						.25921
34						.13925
35						

TABLE II-26. Mortgage Balance Remaining for 15.25%

PERCENTAGE OF
MORTGAGE BALANCE REMAINING FOR 15.25%

AGE OF LOAN \ ORIGINAL TERM	10 YEARS	15 YEARS	20 YEARS	25 YEARS	30 YEARS	35 YEARS
1	.95392	.98121	.99170	.99621	.99825	.99918
2	.90031	.95935	.98204	.99180	.99620	.99823
3	.83792	.93391	.97080	.98667	.99383	.99712
4	.76533	.90431	.95773	.98070	.99107	.99584
5	.68085	.86987	.94251	.97376	.98785	.99434
6	.58256	.82979	.92480	.96568	.98411	.99259
7	.46818	.78315	.90420	.95627	.97975	.99056
8	.33508	.72888	.88022	.94533	.97468	.98820
9	.18021	.66573	.85232	.93259	.96879	.98545
10		.59225	.81986	.91778	.96193	.98225
11		.50675	.78208	.90053	.95394	.97853
12		.40725	.73813	.88047	.94465	.97420
13		.29148	.68698	.85712	.93384	.96916
14		.15676	.62746	.82996	.92126	.96330
15			.55820	.79834	.90662	.95648
16			.47761	.76156	.88959	.94854
17			.38384	.71876	.86977	.93930
18			.27472	.66895	.84671	.92855
19			.14775	.61099	.81987	.91604
20				.54356	.78864	.90149
21				.46508	.75231	.88455
22				.37377	.71002	.86484
23				.26751	.66082	.84191
24				.14387	.60357	.81523
25					.53695	.78418
26					.45943	.74805
27					.36923	.70600
28					.26426	.65708
29					.14212	.60015
30						.53391
31						.45683
32						.36713
33						.26277
34						.14132
35						

TABLE II-27. Mortgage Balance Remaining for 15.50%

	PERCENTAGE OF MORTGAGE BALANCE REMAINING FOR 15.50%					
AGE OF LOAN / ORIGINAL TERM	10 YEARS	15 YEARS	20 YEARS	25 YEARS	30 YEARS	35 YEARS
1	.95457	.98165	.99198	.99638	.99834	.99924
2	.90158	.96025	.98263	.99216	.99641	.99835
3	.83976	.93529	.97171	.98723	.99416	.99731
4	.76765	.90617	.95898	.98149	.99153	.99610
5	.68353	.87220	.94414	.97479	.98846	.99469
6	.58541	.83258	.92681	.96697	.98488	.99304
7	.47095	.78635	.90661	.95785	.98071	.99112
8	.33743	.73244	.88304	.94721	.97584	.98887
9	.18168	.66954	.85555	.93480	.97016	.98626
10		.59617	.82348	.92033	.96354	.98321
11		.51059	.78606	.90345	.95581	.97965
12		.41076	.74243	.88375	.94680	.97550
13		.29431	.69152	.86078	.93628	.97066
14		.15846	.63214	.83398	.92402	.96501
15			.56287	.80271	.90971	.95842
16			.48207	.76625	.89302	.95073
17			.38781	.72371	.87355	.94177
18			.27786	.67408	.85084	.93131
19			.14961	.61620	.82435	.91911
20				.54868	.79345	.90488
21				.46991	.75740	.88828
22				.37803	.71536	.86891
23				.27086	.66631	.84632
24				.14584	.60909	.81997
25					.54235	.78923
26					.46449	.75338
27					.37367	.71155
28					.26773	.66277
29					.14415	.60585
30						.53946
31						.46202
32						.37169
33						.26631
34						.14339
35						

TABLE II-28. Mortgage Balance Remaining for 15.75%

PERCENTAGE OF
MORTGAGE BALANCE REMAINING FOR 15.75%

AGE OF LOAN / ORIGINAL TERM	10 YEARS	15 YEARS	20 YEARS	25 YEARS	30 YEARS	35 YEARS
1	.95521	.98209	.99225	.99654	.99844	.99929
2	.90283	.96114	.98319	.99250	.99661	.99846
3	.84158	.93664	.97260	.98777	.99447	.99748
4	.76995	.90800	.96021	.98224	.99197	.99635
5	.68619	.87450	.94572	.97578	.98904	.99501
6	.58825	.83533	.92878	.96822	.98563	.99346
7	.47371	.78952	.90897	.95938	.98163	.99164
8	.33977	.73596	.88580	.94904	.97695	.98951
9	.18315	.67332	.85871	.93695	.97148	.98702
10		.60008	.82703	.92282	.96509	.98411
11		.51442	.78999	.90628	.95761	.98071
12		.41426	.74667	.88695	.94887	.97673
13		.29713	.69601	.86435	.93864	.97208
14		.16017	.63678	.83791	.92669	.96664
15			.56750	.80700	.91271	.96028
16			.48650	.77086	.89636	.95284
17			.39177	.72859	.87724	.94414
18			.28101	.67915	.85488	.93396
19			.15147	.62135	.82873	.92207
20				.55376	.79816	.90816
21				.47472	.76241	.89189
22				.38229	.72060	.87286
23				.27420	.67171	.85062
24				.14780	.61455	.82460
25					.54769	.79418
26					.46952	.75861
27					.37810	.71701
28					.27119	.66837
29					.14618	.61148
30						.54496
31						.46718
32						.37621
33						.26984
34						.14546
35						

TABLE II-29. Mortgage Balance Remaining for 16.00%

AGE OF LOAN / ORIGINAL TERM	PERCENTAGE OF MORTGAGE BALANCE REMAINING FOR 16.00%					
	10 YEARS	15 YEARS	20 YEARS	25 YEARS	30 YEARS	35 YEARS
1	.95584	.98251	.99252	.99670	.99852	.99934
2	.90407	.96201	.98374	.99283	.99679	.99856
3	.84338	.93797	.97346	.98829	.99477	.99765
4	.77224	.90980	.96140	.98297	.99239	.99658
5	.68884	.87677	.94727	.97674	.98960	.99532
6	.59108	.83805	.93070	.96943	.98633	.99386
7	.47647	.79266	.91128	.96086	.98250	.99213
8	.34212	.73945	.88851	.95081	.97801	.99011
9	.18463	.67708	.86182	.93904	.97275	.98775
10		.60395	.83054	.92523	.96658	.98497
11		.51824	.79386	.90905	.95934	.98172
12		.41775	.75086	.89008	.95086	.97791
13		.29996	.70046	.86784	.94092	.97344
14		.16187	.64137	.84177	.92927	.96820
15			.57211	.81121	.91561	.96206
16			.49091	.77539	.89960	.95486
17			.39573	.73339	.88082	.94642
18			.28414	.68416	.85882	.93652
19			.15334	.62645	.83302	.92493
20				.55880	.80278	.91133
21				.47949	.76733	.89539
22				.38652	.72577	.87670
23				.27753	.67705	.85480
24				.14977	.61994	.82912
25					.55299	.79902
26					.47450	.76374
27					.38250	.72237
28					.27465	.67388
29					.14821	.61704
30						.55040
31						.47229
32						.38071
33						.27336
34						.14752
35						

TABLE II-30. Mortgage Balance Remaining for 16.25%

PERCENTAGE OF
MORTGAGE BALANCE REMAINING FOR 16.25%

AGE OF LOAN \ ORIGINAL TERM	10 YEARS	15 YEARS	20 YEARS	25 YEARS	30 YEARS	35 YEARS
1	.95646	.98293	.99277	.99685	.99861	.99938
2	.90530	.96286	.98428	.99314	.99697	.99865
3	.84517	.93928	.97430	.98879	.99505	.99780
4	.77451	.91157	.96256	.98367	.99279	.99680
5	.69148	.87900	.94878	.97766	.99013	.99562
6	.59390	.84073	.93258	.97059	.98701	.99423
7	.47923	.79576	.91354	.96229	.98334	.99260
8	.34447	.74291	.89117	.95253	.97903	.99068
9	.18610	.68080	.86488	.94106	.97396	.98843
10		.60781	.83398	.92758	.96801	.98579
11		.52204	.79767	.91174	.96101	.98268
12		.42124	.75500	.89313	.95279	.97903
13		.30279	.70486	.87126	.94313	.97474
14		.16359	.64593	.84555	.93177	.96969
15			.57668	.81535	.91843	.96376
16			.49530	.77985	.90274	.95680
17			.39967	.73813	.88431	.94861
18			.28728	.68911	.86266	.93899
19			.15521	.63150	.83721	.92768
20				.56380	.80730	.91440
21				.48423	.77215	.89879
22				.39074	.73085	.88044
23				.28086	.68231	.85888
24				.15174	.62526	.83354
25					.55823	.80376
26					.47945	.76876
27					.38688	.72764
28					.27809	.67931
29					.15024	.62252
30						.55578
31						.47735
32						.38518
33						.27687
34						.14958
35						

TABLE II-31. Mortgage Balance Remaining for 16.50%

PERCENTAGE OF
MORTGAGE BALANCE REMAINING FOR 16.50%

ORIGINAL TERM / AGE OF LOAN	10 YEARS	15 YEARS	20 YEARS	25 YEARS	30 YEARS	35 YEARS
1	.95708	.98333	.99302	.99699	.99869	.99942
2	.90652	.96370	.98480	.99344	.99714	.99874
3	.84695	.94056	.97511	.98927	.99531	.99794
4	.77677	.91331	.96370	.98434	.99316	.99700
5	.69410	.88121	.95025	.97855	.99063	.99589
6	.59671	.84338	.93441	.97172	.98765	.99458
7	.48198	.79883	.91575	.96367	.98414	.99304
8	.34682	.74634	.89377	.95419	.98000	.99122
9	.18759	.68450	.86787	.94302	.97512	.98908
10		.61165	.83737	.92986	.96938	.98656
11		.52583	.80143	.91436	.96261	.98359
12		.42472	.75909	.89611	.95464	.98009
13		.30562	.70921	.87460	.94525	.97597
14		.16530	.65044	.84925	.93419	.97112
15			.58122	.81940	.92115	.96540
16			.49967	.78423	.90580	.95866
17			.40359	.74280	.88771	.95072
18			.29041	.69399	.86640	.94137
19			.15708	.63649	.84130	.93035
20				.56875	.81173	.91737
21				.48895	.77689	.90208
22				.39494	.73584	.88406
23				.28418	.68749	.86284
24				.15371	.63053	.83784
25					.56342	.80839
26					.48437	.77369
27					.39124	.73282
28					.28152	.68466
29					.15227	.62794
30						.56111
31						.48238
32						.38963
33						.28036
34						.15164
35						

TABLE II-32. Mortgage Balance Remaining for 16.75%

PERCENTAGE OF
MORTGAGE BALANCE REMAINING FOR 16.75%

AGE OF LOAN \ ORIGINAL TERM	10 YEARS	15 YEARS	20 YEARS	25 YEARS	30 YEARS	35 YEARS
1	.95769	.98373	.99326	.99713	.99876	.99946
2	.90772	.96452	.98530	.99373	.99730	.99883
3	.84871	.94182	.97590	.98972	.99557	.99808
4	.77902	.91502	.96480	.98499	.99352	.99719
5	.69672	.88338	.95169	.97940	.99111	.99615
6	.59952	.84600	.93620	.97280	.98827	.99491
7	.48473	.80186	.91792	.96500	.98490	.99345
8	.34917	.74973	.89632	.95580	.98093	.99173
9	.18907	.68817	.87082	.94492	.97624	.98970
10		.61546	.84070	.93208	.97070	.98729
11		.52960	.80513	.91692	.96416	.98446
12		.42820	.76312	.89901	.95643	.98111
13		.30845	.71351	.87786	.94730	.97715
14		.16702	.65492	.85288	.93653	.97248
15			.58573	.82338	.92380	.96696
16			.50401	.78854	.90877	.96044
17			.40751	.74740	.89102	.95274
18			.29354	.69881	.87006	.94365
19			.15895	.64143	.84530	.93292
20				.57366	.81606	.92024
21				.49363	.78153	.90527
22				.39912	.74076	.88759
23				.28750	.69260	.86670
24				.15568	.63573	.84204
25					.56856	.81292
26					.48924	.77852
27					.39557	.73790
28					.28494	.68993
29					.15429	.63328
30						.56637
31						.48736
32						.39404
33						.28384
34						.15370
35						

TABLE II-33. Mortgage Balance Remaining for 17.00%

PERCENTAGE OF MORTGAGE BALANCE REMAINING FOR 17.00%

AGE OF LOAN \ ORIGINAL TERM	10 YEARS	15 YEARS	20 YEARS	25 YEARS	30 YEARS	35 YEARS
1	.95829	.98412	.99349	.99726	.99883	.99950
2	.90891	.96532	.98579	.99401	.99745	.99891
3	.85046	.94306	.97667	.99017	.99581	.99820
4	.78125	.91671	.96587	.98561	.99387	.99737
5	.69931	.88552	.95308	.98023	.99157	.99639
6	.60231	.84858	.93795	.97385	.98885	.99522
7	.48747	.80486	.92003	.96630	.98563	.99384
8	.35152	.75309	.89882	.95735	.98182	.99221
9	.19056	.69181	.87370	.94677	.97731	.99028
10		.61925	.84397	.93424	.97196	.98799
11		.53336	.80877	.91940	.96564	.98528
12		.43167	.76710	.90184	.95815	.98207
13		.31127	.71776	.88104	.94928	.97827
14		.16874	.65935	.85643	.93879	.97378
15			.59020	.82728	.92636	.96845
16			.50833	.79278	.91165	.96215
17			.41141	.75193	.89424	.95469
18			.29667	.70357	.87362	.94586
19			.16083	.64631	.84921	.93540
20				.57853	.82031	.92302
21				.49828	.78609	.90836
22				.40328	.74559	.89101
23				.29080	.69764	.87046
24				.15764	.64086	.84614
25					.57365	.81734
26					.49408	.78326
27					.39988	.74290
28					.28835	.69512
29					.15632	.63855
30						.57158
31						.49230
32						.39843
33						.28731
34						.15575
35						

TABLE II-34. Mortgage Balance Remaining for 17.25%

PERCENTAGE OF
MORTGAGE BALANCE REMAINING FOR 17.25%

AGE OF LOAN \ ORIGINAL TERM	10 YEARS	15 YEARS	20 YEARS	25 YEARS	30 YEARS	35 YEARS
1	.95889	.98450	.99372	.99738	.99890	.99953
2	.91010	.96611	.98626	.99428	.99759	.99898
3	.85219	.94428	.97741	.99059	.99604	.99832
4	.78346	.91837	.96691	.98621	.99419	.99754
5	.70190	.88762	.95445	.98102	.99200	.99662
6	.60510	.85113	.93965	.97486	.98941	.99552
7	.49021	.80782	.92210	.96754	.98633	.99421
8	.35387	.75642	.90126	.95886	.98267	.99266
9	.19205	.69542	.87654	.94856	.97833	.99083
10		.62302	.84719	.93633	.97318	.98865
11		.53710	.81236	.92182	.96706	.98606
12		.43512	.77102	.90460	.95981	.98299
13		.31410	.72196	.88416	.95119	.97934
14		.17047	.66374	.85990	.94097	.97502
15			.59464	.83111	.92884	.96988
16			.51263	.79694	.91445	.96379
17			.41530	.75639	.89736	.95656
18			.29979	.70826	.87709	.94798
19			.16270	.65114	.85302	.93779
20				.58336	.82446	.92570
21				.50290	.79057	.91135
22				.40742	.75034	.89433
23				.29410	.70260	.87412
24				.15961	.64594	.85014
25					.57869	.82167
26					.49888	.78789
27					.40416	.74780
28					.29175	.70022
29					.15834	.64375
30						.57673
31						.49719
32						.40280
33						.29076
34						.15780
35						

TABLE II-35. Mortgage Balance Remaining for 17.50%

PERCENTAGE OF MORTGAGE BALANCE REMAINING FOR 17.50%

AGE OF LOAN \ ORIGINAL TERM	10 YEARS	15 YEARS	20 YEARS	25 YEARS	30 YEARS	35 YEARS
1	.95948	.98488	.99394	.99750	.99896	.99957
2	.91127	.96688	.98672	.99453	.99772	.99905
3	.85391	.94547	.97814	.99100	.99625	.99843
4	.78566	.92000	.96792	.98679	.99450	.99770
5	.70447	.88970	.95577	.98179	.99242	.99683
6	.60787	.85365	.94132	.97583	.98994	.99579
7	.49295	.81075	.92412	.96875	.98699	.99456
8	.35622	.75972	.90366	.96032	.98348	.99309
9	.19354	.69900	.87931	.95029	.97931	.99135
10		.62677	.85035	.93837	.97434	.98927
11		.54083	.81589	.92417	.96843	.98680
12		.43858	.77490	.90729	.96140	.98386
13		.31693	.72612	.88720	.95304	.98036
14		.17219	.66809	.86330	.94309	.97620
15			.59905	.83486	.93125	.97125
16			.51691	.80103	.91716	.96536
17			.41918	.76078	.90041	.95835
18			.30291	.71289	.88047	.95002
19			.16458	.65592	.85675	.94010
20				.58814	.82853	.92830
21				.50749	.79496	.91426
22				.41154	.75501	.89755
23				.29739	.70749	.87768
24				.16158	.65095	.85403
25					.58368	.82590
26					.50364	.79244
27					.40842	.75262
28					.29514	.70524
29					.16036	.64888
30						.58183
31						.50205
32						.40713
33						.29420
34						.15985
35						

TABLE II-36. Mortgage Balance Remaining for 17.75%

PERCENTAGE OF MORTGAGE BALANCE REMAINING FOR 17.75%

AGE OF LOAN \ ORIGINAL TERM	10 YEARS	15 YEARS	20 YEARS	25 YEARS	30 YEARS	35 YEARS
1	.96006	.98524	.99415	.99762	.99902	.99960
2	.91242	.96764	.98717	.99478	.99785	.99911
3	.85561	.94665	.97884	.99139	.99646	.99854
4	.78785	.92161	.96891	.98734	.99479	.99785
5	.70703	.89174	.95707	.98252	.99281	.99703
6	.61064	.85613	.94294	.97677	.99044	.99605
7	.49568	.81365	.92610	.96991	.98762	.99489
8	.35857	.76298	.90600	.96173	.98426	.99350
9	.19504	.70256	.88204	.95198	.98024	.99184
10		.63049	.85346	.94034	.97546	.98986
11		.54453	.81937	.92646	.96975	.98750
12		.44202	.77872	.90991	.96294	.98469
13		.31975	.73023	.89017	.95482	.98133
14		.17392	.67240	.86662	.94513	.97733
15			.60342	.83854	.93358	.97256
16			.52116	.80505	.91980	.96687
17			.42304	.76511	.90337	.96008
18			.30602	.71746	.88377	.95198
19			.16646	.66064	.86039	.94232
20				.59287	.83251	.93080
21				.51205	.79926	.91707
22				.41565	.75960	.90068
23				.30067	.71231	.88114
24				.16355	.65589	.85784
25					.58861	.83004
26					.50837	.79689
27					.41266	.75735
28					.29851	.71019
29					.16237	.65394
30						.58686
31						.50686
32						.41143
33						.29763
34						.16189
35						

TABLE II-37. Mortgage Balance Remaining for 18.00%

PERCENTAGE OF
MORTGAGE BALANCE REMAINING FOR 18.00%

ORIGINAL TERM / AGE OF LOAN	10 YEARS	15 YEARS	20 YEARS	25 YEARS	30 YEARS	35 YEARS
1	.96063	.98560	.99435	.99773	.99908	.99962
2	.91357	.96838	.98760	.99501	.99797	.99917
3	.85730	.94780	.97952	.99176	.99665	.99863
4	.79002	.92319	.96987	.98787	.99507	.99799
5	.70957	.89376	.95833	.98323	.99318	.99722
6	.61340	.85858	.94453	.97768	.99093	.99630
7	.49840	.81651	.92803	.97104	.98823	.99519
8	.36092	.76622	.90830	.96310	.98500	.99388
9	.19654	.70608	.88471	.95361	.98114	.99230
10		.63419	.85651	.94226	.97653	.99042
11		.54823	.82280	.92869	.97101	.98817
12		.44545	.78248	.91246	.96442	.98548
13		.32257	.73429	.89307	.95653	.98226
14		.17566	.67666	.86988	.94710	.97841
15			.60776	.84215	.93583	.97381
16			.52538	.80900	.92236	.96831
17			.42689	.76936	.90624	.96173
18			.30913	.72197	.88698	.95387
19			.16834	.66531	.86395	.94447
20				.59757	.83641	.93323
21				.51657	.80348	.91979
22				.41973	.76412	.90372
23				.30395	.71705	.88451
24				.16551	.66078	.86154
25					.59349	.83408
26					.51305	.80125
27					.41687	.76199
28					.30188	.71506
29					.16439	.65894
30						.59184
31						.51162
32						.41571
33						.30104
34						.16393
35						

TABLE II-38. Mortgage Balance Remaining for 18.25%

PERCENTAGE OF MORTGAGE BALANCE REMAINING FOR 18.25%

AGE OF LOAN \ ORIGINAL TERM	10 YEARS	15 YEARS	20 YEARS	25 YEARS	30 YEARS	35 YEARS
1	.96120	.98595	.99455	.99783	.99913	.99965
2	.91470	.96911	.98802	.99523	.99809	.99923
3	.85897	.94893	.98019	.99212	.99683	.99872
4	.79217	.92474	.97080	.98839	.99533	.99812
5	.71211	.89574	.95955	.98391	.99354	.99739
6	.61614	.86099	.94607	.97855	.99138	.99653
7	.50113	.81934	.92992	.97212	.98880	.99548
8	.36327	.76942	.91055	.96442	.98571	.99424
9	.19804	.70958	.88734	.95518	.98200	.99274
10		.63786	.85951	.94412	.97755	.99095
11		.55191	.82617	.93085	.97223	.98880
12		.44888	.78620	.91495	.96584	.98623
13		.32540	.73830	.89590	.95819	.98314
14		.17739	.68088	.87306	.94901	.97944
15			.61206	.84569	.93802	.97501
16			.52958	.81288	.92484	.96969
17			.43072	.77355	.90904	.96332
18			.31223	.72642	.89011	.95569
19			.17022	.66993	.86742	.94654
20				.60222	.84022	.93557
21				.52106	.80762	.92243
22				.42379	.76855	.90667
23				.30721	.72172	.88779
24				.16748	.66560	.86516
25					.59833	.83803
26					.51770	.80552
27					.42106	.76655
28					.30523	.71984
29					.16640	.66386
30						.59677
31						.51635
32						.41996
33						.30443
34						.16596
35						

TABLE II-39. Mortgage Balance Remaining for 18.50%

PERCENTAGE OF
MORTGAGE BALANCE REMAINING FOR 18.50%

AGE OF LOAN / ORIGINAL TERM	10 YEARS	15 YEARS	20 YEARS	25 YEARS	30 YEARS	35 YEARS
1	.96177	.98629	.99474	.99793	.99918	.99967
2	.91583	.96982	.98842	.99545	.99819	.99928
3	.86063	.95004	.98083	.99246	.99701	.99881
4	.79431	.92626	.97171	.98888	.99559	.99824
5	.71462	.89770	.96075	.98457	.99387	.99756
6	.61888	.86337	.94758	.97939	.99182	.99674
7	.50384	.82213	.93176	.97317	.98935	.99576
8	.36562	.77258	.91275	.96569	.98638	.99458
9	.19954	.71305	.88991	.95671	.98282	.99316
10		.64151	.86246	.94592	.97854	.99145
11		.55557	.82949	.93296	.97339	.98940
12		.45230	.78986	.91738	.96721	.98694
13		.32821	.74226	.89866	.95978	.98398
14		.17913	.68506	.87617	.95085	.98042
15			.61633	.84915	.94013	.97615
16			.53376	.81668	.92724	.97102
17			.43454	.77768	.91176	.96485
18			.31533	.73080	.89316	.95744
19			.17210	.67449	.87081	.94853
20				.60682	.84395	.93784
21				.52552	.81168	.92498
22				.42784	.77291	.90954
23				.31047	.72633	.89098
24				.16944	.67036	.86868
25					.60311	.84189
26					.52230	.80970
27					.42522	.77103
28					.30856	.72456
29					.16840	.66872
30						.60163
31						.52103
32						.42418
33						.30781
34						.16799
35						

TABLE II-40. Mortgage Balance Remaining for 18.75%

PERCENTAGE OF
MORTGAGE BALANCE REMAINING FOR 18.75%

AGE OF LOAN / ORIGINAL TERM	10 YEARS	15 YEARS	20 YEARS	25 YEARS	30 YEARS	35 YEARS
1	.96232	.98663	.99493	.99803	.99923	.99970
2	.91694	.97052	.98882	.99565	.99830	.99933
3	.86227	.95113	.98146	.99279	.99717	.99889
4	.79643	.92776	.97259	.98935	.99582	.99836
5	.71713	.89962	.96191	.98520	.99420	.99772
6	.62160	.86572	.94905	.98020	.99224	.99694
7	.50655	.82489	.93356	.97418	.98987	.99602
8	.36797	.77572	.91490	.96693	.98703	.99490
9	.20105	.71649	.89243	.95819	.98361	.99355
10		.64514	.86536	.94767	.97948	.99192
11		.55921	.83275	.93500	.97451	.98997
12		.45570	.79348	.91974	.96853	.98761
13		.33103	.74617	.90136	.96132	.98478
14		.18087	.68920	.87922	.95263	.98136
15			.62057	.85255	.94217	.97724
16			.53791	.82042	.92958	.97228
17			.43835	.78173	.91440	.96631
18			.31842	.73513	.89613	.95912
19			.17398	.67900	.87411	.95046
20				.61138	.84760	.94002
21				.52995	.81566	.92745
22				.43186	.77719	.91231
23				.31371	.73086	.89408
24				.17140	.67505	.87212
25					.60784	.84566
26					.52687	.81380
27					.42935	.77542
28					.31189	.72919
29					.17041	.67351
30						.60645
31						.52567
32						.42837
33						.31118
34						.17002
35						

TABLE II-41. Mortgage Balance Remaining for 19.00%

PERCENTAGE OF
MORTGAGE BALANCE REMAINING FOR 19.00%

AGE OF LOAN \ ORIGINAL TERM	10 YEARS	15 YEARS	20 YEARS	25 YEARS	30 YEARS	35 YEARS
1	.96287	.98696	.99511	.99812	.99927	.99972
2	.91804	.97121	.98920	.99585	.99839	.99937
3	.86390	.95220	.98206	.99311	.99733	.99896
4	.79854	.92924	.97345	.98980	.99605	.99846
5	.71962	.90151	.96304	.98581	.99450	.99786
6	.62432	.86804	.95048	.98098	.99263	.99713
7	.50925	.82762	.93532	.97516	.99037	.99626
8	.37032	.77882	.91701	.96812	.98765	.99520
9	.20256	.71989	.89490	.95963	.98436	.99392
10		.64874	.86820	.94937	.98038	.99237
11		.56283	.83596	.93699	.97559	.99051
12		.45910	.79704	.92204	.96979	.98826
13		.33385	.75004	.90399	.96280	.98554
14		.18261	.69329	.88219	.95435	.98225
15			.62477	.85587	.94415	.97829
16			.54203	.82410	.93184	.97350
17			.44213	.78572	.91697	.96772
18			.32151	.73939	.89902	.96074
19			.17586	.68345	.87734	.95231
20				.61590	.85117	.94213
21				.53434	.81956	.92985
22				.43586	.78140	.91501
23				.31695	.73533	.89710
24				.17337	.67969	.87546
25					.61251	.84935
26					.53140	.81781
27					.43346	.77973
28					.31520	.73375
29					.17241	.67824
30						.61120
31						.53026
32						.43253
33						.31453
34						.17204
35						

TABLE II-42. Mortgage Balance Remaining for 19.25%

PERCENTAGE OF MORTGAGE BALANCE REMAINING FOR 19.25%

AGE OF LOAN / ORIGINAL TERM	10 YEARS	15 YEARS	20 YEARS	25 YEARS	30 YEARS	35 YEARS
1	.96341	.98728	.99528	.99821	.99931	.99974
2	.91912	.97188	.98957	.99604	.99848	.99942
3	.86552	.95324	.98265	.99341	.99748	.99903
4	.80063	.93068	.97428	.99024	.99626	.99856
5	.72209	.90338	.96415	.98639	.99479	.99800
6	.62702	.87032	.95188	.98173	.99301	.99731
7	.51195	.83032	.93704	.97610	.99085	.99648
8	.37267	.78189	.91907	.96928	.98824	.99548
9	.20407	.72327	.89732	.96102	.98508	.99427
10		.65232	.87099	.95102	.98125	.99280
11		.56644	.83912	.93893	.97662	.99102
12		.46249	.80055	.92428	.97101	.98887
13		.33666	.75386	.90656	.96422	.98626
14		.18435	.69734	.88510	.95601	.98310
15			.62893	.85913	.94607	.97928
16			.54613	.82770	.93403	.97466
17			.44590	.78965	.91947	.96907
18			.32459	.74360	.90183	.96229
19			.17774	.68785	.88049	.95410
20				.62037	.85466	.94417
21				.53870	.82339	.93216
22				.43984	.78554	.91763
23				.32017	.73972	.90003
24				.17532	.68427	.87873
25					.61714	.85295
26					.53589	.82174
27					.43754	.78396
28					.31850	.73824
29					.17441	.68290
30						.61590
31						.53482
32						.43667
33						.31786
34						.17406
35						

TABLE II-43. Mortgage Balance Remaining for 19.50%

PERCENTAGE OF
MORTGAGE BALANCE REMAINING FOR 19.50%

ORIGINAL TERM / AGE OF LOAN	10 YEARS	15 YEARS	20 YEARS	25 YEARS	30 YEARS	35 YEARS
1	.96395	.98759	.99545	.99829	.99935	.99975
2	.92020	.97254	.98992	.99622	.99857	.99946
3	.86712	.95427	.98322	.99370	.99762	.99910
4	.80271	.93211	.97509	.99065	.99646	.99866
5	.72455	.90521	.96522	.98695	.99506	.99813
6	.62972	.87258	.95324	.98246	.99336	.99748
7	.51465	.83298	.93871	.97701	.99130	.99670
8	.37502	.78493	.92108	.97039	.98880	.99575
9	.20559	.72662	.89969	.96236	.98576	.99460
10		.65587	.87373	.95262	.98208	.99320
11		.57003	.84223	.94080	.97761	.99150
12		.46586	.80401	.92646	.97218	.98944
13		.33947	.75763	.90906	.96560	.98695
14		.18610	.70135	.88795	.95761	.98392
15			.63306	.86233	.94792	.98024
16			.55020	.83124	.93616	.97578
17			.44966	.79351	.92189	.97036
18			.32766	.74774	.90457	.96379
19			.17963	.69220	.88356	.95582
20				.62480	.85807	.94614
21				.54302	.82713	.93441
22				.44379	.78960	.92016
23				.32339	.74405	.90288
24				.17728	.68878	.88191
25					.62172	.85646
26					.54034	.82558
27					.44160	.78812
28					.32179	.74265
29					.17641	.68749
30						.62055
31						.53933
32						.44077
33						.32119
34						.17608
35						

TABLE II-44. Mortgage Balance Remaining for 19.75%

PERCENTAGE OF
MORTGAGE BALANCE REMAINING FOR 19.75%

AGE OF LOAN / ORIGINAL TERM	10 YEARS	15 YEARS	20 YEARS	25 YEARS	30 YEARS	35 YEARS
1	.96448	.98790	.99561	.99837	.99939	.99977
2	.92127	.97318	.99027	.99639	.99865	.99949
3	.86871	.95528	.98377	.99398	.99775	.99916
4	.80477	.93351	.97587	.99105	.99666	.99875
5	.72700	.90702	.96626	.98749	.99532	.99825
6	.63240	.87480	.95457	.98315	.99370	.99764
7	.51733	.83560	.94035	.97788	.99173	.99690
8	.37736	.78793	.92305	.97147	.98934	.99600
9	.20710	.72994	.90201	.96366	.98642	.99491
10		.65940	.87642	.95417	.98287	.99358
11		.57360	.84528	.94263	.97856	.99196
12		.46923	.80741	.92859	.97331	.98999
13		.34227	.76135	.91150	.96692	.98760
14		.18785	.70531	.89073	.95916	.98469
15			.63716	.86545	.94971	.98115
16			.55425	.83471	.93822	.97684
17			.45340	.79731	.92424	.97160
18			.33073	.75182	.90724	.96523
19			.18151	.69649	.88656	.95748
20				.62918	.86141	.94805
21				.54731	.83081	.93658
22				.44773	.79358	.92262
23				.32659	.74831	.90565
24				.17924	.69323	.88501
25					.62624	.85990
26					.54475	.82935
27					.44563	.79219
28					.32506	.74700
29					.17840	.69202
30						.62515
31						.54380
32						.44485
33						.32449
34						.17809
35						

TABLE II-45. Mortgage Balance Remaining for 20.00%

PERCENTAGE OF
MORTGAGE BALANCE REMAINING FOR 20.00%

AGE OF LOAN \ ORIGINAL TERM	10 YEARS	15 YEARS	20 YEARS	25 YEARS	30 YEARS	35 YEARS
1	.96500	.98820	.99577	.99845	.99943	.99979
2	.92232	.97381	.99061	.99656	.99873	.99953
3	.87028	.95627	.98431	.99425	.99788	.99921
4	.80682	.93488	.97664	.99144	.99684	.99883
5	.72944	.90879	.96728	.98801	.99557	.99836
6	.63508	.87699	.95586	.98383	.99403	.99779
7	.52001	.83820	.94195	.97873	.99214	.99709
8	.37971	.79090	.92498	.97251	.98985	.99624
9	.20862	.73323	.90429	.96492	.98705	.99520
10		.66291	.87906	.95568	.98363	.99394
11		.57715	.84829	.94440	.97947	.99240
12		.47259	.81077	.93065	.97439	.99052
13		.34508	.76502	.91389	.96820	.98822
14		.18959	.70924	.89344	.96065	.98543
15			.64121	.86851	.95144	.98202
16			.55827	.83812	.94022	.97786
17			.45712	.80105	.92653	.97279
18			.33378	.75585	.90984	.96661
19			.18339	.70073	.88949	.95907
20				.63352	.86467	.94988
21				.55157	.83440	.93868
22				.45164	.79750	.92501
23				.32978	.75250	.90835
24				.18119	.69763	.88803
25					.63072	.86325
26					.54913	.83304
27					.44964	.79619
28					.32832	.75127
29					.18039	.69648
30						.62968
31						.54823
32						.44890
33						.32778
34						.18009
35						

TABLE II-46. Mortgage Balance Remaining for 20.25%

PERCENTAGE OF
MORTGAGE BALANCE REMAINING FOR 20.25%

AGE OF LOAN \ ORIGINAL TERM	10 YEARS	15 YEARS	20 YEARS	25 YEARS	30 YEARS	35 YEARS
1	.96552	.98850	.99592	.99852	.99946	.99980
2	.92336	.97443	.99093	.99671	.99880	.99956
3	.87184	.95724	.98483	.99451	.99800	.99927
4	.80885	.93623	.97738	.99181	.99701	.99891
5	.73185	.91054	.96826	.98851	.99581	.99847
6	.63774	.87914	.95712	.98447	.99433	.99793
7	.52269	.84076	.94351	.97954	.99253	.99727
8	.38205	.79384	.92686	.97351	.99034	.99646
9	.21014	.73649	.90652	.96614	.98765	.99548
10		.66638	.88165	.95713	.98436	.99428
11		.58069	.85124	.94612	.98034	.99281
12		.47593	.81408	.93266	.97543	.99101
13		.34788	.76865	.91621	.96943	.98882
14		.19134	.71312	.89610	.96209	.98613
15			.64524	.87151	.95312	.98285
16			.56226	.84146	.94216	.97884
17			.46083	.80472	.92875	.97394
18			.33684	.75981	.91237	.96794
19			.18527	.70492	.89234	.96061
20				.63782	.86786	.95166
21				.55580	.83793	.94071
22				.45553	.80135	.92733
23				.33296	.75663	.91097
24				.18314	.70196	.89097
25					.63514	.86653
26					.55346	.83664
27					.45362	.80012
28					.33157	.75547
29					.18237	.70089
30						.63417
31						.55262
32						.45292
33						.33106
34						.18209
35						

TABLE II-47. Mortgage Balance Remaining for 20.50%

PERCENTAGE OF
MORTGAGE BALANCE REMAINING FOR 20.50%

AGE OF LOAN \ ORIGINAL TERM	10 YEARS	15 YEARS	20 YEARS	25 YEARS	30 YEARS	35 YEARS
1	.96603	.98878	.99607	.99859	.99949	.99982
2	.92439	.97504	.99124	.99687	.99887	.99959
3	.87338	.95819	.98534	.99475	.99811	.99932
4	.81086	.93755	.97810	.99216	.99717	.99898
5	.73426	.91226	.96922	.98898	.99603	.99856
6	.64039	.88127	.95835	.98509	.99463	.99806
7	.52536	.84329	.94503	.98032	.99291	.99744
8	.38440	.79675	.92870	.97448	.99080	.99668
9	.21167	.73972	.90870	.96732	.98822	.99574
10		.66984	.88419	.95855	.98506	.99460
11		.58420	.85415	.94780	.98118	.99320
12		.47926	.81734	.93462	.97643	.99148
13		.35067	.77223	.91847	.97061	.98938
14		.19309	.71696	.89869	.96348	.98680
15			.64922	.87445	.95474	.98364
16			.56622	.84474	.94403	.97977
17			.46451	.80833	.93091	.97503
18			.33988	.76372	.91483	.96922
19			.18715	.70906	.89512	.96210
20				.64207	.87097	.95337
21				.55998	.84138	.94268
22				.45940	.80512	.92957
23				.33613	.76069	.91351
24				.18509	.70624	.89384
25					.63952	.86972
26					.55776	.84018
27					.45757	.80397
28					.33480	.75960
29					.18436	.70523
30						.63860
31						.55696
32						.45692
33						.33432
34						.18409
35						

TABLE II-48. Mortgage Balance Remaining for 20.75%

PERCENTAGE OF MORTGAGE BALANCE REMAINING FOR 20.75%

AGE OF LOAN \ ORIGINAL TERM	10 YEARS	15 YEARS	20 YEARS	25 YEARS	30 YEARS	35 YEARS
1	.96653	.98906	.99621	.99866	.99952	.99983
2	.92541	.97563	.99155	.99701	.99894	.99962
3	.87491	.95913	.98582	.99499	.99821	.99936
4	.81287	.93886	.97879	.99250	.99733	.99905
5	.73665	.91395	.97016	.98944	.99624	.99866
6	.64303	.88336	.95955	.98569	.99490	.99818
7	.52802	.84579	.94651	.98108	.99326	.99759
8	.38674	.79963	.93051	.97542	.99125	.99687
9	.21319	.74292	.91084	.96846	.98877	.99599
10		.67327	.88668	.95992	.98572	.99490
11		.58770	.85700	.94942	.98199	.99357
12		.48258	.82055	.93652	.97739	.99193
13		.35346	.77576	.92068	.97175	.98991
14		.19485	.72075	.90122	.96482	.98744
15			.65317	.87732	.95631	.98440
16			.57016	.84796	.94585	.98067
17			.46818	.81188	.93300	.97608
18			.34291	.76757	.91722	.97045
19			.18903	.71314	.89784	.96353
20				.64628	.87402	.95502
21				.56414	.84477	.94458
22				.46324	.80883	.93175
23				.33929	.76469	.91599
24				.18704	.71046	.89663
25					.64385	.87285
26					.56202	.84363
27					.46150	.80775
28					.33802	.76366
29					.18633	.70951
30						.64298
31						.56127
32						.46088
33						.33757
34						.18608
35						

TABLE III-1. Annual Percentage Rate with a 10-Year Mortgage

ANNUAL PERCENTAGE RATE TABLE
TERM OF MORTGAGE 10 YEARS

CONTRACT INTEREST RATE \ POINTS CHARGED	0.50	1.00	1.50	2.00	2.50	3.00
8.000	0.081152	0.082313	0.083482	0.084660	0.085846	0.087041
8.125	0.082405	0.083568	0.084740	0.085921	0.087110	0.088308
8.250	0.083658	0.084824	0.085999	0.087182	0.088374	0.089575
8.375	0.084911	0.086080	0.087257	0.088443	0.089638	0.090842
8.500	0.086163	0.087335	0.088516	0.089705	0.090903	0.092110
8.625	0.087416	0.088591	0.089774	0.090966	0.092167	0.093377
8.750	0.088669	0.089846	0.091033	0.092228	0.093431	0.094644
8.875	0.089922	0.091102	0.092291	0.093489	0.094696	0.095912
9.000	0.091175	0.092358	0.093550	0.094750	0.095960	0.097179
9.125	0.092427	0.093614	0.094808	0.096012	0.097225	0.098447
9.250	0.093680	0.094869	0.096067	0.097274	0.098489	0.099714
9.375	0.094933	0.096125	0.097326	0.098535	0.099754	0.100982
9.500	0.096186	0.097381	0.098584	0.099797	0.101019	0.102249
9.625	0.097439	0.098637	0.099843	0.101059	0.102283	0.103517
9.750	0.098692	0.099892	0.101102	0.102320	0.103548	0.104785
9.875	0.099945	0.101148	0.102361	0.103582	0.104813	0.106053
10.000	0.101198	0.102404	0.103620	0.104844	0.106078	0.107321
10.125	0.102451	0.103660	0.104878	0.106106	0.107343	0.108589
10.250	0.103703	0.104916	0.106137	0.107368	0.108608	0.109857
10.375	0.104956	0.106172	0.107396	0.108630	0.109873	0.111125
10.500	0.106209	0.107428	0.108655	0.109892	0.111138	0.112393
10.625	0.107462	0.108684	0.109914	0.111154	0.112403	0.113662
10.750	0.108715	0.109940	0.111173	0.112416	0.113668	0.114930
10.875	0.109968	0.111196	0.112432	0.113678	0.114933	0.116198
11.000	0.111221	0.112452	0.113691	0.114940	0.116199	0.117467
11.125	0.112474	0.113708	0.114950	0.116202	0.117464	0.118735
11.250	0.113727	0.114964	0.116209	0.117465	0.118729	0.120004
11.375	0.114980	0.116220	0.117469	0.118727	0.119995	0.121272
11.500	0.116233	0.117476	0.118728	0.119989	0.121260	0.122541
11.625	0.117486	0.118732	0.119987	0.121252	0.122526	0.123810
11.750	0.118739	0.119988	0.121246	0.122514	0.123791	0.125079
11.875	0.119992	0.121244	0.122506	0.123776	0.125057	0.126348
12.000	0.121246	0.122501	0.123765	0.125039	0.126323	0.127617
12.125	0.122499	0.123757	0.125024	0.126301	0.127589	0.128886
12.250	0.123752	0.125013	0.126284	0.127564	0.128854	0.130155
12.375	0.125005	0.126269	0.127543	0.128827	0.130120	0.131424
12.500	0.126258	0.127525	0.128802	0.130089	0.131386	0.132693
12.625	0.127511	0.128782	0.130062	0.131352	0.132652	0.133962
12.750	0.128764	0.130038	0.131321	0.132615	0.133918	0.135231
12.875	0.130017	0.131294	0.132581	0.133878	0.135184	0.136501

TABLE III-2. Annual Percentage Rate with a 10-Year Mortgage

ANNUAL PERCENTAGE RATE TABLE
TERM OF MORTGAGE 10 YEARS

CONTRACT INTEREST RATE \ POINTS CHARGED	0.50	1.00	1.50	2.00	2.50	3.00
13.000	0.131270	0.132551	0.133841	0.135140	0.136450	0.137770
13.125	0.132524	0.133807	0.135100	0.136403	0.137716	0.139040
13.250	0.133777	0.135063	0.136360	0.137666	0.138983	0.140309
13.375	0.135030	0.136320	0.137619	0.138929	0.140249	0.141579
13.500	0.136283	0.137576	0.138879	0.140192	0.141515	0.142849
13.625	0.137536	0.138833	0.140139	0.141455	0.142782	0.144118
13.750	0.138790	0.140089	0.141399	0.142718	0.144048	0.145388
13.875	0.140043	0.141346	0.142658	0.143981	0.145314	0.146658
14.000	0.141296	0.142602	0.143918	0.145244	0.146581	0.147928
14.125	0.142549	0.143859	0.145178	0.146508	0.147848	0.149198
14.250	0.143803	0.145115	0.146438	0.147771	0.149114	0.150468
14.375	0.145056	0.146372	0.147698	0.149034	0.150381	0.151738
14.500	0.146309	0.147628	0.148958	0.150297	0.151648	0.153008
14.625	0.147562	0.148885	0.150218	0.151561	0.152914	0.154279
14.750	0.148816	0.150142	0.151478	0.152824	0.154181	0.155549
14.875	0.150069	0.151398	0.152738	0.154088	0.155448	0.156819
15.000	0.151322	0.152655	0.153998	0.155351	0.156715	0.158090
15.125	0.152576	0.153912	0.155258	0.156615	0.157982	0.159360
15.250	0.153829	0.155168	0.156518	0.157878	0.159249	0.160631
15.375	0.155082	0.156425	0.157778	0.159142	0.160516	0.161902
15.500	0.156336	0.157682	0.159038	0.160405	0.161783	0.163172
15.625	0.157589	0.158938	0.160298	0.161669	0.163051	0.164443
15.750	0.158842	0.160195	0.161559	0.162933	0.164318	0.165714
15.875	0.160096	0.161452	0.162819	0.164197	0.165585	0.166985
16.000	0.161349	0.162709	0.164079	0.165460	0.166852	0.168256
16.125	0.162603	0.163966	0.165340	0.166724	0.168120	0.169527
16.250	0.163856	0.165223	0.166600	0.167988	0.169387	0.170798
16.375	0.165109	0.166479	0.167860	0.169252	0.170655	0.172069
16.500	0.166363	0.167736	0.169121	0.170516	0.171922	0.173340
16.625	0.167616	0.168993	0.170381	0.171780	0.173190	0.174611
16.750	0.168870	0.170250	0.171642	0.173044	0.174458	0.175883
16.875	0.170123	0.171507	0.172902	0.174308	0.175725	0.177154
17.000	0.171377	0.172764	0.174163	0.175572	0.176993	0.178426
17.125	0.172630	0.174021	0.175423	0.176837	0.178261	0.179697
17.250	0.173884	0.175278	0.176684	0.178101	0.179529	0.180969
17.375	0.175137	0.176535	0.177945	0.179365	0.180797	0.182240
17.500	0.176391	0.177792	0.179205	0.180629	0.182065	0.183512
17.625	0.177644	0.179050	0.180466	0.181894	0.183333	0.104784
17.750	0.178898	0.180307	0.181727	0.183158	0.184601	0.186056
17.875	0.180151	0.181564	0.182987	0.184423	0.185869	0.187328

TABLE III-3. Annual Percentage Rate with a 10-Year Mortgage

ANNUAL PERCENTAGE RATE TABLE
TERM OF MORTGAGE 10 YEARS

CONTRACT INTEREST RATE / POINTS CHARGED	0.50	1.00	1.50	2.00	2.50	3.00
18.000	0.181405	0.182821	0.184248	0.185687	0.187137	0.188599
18.125	0.182658	0.184078	0.185509	0.186952	0.188406	0.189871
18.250	0.183912	0.185335	0.186770	0.188216	0.189674	0.191144
18.375	0.185166	0.186593	0.188031	0.189481	0.190942	0.192416
18.500	0.186419	0.187850	0.189292	0.190745	0.192211	0.193688
18.625	0.187673	0.189107	0.190553	0.192010	0.193479	0.194960
18.750	0.188926	0.190364	0.191814	0.193275	0.194748	0.196233
18.875	0.190180	0.191622	0.193075	0.194539	0.196016	0.197505
19.000	0.191434	0.192879	0.194336	0.195804	0.197285	0.198777
19.125	0.192687	0.194136	0.195597	0.197069	0.198553	0.200050
19.250	0.193941	0.195394	0.196858	0.198334	0.199822	0.201322
19.375	0.195195	0.196651	0.198119	0.199599	0.201091	0.202595
19.500	0.196448	0.197908	0.199380	0.200864	0.202360	0.203868
19.625	0.197702	0.199166	0.200641	0.202129	0.203629	0.205141
19.750	0.198956	0.200423	0.201903	0.203394	0.204898	0.206413
19.875	0.200209	0.201681	0.203164	0.204659	0.206166	0.207686
20.000	0.201463	0.202938	0.204425	0.205924	0.207435	0.208959
20.125	0.202717	0.204196	0.205686	0.207189	0.208705	0.210232
20.250	0.203971	0.205453	0.206948	0.208455	0.209974	0.211505
20.375	0.205224	0.206711	0.208209	0.209720	0.211243	0.212778
20.500	0.206478	0.207968	0.209471	0.210985	0.212512	0.214052
20.625	0.207732	0.209226	0.210732	0.212250	0.213781	0.215325
20.750	0.208986	0.210484	0.211993	0.213516	0.215051	0.216598
20.875	0.210240	0.211741	0.213255	0.214781	0.216320	0.217872
21.000	0.211493	0.212999	0.214516	0.216047	0.217589	0.219145
21.125	0.212747	0.214256	0.215778	0.217312	0.218859	0.220419
21.250	0.214001	0.215514	0.217040	0.218578	0.220128	0.221692
21.375	0.215255	0.216772	0.218301	0.219843	0.221398	0.222966
21.500	0.216509	0.218029	0.219563	0.221109	0.222668	0.224240
21.625	0.217762	0.219287	0.220825	0.222375	0.223937	0.225513
21.750	0.219016	0.220545	0.222086	0.223640	0.225207	0.226787
21.875	0.220270	0.221803	0.223348	0.224906	0.226477	0.228061
22.000	0.221524	0.223061	0.224610	0.226172	0.227747	0.229335
22.125	0.222778	0.224318	0.225872	0.227438	0.229017	0.230609
22.250	0.224032	0.225576	0.227133	0.228703	0.230287	0.231883
22.375	0.225286	0.226834	0.228395	0.229969	0.231557	0.233157
22.500	0.226540	0.228092	0.229657	0.231235	0.232827	0.234431
22.625	0.227794	0.229350	0.230919	0.232501	0.234097	0.235706
22.750	0.229048	0.230608	0.232181	0.233767	0.235367	0.236980
22.875	0.230301	0.231866	0.233443	0.235033	0.236637	0.238254

TABLE III-4. Annual Percentage Rate with a 10-Year Mortgage

ANNUAL PERCENTAGE RATE TABLE
TERM OF MORTGAGE 10 YEARS

CONTRACT INTEREST RATE \ POINTS CHARGED	3.50	4.00	4.50	5.00	5.50	6.00
8.000	0.088245	0.089459	0.090681	0.091913	0.093154	0.094405
8.125	0.089515	0.090731	0.091957	0.093192	0.094436	0.095690
8.250	0.090785	0.092004	0.093233	0.094471	0.095718	0.096975
8.375	0.092055	0.093278	0.094509	0.095750	0.097001	0.098261
8.500	0.093326	0.094551	0.095785	0.097029	0.098283	0.099546
8.625	0.094596	0.095824	0.097062	0.098309	0.099566	0.100832
8.750	0.095866	0.097097	0.098338	0.099588	0.100848	0.102118
8.875	0.097137	0.098371	0.099615	0.100868	0.102131	0.103404
9.000	0.098407	0.099644	0.100891	0.102148	0.103414	0.104690
9.125	0.099678	0.100918	0.102168	0.103428	0.104697	0.105976
9.250	0.100948	0.102192	0.103445	0.104708	0.105980	0.107263
9.375	0.102219	0.103466	0.104722	0.105988	0.107263	0.108549
9.500	0.103490	0.104739	0.105999	0.107268	0.108547	0.109836
9.625	0.104761	0.106013	0.107276	0.108548	0.109830	0.111122
9.750	0.106031	0.107287	0.108553	0.109828	0.111114	0.112409
9.875	0.107302	0.108561	0.109830	0.111109	0.112397	0.113696
10.000	0.108573	0.109836	0.111108	0.112389	0.113681	0.114983
10.125	0.109845	0.111110	0.112385	0.113670	0.114965	0.116271
10.250	0.111116	0.112384	0.113663	0.114951	0.116249	0.117558
10.375	0.112387	0.113659	0.114940	0.116232	0.117533	0.118845
10.500	0.113658	0.114933	0.116218	0.117513	0.118818	0.120133
10.625	0.114930	0.116208	0.117496	0.118794	0.120102	0.121421
10.750	0.116201	0.117483	0.118774	0.120075	0.121387	0.122709
10.875	0.117473	0.118757	0.120052	0.121356	0.122671	0.123997
11.000	0.118745	0.120032	0.121330	0.122638	0.123956	0.125285
11.125	0.120016	0.121307	0.122608	0.123919	0.125241	0.126573
11.250	0.121288	0.122582	0.123887	0.125201	0.126526	0.127862
11.375	0.122560	0.123857	0.125165	0.126483	0.127811	0.129150
11.500	0.123832	0.125133	0.126443	0.127765	0.129096	0.130439
11.625	0.125104	0.126408	0.127722	0.129047	0.130382	0.131728
11.750	0.126376	0.127683	0.129001	0.130329	0.131667	0.133016
11.875	0.127648	0.128959	0.130280	0.131611	0.132953	0.134305
12.000	0.128920	0.130234	0.131558	0.132893	0.134239	0.135595
12.125	0.130193	0.131510	0.132837	0.134176	0.135524	0.136884
12.250	0.131465	0.132786	0.134117	0.135458	0.136810	0.138173
12.375	0.132737	0.134061	0.135396	0.136741	0.138096	0.139463
12.500	0.134010	0.135337	0.136675	0.138023	0.139383	0.140753
12.625	0.135282	0.136613	0.137954	0.139306	0.140669	0.142043
12.750	0.136555	0.137889	0.139234	0.140589	0.141955	0.143333
12.875	0.137828	0.139165	0.140513	0.141872	0.143242	0.144623

TABLE III-5. Annual Percentage Rate with a 10-Year Mortgage

ANNUAL PERCENTAGE RATE TABLE
TERM OF MORTGAGE 10 YEARS

CONTRACT INTEREST RATE \ POINTS CHARGED	3.50	4.00	4.50	5.00	5.50	6.00
13.000	0.139101	0.140442	0.141793	0.143155	0.144529	0.145913
13.125	0.140374	0.141718	0.143073	0.144439	0.145815	0.147203
13.250	0.141647	0.142994	0.144353	0.145722	0.147102	0.148494
13.375	0.142920	0.144271	0.145633	0.147005	0.148389	0.149784
13.500	0.144193	0.145547	0.146913	0.148289	0.149676	0.151075
13.625	0.145466	0.146824	0.148193	0.149573	0.150964	0.152366
13.750	0.146739	0.148101	0.149473	0.150856	0.152251	0.153657
13.875	0.148012	0.149377	0.150753	0.152140	0.153538	0.154948
14.000	0.149286	0.150654	0.152034	0.153424	0.154826	0.156239
14.125	0.150559	0.151931	0.153314	0.154708	0.156114	0.157531
14.250	0.151833	0.153208	0.154595	0.155993	0.157402	0.158822
14.375	0.153106	0.154485	0.155876	0.157277	0.158690	0.160114
14.500	0.154380	0.155763	0.157156	0.158561	0.159978	0.161406
14.625	0.155654	0.157040	0.158437	0.159846	0.161266	0.162698
14.750	0.156928	0.158317	0.159718	0.161131	0.162554	0.163990
14.875	0.158202	0.159595	0.160999	0.162415	0.163843	0.165282
15.000	0.159476	0.160872	0.162281	0.163700	0.165131	0.166574
15.125	0.160750	0.162150	0.163562	0.164985	0.166420	0.167867
15.250	0.162024	0.163428	0.164843	0.166270	0.167709	0.169159
15.375	0.163298	0.164706	0.166125	0.167555	0.168998	0.170452
15.500	0.164572	0.165984	0.167406	0.168841	0.170287	0.171745
15.625	0.165847	0.167262	0.168688	0.170126	0.171576	0.173038
15.750	0.167121	0.168540	0.169970	0.171412	0.172865	0.174331
15.875	0.168396	0.169818	0.171252	0.172697	0.174155	0.175624
16.000	0.169670	0.171096	0.172534	0.173983	0.175444	0.176917
16.125	0.170945	0.172374	0.173816	0.175269	0.176734	0.178211
16.250	0.172220	0.173653	0.175098	0.176555	0.178024	0.179505
16.375	0.173494	0.174931	0.176380	0.177841	0.179313	0.180798
16.500	0.174769	0.176210	0.177662	0.179127	0.180603	0.182092
16.625	0.176044	0.177489	0.178945	0.180413	0.181894	0.183386
16.750	0.177319	0.178767	0.180227	0.181700	0.183184	0.184680
16.875	0.178594	0.180046	0.181510	0.182986	0.184474	0.185975
17.000	0.179869	0.181325	0.182793	0.184273	0.185765	0.187269
17.125	0.181145	0.182604	0.184076	0.185559	0.187055	0.188564
17.250	0.182420	0.183883	0.185359	0.186846	0.188346	0.189858
17.375	0.183695	0.185162	0.186642	0.188133	0.189637	0.191153
17.500	0.184971	0.186442	0.187925	0.189420	0.190928	0.192448
17.625	0.186246	0.187721	0.189208	0.190707	0.192219	0.193743
17.750	0.187522	0.189001	0.190491	0.191994	0.193510	0.195038
17.875	0.188798	0.190280	0.191775	0.193282	0.194801	0.196334

TABLE III-6. Annual Percentage Rate with a 10-Year Mortgage

ANNUAL PERCENTAGE RATE TABLE
TERM OF MORTGAGE 10 YEARS

CONTRACT INTEREST RATE \ POINTS CHARGED	3.50	4.00	4.50	5.00	5.50	6.00
18.000	0.190074	0.191560	0.193058	0.194569	0.196093	0.197629
18.125	0.191349	0.192839	0.194342	0.195857	0.197384	0.198925
18.250	0.192625	0.194119	0.195625	0.197144	0.198676	0.200221
18.375	0.193901	0.195399	0.196909	0.198432	0.199968	0.201516
18.500	0.195177	0.196679	0.198193	0.199720	0.201260	0.202812
18.625	0.196453	0.197959	0.199477	0.201008	0.202552	0.204108
18.750	0.197730	0.199239	0.200761	0.202296	0.203844	0.205405
18.875	0.199006	0.200519	0.202045	0.203584	0.205136	0.206701
19.000	0.200282	0.201800	0.203330	0.204873	0.206428	0.207998
19.125	0.201559	0.203080	0.204614	0.206161	0.207721	0.209294
19.250	0.202835	0.204360	0.205899	0.207449	0.209014	0.210591
19.375	0.204112	0.205641	0.207183	0.208738	0.210306	0.211888
19.500	0.205388	0.206922	0.208468	0.210027	0.211599	0.213185
19.625	0.206665	0.208202	0.209752	0.211316	0.212892	0.214482
19.750	0.207942	0.209483	0.211037	0.212605	0.214185	0.215779
19.875	0.209219	0.210764	0.212322	0.213894	0.215478	0.217077
20.000	0.210496	0.212045	0.213607	0.215183	0.216772	0.218374
20.125	0.211773	0.213326	0.214892	0.216472	0.218065	0.219672
20.250	0.213050	0.214607	0.216178	0.217761	0.219359	0.220970
20.375	0.214327	0.215888	0.217463	0.219051	0.220652	0.222268
20.500	0.215604	0.217170	0.218748	0.220340	0.221946	0.223566
20.625	0.216881	0.218451	0.220034	0.221630	0.223240	0.224864
20.750	0.218159	0.219732	0.221319	0.222920	0.224534	0.226162
20.875	0.219436	0.221014	0.222605	0.224210	0.225828	0.227461
21.000	0.220714	0.222296	0.223891	0.225500	0.227123	0.228759
21.125	0.221991	0.223577	0.225177	0.226790	0.228417	0.230058
21.250	0.223269	0.224859	0.226463	0.228080	0.229711	0.231357
21.375	0.224547	0.226141	0.227749	0.229371	0.231006	0.232656
21.500	0.225825	0.227423	0.229035	0.230661	0.232301	0.233955
21.625	0.227102	0.228705	0.230321	0.231951	0.233596	0.235254
21.750	0.228380	0.229987	0.231608	0.233242	0.234891	0.236553
21.875	0.229658	0.231269	0.232894	0.234533	0.236186	0.237853
22.000	0.230936	0.232552	0.234181	0.235824	0.237481	0.239153
22.125	0.232215	0.233834	0.235467	0.237115	0.238776	0.240452
22.250	0.233493	0.235117	0.236754	0.238406	0.240072	0.241752
22.375	0.234771	0.236399	0.238041	0.239697	0.241367	0.243052
22.500	0.236050	0.237682	0.239328	0.240988	0.242663	0.244352
22.625	0.237328	0.238964	0.240615	0.242279	0.243959	0.245652
22.750	0.238607	0.240247	0.241902	0.243571	0.245255	0.246953
22.875	0.239885	0.241530	0.243189	0.244862	0.246550	0.248253

TABLE III-7. Annual Percentage Rate with a 10-Year Mortgage

ANNUAL PERCENTAGE RATE TABLE
TERM OF MORTGAGE 10 YEARS

CONTRACT INTEREST RATE \ POINTS CHARGED	6.50	7.00	7.50	8.00	8.50	9.00
8.000	0.095665	0.096936	0.098216	0.099507	0.100808	0.102119
8.125	0.096954	0.098227	0.099511	0.100805	0.102109	0.103424
8.250	0.098242	0.099519	0.100806	0.102103	0.103411	0.104729
8.375	0.099531	0.100811	0.102101	0.103401	0.104712	0.106034
8.500	0.100820	0.102103	0.103396	0.104700	0.106014	0.107339
8.625	0.102109	0.103395	0.104692	0.105999	0.107316	0.108644
8.750	0.103398	0.104687	0.105987	0.107298	0.108618	0.109950
8.875	0.104687	0.105980	0.107283	0.108597	0.109921	0.111256
9.000	0.105976	0.107272	0.108579	0.109896	0.111223	0.112562
9.125	0.107266	0.108565	0.109875	0.111195	0.112526	0.113868
9.250	0.108555	0.109858	0.111171	0.112495	0.113829	0.115175
9.375	0.109845	0.111151	0.112467	0.113795	0.115132	0.116481
9.500	0.111135	0.112444	0.113764	0.115095	0.116436	0.117788
9.625	0.112425	0.113737	0.115061	0.116395	0.117739	0.119095
9.750	0.113715	0.115031	0.116358	0.117695	0.119043	0.120402
9.875	0.115005	0.116325	0.117655	0.118995	0.120347	0.121710
10.000	0.116296	0.117618	0.118952	0.120296	0.121651	0.123017
10.125	0.117586	0.118912	0.120249	0.121597	0.122955	0.124325
10.250	0.118877	0.120206	0.121547	0.122898	0.124260	0.125633
10.375	0.120168	0.121501	0.122844	0.124199	0.125565	0.126941
10.500	0.121459	0.122795	0.124142	0.125500	0.126869	0.128250
10.625	0.122750	0.124090	0.125440	0.126802	0.128174	0.129558
10.750	0.124041	0.125384	0.126738	0.128103	0.129480	0.130867
10.875	0.125333	0.126679	0.128037	0.129405	0.130785	0.132176
11.000	0.126624	0.127974	0.129335	0.130707	0.132091	0.133486
11.125	0.127916	0.129269	0.130634	0.132010	0.133397	0.134795
11.250	0.129208	0.130565	0.131933	0.133312	0.134703	0.136105
11.375	0.130500	0.131860	0.133232	0.134615	0.136009	0.137415
11.500	0.131792	0.133156	0.134531	0.135917	0.137315	0.138725
11.625	0.133084	0.134452	0.135830	0.137220	0.138622	0.140035
11.750	0.134376	0.135748	0.137130	0.138523	0.139928	0.141345
11.875	0.135669	0.137044	0.138429	0.139827	0.141235	0.142656
12.000	0.136962	0.138340	0.139729	0.141130	0.142543	0.143967
12.125	0.138255	0.139636	0.141029	0.142434	0.143850	0.145278
12.250	0.139548	0.140933	0.142329	0.143738	0.145157	0.146589
12.375	0.140841	0.142230	0.143630	0.145042	0.146465	0.147901
12.500	0.142134	0.143526	0.144930	0.146346	0.147773	0.149212
12.625	0.143427	0.144823	0.146231	0.147650	0.149081	0.150524
12.750	0.144721	0.146121	0.147532	0.148955	0.150389	0.151836
12.875	0.146015	0.147418	0.148833	0.150259	0.151698	0.153149

TABLE III-8. Annual Percentage Rate with a 10-Year Mortgage

ANNUAL PERCENTAGE RATE TABLE
TERM OF MORTGAGE 10 YEARS

CONTRACT INTEREST RATE \ POINTS CHARGED	6.50	7.00	7.50	8.00	8.50	9.00
13.000	0.147308	0.148715	0.150134	0.151564	0.153007	0.154461
13.125	0.148602	0.150013	0.151435	0.152869	0.154316	0.155774
13.250	0.149896	0.151311	0.152737	0.154175	0.155625	0.157087
13.375	0.151191	0.152609	0.154038	0.155480	0.156934	0.158400
13.500	0.152485	0.153907	0.155340	0.156786	0.158243	0.159713
13.625	0.153780	0.155205	0.156642	0.158092	0.159553	0.161027
13.750	0.155074	0.156504	0.157944	0.159397	0.160863	0.162340
13.875	0.156369	0.157802	0.159247	0.160704	0.162173	0.163654
14.000	0.157664	0.159101	0.160549	0.162010	0.163483	0.164968
14.125	0.158959	0.160400	0.161852	0.163316	0.164793	0.166283
14.250	0.160255	0.161699	0.163155	0.164623	0.166104	0.167597
14.375	0.161550	0.162998	0.164458	0.165930	0.167415	0.168912
14.500	0.162845	0.164297	0.165761	0.167237	0.168726	0.170227
14.625	0.164141	0.165597	0.167064	0.168544	0.170037	0.171542
14.750	0.165437	0.166896	0.168368	0.169852	0.171348	0.172858
14.875	0.166733	0.168196	0.169671	0.171159	0.172660	0.174173
15.000	0.168029	0.169496	0.170975	0.172467	0.173972	0.175489
15.125	0.169325	0.170796	0.172279	0.173775	0.175283	0.176805
15.250	0.170622	0.172096	0.173584	0.175083	0.176596	0.178121
15.375	0.171918	0.173397	0.174888	0.176392	0.177908	0.179437
15.500	0.173215	0.174697	0.176192	0.177700	0.179220	0.180754
15.625	0.174512	0.175998	0.177497	0.179009	0.180533	0.182071
15.750	0.175809	0.177299	0.178802	0.180317	0.181846	0.183388
15.875	0.177106	0.178600	0.180107	0.181627	0.183159	0.184705
16.000	0.178403	0.179901	0.181412	0.182936	0.184472	0.186022
16.125	0.179701	0.181203	0.182717	0.184245	0.185786	0.187340
16.250	0.180998	0.182504	0.184023	0.185555	0.187100	0.188658
16.375	0.182296	0.183806	0.185329	0.186864	0.188413	0.189976
16.500	0.183594	0.185108	0.186634	0.188174	0.189728	0.191294
16.625	0.184892	0.186410	0.187940	0.189484	0.191042	0.192613
16.750	0.186190	0.187712	0.189247	0.190795	0.192356	0.193931
16.875	0.187488	0.189014	0.190553	0.192105	0.193671	0.195250
17.000	0.188786	0.190316	0.191859	0.193416	0.194986	0.196569
17.125	0.190085	0.191619	0.193166	0.194727	0.196301	0.197888
17.250	0.191384	0.192922	0.194473	0.196038	0.197616	0.199208
17.375	0.192682	0.194225	0.195780	0.197349	0.198931	0.200528
17.500	0.193981	0.195528	0.197087	0.198660	0.200247	0.201847
17.625	0.195281	0.196831	0.198395	0.199972	0.201563	0.203168
17.750	0.196580	0.198134	0.199702	0.201283	0.202879	0.204488
17.875	0.197879	0.199438	0.201010	0.202595	0.204195	0.205808

TABLE III-9. Annual Percentage Rate with a 10-Year Mortgage

ANNUAL PERCENTAGE RATE TABLE
TERM OF MORTGAGE 10 YEARS

CONTRACT INTEREST RATE \ POINTS CHARGED	6.50	7.00	7.50	8.00	8.50	9.00
18.000	0.199179	0.200741	0.202318	0.203907	0.205511	C.207129
18.125	0.200478	0.202045	0.203626	0.205220	0.206828	0.208450
18.250	0.201778	0.203349	0.204934	0.206532	0.208145	0.209771
18.375	0.203078	0.204653	0.206242	0.207845	0.209461	0.211092
18.500	0.204378	0.205958	0.207551	0.209158	0.210779	0.212414
18.625	0.205679	0.207262	0.208859	0.210471	0.212096	0.213736
18.750	0.206979	0.208567	0.210168	0.211784	0.213413	C.215057
18.875	0.208279	0.209871	0.211477	0.213097	0.214731	0.216380
19.000	0.209580	0.211176	0.212786	0.214411	0.216049	0.217702
19.125	0.210881	0.212481	0.214096	0.215724	0.217367	0.219024
19.250	0.212182	0.213787	0.215405	0.217038	0.218685	C.220347
19.375	0.213483	0.215092	0.216715	0.218352	0.220004	0.221670
19.500	0.214784	0.216398	0.218025	0.219666	0.221322	C.222993
19.625	0.216086	0.217703	0.219335	0.220981	0.222641	0.224317
19.750	0.217387	0.2190C9	0.220645	0.222295	0.223960	0.225640
19.875	0.218689	0.220315	0.221955	0.223610	0.225280	C.226964
20.000	0.219991	0.221621	0.223266	0.224925	0.226599	0.228288
20.125	0.221293	0.222927	0.224577	0.226240	0.227919	0.229612
20.250	0.222595	0.224234	0.225887	0.227555	0.229238	C.230936
20.375	0.223897	0.225540	0.227198	0.228871	0.230558	C.232261
20.500	0.225199	0.226847	0.228510	0.230187	0.231879	0.233586
20.625	0.226502	0.228154	0.229821	0.231502	0.233199	0.234911
20.750	0.227805	0.229461	0.231132	0.232818	0.234519	C.236236
20.875	0.229107	0.230768	0.232444	0.234135	0.235840	0.237561
21.000	0.230410	0.232076	0.233756	0.235451	0.237161	C.238887
21.125	0.231713	0.233383	0.235068	0.236767	0.238482	0.240212
21.250	0.233017	0.234691	0.236380	0.238084	0.239804	0.241538
21.375	0.234320	0.235999	0.237692	0.239401	0.241125	C.242865
21.500	0.235623	0.237307	0.239005	0.240718	0.242447	0.244191
21.625	0.236927	0.238615	0.240317	0.242035	0.243769	0.245518
21.750	0.238231	0.239923	0.241630	0.243353	0.245091	0.246844
21.875	0.239535	0.241231	0.242943	0.244670	0.246413	C.248171
22.000	0.240839	0.242540	0.244256	0.245988	0.247735	0.249498
22.125	0.242143	0.243849	0.245570	0.247306	0.249058	C.250826
22.250	0.243447	0.245158	0.246883	0.248624	0.250381	C.252153
22.375	0.244752	0.246467	0.248197	0.249942	0.251704	0.253481
22.500	0.246056	0.247776	0.249510	0.251261	0.253027	0.254809
22.625	0.247361	0.249085	0.250824	0.252579	0.254350	C.256137
22.750	0.248666	0.250395	0.252139	0.253898	0.255674	C.257466
22.875	0.249971	0.251704	0.253453	0.255217	0.256998	C.258794

TABLE III-10. Annual Percentage Rate with a 10-Year Mortgage

ANNUAL PERCENTAGE RATE TABLE
TERM OF MORTGAGE 10 YEARS

CONTRACT INTEREST RATE / POINTS CHARGED	9.50	10.00	10.50	11.00	11.50	12.00
8.000	0.103441	0.104774	0.106118	0.107472	0.108838	0.110216
8.125	0.104749	0.106085	0.107432	0.108791	0.110160	0.111541
8.250	0.106057	0.107397	0.108748	0.110109	0.111483	0.112867
8.375	0.107366	0.108709	0.110063	0.111428	0.112805	0.114193
8.500	0.108674	0.110021	0.111379	0.112747	0.114128	0.115520
8.625	0.109983	0.111333	0.112694	0.114067	0.115451	0.116846
8.750	0.111292	0.112646	0.114010	0.115386	0.116774	0.118173
8.875	0.112602	0.113959	0.115327	0.116706	0.118097	0.119500
9.000	0.113911	0.115272	0.116643	0.118026	0.119421	0.120828
9.125	0.115221	0.116585	0.117960	0.119347	0.120745	0.122155
9.250	0.116531	0.117898	0.119277	0.120667	0.122069	0.123483
9.375	0.117841	0.119212	0.120594	0.121988	0.123394	0.124811
9.500	0.119151	0.120526	0.121912	0.123309	0.124719	0.126140
9.625	0.120462	0.121840	0.123229	0.124631	0.126044	0.127469
9.750	0.121773	0.123154	0.124547	0.125952	0.127369	0.128798
9.875	0.123084	0.124469	0.125866	0.127274	0.128695	0.130127
10.000	0.124395	0.125784	0.127184	0.128596	0.130021	0.131457
10.125	0.125706	0.127099	0.128503	0.129919	0.131347	0.132787
10.250	0.127018	0.128414	0.129822	0.131241	0.132673	0.134117
10.375	0.128330	0.129729	0.131141	0.132564	0.134000	0.135448
10.500	0.129642	0.131045	0.132460	0.133887	0.135327	0.136778
10.625	0.130954	0.132361	0.133780	0.135211	0.136654	0.138109
10.750	0.132266	0.133677	0.135100	0.136534	0.137981	0.139441
10.875	0.133579	0.134994	0.136420	0.137858	0.139309	0.140772
11.000	0.134892	0.136310	0.137740	0.139183	0.140637	0.142104
11.125	0.136205	0.137627	0.139061	0.140507	0.141965	0.143436
11.250	0.137518	0.138944	0.140382	0.141832	0.143294	0.144769
11.375	0.138832	0.140261	0.141703	0.143157	0.144623	0.146102
11.500	0.140146	0.141579	0.143024	0.144482	0.145952	0.147435
11.625	0.141460	0.142897	0.144346	0.145807	0.147281	0.148768
11.750	0.142774	0.144215	0.145668	0.147133	0.148611	0.150101
11.875	0.144088	0.145533	0.146990	0.148459	0.149941	0.151435
12.000	0.145403	0.146851	0.148312	0.149785	0.151271	0.152770
12.125	0.146718	0.148170	0.149634	0.151111	0.152601	0.154104
12.250	0.148033	0.149489	0.150957	0.152438	0.153932	0.155439
12.375	0.149348	0.150808	0.152280	0.153765	0.155263	0.156774
12.500	0.150664	0.152127	0.153603	0.155092	0.156594	0.158109
12.625	0.151979	0.153447	0.154927	0.156420	0.157926	0.159445
12.750	0.153295	0.154767	0.156251	0.157748	0.159257	0.160780
12.875	0.154611	0.156087	0.157575	0.159076	0.160589	0.162117

TABLE III-11. Annual Percentage Rate with a 10-Year Mortgage

ANNUAL PERCENTAGE RATE TABLE
TERM OF MORTGAGE 10 YEARS

CONTRACT INTEREST RATE \ POINTS CHARGED	9.50	10.00	10.50	11.00	11.50	12.00
13.000	0.155928	0.157407	0.158899	0.160404	0.161922	0.163453
13.125	0.157244	0.158728	0.160223	0.161732	0.163254	0.164790
13.250	0.158561	0.160048	0.161548	0.163061	0.164587	0.166127
13.375	0.159878	0.161369	0.162873	0.164390	0.165920	0.167464
13.500	0.161195	0.162691	0.164198	0.165719	0.167254	0.168802
13.625	0.162513	0.164012	0.165524	0.167049	0.168587	0.170139
13.750	0.163831	0.165334	0.166850	0.168379	0.169921	0.171478
13.875	0.165148	0.166655	0.168176	0.169709	0.171256	0.172816
14.000	0.166467	0.167978	0.169502	0.171039	0.172590	0.174155
14.125	0.167785	0.169300	0.170828	0.172370	0.173925	0.175494
14.250	0.169103	0.170623	0.172155	0.173701	0.175260	0.176833
14.375	0.170422	0.171945	0.173482	0.175032	0.176595	0.178172
14.500	0.171741	0.173268	0.174809	0.176363	0.177931	0.179512
14.625	0.173060	0.174592	0.176136	0.177695	0.179267	0.180852
14.750	0.174380	0.175915	0.177464	0.179026	0.180603	0.182193
14.875	0.175699	0.177239	0.178792	0.180359	0.181939	0.183534
15.000	0.177019	0.178563	0.180120	0.181691	0.183276	0.184875
15.125	0.178339	0.179887	0.181448	0.183024	0.184613	0.186216
15.250	0.179660	0.181212	0.182777	0.184356	0.185950	0.187557
15.375	0.180980	0.182536	0.184106	0.185690	0.187287	0.188899
15.500	0.182301	0.183861	0.185435	0.187023	0.188625	0.190241
15.625	0.183622	0.185186	0.186765	0.188357	0.189963	0.191584
15.750	0.184943	0.186512	0.188094	0.189691	0.191301	0.192927
15.875	0.186264	0.187837	0.189424	0.191025	0.192640	0.194270
16.000	0.187586	0.189163	0.190754	0.192359	0.193979	0.195613
16.125	0.188908	0.190489	0.192084	0.193694	0.195318	0.196956
16.250	0.190230	0.191815	0.193415	0.195029	0.196657	0.198300
16.375	0.191552	0.193142	0.194746	0.196364	0.197997	0.199644
16.500	0.192874	0.194469	0.196077	0.197700	0.199337	0.200989
16.625	0.194197	0.195796	0.197408	0.199035	0.200677	0.202333
16.750	0.195520	0.197123	0.198740	0.200371	0.202017	0.203678
16.875	0.196843	0.198450	0.200072	0.201708	0.203358	0.205024
17.000	0.198167	0.199778	0.201404	0.203044	0.204699	0.206369
17.125	0.199490	0.201106	0.202736	0.204381	0.206040	0.207715
17.250	0.200814	0.202434	0.204069	0.205718	0.207382	0.209061
17.375	0.202138	0.203762	0.205401	0.207055	0.208724	0.210408
17.500	0.203462	0.205091	0.206734	0.208393	0.210066	0.211754
17.625	0.204787	0.206420	0.208068	0.209731	0.211408	0.213101
17.750	0.206111	0.207749	0.209401	0.211069	0.212751	0.214449
17.875	0.207436	0.209078	0.210735	0.212407	0.214094	0.215796

TABLE III-12. Annual Percentage Rate with a 10-Year Mortgage

ANNUAL PERCENTAGE RATE TABLE
TERM OF MORTGAGE 10 YEARS

CONTRACT INTEREST RATE \ POINTS CHARGED	9.50	10.00	10.50	11.00	11.50	12.00
18.000	0.208761	0.210408	0.212069	0.213745	0.215437	0.217144
18.125	0.210086	0.211737	0.213403	0.215084	0.216781	0.218492
18.250	0.211412	0.213067	0.214738	0.216423	0.218124	0.219841
18.375	0.212738	0.214398	0.216073	0.217763	0.219468	0.221189
18.500	0.214064	0.215728	0.217408	0.219102	0.220812	0.222538
18.625	0.215390	0.217059	0.218743	0.220442	0.222157	0.223888
18.750	0.216716	0.218390	0.220078	0.221782	0.223502	0.225237
18.875	0.218043	0.219721	0.221414	0.223123	0.224847	0.226587
19.000	0.219370	0.221052	0.222750	0.224463	0.226192	0.227937
19.125	0.220697	0.222384	0.224086	0.225804	0.227538	0.229287
19.250	0.222024	0.223716	0.225423	0.227145	0.228884	0.230638
19.375	0.223351	0.225048	0.226759	0.228487	0.230230	0.231989
19.500	0.224679	0.226380	0.228096	0.229828	0.231576	0.233340
19.625	0.226007	0.227712	0.229433	0.231170	0.232923	0.234692
19.750	0.227335	0.229045	0.230771	0.232512	0.234270	0.236044
19.875	0.228663	0.230378	0.232108	0.233855	0.235617	0.237396
20.000	0.229992	0.231711	0.233446	0.235197	0.236965	0.238748
20.125	0.231321	0.233045	0.234785	0.236540	0.238312	0.240101
20.250	0.232650	0.234378	0.236123	0.237883	0.239660	0.241454
20.375	0.233979	0.235712	0.237462	0.239227	0.241009	0.242807
20.500	0.235308	0.237046	0.238800	0.240571	0.242357	0.244161
20.625	0.236638	0.238381	0.240139	0.241915	0.243706	0.245514
20.750	0.237968	0.239715	0.241479	0.243259	0.245055	0.246868
20.875	0.239298	0.241050	0.242818	0.244603	0.246405	0.248223
21.000	0.240628	0.242385	0.244158	0.245948	0.247754	0.249577
21.125	0.241958	0.243720	0.245498	0.247293	0.249104	0.250932
21.250	0.243289	0.245056	0.246839	0.248638	0.250454	0.252288
21.375	0.244620	0.246391	0.248179	0.249983	0.251805	0.253643
21.500	0.245951	0.247727	0.249520	0.251329	0.253155	0.254999
21.625	0.247282	0.249063	0.250861	0.252675	0.254506	0.256355
21.750	0.248614	0.250400	0.252202	0.254021	0.255858	0.257711
21.875	0.249946	0.251736	0.253544	0.255368	0.257209	0.259068
22.000	0.251278	0.253073	0.254885	0.256715	0.258561	0.260425
22.125	0.252610	0.254410	0.256227	0.258061	0.259913	0.261782
22.250	0.253942	0.255748	0.257570	0.259409	0.261265	0.263139
22.375	0.255275	0.257085	0.258912	0.260756	0.262618	0.264497
22.500	0.256608	0.258423	0.260255	0.262104	0.263970	0.265855
22.625	0.257941	0.259761	0.261598	0.263452	0.265323	0.267213
22.750	0.259274	0.261099	0.262941	0.264800	0.266677	0.268571
22.875	0.260607	0.262437	0.264284	0.266148	0.268030	0.269930

TABLE III-13. Annual Percentage Rate with a 20-Year Mortgage

ANNUAL PERCENTAGE RATE TABLE
TERM OF MORTGAGE 20 YEARS

CONTRACT INTEREST RATE \ POINTS CHARGED	0.50	1.00	1.50	2.00	2.50	3.00
8.000	0.080675	0.081354	0.082040	0.082730	0.083426	0.084128
8.125	0.081928	0.082611	0.083300	0.083994	0.084693	0.085398
8.250	0.083181	0.083868	0.084560	0.085258	0.085961	0.086669
8.375	0.084435	0.085125	0.085821	0.086522	0.087228	0.087941
8.500	0.085688	0.086382	0.087081	0.087786	0.088496	0.089212
8.625	0.086942	0.087639	0.088341	0.089050	0.089764	0.090483
8.750	0.088195	0.088896	0.089602	0.090314	0.091031	0.091755
8.875	0.089449	0.090153	0.090863	0.091578	0.092299	0.093026
9.000	0.090702	0.091410	0.092123	0.092842	0.093567	0.094298
9.125	0.091956	0.092667	0.093384	0.094107	0.094836	0.095570
9.250	0.093209	0.093924	0.094645	0.095371	0.096104	0.096842
9.375	0.094463	0.095182	0.095906	0.096636	0.097372	0.098114
9.500	0.095717	0.096439	0.097167	0.097901	0.098641	0.099386
9.625	0.096970	0.097696	0.098428	0.099165	0.099909	0.100659
9.750	0.098224	0.098953	0.099689	0.100430	0.101178	0.101931
9.875	0.099477	0.100211	0.100950	0.101695	0.102447	0.103204
10.000	0.100731	0.101468	0.102211	0.102960	0.103715	0.104477
10.125	0.101985	0.102726	0.103472	0.104225	0.104984	0.105750
10.250	0.103239	0.103983	0.104734	0.105491	0.106253	0.107023
10.375	0.104492	0.105241	0.105995	0.106756	0.107523	0.108296
10.500	0.105746	0.106498	0.107257	0.108021	0.108792	0.109569
10.625	0.107000	0.107756	0.108518	0.109287	0.110061	0.110843
10.750	0.108254	0.109014	0.109780	0.110552	0.111331	0.112116
10.875	0.109508	0.110271	0.111041	0.111818	0.112600	0.113390
11.000	0.110761	0.111529	0.112303	0.113083	0.113870	0.114663
11.125	0.112015	0.112787	0.113565	0.114349	0.115140	0.115937
11.250	0.113269	0.114045	0.114827	0.115615	0.116410	0.117211
11.375	0.114523	0.115303	0.116088	0.116881	0.117680	0.118486
11.500	0.115777	0.116560	0.117350	0.118147	0.118950	0.119760
11.625	0.117031	0.117818	0.118612	0.119413	0.120220	0.121034
11.750	0.118285	0.119076	0.119874	0.120679	0.121490	0.122309
11.875	0.119539	0.120334	0.121136	0.121945	0.122761	0.123583
12.000	0.120793	0.121592	0.122399	0.123212	0.124031	0.124858
12.125	0.122047	0.122851	0.123661	0.124478	0.125302	0.126133
12.250	0.123301	0.124109	0.124923	0.125744	0.126573	0.127408
12.375	0.124555	0.125367	0.126185	0.127011	0.127843	0.128683
12.500	0.125809	0.126625	0.127448	0.128278	0.129114	0.129958
12.625	0.127063	0.127883	0.128710	0.129544	0.130385	0.131234
12.750	0.128317	0.129142	0.129973	0.130811	0.131657	0.132509
12.875	0.129572	0.130400	0.131235	0.132078	0.132928	0.133785

TABLE III-14. Annual Percentage Rate with a 20-Year Mortgage

ANNUAL PERCENTAGE RATE TABLE
TERM OF MORTGAGE 20 YEARS

CONTRACT INTEREST RATE \ POINTS CHARGED	0.50	1.00	1.50	2.00	2.50	3.00
13.000	0.130826	0.131658	0.132498	0.133345	0.134199	0.135061
13.125	0.132080	0.132917	0.133761	0.134612	0.135470	0.136336
13.250	0.133334	0.134175	0.135024	0.135879	0.136742	0.137612
13.375	0.134588	0.135434	0.136286	0.137146	0.138014	0.138888
13.500	0.135843	0.136692	0.137549	0.138413	0.139285	0.140165
13.625	0.137097	0.137951	0.138812	0.139681	0.140557	0.141441
13.750	0.138351	0.139209	0.140075	0.140948	0.141829	0.142717
13.875	0.139605	0.140468	0.141338	0.142216	0.143101	0.143994
14.000	0.140860	0.141727	0.142601	0.143483	0.144373	0.145270
14.125	0.142114	0.142985	0.143864	0.144751	0.145645	0.146547
14.250	0.143368	0.144244	0.145128	0.146019	0.146917	0.147824
14.375	0.144623	0.145503	0.146391	0.147286	0.148190	0.149101
14.500	0.145877	0.146762	0.147654	0.148554	0.149462	0.150378
14.625	0.147132	0.148021	0.148918	0.149822	0.150735	0.151655
14.750	0.148386	0.149280	0.150181	0.151090	0.152007	0.152933
14.875	0.149640	0.150539	0.151444	0.152358	0.153280	0.154210
15.000	0.150895	0.151798	0.152708	0.153626	0.154553	0.155488
15.125	0.152149	0.153057	0.153972	0.154895	0.155826	0.156766
15.250	0.153404	0.154316	0.155235	0.156163	0.157099	0.158043
15.375	0.154658	0.155575	0.156499	0.157431	0.158372	0.159321
15.500	0.155913	0.156834	0.157763	0.158700	0.159645	0.160599
15.625	0.157167	0.158093	0.159027	0.159968	0.160919	0.161877
15.750	0.158422	0.159352	0.160290	0.161237	0.162192	0.163156
15.875	0.159677	0.160611	0.161554	0.162506	0.163465	0.164434
16.000	0.160931	0.161871	0.162818	0.163774	0.164739	0.165712
16.125	0.162186	0.163130	0.164082	0.165043	0.166013	0.166991
16.250	0.163440	0.164389	0.165346	0.166312	0.167286	0.168269
16.375	0.164695	0.165649	0.166611	0.167581	0.168560	0.169548
16.500	0.165950	0.166908	0.167875	0.168850	0.169834	0.170827
16.625	0.167205	0.168167	0.169139	0.170119	0.171108	0.172106
16.750	0.168459	0.169427	0.170403	0.171388	0.172382	0.173385
16.875	0.169714	0.170686	0.171668	0.172657	0.173656	0.174664
17.000	0.170969	0.171946	0.172932	0.173927	0.174931	0.175944
17.125	0.172223	0.173206	0.174196	0.175196	0.176205	0.177223
17.250	0.173478	0.174465	0.175461	0.176466	0.177479	0.178502
17.375	0.174733	0.175725	0.176725	0.177735	0.178754	0.179782
17.500	0.175988	0.176984	0.177990	0.179005	0.180028	0.181062
17.625	0.177243	0.178244	0.179255	0.180274	0.181303	0.182341
17.750	0.178497	0.179504	0.180519	0.181544	0.182578	0.183621
17.875	0.179752	0.180764	0.181784	0.182814	0.183853	0.184901

TABLE III-15. Annual Percentage Rate with a 20-Year Mortgage

ANNUAL PERCENTAGE RATE TABLE
TERM OF MORTGAGE 20 YEARS

CONTRACT INTEREST RATE / POINTS CHARGED	0.50	1.00	1.50	2.00	2.50	3.00
18.000	0.181007	0.182023	0.183049	0.184083	0.185128	0.186181
18.125	0.182262	0.183283	0.184314	0.185353	0.186403	0.187461
18.250	0.183517	0.184543	0.185578	0.186623	0.187678	0.188742
18.375	0.184772	0.185803	0.186843	0.187893	0.188953	0.190022
18.500	0.186027	0.187063	0.188108	0.189163	0.190228	0.191303
18.625	0.187282	0.188323	0.189373	0.190433	0.191503	0.192583
18.750	0.188537	0.189583	0.190638	0.191704	0.192779	0.193864
18.875	0.189792	0.190843	0.191903	0.192974	0.194054	0.195144
19.000	0.191047	0.192103	0.193169	0.194244	0.195330	0.196425
19.125	0.192302	0.193363	0.194434	0.195514	0.196605	0.197706
19.250	0.193557	0.194623	0.195699	0.196785	0.197881	0.198987
19.375	0.194812	0.195883	0.196964	0.198055	0.199157	0.200268
19.500	0.196067	0.197143	0.198230	0.199326	0.200433	0.201549
19.625	0.197322	0.198403	0.199495	0.200597	0.201708	0.202831
19.750	0.198577	0.199664	0.200760	0.201867	0.202984	0.204112
19.875	0.199832	0.200924	0.202026	0.203138	0.204260	0.205393
20.000	0.201087	0.202184	0.203291	0.204409	0.205537	0.206675
20.125	0.202342	0.203444	0.204557	0.205680	0.206813	0.207957
20.250	0.203597	0.204705	0.205822	0.206950	0.208089	0.209238
20.375	0.204852	0.205965	0.207088	0.208221	0.209365	0.210520
20.500	0.206108	0.207225	0.208354	0.209492	0.210642	0.211802
20.625	0.207363	0.208486	0.209619	0.210763	0.211918	0.213084
20.750	0.208618	0.209746	0.210885	0.212035	0.213195	0.214366
20.875	0.209873	0.211007	0.212151	0.213306	0.214471	0.215648
21.000	0.211128	0.212267	0.213417	0.214577	0.215748	0.216930
21.125	0.212384	0.213528	0.214683	0.215848	0.217025	0.218213
21.250	0.213639	0.214788	0.215948	0.217119	0.218302	0.219495
21.375	0.214894	0.216049	0.217214	0.218391	0.219578	0.220777
21.500	0.216149	0.217309	0.218480	0.219662	0.220855	0.222060
21.625	0.217405	0.218570	0.219746	0.220934	0.222132	0.223342
21.750	0.218660	0.219831	0.221012	0.222205	0.223409	0.224625
21.875	0.219915	0.221091	0.222278	0.223477	0.224687	0.225908
22.000	0.221171	0.222352	0.223545	0.224748	0.225964	0.227191
22.125	0.222426	0.223613	0.224811	0.226020	0.227241	0.228473
22.250	0.223681	0.224873	0.226077	0.227292	0.228518	0.229756
22.375	0.224937	0.226134	0.227343	0.228564	0.229796	0.231039
22.500	0.226192	0.227395	0.228609	0.229835	0.231073	0.232323
22.625	0.227447	0.228656	0.229876	0.231107	0.232351	0.233606
22.750	0.228703	0.229917	0.231142	0.232379	0.233628	0.234889
22.875	0.229958	0.231178	0.232408	0.233651	0.234906	0.236172

TABLE III-16. Annual Percentage Rate with a 20-Year Mortgage

ANNUAL PERCENTAGE RATE TABLE
TERM OF MORTGAGE 20 YEARS

CONTRACT INTEREST RATE / POINTS CHARGED	3.50	4.00	4.50	5.00	5.50	6.00
8.000	0.084835	0.085548	0.086266	0.086991	0.087721	0.088458
8.125	0.086109	0.086826	0.087548	0.088276	0.089010	0.089751
8.250	0.087384	0.088104	0.088830	0.089562	0.090300	0.091044
8.375	0.088659	0.089382	0.090112	0.090848	0.091590	0.092338
8.500	0.089934	0.090661	0.091395	0.092134	0.092880	0.093632
8.625	0.091209	0.091940	0.092677	0.093421	0.094170	0.094926
8.750	0.092484	0.093219	0.093960	0.094707	0.095461	0.096221
8.875	0.093759	0.094498	0.095243	0.095994	0.096752	0.097516
9.000	0.095035	0.095778	0.096526	0.097281	0.098043	0.098811
9.125	0.096310	0.097057	0.097810	0.098569	0.099334	0.100106
9.250	0.097586	0.098337	0.099093	0.099856	0.100626	0.101402
9.375	0.098862	0.099617	0.100377	0.101144	0.101918	0.102698
9.500	0.100138	0.100897	0.101661	0.102432	0.103210	0.103994
9.625	0.101415	0.102177	0.102945	0.103720	0.104502	0.105290
9.750	0.102691	0.103457	0.104230	0.105009	0.105794	0.106587
9.875	0.103968	0.104738	0.105514	0.106297	0.107087	0.107884
10.000	0.105244	0.106019	0.106799	0.107586	0.108380	0.109181
10.125	0.106521	0.107299	0.108084	0.108875	0.109673	0.110478
10.250	0.107798	0.108580	0.109369	0.110165	0.110967	0.111776
10.375	0.109076	0.109862	0.110655	0.111454	0.112260	0.113074
10.500	0.110353	0.111143	0.111940	0.112744	0.113554	0.114372
10.625	0.111630	0.112425	0.113226	0.114034	0.114849	0.115671
10.750	0.112908	0.113706	0.114512	0.115324	0.116143	0.116969
10.875	0.114186	0.114988	0.115798	0.116614	0.117438	0.118268
11.000	0.115464	0.116270	0.117084	0.117905	0.118733	0.119568
11.125	0.116742	0.117553	0.118371	0.119196	0.120028	0.120867
11.250	0.118020	0.118835	0.119657	0.120487	0.121323	0.122167
11.375	0.119298	0.120118	0.120944	0.121778	0.122619	0.123467
11.500	0.120577	0.121400	0.122231	0.123069	0.123914	0.124767
11.625	0.121855	0.122683	0.123518	0.124361	0.125211	0.126068
11.750	0.123134	0.123966	0.124806	0.125653	0.126507	0.127369
11.875	0.124413	0.125250	0.126093	0.126945	0.127803	0.128670
12.000	0.125692	0.126533	0.127381	0.128237	0.129100	0.129971
12.125	0.126971	0.127816	0.128669	0.129529	0.130397	0.131272
12.250	0.128250	0.129100	0.129957	0.130822	0.131694	0.132574
12.375	0.129530	0.130384	0.131246	0.132115	0.132992	0.133876
12.500	0.130810	0.131668	0.132534	0.133408	0.134289	0.135179
12.625	0.132089	0.132952	0.133823	0.134701	0.135587	0.136481
12.750	0.133369	0.134237	0.135112	0.135995	0.136885	0.137784
12.875	0.134649	0.135521	0.136401	0.137288	0.138184	0.139087

TABLE III-17. Annual Percentage Rate with a 20-Year Mortgage

ANNUAL PERCENTAGE RATE TABLE
TERM OF MORTGAGE 20 YEARS

CONTRACT INTEREST RATE \ POINTS CHARGED	3.50	4.00	4.50	5.00	5.50	6.00
13.000	0.135929	0.136806	0.137690	0.138582	0.139482	0.140390
13.125	0.137210	0.138091	0.138980	0.139876	0.140781	0.141694
13.250	0.138490	0.139376	0.140269	0.141171	0.142080	0.142998
13.375	0.139771	0.140661	0.141559	0.142465	0.143379	0.144302
13.500	0.141052	0.141946	0.142849	0.143760	0.144679	0.145606
13.625	0.142332	0.143232	0.144139	0.145055	0.145979	0.146911
13.750	0.143613	0.144518	0.145430	0.146350	0.147278	0.148215
13.875	0.144895	0.145803	0.146720	0.147645	0.148579	0.149520
14.000	0.146176	0.147089	0.148011	0.148941	0.149879	0.150826
14.125	0.147457	0.148375	0.149302	0.150236	0.151179	0.152131
14.250	0.148739	0.149662	0.150593	0.151532	0.152480	0.153437
14.375	0.150021	0.150948	0.151884	0.152828	0.153781	0.154743
14.500	0.151302	0.152235	0.153175	0.154125	0.155082	0.156049
14.625	0.152584	0.153521	0.154467	0.155421	0.156384	0.157356
14.750	0.153866	0.154808	0.155759	0.156718	0.157686	0.158662
14.875	0.155149	0.156095	0.157051	0.158015	0.158987	0.159969
15.000	0.156431	0.157383	0.158343	0.159312	0.160289	0.161276
15.125	0.157713	0.158670	0.159635	0.160609	0.161592	0.162584
15.250	0.158996	0.159957	0.160927	0.161906	0.162894	0.163891
15.375	0.160279	0.161245	0.162220	0.163204	0.164197	0.165199
15.500	0.161562	0.162533	0.163513	0.164502	0.165500	0.166507
15.625	0.162845	0.163821	0.164806	0.165800	0.166803	0.167815
15.750	0.164128	0.165109	0.166099	0.167098	0.168106	0.169124
15.875	0.165411	0.166397	0.167392	0.168396	0.169410	0.170433
16.000	0.166694	0.167685	0.168685	0.169695	0.170713	0.171742
16.125	0.167978	0.168974	0.169979	0.170994	0.172017	0.173051
16.250	0.169261	0.170263	0.171273	0.172292	0.173321	0.174360
16.375	0.170545	0.171551	0.172567	0.173591	0.174626	0.175670
16.500	0.171829	0.172840	0.173861	0.174891	0.175930	0.176980
16.625	0.173113	0.174129	0.175155	0.176190	0.177235	0.178290
16.750	0.174397	0.175419	0.176449	0.177490	0.178540	0.179600
16.875	0.175681	0.176708	0.177744	0.178790	0.179845	0.180910
17.000	0.176966	0.177997	0.179039	0.180090	0.181150	0.182221
17.125	0.178250	0.179287	0.180333	0.181390	0.182456	0.183532
17.250	0.179535	0.180577	0.181628	0.182690	0.183761	0.184843
17.375	0.180820	0.181867	0.182924	0.183990	0.185067	0.186154
17.500	0.182104	0.183157	0.184219	0.185291	0.186373	0.187466
17.625	0.183389	0.184447	0.185514	0.186592	0.187680	0.188778
17.750	0.184674	0.185737	0.186810	0.187893	0.188986	0.190090
17.875	0.185960	0.187028	0.188106	0.189194	0.190293	0.191402

TABLE III-18. Annual Percentage Rate with a 20-Year Mortgage

ANNUAL PERCENTAGE RATE TABLE
TERM OF MORTGAGE 20 YEARS

CONTRACT INTEREST RATE \ POINTS CHARGED	3.50	4.00	4.50	5.00	5.50	6.00
18.000	0.187245	0.188318	0.189402	0.190495	0.191599	0.192714
18.125	0.188530	0.189609	0.190698	0.191797	0.192906	0.194027
18.250	0.189816	0.190900	0.191994	0.193099	0.194214	0.195339
18.375	0.191101	0.192191	0.193290	0.194400	0.195521	0.196652
18.500	0.192387	0.193482	0.194587	0.195702	0.196828	0.197965
18.625	0.193673	0.194773	0.195883	0.197004	0.198136	0.199279
18.750	0.194959	0.196064	0.197180	0.198307	0.199444	0.200592
18.875	0.196245	0.197356	0.198477	0.199609	0.200752	0.201906
19.000	0.197531	0.198647	0.199774	0.200912	0.202060	0.203220
19.125	0.198817	0.199939	0.201071	0.202215	0.203369	0.204534
19.250	0.200104	0.201231	0.202369	0.203517	0.204677	0.205848
19.375	0.201390	0.202523	0.203666	0.204820	0.205986	0.207163
19.500	0.202677	0.203815	0.204964	0.206124	0.207295	0.208477
19.625	0.203964	0.205107	0.206262	0.207427	0.208604	0.209792
19.750	0.205250	0.206399	0.207559	0.208731	0.209913	0.211107
19.875	0.206537	0.207692	0.208857	0.210034	0.211222	0.212422
20.000	0.207824	0.208984	0.210156	0.211338	0.212532	0.213738
20.125	0.209111	0.210277	0.211454	0.212642	0.213842	0.215053
20.250	0.210399	0.211570	0.212752	0.213946	0.215152	0.216369
20.375	0.211686	0.212863	0.214051	0.215250	0.216462	0.217685
20.500	0.212973	0.214156	0.215349	0.216555	0.217772	0.219001
20.625	0.214261	0.215449	0.216648	0.217859	0.219082	0.220317
20.750	0.215548	0.216742	0.217947	0.219164	0.220393	0.221633
20.875	0.216836	0.218035	0.219246	0.220469	0.221703	0.222950
21.000	0.218124	0.219329	0.220545	0.221774	0.223014	0.224267
21.125	0.219412	0.220622	0.221845	0.223079	0.224325	0.225584
21.250	0.220700	0.221916	0.223144	0.224384	0.225636	0.226901
21.375	0.221988	0.223210	0.224443	0.225689	0.226947	0.228218
21.500	0.223276	0.224504	0.225743	0.226995	0.228259	0.229535
21.625	0.224564	0.225797	0.227043	0.228300	0.229570	0.230853
21.750	0.225852	0.227092	0.228343	0.229606	0.230882	0.232171
21.875	0.227141	0.228386	0.229643	0.230912	0.232194	0.233488
22.000	0.228429	0.229680	0.230943	0.232218	0.233506	0.234806
22.125	0.229718	0.230974	0.232243	0.233524	0.234818	0.236125
22.250	0.231007	0.232269	0.233543	0.234830	0.236130	0.237443
22.375	0.232295	0.233563	0.234844	0.236137	0.237443	0.238761
22.500	0.233584	0.234858	0.236144	0.237443	0.238755	0.240080
22.625	0.234873	0.236153	0.237445	0.238750	0.240068	0.241399
22.750	0.236162	0.237448	0.238746	0.240057	0.241381	0.242718
22.875	0.237451	0.238743	0.240047	0.241364	0.242693	0.244037

TABLE III-19. Annual Percentage Rate with a 20-Year Mortgage

ANNUAL PERCENTAGE RATE TABLE
TERM OF MORTGAGE 20 YEARS

CONTRACT INTEREST RATE \ POINTS CHARGED	6.50	7.00	7.50	8.00	8.50	9.00
8.000	0.089200	0.089949	0.090704	0.091466	0.092234	0.C93008
8.125	0.090497	0.091250	0.092009	0.092775	0.093547	0.094326
8.250	0.091795	0.092551	0.093314	0.094084	0.094860	0.095643
8.375	0.093092	0.093853	0.094620	0.095394	0.096174	0.C96961
8.500	0.094390	0.095155	0.095926	0.096704	0.097488	0.C98280
8.625	0.095689	0.096457	0.097232	0.098014	0.098803	0.099599
8.750	0.096987	0.097760	0.098539	0.099325	0.100118	0.100918
8.875	0.098286	0.099063	0.099846	0.100636	0.101433	0.102238
9.000	0.099585	0.100366	0.101154	0.101948	0.102749	0.103558
9.125	0.100884	0.101669	0.102461	0.103260	0.104065	0.104878
9.250	0.102184	0.102973	0.103769	0.104572	0.105382	0.106199
9.375	0.103484	0.104277	0.105078	0.105885	0.106699	0.107520
9.500	0.104784	0.105582	0.106386	0.107198	0.108016	0.108842
9.625	0.106085	0.106887	0.107695	0.108511	0.109334	0.110164
9.750	0.107386	0.108192	0.109005	0.109825	0.110652	0.111487
9.875	0.108687	0.109497	0.110314	0.111139	0.111971	0.112810
10.000	0.109988	0.110803	0.111624	0.112453	0.113290	0.114133
10.125	0.111290	0.112109	0.112935	0.113768	0.114609	0.115457
10.250	0.112592	0.113415	0.114246	0.115083	0.115928	0.116781
10.375	0.113894	0.114722	0.115557	0.116399	0.117249	0.118106
10.500	0.115197	0.116029	0.116868	0.117715	0.118569	0.119431
10.625	0.116500	0.117336	0.118180	0.119031	0.119890	0.120756
10.750	0.117803	0.118644	0.119492	0.120347	0.121211	0.122082
10.875	0.119106	0.119951	0.120804	0.121664	0.122532	0.123408
11.000	0.120410	0.121260	0.122117	0.122982	0.123854	0.124735
11.125	0.121714	0.122568	0.123430	0.124299	0.125177	0.126062
11.250	0.123018	0.123877	0.124743	0.125617	0.126499	0.127390
11.375	0.124323	0.125186	0.126057	0.126936	0.127823	0.128717
11.500	0.125627	0.126495	0.127371	0.128254	0.129146	0.130046
11.625	0.126932	0.127805	0.128685	0.129573	0.130470	0.131374
11.750	0.128238	0.129115	0.130000	0.130893	0.131794	0.132703
11.875	0.129543	0.130425	0.131315	0.132213	0.133119	0.134033
12.000	0.130849	0.131736	0.132630	0.133533	0.134444	0.135363
12.125	0.132156	0.133047	0.133946	0.134853	0.135769	0.136693
12.250	0.133462	0.134358	0.135262	0.136174	0.137095	0.138024
12.375	0.134769	0.135669	0.136578	0.137495	0.138421	0.139355
12.500	0.136076	0.136981	0.137895	0.138817	0.139747	0.140686
12.625	0.137383	0.138293	0.139212	0.140138	0.141074	0.142018
12.750	0.138691	0.139606	0.140529	0.141461	0.142401	0.143350
12.875	0.139999	0.140918	0.141846	0.142783	0.143728	0.144683

TABLE III-20. Annual Percentage Rate with a 20-Year Mortgage

ANNUAL PERCENTAGE RATE TABLE
TERM OF MORTGAGE 20 YEARS

CONTRACT INTEREST RATE \ POINTS CHARGED	6.50	7.00	7.50	8.00	8.50	9.00
13.000	0.141307	0.142231	0.143164	0.144106	0.145056	0.146016
13.125	0.142615	0.143545	0.144483	0.145429	0.146385	0.147349
13.250	0.143924	0.144858	0.145801	0.146753	0.147713	0.148683
13.375	0.145233	0.146172	0.147120	0.148077	0.149042	0.150017
13.500	0.146542	0.147486	0.148439	0.149401	0.150371	0.151351
13.625	0.147851	0.148800	0.149758	0.150725	0.151701	0.152686
13.750	0.149161	0.150115	0.151078	0.152050	0.153031	0.154022
13.875	0.150471	0.151430	0.152398	0.153375	0.154362	0.155357
14.000	0.151781	0.152745	0.153719	0.154701	0.155692	0.156693
14.125	0.153092	0.154061	0.155039	0.156027	0.157023	0.158030
14.250	0.154402	0.155377	0.156360	0.157353	0.158355	0.159366
14.375	0.155713	0.156693	0.157681	0.158679	0.159687	0.160704
14.500	0.157025	0.158009	0.159003	0.160006	0.161019	0.162041
14.625	0.158336	0.159326	0.160325	0.161333	0.162351	0.163379
14.750	0.159648	0.160643	0.161647	0.162661	0.163684	0.164717
14.875	0.160960	0.161960	0.162970	0.163989	0.165017	0.166056
15.000	0.162272	0.163278	0.164292	0.165317	0.166351	0.167395
15.125	0.163585	0.164595	0.165615	0.166645	0.167685	0.168734
15.250	0.164898	0.165913	0.166939	0.167974	0.169019	0.170074
15.375	0.166211	0.167232	0.168262	0.169303	0.170353	0.171414
15.500	0.167524	0.168550	0.169586	0.170632	0.171688	0.172754
15.625	0.168837	0.169869	0.170910	0.171962	0.173023	0.174095
15.750	0.170151	0.171188	0.172235	0.173292	0.174359	0.175436
15.875	0.171465	0.172508	0.173560	0.174622	0.175695	0.176777
16.000	0.172779	0.173827	0.174885	0.175953	0.177031	0.178119
16.125	0.174094	0.175147	0.176210	0.177283	0.178367	0.179461
16.250	0.175409	0.176467	0.177536	0.178615	0.179704	0.180804
16.375	0.176724	0.177788	0.178862	0.179946	0.181041	0.182147
16.500	0.178039	0.179108	0.180188	0.181278	0.182378	0.183490
16.625	0.179354	0.180429	0.181514	0.182610	0.183716	0.184833
16.750	0.180670	0.181750	0.182841	0.183942	0.185054	0.186177
16.875	0.181986	0.183072	0.184168	0.185275	0.186393	0.187521
17.000	0.183302	0.184393	0.185495	0.186608	0.187731	0.188866
17.125	0.184619	0.185715	0.186823	0.187941	0.189070	0.190211
17.250	0.185935	0.187038	0.188151	0.189275	0.190410	0.191556
17.375	0.187252	0.188360	0.189479	0.190608	0.191749	0.192901
17.500	0.188569	0.189683	0.190807	0.191943	0.193089	0.194247
17.625	0.189886	0.191006	0.192136	0.193277	0.194429	0.195593
17.750	0.191204	0.192329	0.193465	0.194612	0.195770	0.196940
17.875	0.192522	0.193652	0.194794	0.195946	0.197111	0.198286

TABLE III-21. Annual Percentage Rate with a 20-Year Mortgage

ANNUAL PERCENTAGE RATE TABLE
TERM OF MORTGAGE 20 YEARS

CONTRACT INTEREST RATE \ POINTS CHARGED	6.50	7.00	7.50	8.00	8.50	9.00
18.000	0.193839	0.194976	0.196123	0.197282	0.198452	0.199633
18.125	0.195158	0.196300	0.197453	0.198617	0.199793	0.200981
18.250	0.196476	0.197624	0.198783	0.199953	0.201135	0.202328
18.375	0.197795	0.198948	0.200113	0.201289	0.202477	0.203676
18.500	0.199113	0.200273	0.201443	0.202625	0.203819	0.205025
18.625	0.200432	0.201597	0.202774	0.203962	0.205161	0.206373
18.750	0.201752	0.202922	0.204105	0.205298	0.206504	0.207722
18.875	0.203071	0.204248	0.205436	0.206635	0.207847	0.209071
19.000	0.204391	0.205573	0.206767	0.207973	0.209191	0.210421
19.125	0.205711	0.206899	0.208099	0.209310	0.210534	0.211770
19.250	0.207031	0.208225	0.209430	0.210648	0.211878	0.213121
19.375	0.208351	0.209551	0.210762	0.211986	0.213222	0.214471
19.500	0.209671	0.210877	0.212095	0.213325	0.214567	0.215821
19.625	0.210992	0.212204	0.213427	0.214663	0.215911	0.217172
19.750	0.212313	0.213530	0.214760	0.216002	0.217256	0.218524
19.875	0.213634	0.214857	0.216093	0.217341	0.218602	0.219875
20.000	0.214955	0.216185	0.217426	0.218680	0.219947	0.221227
20.125	0.216277	0.217512	0.218760	0.220020	0.221293	0.222579
20.250	0.217598	0.218840	0.220093	0.221360	0.222639	0.223931
20.375	0.218920	0.220167	0.221427	0.222700	0.223985	0.225284
20.500	0.220242	0.221495	0.222761	0.224040	0.225332	0.226636
20.625	0.221564	0.222824	0.224096	0.225381	0.226678	0.227990
20.750	0.222887	0.224152	0.225430	0.226721	0.228025	0.229343
20.875	0.224209	0.225481	0.226765	0.228062	0.229373	0.230697
21.000	0.225532	0.226809	0.228100	0.229403	0.230720	0.232050
21.125	0.226855	0.228138	0.229435	0.230745	0.232068	0.233405
21.250	0.228178	0.229468	0.230770	0.232086	0.233416	0.234759
21.375	0.229501	0.230797	0.232106	0.233428	0.234764	0.236113
21.500	0.230825	0.232127	0.233442	0.234770	0.236112	0.237468
21.625	0.232148	0.233456	0.234778	0.236113	0.237461	0.238824
21.750	0.233472	0.234786	0.236114	0.237455	0.238810	0.240179
21.875	0.234796	0.236116	0.237450	0.238798	0.240159	0.241534
22.000	0.236120	0.237447	0.238787	0.240141	0.241509	0.242890
22.125	0.237444	0.238777	0.240124	0.241484	0.242858	0.244246
22.250	0.238769	0.240108	0.241461	0.242827	0.244208	0.245603
22.375	0.240093	0.241439	0.242798	0.244171	0.245558	0.246959
22.500	0.241418	0.242770	0.244135	0.245515	0.246908	0.248316
22.625	0.242743	0.244101	0.245473	0.246859	0.248259	0.249673
22.750	0.244068	0.245432	0.246810	0.248203	0.249609	0.251030
22.875	0.245393	0.246764	0.248148	0.249547	0.250960	0.252388

TABLE III-22. Annual Percentage Rate with a 20-Year Mortgage

ANNUAL PERCENTAGE RATE TABLE
TERM OF MORTGAGE 20 YEARS

CONTRACT INTEREST RATE / POINTS CHARGED	9.50	10.00	10.50	11.00	11.50	12.00
8.000	0.093790	0.094578	0.095373	0.096175	0.096985	0.097801
8.125	0.095111	0.095904	0.096703	0.097510	0.098323	0.099144
8.250	0.096433	0.097230	0.098033	0.098844	0.099662	0.100488
8.375	0.097755	0.098556	0.099364	0.100180	0.101002	0.101832
8.500	0.099078	0.099883	0.100696	0.101515	0.102342	0.103177
8.625	0.100401	0.101211	0.102027	0.102852	0.103683	0.104522
8.750	0.101725	0.102539	0.103360	0.104188	0.105024	0.105868
8.875	0.103049	0.103867	0.104693	0.105526	0.106366	0.107214
9.000	0.104373	0.105196	0.106026	0.106863	0.107709	0.108561
9.125	0.105698	0.106525	0.107360	0.108202	0.109051	0.109909
9.250	0.107023	0.107855	0.108694	0.109541	0.110395	0.111257
9.375	0.108349	0.109185	0.110029	0.110880	0.111739	0.112606
9.500	0.109675	0.110516	0.111364	0.112220	0.113084	0.113955
9.625	0.111002	0.111847	0.112700	0.113560	0.114429	0.115305
9.750	0.112329	0.113179	0.114036	0.114901	0.115774	0.116656
9.875	0.113656	0.114511	0.115373	0.116243	0.117121	0.118007
10.000	0.114984	0.115843	0.116710	0.117585	0.118467	0.119358
10.125	0.116313	0.117176	0.118048	0.118927	0.119815	0.120710
10.250	0.117642	0.118510	0.119386	0.120270	0.121163	0.122063
10.375	0.118971	0.119844	0.120725	0.121614	0.122511	0.123417
10.500	0.120301	0.121178	0.122064	0.122958	0.123860	0.124770
10.625	0.121631	0.122513	0.123404	0.124302	0.125209	0.126125
10.750	0.122961	0.123848	0.124744	0.125647	0.126559	0.127480
10.875	0.124292	0.125184	0.126084	0.126993	0.127910	0.128836
11.000	0.125624	0.126520	0.127425	0.128339	0.129261	0.130192
11.125	0.126955	0.127857	0.128767	0.129685	0.130613	0.131548
11.250	0.128288	0.129194	0.130109	0.131033	0.131965	0.132906
11.375	0.129620	0.130532	0.131452	0.132380	0.133317	0.134263
11.500	0.130954	0.131870	0.132795	0.133728	0.134671	0.135622
11.625	0.132287	0.133208	0.134138	0.135077	0.136024	0.136981
11.750	0.133621	0.134547	0.135482	0.136426	0.137379	0.138340
11.875	0.134955	0.135887	0.136827	0.137776	0.138733	0.139700
12.000	0.136290	0.137227	0.138172	0.139126	0.140089	0.141061
12.125	0.137625	0.138567	0.139517	0.140476	0.141445	0.142422
12.250	0.138961	0.139908	0.140863	0.141827	0.142801	0.143784
12.375	0.140297	0.141249	0.142209	0.143179	0.144158	0.145146
12.500	0.141634	0.142590	0.143556	0.144531	0.145515	0.146509
12.625	0.142971	0.143932	0.144903	0.145884	0.146873	0.147872
12.750	0.144308	0.145275	0.146251	0.147237	0.148232	0.149236
12.875	0.145646	0.146618	0.147599	0.148590	0.149591	0.150601

TABLE III-23. Annual Percentage Rate with a 20-Year Mortgage

ANNUAL PERCENTAGE RATE TABLE
TERM OF MORTGAGE 20 YEARS

CONTRACT INTEREST RATE \ POINTS CHARGED	9.50	10.00	10.50	11.00	11.50	12.00
13.000	0.146984	0.147961	0.148948	0.149944	0.150950	0.151966
13.125	0.148322	0.149305	0.150297	0.151299	0.152310	0.153331
13.250	0.149661	0.150649	0.151647	0.152654	0.153670	0.154697
13.375	0.151001	0.151994	0.152997	0.154009	0.155031	0.156064
13.500	0.152341	0.153339	0.154347	0.155365	0.156393	0.157431
13.625	0.153681	0.154685	0.155698	0.156722	0.157755	0.158798
13.750	0.155021	0.156031	0.157050	0.158078	0.159117	0.160167
13.875	0.156362	0.157377	0.158401	0.159436	0.160480	0.161535
14.000	0.157704	0.158724	0.159754	0.160794	0.161844	0.162905
14.125	0.159045	0.160071	0.161106	0.162152	0.163208	0.164274
14.250	0.160388	0.161419	0.162460	0.163511	0.164572	0.165644
14.375	0.161730	0.162767	0.163813	0.164870	0.165937	0.167015
14.500	0.163073	0.164115	0.165167	0.166230	0.167303	0.168386
14.625	0.164416	0.165464	0.166522	0.167590	0.168669	0.169758
14.750	0.165760	0.166813	0.167877	0.168951	0.170035	0.171131
14.875	0.167104	0.168163	0.169232	0.170312	0.171402	0.172503
15.000	0.168449	0.169513	0.170588	0.171673	0.172769	0.173877
15.125	0.169794	0.170864	0.171944	0.173035	0.174137	0.175250
15.250	0.171139	0.172215	0.173301	0.174398	0.175506	0.176625
15.375	0.172485	0.173566	0.174658	0.175761	0.176874	0.177999
15.500	0.173831	0.174918	0.176015	0.177124	0.178244	0.179375
15.625	0.175177	0.176270	0.177373	0.178488	0.179613	0.180750
15.750	0.176524	0.177622	0.178732	0.179852	0.180984	0.182127
15.875	0.177871	0.178975	0.180090	0.181217	0.182354	0.183503
16.000	0.179218	0.180328	0.181450	0.182582	0.183725	0.184881
16.125	0.180566	0.181682	0.182809	0.183947	0.185097	0.186258
16.250	0.181915	0.183036	0.184169	0.185313	0.186469	0.187636
16.375	0.183263	0.184391	0.185529	0.186680	0.187841	0.189015
16.500	0.184612	0.185746	0.186890	0.188046	0.189214	0.190394
16.625	0.185961	0.187101	0.188251	0.189414	0.190588	0.191774
16.750	0.187311	0.188456	0.189613	0.190781	0.191961	0.193154
16.875	0.188661	0.189812	0.190975	0.192149	0.193336	0.194534
17.000	0.190011	0.191169	0.192337	0.193518	0.194710	0.195915
17.125	0.191362	0.192525	0.193700	0.194887	0.196085	0.197297
17.250	0.192713	0.193882	0.195063	0.196256	0.197461	0.198678
17.375	0.194065	0.195240	0.196427	0.197626	0.198837	0.200061
17.500	0.195416	0.196598	0.197791	0.198996	0.200213	0.201443
17.625	0.196769	0.197956	0.199155	0.200366	0.201590	0.202827
17.750	0.198121	0.199314	0.200520	0.201737	0.202967	0.204210
17.875	0.199474	0.200673	0.201885	0.203109	0.204345	0.205594

TABLE III-24. Annual Percentage Rate with a 20-Year Mortgage

ANNUAL PERCENTAGE RATE TABLE
TERM OF MORTGAGE 20 YEARS

CONTRACT INTEREST RATE \ POINTS CHARGED	9.50	10.00	10.50	11.00	11.50	12.00
18.000	0.200827	0.202032	0.203250	0.204480	0.205723	0.206979
18.125	0.202180	0.203392	0.204616	0.205852	0.207101	C.208364
18.250	0.203534	0.204752	0.205982	0.207225	0.208480	C.209749
18.375	0.204888	0.206112	0.207348	0.208598	0.209860	C.211135
18.500	0.206242	0.207473	0.208715	0.209971	0.211239	C.212521
18.625	0.207597	0.208834	0.210083	0.211344	0.212619	C.213908
18.750	0.208952	0.210195	0.211450	0.212718	0.214000	C.215294
18.875	0.210308	0.211556	0.212818	0.214093	0.215381	0.216682
19.000	0.211663	0.212918	0.214186	0.215467	0.216762	0.218070
19.125	0.213019	0.214281	0.215555	0.216842	0.218143	0.219458
19.250	0.214375	0.215643	0.216924	0.218218	0.219525	C.220847
19.375	0.215732	0.217006	0.218293	0.219594	0.220908	0.222236
19.500	0.217089	0.218369	0.219663	0.220970	0.222291	0.223625
19.625	0.218446	0.219733	0.221033	0.222346	0.223674	C.225015
19.750	0.219804	0.221097	0.222403	0.223723	0.225057	0.226405
19.875	0.221161	0.222461	0.223774	0.225100	0.226441	C.227796
20.000	0.222519	0.223825	0.225145	0.226478	0.227825	0.229187
20.125	0.223878	0.225190	0.226516	0.227856	0.229210	C.230578
20.250	0.225236	0.226555	0.227888	0.229234	0.230595	C.231970
20.375	0.226595	0.227921	0.229260	0.230613	0.231980	0.233362
20.500	0.227955	0.229286	0.230632	0.231992	0.233366	C.234754
20.625	0.229314	0.230652	0.232005	0.233371	0.234752	C.236147
20.750	0.230674	0.232019	0.233377	0.234750	0.236138	0.237540
20.875	0.232034	0.233385	0.234751	0.236130	0.237525	0.238934
21.000	0.233394	0.234752	0.236124	0.237511	0.238912	C.240328
21.125	0.234755	0.236119	0.237498	0.238891	0.240299	C.241722
21.250	0.236116	0.237487	0.238872	0.240272	0.241687	0.243116
21.375	0.237477	0.238854	0.240246	0.241653	0.243075	C.244511
21.500	0.238838	0.240222	0.241621	0.243034	0.244463	0.245907
21.625	0.240200	0.241591	0.242996	0.244416	0.245852	0.247302
21.750	0.241562	0.242959	0.244371	0.245798	0.247240	C.248698
21.875	0.242924	0.244328	0.245747	0.247181	0.248630	0.250094
22.000	0.244286	0.245697	0.247123	0.248563	0.250019	0.251491
22.125	0.245649	0.247067	0.248499	0.249946	0.251409	C.252888
22.250	0.247012	0.248436	0.249875	0.251330	0.252799	C.254285
22.375	0.248375	0.249806	0.251252	0.252713	0.254190	0.255683
22.500	0.249739	0.251176	0.252629	0.254097	0.255581	0.257080
22.625	0.251102	0.252547	0.254006	0.255481	0.256972	C.258479
22.750	0.252466	0.253917	0.255384	0.256865	0.258363	0.259877
22.875	0.253830	0.255288	0.256761	0.258250	0.259755	C.261276

TABLE III-25. Annual Percentage Rate with a 30-Year Mortgage

ANNUAL PERCENTAGE RATE TABLE
TERM OF MORTGAGE 30 YEARS

CONTRACT INTEREST RATE / POINTS CHARGED	0.50	1.00	1.50	2.00	2.50	3.00
8.000	0.080528	0.081061	0.081599	0.082140	0.082687	0.083238
8.125	0.081782	0.082319	0.082861	0.083407	0.083957	0.084512
8.250	0.083037	0.083578	0.084123	0.084673	0.085228	0.085788
8.375	0.084291	0.084836	0.085385	0.085940	0.086499	0.087063
8.500	0.085545	0.086094	0.086648	0.087207	0.087770	0.088338
8.625	0.086799	0.087352	0.087911	0.088473	0.089041	0.089614
8.750	0.088053	0.088611	0.089173	0.089740	0.090313	0.090890
8.875	0.089307	0.089869	0.090436	0.091008	0.091584	0.092165
9.000	0.090561	0.091128	0.091699	0.092275	0.092856	0.093442
9.125	0.091816	0.092386	0.092962	0.093542	0.094127	0.094718
9.250	0.093070	0.093645	0.094225	0.094810	0.095399	0.095994
9.375	0.094324	0.094904	0.095488	0.096077	0.096671	0.097271
9.500	0.095579	0.096162	0.096751	0.097345	0.097944	0.098548
9.625	0.096833	0.097421	0.098014	0.098613	0.099216	0.099825
9.750	0.098087	0.098680	0.099278	0.099880	0.100489	0.101102
9.875	0.099342	0.099939	0.100541	0.101148	0.101761	0.102379
10.000	0.100596	0.101198	0.101805	0.102417	0.103034	0.103657
10.125	0.101851	0.102457	0.103068	0.103685	0.104307	0.104935
10.250	0.103105	0.103716	0.104332	0.104953	0.105580	0.106212
10.375	0.104360	0.104975	0.105596	0.106222	0.106853	0.107490
10.500	0.105614	0.106234	0.106859	0.107490	0.108127	0.108769
10.625	0.106869	0.107493	0.108123	0.108759	0.109400	0.110047
10.750	0.108124	0.108753	0.109387	0.110028	0.110674	0.111325
10.875	0.109378	0.110012	0.110651	0.111296	0.111947	0.112604
11.000	0.110633	0.111271	0.111916	0.112565	0.113221	0.113883
11.125	0.111888	0.112531	0.113180	0.113835	0.114495	0.115162
11.250	0.113142	0.113790	0.114444	0.115104	0.115769	0.116441
11.375	0.114397	0.115050	0.115708	0.116373	0.117044	0.117720
11.500	0.115652	0.116309	0.116973	0.117642	0.118318	0.119000
11.625	0.116907	0.117569	0.118237	0.118912	0.119592	0.120279
11.750	0.118161	0.118829	0.119502	0.120181	0.120867	0.121559
11.875	0.119416	0.120088	0.120767	0.121451	0.122142	0.122839
12.000	0.120671	0.121348	0.122032	0.122721	0.123417	0.124119
12.125	0.121926	0.122608	0.123296	0.123991	0.124692	0.125399
12.250	0.123181	0.123868	0.124561	0.125261	0.125967	0.126679
12.375	0.124436	0.125128	0.125826	0.126531	0.127242	0.127960
12.500	0.125691	0.126388	0.127091	0.127801	0.128517	0.129240
12.625	0.126946	0.127648	0.128356	0.129071	0.129793	0.130521
12.750	0.128201	0.128908	0.129621	0.130342	0.131068	0.131802
12.875	0.129456	0.130168	0.130887	0.131612	0.132344	0.133083

TABLE III-26. Annual Percentage Rate with a 30-Year Mortgage

ANNUAL PERCENTAGE RATE TABLE
TERM OF MORTGAGE 30 YEARS

CONTRACT INTEREST RATE \ POINTS CHARGED	0.50	1.00	1.50	2.00	2.50	3.00
13.000	0.130711	0.131428	0.132152	0.132883	0.133620	0.134364
13.125	0.131966	0.132688	0.133417	0.134153	0.134896	0.135646
13.250	0.133221	0.133949	0.134683	0.135424	0.136172	0.136927
13.375	0.134476	0.135209	0.135948	0.136695	0.137448	0.138208
13.500	0.135731	0.136469	0.137214	0.137966	0.138724	0.139490
13.625	0.136986	0.137730	0.138480	0.139237	0.140001	0.140772
13.750	0.138242	0.138990	0.139745	0.140508	0.141277	0.142054
13.875	0.139497	0.140250	0.141011	0.141779	0.142554	0.143336
14.000	0.140752	0.141511	0.142277	0.143050	0.143830	0.144618
14.125	0.142007	0.142771	0.143543	0.144321	0.145107	0.145900
14.250	0.143262	0.144032	0.144809	0.145593	0.146384	0.147183
14.375	0.144518	0.145292	0.146075	0.146864	0.147661	0.148465
14.500	0.145773	0.146553	0.147341	0.148135	0.148938	0.149748
14.625	0.147028	0.147814	0.148607	0.149407	0.150215	0.151031
14.750	0.148284	0.149074	0.149873	0.150679	0.151492	0.152314
14.875	0.149539	0.150335	0.151139	0.151950	0.152770	0.153597
15.000	0.150794	0.151596	0.152405	0.153222	0.154047	0.154880
15.125	0.152050	0.152857	0.153672	0.154494	0.155325	0.156163
15.250	0.153305	0.154118	0.154938	0.155766	0.156602	0.157446
15.375	0.154560	0.155379	0.156204	0.157038	0.157880	0.158730
15.500	0.155816	0.156639	0.157471	0.158310	0.159158	0.160013
15.625	0.157071	0.157900	0.158737	0.159582	0.160435	0.161297
15.750	0.158327	0.159161	0.160004	0.160855	0.161713	0.162580
15.875	0.159582	0.160422	0.161271	0.162127	0.162991	0.163864
16.000	0.160838	0.161683	0.162537	0.163399	0.164269	0.165148
16.125	0.162093	0.162945	0.163804	0.164672	0.165548	0.166432
16.250	0.163349	0.164206	0.165071	0.165944	0.166826	0.167716
16.375	0.164604	0.165467	0.166338	0.167217	0.168104	0.169001
16.500	0.165860	0.166728	0.167604	0.168489	0.169383	0.170285
16.625	0.167115	0.167989	0.168871	0.169762	0.170661	0.171569
16.750	0.168371	0.169250	0.170138	0.171035	0.171940	0.172854
16.875	0.169627	0.170512	0.171405	0.172307	0.173218	0.174138
17.000	0.170882	0.171773	0.172672	0.173580	0.174497	0.175423
17.125	0.172138	0.173034	0.173939	0.174853	0.175776	0.176708
17.250	0.173394	0.174296	0.175206	0.176126	0.177055	0.177992
17.375	0.174649	0.175557	0.176474	0.177399	0.178334	0.179277
17.500	0.175905	0.176818	0.177741	0.178672	0.179613	0.180562
17.625	0.177161	0.178080	0.179008	0.179945	0.180892	0.181847
17.750	0.178416	0.179341	0.180275	0.181218	0.182171	0.183132
17.875	0.179672	0.180603	0.181543	0.182492	0.183450	0.184418

TABLE III-27. Annual Percentage Rate with a 30-Year Mortgage

ANNUAL PERCENTAGE RATE TABLE
TERM OF MORTGAGE 30 YEARS

CONTRACT INTEREST RATE / POINTS CHARGED	0.50	1.00	1.50	2.00	2.50	3.00
18.000	0.180928	0.181864	0.182810	0.183765	0.184729	0.185703
18.125	0.182183	0.183126	0.184077	0.185038	0.186008	0.186988
18.250	0.183439	0.184387	0.185345	0.186311	0.187288	0.188274
18.375	0.184695	0.185649	0.186612	0.187585	0.188567	0.189559
18.500	0.185951	0.186910	0.187880	0.188858	0.189847	0.190845
18.625	0.187206	0.188172	0.189147	0.190132	0.191126	0.192130
18.750	0.188462	0.189434	0.190415	0.191405	0.192406	0.193416
18.875	0.189718	0.190695	0.191682	0.192679	0.193685	0.194702
19.000	0.190974	0.191957	0.192950	0.193953	0.194965	0.195988
19.125	0.192230	0.193219	0.194218	0.195226	0.196245	0.197274
19.250	0.193485	0.194480	0.195485	0.196500	0.197525	0.198560
19.375	0.194741	0.195742	0.196753	0.197774	0.198804	0.199846
19.500	0.195997	0.197004	0.198021	0.199047	0.200084	0.201132
19.625	0.197253	0.198266	0.199288	0.200321	0.201364	0.202418
19.750	0.198509	0.199528	0.200556	0.201595	0.202644	0.203704
19.875	0.199765	0.200789	0.201824	0.202869	0.203924	0.204990
20.000	0.201021	0.202051	0.203092	0.204143	0.205204	0.206277
20.125	0.202277	0.203313	0.204360	0.205417	0.206485	0.207563
20.250	0.203532	0.204575	0.205628	0.206691	0.207765	0.208849
20.375	0.204788	0.205837	0.206896	0.207965	0.209045	0.210136
20.500	0.206044	0.207099	0.208164	0.209239	0.210325	0.211422
20.625	0.207300	0.208361	0.209432	0.210513	0.211606	0.212709
20.750	0.208556	0.209623	0.210700	0.211787	0.212886	0.213996
20.875	0.209812	0.210885	0.211968	0.213061	0.214166	0.215282
21.000	0.211068	0.212146	0.213236	0.214336	0.215447	0.216569
21.125	0.212324	0.213408	0.214504	0.215610	0.216727	0.217856
21.250	0.213580	0.214670	0.215772	0.216884	0.218008	0.219142
21.375	0.214836	0.215932	0.217040	0.218158	0.219288	0.220429
21.500	0.216092	0.217195	0.218308	0.219433	0.220569	0.221716
21.625	0.217348	0.218457	0.219576	0.220707	0.221849	0.223003
21.750	0.218604	0.219719	0.220844	0.221982	0.223130	0.224290
21.875	0.219860	0.220981	0.222113	0.223256	0.224411	0.225577
22.000	0.221116	0.222243	0.223381	0.224530	0.225691	0.226864
22.125	0.222372	0.223505	0.224649	0.225805	0.226972	0.228151
22.250	0.223628	0.224767	0.225917	0.227079	0.228253	0.229438
22.375	0.224884	0.226029	0.227186	0.228354	0.229534	0.230726
22.500	0.226140	0.227291	0.228454	0.229628	0.230815	0.232013
22.625	0.227396	0.228553	0.229722	0.230903	0.232095	0.233300
22.750	0.228652	0.229816	0.230991	0.232177	0.233376	0.234587
22.875	0.229908	0.231078	0.232259	0.233452	0.234657	0.235875

TABLE III-28. Annual Percentage Rate with a 30-Year Mortgage

ANNUAL PERCENTAGE RATE TABLE
TERM OF MORTGAGE 30 YEARS

CONTRACT INTEREST RATE / POINTS CHARGED	3.50	4.00	4.50	5.00	5.50	6.00
8.000	0.083793	0.084354	0.084919	0.085489	0.086065	0.086645
8.125	0.085072	0.085637	0.086207	0.086782	0.087361	0.087946
8.250	0.086352	0.086921	0.087495	0.088074	0.088659	0.089248
8.375	0.087631	0.088205	0.088784	0.089368	0.089956	0.090551
8.500	0.088911	0.089489	0.090073	0.090661	0.091254	0.091853
8.625	0.090191	0.090774	0.091362	0.091955	0.092553	0.093156
8.750	0.091472	0.092059	0.092651	0.093249	0.093851	0.094460
8.875	0.092752	0.093344	0.093941	0.094543	0.095150	0.095764
9.000	0.094033	0.094629	0.095231	0.095837	0.096450	0.097068
9.125	0.095314	0.095914	0.096521	0.097132	0.097749	0.098372
9.250	0.096595	0.097200	0.097811	0.098428	0.099050	0.099677
9.375	0.097876	0.098486	0.099102	0.099723	0.100350	0.100982
9.500	0.099157	0.099772	0.100393	0.101019	0.101651	0.102288
9.625	0.100439	0.101059	0.101684	0.102315	0.102952	0.103594
9.750	0.101721	0.102345	0.102976	0.103611	0.104253	0.104900
9.875	0.103003	0.103632	0.104267	0.104908	0.105555	0.106207
10.000	0.104285	0.104919	0.105559	0.106205	0.106856	0.107514
10.125	0.105568	0.106207	0.106852	0.107502	0.108159	0.108821
10.250	0.106851	0.107494	0.108144	0.108800	0.109461	0.110129
10.375	0.108133	0.108782	0.109437	0.110097	0.110764	0.111437
10.500	0.109416	0.110070	0.110730	0.111396	0.112067	0.112746
10.625	0.110700	0.111358	0.112023	0.112694	0.113371	0.114054
10.750	0.111983	0.112647	0.113317	0.113993	0.114675	0.115363
10.875	0.113267	0.113935	0.114610	0.115291	0.115979	0.116673
11.000	0.114551	0.115224	0.115904	0.116591	0.117283	0.117983
11.125	0.115835	0.116513	0.117199	0.117890	0.118588	0.119293
11.250	0.117119	0.117803	0.118493	0.119190	0.119893	0.120603
11.375	0.118403	0.119092	0.119788	0.120490	0.121198	0.121914
11.500	0.119688	0.120382	0.121083	0.121790	0.122504	0.123225
11.625	0.120972	0.121672	0.122378	0.123091	0.123810	0.124536
11.750	0.122257	0.122962	0.123673	0.124391	0.125116	0.125848
11.875	0.123542	0.124252	0.124969	0.125692	0.126423	0.127160
12.000	0.124828	0.125543	0.126265	0.126994	0.127729	0.128472
12.125	0.126113	0.126834	0.127561	0.128295	0.129036	0.129785
12.250	0.127399	0.128124	0.128857	0.129597	0.130344	0.131097
12.375	0.128684	0.129416	0.130154	0.130899	0.131651	0.132411
12.500	0.129970	0.130707	0.131450	0.132201	0.132959	0.133724
12.625	0.131256	0.131998	0.132747	0.133503	0.134267	0.135038
12.750	0.132543	0.133290	0.134044	0.134806	0.135575	0.136352
12.875	0.133829	0.134582	0.135342	0.136109	0.136884	0.137666

TABLE III-29. Annual Percentage Rate with a 30-Year Mortgage

ANNUAL PERCENTAGE RATE TABLE
TERM OF MORTGAGE 30 YEARS

POINTS CHARGED / CONTRACT INTEREST RATE	3.50	4.00	4.50	5.00	5.50	6.00
13.000	0.135115	0.135874	0.136639	0.137412	0.138193	0.138981
13.125	0.136402	0.137166	0.137937	0.138716	0.139502	0.140295
13.250	0.137689	0.138458	0.139235	0.140019	0.140811	0.141611
13.375	0.138976	0.139751	0.140533	0.141323	0.142121	0.142926
13.500	0.140263	0.141044	0.141832	0.142627	0.143431	0.144242
13.625	0.141551	0.142337	0.143130	0.143932	0.144741	0.145558
13.750	0.142838	0.143630	0.144429	0.145236	0.146051	0.146874
13.875	0.144126	0.144923	0.145728	0.146541	0.147361	0.148190
14.000	0.145413	0.146216	0.147027	0.147846	0.148672	0.149507
14.125	0.146701	0.147510	0.148326	0.149151	0.149983	0.150824
14.250	0.147989	0.148804	0.149626	0.150456	0.151294	0.152141
14.375	0.149278	0.150098	0.150926	0.151762	0.152606	0.153458
14.500	0.150566	0.151392	0.152225	0.153067	0.153917	0.154776
14.625	0.151854	0.152686	0.153525	0.154373	0.155229	0.156094
14.750	0.153143	0.153980	0.154826	0.155679	0.156541	0.157412
14.875	0.154432	0.155275	0.156126	0.156986	0.157854	0.158731
15.000	0.155720	0.156569	0.157426	0.158292	0.159166	0.160049
15.125	0.157009	0.157864	0.158727	0.159599	0.160479	0.161368
15.250	0.158298	0.159159	0.160028	0.160906	0.161792	0.162687
15.375	0.159588	0.160454	0.161329	0.162213	0.163105	0.164006
15.500	0.160877	0.161749	0.162630	0.163520	0.164418	0.165326
15.625	0.162166	0.163045	0.163932	0.164827	0.165732	0.166645
15.750	0.163456	0.164340	0.165233	0.166135	0.167045	0.167965
15.875	0.164746	0.165636	0.166535	0.167442	0.168359	0.169285
16.000	0.166035	0.166932	0.167836	0.168750	0.169673	0.170606
16.125	0.167325	0.168227	0.169138	0.170058	0.170987	0.171926
16.250	0.168615	0.169523	0.170440	0.171367	0.172302	0.173247
16.375	0.169906	0.170820	0.171743	0.172675	0.173616	0.174568
16.500	0.171196	0.172116	0.173045	0.173983	0.174931	0.175889
16.625	0.172486	0.173412	0.174347	0.175292	0.176246	0.177210
16.750	0.173777	0.174709	0.175650	0.176601	0.177561	0.178531
16.875	0.175067	0.176005	0.176953	0.177910	0.178876	0.179853
17.000	0.176358	0.177302	0.178256	0.179219	0.180192	0.181175
17.125	0.177649	0.178599	0.179559	0.180528	0.181507	0.182497
17.250	0.178939	0.179896	0.180862	0.181838	0.182823	0.183819
17.375	0.180230	0.181193	0.182165	0.183147	0.184139	0.185141
17.500	0.181521	0.182490	0.183468	0.184457	0.185455	0.186463
17.625	0.182813	0.183787	0.184772	0.185766	0.186771	0.187786
17.750	0.184104	0.185085	0.186076	0.187076	0.188087	0.189109
17.875	0.185395	0.186382	0.187379	0.188386	0.189404	0.190432

TABLE III-30. Annual Percentage Rate with a 30-Year Mortgage

ANNUAL PERCENTAGE RATE TABLE
TERM OF MORTGAGE 30 YEARS

CONTRACT INTEREST RATE \ POINTS CHARGED	3.50	4.00	4.50	5.00	5.50	6.00
18.000	0.186686	0.187680	0.188683	0.189697	0.190720	0.191755
18.125	0.187978	0.188977	0.189987	0.191007	0.192037	0.193078
18.250	0.189270	0.190275	0.191291	0.192317	0.193354	0.194401
18.375	0.190561	0.191573	0.192595	0.193628	0.194671	0.195725
18.500	0.191853	0.192871	0.193900	0.194939	0.195988	0.197048
18.625	0.193145	0.194169	0.195204	0.196249	0.197305	0.198372
18.750	0.194437	0.195467	0.196508	0.197560	0.198623	0.199696
18.875	0.195729	0.196766	0.197813	0.198871	0.199940	0.201020
19.000	0.197021	0.198064	0.199118	0.200182	0.201258	0.202344
19.125	0.198313	0.199362	0.200423	0.201494	0.202576	0.203669
19.250	0.199605	0.200661	0.201727	0.202805	0.203893	0.204993
19.375	0.200897	0.201959	0.203032	0.204116	0.205211	0.206318
19.500	0.202190	0.203258	0.204337	0.205428	0.206529	0.207642
19.625	0.203482	0.204557	0.205643	0.206739	0.207848	0.208967
19.750	0.204774	0.205856	0.206948	0.208051	0.209166	0.210292
19.875	0.206067	0.207154	0.208253	0.209363	0.210484	0.211617
20.000	0.207360	0.208453	0.209558	0.210675	0.211803	0.212942
20.125	0.208652	0.209752	0.210864	0.211987	0.213121	0.214268
20.250	0.209945	0.211052	0.212169	0.213299	0.214440	0.215593
20.375	0.211238	0.212351	0.213475	0.214611	0.215759	0.216918
20.500	0.212531	0.213650	0.214781	0.215923	0.217078	0.218244
20.625	0.213823	0.214949	0.216087	0.217236	0.218397	0.219570
20.750	0.215116	0.216249	0.217392	0.218548	0.219716	0.220895
20.875	0.216409	0.217548	0.218698	0.219861	0.221035	0.222221
21.000	0.217702	0.218848	0.220004	0.221173	0.222354	0.223547
21.125	0.218996	0.220147	0.221310	0.222486	0.223673	0.224873
21.250	0.220289	0.221447	0.222617	0.223799	0.224993	0.226199
21.375	0.221582	0.222746	0.223923	0.225111	0.226312	0.227526
21.500	0.222875	0.224046	0.225229	0.226424	0.227632	0.228852
21.625	0.224169	0.225346	0.226535	0.227737	0.228951	0.230178
21.750	0.225462	0.226646	0.227842	0.229050	0.230271	0.231505
21.875	0.226755	0.227946	0.229148	0.230363	0.231591	0.232831
22.000	0.228049	0.229246	0.230455	0.231676	0.232911	0.234158
22.125	0.229342	0.230546	0.231761	0.232990	0.234231	0.235485
22.250	0.230636	0.231846	0.233068	0.234303	0.235551	0.236811
22.375	0.231930	0.233146	0.234375	0.235616	0.236871	0.238138
22.500	0.233223	0.234446	0.235681	0.236930	0.238191	0.239465
22.625	0.234517	0.235746	0.236988	0.238243	0.239511	0.240792
22.750	0.235811	0.237046	0.238295	0.239557	0.240831	0.242119
22.875	0.237104	0.238347	0.239602	0.240870	0.242152	0.243447

TABLE III-31. Annual Percentage Rate with a 30-Year Mortgage

ANNUAL PERCENTAGE RATE TABLE
TERM OF MORTGAGE 30 YEARS

CONTRACT INTEREST RATE / POINTS CHARGED	6.50	7.00	7.50	8.00	8.50	9.00
8.000	0.087230	0.087821	0.088417	0.089018	0.089625	0.090238
8.125	0.088536	0.089132	0.089733	0.090339	0.090951	0.091568
8.250	0.089843	0.090443	0.091049	0.091660	0.092277	0.092899
8.375	0.091150	0.091755	0.092365	0.092981	0.093603	0.094230
8.500	0.092457	0.093067	0.093682	0.094303	0.094930	0.095562
8.625	0.093765	0.094380	0.095000	0.095626	0.096257	0.096895
8.750	0.095074	0.095693	0.096318	0.096949	0.097585	0.098228
8.875	0.096382	0.097006	0.097636	0.098272	0.098914	0.099562
9.000	0.097691	0.098320	0.098955	0.099596	0.100243	0.100896
9.125	0.099001	0.099635	0.100275	0.100921	0.101573	0.102231
9.250	0.100310	0.100950	0.101595	0.102246	0.102903	0.103566
9.375	0.101621	0.102265	0.102915	0.103571	0.104234	0.104902
9.500	0.102931	0.103581	0.104236	0.104897	0.105565	0.106239
9.625	0.104242	0.104897	0.105557	0.106224	0.106897	0.107576
9.750	0.105554	0.106213	0.106879	0.107551	0.108229	0.108914
9.875	0.106866	0.107530	0.108201	0.108878	0.109562	0.110252
10.000	0.108178	0.108848	0.109524	0.110206	0.110895	0.111591
10.125	0.109490	0.110165	0.110847	0.111535	0.112229	0.112930
10.250	0.110803	0.111483	0.112170	0.112864	0.113563	0.114270
10.375	0.112116	0.112802	0.113494	0.114193	0.114898	0.115611
10.500	0.113430	0.114121	0.114819	0.115523	0.116234	0.116952
10.625	0.114744	0.115440	0.116143	0.116853	0.117570	0.118293
10.750	0.116059	0.116760	0.117469	0.118184	0.118906	0.119635
10.875	0.117373	0.118080	0.118794	0.119515	0.120243	0.120977
11.000	0.118688	0.119401	0.120120	0.120847	0.121580	0.122320
11.125	0.120004	0.120722	0.121447	0.122179	0.122918	0.123664
11.250	0.121320	0.122043	0.122774	0.123511	0.124256	0.125008
11.375	0.122636	0.123365	0.124101	0.124844	0.125595	0.126353
11.500	0.123952	0.124687	0.125429	0.126178	0.126934	0.127698
11.625	0.125269	0.126009	0.126757	0.127511	0.128273	0.129043
11.750	0.126586	0.127332	0.128085	0.128846	0.129614	0.130389
11.875	0.127904	0.128655	0.129414	0.130180	0.130954	0.131736
12.000	0.129222	0.129979	0.130743	0.131515	0.132295	0.133082
12.125	0.130540	0.131303	0.132073	0.132851	0.133637	0.134430
12.250	0.131859	0.132627	0.133403	0.134187	0.134978	0.135778
12.375	0.133177	0.133952	0.134734	0.135523	0.136321	0.137126
12.500	0.134497	0.135277	0.136064	0.136860	0.137663	0.138475
12.625	0.135816	0.136602	0.137396	0.138197	0.139006	0.139824
12.750	0.137136	0.137928	0.138727	0.139535	0.140350	0.141174
12.875	0.138456	0.139253	0.140059	0.140872	0.141694	0.142524

TABLE III-32. Annual Percentage Rate with a 30-Year Mortgage

ANNUAL PERCENTAGE RATE TABLE
TERM OF MORTGAGE 30 YEARS

CONTRACT INTEREST RATE \ POINTS CHARGED	6.50	7.00	7.50	8.00	8.50	9.00
13.000	0.139776	0.140580	0.141391	0.142211	0.143038	0.143874
13.125	0.141097	0.141906	0.142724	0.143549	0.144383	0.145225
13.250	0.142418	0.143233	0.144057	0.144888	0.145728	0.146577
13.375	0.143739	0.144560	0.145390	0.146228	0.147074	0.147929
13.500	0.145061	0.145888	0.146724	0.147567	0.148420	0.149281
13.625	0.146383	0.147216	0.148057	0.148907	0.149766	0.150633
13.750	0.147705	0.148544	0.149392	0.150248	0.151113	0.151986
13.875	0.149027	0.149873	0.150726	0.151589	0.152460	0.153340
14.000	0.150350	0.151201	0.152061	0.152930	0.153807	0.154694
14.125	0.151673	0.152530	0.153396	0.154271	0.155155	0.156048
14.250	0.152996	0.153860	0.154732	0.155613	0.156503	0.157402
14.375	0.154320	0.155189	0.156068	0.156955	0.157852	0.158757
14.500	0.155643	0.156519	0.157404	0.158298	0.159201	0.160113
14.625	0.156967	0.157849	0.158740	0.159640	0.160550	0.161468
14.750	0.158292	0.159180	0.160077	0.160984	0.161899	0.162824
14.875	0.159616	0.160511	0.161414	0.162327	0.163249	0.164181
15.000	0.160941	0.161842	0.162751	0.163671	0.164599	0.165538
15.125	0.162266	0.163173	0.164089	0.165015	0.165950	0.166895
15.250	0.163591	0.164504	0.165427	0.166359	0.167301	0.168252
15.375	0.164917	0.165836	0.166765	0.167704	0.168652	0.169610
15.500	0.166242	0.167168	0.168104	0.169049	0.170003	0.170968
15.625	0.167568	0.168500	0.169442	0.170394	0.171355	0.172326
15.750	0.168894	0.169833	0.170781	0.171739	0.172707	0.173685
15.875	0.170221	0.171166	0.172120	0.173085	0.174059	0.175044
16.000	0.171547	0.172499	0.173460	0.174431	0.175412	0.176403
16.125	0.172874	0.173832	0.174800	0.175777	0.176765	0.177763
16.250	0.174201	0.175165	0.176139	0.177124	0.178118	0.179123
16.375	0.175528	0.176499	0.177480	0.178470	0.179472	0.180483
16.500	0.176856	0.177833	0.178820	0.179817	0.180825	0.181844
16.625	0.178183	0.179167	0.180161	0.181165	0.182179	0.183204
16.750	0.179511	0.180501	0.181502	0.182512	0.183534	0.184566
16.875	0.180839	0.181836	0.182843	0.183860	0.184888	0.185927
17.000	0.182168	0.183171	0.184184	0.185208	0.186243	0.187289
17.125	0.183496	0.184506	0.185526	0.186556	0.187598	0.188650
17.250	0.184825	0.185841	0.186867	0.187905	0.188953	0.190013
17.375	0.186153	0.187176	0.188209	0.189254	0.190309	0.191375
17.500	0.187482	0.188512	0.189552	0.190602	0.191664	0.192738
17.625	0.188811	0.189847	0.190894	0.191952	0.193020	0.194100
17.750	0.190141	0.191183	0.192237	0.193301	0.194377	0.195464
17.875	0.191470	0.192519	0.193579	0.194650	0.195733	0.196827

TABLE III-33. Annual Percentage Rate with a 30-Year Mortgage

ANNUAL PERCENTAGE RATE TABLE
TERM OF MORTGAGE 30 YEARS

CONTRACT INTEREST RATE / POINTS CHARGED	6.50	7.00	7.50	8.00	8.50	9.00
18.000	0.192800	0.193855	0.194922	0.196000	0.197090	0.198191
18.125	0.194129	0.195192	0.196265	0.197350	0.198446	0.199554
18.250	0.195459	0.196528	0.197609	0.198700	0.199804	0.200918
18.375	0.196789	0.197865	0.198952	0.200051	0.201161	0.202283
18.500	0.198120	0.199202	0.200296	0.201401	0.202518	0.203647
18.625	0.199450	0.200539	0.201640	0.202752	0.203876	0.205012
18.750	0.200781	0.201877	0.202984	0.204103	0.205234	0.206377
18.875	0.202111	0.203214	0.204328	0.205454	0.206592	0.207742
19.000	0.203442	0.204552	0.205672	0.206805	0.207950	0.209107
19.125	0.204773	0.205889	0.207017	0.208157	0.209309	0.210473
19.250	0.206104	0.207227	0.208362	0.209508	0.210667	0.211838
19.375	0.207436	0.208565	0.209707	0.210860	0.212026	0.213204
19.500	0.208767	0.209903	0.211052	0.212212	0.213385	0.214570
19.625	0.210098	0.211242	0.212397	0.213564	0.214744	0.215936
19.750	0.211430	0.212580	0.213742	0.214916	0.216103	0.217303
19.875	0.212762	0.213919	0.215087	0.216269	0.217463	0.218669
20.000	0.214094	0.215257	0.216433	0.217621	0.218822	0.220036
20.125	0.215426	0.216596	0.217779	0.218974	0.220182	0.221403
20.250	0.216758	0.217935	0.219125	0.220327	0.221542	0.222770
20.375	0.218090	0.219274	0.220471	0.221680	0.222902	0.224137
20.500	0.219422	0.220613	0.221817	0.223033	0.224262	0.225505
20.625	0.220755	0.221953	0.223163	0.224386	0.225623	0.226872
20.750	0.222087	0.223292	0.224509	0.225740	0.226983	0.228240
20.875	0.223420	0.224632	0.225856	0.227093	0.228344	0.229608
21.000	0.224753	0.225971	0.227202	0.228447	0.229705	0.230976
21.125	0.226086	0.227311	0.228549	0.229801	0.231065	0.232344
21.250	0.227419	0.228651	0.229896	0.231154	0.232427	0.233712
21.375	0.228752	0.229991	0.231243	0.232508	0.233788	0.235081
21.500	0.230085	0.231331	0.232590	0.233863	0.235149	0.236449
21.625	0.231418	0.232671	0.233937	0.235217	0.236510	0.237818
21.750	0.232751	0.234011	0.235284	0.236571	0.237872	0.239187
21.875	0.234085	0.235352	0.236632	0.237926	0.239234	0.240555
22.000	0.235418	0.236692	0.237979	0.239280	0.240595	0.241924
22.125	0.236752	0.238033	0.239327	0.240635	0.241957	0.243294
22.250	0.238086	0.239373	0.240674	0.241990	0.243319	0.244663
22.375	0.239419	0.240714	0.242022	0.243345	0.244681	0.246032
22.500	0.240753	0.242055	0.243370	0.244699	0.246043	0.247402
22.625	0.242087	0.243395	0.244718	0.246055	0.247406	0.248771
22.750	0.243421	0.244736	0.246066	0.247410	0.248768	0.250141
22.875	0.244755	0.246077	0.247414	0.248765	0.250130	0.251511

TABLE III-34. Annual Percentage Rate with a 30-Year Mortgage

ANNUAL PERCENTAGE RATE TABLE
TERM OF MORTGAGE 30 YEARS

CONTRACT INTEREST RATE \ POINTS CHARGED	9.50	10.00	10.50	11.00	11.50	12.00
8.000	0.090856	0.091480	0.092110	0.092745	0.093387	0.094035
8.125	0.092191	0.092820	0.093455	0.094096	0.094743	0.095396
8.250	0.093527	0.094161	0.094801	0.095447	0.096100	0.096758
8.375	0.094864	0.095503	0.096148	0.096799	0.097457	0.098121
8.500	0.096201	0.096845	0.097495	0.098152	0.098815	0.099485
8.625	0.097538	0.098188	0.098844	0.099506	0.100174	0.100849
8.750	0.098877	0.099532	0.100193	0.100860	0.101534	0.102214
8.875	0.100216	0.100876	0.101542	0.102215	0.102894	0.103580
9.000	0.101555	0.102221	0.102892	0.103571	0.104256	0.104947
9.125	0.102895	0.103566	0.104243	0.104927	0.105618	0.106315
9.250	0.104236	0.104912	0.105595	0.106284	0.106980	0.107683
9.375	0.105578	0.106259	0.106947	0.107642	0.108344	0.109052
9.500	0.106920	0.107607	0.108300	0.109001	0.109708	0.110422
9.625	0.108262	0.108955	0.109654	0.110360	0.111073	0.111793
9.750	0.109605	0.110303	0.111008	0.111720	0.112439	0.113165
9.875	0.110949	0.111653	0.112363	0.113081	0.113805	0.114537
10.000	0.112293	0.113003	0.113719	0.114442	0.115172	0.115910
10.125	0.113638	0.114353	0.115075	0.115804	0.116540	0.117284
10.250	0.114984	0.115704	0.116432	0.117167	0.117909	0.118658
10.375	0.116330	0.117056	0.117789	0.118530	0.119278	0.120034
10.500	0.117676	0.118408	0.119147	0.119894	0.120648	0.121410
10.625	0.119024	0.119761	0.120506	0.121259	0.122019	0.122786
10.750	0.120371	0.121115	0.121866	0.122624	0.123390	0.124164
10.875	0.121719	0.122469	0.123226	0.123990	0.124762	0.125542
11.000	0.123068	0.123824	0.124586	0.125357	0.126135	0.126921
11.125	0.124418	0.125179	0.125947	0.126724	0.127508	0.128301
11.250	0.125768	0.126535	0.127309	0.128092	0.128882	0.129681
11.375	0.127118	0.127891	0.128672	0.129460	0.130257	0.131062
11.500	0.128469	0.129248	0.130035	0.130830	0.131632	0.132444
11.625	0.129820	0.130605	0.131398	0.132199	0.133008	0.133826
11.750	0.131172	0.131963	0.132762	0.133570	0.134385	0.135209
11.875	0.132525	0.133322	0.134127	0.134941	0.135762	0.136593
12.000	0.133878	0.134681	0.135492	0.136312	0.137140	0.137977
12.125	0.135231	0.136041	0.136858	0.137684	0.138519	0.139362
12.250	0.136585	0.137401	0.138225	0.139057	0.139898	0.140748
12.375	0.137940	0.138761	0.139592	0.140430	0.141278	0.142134
12.500	0.139295	0.140123	0.140959	0.141804	0.142658	0.143521
12.625	0.140650	0.141484	0.142327	0.143179	0.144039	0.144908
12.750	0.142006	0.142846	0.143696	0.144554	0.145420	0.146296
12.875	0.143362	0.144209	0.145065	0.145929	0.146802	0.147685

TABLE III-35. Annual Percentage Rate with a 30-Year Mortgage

ANNUAL PERCENTAGE RATE TABLE
TERM OF MORTGAGE 30 YEARS

CONTRACT INTEREST RATE / POINTS CHARGED	9.50	10.00	10.50	11.00	11.50	12.00
13.000	0.144719	0.145572	0.146434	0.147305	0.148185	0.149074
13.125	0.146076	0.146936	0.147804	0.148682	0.149568	0.150464
13.250	0.147434	0.148300	0.149175	0.150059	0.150952	0.151855
13.375	0.148792	0.149664	0.150546	0.151436	0.152336	0.153246
13.500	0.150151	0.151029	0.151917	0.152815	0.153721	0.154637
13.625	0.151510	0.152395	0.153289	0.154193	0.155107	0.156030
13.750	0.152869	0.153761	0.154662	0.155572	0.156492	0.157422
13.875	0.154229	0.155127	0.156035	0.156952	0.157879	0.158816
14.000	0.155589	0.156494	0.157408	0.158332	0.159266	0.160209
14.125	0.156950	0.157861	0.158782	0.159713	0.160653	0.161604
14.250	0.158311	0.159229	0.160157	0.161094	0.162041	0.162999
14.375	0.159672	0.160597	0.161531	0.162475	0.163430	0.164394
14.500	0.161034	0.161966	0.162906	0.163857	0.164818	0.165790
14.625	0.162397	0.163334	0.164282	0.165240	0.166208	0.167186
14.750	0.163759	0.164704	0.165658	0.166623	0.167598	0.168583
14.875	0.165122	0.166073	0.167035	0.168006	0.168988	0.169980
15.000	0.166486	0.167444	0.168412	0.169390	0.170379	0.171378
15.125	0.167849	0.168814	0.169789	0.170774	0.171770	0.172776
15.250	0.169213	0.170185	0.171167	0.172159	0.173162	0.174175
15.375	0.170578	0.171556	0.172545	0.173544	0.174554	0.175574
15.500	0.171943	0.172928	0.173923	0.174929	0.175946	0.176974
15.625	0.173308	0.174300	0.175302	0.176315	0.177339	0.178374
15.750	0.174673	0.175672	0.176681	0.177701	0.178732	0.179775
15.875	0.176039	0.177045	0.178061	0.179088	0.180126	0.181176
16.000	0.177405	0.178418	0.179441	0.180475	0.181520	0.182577
16.125	0.178772	0.179791	0.180821	0.181862	0.182915	0.183979
16.250	0.180138	0.181165	0.182202	0.183250	0.184310	0.185381
16.375	0.181505	0.182539	0.183583	0.184638	0.185705	0.186784
16.500	0.182873	0.183913	0.184964	0.186027	0.187101	0.188187
16.625	0.184241	0.185288	0.186346	0.187416	0.188497	0.189590
16.750	0.185608	0.186663	0.187728	0.188805	0.189893	0.190994
16.875	0.186977	0.188038	0.189110	0.190194	0.191290	0.192398
17.000	0.188345	0.189413	0.190493	0.191584	0.192687	0.193802
17.125	0.189714	0.190789	0.191876	0.192974	0.194085	0.195207
17.250	0.191083	0.192165	0.193259	0.194365	0.195482	0.196612
17.375	0.192453	0.193542	0.194643	0.195756	0.196881	0.198018
17.500	0.193822	0.194918	0.196027	0.197147	0.198279	0.199424
17.625	0.195192	0.196295	0.197411	0.198538	0.199678	0.200830
17.750	0.196562	0.197673	0.198795	0.199930	0.201077	0.202236
17.875	0.197933	0.199050	0.200180	0.201322	0.202476	0.203643

TABLE III-36. Annual Percentage Rate with a 30-Year Mortgage

ANNUAL PERCENTAGE RATE TABLE
TERM OF MORTGAGE 30 YEARS

CONTRACT INTEREST RATE / POINTS CHARGED	9.50	10.00	10.50	11.00	11.50	12.00
18.000	0.199303	0.200428	0.201565	0.202714	0.203876	C.205050
18.125	0.200674	0.201806	0.202950	0.204107	0.205276	0.206458
18.250	0.202045	0.203184	0.204336	0.205499	0.206676	C.207866
18.375	0.203417	0.204563	0.205721	0.206893	0.208077	0.209274
18.500	0.204788	0.205941	0.207107	0.208286	0.209477	C.210682
18.625	0.206160	0.207320	0.208494	0.209680	0.210879	0.212091
18.750	0.207532	0.2087C0	0.209880	0.211073	0.212280	0.213500
18.875	0.208904	0.210079	0.211267	0.212468	0.213682	C.214909
19.0C0	0.210277	0.211459	0.212654	0.213862	0.215083	0.216318
19.125	0.211649	0.212839	0.214041	0.215257	0.216486	C.217728
19.250	0.213022	0.214219	0.215429	0.216651	0.217888	0.219138
19.375	0.214395	0.215599	0.216816	0.218047	0.219291	0.220548
19.5C0	0.215768	0.216980	0.218204	0.219442	0.220693	C.221959
19.625	0.217142	0.218360	0.219592	0.220837	0.222096	0.223370
19.750	0.218515	0.219741	0.220980	0.222233	0.223500	C.224780
19.875	0.219889	0.221122	0.222369	0.223629	0.224903	C.226192
20.000	0.221263	0.222504	0.223758	0.225025	0.226307	0.227603
20.125	0.222637	0.223885	0.225146	0.226422	0.227711	C.229015
20.250	0.224012	0.225267	0.226535	0.227818	0.229115	0.230427
20.375	0.225386	0.226649	0.227925	0.229215	0.230520	C.231839
20.5C0	0.226761	0.228031	0.229314	0.230612	0.231924	0.233251
20.625	0.228136	0.229413	0.2307C4	0.232009	0.233329	C.234663
20.750	0.229511	0.230795	0.232094	0.233406	0.234734	0.236076
20.875	0.230886	0.232178	0.233484	0.234804	0.236139	0.237489
21.000	0.232261	0.233560	0.234874	0.236202	0.237544	0.238902
21.125	0.233636	0.234943	0.236264	0.237599	0.238950	C.240315
21.250	0.235012	0.236326	0.237654	0.238997	0.240355	C.241729
21.375	0.236388	0.237709	0.239045	0.240396	0.241761	0.243142
21.500	0.237764	0.239092	0.240436	0.241794	0.243167	0.244556
21.625	0.239140	0.240476	0.241827	0.243192	0.244574	0.245970
21.750	0.240516	0.241859	0.243218	0.244591	0.245980	0.247384
21.875	0.241892	0.243243	0.244609	0.245990	0.247386	C.248798
22.000	0.243268	0.244627	0.246000	0.247389	0.248793	C.250213
22.125	0.244645	0.246011	0.247392	0.248788	0.250200	C.251628
22.250	0.246021	0.247395	0.248783	0.250187	0.251607	0.253042
22.375	0.247398	0.248779	0.250175	0.251586	0.253014	0.254457
22.5C0	0.248775	0.250163	0.251567	0.252986	0.254421	0.255872
22.625	0.250152	0.251548	0.252959	0.254386	0.255828	0.257287
22.750	0.251529	0.252932	0.254351	0.255785	0.257236	0.258703
22.875	0.252906	0.254317	0.255743	0.257185	0.258643	C.260118

TABLE IV-1. **Graduated Payment Mortgage, FHA Plan I at 12.0% Interest, Graduated at 2.5%**

FHA GRADUATED PAYMENT PLAN I
TERM:30 YEARS INTEREST:12.00% GRADUATED AT 2.50%

PAYMENT AMOUNT	YEAR 1	YEAR 2	YEAR 3	YEAR 4	YEAR 5	YEARS 6-30
50	0.47	0.48	0.50	0.51	0.52	0.53
100	0.94	0.97	0.99	1.01	1.04	1.07
200	1.88	1.93	1.98	2.03	2.08	2.13
300	2.83	2.90	2.97	3.04	3.12	3.20
400	3.77	3.86	3.96	4.06	4.16	4.26
500	4.71	4.83	4.95	5.07	5.20	5.33
600	5.65	5.80	5.94	6.09	6.24	6.40
700	6.60	6.76	6.93	7.10	7.28	7.46
800	7.54	7.73	7.92	8.12	8.32	8.53
900	8.48	8.69	8.91	9.13	9.36	9.60
1,000	9.42	9.66	9.90	10.15	10.40	10.66
2,000	18.85	19.32	19.80	20.30	20.80	21.32
3,000	28.27	28.98	29.70	30.45	31.21	31.99
4,000	37.70	38.64	39.60	40.59	41.61	42.65
5,000	47.12	48.30	49.50	50.74	52.01	53.31
6,000	56.54	57.96	59.41	60.89	62.41	63.97
7,000	65.97	67.62	69.31	71.04	72.81	74.64
8,000	75.39	77.28	79.21	81.19	83.22	85.30
9,000	84.81	86.93	89.11	91.34	93.62	95.96
10,000	94.24	96.59	99.01	101.48	104.02	106.62
15,000	141.36	144.89	148.51	152.23	156.03	159.93
20,000	188.48	193.19	198.02	202.97	208.04	213.24
25,000	235.60	241.49	247.52	253.71	260.05	266.55
30,000	282.71	289.78	297.03	304.45	312.06	319.87
35,000	329.83	338.08	346.53	355.19	364.07	373.18
40,000	376.95	386.38	396.04	405.94	416.08	426.49
45,000	424.07	434.67	445.54	456.68	468.10	479.80
50,000	471.19	482.97	495.04	507.42	520.11	533.11
55,000	518.31	531.27	544.55	558.16	572.12	586.42
60,000	565.43	579.56	594.05	608.90	624.13	639.73
65,000	612.55	627.86	643.56	659.65	676.14	693.04
70,000	659.67	676.16	693.06	710.39	728.15	746.35
75,000	706.79	724.46	742.57	761.13	780.16	799.66
80,000	753.90	772.75	792.07	811.87	832.17	852.97
85,000	801.02	821.05	841.58	862.62	884.18	906.28
90,000	848.14	869.35	891.08	913.36	936.19	959.60
95,000	895.26	917.64	940.58	964.10	988.20	1,012.91
100,000	942.38	965.94	990.09	1,014.84	1,040.21	1,066.22
110,000	1,036.62	1,062.53	1,089.10	1,116.33	1,144.23	1,172.84
120,000	1,130.86	1,159.13	1,188.11	1,217.81	1,248.25	1,279.46
130,000	1,225.10	1,255.72	1,287.12	1,319.29	1,352.28	1,386.08
140,000	1,319.33	1,352.32	1,386.12	1,420.78	1,456.30	1,492.70
150,000	1,413.57	1,448.91	1,485.13	1,522.26	1,560.32	1,599.33
160,000	1,507.81	1,545.50	1,584.14	1,623.75	1,664.34	1,705.95
170,000	1,602.05	1,642.10	1,683.15	1,725.23	1,768.36	1,812.57
180,000	1,696.29	1,738.69	1,782.16	1,826.71	1,872.38	1,919.19
190,000	1,790.52	1,835.29	1,881.17	1,928.20	1,976.40	2,025.81
200,000	1,884.76	1,931.88	1,980.18	2,029.68	2,080.42	2,132.44

TABLE IV-2. **Graduated Payment Mortgage, FHA Plan I at 12.5% Interest, Graduated at 2.5%**

FHA GRADUATED PAYMENT PLAN I
TERM:30 YEARS INTEREST:12.50% GRADUATED AT 2.50%

PAYMENT AMOUNT	YEAR 1	YEAR 2	YEAR 3	YEAR 4	YEAR 5	YEARS 6-30
50	0.49	0.50	0.51	0.53	0.54	0.55
100	0.98	1.00	1.03	1.05	1.08	1.11
200	1.96	2.01	2.06	2.11	2.16	2.21
300	2.94	3.01	3.09	3.16	3.24	3.32
400	3.92	4.01	4.11	4.22	4.32	4.43
500	4.89	5.02	5.14	5.27	5.40	5.54
600	5.87	6.02	6.17	6.32	6.48	6.64
700	6.85	7.02	7.20	7.38	7.56	7.75
800	7.83	8.03	8.23	8.43	8.64	8.86
900	8.81	9.03	9.26	9.49	9.72	9.97
1,000	9.79	10.03	10.28	10.54	10.80	11.07
2,000	19.58	20.07	20.57	21.08	21.61	22.15
3,000	29.36	30.10	30.85	31.62	32.41	33.22
4,000	39.15	40.13	41.13	42.16	43.22	44.30
5,000	48.94	50.16	51.42	52.70	54.02	55.37
6,000	58.73	60.20	61.70	63.24	64.83	66.45
7,000	68.52	70.23	71.99	73.79	75.63	77.52
8,000	78.31	80.26	82.27	84.33	86.43	88.60
9,000	88.09	90.30	92.55	94.87	97.24	99.67
10,000	97.88	100.33	102.84	105.41	108.04	110.74
15,000	146.82	150.49	154.26	158.11	162.07	166.12
20,000	195.76	200.66	205.67	210.82	216.09	221.49
25,000	244.70	250.82	257.09	263.52	270.11	276.86
30,000	293.65	300.99	308.51	316.22	324.13	332.23
35,000	342.59	351.15	359.93	368.93	378.15	387.61
40,000	391.53	401.32	411.35	421.63	432.17	442.98
45,000	440.47	451.48	462.77	474.34	486.20	498.35
50,000	489.41	501.64	514.19	527.04	540.22	553.72
55,000	538.35	551.81	565.60	579.74	594.24	609.09
60,000	587.29	601.97	617.02	632.45	648.26	664.47
65,000	636.23	652.14	668.44	685.15	702.28	719.84
70,000	685.17	702.30	719.86	737.86	756.30	775.21
75,000	734.11	752.47	771.28	790.56	810.33	830.58
80,000	783.06	802.63	822.70	843.27	864.35	885.96
85,000	832.00	852.80	874.12	895.97	918.37	941.33
90,000	880.94	902.96	925.54	948.67	972.39	996.70
95,000	929.88	953.13	976.95	1,001.38	1,026.41	1,052.07
100,000	978.82	1,003.29	1,028.37	1,054.08	1,080.43	1,107.44
110,000	1,076.70	1,103.62	1,131.21	1,159.49	1,188.48	1,218.19
120,000	1,174.58	1,203.95	1,234.05	1,264.90	1,296.52	1,328.93
130,000	1,272.47	1,304.28	1,336.88	1,370.31	1,404.56	1,439.68
140,000	1,370.35	1,404.61	1,439.72	1,475.71	1,512.61	1,550.42
150,000	1,468.23	1,504.93	1,542.56	1,581.12	1,620.65	1,661.17
160,000	1,566.11	1,605.26	1,645.40	1,686.53	1,728.69	1,771.91
170,000	1,663.99	1,705.59	1,748.23	1,791.94	1,836.74	1,882.66
180,000	1,761.88	1,805.92	1,851.07	1,897.35	1,944.78	1,993.40
190,000	1,859.76	1,906.25	1,953.91	2,002.75	2,052.82	2,104.14
200,000	1,957.64	2,006.58	2,056.74	2,108.16	2,160.87	2,214.89

TABLE IV-3. Graduated Payment Mortgage, FHA Plan I at 13.0% Interest, Graduated at 2.5%

FHA GRADUATED PAYMENT PLAN I
TERM:30 YEARS INTEREST:13.00% GRADUATED AT 2.50%

PAYMENT AMOUNT	YEAR 1	YEAR 2	YEAR 3	YEAR 4	YEAR 5	YEARS 6-30
50	0.51	0.52	0.53	0.55	0.56	0.57
100	1.02	1.04	1.07	1.09	1.12	1.15
200	2.03	2.08	2.13	2.19	2.24	2.30
300	3.05	3.12	3.20	3.28	3.36	3.45
400	4.06	4.16	4.27	4.37	4.48	4.60
500	5.08	5.20	5.34	5.47	5.61	5.75
600	6.09	6.25	6.40	6.56	6.73	6.89
700	7.11	7.29	7.47	7.66	7.85	8.04
800	8.12	8.33	8.54	8.75	8.97	9.19
900	9.14	9.37	9.60	9.84	10.09	10.34
1,000	10.16	10.41	10.67	10.94	11.21	11.49
2,000	20.31	20.82	21.34	21.87	22.42	22.98
3,000	30.47	31.23	32.01	32.81	33.63	34.47
4,000	40.62	41.64	42.68	43.75	44.84	45.96
5,000	50.78	52.05	53.35	54.68	56.05	57.45
6,000	60.94	62.46	64.02	65.62	67.26	68.94
7,000	71.09	72.87	74.69	76.56	78.47	80.43
8,000	81.25	83.28	85.36	87.50	89.68	91.92
9,000	91.40	93.69	96.03	98.43	100.89	103.42
10,000	101.56	104.10	106.70	109.37	112.10	114.91
15,000	152.34	156.15	160.05	164.05	168.15	172.36
20,000	203.12	208.20	213.40	218.74	224.21	229.81
25,000	253.90	260.25	266.75	273.42	280.26	287.26
30,000	304.68	312.30	320.10	328.11	336.31	344.72
35,000	355.46	364.35	373.45	382.79	392.36	402.17
40,000	406.24	416.40	426.81	437.48	448.41	459.62
45,000	457.02	468.44	480.16	492.16	504.46	517.08
50,000	507.80	520.49	533.51	546.84	560.52	574.53
55,000	558.58	572.54	586.86	601.53	616.57	631.98
60,000	609.36	624.59	640.21	656.21	672.62	689.43
65,000	660.14	676.64	693.56	710.90	728.67	746.89
70,000	710.92	728.69	746.91	765.58	784.72	804.34
75,000	761.70	780.74	800.26	820.27	840.77	861.79
80,000	812.48	832.79	853.61	874.95	896.82	919.25
85,000	863.26	884.84	906.96	929.64	952.88	976.70
90,000	914.04	936.89	960.31	984.32	1,008.93	1,034.15
95,000	964.82	988.94	1,013.66	1,039.00	1,064.98	1,091.60
100,000	1,015.60	1,040.99	1,067.01	1,093.69	1,121.03	1,149.06
110,000	1,117.16	1,145.09	1,173.71	1,203.06	1,233.13	1,263.96
120,000	1,218.72	1,249.19	1,280.42	1,312.43	1,345.24	1,378.87
130,000	1,320.28	1,353.29	1,387.12	1,421.80	1,457.34	1,493.77
140,000	1,421.84	1,457.38	1,493.82	1,531.16	1,569.44	1,608.68
150,000	1,523.40	1,561.48	1,600.52	1,640.53	1,681.55	1,723.59
160,000	1,624.96	1,665.58	1,707.22	1,749.90	1,793.65	1,838.49
170,000	1,726.52	1,769.68	1,813.92	1,859.27	1,905.75	1,953.40
180,000	1,828.08	1,873.78	1,920.62	1,968.64	2,017.86	2,068.30
190,000	1,929.64	1,977.88	2,027.33	2,078.01	2,129.96	2,183.21
200,000	2,031.20	2,081.98	2,134.03	2,187.38	2,242.06	2,298.11

TABLE IV-4. Graduated Payment Mortgage, FHA Plan I at 13.5% Interest, Graduated at 2.5%

FHA GRADUATED PAYMENT PLAN I
TERM: 30 YEARS INTEREST: 13.50% GRADUATED AT 2.50%

PAYMENT AMOUNT	YEAR 1	YEAR 2	YEAR 3	YEAR 4	YEAR 5	YEARS 6-30
50	0.53	0.54	0.55	0.57	0.58	0.60
100	1.05	1.08	1.11	1.13	1.16	1.19
200	2.11	2.16	2.21	2.27	2.32	2.38
300	3.16	3.24	3.32	3.40	3.49	3.57
400	4.21	4.32	4.42	4.53	4.65	4.76
500	5.26	5.40	5.53	5.67	5.81	5.96
600	6.32	6.47	6.64	6.80	6.97	7.15
700	7.37	7.55	7.74	7.94	8.13	8.34
800	8.42	8.63	8.85	9.07	9.30	9.53
900	9.47	9.71	9.95	10.20	10.46	10.72
1,000	10.53	10.79	11.06	11.34	11.62	11.91
2,000	21.05	21.58	22.12	22.67	23.24	23.82
3,000	31.58	32.37	33.18	34.01	34.86	35.73
4,000	42.11	43.16	44.24	45.35	46.48	47.64
5,000	52.63	53.95	55.30	56.68	58.10	59.55
6,000	63.16	64.74	66.36	68.02	69.72	71.46
7,000	73.69	75.53	77.42	79.35	81.34	83.37
8,000	84.22	86.32	88.48	90.69	92.96	95.28
9,000	94.74	97.11	99.54	102.03	104.58	107.19
10,000	105.27	107.90	110.60	113.36	116.20	119.10
15,000	157.90	161.85	165.90	170.05	174.30	178.65
20,000	210.54	215.80	221.20	226.73	232.40	238.21
25,000	263.17	269.75	276.50	283.41	290.49	297.76
30,000	315.81	323.70	331.80	340.09	348.59	357.31
35,000	368.44	377.65	387.10	396.77	406.69	416.86
40,000	421.08	431.60	442.40	453.45	464.79	476.41
45,000	473.71	485.56	497.69	510.14	522.89	535.96
50,000	526.35	539.51	552.99	566.82	580.99	595.51
55,000	578.98	593.46	608.29	623.50	639.09	655.07
60,000	631.62	647.41	663.59	680.18	697.19	714.62
65,000	684.25	701.36	718.89	736.86	755.29	774.17
70,000	736.89	755.31	774.19	793.55	813.38	833.72
75,000	789.52	809.26	829.49	850.23	871.48	893.27
80,000	842.16	863.21	884.79	906.91	929.58	952.82
85,000	894.79	917.16	940.09	963.59	987.68	1,012.37
90,000	947.43	971.11	995.39	1,020.27	1,045.78	1,071.92
95,000	1,000.06	1,025.06	1,050.69	1,076.96	1,103.88	1,131.48
100,000	1,052.69	1,079.01	1,105.99	1,133.64	1,161.98	1,191.03
110,000	1,157.96	1,186.91	1,216.59	1,247.00	1,278.18	1,310.13
120,000	1,263.23	1,294.81	1,327.19	1,360.36	1,394.37	1,429.23
130,000	1,368.50	1,402.72	1,437.78	1,473.73	1,510.57	1,548.34
140,000	1,473.77	1,510.62	1,548.38	1,587.09	1,626.77	1,667.44
150,000	1,579.04	1,618.52	1,658.98	1,700.46	1,742.97	1,786.54
160,000	1,684.31	1,726.42	1,769.58	1,813.82	1,859.17	1,905.64
170,000	1,789.58	1,834.32	1,880.18	1,927.18	1,975.36	2,024.75
180,000	1,894.85	1,942.22	1,990.78	2,040.55	2,091.56	2,143.85
190,000	2,000.12	2,050.12	2,101.38	2,153.91	2,207.76	2,262.95
200,000	2,105.39	2,158.02	2,211.98	2,267.27	2,323.96	2,382.06

TABLE IV-5. Graduated Payment Mortgage, FHA Plan I at 14.0% Interest, Graduated at 2.5%

FHA GRADUATED PAYMENT PLAN I
TERM:30 YEARS INTEREST:14.00% GRADUATED AT 2.50%

PAYMENT AMOUNT	YEAR 1	YEAR 2	YEAR 3	YEAR 4	YEAR 5	YEARS 6-30
50	0.55	0.56	0.57	0.59	0.60	0.62
100	1.09	1.12	1.15	1.17	1.20	1.23
200	2.18	2.23	2.29	2.35	2.41	2.47
300	3.27	3.35	3.44	3.52	3.61	3.70
400	4.36	4.47	4.58	4.70	4.81	4.93
500	5.45	5.59	5.73	5.87	6.02	6.17
600	6.54	6.70	6.87	7.04	7.22	7.40
700	7.63	7.82	8.02	8.22	8.42	8.63
800	8.72	8.94	9.16	9.39	9.63	9.87
900	9.81	10.06	10.31	10.57	10.83	11.10
1,000	10.90	11.17	11.45	11.74	12.03	12.33
2,000	21.80	22.35	22.91	23.48	24.06	24.67
3,000	32.70	33.52	34.36	35.22	36.10	37.00
4,000	43.60	44.69	45.81	46.96	48.13	49.33
5,000	54.50	55.87	57.26	58.70	60.16	61.67
6,000	65.41	67.04	68.72	70.43	72.19	74.00
7,000	76.31	78.21	80.17	82.17	84.23	86.33
8,000	87.21	89.39	91.62	93.91	96.26	98.67
9,000	98.11	100.56	103.07	105.65	108.29	111.00
10,000	109.01	111.73	114.53	117.39	120.32	123.33
15,000	163.51	167.60	171.79	176.09	180.49	185.00
20,000	218.02	223.47	229.05	234.78	240.65	246.67
25,000	272.52	279.33	286.32	293.48	300.81	308.33
30,000	327.03	335.20	343.58	352.17	360.97	370.00
35,000	381.53	391.07	400.84	410.87	421.14	431.67
40,000	436.03	446.93	458.11	469.56	481.30	493.33
45,000	490.54	502.80	515.37	528.26	541.46	555.00
50,000	545.04	558.67	572.64	586.95	601.62	616.67
55,000	599.55	614.54	629.90	645.65	661.79	678.33
60,000	654.05	670.40	687.16	704.34	721.95	740.00
65,000	708.56	726.27	744.43	763.04	782.11	801.66
70,000	763.06	782.14	801.69	821.73	842.27	863.33
75,000	817.56	838.00	858.95	880.43	902.44	925.00
80,000	872.07	893.87	916.22	939.12	962.60	986.66
85,000	926.57	949.74	973.48	997.82	1,022.76	1,048.33
90,000	981.08	1,005.60	1,030.74	1,056.51	1,082.92	1,110.00
95,000	1,035.58	1,061.47	1,088.01	1,115.21	1,143.09	1,171.66
100,000	1,090.08	1,117.34	1,145.27	1,173.90	1,203.25	1,233.33
110,000	1,199.09	1,229.07	1,259.80	1,291.29	1,323.57	1,356.66
120,000	1,308.10	1,340.80	1,374.32	1,408.68	1,443.90	1,480.00
130,000	1,417.11	1,452.54	1,488.85	1,526.07	1,564.22	1,603.33
140,000	1,526.12	1,564.27	1,603.38	1,643.46	1,684.55	1,726.66
150,000	1,635.13	1,676.01	1,717.91	1,760.85	1,804.87	1,850.00
160,000	1,744.14	1,787.74	1,832.43	1,878.24	1,925.20	1,973.33
170,000	1,853.14	1,899.47	1,946.96	1,995.63	2,045.52	2,096.66
180,000	1,962.15	2,011.21	2,061.49	2,113.02	2,165.85	2,220.00
190,000	2,071.16	2,122.94	2,176.01	2,230.41	2,286.17	2,343.33
200,000	2,180.17	2,234.67	2,290.54	2,347.80	2,406.50	2,466.66

TABLE IV-6. Graduated Payment Mortgage, FHA Plan I at 14.5% Interest, Graduated at 2.5%

FHA GRADUATED PAYMENT PLAN I
TERM: 30 YEARS INTEREST: 14.50% GRADUATED AT 2.50%

PAYMENT AMOUNT	YEAR 1	YEAR 2	YEAR 3	YEAR 4	YEAR 5	YEARS 6-30
50	0.56	0.58	0.59	0.61	0.62	0.64
100	1.13	1.16	1.18	1.21	1.24	1.28
200	2.26	2.31	2.37	2.43	2.49	2.55
300	3.38	3.47	3.55	3.64	3.73	3.83
400	4.51	4.62	4.74	4.86	4.98	5.10
500	5.64	5.78	5.92	6.07	6.22	6.38
600	6.77	6.94	7.11	7.29	7.47	7.66
700	7.89	8.09	8.29	8.50	8.71	8.93
800	9.02	9.25	9.48	9.72	9.96	10.21
900	10.15	10.40	10.66	10.93	11.20	11.48
1,000	11.28	11.56	11.85	12.14	12.45	12.76
2,000	22.55	23.12	23.70	24.29	24.90	25.52
3,000	33.83	34.68	35.55	36.43	37.34	38.28
4,000	45.11	46.24	47.39	48.58	49.79	51.04
5,000	56.39	57.80	59.24	60.72	62.24	63.80
6,000	67.66	69.36	71.09	72.87	74.69	76.56
7,000	78.94	80.92	82.94	85.01	87.14	89.32
8,000	90.22	92.48	94.79	97.16	99.59	102.08
9,000	101.50	104.03	106.64	109.30	112.03	114.83
10,000	112.77	115.59	118.48	121.45	124.48	127.59
15,000	169.16	173.39	177.73	182.17	186.72	191.39
20,000	225.55	231.19	236.97	242.89	248.96	255.19
25,000	281.94	288.99	296.21	303.61	311.21	318.99
30,000	338.32	346.78	355.45	364.34	373.45	382.78
35,000	394.71	404.58	414.69	425.06	435.69	446.58
40,000	451.10	462.38	473.94	485.78	497.93	510.38
45,000	507.49	520.17	533.18	546.51	560.17	574.17
50,000	563.87	577.97	592.42	607.23	622.41	637.97
55,000	620.26	635.77	651.66	667.95	684.65	701.77
60,000	676.65	693.56	710.90	728.68	746.89	765.57
65,000	733.04	751.36	770.15	789.40	809.13	829.36
70,000	789.42	809.16	829.39	850.12	871.37	893.16
75,000	845.81	866.96	888.63	910.84	933.62	956.96
80,000	902.20	924.75	947.87	971.57	995.86	1,020.75
85,000	958.58	982.55	1,007.11	1,032.29	1,058.10	1,084.55
90,000	1,014.97	1,040.35	1,066.36	1,093.01	1,120.34	1,148.35
95,000	1,071.36	1,098.14	1,125.60	1,153.74	1,182.58	1,212.14
100,000	1,127.75	1,155.94	1,184.84	1,214.46	1,244.82	1,275.94
110,000	1,240.52	1,271.53	1,303.32	1,335.91	1,369.30	1,403.54
120,000	1,353.30	1,387.13	1,421.81	1,457.35	1,493.79	1,531.13
130,000	1,466.07	1,502.72	1,540.29	1,578.80	1,618.27	1,658.72
140,000	1,578.85	1,618.32	1,658.77	1,700.24	1,742.75	1,786.32
150,000	1,691.62	1,733.91	1,777.26	1,821.69	1,867.23	1,913.91
160,000	1,804.39	1,849.50	1,895.74	1,943.14	1,991.71	2,041.51
170,000	1,917.17	1,965.10	2,014.23	2,064.58	2,116.20	2,169.10
180,000	2,029.94	2,080.69	2,132.71	2,186.03	2,240.68	2,296.70
190,000	2,142.72	2,196.29	2,251.19	2,307.47	2,365.16	2,424.29
200,000	2,255.49	2,311.88	2,369.68	2,428.92	2,489.64	2,551.88

TABLE IV-7. Graduated Payment Mortgage, FHA Plan I at 15.0% Interest, Graduated at 2.5%

FHA GRADUATED PAYMENT PLAN I
TERM:30 YEARS INTEREST:15.00% GRADUATED AT 2.50%

PAYMENT AMCUNT	YEAR 1	YEAR 2	YEAR 3	YEAR 4	YEAR 5	YEARS 6-30
50	0.58	0.60	0.61	0.63	0.64	0.66
100	1.17	1.19	1.22	1.26	1.29	1.32
200	2.33	2.39	2.45	2.51	2.57	2.64
300	3.50	3.58	3.67	3.77	3.86	3.96
400	4.66	4.78	4.90	5.02	5.15	5.28
500	5.83	5.97	6.12	6.28	6.43	6.59
600	6.99	7.17	7.35	7.53	7.72	7.91
700	8.16	8.36	8.57	8.79	9.01	9.23
800	9.33	9.56	9.80	10.04	10.29	10.55
900	10.49	10.75	11.02	11.30	11.58	11.87
1,000	11.66	11.95	12.25	12.55	12.87	13.19
2,000	23.31	23.90	24.49	25.11	25.73	26.38
3,000	34.97	35.84	36.74	37.66	38.60	39.57
4,000	46.63	47.79	48.99	50.21	51.47	52.75
5,000	58.28	59.74	61.23	62.76	64.33	65.94
6,000	69.94	71.69	73.48	75.32	77.20	79.13
7,000	81.60	83.64	85.73	87.87	90.07	92.32
8,000	93.25	95.58	97.97	100.42	102.93	105.51
9,000	104.91	107.53	110.22	112.98	115.80	118.70
10,000	116.57	119.48	122.47	125.53	128.67	131.88
15,000	174.85	179.22	183.70	188.29	193.00	197.83
20,000	233.13	238.96	244.93	251.06	257.33	263.77
25,000	291.42	298.70	306.17	313.82	321.67	329.71
30,000	349.70	358.44	367.40	376.59	386.00	395.65
35,000	407.98	418.18	428.64	439.35	450.34	461.59
40,000	466.26	477.92	489.87	502.12	514.67	527.54
45,000	524.55	537.66	551.10	564.88	579.00	593.48
50,000	582.83	597.40	612.34	627.64	643.34	659.42
55,000	641.11	657.14	673.57	690.41	707.67	725.36
60,000	699.40	716.88	734.80	753.17	772.00	791.30
65,000	757.68	776.62	796.04	815.94	836.34	857.25
70,000	815.96	836.36	857.27	878.70	900.67	923.19
75,000	874.25	896.10	918.50	941.47	965.00	989.13
80,000	932.53	955.84	979.74	1,004.23	1,029.34	1,055.07
85,000	990.81	1,015.58	1,040.97	1,067.00	1,093.67	1,121.01
90,000	1,049.10	1,075.32	1,102.21	1,129.76	1,158.00	1,186.95
95,000	1,107.38	1,135.06	1,163.44	1,192.53	1,222.34	1,252.90
100,000	1,165.66	1,194.80	1,224.67	1,255.29	1,286.67	1,318.84
110,000	1,282.23	1,314.28	1,347.14	1,380.82	1,415.34	1,450.72
120,000	1,398.79	1,433.76	1,469.61	1,506.35	1,544.01	1,582.61
130,000	1,515.36	1,553.24	1,592.07	1,631.88	1,672.67	1,714.49
140,000	1,631.93	1,672.72	1,714.54	1,757.41	1,801.34	1,846.37
150,000	1,748.49	1,792.20	1,837.01	1,882.93	1,930.01	1,978.26
160,000	1,865.06	1,911.68	1,959.48	2,008.46	2,058.67	2,110.14
170,000	1,981.62	2,031.16	2,081.94	2,133.99	2,187.34	2,242.03
180,000	2,098.19	2,150.64	2,204.41	2,259.52	2,316.01	2,373.91
190,000	2,214.76	2,270.13	2,326.88	2,385.05	2,444.68	2,505.79
200,000	2,331.32	2,389.61	2,449.35	2,510.58	2,573.34	2,637.68

TABLE IV-8. Graduated Payment Mortgage, FHA Plan I at 15.5% Interest, Graduated at 2.5%

FHA GRADUATED PAYMENT PLAN I
TERM:30 YEARS INTEREST:15.50% GRADUATED AT 2.50%

PAYMENT AMOUNT	YEAR 1	YEAR 2	YEAR 3	YEAR 4	YEAR 5	YEARS 6-30
50	0.60	0.62	0.63	0.65	0.66	0.68
100	1.20	1.23	1.26	1.30	1.33	1.36
200	2.41	2.47	2.53	2.59	2.66	2.72
300	3.61	3.70	3.79	3.89	3.99	4.09
400	4.82	4.94	5.06	5.19	5.32	5.45
500	6.02	6.17	6.32	6.48	6.64	6.81
600	7.22	7.40	7.59	7.78	7.97	8.17
700	8.43	8.64	8.85	9.07	9.30	9.53
800	9.63	9.87	10.12	10.37	10.63	10.90
900	10.83	11.11	11.38	11.67	11.96	12.26
1,000	12.04	12.34	12.65	12.96	13.29	13.62
2,000	24.08	24.68	25.30	25.93	26.58	27.24
3,000	36.11	37.02	37.94	38.89	39.86	40.86
4,000	48.15	49.36	50.59	51.85	53.15	54.48
5,000	60.19	61.70	63.24	64.82	66.44	68.10
6,000	72.23	74.03	75.89	77.78	79.73	81.72
7,000	84.27	86.37	88.53	90.75	93.01	95.34
8,000	96.30	98.71	101.18	103.71	106.30	108.96
9,000	108.34	111.05	113.83	116.67	119.59	122.58
10,000	120.38	123.39	126.48	129.64	132.88	136.20
15,000	180.57	185.09	189.71	194.46	199.32	204.30
20,000	240.76	246.78	252.95	259.27	265.76	272.40
25,000	300.95	308.48	316.19	324.09	332.20	340.50
30,000	361.14	370.17	379.43	388.91	398.63	408.60
35,000	421.33	431.87	442.66	453.73	465.07	476.70
40,000	481.52	493.56	505.90	518.55	531.51	544.80
45,000	541.71	555.26	569.14	583.37	597.95	612.90
50,000	601.90	616.95	632.38	648.19	664.39	681.00
55,000	662.10	678.65	695.61	713.00	730.83	749.10
60,000	722.29	740.34	758.85	777.82	797.27	817.20
65,000	782.48	802.04	822.09	842.64	863.71	885.30
70,000	842.67	863.73	885.33	907.46	930.15	953.40
75,000	902.86	925.43	948.56	972.28	996.59	1,021.50
80,000	963.05	987.12	1,011.80	1,037.10	1,063.02	1,089.60
85,000	1,023.24	1,048.82	1,075.04	1,101.92	1,129.46	1,157.70
90,000	1,083.43	1,110.51	1,138.28	1,166.73	1,195.90	1,225.80
95,000	1,143.62	1,172.21	1,201.51	1,231.55	1,262.34	1,293.90
100,000	1,203.81	1,233.90	1,264.75	1,296.37	1,328.78	1,362.00
110,000	1,324.19	1,357.29	1,391.23	1,426.01	1,461.66	1,498.20
120,000	1,444.57	1,480.69	1,517.70	1,555.64	1,594.54	1,634.40
130,000	1,564.95	1,604.08	1,644.18	1,685.28	1,727.41	1,770.60
140,000	1,685.33	1,727.47	1,770.65	1,814.92	1,860.29	1,906.80
150,000	1,805.71	1,850.86	1,897.13	1,944.56	1,993.17	2,043.00
160,000	1,926.09	1,974.25	2,023.60	2,074.19	2,126.05	2,179.20
170,000	2,046.48	2,097.64	2,150.08	2,203.83	2,258.93	2,315.40
180,000	2,166.86	2,221.03	2,276.55	2,333.47	2,391.80	2,451.60
190,000	2,287.24	2,344.42	2,403.03	2,463.10	2,524.68	2,587.80
200,000	2,407.62	2,467.81	2,529.50	2,592.74	2,657.56	2,724.00

TABLE IV-9. Graduated Payment Mortgage, FHA Plan I at 16.0% Interest, Graduated at 2.5%

FHA GRADUATED PAYMENT PLAN I
TERM:30 YEARS INTEREST:16.00% GRADUATED AT 2.50%

PAYMENT AMCUNT	YEAR 1	YEAR 2	YEAR 3	YEAR 4	YEAR 5	YEARS 6-30
50	0.62	0.64	0.65	0.67	0.69	0.70
100	1.24	1.27	1.31	1.34	1.37	1.41
200	2.48	2.55	2.61	2.68	2.74	2.81
300	3.73	3.82	3.92	4.01	4.11	4.22
400	4.97	5.09	5.22	5.35	5.48	5.62
500	6.21	6.37	6.53	6.69	6.86	7.03
600	7.45	7.64	7.83	8.03	8.23	8.43
700	8.70	8.91	9.14	9.36	9.60	9.84
800	9.94	10.19	10.44	10.70	10.97	11.24
900	11.18	11.46	11.75	12.04	12.34	12.65
1,000	12.42	12.73	13.05	13.38	13.71	14.05
2,000	24.84	25.46	26.10	26.75	27.42	28.11
3,000	37.27	38.20	39.15	40.13	41.13	42.16
4,000	49.69	50.93	52.20	53.51	54.85	56.22
5,000	62.11	63.66	65.25	66.88	68.56	70.27
6,000	74.53	76.39	78.30	80.26	82.27	84.32
7,000	86.95	89.13	91.35	93.64	95.98	98.38
8,000	99.37	101.86	104.40	107.01	109.69	112.43
9,000	111.80	114.59	117.46	120.39	123.40	126.49
10,000	124.22	127.32	130.51	133.77	137.11	140.54
15,000	186.33	190.98	195.76	200.65	205.67	210.81
20,000	248.43	254.65	261.01	267.54	274.23	281.08
25,000	310.54	318.31	326.26	334.42	342.78	351.35
30,000	372.65	381.97	391.52	401.31	411.34	421.62
35,000	434.76	445.63	456.77	468.19	479.89	491.89
40,000	496.87	509.29	522.02	535.07	548.45	562.16
45,000	558.98	572.95	587.28	601.96	617.01	632.43
50,000	621.09	636.61	652.53	668.84	685.56	702.70
55,000	683.20	700.28	717.78	735.73	754.12	772.97
60,000	745.30	763.94	783.04	802.61	822.68	843.24
65,000	807.41	827.60	848.29	869.50	891.23	913.51
70,000	869.52	891.26	913.54	936.38	959.79	983.78
75,000	931.63	954.92	978.79	1,003.26	1,028.35	1,054.05
80,000	993.74	1,018.58	1,044.05	1,070.15	1,096.90	1,124.32
85,000	1,055.85	1,082.24	1,109.30	1,137.03	1,165.46	1,194.59
90,000	1,117.96	1,145.91	1,174.55	1,203.92	1,234.01	1,264.86
95,000	1,180.06	1,209.57	1,239.81	1,270.80	1,302.57	1,335.14
100,000	1,242.17	1,273.23	1,305.06	1,337.69	1,371.13	1,405.41
110,000	1,366.39	1,400.55	1,435.56	1,471.45	1,508.24	1,545.95
120,000	1,490.61	1,527.87	1,566.07	1,605.22	1,645.35	1,686.49
130,000	1,614.83	1,655.20	1,696.58	1,738.99	1,782.47	1,827.03
140,000	1,739.04	1,782.52	1,827.08	1,872.76	1,919.58	1,967.57
150,000	1,863.26	1,909.84	1,957.59	2,006.53	2,056.69	2,108.11
160,000	1,987.48	2,037.16	2,088.09	2,140.30	2,193.80	2,248.65
170,000	2,111.69	2,164.49	2,218.60	2,274.06	2,330.92	2,389.19
180,000	2,235.91	2,291.81	2,349.11	2,407.83	2,468.03	2,529.73
190,000	2,360.13	2,419.13	2,479.61	2,541.60	2,605.14	2,670.27
200,000	2,484.35	2,546.46	2,610.12	2,675.37	2,742.25	2,810.81

TABLE IV-10. Graduated Payment Mortgage, FHA Plan I at 16.5% Interest, Graduated at 2.5%

FHA GRADUATED PAYMENT PLAN I
TERM:30 YEARS INTEREST:16.50% GRADUATED AT 2.50%

PAYMENT AMOUNT	YEAR 1	YEAR 2	YEAR 3	YEAR 4	YEAR 5	YEARS 6-30
50	0.64	0.66	0.67	0.69	0.71	0.72
100	1.28	1.31	1.35	1.38	1.41	1.45
200	2.56	2.63	2.69	2.76	2.83	2.90
300	3.84	3.94	4.04	4.14	4.24	4.35
400	5.12	5.25	5.38	5.52	5.65	5.80
500	6.40	6.56	6.73	6.90	7.07	7.25
600	7.68	7.88	8.07	8.28	8.48	8.69
700	8.97	9.19	9.42	9.65	9.90	10.14
800	10.25	10.50	10.76	11.03	11.31	11.59
900	11.53	11.81	12.11	12.41	12.72	13.04
1,000	12.81	13.13	13.46	13.79	14.14	14.49
2,000	25.61	26.26	26.91	27.58	28.27	28.98
3,000	38.42	39.38	40.37	41.38	42.41	43.47
4,000	51.23	52.51	53.82	55.17	56.55	57.96
5,000	64.04	65.64	67.28	68.96	70.68	72.45
6,000	76.84	78.77	80.73	82.75	84.82	86.94
7,000	89.65	91.89	94.19	96.55	98.96	101.43
8,000	102.46	105.02	107.65	110.34	113.10	115.92
9,000	115.27	118.15	121.10	124.13	127.23	130.41
10,000	128.07	131.28	134.56	137.92	141.37	144.90
15,000	192.11	196.91	201.84	206.88	212.05	217.36
20,000	256.15	262.55	269.12	275.84	282.74	289.81
25,000	320.18	328.19	336.39	344.80	353.42	362.26
30,000	384.22	393.83	403.67	413.76	424.11	434.71
35,000	448.26	459.46	470.95	482.73	494.79	507.16
40,000	512.30	525.10	538.23	551.69	565.48	579.62
45,000	576.33	590.74	605.51	620.65	636.16	652.07
50,000	640.37	656.38	672.79	689.61	706.85	724.52
55,000	704.41	722.02	740.07	758.57	777.53	796.97
60,000	768.44	787.65	807.35	827.53	848.22	869.42
65,000	832.48	853.29	874.62	896.49	918.90	941.87
70,000	896.52	918.93	941.90	965.45	989.59	1,014.33
75,000	960.55	984.57	1,009.18	1,034.41	1,060.27	1,086.78
80,000	1,024.59	1,050.21	1,076.46	1,103.37	1,130.96	1,159.23
85,000	1,088.63	1,115.84	1,143.74	1,172.33	1,201.64	1,231.68
90,000	1,152.66	1,181.48	1,211.02	1,241.29	1,272.33	1,304.13
95,000	1,216.70	1,247.12	1,278.30	1,310.25	1,343.01	1,376.59
100,000	1,280.74	1,312.76	1,345.58	1,379.21	1,413.70	1,449.04
110,000	1,408.81	1,444.03	1,480.13	1,517.14	1,555.06	1,593.94
120,000	1,536.89	1,575.31	1,614.69	1,655.06	1,696.43	1,738.85
130,000	1,664.96	1,706.58	1,749.25	1,792.98	1,837.80	1,883.75
140,000	1,793.03	1,837.86	1,883.81	1,930.90	1,979.17	2,028.65
150,000	1,921.11	1,969.13	2,018.36	2,068.82	2,120.54	2,173.56
160,000	2,049.18	2,100.41	2,152.92	2,206.74	2,261.91	2,318.46
170,000	2,177.25	2,231.69	2,287.48	2,344.67	2,403.28	2,463.36
180,000	2,305.33	2,362.96	2,422.04	2,482.59	2,544.65	2,608.27
190,000	2,433.40	2,494.24	2,556.59	2,620.51	2,686.02	2,753.17
200,000	2,561.48	2,625.51	2,691.15	2,758.43	2,827.39	2,898.08

TABLE IV-11. Graduated Payment Mortgage, FHA Plan I at 17.0% Interest, Graduated at 2.5%

FHA GRADUATED PAYMENT PLAN I
TERM:30 YEARS INTEREST:17.00% GRADUATED AT 2.50%

PAYMENT AMCUNT	YEAR 1	YEAR 2	YEAR 3	YEAR 4	YEAR 5	YEARS 6-30
50	0.66	0.68	0.69	0.71	0.73	0.75
100	1.32	1.35	1.39	1.42	1.46	1.49
200	2.64	2.70	2.77	2.84	2.91	2.99
300	3.96	4.06	4.16	4.26	4.37	4.48
400	5.28	5.41	5.55	5.68	5.83	5.97
500	6.60	6.76	6.93	7.10	7.28	7.46
600	7.92	8.11	8.32	8.53	8.74	8.96
700	9.24	9.47	9.70	9.95	10.20	10.45
800	10.56	10.82	11.09	11.37	11.65	11.94
900	11.88	12.17	12.48	12.79	13.11	13.44
1,000	13.19	13.52	13.86	14.21	14.56	14.93
2,000	26.39	27.05	27.73	28.42	29.13	29.86
3,000	39.58	40.57	41.59	42.63	43.69	44.79
4,000	52.78	54.10	55.45	56.84	58.26	59.72
5,000	65.97	67.62	69.31	71.05	72.82	74.64
6,000	79.17	81.15	83.18	85.26	87.39	89.57
7,000	92.36	94.67	97.04	99.47	101.95	104.50
8,000	105.56	108.20	110.90	113.68	116.52	119.43
9,000	118.75	121.72	124.77	127.88	131.08	134.36
10,000	131.95	135.25	138.63	142.09	145.65	149.29
15,000	197.92	202.87	207.94	213.14	218.47	223.93
20,000	263.90	270.50	277.26	284.19	291.29	298.58
25,000	329.87	338.12	346.57	355.24	364.12	373.22
30,000	395.85	405.74	415.89	426.28	436.94	447.86
35,000	461.82	473.37	485.20	497.33	509.76	522.51
40,000	527.80	540.99	554.51	568.38	582.59	597.15
45,000	593.77	608.61	623.83	639.42	655.41	671.80
50,000	659.74	676.24	693.14	710.47	728.23	746.44
55,000	725.72	743.86	762.46	781.52	801.06	821.08
60,000	791.69	811.49	831.77	852.57	873.88	895.73
65,000	857.67	879.11	901.09	923.61	946.70	970.37
70,000	923.64	946.73	970.40	994.66	1,019.53	1,045.02
75,000	989.62	1,014.36	1,039.72	1,065.71	1,092.35	1,119.66
80,000	1,055.59	1,081.98	1,109.03	1,136.76	1,165.17	1,194.30
85,000	1,121.56	1,149.60	1,178.34	1,207.80	1,238.00	1,268.95
90,000	1,187.54	1,217.23	1,247.66	1,278.85	1,310.82	1,343.59
95,000	1,253.51	1,284.85	1,316.97	1,349.90	1,383.64	1,418.24
100,000	1,319.49	1,352.48	1,386.29	1,420.94	1,456.47	1,492.88
110,000	1,451.44	1,487.72	1,524.92	1,563.04	1,602.11	1,642.17
120,000	1,583.39	1,622.97	1,663.54	1,705.13	1,747.76	1,791.46
130,000	1,715.33	1,758.22	1,802.17	1,847.23	1,893.41	1,940.74
140,000	1,847.28	1,893.47	1,940.80	1,989.32	2,039.05	2,090.03
150,000	1,979.23	2,028.71	2,079.43	2,131.42	2,184.70	2,239.32
160,000	2,111.18	2,163.96	2,218.06	2,273.51	2,330.35	2,388.61
170,000	2,243.13	2,299.21	2,356.69	2,415.60	2,476.00	2,537.89
180,000	2,375.08	2,434.46	2,495.32	2,557.70	2,621.64	2,687.18
190,000	2,507.03	2,569.70	2,633.95	2,699.79	2,767.29	2,836.47
200,000	2,638.98	2,704.95	2,772.57	2,841.89	2,912.94	2,985.76

TABLE IV-12. Graduated Payment Mortgage, FHA Plan I at 17.5% Interest, Graduated at 2.5%

FHA GRADUATED PAYMENT PLAN I
TERM:30 YEARS INTEREST:17.50% GRADUATED AT 2.50%

PAYMENT AMOUNT	YEAR 1	YEAR 2	YEAR 3	YEAR 4	YEAR 5	YEARS 6-30
50	0.68	0.70	0.71	0.73	0.75	0.77
100	1.36	1.39	1.43	1.46	1.50	1.54
200	2.72	2.78	2.85	2.93	3.00	3.07
300	4.08	4.18	4.28	4.39	4.50	4.61
400	5.43	5.57	5.71	5.85	6.00	6.15
500	6.79	6.96	7.14	7.31	7.50	7.68
600	8.15	8.35	8.56	8.78	9.00	9.22
700	9.51	9.75	9.99	10.24	10.50	10.76
800	10.87	11.14	11.42	11.70	12.00	12.30
900	12.23	12.53	12.84	13.17	13.49	13.83
1,000	13.58	13.92	14.27	14.63	14.99	15.37
2,000	27.17	27.85	28.54	29.26	29.99	30.74
3,000	40.75	41.77	42.82	43.89	44.98	46.11
4,000	54.34	55.69	57.09	58.51	59.98	61.48
5,000	67.92	69.62	71.36	73.14	74.97	76.85
6,000	81.50	83.54	85.63	87.77	89.97	92.21
7,000	95.09	97.47	99.90	102.40	104.96	107.58
8,000	108.67	111.39	114.17	117.03	119.95	122.95
9,000	122.26	125.31	128.45	131.66	134.95	138.32
10,000	135.84	139.24	142.72	146.29	149.94	153.69
15,000	203.76	208.86	214.08	219.43	224.91	230.54
20,000	271.68	278.47	285.44	292.57	299.89	307.38
25,000	339.60	348.09	356.79	365.71	374.86	384.23
30,000	407.52	417.71	428.15	438.86	449.83	461.07
35,000	475.44	487.33	499.51	512.00	524.80	537.92
40,000	543.36	556.95	570.87	585.14	599.77	614.77
45,000	611.28	626.57	642.23	658.29	674.74	691.61
50,000	679.20	696.18	713.59	731.43	749.71	768.46
55,000	747.13	765.80	784.95	804.57	824.69	845.30
60,000	815.05	835.42	856.31	877.71	899.66	922.15
65,000	882.97	905.04	927.67	950.86	974.63	998.99
70,000	950.89	974.66	999.03	1,024.00	1,049.60	1,075.84
75,000	1,018.81	1,044.28	1,070.38	1,097.14	1,124.57	1,152.69
80,000	1,086.73	1,113.90	1,141.74	1,170.29	1,199.54	1,229.53
85,000	1,154.65	1,183.51	1,213.10	1,243.43	1,274.52	1,306.38
90,000	1,222.57	1,253.13	1,284.46	1,316.57	1,349.49	1,383.22
95,000	1,290.49	1,322.75	1,355.82	1,389.72	1,424.46	1,460.07
100,000	1,358.41	1,392.37	1,427.18	1,462.86	1,499.43	1,536.92
110,000	1,494.25	1,531.61	1,569.90	1,609.14	1,649.37	1,690.61
120,000	1,630.09	1,670.84	1,712.61	1,755.43	1,799.32	1,844.30
130,000	1,765.93	1,810.08	1,855.33	1,901.72	1,949.26	1,997.99
140,000	1,901.77	1,949.32	1,998.05	2,048.00	2,099.20	2,151.68
150,000	2,037.61	2,088.55	2,140.77	2,194.29	2,249.14	2,305.37
160,000	2,173.45	2,227.79	2,283.49	2,340.57	2,399.09	2,459.06
170,000	2,309.30	2,367.03	2,426.20	2,486.86	2,549.03	2,612.76
180,000	2,445.14	2,506.26	2,568.92	2,633.14	2,698.97	2,766.45
190,000	2,580.98	2,645.50	2,711.64	2,779.43	2,848.92	2,920.14
200,000	2,716.82	2,784.74	2,854.36	2,925.72	2,998.86	3,073.83

TABLE IV-13. Graduated Payment Mortgage, FHA Plan I at 18.0% Interest, Graduated at 2.5%

FHA GRADUATED PAYMENT PLAN I
TERM:30 YEARS INTEREST:18.00% GRADUATED AT 2.50%

PAYMENT AMOUNT	YEAR 1	YEAR 2	YEAR 3	YEAR 4	YEAR 5	YEARS 6-30
50	0.70	0.72	0.73	0.75	0.77	0.79
100	1.40	1.43	1.47	1.50	1.54	1.58
200	2.79	2.86	2.94	3.01	3.09	3.16
300	4.19	4.30	4.40	4.51	4.63	4.74
400	5.59	5.73	5.87	6.02	6.17	6.32
500	6.99	7.16	7.34	7.52	7.71	7.91
600	8.38	8.59	8.81	9.03	9.26	9.49
700	9.78	10.03	10.28	10.53	10.80	11.07
800	11.18	11.46	11.75	12.04	12.34	12.65
900	12.58	12.89	13.21	13.54	13.88	14.23
1,000	13.97	14.32	14.68	15.05	15.43	15.81
2,000	27.95	28.65	29.36	30.10	30.85	31.62
3,000	41.92	42.97	44.05	45.15	46.28	47.43
4,000	55.90	57.30	58.73	60.20	61.70	63.25
5,000	69.87	71.62	73.41	75.25	77.13	79.06
6,000	83.85	85.95	88.09	90.30	92.55	94.87
7,000	97.82	100.27	102.78	105.35	107.98	110.68
8,000	111.80	114.59	117.46	120.40	123.41	126.49
9,000	125.77	128.92	132.14	135.44	138.83	142.30
10,000	139.75	143.24	146.82	150.49	154.26	158.11
15,000	209.62	214.86	220.24	225.74	231.39	237.17
20,000	279.50	286.49	293.65	300.99	308.51	316.23
25,000	349.37	358.11	367.06	376.24	385.64	395.28
30,000	419.25	429.73	440.47	451.48	462.77	474.34
35,000	489.12	501.35	513.88	526.73	539.90	553.40
40,000	559.00	572.97	587.29	601.98	617.03	632.45
45,000	628.87	644.59	660.71	677.22	694.16	711.51
50,000	698.74	716.21	734.12	752.47	771.28	790.57
55,000	768.62	787.83	807.53	827.72	848.41	869.62
60,000	838.49	859.46	880.94	902.97	925.54	948.68
65,000	908.37	931.08	954.35	978.21	1,002.67	1,027.74
70,000	978.24	1,002.70	1,027.77	1,053.46	1,079.80	1,106.79
75,000	1,048.12	1,074.32	1,101.18	1,128.71	1,156.93	1,185.85
80,000	1,117.99	1,145.94	1,174.59	1,203.95	1,234.05	1,264.90
85,000	1,187.87	1,217.56	1,248.00	1,279.20	1,311.18	1,343.96
90,000	1,257.74	1,289.18	1,321.41	1,354.45	1,388.31	1,423.02
95,000	1,327.61	1,360.81	1,394.83	1,429.70	1,465.44	1,502.07
100,000	1,397.49	1,432.43	1,468.24	1,504.94	1,542.57	1,581.13
110,000	1,537.24	1,575.67	1,615.06	1,655.44	1,696.82	1,739.24
120,000	1,676.99	1,718.91	1,761.88	1,805.93	1,851.08	1,897.36
130,000	1,816.74	1,862.15	1,908.71	1,956.43	2,005.34	2,055.47
140,000	1,956.49	2,005.40	2,055.53	2,106.92	2,159.59	2,213.58
150,000	2,096.23	2,148.64	2,202.36	2,257.41	2,313.85	2,371.70
160,000	2,235.98	2,291.88	2,349.18	2,407.91	2,468.11	2,529.81
170,000	2,375.73	2,435.13	2,496.00	2,558.40	2,622.36	2,687.92
180,000	2,515.48	2,578.37	2,642.83	2,708.90	2,776.62	2,846.04
190,000	2,655.23	2,721.61	2,789.65	2,859.39	2,930.88	3,004.15
200,000	2,794.98	2,864.85	2,936.47	3,009.89	3,085.13	3,162.26

TABLE IV-14. Graduated Payment Mortgage, FHA Plan I at 18.5% Interest, Graduated at 2.5%

FHA GRADUATED PAYMENT PLAN I
TERM:30 YEARS INTEREST:18.50% GRADUATED AT 2.50%

PAYMENT AMOUNT	YEAR 1	YEAR 2	YEAR 3	YEAR 4	YEAR 5	YEARS 6-30
50	0.72	0.74	0.75	0.77	0.79	0.81
100	1.44	1.47	1.51	1.55	1.59	1.63
200	2.87	2.95	3.02	3.09	3.17	3.25
300	4.31	4.42	4.53	4.64	4.76	4.88
400	5.75	5.89	6.04	6.19	6.34	6.50
500	7.18	7.36	7.55	7.74	7.93	8.13
600	8.62	8.84	9.06	9.28	9.52	9.75
700	10.06	10.31	10.57	10.83	11.10	11.38
800	11.49	11.78	12.08	12.38	12.69	13.00
900	12.93	13.25	13.59	13.92	14.27	14.63
1,000	14.37	14.73	15.09	15.47	15.86	16.26
2,000	28.73	29.45	30.19	30.94	31.72	32.51
3,000	43.10	44.18	45.28	46.42	47.58	48.77
4,000	57.47	58.91	60.38	61.89	63.43	65.02
5,000	71.84	73.63	75.47	77.36	79.29	81.28
6,000	86.20	88.36	90.57	92.83	95.15	97.53
7,000	100.57	103.08	105.66	108.30	111.01	113.79
8,000	114.94	117.81	120.76	123.77	126.87	130.04
9,000	129.30	132.54	135.85	139.25	142.73	146.30
10,000	143.67	147.26	150.95	154.72	158.59	162.55
15,000	215.51	220.90	226.42	232.08	237.88	243.83
20,000	287.34	294.53	301.89	309.44	317.17	325.10
25,000	359.18	368.16	377.36	386.80	396.47	406.38
30,000	431.02	441.79	452.84	464.16	475.76	487.65
35,000	502.85	515.42	528.31	541.52	555.05	568.93
40,000	574.69	589.05	603.78	618.87	634.35	650.21
45,000	646.52	662.69	679.25	696.23	713.64	731.48
50,000	718.36	736.32	754.73	773.59	792.93	812.76
55,000	790.19	809.95	830.20	850.95	872.23	894.03
60,000	862.03	883.58	905.67	928.31	951.52	975.31
65,000	933.87	957.21	981.14	1,005.67	1,030.81	1,056.58
70,000	1,005.70	1,030.84	1,056.62	1,083.03	1,110.11	1,137.86
75,000	1,077.54	1,104.48	1,132.09	1,160.39	1,189.40	1,219.13
80,000	1,149.37	1,178.11	1,207.56	1,237.75	1,268.69	1,300.41
85,000	1,221.21	1,251.74	1,283.03	1,315.11	1,347.99	1,381.69
90,000	1,293.05	1,325.37	1,358.51	1,392.47	1,427.28	1,462.96
95,000	1,364.88	1,399.00	1,433.98	1,469.83	1,506.57	1,544.24
100,000	1,436.72	1,472.63	1,509.45	1,547.19	1,585.87	1,625.51
110,000	1,580.39	1,619.90	1,660.40	1,701.91	1,744.45	1,788.06
120,000	1,724.06	1,767.16	1,811.34	1,856.62	1,903.04	1,950.62
130,000	1,867.73	1,914.42	1,962.29	2,011.34	2,061.63	2,113.17
140,000	2,011.40	2,061.69	2,113.23	2,166.06	2,220.21	2,275.72
150,000	2,155.08	2,208.95	2,264.18	2,320.78	2,378.80	2,438.27
160,000	2,298.75	2,356.22	2,415.12	2,475.50	2,537.39	2,600.82
170,000	2,442.42	2,503.48	2,566.07	2,630.22	2,695.97	2,763.37
180,000	2,586.09	2,650.74	2,717.01	2,784.94	2,854.56	2,925.92
190,000	2,729.76	2,798.01	2,867.96	2,939.65	3,013.15	3,088.47
200,000	2,873.43	2,945.27	3,018.90	3,094.37	3,171.73	3,251.03

TABLE IV-15. Graduated Payment Mortgage, FHA Plan I at 19.0% Interest, Graduated at 2.5%

FHA GRADUATED PAYMENT PLAN I
TERM:30 YEARS INTEREST:19.00% GRADUATED AT 2.50%

PAYMENT AMOUNT	YEAR 1	YEAR 2	YEAR 3	YEAR 4	YEAR 5	YEARS 6-30
50	0.74	0.76	0.78	0.79	0.81	0.84
100	1.48	1.51	1.55	1.59	1.63	1.67
200	2.95	3.03	3.10	3.18	3.26	3.34
300	4.43	4.54	4.65	4.77	4.89	5.01
400	5.90	6.05	6.20	6.36	6.52	6.68
500	7.38	7.56	7.75	7.95	8.15	8.35
600	8.86	9.08	9.30	9.54	9.78	10.02
700	10.33	10.59	10.86	11.13	11.41	11.69
800	11.81	12.10	12.41	12.72	13.03	13.36
900	13.28	13.62	13.96	14.31	14.66	15.03
1,000	14.76	15.13	15.51	15.90	16.29	16.70
2,000	29.52	30.26	31.02	31.79	32.59	33.40
3,000	44.28	45.39	46.52	47.69	48.88	50.10
4,000	59.04	60.52	62.03	63.58	65.17	66.80
5,000	73.80	75.65	77.54	79.48	81.47	83.50
6,000	88.56	90.78	93.05	95.37	97.76	100.20
7,000	103.33	105.91	108.56	111.27	114.05	116.90
8,000	118.09	121.04	124.06	127.17	130.35	133.60
9,000	132.85	136.17	139.57	143.06	146.64	150.30
10,000	147.61	151.30	155.08	158.96	162.93	167.00
15,000	221.41	226.95	232.62	238.44	244.40	250.51
20,000	295.22	302.60	310.16	317.92	325.86	334.01
25,000	369.02	378.25	387.70	397.39	407.33	417.51
30,000	442.82	453.89	465.24	476.87	488.79	501.01
35,000	516.63	529.54	542.78	556.35	570.26	584.52
40,000	590.43	605.19	620.32	635.83	651.73	668.02
45,000	664.24	680.84	697.86	715.31	733.19	751.52
50,000	738.04	756.49	775.40	794.79	814.66	835.02
55,000	811.84	832.14	852.94	874.27	896.12	918.53
60,000	885.65	907.79	930.48	953.75	977.59	1,002.03
65,000	959.45	983.44	1,008.02	1,033.23	1,059.06	1,085.53
70,000	1,033.26	1,059.09	1,085.56	1,112.70	1,140.52	1,169.03
75,000	1,107.06	1,134.74	1,163.11	1,192.18	1,221.99	1,252.54
80,000	1,180.86	1,210.39	1,240.65	1,271.66	1,303.45	1,336.04
85,000	1,254.67	1,286.04	1,318.19	1,351.14	1,384.92	1,419.54
90,000	1,328.47	1,361.68	1,395.73	1,430.62	1,466.38	1,503.04
95,000	1,402.28	1,437.33	1,473.27	1,510.10	1,547.85	1,586.55
100,000	1,476.08	1,512.98	1,550.81	1,589.58	1,629.32	1,670.05
110,000	1,623.69	1,664.28	1,705.89	1,748.53	1,792.25	1,837.05
120,000	1,771.30	1,815.58	1,860.97	1,907.49	1,955.18	2,004.06
130,000	1,918.90	1,966.88	2,016.05	2,066.45	2,118.11	2,171.06
140,000	2,066.51	2,118.18	2,171.13	2,225.41	2,281.04	2,338.07
150,000	2,214.12	2,269.47	2,326.21	2,384.37	2,443.97	2,505.07
160,000	2,361.73	2,420.77	2,481.29	2,543.32	2,606.91	2,672.08
170,000	2,509.34	2,572.07	2,636.37	2,702.28	2,769.84	2,839.08
180,000	2,656.94	2,723.37	2,791.45	2,861.24	2,932.77	3,006.09
190,000	2,804.55	2,874.67	2,946.53	3,020.20	3,095.70	3,173.09
200,000	2,952.16	3,025.96	3,101.61	3,179.15	3,258.63	3,340.10

TABLE IV-16. Graduated Payment Mortgage, FHA Plan I at 19.5% Interest, Graduated at 2.5%

FHA GRADUATED PAYMENT PLAN I
TERM:30 YEARS INTEREST:19.50% GRADUATED AT 2.50%

PAYMENT AMCUNT	YEAR 1	YEAR 2	YEAR 3	YEAR 4	YEAR 5	YEARS 6-3C
50	0.76	0.78	0.80	0.82	0.84	C.86
100	1.52	1.55	1.59	1.63	1.67	1.71
200	3.03	3.11	3.18	3.26	3.35	3.43
300	4.55	4.66	4.78	4.90	5.02	5.14
400	6.06	6.21	6.37	6.53	6.69	6.86
500	7.58	7.77	7.96	8.16	8.36	8.57
600	9.09	9.32	9.55	9.79	10.04	10.29
700	10.61	10.87	11.15	11.42	11.71	12.00
800	12.12	12.43	12.74	13.06	13.38	13.72
900	13.64	13.98	14.33	14.69	15.06	15.43
1,000	15.16	15.53	15.92	16.32	16.73	17.15
2,000	30.31	31.07	31.85	32.64	33.46	34.29
3,000	45.47	46.60	47.77	48.96	50.19	51.44
4,000	60.62	62.14	63.69	65.28	66.92	68.59
5,000	75.78	77.67	79.61	81.61	83.65	85.74
6,000	90.93	93.21	95.54	97.93	100.37	102.88
7,000	106.09	108.74	111.46	114.25	117.10	120.03
8,000	121.25	124.28	127.38	130.57	133.83	137.18
9,000	136.40	139.81	143.31	146.89	150.56	154.33
10,000	151.56	155.35	159.23	163.21	167.29	171.47
15,000	227.34	233.02	238.84	244.82	250.94	257.21
20,000	303.11	310.69	318.46	326.42	334.58	342.95
25,000	378.89	388.37	398.07	408.03	418.23	428.68
30,000	454.67	466.04	477.69	489.63	501.87	514.42
35,000	530.45	543.71	557.30	571.24	585.52	600.16
40,000	606.23	621.38	636.92	652.84	669.16	685.89
45,000	682.01	699.06	716.53	734.45	752.81	771.63
50,000	757.79	776.73	796.15	816.05	836.45	857.36
55,000	833.56	854.40	875.76	897.66	920.10	943.10
60,000	909.34	932.08	955.38	979.26	1,003.74	1,028.84
65,000	985.12	1,009.75	1,034.99	1,060.87	1,087.39	1,114.57
70,000	1,060.90	1,087.42	1,114.61	1,142.47	1,171.03	1,200.31
75,000	1,136.68	1,165.10	1,194.22	1,224.08	1,254.68	1,286.05
80,000	1,212.46	1,242.77	1,273.84	1,305.68	1,338.33	1,371.78
85,000	1,288.24	1,320.44	1,353.45	1,387.29	1,421.97	1,457.52
90,000	1,364.01	1,398.11	1,433.07	1,468.89	1,505.62	1,543.26
95,000	1,439.79	1,475.79	1,512.68	1,550.50	1,589.26	1,628.99
100,000	1,515.57	1,553.46	1,592.30	1,632.10	1,672.91	1,714.73
110,000	1,667.13	1,708.81	1,751.53	1,795.31	1,840.20	1,886.20
120,000	1,818.69	1,864.15	1,910.76	1,958.52	2,007.49	2,057.68
130,000	1,970.24	2,019.50	2,069.99	2,121.74	2,174.78	2,229.15
140,000	2,121.80	2,174.84	2,229.22	2,284.95	2,342.07	2,400.62
150,000	2,273.36	2,330.19	2,388.44	2,448.16	2,509.36	2,572.09
160,000	2,424.91	2,485.54	2,547.67	2,611.37	2,676.65	2,743.57
170,000	2,576.47	2,640.88	2,706.90	2,774.58	2,843.94	2,915.04
180,000	2,728.03	2,796.23	2,866.13	2,937.79	3,011.23	3,086.51
190,000	2,879.58	2,951.57	3,025.36	3,101.00	3,178.52	3,257.99
200,000	3,031.14	3,106.92	3,184.59	3,264.21	3,345.81	3,429.46

TABLE IV-17. Graduated Payment Mortgage, FHA Plan I at 20.0% Interest, Graduated at 2.5%

FHA GRADUATED PAYMENT PLAN I
TERM:30 YEARS INTEREST:20.00% GRADUATED AT 2.50%

PAYMENT AMOUNT	YEAR 1	YEAR 2	YEAR 3	YEAR 4	YEAR 5	YEARS 6-30
50	0.78	0.80	0.82	0.84	0.86	0.88
100	1.56	1.59	1.63	1.67	1.72	1.76
200	3.11	3.19	3.27	3.35	3.43	3.52
300	4.67	4.78	4.90	5.02	5.15	5.28
400	6.22	6.38	6.54	6.70	6.87	7.04
500	7.78	7.97	8.17	8.37	8.58	8.80
600	9.33	9.56	9.80	10.05	10.30	10.56
700	10.89	11.16	11.44	11.72	12.02	12.32
800	12.44	12.75	13.07	13.40	13.73	14.08
900	14.00	14.35	14.71	15.07	15.45	15.84
1,000	15.55	15.94	16.34	16.75	17.17	17.60
2,000	31.10	31.88	32.68	33.50	34.33	35.19
3,000	46.66	47.82	49.02	50.24	51.50	52.79
4,000	62.21	63.76	65.36	66.99	68.67	70.38
5,000	77.76	79.70	81.70	83.74	85.83	87.98
6,000	93.31	95.64	98.03	100.49	103.00	105.57
7,000	108.86	111.58	114.37	117.23	120.16	123.17
8,000	124.41	127.52	130.71	133.98	137.33	140.76
9,000	139.97	143.47	147.05	150.73	154.50	158.36
10,000	155.52	159.41	163.39	167.48	171.66	175.95
15,000	233.28	239.11	245.09	251.21	257.49	263.93
20,000	311.04	318.81	326.78	334.95	343.33	351.91
25,000	388.79	398.51	408.48	418.69	429.16	439.89
30,000	466.55	478.22	490.17	502.43	514.99	527.86
35,000	544.31	557.92	571.87	586.17	600.82	615.84
40,000	622.07	637.62	653.56	669.90	686.65	703.82
45,000	699.83	717.33	735.26	753.64	772.48	791.79
50,000	777.59	797.03	816.95	837.38	858.31	879.77
55,000	855.35	876.73	898.65	921.12	944.14	967.75
60,000	933.11	956.43	980.35	1,004.85	1,029.98	1,055.73
65,000	1,010.87	1,036.14	1,062.04	1,088.59	1,115.81	1,143.70
70,000	1,088.63	1,115.84	1,143.74	1,172.33	1,201.64	1,231.68
75,000	1,166.38	1,195.54	1,225.43	1,256.07	1,287.47	1,319.66
80,000	1,244.14	1,275.25	1,307.13	1,339.81	1,373.30	1,407.63
85,000	1,321.90	1,354.95	1,388.82	1,423.54	1,459.13	1,495.61
90,000	1,399.66	1,434.65	1,470.52	1,507.28	1,544.96	1,583.59
95,000	1,477.42	1,514.36	1,552.21	1,591.02	1,630.80	1,671.56
100,000	1,555.18	1,594.06	1,633.91	1,674.76	1,716.63	1,759.54
110,000	1,710.70	1,753.46	1,797.30	1,842.23	1,888.29	1,935.50
120,000	1,866.21	1,912.87	1,960.69	2,009.71	2,059.95	2,111.45
130,000	2,021.73	2,072.28	2,124.08	2,177.18	2,231.61	2,287.40
140,000	2,177.25	2,231.68	2,287.47	2,344.66	2,403.28	2,463.36
150,000	2,332.77	2,391.09	2,450.86	2,512.14	2,574.94	2,639.31
160,000	2,488.29	2,550.49	2,614.26	2,679.61	2,746.60	2,815.27
170,000	2,643.80	2,709.90	2,777.65	2,847.09	2,918.26	2,991.22
180,000	2,799.32	2,869.30	2,941.04	3,014.56	3,089.93	3,167.18
190,000	2,954.84	3,028.71	3,104.43	3,182.04	3,261.59	3,343.13
200,000	3,110.36	3,188.12	3,267.82	3,349.51	3,433.25	3,519.08

TABLE IV-18. Graduated Payment Mortgage, FHA Plan I at 20.5% Interest, Graduated at 2.5%

FHA GRADUATED PAYMENT PLAN I
TERM:30 YEARS INTEREST:20.50% GRADUATED AT 2.50%

PAYMENT AMOUNT	YEAR 1	YEAR 2	YEAR 3	YEAR 4	YEAR 5	YEARS 6-30
50	0.80	0.82	0.84	0.86	0.88	0.90
100	1.59	1.63	1.68	1.72	1.76	1.80
200	3.19	3.27	3.35	3.44	3.52	3.61
300	4.78	4.90	5.03	5.15	5.28	5.41
400	6.38	6.54	6.70	6.87	7.04	7.22
500	7.97	8.17	8.38	8.59	8.80	9.02
600	9.57	9.81	10.05	10.31	10.56	10.83
700	11.16	11.44	11.73	12.02	12.32	12.63
800	12.76	13.08	13.41	13.74	14.08	14.44
900	14.35	14.71	15.08	15.46	15.84	16.24
1,000	15.95	16.35	16.76	17.18	17.60	18.04
2,000	31.90	32.70	33.51	34.35	35.21	36.09
3,000	47.85	49.04	50.27	51.53	52.81	54.13
4,000	63.80	65.39	67.03	68.70	70.42	72.18
5,000	79.74	81.74	83.78	85.88	88.02	90.22
6,000	95.69	98.09	100.54	103.05	105.63	108.27
7,000	111.64	114.43	117.29	120.23	123.23	126.31
8,000	127.59	130.78	134.05	137.40	140.84	144.36
9,000	143.54	147.13	150.81	154.58	158.44	162.40
10,000	159.49	163.48	167.56	171.75	176.05	180.45
15,000	239.23	245.22	251.35	257.63	264.07	270.67
20,000	318.98	326.95	335.13	343.51	352.09	360.90
25,000	398.72	408.69	418.91	429.38	440.12	451.12
30,000	478.47	490.43	502.69	515.26	528.14	541.34
35,000	558.21	572.17	586.47	601.14	616.16	631.57
40,000	637.96	653.91	670.26	687.01	704.19	721.79
45,000	717.70	735.65	754.04	772.89	792.21	812.02
50,000	797.45	817.38	837.82	858.76	880.23	902.24
55,000	877.19	899.12	921.60	944.64	968.26	992.46
60,000	956.94	980.86	1,005.38	1,030.52	1,056.28	1,082.69
65,000	1,036.68	1,062.60	1,089.16	1,116.39	1,144.30	1,172.91
70,000	1,116.43	1,144.34	1,172.95	1,202.27	1,232.33	1,263.13
75,000	1,196.17	1,226.08	1,256.73	1,288.15	1,320.35	1,353.36
80,000	1,275.92	1,307.81	1,340.51	1,374.02	1,408.37	1,443.58
85,000	1,355.66	1,389.55	1,424.29	1,459.90	1,496.40	1,533.81
90,000	1,435.41	1,471.29	1,508.07	1,545.78	1,584.42	1,624.03
95,000	1,515.15	1,553.03	1,591.86	1,631.65	1,672.44	1,714.25
100,000	1,594.90	1,634.77	1,675.64	1,717.53	1,760.47	1,804.48
110,000	1,754.39	1,798.25	1,843.20	1,889.28	1,936.51	1,984.93
120,000	1,913.88	1,961.72	2,010.77	2,061.03	2,112.56	2,165.37
130,000	2,073.36	2,125.20	2,178.33	2,232.79	2,288.61	2,345.82
140,000	2,232.85	2,288.68	2,345.89	2,404.54	2,464.65	2,526.27
150,000	2,392.34	2,452.15	2,513.46	2,576.29	2,640.70	2,706.72
160,000	2,551.83	2,615.63	2,681.02	2,748.05	2,816.75	2,887.17
170,000	2,711.32	2,779.11	2,848.58	2,919.80	2,992.79	3,067.61
180,000	2,870.81	2,942.58	3,016.15	3,091.55	3,168.84	3,248.06
190,000	3,030.30	3,106.06	3,183.71	3,263.30	3,344.89	3,428.51
200,000	3,189.79	3,269.54	3,351.28	3,435.06	3,520.93	3,608.96

TABLE IV-19. Graduated Payment Mortgage, FHA Plan II at 12.0% Interest, Graduated at 5.0%

FHA GRADUATED PAYMENT PLAN II
TERM:30 YEARS INTEREST:12.00% GRADUATED AT 5.00%

PAYMENT AMOUNT	YEAR 1	YEAR 2	YEAR 3	YEAR 4	YEAR 5	YEARS 6-30
50	0.43	0.45	0.48	0.50	0.52	0.55
100	0.86	0.91	0.95	1.00	1.05	1.10
200	1.73	1.81	1.90	2.00	2.10	2.20
300	2.59	2.72	2.86	3.00	3.15	3.31
400	3.45	3.63	3.81	4.00	4.20	4.41
500	4.32	4.53	4.76	5.00	5.25	5.51
600	5.18	5.44	5.71	6.00	6.30	6.61
700	6.04	6.35	6.66	7.00	7.35	7.71
800	6.91	7.25	7.62	8.00	8.40	8.82
900	7.77	8.16	8.57	9.00	9.45	9.92
1,000	8.63	9.07	9.52	10.00	10.50	11.02
2,000	17.27	18.13	19.04	19.99	20.99	22.04
3,000	25.90	27.20	28.56	29.99	31.49	33.06
4,000	34.54	36.27	38.08	39.98	41.98	44.08
5,000	43.17	45.33	47.60	49.98	52.48	55.10
6,000	51.81	54.40	57.12	59.98	62.97	66.12
7,000	60.44	63.47	66.64	69.97	73.47	77.14
8,000	69.08	72.53	76.16	79.97	83.97	88.16
9,000	77.71	81.60	85.68	89.96	94.46	99.18
10,000	86.35	90.67	95.20	99.96	104.96	110.20
15,000	129.52	136.00	142.80	149.94	157.44	165.31
20,000	172.70	181.33	190.40	199.92	209.91	220.41
25,000	215.87	226.66	238.00	249.90	262.39	275.51
30,000	259.04	272.00	285.60	299.88	314.87	330.61
35,000	302.22	317.33	333.20	349.86	367.35	385.72
40,000	345.39	362.66	380.80	399.84	419.83	440.82
45,000	388.57	408.00	428.40	449.81	472.31	495.92
50,000	431.74	453.33	475.99	499.79	524.78	551.02
55,000	474.92	498.66	523.59	549.77	577.26	606.13
60,000	518.09	543.99	571.19	599.75	629.74	661.23
65,000	561.26	589.33	618.79	649.73	682.22	716.33
70,000	604.44	634.66	666.39	699.71	734.70	771.43
75,000	647.61	679.99	713.99	749.69	787.18	826.54
80,000	690.79	725.33	761.59	799.67	839.65	881.64
85,000	733.96	770.66	809.19	849.65	892.13	936.74
90,000	777.13	815.99	856.79	899.63	944.61	991.84
95,000	820.31	861.32	904.39	949.61	997.09	1,046.94
100,000	863.48	906.66	951.99	999.59	1,049.57	1,102.05
110,000	949.83	997.32	1,047.19	1,099.55	1,154.53	1,212.25
120,000	1,036.18	1,087.99	1,142.39	1,199.51	1,259.48	1,322.46
130,000	1,122.53	1,178.65	1,237.59	1,299.47	1,364.44	1,432.66
140,000	1,208.88	1,269.32	1,332.79	1,399.42	1,469.40	1,542.87
150,000	1,295.22	1,359.98	1,427.98	1,499.38	1,574.35	1,653.07
160,000	1,381.57	1,450.65	1,523.18	1,599.34	1,679.31	1,763.27
170,000	1,467.92	1,541.32	1,618.38	1,699.30	1,784.27	1,873.48
180,000	1,554.27	1,631.98	1,713.58	1,799.26	1,889.22	1,983.68
190,000	1,640.62	1,722.65	1,808.78	1,899.22	1,994.18	2,093.89
200,000	1,726.96	1,813.31	1,903.98	1,999.18	2,099.14	2,204.09

TABLE IV-20. Graduated Payment Mortgage, FHA Plan II at 12.5% Interest, Graduated at 5.0%

FHA GRADUATED PAYMENT PLAN II
TERM: 30 YEARS INTEREST: 12.50% GRADUATED AT 5.00%

PAYMENT AMCUNT	YEAR 1	YEAR 2	YEAR 3	YEAR 4	YEAR 5	YEARS 6-30
50	0.45	0.47	0.49	0.52	0.55	0.57
100	0.90	0.94	0.99	1.04	1.09	1.15
200	1.80	1.89	1.98	2.08	2.18	2.29
300	2.69	2.83	2.97	3.12	3.27	3.44
400	3.59	3.77	3.96	4.16	4.36	4.58
500	4.49	4.71	4.95	5.20	5.46	5.73
600	5.39	5.66	5.94	6.24	6.55	6.87
700	6.28	6.60	6.93	7.27	7.64	8.02
800	7.18	7.54	7.92	8.31	8.73	9.17
900	8.08	8.48	8.91	9.35	9.82	10.31
1,000	8.98	9.43	9.90	10.39	10.91	11.46
2,000	17.96	18.85	19.80	20.79	21.82	22.92
3,000	26.93	28.28	29.69	31.18	32.74	34.37
4,000	35.91	37.71	39.59	41.57	43.65	45.83
5,000	44.89	47.13	49.49	51.96	54.56	57.29
6,000	53.87	56.56	59.39	62.36	65.47	68.75
7,000	62.84	65.99	69.29	72.75	76.39	80.21
8,000	71.82	75.41	79.18	83.14	87.30	91.66
9,000	80.80	84.84	89.08	93.54	98.21	103.12
10,000	89.78	94.27	98.98	103.93	109.12	114.58
15,000	134.67	141.40	148.47	155.89	163.69	171.87
20,000	179.55	188.53	197.96	207.86	218.25	229.16
25,000	224.44	235.66	247.45	259.82	272.81	286.45
30,000	269.33	282.80	296.94	311.78	327.37	343.74
35,000	314.22	329.93	346.43	363.75	381.94	401.03
40,000	359.11	377.06	395.92	415.71	436.50	458.32
45,000	404.00	424.20	445.41	467.68	491.06	515.61
50,000	448.88	471.33	494.89	519.64	545.62	572.90
55,000	493.77	518.46	544.38	571.60	600.18	630.19
60,000	538.66	565.59	593.87	623.57	654.75	687.48
65,000	583.55	612.73	643.36	675.53	709.31	744.77
70,000	628.44	659.86	692.85	727.50	763.87	802.06
75,000	673.33	706.99	742.34	779.46	818.43	859.35
80,000	718.21	754.13	791.83	831.42	872.99	916.64
85,000	763.10	801.26	841.32	883.39	927.56	973.93
90,000	807.99	848.39	890.81	935.35	982.12	1,031.22
95,000	852.88	895.52	940.30	987.32	1,036.68	1,088.52
100,000	897.77	942.66	989.79	1,039.28	1,091.24	1,145.81
110,000	987.55	1,036.92	1,088.77	1,143.21	1,200.37	1,260.39
120,000	1,077.32	1,131.19	1,187.75	1,247.14	1,309.49	1,374.97
130,000	1,167.10	1,225.45	1,286.73	1,351.06	1,418.62	1,489.55
140,000	1,256.88	1,319.72	1,385.71	1,454.99	1,527.74	1,604.13
150,000	1,346.65	1,413.99	1,484.68	1,558.92	1,636.86	1,718.71
160,000	1,436.43	1,508.25	1,583.66	1,662.85	1,745.99	1,833.29
170,000	1,526.21	1,602.52	1,682.64	1,766.77	1,855.11	1,947.87
180,000	1,615.98	1,696.78	1,781.62	1,870.70	1,964.24	2,062.45
190,000	1,705.76	1,791.05	1,880.60	1,974.63	2,073.36	2,177.03
200,000	1,795.54	1,885.31	1,979.58	2,078.56	2,182.49	2,291.61

TABLE IV-21. Graduated Payment Mortgage, FHA Plan II at 13.0% Interest, Graduated at 5.0%

FHA GRADUATED PAYMENT PLAN II
TERM:30 YEARS INTEREST:13.00% GRADUATED AT 5.00%

PAYMENT AMOUNT	YEAR 1	YEAR 2	YEAR 3	YEAR 4	YEAR 5	YEARS 6-30
50	0.47	0.49	0.51	0.54	0.57	0.60
100	0.93	0.98	1.03	1.08	1.13	1.19
200	1.86	1.96	2.06	2.16	2.27	2.38
300	2.80	2.94	3.08	3.24	3.40	3.57
400	3.73	3.92	4.11	4.32	4.53	4.76
500	4.66	4.90	5.14	5.40	5.67	5.95
600	5.59	5.87	6.17	6.48	6.80	7.14
700	6.53	6.85	7.20	7.56	7.93	8.33
800	7.46	7.83	8.22	8.64	9.07	9.52
900	8.39	8.81	9.25	9.71	10.20	10.71
1,000	9.32	9.79	10.28	10.79	11.33	11.90
2,000	18.65	19.58	20.56	21.59	22.67	23.80
3,000	27.97	29.37	30.84	32.38	34.00	35.70
4,000	37.30	39.16	41.12	43.18	45.34	47.60
5,000	46.62	48.95	51.40	53.97	56.67	59.50
6,000	55.95	58.74	61.68	64.76	68.00	71.40
7,000	65.27	68.53	71.96	75.56	79.34	83.30
8,000	74.59	78.32	82.24	86.35	90.67	95.20
9,000	83.92	88.11	92.52	97.15	102.00	107.10
10,000	93.24	97.91	102.80	107.94	113.34	119.00
15,000	139.86	146.86	154.20	161.91	170.01	178.51
20,000	186.49	195.81	205.60	215.88	226.68	238.01
25,000	233.11	244.76	257.00	269.85	283.34	297.51
30,000	279.73	293.72	308.40	323.82	340.01	357.01
35,000	326.35	342.67	359.80	377.79	396.68	416.52
40,000	372.97	391.62	411.20	431.76	453.35	476.02
45,000	419.59	440.57	462.60	485.73	510.02	535.52
50,000	466.22	489.53	514.00	539.70	566.69	595.02
55,000	512.84	538.48	565.40	593.67	623.36	654.52
60,000	559.46	587.43	616.80	647.64	680.03	714.03
65,000	606.08	636.38	668.20	701.61	736.69	773.53
70,000	652.70	685.34	719.60	755.58	793.36	833.03
75,000	699.32	734.29	771.00	809.55	850.03	892.53
80,000	745.94	783.24	822.40	863.52	906.70	952.04
85,000	792.57	832.19	873.80	917.49	963.37	1,011.54
90,000	839.19	881.15	925.20	971.46	1,020.04	1,071.04
95,000	885.81	930.10	976.60	1,025.43	1,076.71	1,130.54
100,000	932.43	979.05	1,028.00	1,079.40	1,133.38	1,190.04
110,000	1,025.67	1,076.96	1,130.81	1,187.35	1,246.71	1,309.05
120,000	1,118.92	1,174.86	1,233.61	1,295.29	1,360.05	1,428.05
130,000	1,212.16	1,272.77	1,336.41	1,403.23	1,473.39	1,547.06
140,000	1,305.40	1,370.67	1,439.21	1,511.17	1,586.73	1,666.06
150,000	1,398.65	1,468.58	1,542.01	1,619.11	1,700.06	1,785.07
160,000	1,491.89	1,566.48	1,644.81	1,727.05	1,813.40	1,904.07
170,000	1,585.13	1,664.39	1,747.61	1,834.99	1,926.74	2,023.07
180,000	1,678.38	1,762.29	1,850.41	1,942.93	2,040.08	2,142.08
190,000	1,771.62	1,860.20	1,953.21	2,050.87	2,153.41	2,261.08
200,000	1,864.86	1,958.10	2,056.01	2,158.81	2,266.75	2,380.09

TABLE IV-22. Graduated Payment Mortgage, FHA Plan II at 13.5% Interest, Graduated at 5.0%

FHA GRADUATED PAYMENT PLAN II
TERM: 30 YEARS INTEREST: 13.50% GRADUATED AT 5.00%

PAYMENT AMOUNT	YEAR 1	YEAR 2	YEAR 3	YEAR 4	YEAR 5	YEARS 6-30
50	0.48	0.51	0.53	0.56	0.59	0.62
100	0.97	1.02	1.07	1.12	1.18	1.23
200	1.93	2.03	2.13	2.24	2.35	2.47
300	2.90	3.05	3.20	3.36	3.53	3.70
400	3.87	4.06	4.27	4.48	4.70	4.94
500	4.84	5.08	5.33	5.60	5.88	6.17
600	5.80	6.09	6.40	6.72	7.06	7.41
700	6.77	7.11	7.47	7.84	8.23	8.64
800	7.74	8.13	8.53	8.96	9.41	9.88
900	8.71	9.14	9.60	10.08	10.58	11.11
1,000	9.67	10.16	10.67	11.20	11.76	12.35
2,000	19.35	20.32	21.33	22.40	23.52	24.69
3,000	29.02	30.47	32.00	33.60	35.28	37.04
4,000	38.70	40.63	42.66	44.80	47.04	49.39
5,000	48.37	50.79	53.33	56.00	58.80	61.74
6,000	58.05	60.95	64.00	67.20	70.56	74.08
7,000	67.72	71.11	74.66	78.40	82.32	86.43
8,000	77.40	81.27	85.33	89.60	94.07	98.78
9,000	87.07	91.42	95.99	100.79	105.83	111.13
10,000	96.74	101.58	106.66	111.99	117.59	123.47
15,000	145.12	152.37	159.99	167.99	176.39	185.21
20,000	193.49	203.16	213.32	223.99	235.19	246.95
25,000	241.86	253.95	266.65	279.98	293.98	308.68
30,000	290.23	304.75	319.98	335.98	352.78	370.42
35,000	338.61	355.54	373.31	391.98	411.58	432.16
40,000	386.98	406.33	426.64	447.98	470.37	493.89
45,000	435.35	457.12	479.97	503.97	529.17	555.63
50,000	483.72	507.91	533.30	559.97	587.97	617.37
55,000	532.10	558.70	586.64	615.97	646.77	679.10
60,000	580.47	609.49	639.97	671.96	705.56	740.84
65,000	628.84	660.28	693.30	727.96	764.36	802.58
70,000	677.21	711.07	746.63	783.96	823.16	864.31
75,000	725.58	761.86	799.96	839.95	881.95	926.05
80,000	773.96	812.65	853.29	895.95	940.75	987.79
85,000	822.33	863.45	906.62	951.95	999.55	1,049.52
90,000	870.70	914.24	959.95	1,007.95	1,058.34	1,111.26
95,000	919.07	965.03	1,013.28	1,063.94	1,117.14	1,173.00
100,000	967.45	1,015.82	1,066.61	1,119.94	1,175.94	1,234.73
110,000	1,064.19	1,117.40	1,173.27	1,231.93	1,293.53	1,358.21
120,000	1,160.94	1,218.98	1,279.93	1,343.93	1,411.12	1,481.68
130,000	1,257.68	1,320.56	1,386.59	1,455.92	1,528.72	1,605.15
140,000	1,354.42	1,422.15	1,493.25	1,567.92	1,646.31	1,728.63
150,000	1,451.17	1,523.73	1,599.91	1,679.91	1,763.91	1,852.10
160,000	1,547.91	1,625.31	1,706.57	1,791.90	1,881.50	1,975.57
170,000	1,644.66	1,726.89	1,813.24	1,903.90	1,999.09	2,099.05
180,000	1,741.40	1,828.47	1,919.90	2,015.89	2,116.69	2,222.52
190,000	1,838.15	1,930.05	2,026.56	2,127.89	2,234.28	2,345.99
200,000	1,934.89	2,031.64	2,133.22	2,239.88	2,351.87	2,469.47

TABLE IV-23. Graduated Payment Mortgage, FHA Plan II at 14.0% Interest, Graduated at 5.0%

FHA GRADUATED PAYMENT PLAN II
TERM:30 YEARS INTEREST:14.00% GRADUATED AT 5.00%

PAYMENT AMOUNT	YEAR 1	YEAR 2	YEAR 3	YEAR 4	YEAR 5	YEARS 6-30
50	0.50	0.53	0.55	0.58	0.61	0.64
100	1.00	1.05	1.11	1.16	1.22	1.28
200	2.01	2.11	2.21	2.32	2.44	2.56
300	3.01	3.16	3.32	3.48	3.66	3.84
400	4.01	4.21	4.42	4.64	4.88	5.12
500	5.01	5.26	5.53	5.80	6.09	6.40
600	6.02	6.32	6.63	6.97	7.31	7.68
700	7.02	7.37	7.74	8.13	8.53	8.96
800	8.02	8.42	8.84	9.29	9.75	10.24
900	9.03	9.48	9.95	10.45	10.97	11.52
1,000	10.03	10.53	11.06	11.61	12.19	12.80
2,000	20.06	21.06	22.11	23.22	24.38	25.60
3,000	30.08	31.59	33.17	34.83	36.57	38.40
4,000	40.11	42.12	44.22	46.43	48.76	51.19
5,000	50.14	52.65	55.28	58.04	60.95	63.99
6,000	60.17	63.18	66.33	69.65	73.13	76.79
7,000	70.20	73.71	77.39	81.26	85.32	89.59
8,000	80.22	84.23	88.45	92.87	97.51	102.39
9,000	90.25	94.76	99.50	104.48	109.70	115.19
10,000	100.28	105.29	110.56	116.09	121.89	127.98
15,000	150.42	157.94	165.84	174.13	182.84	191.98
20,000	200.56	210.59	221.12	232.17	243.78	255.97
25,000	250.70	263.23	276.39	290.21	304.73	319.96
30,000	300.84	315.88	331.67	348.26	365.67	383.95
35,000	350.98	368.53	386.95	406.30	426.62	447.95
40,000	401.12	421.17	442.23	464.34	487.56	511.94
45,000	451.26	473.82	497.51	522.39	548.51	575.93
50,000	501.40	526.47	552.79	580.43	609.45	639.92
55,000	551.54	579.11	608.07	638.47	670.40	703.92
60,000	601.68	631.76	663.35	696.52	731.34	767.91
65,000	651.82	684.41	718.63	754.56	792.29	831.90
70,000	701.96	737.05	773.91	812.60	853.23	895.89
75,000	752.10	789.70	829.18	870.64	914.18	959.89
80,000	802.23	842.35	884.46	928.69	975.12	1,023.88
85,000	852.37	894.99	939.74	986.73	1,036.07	1,087.87
90,000	902.51	947.64	995.02	1,044.77	1,097.01	1,151.86
95,000	952.65	1,000.29	1,050.30	1,102.82	1,157.96	1,215.85
100,000	1,002.79	1,052.93	1,105.58	1,160.86	1,218.90	1,279.85
110,000	1,103.07	1,158.23	1,216.14	1,276.94	1,340.79	1,407.83
120,000	1,203.35	1,263.52	1,326.70	1,393.03	1,462.68	1,535.82
130,000	1,303.63	1,368.81	1,437.25	1,509.12	1,584.57	1,663.80
140,000	1,403.91	1,474.11	1,547.81	1,625.20	1,706.46	1,791.79
150,000	1,504.19	1,579.40	1,658.37	1,741.29	1,828.35	1,919.77
160,000	1,604.47	1,684.69	1,768.93	1,857.37	1,950.24	2,047.75
170,000	1,704.75	1,789.99	1,879.49	1,973.46	2,072.13	2,175.74
180,000	1,805.03	1,895.28	1,990.04	2,089.55	2,194.02	2,303.72
190,000	1,905.31	2,000.57	2,100.60	2,205.63	2,315.91	2,431.71
200,000	2,005.59	2,105.87	2,211.16	2,321.72	2,437.80	2,559.69

TABLE IV-24. Graduated Payment Mortgage, FHA Plan II at 14.5% Interest, Graduated at 5.0%

FHA GRADUATED PAYMENT PLAN II
TERM:30 YEARS INTEREST:14.50% GRADUATED AT 5.00%

PAYMENT AMOUNT	YEAR 1	YEAR 2	YEAR 3	YEAR 4	YEAR 5	YEARS 6-30
50	0.52	0.55	0.57	0.60	0.63	0.66
100	1.04	1.09	1.14	1.20	1.26	1.33
200	2.08	2.18	2.29	2.40	2.52	2.65
300	3.12	3.27	3.43	3.61	3.79	3.98
400	4.15	4.36	4.58	4.81	5.05	5.30
500	5.19	5.45	5.72	6.01	6.31	6.63
600	6.23	6.54	6.87	7.21	7.57	7.95
700	7.27	7.63	8.01	8.41	8.84	9.28
800	8.31	8.72	9.16	9.62	10.10	10.60
900	9.35	9.81	10.30	10.82	11.36	11.93
1,000	10.38	10.90	11.45	12.02	12.62	13.25
2,000	20.77	21.81	22.90	24.04	25.24	26.51
3,000	31.15	32.71	34.35	36.06	37.87	39.76
4,000	41.54	43.62	45.80	48.09	50.49	53.01
5,000	51.92	54.52	57.24	60.11	63.11	66.27
6,000	62.31	65.42	68.69	72.13	75.73	79.52
7,000	72.69	76.33	80.14	84.15	88.36	92.78
8,000	83.08	87.23	91.59	96.17	100.98	106.03
9,000	93.46	98.13	103.04	108.19	113.60	119.28
10,000	103.85	109.04	114.49	120.21	126.22	132.54
15,000	155.77	163.56	171.73	180.32	189.34	198.80
20,000	207.69	218.08	228.98	240.43	252.45	265.07
25,000	259.61	272.59	286.22	300.53	315.56	331.34
30,000	311.54	327.11	343.47	360.64	378.67	397.61
35,000	363.46	381.63	400.71	420.75	441.79	463.88
40,000	415.38	436.15	457.96	480.86	504.90	530.14
45,000	467.30	490.67	515.20	540.96	568.01	596.41
50,000	519.23	545.19	572.45	601.07	631.12	662.68
55,000	571.15	599.71	629.69	661.18	694.24	728.95
60,000	623.07	654.23	686.94	721.28	757.35	795.21
65,000	674.99	708.74	744.18	781.39	820.46	861.48
70,000	726.92	763.26	801.43	841.50	883.57	927.75
75,000	778.84	817.78	858.67	901.60	946.68	994.02
80,000	830.76	872.30	915.92	961.71	1,009.80	1,060.29
85,000	882.68	926.82	973.16	1,021.82	1,072.91	1,126.55
90,000	934.61	981.34	1,030.40	1,081.92	1,136.02	1,192.82
95,000	986.53	1,035.86	1,087.65	1,142.03	1,199.13	1,259.09
100,000	1,038.45	1,090.38	1,144.89	1,202.14	1,262.25	1,325.36
110,000	1,142.30	1,199.41	1,259.38	1,322.35	1,388.47	1,457.89
120,000	1,246.14	1,308.45	1,373.87	1,442.57	1,514.69	1,590.43
130,000	1,349.99	1,417.49	1,488.36	1,562.78	1,640.92	1,722.97
140,000	1,453.83	1,526.53	1,602.85	1,682.99	1,767.14	1,855.50
150,000	1,557.68	1,635.56	1,717.34	1,803.21	1,893.37	1,988.04
160,000	1,661.52	1,744.60	1,831.83	1,923.42	2,019.59	2,120.57
170,000	1,765.37	1,853.64	1,946.32	2,043.64	2,145.82	2,253.11
180,000	1,869.21	1,962.68	2,060.81	2,163.85	2,272.04	2,385.64
190,000	1,973.06	2,071.71	2,175.30	2,284.06	2,398.27	2,518.18
200,000	2,076.91	2,180.75	2,289.79	2,404.28	2,524.49	2,650.72

TABLE IV-25. Graduated Payment Mortgage, FHA Plan II at 15.0% Interest, Graduated at 5.0%

FHA GRADUATED PAYMENT PLAN II
TERM:30 YEARS INTEREST:15.00% GRADUATED AT 5.00%

PAYMENT AMCUNT	YEAR 1	YEAR 2	YEAR 3	YEAR 4	YEAR 5	YEARS 6-30
50	0.54	0.56	0.59	0.62	0.65	0.69
100	1.07	1.13	1.18	1.24	1.31	1.37
200	2.15	2.26	2.37	2.49	2.61	2.74
300	3.22	3.38	3.55	3.73	3.92	4.11
400	4.30	4.51	4.74	4.98	5.22	5.48
500	5.37	5.64	5.92	6.22	6.53	6.86
600	6.45	6.77	7.11	7.46	7.84	8.23
700	7.52	7.90	8.29	8.71	9.14	9.60
800	8.60	9.02	9.48	9.95	10.45	10.97
900	9.67	10.15	10.66	11.19	11.75	12.34
1,000	10.74	11.28	11.85	12.44	13.06	13.71
2,000	21.49	22.56	23.69	24.88	26.12	27.42
3,000	32.23	33.84	35.54	37.31	39.18	41.14
4,000	42.98	45.12	47.38	49.75	52.24	54.85
5,000	53.72	56.41	59.23	62.19	65.30	68.56
6,000	64.46	67.69	71.07	74.63	78.36	82.27
7,000	75.21	78.97	82.92	87.06	91.42	95.99
8,000	85.95	90.25	94.76	99.50	104.48	109.70
9,000	96.70	101.53	106.61	111.94	117.54	123.41
10,000	107.44	112.81	118.45	124.38	130.59	137.12
15,000	161.16	169.22	177.68	186.56	195.89	205.69
20,000	214.88	225.62	236.91	248.75	261.19	274.25
25,000	268.60	282.03	296.13	310.94	326.49	342.81
30,000	322.32	338.44	355.36	373.13	391.78	411.37
35,000	376.04	394.84	414.59	435.32	457.08	479.93
40,000	429.76	451.25	473.81	497.50	522.38	548.50
45,000	483.48	507.66	533.04	559.69	587.68	617.06
50,000	537.20	564.06	592.27	621.88	652.97	685.62
55,000	590.92	620.47	651.49	684.07	718.27	754.18
60,000	644.64	676.87	710.72	746.25	783.57	822.75
65,000	698.36	733.28	769.95	808.44	848.86	891.31
70,000	752.08	789.69	829.17	870.63	914.16	959.87
75,000	805.80	846.09	888.40	932.82	979.46	1,028.43
80,000	859.52	902.50	947.62	995.01	1,044.76	1,096.99
85,000	913.24	958.91	1,006.85	1,057.19	1,110.05	1,165.56
90,000	966.96	1,015.31	1,066.08	1,119.38	1,175.35	1,234.12
95,000	1,020.68	1,071.72	1,125.30	1,181.57	1,240.65	1,302.68
100,000	1,074.40	1,128.12	1,184.53	1,243.76	1,305.95	1,371.24
110,000	1,181.84	1,240.94	1,302.98	1,368.13	1,436.54	1,508.37
120,000	1,289.29	1,353.75	1,421.44	1,492.51	1,567.13	1,645.49
130,000	1,396.73	1,466.56	1,539.89	1,616.88	1,697.73	1,782.62
140,000	1,504.17	1,579.37	1,658.34	1,741.26	1,828.32	1,919.74
150,000	1,611.61	1,692.19	1,776.80	1,865.64	1,958.92	2,056.86
160,000	1,719.05	1,805.00	1,895.25	1,990.01	2,089.51	2,193.99
170,000	1,826.49	1,917.81	2,013.70	2,114.39	2,220.11	2,331.11
180,000	1,933.93	2,030.62	2,132.16	2,238.76	2,350.70	2,468.24
190,000	2,041.37	2,143.44	2,250.61	2,363.14	2,481.30	2,605.36
200,000	2,148.81	2,256.25	2,369.06	2,487.51	2,611.89	2,742.49

TABLE IV-26. Graduated Payment Mortgage, FHA Plan II at 15.5% Interest, Graduated at 5.0%

FHA GRADUATED PAYMENT PLAN II
TERM:30 YEARS INTEREST:15.50% GRADUATED AT 5.00%

PAYMENT AMCUNT	YEAR 1	YEAR 2	YEAR 3	YEAR 4	YEAR 5	YEARS 6-30
50	0.56	0.58	0.61	0.64	0.67	0.71
100	1.11	1.17	1.22	1.29	1.35	1.42
200	2.22	2.33	2.45	2.57	2.70	2.83
300	3.33	3.50	3.67	3.86	4.05	4.25
400	4.44	4.66	4.90	5.14	5.40	5.67
500	5.55	5.83	6.12	6.43	6.75	7.C9
600	6.66	7.00	7.35	7.71	8.10	8.50
700	7.77	8.16	8.57	9.00	9.45	9.92
800	8.89	9.33	9.80	10.29	10.80	11.34
900	10.00	10.50	11.02	11.57	12.15	12.76
1,000	11.11	11.66	12.24	12.86	13.50	14.17
2,000	22.21	23.32	24.49	25.71	27.00	28.35
3,000	33.32	34.98	36.73	38.57	40.50	42.52
4,000	44.43	46.65	48.98	51.43	54.00	56.7C
5,000	55.53	58.31	61.22	64.28	67.50	70.87
6,000	66.64	69.97	73.47	77.14	81.00	85.05
7,000	77.74	81.63	85.71	90.00	94.50	99.22
8,000	88.85	93.29	97.96	102.86	108.00	113.4C
9,000	99.96	104.95	110.20	115.71	121.50	127.57
10,000	111.06	116.62	122.45	128.57	135.00	141.75
15,000	166.59	174.92	183.67	192.85	202.50	212.62
20,000	222.13	233.23	244.89	257.14	270.00	283.50
25,000	277.66	291.54	306.12	321.42	337.49	354.37
30,000	333.19	349.85	367.34	385.71	404.99	425.24
35,000	388.72	408.16	428.56	449.99	472.49	496.12
40,000	444.25	466.47	489.79	514.28	539.99	566.99
45,000	499.78	524.77	551.01	578.56	607.49	637.87
50,000	555.32	583.08	612.24	642.85	674.99	708.74
55,000	610.85	641.39	673.46	707.13	742.49	779.61
60,000	666.38	699.70	734.68	771.42	809.99	850.49
65,000	721.91	758.01	795.91	835.70	877.49	921.36
70,000	777.44	816.31	857.13	899.99	944.99	992.23
75,000	832.97	874.62	918.35	964.27	1,012.48	1,063.11
80,000	888.50	932.93	979.58	1,028.56	1,079.98	1,133.98
85,000	944.04	991.24	1,040.80	1,092.84	1,147.48	1,204.86
90,000	999.57	1,049.55	1,102.02	1,157.13	1,214.98	1,275.73
95,000	1,055.10	1,107.85	1,163.25	1,221.41	1,282.48	1,346.60
100,000	1,110.63	1,166.16	1,224.47	1,285.69	1,349.98	1,417.48
110,000	1,221.69	1,282.78	1,346.92	1,414.26	1,484.98	1,559.23
120,000	1,332.76	1,399.40	1,469.37	1,542.83	1,619.98	1,700.97
130,000	1,443.82	1,516.01	1,591.81	1,671.40	1,754.97	1,842.72
140,000	1,554.88	1,632.63	1,714.26	1,799.97	1,889.97	1,984.47
150,000	1,665.95	1,749.24	1,836.71	1,928.54	2,024.97	2,126.22
160,000	1,777.01	1,865.86	1,959.15	2,057.11	2,159.97	2,267.97
170,000	1,888.07	1,982.48	2,081.60	2,185.68	2,294.96	2,409.71
180,000	1,999.14	2,099.09	2,204.05	2,314.25	2,429.96	2,551.46
190,000	2,110.20	2,215.71	2,326.49	2,442.82	2,564.96	2,693.21
200,000	2,221.26	2,332.33	2,448.94	2,571.39	2,699.96	2,834.96

TABLE IV-27. Graduated Payment Mortgage, FHA Plan II at 16.0% Interest, Graduated at 5.0%

FHA GRADUATED PAYMENT PLAN II
TERM: 30 YEARS INTEREST: 16.00% GRADUATED AT 5.00%

PAYMENT AMOUNT	YEAR 1	YEAR 2	YEAR 3	YEAR 4	YEAR 5	YEARS 6-30
50	0.57	0.60	0.63	0.66	0.70	0.73
100	1.15	1.20	1.26	1.33	1.39	1.46
200	2.29	2.41	2.53	2.66	2.79	2.93
300	3.44	3.61	3.79	3.98	4.18	4.39
400	4.59	4.82	5.06	5.31	5.58	5.86
500	5.74	6.02	6.32	6.64	6.97	7.32
600	6.88	7.23	7.59	7.97	8.37	8.78
700	8.03	8.43	8.85	9.30	9.76	10.25
800	9.18	9.64	10.12	10.62	11.15	11.71
900	10.32	10.84	11.38	11.95	12.55	13.18
1,000	11.47	12.04	12.65	13.28	13.94	14.64
2,000	22.94	24.09	25.29	26.56	27.89	29.28
3,000	34.41	36.13	37.94	39.84	41.83	43.92
4,000	45.88	48.18	50.59	53.12	55.77	58.56
5,000	57.36	60.22	63.23	66.40	69.72	73.20
6,000	68.83	72.27	75.88	79.68	83.66	87.84
7,000	80.30	84.31	88.53	92.96	97.60	102.48
8,000	91.77	96.36	101.18	106.23	111.55	117.12
9,000	103.24	108.40	113.82	119.51	125.49	131.76
10,000	114.71	120.45	126.47	132.79	139.43	146.40
15,000	172.07	180.67	189.70	199.19	209.15	219.61
20,000	229.42	240.89	252.94	265.59	278.87	292.81
25,000	286.78	301.12	316.17	331.98	348.58	366.01
30,000	344.13	361.34	379.41	398.38	418.30	439.21
35,000	401.49	421.57	442.64	464.78	488.01	512.42
40,000	458.85	481.79	505.88	531.17	557.73	585.62
45,000	516.20	542.01	569.11	597.57	627.45	658.82
50,000	573.56	602.24	632.35	663.97	697.16	732.02
55,000	630.91	662.46	695.58	730.36	766.88	805.22
60,000	688.27	722.68	758.82	796.76	836.60	878.43
65,000	745.63	782.91	822.05	863.15	906.31	951.63
70,000	802.98	843.13	885.29	929.55	976.03	1,024.83
75,000	860.34	903.35	948.52	995.95	1,045.75	1,098.03
80,000	917.69	963.58	1,011.76	1,062.34	1,115.46	1,171.23
85,000	975.05	1,023.80	1,074.99	1,128.74	1,185.18	1,244.44
90,000	1,032.40	1,084.02	1,138.23	1,195.14	1,254.89	1,317.64
95,000	1,089.76	1,144.25	1,201.46	1,261.53	1,324.61	1,390.84
100,000	1,147.12	1,204.47	1,264.70	1,327.93	1,394.33	1,464.04
110,000	1,261.83	1,324.92	1,391.17	1,460.72	1,533.76	1,610.45
120,000	1,376.54	1,445.37	1,517.63	1,593.52	1,673.19	1,756.85
130,000	1,491.25	1,565.81	1,644.10	1,726.31	1,812.62	1,903.26
140,000	1,605.96	1,686.26	1,770.57	1,859.10	1,952.06	2,049.66
150,000	1,720.67	1,806.71	1,897.04	1,991.90	2,091.49	2,196.06
160,000	1,835.39	1,927.15	2,023.51	2,124.69	2,230.92	2,342.47
170,000	1,950.10	2,047.60	2,149.98	2,257.48	2,370.36	2,488.87
180,000	2,064.81	2,168.05	2,276.45	2,390.27	2,509.79	2,635.28
190,000	2,179.52	2,288.50	2,402.92	2,523.07	2,649.22	2,781.68
200,000	2,294.23	2,408.94	2,529.39	2,655.86	2,788.65	2,928.09

TABLE IV-28. Graduated Payment Mortgage, FHA Plan II at 16.5% Interest, Graduated at 5.0%

FHA GRADUATED PAYMENT PLAN II
TERM:30 YEARS INTEREST:16.50% GRADUATED AT 5.00%

PAYMENT AMOUNT	YEAR 1	YEAR 2	YEAR 3	YEAR 4	YEAR 5	YEARS 6-30
50	0.59	0.62	0.65	0.69	0.72	0.76
100	1.18	1.24	1.31	1.37	1.44	1.51
200	2.37	2.49	2.61	2.74	2.88	3.02
300	3.55	3.73	3.92	4.11	4.32	4.53
400	4.74	4.97	5.22	5.48	5.76	6.04
500	5.92	6.22	6.53	6.85	7.19	7.55
600	7.10	7.46	7.83	8.22	8.63	9.07
700	8.29	8.70	9.14	9.59	10.07	10.58
800	9.47	9.94	10.44	10.96	11.51	12.09
900	10.65	11.19	11.75	12.33	12.95	13.60
1,000	11.84	12.43	13.05	13.70	14.39	15.11
2,000	23.68	24.86	26.10	27.41	28.78	30.22
3,000	35.52	37.29	39.16	41.11	43.17	45.33
4,000	47.35	49.72	52.21	54.82	57.56	60.44
5,000	59.19	62.15	65.26	68.52	71.95	75.55
6,000	71.03	74.58	78.31	82.23	86.34	90.66
7,000	82.87	87.01	91.36	95.93	100.73	105.76
8,000	94.71	99.44	104.41	109.64	115.12	120.87
9,000	106.55	111.87	117.47	123.34	129.51	135.98
10,000	118.38	124.30	130.52	137.04	143.90	151.09
15,000	177.58	186.46	195.78	205.57	215.85	226.64
20,000	236.77	248.61	261.04	274.09	287.79	302.18
25,000	295.96	310.76	326.30	342.61	359.74	377.73
30,000	355.15	372.91	391.56	411.13	431.69	453.28
35,000	414.35	435.06	456.82	479.66	503.64	528.82
40,000	473.54	497.21	522.07	548.18	575.59	604.37
45,000	532.73	559.37	587.33	616.70	647.54	679.91
50,000	591.92	621.52	652.59	685.22	719.48	755.46
55,000	651.11	683.67	717.85	753.75	791.43	831.00
60,000	710.31	745.82	783.11	822.27	863.38	906.55
65,000	769.50	807.97	848.37	890.79	935.33	982.10
70,000	828.69	870.12	913.63	959.31	1,007.28	1,057.64
75,000	887.88	932.28	978.89	1,027.84	1,079.23	1,133.19
80,000	947.07	994.43	1,044.15	1,096.36	1,151.18	1,208.73
85,000	1,006.27	1,056.58	1,109.41	1,164.88	1,223.12	1,284.28
90,000	1,065.46	1,118.73	1,174.67	1,233.40	1,295.07	1,359.83
95,000	1,124.65	1,180.88	1,239.93	1,301.92	1,367.02	1,435.37
100,000	1,183.84	1,243.04	1,305.19	1,370.45	1,438.97	1,510.92
110,000	1,302.23	1,367.34	1,435.71	1,507.49	1,582.87	1,662.01
120,000	1,420.61	1,491.64	1,566.22	1,644.54	1,726.76	1,813.10
130,000	1,539.00	1,615.95	1,696.74	1,781.58	1,870.66	1,964.19
140,000	1,657.38	1,740.25	1,827.26	1,918.63	2,014.56	2,115.28
150,000	1,775.77	1,864.55	1,957.78	2,055.67	2,158.45	2,266.38
160,000	1,894.15	1,988.86	2,088.30	2,192.71	2,302.35	2,417.47
170,000	2,012.53	2,113.16	2,218.82	2,329.76	2,446.25	2,560.56
180,000	2,130.92	2,237.46	2,349.34	2,466.80	2,590.14	2,719.65
190,000	2,249.30	2,361.77	2,479.86	2,603.85	2,734.04	2,870.74
200,000	2,367.69	2,486.07	2,610.37	2,740.89	2,877.94	3,021.83

TABLE IV-29. Graduated Payment Mortgage, FHA Plan II at 17.0% Interest, Graduated at 5.0%

FHA GRADUATED PAYMENT PLAN II
TERM:30 YEARS INTEREST:17.00% GRADUATED AT 5.00%

PAYMENT AMOUNT	YEAR 1	YEAR 2	YEAR 3	YEAR 4	YEAR 5	YEARS 6-30
50	0.61	0.64	0.67	0.71	0.74	0.78
100	1.22	1.28	1.35	1.41	1.48	1.56
200	2.44	2.56	2.69	2.83	2.97	3.12
300	3.66	3.85	4.04	4.24	4.45	4.67
400	4.88	5.13	5.38	5.65	5.94	6.23
500	6.10	6.41	6.73	7.07	7.42	7.79
600	7.32	7.69	8.08	8.48	8.90	9.35
700	8.55	8.97	9.42	9.89	10.39	10.91
800	9.77	10.25	10.77	11.31	11.87	12.46
900	10.99	11.54	12.11	12.72	13.35	14.02
1,000	12.21	12.82	13.46	14.13	14.84	15.58
2,000	24.42	25.64	26.92	28.26	29.68	31.16
3,000	36.62	38.46	40.38	42.40	44.52	46.74
4,000	48.83	51.27	53.84	56.53	59.36	62.32
5,000	61.04	64.09	67.30	70.66	74.19	77.90
6,000	73.25	76.91	80.76	84.79	89.03	93.48
7,000	85.46	89.73	94.22	98.93	103.87	109.07
8,000	97.66	102.55	107.67	113.06	118.71	124.65
9,000	109.87	115.37	121.13	127.19	133.55	140.23
10,000	122.08	128.18	134.59	141.32	148.39	155.81
15,000	183.12	192.28	201.89	211.98	222.58	233.71
20,000	244.16	256.37	269.19	282.65	296.78	311.62
25,000	305.20	320.46	336.48	353.31	370.97	389.52
30,000	366.24	384.55	403.78	423.97	445.17	467.42
35,000	427.28	448.64	471.08	494.63	519.36	545.33
40,000	488.32	512.74	538.37	565.29	593.56	623.23
45,000	549.36	576.83	605.67	635.95	667.75	701.14
50,000	610.40	640.92	672.97	706.61	741.94	779.04
55,000	671.44	705.01	740.26	777.27	816.14	856.95
60,000	732.48	769.10	807.56	847.94	890.33	934.85
65,000	793.52	833.19	874.85	918.60	964.53	1,012.75
70,000	854.56	897.29	942.15	989.26	1,038.72	1,090.66
75,000	915.60	961.38	1,009.45	1,059.92	1,112.92	1,168.56
80,000	976.64	1,025.47	1,076.74	1,130.58	1,187.11	1,246.47
85,000	1,037.68	1,089.56	1,144.04	1,201.24	1,261.30	1,324.37
90,000	1,098.72	1,153.65	1,211.34	1,271.90	1,335.50	1,402.27
95,000	1,159.76	1,217.75	1,278.63	1,342.57	1,409.69	1,480.18
100,000	1,220.80	1,281.84	1,345.93	1,413.23	1,483.89	1,558.08
110,000	1,342.88	1,410.02	1,480.52	1,554.55	1,632.28	1,713.89
120,000	1,464.96	1,538.21	1,615.12	1,695.87	1,780.67	1,869.70
130,000	1,587.04	1,666.39	1,749.71	1,837.19	1,929.05	2,025.51
140,000	1,709.12	1,794.57	1,884.30	1,978.52	2,077.44	2,181.32
150,000	1,831.20	1,922.76	2,018.90	2,119.84	2,225.83	2,337.12
160,000	1,953.28	2,050.94	2,153.49	2,261.16	2,374.22	2,492.93
170,000	2,075.36	2,179.13	2,288.08	2,402.49	2,522.61	2,648.74
180,000	2,197.44	2,307.31	2,422.67	2,543.81	2,671.00	2,804.55
190,000	2,319.52	2,435.49	2,557.27	2,685.13	2,819.39	2,960.36
200,000	2,441.60	2,563.68	2,691.86	2,826.45	2,967.78	3,116.17

TABLE IV-30. Graduated Payment Mortgage, FHA Plan II at 17.5% Interest, Graduated at 5.0%

FHA GRADUATED PAYMENT PLAN II
TERM:30 YEARS INTEREST:17.50% GRADUATED AT 5.00%

PAYMENT AMOUNT	YEAR 1	YEAR 2	YEAR 3	YEAR 4	YEAR 5	YEARS 6-30
50	0.63	0.66	0.69	0.73	0.76	0.80
100	1.26	1.32	1.39	1.46	1.53	1.61
200	2.52	2.64	2.77	2.91	3.06	3.21
300	3.77	3.96	4.16	4.37	4.59	4.82
400	5.03	5.28	5.55	5.83	6.12	6.42
500	6.29	6.60	6.93	7.28	7.65	8.03
600	7.55	7.93	8.32	8.74	9.17	9.63
700	8.81	9.25	9.71	10.19	10.70	11.24
800	10.06	10.57	11.10	11.65	12.23	12.84
900	11.32	11.89	12.48	13.11	13.76	14.45
1,000	12.58	13.21	13.87	14.56	15.29	16.06
2,000	25.16	26.42	27.74	29.13	30.58	32.11
3,000	37.74	39.63	41.61	43.69	45.87	48.17
4,000	50.32	52.83	55.48	58.25	61.16	64.22
5,000	62.90	66.04	69.35	72.81	76.45	80.28
6,000	75.48	79.25	83.21	87.38	91.74	96.33
7,000	88.06	92.46	97.08	101.94	107.03	112.39
8,000	100.64	105.67	110.95	116.50	122.33	128.44
9,000	113.22	118.88	124.82	131.06	137.62	144.50
10,000	125.80	132.09	138.69	145.63	152.91	160.55
15,000	188.70	198.13	208.04	218.44	229.36	240.83
20,000	251.59	264.17	277.38	291.25	305.81	321.10
25,000	314.49	330.22	346.73	364.06	382.27	401.38
30,000	377.39	396.26	416.07	436.88	458.72	481.66
35,000	440.29	462.30	485.42	509.69	535.17	561.93
40,000	503.19	528.35	554.76	582.50	611.63	642.21
45,000	566.09	594.39	624.11	655.31	688.08	722.48
50,000	628.98	660.43	693.45	728.13	764.53	802.76
55,000	691.88	726.48	762.80	800.94	840.99	883.04
60,000	754.78	792.52	832.15	873.75	917.44	963.31
65,000	817.68	858.56	901.49	946.57	993.89	1,043.59
70,000	880.58	924.61	970.84	1,019.38	1,070.35	1,123.86
75,000	943.48	990.65	1,040.18	1,092.19	1,146.80	1,204.14
80,000	1,006.37	1,056.69	1,109.53	1,165.00	1,223.25	1,284.42
85,000	1,069.27	1,122.74	1,178.87	1,237.82	1,299.71	1,364.69
90,000	1,132.17	1,188.78	1,248.22	1,310.63	1,376.16	1,444.97
95,000	1,195.07	1,254.82	1,317.56	1,383.44	1,452.61	1,525.25
100,000	1,257.97	1,320.87	1,386.91	1,456.26	1,529.07	1,605.52
110,000	1,383.76	1,452.95	1,525.60	1,601.88	1,681.97	1,766.07
120,000	1,509.56	1,585.04	1,664.29	1,747.51	1,834.88	1,926.63
130,000	1,635.36	1,717.13	1,802.98	1,893.13	1,987.79	2,087.18
140,000	1,761.16	1,849.21	1,941.67	2,038.76	2,140.69	2,247.73
150,000	1,886.95	1,981.30	2,080.36	2,184.38	2,293.60	2,408.28
160,000	2,012.75	2,113.39	2,219.06	2,330.01	2,446.51	2,568.83
170,000	2,138.55	2,245.47	2,357.75	2,475.63	2,599.42	2,729.39
180,000	2,264.34	2,377.56	2,496.44	2,621.26	2,752.32	2,889.94
190,000	2,390.14	2,509.65	2,635.13	2,766.88	2,905.23	3,050.49
200,000	2,515.94	2,641.73	2,773.82	2,912.51	3,058.14	3,211.04

TABLE IV-31. Graduated Payment Mortgage, FHA Plan II at 18.0% Interest, Graduated at 5.0%

FHA GRADUATED PAYMENT PLAN II
TERM:30 YEARS INTEREST:18.00% GRADUATED AT 5.00%

PAYMENT AMCUNT	YEAR 1	YEAR 2	YEAR 3	YEAR 4	YEAR 5	YEARS 6-30
50	0.65	0.68	0.71	0.75	0.79	0.83
100	1.30	1.36	1.43	1.50	1.57	1.65
200	2.59	2.72	2.86	3.00	3.15	3.31
300	3.89	4.08	4.28	4.50	4.72	4.96
400	5.18	5.44	5.71	6.00	6.30	6.61
500	6.48	6.80	7.14	7.50	7.87	8.27
600	7.77	8.16	8.57	9.00	9.45	9.92
700	9.07	9.52	10.00	10.50	11.02	11.57
800	10.36	10.88	11.42	12.00	12.60	13.23
900	11.66	12.24	12.85	13.50	14.17	14.88
1,000	12.95	13.60	14.28	15.00	15.74	16.53
2,000	25.91	27.20	28.56	29.99	31.49	33.06
3,000	38.86	40.80	42.84	44.99	47.23	49.60
4,000	51.81	54.40	57.12	59.98	62.98	66.13
5,000	64.77	68.01	71.41	74.98	78.72	82.66
6,000	77.72	81.61	85.69	89.97	94.47	99.19
7,000	90.67	95.21	99.97	104.97	110.21	115.73
8,000	103.63	108.81	114.25	119.96	125.96	132.26
9,000	116.58	122.41	128.53	134.96	141.70	148.79
10,000	129.53	136.01	142.81	149.95	157.45	165.32
15,000	194.30	204.02	214.22	224.93	236.17	247.98
20,000	259.07	272.02	285.62	299.90	314.90	330.64
25,000	323.83	340.03	357.03	374.88	393.62	413.30
30,000	388.60	408.03	428.43	449.85	472.35	495.97
35,000	453.37	476.04	499.84	524.83	551.07	578.63
40,000	518.14	544.04	571.24	599.81	629.80	661.29
45,000	582.90	612.05	642.65	674.78	708.52	743.95
50,000	647.67	680.05	714.06	749.76	787.25	826.61
55,000	712.44	748.06	785.46	824.73	865.97	909.27
60,000	777.20	816.06	856.87	899.71	944.70	991.93
65,000	841.97	884.07	928.27	974.69	1,023.42	1,074.59
70,000	906.74	952.07	999.68	1,049.66	1,102.14	1,157.25
75,000	971.50	1,020.08	1,071.08	1,124.64	1,180.87	1,239.91
80,000	1,036.27	1,088.08	1,142.49	1,199.61	1,259.59	1,322.57
85,000	1,101.04	1,156.09	1,213.89	1,274.59	1,338.32	1,405.23
90,000	1,165.80	1,224.10	1,285.30	1,349.56	1,417.04	1,487.90
95,000	1,230.57	1,292.10	1,356.71	1,424.54	1,495.77	1,570.56
100,000	1,295.34	1,360.11	1,428.11	1,499.52	1,574.49	1,653.22
110,000	1,424.87	1,496.12	1,570.92	1,649.47	1,731.94	1,818.54
120,000	1,554.41	1,632.13	1,713.73	1,799.42	1,889.39	1,983.86
130,000	1,683.94	1,768.14	1,856.54	1,949.37	2,046.84	2,149.18
140,000	1,813.47	1,904.15	1,999.36	2,099.32	2,204.29	2,314.50
150,000	1,943.01	2,040.16	2,142.17	2,249.27	2,361.74	2,479.83
160,000	2,072.54	2,176.17	2,284.98	2,399.23	2,519.19	2,645.15
170,000	2,202.08	2,312.18	2,427.79	2,549.18	2,676.64	2,810.47
180,000	2,331.61	2,448.19	2,570.60	2,699.13	2,834.09	2,975.79
190,000	2,461.14	2,584.20	2,713.41	2,849.08	2,991.54	3,141.11
200,000	2,590.68	2,720.21	2,856.22	2,999.03	3,148.98	3,306.43

TABLE IV-32. Graduated Payment Mortgage, FHA Plan II at 18.5% Interest, Graduated at 5.0%

FHA GRADUATED PAYMENT PLAN II
TERM:30 YEARS INTEREST:18.50% GRADUATED AT 5.00%

PAYMENT AMOUNT	YEAR 1	YEAR 2	YEAR 3	YEAR 4	YEAR 5	YEARS 6-30
50	0.67	0.70	0.73	0.77	0.81	0.85
100	1.33	1.40	1.47	1.54	1.62	1.70
200	2.67	2.80	2.94	3.09	3.24	3.40
300	4.00	4.20	4.41	4.63	4.86	5.10
400	5.33	5.60	5.88	6.17	6.48	6.80
500	6.66	7.00	7.35	7.71	8.10	8.51
600	8.00	8.40	8.82	9.26	9.72	10.21
700	9.33	9.80	10.29	10.80	11.34	11.91
800	10.66	11.20	11.76	12.34	12.96	13.61
900	12.00	12.60	13.23	13.89	14.58	15.31
1,000	13.33	14.00	14.70	15.43	16.20	17.01
2,000	26.66	27.99	29.39	30.86	32.40	34.02
3,000	39.99	41.99	44.09	46.29	48.60	51.03
4,000	53.32	55.98	58.78	61.72	64.81	68.05
5,000	66.64	69.98	73.48	77.15	81.01	85.06
6,000	79.97	83.97	88.17	92.58	97.21	102.07
7,000	93.30	97.97	102.87	108.01	113.41	119.08
8,000	106.63	111.96	117.56	123.44	129.61	136.09
9,000	119.96	125.96	132.26	138.87	145.81	153.10
10,000	133.29	139.95	146.95	154.30	162.01	170.12
15,000	199.93	209.93	220.43	231.45	243.02	255.17
20,000	266.58	279.91	293.90	308.60	324.03	340.23
25,000	333.22	349.89	367.38	385.75	405.04	425.29
30,000	399.87	419.86	440.86	462.90	486.04	510.35
35,000	466.51	489.84	514.33	540.05	567.05	595.40
40,000	533.16	559.82	587.81	617.20	648.06	680.46
45,000	599.80	629.80	661.28	694.35	729.07	765.52
50,000	666.45	699.77	734.76	771.50	810.07	850.58
55,000	733.09	769.75	808.24	848.65	891.08	935.64
60,000	799.74	839.73	881.71	925.80	972.09	1,020.69
65,000	866.38	909.70	955.19	1,002.95	1,053.10	1,105.75
70,000	933.03	979.68	1,028.67	1,080.10	1,134.10	1,190.81
75,000	999.67	1,049.66	1,102.14	1,157.25	1,215.11	1,275.87
80,000	1,066.32	1,119.64	1,175.62	1,234.40	1,296.12	1,360.92
85,000	1,132.96	1,189.61	1,249.09	1,311.55	1,377.13	1,445.98
90,000	1,199.61	1,259.59	1,322.57	1,388.70	1,458.13	1,531.04
95,000	1,266.25	1,329.57	1,396.05	1,465.85	1,539.14	1,616.10
100,000	1,332.90	1,399.54	1,469.52	1,543.00	1,620.15	1,701.16
110,000	1,466.19	1,539.50	1,616.47	1,697.30	1,782.16	1,871.27
120,000	1,599.48	1,679.45	1,763.43	1,851.60	1,944.18	2,041.39
130,000	1,732.77	1,819.41	1,910.38	2,005.90	2,106.19	2,211.50
140,000	1,866.06	1,959.36	2,057.33	2,160.20	2,268.21	2,381.62
150,000	1,999.35	2,099.32	2,204.28	2,314.50	2,430.22	2,551.73
160,000	2,132.64	2,239.27	2,351.23	2,468.80	2,592.24	2,721.85
170,000	2,265.93	2,379.23	2,498.19	2,623.10	2,754.25	2,891.96
180,000	2,399.22	2,519.18	2,645.14	2,777.40	2,916.27	3,062.08
190,000	2,532.51	2,659.13	2,792.09	2,931.70	3,078.28	3,232.19
200,000	2,665.80	2,799.09	2,939.04	3,086.00	3,240.30	3,402.31

TABLE IV-33. Graduated Payment Mortgage, FHA Plan II at 19.0% Interest, Graduated at 5.0%

FHA GRADUATED PAYMENT PLAN II
TERM:30 YEARS INTEREST:19.00% GRADUATED AT 5.00%

PAYMENT AMOUNT	YEAR 1	YEAR 2	YEAR 3	YEAR 4	YEAR 5	YEARS 6-30
50	0.69	0.72	0.76	0.79	0.83	0.87
100	1.37	1.44	1.51	1.59	1.67	1.75
200	2.74	2.88	3.02	3.17	3.33	3.50
300	4.11	4.32	4.53	4.76	5.00	5.25
400	5.48	5.76	6.04	6.35	6.66	7.00
500	6.85	7.20	7.56	7.93	8.33	8.75
600	8.22	8.64	9.07	9.52	10.00	10.50
700	9.59	10.07	10.58	11.11	11.66	12.25
800	10.97	11.51	12.09	12.69	13.33	13.99
900	12.34	12.95	13.60	14.28	14.99	15.74
1,000	13.71	14.39	15.11	15.87	16.66	17.49
2,000	27.41	28.78	30.22	31.73	33.32	34.99
3,000	41.12	43.18	45.33	47.60	49.98	52.48
4,000	54.83	57.57	60.45	63.47	66.64	69.97
5,000	68.53	71.96	75.56	79.33	83.30	87.47
6,000	82.24	86.35	90.67	95.20	99.96	104.96
7,000	95.94	100.74	105.78	111.07	116.62	122.45
8,000	109.65	115.13	120.89	126.93	133.28	139.95
9,000	123.36	129.53	136.00	142.80	149.94	157.44
10,000	137.06	143.92	151.11	158.67	166.60	174.93
15,000	205.60	215.88	226.67	238.00	249.90	262.40
20,000	274.13	287.83	302.23	317.34	333.20	349.86
25,000	342.66	359.79	377.78	396.67	416.51	437.33
30,000	411.19	431.75	453.34	476.01	499.81	524.80
35,000	479.72	503.71	528.90	555.34	583.11	612.26
40,000	548.26	575.67	604.45	634.67	666.41	699.73
45,000	616.79	647.63	680.01	714.01	749.71	787.19
50,000	685.32	719.59	755.56	793.34	833.01	874.66
55,000	753.85	791.54	831.12	872.68	916.31	962.13
60,000	822.38	863.50	906.68	952.01	999.61	1,049.59
65,000	890.92	935.46	982.23	1,031.35	1,082.91	1,137.06
70,000	959.45	1,007.42	1,057.79	1,110.68	1,166.21	1,224.53
75,000	1,027.98	1,079.38	1,133.35	1,190.01	1,249.52	1,311.99
80,000	1,096.51	1,151.34	1,208.90	1,269.35	1,332.82	1,399.46
85,000	1,165.04	1,223.30	1,284.46	1,348.68	1,416.12	1,486.92
90,000	1,233.58	1,295.25	1,360.02	1,428.02	1,499.42	1,574.39
95,000	1,302.11	1,367.21	1,435.57	1,507.35	1,582.72	1,661.86
100,000	1,370.64	1,439.17	1,511.13	1,586.69	1,666.02	1,749.32
110,000	1,507.70	1,583.09	1,662.24	1,745.36	1,832.62	1,924.25
120,000	1,644.77	1,727.01	1,813.36	1,904.02	1,999.22	2,099.19
130,000	1,781.83	1,870.92	1,964.47	2,062.69	2,165.83	2,274.12
140,000	1,918.90	2,014.84	2,115.58	2,221.36	2,332.43	2,449.05
150,000	2,055.96	2,158.76	2,266.69	2,380.03	2,499.03	2,623.98
160,000	2,193.02	2,302.67	2,417.81	2,538.70	2,665.63	2,798.91
170,000	2,330.09	2,446.59	2,568.92	2,697.37	2,832.24	2,973.85
180,000	2,467.15	2,590.51	2,720.03	2,856.04	2,998.84	3,148.78
190,000	2,604.21	2,734.43	2,871.15	3,014.70	3,165.44	3,323.71
200,000	2,741.28	2,878.34	3,022.26	3,173.37	3,332.04	3,498.64

TABLE IV-34. Graduated Payment Mortgage, FHA Plan II at 19.5% Interest, Graduated at 5.0%

FHA GRADUATED PAYMENT PLAN II
TERM:30 YEARS INTEREST:19.50% GRADUATED AT 5.00%

PAYMENT AMOUNT	YEAR 1	YEAR 2	YEAR 3	YEAR 4	YEAR 5	YEARS 6-30
50	0.70	0.74	0.78	0.82	0.86	0.90
100	1.41	1.48	1.55	1.63	1.71	1.80
200	2.82	2.96	3.11	3.26	3.42	3.60
300	4.23	4.44	4.66	4.89	5.14	5.39
400	5.63	5.92	6.21	6.52	6.85	7.19
500	7.04	7.39	7.76	8.15	8.56	8.99
600	8.45	8.87	9.32	9.78	10.27	10.79
700	9.86	10.35	10.87	11.41	11.98	12.58
800	11.27	11.83	12.42	13.04	13.70	14.38
900	12.68	13.31	13.98	14.68	15.41	16.18
1,000	14.09	14.79	15.53	16.31	17.12	17.98
2,000	28.17	29.58	31.06	32.61	34.24	35.95
3,000	42.26	44.37	46.59	48.92	51.36	53.93
4,000	56.34	59.16	62.12	65.22	68.48	71.91
5,000	70.43	73.95	77.65	81.53	85.60	89.89
6,000	84.51	88.74	93.18	97.83	102.73	107.86
7,000	98.60	103.53	108.70	114.14	119.85	125.84
8,000	112.68	118.32	124.23	130.45	136.97	143.82
9,000	126.77	133.11	139.76	146.75	154.09	161.79
10,000	140.85	147.90	155.29	163.06	171.21	179.77
15,000	211.28	221.85	232.94	244.59	256.81	269.66
20,000	281.71	295.80	310.58	326.11	342.42	359.54
25,000	352.14	369.74	388.23	407.64	428.02	449.43
30,000	422.56	443.69	465.88	489.17	513.63	539.31
35,000	492.99	517.64	543.52	570.70	599.23	629.20
40,000	563.42	591.59	621.17	652.23	684.84	719.08
45,000	633.85	665.54	698.82	733.76	770.44	808.97
50,000	704.27	739.49	776.46	815.29	856.05	898.85
55,000	774.70	813.44	854.11	896.81	941.65	988.74
60,000	845.13	887.39	931.75	978.34	1,027.26	1,078.62
65,000	915.56	961.33	1,009.40	1,059.87	1,112.86	1,168.51
70,000	985.98	1,035.28	1,087.05	1,141.40	1,198.47	1,258.39
75,000	1,056.41	1,109.23	1,164.69	1,222.93	1,284.07	1,348.28
80,000	1,126.84	1,183.18	1,242.34	1,304.46	1,369.68	1,438.16
85,000	1,197.27	1,257.13	1,319.99	1,385.98	1,455.28	1,528.05
90,000	1,267.69	1,331.08	1,397.63	1,467.51	1,540.89	1,617.93
95,000	1,338.12	1,405.03	1,475.28	1,549.04	1,626.49	1,707.82
100,000	1,408.55	1,478.98	1,552.92	1,630.57	1,712.10	1,797.70
110,000	1,549.40	1,626.87	1,708.22	1,793.63	1,883.31	1,977.47
120,000	1,690.26	1,774.77	1,863.51	1,956.68	2,054.52	2,157.24
130,000	1,831.11	1,922.67	2,018.80	2,119.74	2,225.73	2,337.01
140,000	1,971.97	2,070.57	2,174.09	2,282.80	2,396.94	2,516.79
150,000	2,112.82	2,218.46	2,329.39	2,445.86	2,568.15	2,696.56
160,000	2,253.68	2,366.36	2,484.68	2,608.91	2,739.36	2,876.33
170,000	2,394.53	2,514.26	2,639.97	2,771.97	2,910.57	3,056.10
180,000	2,535.39	2,662.16	2,795.26	2,935.03	3,081.78	3,235.87
190,000	2,676.24	2,810.05	2,950.56	3,098.08	3,252.99	3,415.64
200,000	2,817.10	2,957.95	3,105.85	3,261.14	3,424.20	3,595.41

TABLE IV-35. Graduated Payment Mortgage, FHA Plan II at 20.0% Interest, Graduated at 5.0%

FHA GRADUATED PAYMENT PLAN II
TERM: 30 YEARS INTEREST: 20.00% GRADUATED AT 5.00%

PAYMENT AMOUNT	YEAR 1	YEAR 2	YEAR 3	YEAR 4	YEAR 5	YEARS 6-30
50	0.72	0.76	0.80	0.84	0.88	0.92
100	1.45	1.52	1.59	1.67	1.76	1.85
200	2.89	3.04	3.19	3.35	3.52	3.69
300	4.34	4.56	4.78	5.02	5.28	5.54
400	5.79	6.08	6.38	6.70	7.03	7.39
500	7.23	7.59	7.97	8.37	8.79	9.23
600	8.68	9.11	9.57	10.05	10.55	11.08
700	10.13	10.63	11.16	11.72	12.31	12.92
800	11.57	12.15	12.76	13.40	14.07	14.77
900	13.02	13.67	14.35	15.07	15.83	16.62
1,000	14.47	15.19	15.95	16.75	17.58	18.46
2,000	28.93	30.38	31.90	33.49	35.17	36.93
3,000	43.40	45.57	47.85	50.24	52.75	55.39
4,000	57.86	60.76	63.80	66.99	70.33	73.85
5,000	72.33	75.95	79.74	83.73	87.92	92.31
6,000	86.80	91.14	95.69	100.48	105.50	110.78
7,000	101.26	106.33	111.64	117.22	123.09	129.24
8,000	115.73	121.52	127.59	133.97	140.67	147.70
9,000	130.20	136.71	143.54	150.72	158.25	166.17
10,000	144.66	151.89	159.49	167.46	175.84	184.63
15,000	216.99	227.84	239.23	251.20	263.76	276.94
20,000	289.32	303.79	318.98	334.93	351.67	369.26
25,000	361.65	379.74	398.72	418.66	439.59	461.57
30,000	433.98	455.68	478.47	502.39	527.51	553.89
35,000	506.32	531.63	558.21	586.12	615.43	646.20
40,000	578.65	607.58	637.96	669.86	703.35	738.52
45,000	650.98	683.53	717.70	753.59	791.27	830.83
50,000	723.31	759.47	797.45	837.32	879.19	923.14
55,000	795.64	835.42	877.19	921.05	967.10	1,015.46
60,000	867.97	911.37	956.94	1,004.78	1,055.02	1,107.77
65,000	940.30	987.32	1,036.68	1,088.52	1,142.94	1,200.09
70,000	1,012.63	1,063.26	1,116.43	1,172.25	1,230.86	1,292.40
75,000	1,084.96	1,139.21	1,196.17	1,255.98	1,318.78	1,384.72
80,000	1,157.29	1,215.16	1,275.92	1,339.71	1,406.70	1,477.03
85,000	1,229.62	1,291.10	1,355.66	1,423.44	1,494.62	1,569.35
90,000	1,301.95	1,367.05	1,435.40	1,507.17	1,582.53	1,661.66
95,000	1,374.29	1,443.00	1,515.15	1,590.91	1,670.45	1,753.97
100,000	1,446.62	1,518.95	1,594.89	1,674.64	1,758.37	1,846.29
110,000	1,591.28	1,670.84	1,754.38	1,842.10	1,934.21	2,030.92
120,000	1,735.94	1,822.74	1,913.87	2,009.57	2,110.04	2,215.55
130,000	1,880.60	1,974.63	2,073.36	2,177.03	2,285.88	2,400.18
140,000	2,025.26	2,126.53	2,232.85	2,344.49	2,461.72	2,584.80
150,000	2,169.92	2,278.42	2,392.34	2,511.96	2,637.56	2,769.43
160,000	2,314.59	2,430.31	2,551.83	2,679.42	2,813.39	2,954.06
170,000	2,459.25	2,582.21	2,711.32	2,846.89	2,989.23	3,138.69
180,000	2,603.91	2,734.10	2,870.81	3,014.35	3,165.07	3,323.32
190,000	2,748.57	2,886.00	3,030.30	3,181.81	3,340.90	3,507.95
200,000	2,893.23	3,037.89	3,189.79	3,349.28	3,516.74	3,692.58

TABLE IV-36. Graduated Payment Mortgage, FHA Plan II at 20.5% Interest, Graduated at 5.0%

FHA GRADUATED PAYMENT PLAN II
TERM:30 YEARS INTEREST:20.50% GRADUATED AT 5.00%

PAYMENT AMOUNT	YEAR 1	YEAR 2	YEAR 3	YEAR 4	YEAR 5	YEARS 6-30
50	0.74	0.78	0.82	0.86	0.90	0.95
100	1.48	1.56	1.64	1.72	1.80	1.90
200	2.97	3.12	3.27	3.44	3.61	3.79
300	4.45	4.68	4.91	5.16	5.41	5.69
400	5.94	6.24	6.55	6.88	7.22	7.58
500	7.42	7.80	8.19	8.59	9.02	9.48
600	8.91	9.35	9.82	10.31	10.83	11.37
700	10.39	10.91	11.46	12.03	12.63	13.27
800	11.88	12.47	13.10	13.75	14.44	15.16
900	13.36	14.03	14.73	15.47	16.24	17.06
1,000	14.85	15.59	16.37	17.19	18.05	18.95
2,000	29.70	31.18	32.74	34.38	36.10	37.90
3,000	44.55	46.77	49.11	51.57	54.14	56.85
4,000	59.39	62.36	65.48	68.76	72.19	75.80
5,000	74.24	77.95	81.85	85.94	90.24	94.75
6,000	89.09	93.54	98.22	103.13	108.29	113.70
7,000	103.94	109.14	114.59	120.32	126.34	132.65
8,000	118.79	124.73	130.96	137.51	144.39	151.61
9,000	133.64	140.32	147.33	154.70	162.43	170.56
10,000	148.48	155.91	163.70	171.89	180.48	189.51
15,000	222.73	233.86	245.55	257.83	270.72	284.26
20,000	296.97	311.82	327.41	343.78	360.97	379.01
25,000	371.21	389.77	409.26	429.72	451.21	473.77
30,000	445.45	467.72	491.11	515.66	541.45	568.52
35,000	519.69	545.68	572.96	601.61	631.69	663.27
40,000	593.93	623.63	654.81	687.55	721.93	758.03
45,000	668.18	701.58	736.66	773.50	812.17	852.78
50,000	742.42	779.54	818.52	859.44	902.41	947.53
55,000	816.66	857.49	900.37	945.39	992.65	1,042.29
60,000	890.90	935.45	982.22	1,031.33	1,082.90	1,137.04
65,000	965.14	1,013.40	1,064.07	1,117.27	1,173.14	1,231.79
70,000	1,039.38	1,091.35	1,145.92	1,203.22	1,263.38	1,326.55
75,000	1,113.63	1,169.31	1,227.77	1,289.16	1,353.62	1,421.30
80,000	1,187.87	1,247.26	1,309.62	1,375.11	1,443.86	1,516.05
85,000	1,262.11	1,325.22	1,391.48	1,461.05	1,534.10	1,610.81
90,000	1,336.35	1,403.17	1,473.33	1,546.99	1,624.34	1,705.56
95,000	1,410.59	1,481.12	1,555.18	1,632.94	1,714.58	1,800.31
100,000	1,484.83	1,559.08	1,637.03	1,718.88	1,804.83	1,895.07
110,000	1,633.32	1,714.98	1,800.73	1,890.77	1,985.31	2,084.57
120,000	1,781.80	1,870.89	1,964.44	2,062.66	2,165.79	2,274.08
130,000	1,930.29	2,026.80	2,128.14	2,234.55	2,346.27	2,463.59
140,000	2,078.77	2,182.71	2,291.84	2,406.43	2,526.76	2,653.09
150,000	2,227.25	2,338.61	2,455.55	2,578.32	2,707.24	2,842.60
160,000	2,375.74	2,494.52	2,619.25	2,750.21	2,887.72	3,032.11
170,000	2,524.22	2,650.43	2,782.95	2,922.10	3,068.20	3,221.61
180,000	2,672.70	2,806.34	2,946.65	3,093.99	3,248.69	3,411.12
190,000	2,821.19	2,962.25	3,110.36	3,265.88	3,429.17	3,600.63
200,000	2,969.67	3,118.15	3,274.06	3,437.76	3,609.65	3,790.13

TABLE IV-37. Graduated Payment Mortgage, FHA Plan III at 12.0% Interest, Graduated at 7.5%

FHA GRADUATED PAYMENT PLAN III
TERM:30 YEARS INTEREST:12.00% GRADUATED AT 7.50%

PAYMENT AMOUNT	YEAR 1	YEAR 2	YEAR 3	YEAR 4	YEAR 5	YEARS 6-30
50	0.40	0.43	0.46	0.49	0.53	0.57
100	0.79	0.85	0.91	0.98	1.06	1.14
200	1.58	1.70	1.83	1.97	2.11	2.27
300	2.37	2.55	2.74	2.95	3.17	3.41
400	3.17	3.40	3.66	3.93	4.23	4.54
500	3.96	4.25	4.57	4.92	5.28	5.68
600	4.75	5.10	5.49	5.90	6.34	6.82
700	5.54	5.96	6.40	6.88	7.40	7.95
800	6.33	6.81	7.32	7.86	8.45	9.09
900	7.12	7.66	8.23	8.85	9.51	10.23
1,000	7.91	8.51	9.15	9.83	10.57	11.36
2,000	15.83	17.01	18.29	19.66	21.14	22.72
3,000	23.74	25.52	27.44	29.49	31.71	34.08
4,000	31.66	34.03	36.58	39.32	42.27	45.44
5,000	39.57	42.54	45.73	49.16	52.84	56.81
6,000	47.48	51.04	54.87	58.99	63.41	68.17
7,000	55.40	59.55	64.02	68.82	73.98	79.53
8,000	63.31	68.06	73.16	78.65	84.55	90.89
9,000	71.22	76.57	82.31	88.48	95.12	102.25
10,000	79.14	85.07	91.45	98.31	105.69	113.61
15,000	118.71	127.61	137.18	147.47	158.53	170.42
20,000	158.28	170.15	182.91	196.62	211.37	227.22
25,000	197.84	212.68	228.63	245.78	264.21	284.03
30,000	237.41	255.22	274.36	294.94	317.06	340.84
35,000	276.98	297.75	320.09	344.09	369.90	397.64
40,000	316.55	340.29	365.81	393.25	422.74	454.45
45,000	356.12	382.83	411.54	442.41	475.59	511.25
50,000	395.69	425.36	457.27	491.56	528.43	568.06
55,000	435.26	467.90	502.99	540.72	581.27	624.87
60,000	474.83	510.44	548.72	589.87	634.11	681.67
65,000	514.39	552.97	594.45	639.03	686.96	738.48
70,000	553.96	595.51	640.17	688.19	739.80	795.29
75,000	593.53	638.05	685.90	737.34	792.64	852.09
80,000	633.10	680.58	731.63	786.50	845.49	908.90
85,000	672.67	723.12	777.35	835.65	898.33	965.70
90,000	712.24	765.66	823.08	884.81	951.17	1,022.51
95,000	751.81	808.19	868.81	933.97	1,004.01	1,079.32
100,000	791.38	850.73	914.53	983.12	1,056.86	1,136.12
110,000	870.51	935.80	1,005.99	1,081.44	1,162.54	1,249.73
120,000	949.65	1,020.87	1,097.44	1,179.75	1,268.23	1,363.35
130,000	1,028.79	1,105.95	1,188.89	1,278.06	1,373.91	1,476.96
140,000	1,107.93	1,191.02	1,280.35	1,376.37	1,479.60	1,590.57
150,000	1,187.06	1,276.09	1,371.80	1,474.68	1,585.29	1,704.18
160,000	1,266.20	1,361.17	1,463.25	1,573.00	1,690.97	1,817.79
170,000	1,345.34	1,446.24	1,554.71	1,671.31	1,796.66	1,931.41
180,000	1,424.48	1,531.31	1,646.16	1,769.62	1,902.34	2,045.02
190,000	1,503.61	1,616.38	1,737.61	1,867.93	2,008.03	2,158.63
200,000	1,582.75	1,701.46	1,829.07	1,966.25	2,113.71	2,272.24

TABLE IV-39. Graduated Payment Mortgage, FHA Plan III at 13.0% Interest, Graduated at 7.5%

FHA GRADUATED PAYMENT PLAN III
TERM:30 YEARS INTEREST:13.00% GRADUATED AT 7.50%

PAYMENT AMOUNT	YEAR 1	YEAR 2	YEAR 3	YEAR 4	YEAR 5	YEARS 6-30
50	0.43	0.46	0.49	0.53	0.57	0.61
100	0.86	0.92	0.99	1.06	1.14	1.23
200	1.71	1.84	1.98	2.13	2.29	2.46
300	2.57	2.76	2.97	3.19	3.43	3.69
400	3.42	3.68	3.96	4.25	4.57	4.92
500	4.28	4.60	4.95	5.32	5.72	6.15
600	5.14	5.52	5.94	6.38	6.86	7.37
700	5.99	6.44	6.93	7.45	8.00	8.60
800	6.85	7.36	7.92	8.51	9.15	9.83
900	7.71	8.28	8.90	9.57	10.29	11.06
1,000	8.56	9.20	9.89	10.64	11.43	12.29
2,000	17.12	18.41	19.79	21.27	22.87	24.58
3,000	25.69	27.61	29.68	31.91	34.30	36.87
4,000	34.25	36.82	39.58	42.55	45.74	49.17
5,000	42.81	46.02	49.47	53.18	57.17	61.46
6,000	51.37	55.22	59.37	63.82	68.60	73.75
7,000	59.93	64.43	69.26	74.45	80.04	86.04
8,000	68.49	73.63	79.15	85.09	91.47	98.33
9,000	77.06	82.84	89.05	95.73	102.91	110.62
10,000	85.62	92.04	98.94	106.36	114.34	122.92
15,000	128.43	138.06	148.41	159.55	171.51	184.37
20,000	171.24	184.08	197.89	212.73	228.68	245.83
25,000	214.05	230.10	247.36	265.91	285.85	307.29
30,000	256.86	276.12	296.83	319.09	343.02	368.75
35,000	299.66	322.14	346.30	372.27	400.19	430.21
40,000	342.47	368.16	395.77	425.45	457.36	491.67
45,000	385.28	414.18	445.24	478.64	514.53	553.12
50,000	428.09	460.20	494.71	531.82	571.70	614.58
55,000	470.90	506.22	544.19	585.00	628.87	676.04
60,000	513.71	552.24	593.66	638.18	686.04	737.50
65,000	556.52	598.26	643.13	691.36	743.21	798.96
70,000	599.33	644.28	692.60	744.54	800.38	860.41
75,000	642.14	690.30	742.07	797.73	857.56	921.87
80,000	684.95	736.32	791.54	850.91	914.73	983.33
85,000	727.76	782.34	841.01	904.09	971.90	1,044.79
90,000	770.57	828.36	890.48	957.27	1,029.07	1,106.25
95,000	813.37	874.38	939.96	1,010.45	1,086.24	1,167.70
100,000	856.18	920.40	989.43	1,063.63	1,143.41	1,229.16
110,000	941.80	1,012.44	1,088.37	1,170.00	1,257.75	1,352.08
120,000	1,027.42	1,104.48	1,187.31	1,276.36	1,372.09	1,475.00
130,000	1,113.04	1,196.52	1,286.26	1,382.72	1,486.43	1,597.91
140,000	1,198.66	1,288.56	1,385.20	1,489.09	1,600.77	1,720.83
150,000	1,284.28	1,380.60	1,484.14	1,595.45	1,715.11	1,843.74
160,000	1,369.89	1,472.64	1,583.08	1,701.82	1,829.45	1,966.66
170,000	1,455.51	1,564.68	1,682.03	1,808.18	1,943.79	2,089.58
180,000	1,541.13	1,656.72	1,780.97	1,914.54	2,058.13	2,212.49
190,000	1,626.75	1,748.76	1,879.91	2,020.91	2,172.47	2,335.41
200,000	1,712.37	1,840.80	1,978.85	2,127.27	2,286.81	2,458.33

TABLE IV-38. Graduated Payment Mortgage, FHA Plan III at 12
Graduated at 7.5%

FHA GRADUATED PAYMENT PLAN III
TERM: 30 YEARS INTEREST: 12.50% GRADUATED

PAYMENT AMOUNT	YEAR 1	YEAR 2	YEAR 3	YEAR 4	YEAR 5	
50	0.41	0.44	0.48	0.51	0.55	
100	0.82	0.89	0.95	1.02	1.10	
200	1.65	1.77	1.90	2.05	2.20	
300	2.47	2.66	2.86	3.07	3.30	
400	3.29	3.54	3.81	4.09	4.40	
500	4.12	4.43	4.76	5.12	5.50	
600	4.94	5.31	5.71	6.14	6.60	
700	5.77	6.20	6.66	7.16	7.70	
800	6.59	7.08	7.61	8.19	8.80	
900	7.41	7.97	8.57	9.21	9.90	
1,000	8.24	8.85	9.52	10.23	11.00	
2,000	16.47	17.71	19.03	20.46	22.00	
3,000	24.71	26.56	28.55	30.69	33.00	
4,000	32.94	35.41	38.07	40.93	43.99	
5,000	41.18	44.27	47.59	51.16	54.99	
6,000	49.41	53.12	57.10	61.39	65.99	
7,000	57.65	61.97	66.62	71.62	76.99	
8,000	65.89	70.83	76.14	81.85	87.99	
9,000	74.12	79.68	85.66	92.08	98.99	
10,000	82.36	88.53	95.17	102.31	109.99	
15,000	123.54	132.80	142.76	153.47	164.98	
20,000	164.72	177.07	190.35	204.63	219.97	
25,000	205.89	221.34	237.94	255.78	274.97	
30,000	247.07	265.60	285.52	306.94	329.96	
35,000	288.25	309.87	333.11	358.10	384.95	
40,000	329.43	354.14	380.70	409.25	439.95	
45,000	370.61	398.41	428.29	460.41	494.94	
50,000	411.79	442.67	475.87	511.56	549.93	
55,000	452.97	486.94	523.46	562.72	604.92	
60,000	494.15	531.21	571.05	613.88	659.92	
65,000	535.33	575.48	618.64	665.03	714.91	
70,000	576.50	619.74	666.22	716.19	769.90	
75,000	617.68	664.01	713.81	767.35	824.90	
80,000	658.86	708.28	761.40	818.50	879.89	
85,000	700.04	752.54	808.99	869.66	934.88	1,
90,000	741.22	796.81	856.57	920.82	989.88	1,
95,000	782.40	841.08	904.16	971.97	1,044.87	1,
100,000	823.58	885.35	951.75	1,023.13	1,099.86	1,
110,000	905.94	973.88	1,046.92	1,125.44	1,209.85	1,
120,000	988.29	1,062.42	1,142.10	1,227.75	1,319.84	1,
130,000	1,070.65	1,150.95	1,237.27	1,330.07	1,429.82	1,
140,000	1,153.01	1,239.49	1,332.45	1,432.38	1,539.81	1,
150,000	1,235.37	1,328.02	1,427.62	1,534.69	1,649.79	1,7
160,000	1,317.73	1,416.55	1,522.80	1,637.01	1,759.78	1,8
170,000	1,400.08	1,505.09	1,617.97	1,739.32	1,869.77	2,0
180,000	1,482.44	1,593.62	1,713.15	1,841.63	1,979.75	2,1
190,000	1,564.80	1,682.16	1,808.32	1,943.94	2,089.74	2,2
200,000	1,647.16	1,770.69	1,903.50	2,046.26	2,199.73	2,3

TABLE IV-40. Graduated Payment Mortgage, FHA Plan III at 13.5% Interest, Graduated at 7.5%

FHA GRADUATED PAYMENT PLAN III
TERM: 30 YEARS INTEREST: 13.50% GRADUATED AT 7.50%

PAYMENT AMOUNT	YEAR 1	YEAR 2	YEAR 3	YEAR 4	YEAR 5	YEARS 6-30
50	0.44	0.48	0.51	0.55	0.59	0.64
100	0.89	0.96	1.03	1.10	1.19	1.28
200	1.78	1.91	2.06	2.21	2.37	2.55
300	2.67	2.87	3.08	3.31	3.56	3.83
400	3.56	3.82	4.11	4.42	4.75	5.11
500	4.45	4.78	5.14	5.52	5.94	6.38
600	5.34	5.74	6.17	6.63	7.12	7.66
700	6.22	6.69	7.19	7.73	8.31	8.94
800	7.11	7.65	8.22	8.84	9.50	10.21
900	8.00	8.60	9.25	9.94	10.69	11.49
1,000	8.89	9.56	10.28	11.05	11.87	12.77
2,000	17.78	19.12	20.55	22.09	23.75	25.53
3,000	26.68	28.68	30.83	33.14	35.62	38.30
4,000	35.57	38.23	41.10	44.18	47.50	51.06
5,000	44.46	47.79	51.38	55.23	59.37	63.83
6,000	53.35	57.35	61.65	66.28	71.25	76.59
7,000	62.24	66.91	71.93	77.32	83.12	89.36
8,000	71.13	76.47	82.20	88.37	95.00	102.12
9,000	80.03	86.03	92.48	99.42	106.87	114.89
10,000	88.92	95.59	102.75	110.46	118.75	127.65
15,000	133.38	143.38	154.13	165.69	178.12	191.48
20,000	177.83	191.17	205.51	220.92	237.49	255.30
25,000	222.29	238.96	256.89	276.15	296.87	319.13
30,000	266.75	286.76	308.26	331.38	356.24	382.96
35,000	311.21	334.55	359.64	386.62	415.61	446.78
40,000	355.67	382.34	411.02	441.85	474.98	510.61
45,000	400.13	430.14	462.40	497.08	534.36	574.43
50,000	444.59	477.93	513.77	552.31	593.73	638.26
55,000	489.04	525.72	565.15	607.54	653.10	702.09
60,000	533.50	573.52	616.53	662.77	712.48	765.91
65,000	577.96	621.31	667.91	718.00	771.85	829.74
70,000	622.42	669.10	719.28	773.23	831.22	893.56
75,000	666.88	716.89	770.66	828.46	890.60	957.39
80,000	711.34	764.69	822.04	883.69	949.97	1,021.22
85,000	755.80	812.48	873.42	938.92	1,009.34	1,085.04
90,000	800.25	860.27	924.79	994.15	1,068.71	1,148.87
95,000	844.71	908.07	976.17	1,049.38	1,128.09	1,212.69
100,000	889.17	955.86	1,027.55	1,104.61	1,187.46	1,276.52
110,000	978.09	1,051.45	1,130.30	1,215.08	1,306.21	1,404.17
120,000	1,067.01	1,147.03	1,233.06	1,325.54	1,424.95	1,531.82
130,000	1,155.92	1,242.62	1,335.81	1,436.00	1,543.70	1,659.48
140,000	1,244.84	1,338.20	1,438.57	1,546.46	1,662.45	1,787.13
150,000	1,333.76	1,433.79	1,541.32	1,656.92	1,781.19	1,914.78
160,000	1,422.67	1,529.37	1,644.08	1,767.38	1,899.94	2,042.43
170,000	1,511.59	1,624.96	1,746.83	1,877.85	2,018.68	2,170.08
180,000	1,600.51	1,720.55	1,849.59	1,988.31	2,137.43	2,297.74
190,000	1,689.43	1,816.13	1,952.34	2,098.77	2,256.18	2,425.39
200,000	1,778.34	1,911.72	2,055.10	2,209.23	2,374.92	2,553.04

TABLE IV-41. Graduated Payment Mortgage, FHA Plan III at 14.0% Interest, Graduated at 7.5%

FHA GRADUATED PAYMENT PLAN III
TERM:30 YEARS INTEREST:14.00% GRADUATED AT 7.50%

PAYMENT AMOUNT	YEAR 1	YEAR 2	YEAR 3	YEAR 4	YEAR 5	YEARS 6-30
50	0.46	0.50	0.53	0.57	0.62	0.66
100	0.92	0.99	1.07	1.15	1.23	1.32
200	1.85	1.98	2.13	2.29	2.46	2.65
300	2.77	2.98	3.20	3.44	3.70	3.97
400	3.69	3.97	4.26	4.58	4.93	5.30
500	4.61	4.96	5.33	5.73	6.16	6.62
600	5.54	5.95	6.40	6.88	7.39	7.95
700	6.46	6.94	7.46	8.02	8.62	9.27
800	7.38	7.93	8.53	9.17	9.86	10.60
900	8.30	8.93	9.59	10.31	11.09	11.92
1,000	9.23	9.92	10.66	11.46	12.32	13.24
2,000	18.45	19.83	21.32	22.92	24.64	26.49
3,000	27.68	29.75	31.98	34.38	36.96	39.73
4,000	36.90	39.67	42.64	45.84	49.28	52.98
5,000	46.13	49.59	53.30	57.30	61.60	66.22
6,000	55.35	59.50	63.97	68.76	73.92	79.46
7,000	64.58	69.42	74.63	80.22	86.24	92.71
8,000	73.80	79.34	85.29	91.68	98.56	105.95
9,000	83.03	89.25	95.95	103.14	110.88	119.20
10,000	92.25	99.17	106.61	114.60	123.20	132.44
15,000	138.38	148.76	159.91	171.91	184.80	198.66
20,000	184.50	198.34	213.22	229.21	246.40	264.88
25,000	230.63	247.93	266.52	286.51	308.00	331.10
30,000	276.76	297.51	319.83	343.81	369.60	397.32
35,000	322.88	347.10	373.13	401.12	431.20	463.54
40,000	369.01	396.68	426.44	458.42	492.80	529.76
45,000	415.13	446.27	479.74	515.72	554.40	595.98
50,000	461.26	495.86	533.04	573.02	616.00	662.20
55,000	507.39	545.44	586.35	630.32	677.60	728.42
60,000	553.51	595.03	639.65	687.63	739.20	794.64
65,000	599.64	644.61	692.96	744.93	800.80	860.86
70,000	645.76	694.20	746.26	802.23	862.40	927.08
75,000	691.89	743.78	799.57	859.53	924.00	993.30
80,000	738.02	793.37	852.87	916.84	985.60	1,059.52
85,000	784.14	842.95	906.18	974.14	1,047.20	1,125.74
90,000	830.27	892.54	959.48	1,031.44	1,108.80	1,191.96
95,000	876.39	942.12	1,012.78	1,088.74	1,170.40	1,258.18
100,000	922.52	991.71	1,066.09	1,146.04	1,232.00	1,324.40
110,000	1,014.77	1,090.88	1,172.70	1,260.65	1,355.20	1,456.84
120,000	1,107.03	1,190.05	1,279.31	1,375.25	1,478.40	1,589.28
130,000	1,199.28	1,289.22	1,385.91	1,489.86	1,601.60	1,721.72
140,000	1,291.53	1,388.39	1,492.52	1,604.46	1,724.80	1,854.16
150,000	1,383.78	1,487.57	1,599.13	1,719.07	1,848.00	1,986.60
160,000	1,476.03	1,586.74	1,705.74	1,833.67	1,971.20	2,119.04
170,000	1,568.29	1,685.91	1,812.35	1,948.28	2,094.40	2,251.48
180,000	1,660.54	1,785.08	1,918.96	2,062.88	2,217.60	2,383.92
190,000	1,752.79	1,884.25	2,025.57	2,177.49	2,340.80	2,516.36
200,000	1,845.04	1,983.42	2,132.18	2,292.09	2,464.00	2,648.80

TABLE IV-42. Graduated Payment Mortgage, FHA Plan III at 14.5% Interest, Graduated at 7.5%

FHA GRADUATED PAYMENT PLAN III
TERM:30 YEARS INTEREST:14.50% GRADUATED AT 7.50%

PAYMENT AMOUNT	YEAR 1	YEAR 2	YEAR 3	YEAR 4	YEAR 5	YEARS 6-30
50	0.48	0.51	0.55	0.59	0.64	0.69
100	0.96	1.03	1.11	1.19	1.28	1.37
200	1.91	2.06	2.21	2.38	2.55	2.75
300	2.87	3.08	3.32	3.56	3.83	4.12
400	3.82	4.11	4.42	4.75	5.11	5.49
500	4.78	5.14	5.53	5.94	6.38	6.86
600	5.74	6.17	6.63	7.13	7.66	8.24
700	6.69	7.20	7.74	8.32	8.94	9.61
800	7.65	8.22	8.84	9.50	10.22	10.98
900	8.61	9.25	9.95	10.69	11.49	12.35
1,000	9.56	10.28	11.05	11.88	12.77	13.73
2,000	19.12	20.56	22.10	23.76	25.54	27.46
3,000	28.69	30.84	33.15	35.64	38.31	41.18
4,000	38.25	41.12	44.20	47.52	51.08	54.91
5,000	47.81	51.40	55.25	59.40	63.85	68.64
6,000	57.37	61.68	66.30	71.27	76.62	82.37
7,000	66.93	71.96	77.35	83.15	89.39	96.09
8,000	76.50	82.23	88.40	95.03	102.16	109.82
9,000	86.06	92.51	99.45	106.91	114.93	123.55
10,000	95.62	102.79	110.50	118.79	127.70	137.28
15,000	143.43	154.19	165.75	178.19	191.55	205.92
20,000	191.24	205.59	221.00	237.58	255.40	274.55
25,000	239.05	256.98	276.26	296.98	319.25	343.19
30,000	286.86	308.38	331.51	356.37	383.10	411.83
35,000	334.67	359.78	386.76	415.77	446.95	480.47
40,000	382.49	411.17	442.01	475.16	510.80	549.11
45,000	430.30	462.57	497.26	534.56	574.65	617.75
50,000	478.11	513.97	552.51	593.95	638.50	686.38
55,000	525.92	565.36	607.76	653.35	702.35	755.02
60,000	573.73	616.76	663.01	712.74	766.20	823.66
65,000	621.54	668.15	718.27	772.14	830.05	892.30
70,000	669.35	719.55	773.52	831.53	893.90	960.94
75,000	717.16	770.95	828.77	890.93	957.75	1,029.58
80,000	764.97	822.34	884.02	950.32	1,021.60	1,098.22
85,000	812.78	873.74	939.27	1,009.72	1,085.45	1,166.85
90,000	860.59	925.14	994.52	1,069.11	1,149.30	1,235.49
95,000	908.40	976.53	1,049.77	1,128.51	1,213.14	1,304.13
100,000	956.21	1,027.93	1,105.02	1,187.90	1,276.99	1,372.77
110,000	1,051.84	1,130.72	1,215.53	1,306.69	1,404.69	1,510.05
120,000	1,147.46	1,233.52	1,326.03	1,425.48	1,532.39	1,647.32
130,000	1,243.08	1,336.31	1,436.53	1,544.27	1,660.09	1,784.60
140,000	1,338.70	1,439.10	1,547.03	1,663.06	1,787.79	1,921.88
150,000	1,434.32	1,541.90	1,657.54	1,781.85	1,915.49	2,059.15
160,000	1,529.94	1,644.69	1,768.04	1,900.64	2,043.19	2,196.43
170,000	1,625.56	1,747.48	1,878.54	2,019.43	2,170.89	2,333.71
180,000	1,721.19	1,850.27	1,989.04	2,138.22	2,298.59	2,470.98
190,000	1,816.81	1,953.07	2,099.55	2,257.01	2,426.29	2,608.26
200,000	1,912.43	2,055.86	2,210.05	2,375.80	2,553.99	2,745.54

TABLE IV-43. Graduated Payment Mortgage, FHA Plan III at 15.0% Interest, Graduated at 7.5%

FHA GRADUATED PAYMENT PLAN III
TERM: 30 YEARS INTEREST: 15.00% GRADUATED AT 7.50%

PAYMENT AMCUNT	YEAR 1	YEAR 2	YEAR 3	YEAR 4	YEAR 5	YEARS 6-30
50	0.50	0.53	0.57	0.62	0.66	0.71
100	0.99	1.06	1.14	1.23	1.32	1.42
200	1.98	2.13	2.29	2.46	2.64	2.84
300	2.97	3.19	3.43	3.69	3.97	4.26
400	3.96	4.26	4.58	4.92	5.29	5.69
500	4.95	5.32	5.72	6.15	6.61	7.11
600	5.94	6.39	6.87	7.38	7.93	8.53
700	6.93	7.45	8.01	8.61	9.26	9.95
800	7.92	8.52	9.15	9.84	10.58	11.37
900	8.91	9.58	10.30	11.07	11.90	12.79
1,000	9.90	10.65	11.44	12.30	13.22	14.22
2,000	19.80	21.29	22.89	24.60	26.45	28.43
3,000	29.71	31.94	34.33	36.90	39.67	42.65
4,000	39.61	42.58	45.77	49.21	52.90	56.86
5,000	49.51	53.23	57.22	61.51	66.12	71.08
6,000	59.41	63.87	68.66	73.81	79.35	85.30
7,000	69.32	74.52	80.10	86.11	92.57	99.51
8,000	79.22	85.16	91.55	98.41	105.79	113.73
9,000	89.12	95.81	102.99	110.71	119.02	127.94
10,000	99.02	106.45	114.43	123.02	132.24	142.16
15,000	148.53	159.68	171.65	184.52	198.36	213.24
20,000	198.05	212.90	228.87	246.03	264.49	284.32
25,000	247.56	266.13	286.08	307.54	330.61	355.40
30,000	297.07	319.35	343.30	369.05	396.73	426.48
35,000	346.58	372.58	400.52	430.56	462.85	497.56
40,000	396.09	425.80	457.74	492.07	528.97	568.64
45,000	445.60	479.03	514.95	553.57	595.09	639.72
50,000	495.12	532.25	572.17	615.08	661.21	710.80
55,000	544.63	585.48	629.39	676.59	727.33	781.88
60,000	594.14	638.70	686.60	738.10	793.46	852.96
65,000	643.65	691.93	743.82	799.61	859.58	924.04
70,000	693.16	745.15	801.04	861.11	925.70	995.13
75,000	742.67	798.38	858.25	922.62	991.82	1,066.21
80,000	792.19	851.60	915.47	984.13	1,057.94	1,137.29
85,000	841.70	904.83	972.69	1,045.64	1,124.06	1,208.37
90,000	891.21	958.05	1,029.90	1,107.15	1,190.18	1,279.45
95,000	940.72	1,011.28	1,087.12	1,168.65	1,256.30	1,350.53
100,000	990.23	1,064.50	1,144.34	1,230.16	1,322.43	1,421.61
110,000	1,089.26	1,170.95	1,258.77	1,353.18	1,454.67	1,563.77
120,000	1,188.28	1,277.40	1,373.21	1,476.20	1,586.91	1,705.93
130,000	1,287.30	1,383.85	1,487.64	1,599.21	1,719.15	1,848.09
140,000	1,386.33	1,490.30	1,602.07	1,722.23	1,851.40	1,990.25
150,000	1,485.35	1,596.75	1,716.51	1,845.24	1,983.64	2,132.41
160,000	1,584.37	1,703.20	1,830.94	1,968.26	2,115.88	2,274.57
170,000	1,683.40	1,809.65	1,945.37	2,091.28	2,248.12	2,416.73
180,000	1,782.42	1,916.10	2,059.81	2,214.29	2,380.37	2,558.89
190,000	1,881.44	2,022.55	2,174.24	2,337.31	2,512.61	2,701.05
200,000	1,980.47	2,129.00	2,288.68	2,460.33	2,644.85	2,843.21

TABLE IV-44. Graduated Payment Mortgage, FHA Plan III at 15.5% Interest, Graduated at 7.5%

FHA GRADUATED PAYMENT PLAN III
TERM: 30 YEARS INTEREST: 15.50% GRADUATED AT 7.50%

PAYMENT AMOUNT	YEAR 1	YEAR 2	YEAR 3	YEAR 4	YEAR 5	YEARS 6-30
50	0.51	0.55	0.59	0.64	0.68	0.74
100	1.02	1.10	1.18	1.27	1.37	1.47
200	2.05	2.20	2.37	2.55	2.74	2.94
300	3.07	3.30	3.55	3.82	4.10	4.41
400	4.10	4.41	4.74	5.09	5.47	5.88
500	5.12	5.51	5.92	6.36	6.84	7.35
600	6.15	6.61	7.10	7.64	8.21	8.83
700	7.17	7.71	8.29	8.91	9.58	10.30
800	8.20	8.81	9.47	10.18	10.95	11.77
900	9.22	9.91	10.66	11.46	12.31	13.24
1,000	10.25	11.01	11.84	12.73	13.68	14.71
2,000	20.49	22.03	23.68	25.46	27.37	29.42
3,000	30.74	33.04	35.52	38.18	41.05	44.13
4,000	40.98	44.06	47.36	50.91	54.73	58.84
5,000	51.23	55.07	59.20	63.64	68.41	73.54
6,000	61.47	66.08	71.04	76.37	82.10	88.25
7,000	71.72	77.10	82.88	89.10	95.78	102.96
8,000	81.96	88.11	94.72	101.82	109.46	117.67
9,000	92.21	99.13	106.56	114.55	123.14	132.38
10,000	102.46	110.14	118.40	127.28	136.83	147.09
15,000	153.68	165.21	177.60	190.92	205.24	220.63
20,000	204.91	220.28	236.80	254.56	273.65	294.18
25,000	256.14	275.35	296.00	318.20	342.07	367.72
30,000	307.37	330.42	355.20	381.84	410.48	441.27
35,000	358.60	385.49	414.40	445.48	478.89	514.81
40,000	409.82	440.56	473.60	509.12	547.31	588.36
45,000	461.05	495.63	532.80	572.76	615.72	661.90
50,000	512.28	550.70	592.00	636.40	684.13	735.44
55,000	563.51	605.77	651.20	700.04	752.55	808.99
60,000	614.74	660.84	710.40	763.68	820.96	882.53
65,000	665.96	715.91	769.60	827.33	889.37	956.08
70,000	717.19	770.98	828.81	890.97	957.79	1,029.62
75,000	768.42	826.05	888.01	954.61	1,026.20	1,103.17
80,000	819.65	881.12	947.21	1,018.25	1,094.61	1,176.71
85,000	870.88	936.19	1,006.41	1,081.89	1,163.03	1,250.26
90,000	922.10	991.26	1,065.61	1,145.53	1,231.44	1,323.80
95,000	973.33	1,046.33	1,124.81	1,209.17	1,299.86	1,397.34
100,000	1,024.56	1,101.40	1,184.01	1,272.81	1,368.27	1,470.89
110,000	1,127.02	1,211.54	1,302.41	1,400.09	1,505.10	1,617.98
120,000	1,229.47	1,321.68	1,420.81	1,527.37	1,641.92	1,765.07
130,000	1,331.93	1,431.82	1,539.21	1,654.65	1,778.75	1,912.16
140,000	1,434.38	1,541.96	1,657.61	1,781.93	1,915.58	2,059.24
150,000	1,536.84	1,652.10	1,776.01	1,909.21	2,052.40	2,206.33
160,000	1,639.30	1,762.24	1,894.41	2,036.49	2,189.23	2,353.42
170,000	1,741.75	1,872.38	2,012.81	2,163.77	2,326.06	2,500.51
180,000	1,844.21	1,982.52	2,131.21	2,291.05	2,462.88	2,647.60
190,000	1,946.66	2,092.66	2,249.61	2,418.34	2,599.71	2,794.69
200,000	2,049.12	2,202.80	2,368.02	2,545.62	2,736.54	2,941.78

TABLE IV-45. Graduated Payment Mortgage, FHA Plan III at 16.0% Interest, Graduated at 7.5%

FHA GRADUATED PAYMENT PLAN III
TERM:30 YEARS INTEREST:16.00% GRADUATED AT 7.50%

PAYMENT AMOUNT	YEAR 1	YEAR 2	YEAR 3	YEAR 4	YEAR 5	YEARS 6-30
50	0.53	0.57	0.61	0.66	0.71	0.76
100	1.06	1.14	1.22	1.32	1.41	1.52
200	2.12	2.28	2.45	2.63	2.83	3.04
300	3.18	3.42	3.67	3.95	4.24	4.56
400	4.24	4.55	4.90	5.26	5.66	6.08
500	5.30	5.69	6.12	6.58	7.07	7.60
600	6.36	6.83	7.34	7.89	8.49	9.12
700	7.41	7.97	8.57	9.21	9.90	10.64
800	8.47	9.11	9.79	10.53	11.32	12.16
900	9.53	10.25	11.02	11.84	12.73	13.69
1,000	10.59	11.39	12.24	13.16	14.15	15.21
2,000	21.18	22.77	24.48	26.32	28.29	30.41
3,000	31.78	34.16	36.72	39.47	42.44	45.62
4,000	42.37	45.54	48.96	52.63	56.58	60.82
5,000	52.96	56.93	61.20	65.79	70.73	76.03
6,000	63.55	68.32	73.44	78.95	84.87	91.24
7,000	74.14	79.70	85.68	92.11	99.02	106.44
8,000	84.73	91.09	97.92	105.27	113.16	121.65
9,000	95.33	102.48	110.16	118.42	127.31	136.85
10,000	105.92	113.86	122.40	131.58	141.45	152.06
15,000	158.88	170.79	183.60	197.37	212.18	228.09
20,000	211.84	227.72	244.80	263.16	282.90	304.12
25,000	264.80	284.65	306.00	328.95	353.63	380.15
30,000	317.75	341.59	367.20	394.75	424.35	456.18
35,000	370.71	398.52	428.41	460.54	495.08	532.21
40,000	423.67	455.45	489.61	526.33	565.80	608.24
45,000	476.63	512.38	550.81	592.12	636.53	684.27
50,000	529.59	569.31	612.01	657.91	707.25	760.30
55,000	582.55	626.24	673.21	723.70	777.98	836.32
60,000	635.51	683.17	734.41	789.49	848.70	912.35
65,000	688.47	740.10	795.61	855.28	919.43	988.38
70,000	741.43	797.03	856.81	921.07	990.15	1,064.41
75,000	794.39	853.96	918.01	986.86	1,060.88	1,140.44
80,000	847.34	910.90	979.21	1,052.65	1,131.60	1,216.47
85,000	900.30	967.83	1,040.41	1,118.44	1,202.33	1,292.50
90,000	953.26	1,024.76	1,101.61	1,184.24	1,273.05	1,368.53
95,000	1,006.22	1,081.69	1,162.81	1,250.03	1,343.78	1,444.56
100,000	1,059.18	1,138.62	1,224.02	1,315.82	1,414.50	1,520.59
110,000	1,165.10	1,252.48	1,346.42	1,447.40	1,555.95	1,672.65
120,000	1,271.02	1,366.34	1,468.82	1,578.98	1,697.40	1,824.71
130,000	1,376.93	1,480.21	1,591.22	1,710.56	1,838.85	1,976.77
140,000	1,482.85	1,594.07	1,713.62	1,842.14	1,980.30	2,128.83
150,000	1,588.77	1,707.93	1,836.02	1,973.73	2,121.75	2,280.89
160,000	1,694.69	1,821.79	1,958.43	2,105.31	2,263.21	2,432.95
170,000	1,800.61	1,935.65	2,080.83	2,236.89	2,404.66	2,585.00
180,000	1,906.53	2,049.51	2,203.23	2,368.47	2,546.11	2,737.06
190,000	2,012.44	2,163.38	2,325.63	2,500.05	2,687.56	2,889.12
200,000	2,118.36	2,277.24	2,448.03	2,631.63	2,829.01	3,041.18

TABLE IV-46. Graduated Payment Mortgage, FHA Plan III at 16.5% Interest, Graduated at 7.5%

FHA GRADUATED PAYMENT PLAN III
TERM:30 YEARS INTEREST:16.50% GRADUATED AT 7.50%

PAYMENT AMOUNT	YEAR 1	YEAR 2	YEAR 3	YEAR 4	YEAR 5	YEARS 6-30
50	0.55	0.59	0.63	0.68	0.73	0.79
100	1.09	1.18	1.26	1.36	1.46	1.57
200	2.19	2.35	2.53	2.72	2.92	3.14
300	3.28	3.53	3.79	4.08	4.38	4.71
400	4.38	4.70	5.06	5.44	5.84	6.28
500	5.47	5.88	6.32	6.80	7.31	7.85
600	6.56	7.06	7.59	8.16	8.77	9.42
700	7.66	8.23	8.85	9.51	10.23	10.99
800	8.75	9.41	10.11	10.87	11.69	12.57
900	9.85	10.59	11.38	12.23	13.15	14.14
1,000	10.94	11.76	12.64	13.59	14.61	15.71
2,000	21.88	23.52	25.29	27.18	29.22	31.41
3,000	32.82	35.28	37.93	40.78	43.83	47.12
4,000	43.76	47.05	50.57	54.37	58.44	62.83
5,000	54.70	58.81	63.22	67.96	73.06	78.53
6,000	65.64	70.57	75.86	81.55	87.67	94.24
7,000	76.59	82.33	88.50	95.14	102.28	109.95
8,000	87.53	94.09	101.15	108.73	116.89	125.66
9,000	98.47	105.85	113.79	122.33	131.50	141.36
10,000	109.41	117.61	126.43	135.92	146.11	157.07
15,000	164.11	176.42	189.65	203.88	219.17	235.60
20,000	218.82	235.23	252.87	271.83	292.22	314.14
25,000	273.52	294.03	316.09	339.79	365.28	392.67
30,000	328.22	352.84	379.30	407.75	438.33	471.21
35,000	382.93	411.65	442.52	475.71	511.39	549.74
40,000	437.63	470.45	505.74	543.67	584.44	628.28
45,000	492.34	529.26	568.96	611.63	657.50	706.81
50,000	547.04	588.07	632.17	679.59	730.55	785.35
55,000	601.74	646.87	695.39	747.54	803.61	863.88
60,000	656.45	705.68	758.61	815.50	876.67	942.42
65,000	711.15	764.49	821.82	883.46	949.72	1,020.95
70,000	765.86	823.29	885.04	951.42	1,022.78	1,099.48
75,000	820.56	882.10	948.26	1,019.38	1,095.83	1,178.02
80,000	875.26	940.91	1,011.48	1,087.34	1,168.89	1,256.55
85,000	929.97	999.71	1,074.69	1,155.30	1,241.94	1,335.09
90,000	984.67	1,058.52	1,137.91	1,223.25	1,315.00	1,413.62
95,000	1,039.38	1,117.33	1,201.13	1,291.21	1,388.05	1,492.16
100,000	1,094.08	1,176.13	1,264.35	1,359.17	1,461.11	1,570.69
110,000	1,203.49	1,293.75	1,390.78	1,495.09	1,607.22	1,727.76
120,000	1,312.89	1,411.36	1,517.21	1,631.01	1,753.33	1,884.83
130,000	1,422.30	1,528.98	1,643.65	1,766.92	1,899.44	2,041.90
140,000	1,531.71	1,646.59	1,770.08	1,902.84	2,045.55	2,198.97
150,000	1,641.12	1,764.20	1,896.52	2,038.76	2,191.66	2,356.04
160,000	1,750.53	1,881.82	2,022.95	2,174.67	2,337.77	2,513.11
170,000	1,859.93	1,999.43	2,149.39	2,310.59	2,483.89	2,670.18
180,000	1,969.34	2,117.04	2,275.82	2,446.51	2,630.00	2,827.25
190,000	2,078.75	2,234.66	2,402.26	2,582.42	2,776.11	2,984.31
200,000	2,188.16	2,352.27	2,528.69	2,718.34	2,922.22	3,141.38

TABLE IV-47. Graduated Payment Mortgage, FHA Plan III at 17.0% Interest, Graduated at 7.5%

FHA GRADUATED PAYMENT PLAN III
TERM:30 YEARS INTEREST:17.00% GRADUATED AT 7.50%

PAYMENT AMOUNT	YEAR 1	YEAR 2	YEAR 3	YEAR 4	YEAR 5	YEARS 6-30
50	0.56	0.61	0.65	0.70	0.75	0.81
100	1.13	1.21	1.30	1.40	1.51	1.62
200	2.26	2.43	2.61	2.81	3.02	3.24
300	3.39	3.64	3.91	4.21	4.52	4.86
400	4.52	4.86	5.22	5.61	6.03	6.48
500	5.65	6.07	6.52	7.01	7.54	8.11
600	6.78	7.28	7.83	8.42	9.05	9.73
700	7.90	8.50	9.13	9.82	10.56	11.35
800	9.03	9.71	10.44	11.22	12.06	12.97
900	10.16	10.93	11.74	12.63	13.57	14.59
1,000	11.29	12.14	13.05	14.03	15.08	16.21
2,000	22.58	24.28	26.10	28.06	30.16	32.42
3,000	33.88	36.42	39.15	42.09	45.24	48.64
4,000	45.17	48.56	52.20	56.11	60.32	64.85
5,000	56.46	60.70	65.25	70.14	75.40	81.06
6,000	67.75	72.84	78.30	84.17	90.48	97.27
7,000	79.05	84.98	91.35	98.20	105.56	113.48
8,000	90.34	97.11	104.40	112.23	120.65	129.69
9,000	101.63	109.25	117.45	126.26	135.73	145.91
10,000	112.92	121.39	130.50	140.29	150.81	162.12
15,000	169.39	182.09	195.75	210.43	226.21	243.18
20,000	225.85	242.79	261.00	280.57	301.61	324.23
25,000	282.31	303.48	326.24	350.71	377.02	405.29
30,000	338.77	364.18	391.49	420.86	452.42	486.35
35,000	395.23	424.88	456.74	491.00	527.82	567.41
40,000	451.70	485.57	521.99	561.14	603.23	648.47
45,000	508.16	546.27	587.24	631.28	678.63	729.53
50,000	564.62	606.97	652.49	701.43	754.03	810.59
55,000	621.08	667.66	717.74	771.57	829.44	891.64
60,000	677.54	728.36	782.99	841.71	904.84	972.70
65,000	734.01	789.06	848.24	911.85	980.24	1,053.76
70,000	790.47	849.75	913.49	982.00	1,055.65	1,134.82
75,000	846.93	910.45	978.73	1,052.14	1,131.05	1,215.88
80,000	903.39	971.15	1,043.98	1,122.28	1,206.45	1,296.94
85,000	959.86	1,031.84	1,109.23	1,192.43	1,281.86	1,378.00
90,000	1,016.32	1,092.54	1,174.48	1,262.57	1,357.26	1,459.05
95,000	1,072.78	1,153.24	1,239.73	1,332.71	1,432.66	1,540.11
100,000	1,129.24	1,213.93	1,304.98	1,402.85	1,508.07	1,621.17
110,000	1,242.17	1,335.33	1,435.48	1,543.14	1,658.87	1,783.29
120,000	1,355.09	1,456.72	1,565.98	1,683.42	1,809.68	1,945.41
130,000	1,468.01	1,578.11	1,696.47	1,823.71	1,960.49	2,107.52
140,000	1,580.94	1,699.51	1,826.97	1,963.99	2,111.29	2,269.64
150,000	1,693.86	1,820.90	1,957.47	2,104.28	2,262.10	2,431.76
160,000	1,806.79	1,942.30	2,087.97	2,244.56	2,412.91	2,593.88
170,000	1,919.71	2,063.69	2,218.47	2,384.85	2,563.71	2,755.99
180,000	2,032.63	2,185.08	2,348.96	2,525.14	2,714.52	2,918.11
190,000	2,145.56	2,306.48	2,479.46	2,665.42	2,865.33	3,080.23
200,000	2,258.48	2,427.87	2,609.96	2,805.71	3,016.13	3,242.34

TABLE IV-48. Graduated Payment Mortgage, FHA Plan III at 17.5% Interest, Graduated at 7.5%

FHA GRADUATED PAYMENT PLAN III
TERM:30 YEARS INTEREST:17.50% GRADUATED AT 7.50%

PAYMENT AMOUNT	YEAR 1	YEAR 2	YEAR 3	YEAR 4	YEAR 5	YEARS 6-30
50	0.58	0.63	0.67	0.72	0.78	0.84
100	1.16	1.25	1.35	1.45	1.56	1.67
200	2.33	2.50	2.69	2.89	3.11	3.34
300	3.49	3.76	4.04	4.34	4.67	5.02
400	4.66	5.01	5.38	5.79	6.22	6.69
500	5.82	6.26	6.73	7.23	7.78	8.36
600	6.99	7.51	8.08	8.68	9.33	10.03
700	8.15	8.76	9.42	10.13	10.89	11.70
800	9.32	10.02	10.77	11.57	12.44	13.38
900	10.48	11.27	12.11	13.02	14.00	15.05
1,000	11.65	12.52	13.46	14.47	15.55	16.72
2,000	23.29	25.04	26.92	28.94	31.11	33.44
3,000	34.94	37.56	40.38	43.41	46.66	50.16
4,000	46.59	50.08	53.84	57.87	62.21	66.88
5,000	58.23	62.60	67.30	72.34	77.77	83.60
6,000	69.88	75.12	80.75	86.81	93.32	100.32
7,000	81.53	87.64	94.21	101.28	108.88	117.04
8,000	93.17	100.16	107.67	115.75	124.43	133.76
9,000	104.82	112.68	121.13	130.22	139.98	150.48
10,000	116.47	125.20	134.59	144.68	155.54	167.20
15,000	174.70	187.80	201.89	217.03	233.30	250.80
20,000	232.93	250.40	269.18	289.37	311.07	334.40
25,000	291.16	313.00	336.48	361.71	388.84	418.00
30,000	349.40	375.60	403.77	434.05	466.61	501.60
35,000	407.63	438.20	471.07	506.40	544.38	585.20
40,000	465.86	500.80	538.36	578.74	622.14	668.80
45,000	524.09	563.40	605.66	651.08	699.91	752.41
50,000	582.33	626.00	672.95	723.42	777.68	836.01
55,000	640.56	688.60	740.25	795.77	855.45	919.61
60,000	698.79	751.20	807.54	868.11	933.22	1,003.21
65,000	757.03	813.80	874.84	940.45	1,010.98	1,086.81
70,000	815.26	876.40	942.13	1,012.79	1,088.75	1,170.41
75,000	873.49	939.00	1,009.43	1,085.13	1,166.52	1,254.01
80,000	931.72	1,001.60	1,076.72	1,157.48	1,244.29	1,337.61
85,000	989.96	1,064.20	1,144.02	1,229.82	1,322.06	1,421.21
90,000	1,048.19	1,126.80	1,211.31	1,302.16	1,399.82	1,504.81
95,000	1,106.42	1,189.40	1,278.61	1,374.50	1,477.59	1,588.41
100,000	1,164.65	1,252.00	1,345.90	1,446.85	1,555.36	1,672.01
110,000	1,281.12	1,377.20	1,480.49	1,591.53	1,710.90	1,839.21
120,000	1,397.59	1,502.40	1,615.08	1,736.22	1,866.43	2,006.41
130,000	1,514.05	1,627.60	1,749.67	1,880.90	2,021.97	2,173.62
140,000	1,630.52	1,752.81	1,884.27	2,025.59	2,177.50	2,340.82
150,000	1,746.98	1,878.01	2,018.86	2,170.27	2,333.04	2,508.02
160,000	1,863.45	2,003.21	2,153.45	2,314.95	2,488.58	2,675.22
170,000	1,979.91	2,128.41	2,288.04	2,459.64	2,644.11	2,842.42
180,000	2,096.38	2,253.61	2,422.63	2,604.32	2,799.65	3,009.62
190,000	2,212.84	2,378.81	2,557.22	2,749.01	2,955.18	3,176.82
200,000	2,329.31	2,504.01	2,691.81	2,893.69	3,110.72	3,344.02

TABLE IV-49. Graduated Payment Mortgage, FHA Plan III at 18.0% Interest, Graduated at 7.5%

FHA GRADUATED PAYMENT PLAN III
TERM:30 YEARS INTEREST:18.00% GRADUATED AT 7.50%

PAYMENT AMOUNT	YEAR 1	YEAR 2	YEAR 3	YEAR 4	YEAR 5	YEARS 6-30
50	0.60	0.65	0.69	0.75	0.80	0.86
100	1.20	1.29	1.39	1.49	1.60	1.72
200	2.40	2.58	2.77	2.98	3.21	3.45
300	3.60	3.87	4.16	4.47	4.81	5.17
400	4.80	5.16	5.55	5.96	6.41	6.89
500	6.00	6.45	6.94	7.46	8.01	8.62
600	7.20	7.74	8.32	8.95	9.62	10.34
700	8.40	9.03	9.71	10.44	11.22	12.06
800	9.60	10.32	11.10	11.93	12.82	13.79
900	10.80	11.61	12.48	13.42	14.43	15.51
1,000	12.00	12.90	13.87	14.91	16.03	17.23
2,000	24.01	25.81	27.74	29.82	32.06	34.46
3,000	36.01	38.71	41.61	44.73	48.09	51.70
4,000	48.01	51.61	55.48	59.65	64.12	68.93
5,000	60.02	64.52	69.36	74.56	80.15	86.16
6,000	72.02	77.42	83.23	89.47	96.18	103.39
7,000	84.02	90.32	97.10	104.38	112.21	120.62
8,000	96.02	103.23	110.97	119.29	128.24	137.86
9,000	108.03	116.13	124.84	134.20	144.27	155.09
10,000	120.03	129.03	138.71	149.11	160.30	172.32
15,000	180.05	193.55	208.07	223.67	240.45	258.48
20,000	240.06	258.07	277.42	298.23	320.59	344.64
25,000	300.08	322.58	346.78	372.78	400.74	430.80
30,000	360.09	387.10	416.13	447.34	480.89	516.96
35,000	420.11	451.62	485.49	521.90	561.04	603.12
40,000	480.12	516.13	554.84	596.45	641.19	689.28
45,000	540.14	580.65	624.20	671.01	721.34	775.44
50,000	600.15	645.16	693.55	745.57	801.49	861.60
55,000	660.17	709.68	762.91	820.13	881.63	947.76
60,000	720.18	774.20	832.26	894.68	961.78	1,033.92
65,000	780.20	838.71	901.62	969.24	1,041.93	1,120.08
70,000	840.21	903.23	970.97	1,043.80	1,122.08	1,206.24
75,000	900.23	967.75	1,040.33	1,118.35	1,202.23	1,292.40
80,000	960.24	1,032.26	1,109.68	1,192.91	1,282.38	1,378.56
85,000	1,020.26	1,096.78	1,179.04	1,267.47	1,362.53	1,464.72
90,000	1,080.28	1,161.30	1,248.39	1,342.02	1,442.67	1,550.88
95,000	1,140.29	1,225.81	1,317.75	1,416.58	1,522.82	1,637.03
100,000	1,200.31	1,290.33	1,387.10	1,491.14	1,602.97	1,723.19
110,000	1,320.34	1,419.36	1,525.81	1,640.25	1,763.27	1,895.51
120,000	1,440.37	1,548.39	1,664.52	1,789.36	1,923.57	2,067.83
130,000	1,560.40	1,677.43	1,803.23	1,938.48	2,083.86	2,240.15
140,000	1,680.43	1,806.46	1,941.95	2,087.59	2,244.16	2,412.47
150,000	1,800.46	1,935.49	2,080.66	2,236.70	2,404.46	2,584.79
160,000	1,920.49	2,064.53	2,219.37	2,385.82	2,564.75	2,757.11
170,000	2,040.52	2,193.56	2,358.08	2,534.93	2,725.05	2,929.43
180,000	2,160.55	2,322.59	2,496.79	2,684.05	2,885.35	3,101.75
190,000	2,280.58	2,451.63	2,635.50	2,833.16	3,045.65	3,274.07
200,000	2,400.61	2,580.66	2,774.21	2,982.27	3,205.94	3,446.39

TABLE IV-50. Graduated Payment Mortgage, FHA Plan III at 18.5% Interest, Graduated at 7.5%

FHA GRADUATED PAYMENT PLAN III
TERM:30 YEARS INTEREST:18.50% GRADUATED AT 7.50%

PAYMENT AMOUNT	YEAR 1	YEAR 2	YEAR 3	YEAR 4	YEAR 5	YEARS 6-30
50	0.62	0.66	0.71	0.77	0.83	0.89
100	1.24	1.33	1.43	1.54	1.65	1.77
200	2.47	2.66	2.86	3.07	3.30	3.55
300	3.71	3.99	4.29	4.61	4.95	5.32
400	4.94	5.32	5.71	6.14	6.60	7.10
500	6.18	6.64	7.14	7.68	8.25	8.87
600	7.42	7.97	8.57	9.21	9.91	10.65
700	8.65	9.30	10.00	10.75	11.56	12.42
800	9.89	10.63	11.43	12.29	13.21	14.20
900	11.13	11.96	12.86	13.82	14.86	15.97
1,000	12.36	13.29	14.29	15.36	16.51	17.75
2,000	24.72	26.58	28.57	30.71	33.02	35.49
3,000	37.09	39.87	42.86	46.07	49.53	53.24
4,000	49.45	53.16	57.14	61.43	66.04	70.99
5,000	61.81	66.44	71.43	76.79	82.54	88.74
6,000	74.17	79.73	85.71	92.14	99.05	106.48
7,000	86.53	93.02	100.00	107.50	115.56	124.23
8,000	98.89	106.31	114.29	122.86	132.07	141.98
9,000	111.26	119.60	128.57	138.21	148.58	159.72
10,000	123.62	132.89	142.86	153.57	165.09	177.47
15,000	185.43	199.33	214.28	230.36	247.63	266.21
20,000	247.24	265.78	285.71	307.14	330.18	354.94
25,000	309.05	332.22	357.14	383.93	412.72	443.68
30,000	370.86	398.67	428.57	460.71	495.27	532.41
35,000	432.66	465.11	500.00	537.50	577.81	621.15
40,000	494.47	531.56	571.43	614.28	660.35	709.88
45,000	556.28	598.00	642.85	691.07	742.90	798.62
50,000	618.09	664.45	714.28	767.85	825.44	887.35
55,000	679.90	730.89	785.71	844.64	907.99	976.09
60,000	741.71	797.34	857.14	921.42	990.53	1,064.82
65,000	803.52	863.78	928.57	998.21	1,073.08	1,153.56
70,000	865.33	930.23	1,000.00	1,075.00	1,155.62	1,242.29
75,000	927.14	996.67	1,071.42	1,151.78	1,238.16	1,331.03
80,000	988.95	1,063.12	1,142.85	1,228.57	1,320.71	1,419.76
85,000	1,050.76	1,129.56	1,214.28	1,305.35	1,403.25	1,508.50
90,000	1,112.57	1,196.01	1,285.71	1,382.14	1,485.80	1,597.23
95,000	1,174.38	1,262.45	1,357.14	1,458.92	1,568.34	1,685.97
100,000	1,236.18	1,328.90	1,428.57	1,535.71	1,650.89	1,774.70
110,000	1,359.80	1,461.79	1,571.42	1,689.28	1,815.97	1,952.17
120,000	1,483.42	1,594.68	1,714.28	1,842.85	1,981.06	2,129.64
130,000	1,607.04	1,727.57	1,857.14	1,996.42	2,146.15	2,307.11
140,000	1,730.66	1,860.46	1,999.99	2,149.99	2,311.24	2,484.58
150,000	1,854.28	1,993.35	2,142.85	2,303.56	2,476.33	2,662.05
160,000	1,977.90	2,126.24	2,285.71	2,457.13	2,641.42	2,839.52
170,000	2,101.51	2,259.13	2,428.56	2,610.70	2,806.51	3,016.99
180,000	2,225.13	2,392.02	2,571.42	2,764.27	2,971.60	3,194.47
190,000	2,348.75	2,524.91	2,714.27	2,917.85	3,136.68	3,371.94
200,000	2,472.37	2,657.80	2,857.13	3,071.42	3,301.77	3,549.41

TABLE IV-51. Graduated Payment Mortgage, FHA Plan III at 19.0% Interest, Graduated at 7.5%

FHA GRADUATED PAYMENT PLAN III
TERM:30 YEARS INTEREST:19.00% GRADUATED AT 7.50%

PAYMENT AMOUNT	YEAR 1	YEAR 2	YEAR 3	YEAR 4	YEAR 5	YEARS 6-30
50	0.64	0.68	0.74	0.79	0.85	0.91
100	1.27	1.37	1.47	1.58	1.70	1.83
200	2.54	2.74	2.94	3.16	3.40	3.65
300	3.82	4.10	4.41	4.74	5.10	5.48
400	5.09	5.47	5.88	6.32	6.80	7.31
500	6.36	6.84	7.35	7.90	8.50	9.13
600	7.63	8.21	8.82	9.48	10.19	10.96
700	8.91	9.57	10.29	11.06	11.89	12.79
800	10.18	10.94	11.76	12.64	13.59	14.61
900	11.45	12.31	13.23	14.22	15.29	16.44
1,000	12.72	13.68	14.70	15.81	16.99	18.27
2,000	25.45	27.35	29.41	31.61	33.98	36.53
3,000	38.17	41.03	44.11	47.42	50.97	54.80
4,000	50.89	54.71	58.81	63.22	67.96	73.06
5,000	63.61	68.39	73.51	79.03	84.95	91.33
6,000	76.34	82.06	88.22	94.83	101.95	109.59
7,000	89.06	95.74	102.92	110.64	118.94	127.86
8,000	101.78	109.42	117.62	126.44	135.93	146.12
9,000	114.51	123.09	132.32	142.25	152.92	164.39
10,000	127.23	136.77	147.03	158.05	169.91	182.65
15,000	190.84	205.16	220.54	237.08	254.86	273.98
20,000	254.46	273.54	294.06	316.11	339.82	365.30
25,000	318.07	341.93	367.57	395.14	424.77	456.63
30,000	381.68	410.31	441.08	474.16	509.73	547.96
35,000	445.30	478.70	514.60	553.19	594.68	639.28
40,000	508.91	547.08	588.11	632.22	679.64	730.61
45,000	572.53	615.47	661.62	711.25	764.59	821.93
50,000	636.14	683.85	735.14	790.27	849.54	913.26
55,000	699.75	752.24	808.65	869.30	934.50	1,004.59
60,000	763.37	820.62	882.17	948.33	1,019.45	1,095.91
65,000	826.98	889.01	955.68	1,027.36	1,104.41	1,187.24
70,000	890.60	957.39	1,029.19	1,106.38	1,189.36	1,278.56
75,000	954.21	1,025.78	1,102.71	1,185.41	1,274.32	1,369.89
80,000	1,017.82	1,094.16	1,176.22	1,264.44	1,359.27	1,461.22
85,000	1,081.44	1,162.55	1,249.74	1,343.47	1,444.23	1,552.54
90,000	1,145.05	1,230.93	1,323.25	1,422.49	1,529.18	1,643.87
95,000	1,208.67	1,299.32	1,396.76	1,501.52	1,614.14	1,735.20
100,000	1,272.28	1,367.70	1,470.28	1,580.55	1,699.09	1,826.52
110,000	1,399.51	1,504.47	1,617.31	1,738.60	1,869.00	2,009.17
120,000	1,526.74	1,641.24	1,764.33	1,896.66	2,038.91	2,191.83
130,000	1,653.96	1,778.01	1,911.36	2,054.71	2,208.82	2,374.48
140,000	1,781.19	1,914.78	2,058.39	2,212.77	2,378.73	2,557.13
150,000	1,908.42	2,051.55	2,205.42	2,370.82	2,548.63	2,739.78
160,000	2,035.65	2,188.32	2,352.44	2,528.88	2,718.54	2,922.43
170,000	2,162.87	2,325.09	2,499.47	2,686.93	2,888.45	3,105.09
180,000	2,290.10	2,461.86	2,646.50	2,844.99	3,058.36	3,287.74
190,000	2,417.33	2,598.63	2,793.53	3,003.04	3,228.27	3,470.39
200,000	2,544.56	2,735.40	2,940.56	3,161.10	3,398.18	3,653.04

TABLE IV-52. Graduated Payment Mortgage, FHA Plan III at 19.5% Interest, Graduated at 7.5%

FHA GRADUATED PAYMENT PLAN III
TERM:30 YEARS INTEREST:19.50% GRADUATED AT 7.50%

PAYMENT AMOUNT	YEAR 1	YEAR 2	YEAR 3	YEAR 4	YEAR 5	YEARS 6-30
50	0.65	0.70	0.76	0.81	0.87	0.94
100	1.31	1.41	1.51	1.63	1.75	1.88
200	2.62	2.81	3.02	3.25	3.50	3.76
300	3.93	4.22	4.54	4.88	5.24	5.64
400	5.23	5.63	6.05	6.50	6.99	7.51
500	6.54	7.03	7.56	8.13	8.74	9.39
600	7.85	8.44	9.07	9.75	10.49	11.27
700	9.16	9.85	10.59	11.38	12.23	13.15
800	10.47	11.25	12.10	13.01	13.98	15.03
900	11.78	12.66	13.61	14.63	15.73	16.91
1,000	13.09	14.07	15.12	16.26	17.48	18.79
2,000	26.17	28.13	30.24	32.51	34.95	37.57
3,000	39.26	42.20	45.37	48.77	52.43	56.36
4,000	52.34	56.27	60.49	65.03	69.90	75.15
5,000	65.43	70.34	75.61	81.28	87.38	93.93
6,000	78.51	84.40	90.73	97.54	104.85	112.72
7,000	91.60	98.47	105.86	113.80	122.33	131.50
8,000	104.69	112.54	120.98	130.05	139.81	150.29
9,000	117.77	126.61	136.10	146.31	157.28	169.08
10,000	130.86	140.67	151.22	162.56	174.76	187.86
15,000	196.29	211.01	226.83	243.85	262.14	281.80
20,000	261.72	281.34	302.45	325.13	349.51	375.73
25,000	327.14	351.68	378.06	406.41	436.89	469.66
30,000	392.57	422.02	453.67	487.69	524.27	563.59
35,000	458.00	492.35	529.28	568.98	611.65	657.52
40,000	523.43	562.69	604.89	650.26	699.03	751.45
45,000	588.86	633.03	680.50	731.54	786.41	845.39
50,000	654.29	703.36	756.11	812.82	873.78	939.32
55,000	719.72	773.70	831.73	894.10	961.16	1,033.25
60,000	785.15	844.03	907.34	975.39	1,048.54	1,127.18
65,000	850.58	914.37	982.95	1,056.67	1,135.92	1,221.11
70,000	916.01	984.71	1,058.56	1,137.95	1,223.30	1,315.04
75,000	981.43	1,055.04	1,134.17	1,219.23	1,310.68	1,408.98
80,000	1,046.86	1,125.38	1,209.78	1,300.52	1,398.05	1,502.91
85,000	1,112.29	1,195.71	1,285.39	1,381.80	1,485.43	1,596.84
90,000	1,177.72	1,266.05	1,361.00	1,463.08	1,572.81	1,690.77
95,000	1,243.15	1,336.39	1,436.62	1,544.36	1,660.19	1,784.70
100,000	1,308.58	1,406.72	1,512.23	1,625.64	1,747.57	1,878.64
110,000	1,439.44	1,547.40	1,663.45	1,788.21	1,922.32	2,066.50
120,000	1,570.30	1,688.07	1,814.67	1,950.77	2,097.08	2,254.36
130,000	1,701.15	1,828.74	1,965.90	2,113.34	2,271.84	2,442.23
140,000	1,832.01	1,969.41	2,117.12	2,275.90	2,446.60	2,630.09
150,000	1,962.87	2,110.09	2,268.34	2,438.47	2,621.35	2,817.95
160,000	2,093.73	2,250.76	2,419.56	2,601.03	2,796.11	3,005.82
170,000	2,224.59	2,391.43	2,570.79	2,763.60	2,970.87	3,193.68
180,000	2,355.44	2,532.10	2,722.01	2,926.16	3,145.62	3,381.54
190,000	2,486.30	2,672.77	2,873.23	3,088.72	3,320.38	3,569.41
200,000	2,617.16	2,813.45	3,024.46	3,251.29	3,495.14	3,757.27

TABLE IV-53. Graduated Payment Mortgage, FHA Plan III at 20.0% Interest, Graduated at 7.5%

FHA GRADUATED PAYMENT PLAN III
TERM:30 YEARS INTEREST:20.00% GRADUATED AT 7.50%

PAYMENT AMOUNT	YEAR 1	YEAR 2	YEAR 3	YEAR 4	YEAR 5	YEARS 6-30
50	0.67	0.72	0.78	0.84	0.90	0.97
100	1.35	1.45	1.55	1.67	1.80	1.93
200	2.69	2.89	3.11	3.34	3.59	3.86
300	4.04	4.34	4.66	5.01	5.39	5.79
400	5.38	5.78	6.22	6.68	7.19	7.72
500	6.73	7.23	7.77	8.35	8.98	9.66
600	8.07	8.68	9.33	10.03	10.78	11.59
700	9.42	10.12	10.88	11.70	12.57	13.52
800	10.76	11.57	12.44	13.37	14.37	15.45
900	12.11	13.01	13.99	15.04	16.17	17.38
1,000	13.45	14.46	15.54	16.71	17.96	19.31
2,000	26.90	28.92	31.09	33.42	35.93	38.62
3,000	40.35	43.38	46.63	50.13	53.89	57.93
4,000	53.80	57.84	62.18	66.84	71.85	77.24
5,000	67.25	72.30	77.72	83.55	89.82	96.55
6,000	80.70	86.76	93.26	100.26	107.78	115.86
7,000	94.16	101.22	108.81	116.97	125.74	135.17
8,000	107.61	115.68	124.35	133.68	143.70	154.48
9,000	121.06	130.14	139.90	150.39	161.67	173.79
10,000	134.51	144.60	155.44	167.10	179.63	193.10
15,000	201.76	216.89	233.16	250.65	269.45	289.65
20,000	269.02	289.19	310.88	334.20	359.26	386.21
25,000	336.27	361.49	388.60	417.75	449.08	482.76
30,000	403.52	433.79	466.32	501.30	538.89	579.31
35,000	470.78	506.09	544.04	584.84	628.71	675.86
40,000	538.03	578.38	621.76	668.39	718.52	772.41
45,000	605.28	650.68	699.48	751.94	808.34	868.96
50,000	672.54	722.98	777.20	835.49	898.15	965.52
55,000	739.79	795.28	854.92	919.04	987.97	1,062.07
60,000	807.05	867.57	932.64	1,002.59	1,077.79	1,158.62
65,000	874.30	939.87	1,010.36	1,086.14	1,167.60	1,255.17
70,000	941.55	1,012.17	1,088.08	1,169.69	1,257.42	1,351.72
75,000	1,008.81	1,084.47	1,165.80	1,253.24	1,347.23	1,448.27
80,000	1,076.06	1,156.77	1,243.52	1,336.79	1,437.05	1,544.83
85,000	1,143.32	1,229.06	1,321.24	1,420.34	1,526.86	1,641.38
90,000	1,210.57	1,301.36	1,398.96	1,503.89	1,616.68	1,737.93
95,000	1,277.82	1,373.66	1,476.68	1,587.44	1,706.49	1,834.48
100,000	1,345.08	1,445.96	1,554.40	1,670.99	1,796.31	1,931.03
110,000	1,479.58	1,590.55	1,709.85	1,838.08	1,975.94	2,124.14
120,000	1,614.09	1,735.15	1,865.29	2,005.18	2,155.57	2,317.24
130,000	1,748.60	1,879.75	2,020.73	2,172.28	2,335.20	2,510.34
140,000	1,883.11	2,024.34	2,176.17	2,339.38	2,514.83	2,703.45
150,000	2,017.62	2,168.94	2,331.61	2,506.48	2,694.46	2,896.55
160,000	2,152.12	2,313.53	2,487.05	2,673.58	2,874.09	3,089.65
170,000	2,286.63	2,458.13	2,642.49	2,840.67	3,053.73	3,282.75
180,000	2,421.14	2,602.72	2,797.93	3,007.77	3,233.36	3,475.86
190,000	2,555.65	2,747.32	2,953.37	3,174.87	3,412.99	3,668.96
200,000	2,690.15	2,891.92	3,108.81	3,341.97	3,592.62	3,862.06

TABLE IV-54. Graduated Payment Mortgage, FHA Plan III at 20.5% Interest, Graduated at 7.5%

FHA GRADUATED PAYMENT PLAN III
TERM: 30 YEARS INTEREST: 20.50% GRADUATED AT 7.50%

PAYMENT AMOUNT	YEAR 1	YEAR 2	YEAR 3	YEAR 4	YEAR 5	YEARS 6-30
50	0.69	0.74	0.80	0.86	0.92	0.99
100	1.38	1.49	1.60	1.72	1.85	1.98
200	2.76	2.97	3.19	3.43	3.69	3.97
300	4.15	4.46	4.79	5.15	5.54	5.95
400	5.53	5.94	6.39	6.87	7.38	7.93
500	6.91	7.43	7.98	8.58	9.23	9.92
600	8.29	8.91	9.58	10.30	11.07	11.90
700	9.67	10.40	11.18	12.02	12.92	13.89
800	11.05	11.88	12.77	13.73	14.76	15.87
900	12.44	13.37	14.37	15.45	16.61	17.85
1,000	13.82	14.85	15.97	17.17	18.45	19.84
2,000	27.64	29.71	31.94	34.33	36.91	39.67
3,000	41.45	44.56	47.90	51.50	55.36	59.51
4,000	55.27	59.42	63.87	68.66	73.81	79.35
5,000	69.09	74.27	79.84	85.83	92.27	99.18
6,000	82.91	89.12	95.81	102.99	110.72	119.02
7,000	96.72	103.98	111.78	120.16	129.17	138.86
8,000	110.54	118.83	127.74	137.32	147.62	158.70
9,000	124.36	133.69	143.71	154.49	166.08	178.53
10,000	138.18	148.54	159.68	171.66	184.53	198.37
15,000	207.26	222.81	239.52	257.48	276.80	297.55
20,000	276.35	297.08	319.36	343.31	369.06	396.74
25,000	345.44	371.35	399.20	429.14	461.33	495.92
30,000	414.53	445.62	479.04	514.97	553.59	595.11
35,000	483.62	519.89	558.88	600.80	645.86	694.29
40,000	552.70	594.16	638.72	686.62	738.12	793.48
45,000	621.79	668.43	718.56	772.45	830.39	892.66
50,000	690.88	742.70	798.40	858.28	922.65	991.85
55,000	759.97	816.97	878.24	944.11	1,014.92	1,091.03
60,000	829.06	891.24	958.08	1,029.94	1,107.18	1,190.22
65,000	898.15	965.51	1,037.92	1,115.76	1,199.45	1,289.40
70,000	967.23	1,039.78	1,117.76	1,201.59	1,291.71	1,388.59
75,000	1,036.32	1,114.05	1,197.60	1,287.42	1,383.98	1,487.77
80,000	1,105.41	1,188.32	1,277.44	1,373.25	1,476.24	1,586.96
85,000	1,174.50	1,262.59	1,357.28	1,459.08	1,568.51	1,686.14
90,000	1,243.59	1,336.86	1,437.12	1,544.90	1,660.77	1,785.33
95,000	1,312.67	1,411.12	1,516.96	1,630.73	1,753.04	1,884.51
100,000	1,381.76	1,485.39	1,596.80	1,716.56	1,845.30	1,983.70
110,000	1,519.94	1,633.93	1,756.48	1,888.22	2,029.83	2,182.07
120,000	1,658.11	1,782.47	1,916.16	2,059.87	2,214.36	2,380.44
130,000	1,796.29	1,931.01	2,075.84	2,231.53	2,398.89	2,578.81
140,000	1,934.47	2,079.55	2,235.52	2,403.18	2,583.42	2,777.18
150,000	2,072.64	2,228.09	2,395.20	2,574.84	2,767.95	2,975.55
160,000	2,210.82	2,376.63	2,554.88	2,746.49	2,952.48	3,173.92
170,000	2,349.00	2,525.17	2,714.56	2,918.15	3,137.01	3,372.29
180,000	2,487.17	2,673.71	2,874.24	3,089.81	3,321.54	3,570.66
190,000	2,625.35	2,822.25	3,033.92	3,261.46	3,506.07	3,769.03
200,000	2,763.52	2,970.79	3,193.60	3,433.12	3,690.60	3,967.40

TABLE IV-55. Graduated Payment Mortgage, FHA Plan IV at 12.0% Interest, Graduated at 2.0%

FHA GRADUATED PAYMENT PLAN IV
TERM:30 YEARS INTEREST:12.00% GRADUATED AT 2.00%

PAYMENT AMOUNT	YEAR 1	YEAR 2	YEAR 3	YEAR 4	YEAR 5	YEAR 6
50	0.46	0.47	0.48	0.49	0.50	0.51
100	0.92	0.94	0.96	0.98	1.00	1.02
200	1.84	1.88	1.92	1.96	2.00	2.04
300	2.77	2.82	2.88	2.94	3.00	3.06
400	3.69	3.76	3.84	3.92	3.99	4.07
500	4.61	4.70	4.80	4.89	4.99	5.09
600	5.53	5.64	5.76	5.87	5.99	6.11
700	6.46	6.59	6.72	6.85	6.99	7.13
800	7.38	7.53	7.68	7.83	7.99	8.15
900	8.30	8.47	8.64	8.81	8.99	9.17
1,000	9.22	9.41	9.60	9.79	9.98	10.18
2,000	18.45	18.82	19.19	19.58	19.97	20.37
3,000	27.67	28.22	28.79	29.36	29.95	30.55
4,000	36.89	37.63	38.39	39.15	39.94	40.73
5,000	46.12	47.04	47.98	48.94	49.92	50.92
6,000	55.34	56.45	57.58	58.73	59.90	61.10
7,000	64.57	65.86	67.17	68.52	69.89	71.29
8,000	73.79	75.27	76.77	78.31	79.87	81.47
9,000	83.01	84.67	86.37	88.09	89.86	91.65
10,000	92.24	94.08	95.96	97.88	99.84	101.84
15,000	138.36	141.12	143.95	146.82	149.76	152.76
20,000	184.47	188.16	191.93	195.77	199.68	203.67
25,000	230.59	235.20	239.91	244.71	249.60	254.59
30,000	276.71	282.25	287.89	293.65	299.52	305.51
35,000	322.83	329.29	335.87	342.59	349.44	356.43
40,000	368.95	376.33	383.85	391.53	399.36	407.35
45,000	415.07	423.37	431.84	440.47	449.28	458.27
50,000	461.19	470.41	479.82	489.41	499.20	509.19
55,000	507.30	517.45	527.80	538.35	549.12	560.10
60,000	553.42	564.49	575.78	587.30	599.04	611.02
65,000	599.54	611.53	623.76	636.24	648.96	661.94
70,000	645.66	658.57	671.74	685.18	698.88	712.86
75,000	691.78	705.61	719.73	734.12	748.80	763.78
80,000	737.90	752.65	767.71	783.06	798.72	814.70
85,000	784.01	799.69	815.69	832.00	848.64	865.62
90,000	830.13	846.74	863.67	880.94	898.56	916.53
95,000	876.25	893.78	911.65	929.89	948.48	967.45
100,000	922.37	940.82	959.63	978.83	998.40	1,018.37
110,000	1,014.61	1,034.90	1,055.60	1,076.71	1,098.24	1,120.21
120,000	1,106.84	1,128.98	1,151.56	1,174.59	1,198.08	1,222.05
130,000	1,199.08	1,223.06	1,247.52	1,272.47	1,297.92	1,323.88
140,000	1,291.32	1,317.14	1,343.49	1,370.36	1,397.76	1,425.72
150,000	1,383.56	1,411.23	1,439.45	1,468.24	1,497.60	1,527.56
160,000	1,475.79	1,505.31	1,535.41	1,566.12	1,597.45	1,629.39
170,000	1,568.03	1,599.39	1,631.38	1,664.01	1,697.29	1,731.23
180,000	1,660.27	1,693.47	1,727.34	1,761.89	1,797.13	1,833.07
190,000	1,752.50	1,787.55	1,823.30	1,859.77	1,896.97	1,934.91
200,000	1,844.74	1,881.64	1,919.27	1,957.65	1,996.81	2,036.74

TABLE IV-55. (*Continued*)

FHA GRADUATED PAYMENT PLAN IV
TERM:30 YEARS INTEREST:12.00% GRADUATED AT 2.00%

PAYMENT AMOUNT	YEAR 7	YEAR 8	YEAR 9	YEAR 10	YEARS 11-30
50	0.52	0.53	0.54	0.55	0.56
100	1.04	1.06	1.08	1.10	1.12
200	2.08	2.12	2.16	2.20	2.25
300	3.12	3.18	3.24	3.31	3.37
400	4.15	4.24	4.32	4.41	4.50
500	5.19	5.30	5.40	5.51	5.62
600	6.23	6.36	6.48	6.61	6.75
700	7.27	7.42	7.56	7.72	7.87
800	8.31	8.48	8.65	8.82	8.99
900	9.35	9.54	9.73	9.92	10.12
1,000	10.39	10.60	10.81	11.02	11.24
2,000	20.77	21.19	21.61	22.05	22.49
3,000	31.16	31.79	32.42	33.07	33.73
4,000	41.55	42.38	43.23	44.09	44.97
5,000	51.94	52.98	54.04	55.12	56.22
6,000	62.32	63.57	64.84	66.14	67.46
7,000	72.71	74.17	75.65	77.16	78.71
8,000	83.10	84.76	86.46	88.19	89.95
9,000	93.49	95.36	97.26	99.21	101.19
10,000	103.87	105.95	108.07	110.23	112.44
15,000	155.81	158.93	162.11	165.35	168.65
20,000	207.75	211.90	216.14	220.46	224.87
25,000	259.68	264.88	270.18	275.58	281.09
30,000	311.62	317.85	324.21	330.70	337.31
35,000	363.56	370.83	378.25	385.81	393.53
40,000	415.50	423.81	432.28	440.93	449.75
45,000	467.43	476.78	486.32	496.04	505.96
50,000	519.37	529.76	540.35	551.16	562.18
55,000	571.31	582.73	594.39	606.27	618.40
60,000	623.24	635.71	648.42	661.39	674.62
65,000	675.18	688.68	702.46	716.51	730.84
70,000	727.12	741.66	756.49	771.62	787.05
75,000	779.05	794.64	810.53	826.74	843.27
80,000	830.99	847.61	864.56	881.85	899.49
85,000	882.93	900.59	918.60	936.97	955.71
90,000	934.86	953.56	972.63	992.09	1,011.93
95,000	986.80	1,006.54	1,026.67	1,047.20	1,068.15
100,000	1,038.74	1,059.51	1,080.70	1,102.32	1,124.36
110,000	1,142.61	1,165.46	1,188.77	1,212.55	1,236.80
120,000	1,246.49	1,271.42	1,296.84	1,322.78	1,349.24
130,000	1,350.36	1,377.37	1,404.91	1,433.01	1,461.67
140,000	1,454.23	1,483.32	1,512.99	1,543.24	1,574.11
150,000	1,558.11	1,589.27	1,621.06	1,653.48	1,686.55
160,000	1,661.98	1,695.22	1,729.13	1,763.71	1,798.98
170,000	1,765.86	1,801.17	1,837.20	1,073.94	1,911.42
180,000	1,869.73	1,907.12	1,945.27	1,984.17	2,023.86
190,000	1,973.60	2,013.08	2,053.34	2,094.40	2,136.29
200,000	2,077.48	2,119.03	2,161.41	2,204.64	2,248.73

TABLE IV-56. **Graduated Payment Mortgage, FHA Plan IV at 12.5% Interest, Graduated at 2.0%**

FHA GRADUATED PAYMENT PLAN IV
TERM:30 YEARS INTEREST:12.50% GRADUATED AT 2.00%

PAYMENT AMOUNT	YEAR 1	YEAR 2	YEAR 3	YEAR 4	YEAR 5	YEAR 6
50	0.48	0.49	0.50	0.51	0.52	0.53
100	0.96	0.98	1.00	1.02	1.04	1.06
200	1.92	1.96	2.00	2.04	2.08	2.12
300	2.88	2.93	2.99	3.05	3.11	3.18
400	3.84	3.91	3.99	4.07	4.15	4.24
500	4.80	4.89	4.99	5.09	5.19	5.29
600	5.75	5.87	5.99	6.11	6.23	6.35
700	6.71	6.85	6.98	7.12	7.27	7.41
800	7.67	7.83	7.98	8.14	8.30	8.47
900	8.63	8.80	8.98	9.16	9.34	9.53
1,000	9.59	9.78	9.98	10.18	10.38	10.59
2,000	19.18	19.56	19.96	20.36	20.76	21.18
3,000	28.77	29.35	29.93	30.53	31.14	31.77
4,000	38.36	39.13	39.91	40.71	41.52	42.35
5,000	47.95	48.91	49.89	50.89	51.91	52.94
6,000	57.54	58.69	59.87	61.07	62.29	63.53
7,000	67.13	68.48	69.85	71.24	72.67	74.12
8,000	76.72	78.26	79.82	81.42	83.05	84.71
9,000	86.31	88.04	89.80	91.60	93.43	95.30
10,000	95.91	97.82	99.78	101.78	103.81	105.89
15,000	143.86	146.73	149.67	152.66	155.72	158.83
20,000	191.81	195.65	199.56	203.55	207.62	211.77
25,000	239.76	244.56	249.45	254.44	259.53	264.72
30,000	287.72	293.47	299.34	305.33	311.43	317.66
35,000	335.67	342.38	349.23	356.21	363.34	370.60
40,000	383.62	391.29	399.12	407.10	415.24	423.55
45,000	431.57	440.20	449.01	457.99	467.15	476.49
50,000	479.53	489.12	498.90	508.88	519.05	529.43
55,000	527.48	538.03	548.79	559.76	570.96	582.38
60,000	575.43	586.94	598.68	610.65	622.86	635.32
65,000	623.38	635.85	648.57	661.54	674.77	688.27
70,000	671.34	684.76	698.46	712.43	726.68	741.21
75,000	719.29	733.67	748.35	763.31	778.58	794.15
80,000	767.24	782.59	798.24	814.20	830.49	847.10
85,000	815.19	831.50	848.13	865.09	882.39	900.04
90,000	863.15	880.41	898.02	915.98	934.30	952.98
95,000	911.10	929.32	947.91	966.86	986.20	1,005.93
100,000	959.05	978.23	997.80	1,017.75	1,038.11	1,058.87
110,000	1,054.96	1,076.06	1,097.58	1,119.53	1,141.92	1,164.76
120,000	1,150.86	1,173.88	1,197.36	1,221.30	1,245.73	1,270.64
130,000	1,246.77	1,271.70	1,297.14	1,323.08	1,349.54	1,376.53
140,000	1,342.67	1,369.52	1,396.92	1,424.85	1,453.35	1,482.42
150,000	1,438.58	1,467.35	1,496.69	1,526.63	1,557.16	1,588.30
160,000	1,534.48	1,565.17	1,596.47	1,628.40	1,660.97	1,694.19
170,000	1,630.39	1,662.99	1,696.25	1,730.18	1,764.78	1,800.08
180,000	1,726.29	1,760.82	1,796.03	1,831.95	1,868.59	1,905.97
190,000	1,822.20	1,858.64	1,895.81	1,933.73	1,972.40	2,011.85
200,000	1,918.10	1,956.46	1,995.59	2,035.51	2,076.22	2,117.74

TABLE IV-56. (*Continued*)

FHA GRADUATED PAYMENT PLAN IV
TERM:30 YEARS INTEREST:12.50% GRADUATED AT 2.00%

PAYMENT AMOUNT	YEAR 7	YEAR 8	YEAR 9	YEAR 10	YEARS 11-30
50	0.54	0.55	0.56	0.57	0.58
100	1.08	1.10	1.12	1.15	1.17
200	2.16	2.20	2.25	2.29	2.34
300	3.24	3.30	3.37	3.44	3.51
400	4.32	4.41	4.49	4.58	4.68
500	5.40	5.51	5.62	5.73	5.85
600	6.48	6.61	6.74	6.88	7.01
700	7.56	7.71	7.87	8.02	8.18
800	8.64	8.81	8.99	9.17	9.35
900	9.72	9.91	10.11	10.32	10.52
1,000	10.80	11.02	11.24	11.46	11.69
2,000	21.60	22.03	22.47	22.92	23.38
3,000	32.40	33.05	33.71	34.38	35.07
4,000	43.20	44.07	44.95	45.85	46.76
5,000	54.00	55.08	56.18	57.31	58.45
6,000	64.80	66.10	67.42	68.77	70.14
7,000	75.60	77.12	78.66	80.23	81.84
8,000	86.40	88.13	89.89	91.69	93.53
9,000	97.20	99.15	101.13	103.15	105.22
10,000	108.00	110.16	112.37	114.62	116.91
15,000	162.01	165.25	168.55	171.92	175.36
20,000	216.01	220.33	224.74	229.23	233.82
25,000	270.01	275.41	280.92	286.54	292.27
30,000	324.01	330.49	337.10	343.85	350.72
35,000	378.02	385.58	393.29	401.15	409.18
40,000	432.02	440.66	449.47	458.46	467.63
45,000	486.02	495.74	505.66	515.77	526.09
50,000	540.02	550.82	561.84	573.08	584.54
55,000	594.03	605.91	618.02	630.39	642.99
60,000	648.03	660.99	674.21	687.69	701.45
65,000	702.03	716.07	730.39	745.00	759.90
70,000	756.03	771.15	786.58	802.31	818.35
75,000	810.04	826.24	842.76	859.62	876.81
80,000	864.04	881.32	898.94	916.92	935.26
85,000	918.04	936.40	955.13	974.23	993.72
90,000	972.04	991.48	1,011.31	1,031.54	1,052.17
95,000	1,026.04	1,046.57	1,067.50	1,088.85	1,110.62
100,000	1,080.05	1,101.65	1,123.68	1,146.15	1,169.08
110,000	1,188.05	1,211.81	1,236.05	1,260.77	1,285.99
120,000	1,296.06	1,321.98	1,348.42	1,375.39	1,402.89
130,000	1,404.06	1,432.14	1,460.79	1,490.00	1,519.80
140,000	1,512.07	1,542.31	1,573.15	1,604.62	1,636.71
150,000	1,620.07	1,652.47	1,685.52	1,719.23	1,753.62
160,000	1,728.08	1,762.64	1,797.89	1,833.85	1,870.52
170,000	1,836.08	1,872.80	1,910.26	1,948.46	1,987.43
180,000	1,944.08	1,982.97	2,022.63	2,063.08	2,104.34
190,000	2,052.09	2,093.13	2,134.99	2,177.69	2,221.25
200,000	2,160.09	2,203.30	2,247.36	2,292.31	2,338.16

TABLE IV-57. Graduated Payment Mortgage, FHA Plan IV at 13.0% Interest, Graduated at 2.0%

FHA GRADUATED PAYMENT PLAN IV
TERM:30 YEARS INTEREST:13.00% GRADUATED AT 2.00%

PAYMENT AMOUNT	YEAR 1	YEAR 2	YEAR 3	YEAR 4	YEAR 5	YEAR 6
50	0.50	0.51	0.52	0.53	0.54	0.55
100	1.00	1.02	1.04	1.06	1.08	1.10
200	1.99	2.03	2.07	2.11	2.16	2.20
300	2.99	3.05	3.11	3.17	3.23	3.30
400	3.98	4.06	4.15	4.23	4.31	4.40
500	4.98	5.08	5.18	5.29	5.39	5.50
600	5.98	6.10	6.22	6.34	6.47	6.60
700	6.97	7.11	7.25	7.40	7.55	7.70
800	7.97	8.13	8.29	8.46	8.63	8.80
900	8.97	9.14	9.33	9.51	9.70	9.90
1,000	9.96	10.16	10.36	10.57	10.78	11.00
2,000	19.92	20.32	20.73	21.14	21.56	22.00
3,000	29.88	30.48	31.09	31.71	32.35	32.99
4,000	39.84	40.64	41.45	42.28	43.13	43.99
5,000	49.81	50.80	51.82	52.85	53.91	54.99
6,000	59.77	60.96	62.18	63.43	64.69	65.99
7,000	69.73	71.12	72.54	74.00	75.48	76.99
8,000	79.69	81.28	82.91	84.57	86.26	87.98
9,000	89.65	91.44	93.27	95.14	97.04	98.98
10,000	99.61	101.60	103.64	105.71	107.82	109.98
15,000	149.42	152.41	155.45	158.56	161.73	164.97
20,000	199.22	203.21	207.27	211.42	215.65	219.96
25,000	249.03	254.01	259.09	264.27	269.56	274.95
30,000	298.83	304.81	310.91	317.13	323.47	329.94
35,000	348.64	355.61	362.72	369.98	377.38	384.93
40,000	398.45	406.41	414.54	422.83	431.29	439.92
45,000	448.25	457.22	466.36	475.69	485.20	494.91
50,000	498.06	508.02	518.18	528.54	539.11	549.89
55,000	547.86	558.82	570.00	581.40	593.02	604.88
60,000	597.67	609.62	621.81	634.25	646.94	659.87
65,000	647.47	660.42	673.63	687.10	700.85	714.86
70,000	697.28	711.23	725.45	739.96	754.76	769.85
75,000	747.09	762.03	777.27	792.81	808.67	824.84
80,000	796.89	812.83	829.09	845.67	862.58	879.83
85,000	846.70	863.63	880.90	898.52	916.49	934.82
90,000	896.50	914.43	932.72	951.38	970.40	989.81
95,000	946.31	965.23	984.54	1,004.23	1,024.31	1,044.80
100,000	996.11	1,016.04	1,036.36	1,057.08	1,078.23	1,099.79
110,000	1,095.72	1,117.64	1,139.99	1,162.79	1,186.05	1,209.77
120,000	1,195.34	1,219.24	1,243.63	1,268.50	1,293.87	1,319.75
130,000	1,294.95	1,320.85	1,347.26	1,374.21	1,401.69	1,429.73
140,000	1,394.56	1,422.45	1,450.90	1,479.92	1,509.52	1,539.71
150,000	1,494.17	1,524.05	1,554.53	1,585.63	1,617.34	1,649.68
160,000	1,593.78	1,625.66	1,658.17	1,691.33	1,725.16	1,759.66
170,000	1,693.39	1,727.26	1,761.81	1,797.04	1,832.98	1,869.64
180,000	1,793.00	1,828.86	1,865.44	1,902.75	1,940.81	1,979.62
190,000	1,892.62	1,930.47	1,969.08	2,008.46	2,048.63	2,089.60
200,000	1,992.23	2,032.07	2,072.71	2,114.17	2,156.45	2,199.58

TABLE IV-57. (*Continued*)

FHA GRADUATED PAYMENT PLAN IV
TERM:30 YEARS INTEREST:13.00% GRADUATED AT 2.00%

PAYMENT AMOUNT	YEAR 7	YEAR 8	YEAR 9	YEAR 10	YEARS 11-30
50	0.56	0.57	0.58	0.60	0.61
100	1.12	1.14	1.17	1.19	1.21
200	2.24	2.29	2.33	2.38	2.43
300	3.37	3.43	3.50	3.57	3.64
400	4.49	4.58	4.67	4.76	4.86
500	5.61	5.72	5.84	5.95	6.07
600	6.73	6.87	7.00	7.14	7.29
700	7.85	8.01	8.17	8.33	8.50
800	8.97	9.15	9.34	9.52	9.71
900	10.10	10.30	10.50	10.71	10.93
1,000	11.22	11.44	11.67	11.90	12.14
2,000	22.44	22.88	23.34	23.81	24.29
3,000	33.65	34.33	35.01	35.71	36.43
4,000	44.87	45.77	46.68	47.62	48.57
5,000	56.09	57.21	58.36	59.52	60.71
6,000	67.31	68.65	70.03	71.43	72.86
7,000	78.52	80.10	81.70	83.33	85.00
8,000	89.74	91.54	93.37	95.24	97.14
9,000	100.96	102.98	105.04	107.14	109.28
10,000	112.18	114.42	116.71	119.04	121.43
15,000	168.27	171.63	175.07	178.57	182.14
20,000	224.36	228.84	233.42	238.09	242.85
25,000	280.45	286.06	291.78	297.61	303.56
30,000	336.54	343.27	350.13	357.13	364.28
35,000	392.62	400.48	408.49	416.66	424.99
40,000	448.71	457.69	466.84	476.18	485.70
45,000	504.80	514.90	525.20	535.70	546.42
50,000	560.89	572.11	583.55	595.22	607.13
55,000	616.98	629.32	641.91	654.75	667.84
60,000	673.07	686.53	700.26	714.27	728.55
65,000	729.16	743.74	758.62	773.79	789.27
70,000	785.25	800.95	816.97	833.31	849.98
75,000	841.34	858.17	875.33	892.84	910.69
80,000	897.43	915.38	933.68	952.36	971.41
85,000	953.52	972.59	992.04	1,011.88	1,032.12
90,000	1,009.61	1,029.80	1,050.40	1,071.40	1,092.83
95,000	1,065.70	1,087.01	1,108.75	1,130.93	1,153.54
100,000	1,121.79	1,144.22	1,167.11	1,190.45	1,214.26
110,000	1,233.96	1,258.64	1,283.82	1,309.49	1,335.68
120,000	1,346.14	1,373.07	1,400.53	1,428.54	1,457.11
130,000	1,458.32	1,487.49	1,517.24	1,547.58	1,578.53
140,000	1,570.50	1,601.91	1,633.95	1,666.63	1,699.96
150,000	1,682.68	1,716.33	1,750.66	1,785.67	1,821.39
160,000	1,794.86	1,830.75	1,867.37	1,904.72	1,942.81
170,000	1,907.04	1,945.18	1,984.08	2,023.76	2,064.24
180,000	2,019.21	2,059.60	2,100.79	2,142.81	2,185.66
190,000	2,131.39	2,174.02	2,217.50	2,261.85	2,307.09
200,000	2,243.57	2,288.44	2,334.21	2,380.90	2,428.51

TABLE IV-58. Graduated Payment Mortgage, FHA Plan IV at 13.5% Interest, Graduated at 2.0%

FHA GRADUATED PAYMENT PLAN IV
TERM:30 YEARS INTEREST:13.50% GRADUATED AT 2.00%

PAYMENT AMOUNT	YEAR 1	YEAR 2	YEAR 3	YEAR 4	YEAR 5	YEAR 6
50	0.52	0.53	0.54	0.55	0.56	0.57
100	1.03	1.05	1.08	1.10	1.12	1.14
200	2.07	2.11	2.15	2.19	2.24	2.28
300	3.10	3.16	3.23	3.29	3.36	3.42
400	4.13	4.22	4.30	4.39	4.47	4.56
500	5.17	5.27	5.38	5.48	5.59	5.71
600	6.20	6.33	6.45	6.58	6.71	6.85
700	7.23	7.38	7.53	7.68	7.83	7.99
800	8.27	8.43	8.60	8.77	8.95	9.13
900	9.30	9.49	9.68	9.87	10.07	10.27
1,000	10.34	10.54	10.75	10.97	11.19	11.41
2,000	20.67	21.08	21.51	21.94	22.37	22.82
3,000	31.01	31.63	32.26	32.90	33.56	34.23
4,000	41.34	42.17	43.01	43.87	44.75	45.64
5,000	51.68	52.71	53.76	54.84	55.94	57.06
6,000	62.01	63.25	64.52	65.81	67.12	68.47
7,000	72.35	73.79	75.27	76.78	78.31	79.88
8,000	82.68	84.34	86.02	87.74	89.50	91.29
9,000	93.02	94.88	96.78	98.71	100.69	102.70
10,000	103.35	105.42	107.53	109.68	111.87	114.11
15,000	155.03	158.13	161.29	164.52	167.81	171.17
20,000	206.71	210.84	215.06	219.36	223.75	228.22
25,000	258.38	263.55	268.82	274.20	279.68	285.28
30,000	310.06	316.26	322.59	329.04	335.62	342.33
35,000	361.74	368.97	376.35	383.88	391.55	399.39
40,000	413.41	421.68	430.11	438.72	447.49	456.44
45,000	465.09	474.39	483.88	493.56	503.43	513.50
50,000	516.77	527.10	537.64	548.40	559.36	570.55
55,000	568.44	579.81	591.41	603.24	615.30	627.61
60,000	620.12	632.52	645.17	658.08	671.24	684.66
65,000	671.80	685.23	698.94	712.91	727.17	741.72
70,000	723.47	737.94	752.70	767.75	783.11	798.77
75,000	775.15	790.65	806.46	822.59	839.05	855.83
80,000	826.83	843.36	860.23	877.43	894.98	912.88
85,000	878.50	896.07	913.99	932.27	950.92	969.94
90,000	930.18	948.78	967.76	987.11	1,006.86	1,026.99
95,000	981.85	1,001.49	1,021.52	1,041.95	1,062.79	1,084.05
100,000	1,033.53	1,054.20	1,075.29	1,096.79	1,118.73	1,141.10
110,000	1,136.88	1,159.62	1,182.81	1,206.47	1,230.60	1,255.21
120,000	1,240.24	1,265.04	1,290.34	1,316.15	1,342.47	1,369.32
130,000	1,343.59	1,370.46	1,397.87	1,425.83	1,454.35	1,483.43
140,000	1,446.94	1,475.88	1,505.40	1,535.51	1,566.22	1,597.54
150,000	1,550.30	1,581.30	1,612.93	1,645.19	1,678.09	1,711.65
160,000	1,653.65	1,686.72	1,720.46	1,754.87	1,789.96	1,825.76
170,000	1,757.00	1,792.14	1,827.99	1,864.55	1,901.84	1,939.87
180,000	1,860.36	1,897.56	1,935.52	1,974.23	2,013.71	2,053.98
190,000	1,963.71	2,002.98	2,043.04	2,083.90	2,125.58	2,168.09
200,000	2,067.06	2,108.40	2,150.57	2,193.58	2,237.46	2,282.20

TABLE IV-58. (*Continued*)

FHA GRADUATED PAYMENT PLAN IV
TERM:30 YEARS INTEREST:13.50% GRADUATED AT 2.00%

PAYMENT AMOUNT	YEAR 7	YEAR 8	YEAR 9	YEAR 10	YEARS 11-30
50	0.58	0.59	0.61	0.62	0.63
100	1.16	1.19	1.21	1.24	1.26
200	2.33	2.37	2.42	2.47	2.52
300	3.49	3.56	3.63	3.71	3.78
400	4.66	4.75	4.84	4.94	5.04
500	5.82	5.94	6.05	6.18	6.30
600	6.98	7.12	7.27	7.41	7.56
700	8.15	8.31	8.48	8.65	8.82
800	9.31	9.50	9.69	9.88	10.08
900	10.48	10.68	10.90	11.12	11.34
1,000	11.64	11.87	12.11	12.35	12.60
2,000	23.28	23.74	24.22	24.70	25.20
3,000	34.92	35.62	36.33	37.05	37.80
4,000	46.56	47.49	48.44	49.41	50.39
5,000	58.20	59.36	60.55	61.76	62.99
6,000	69.84	71.23	72.66	74.11	75.59
7,000	81.47	83.10	84.77	86.46	88.19
8,000	93.11	94.98	96.88	98.81	100.79
9,000	104.75	106.85	108.99	111.16	113.39
10,000	116.39	118.72	121.09	123.52	125.99
15,000	174.59	178.08	181.64	185.27	188.98
20,000	232.78	237.44	242.19	247.03	251.97
25,000	290.98	296.80	302.74	308.79	314.97
30,000	349.18	356.16	363.28	370.55	377.96
35,000	407.37	415.52	423.83	432.31	440.95
40,000	465.57	474.88	484.38	494.07	503.95
45,000	523.77	534.24	544.93	555.82	566.94
50,000	581.96	593.60	605.47	617.58	629.93
55,000	640.16	652.96	666.02	679.34	692.93
60,000	698.35	712.32	726.57	741.10	755.92
65,000	756.55	771.68	787.12	802.86	818.91
70,000	814.75	831.04	847.66	864.62	881.91
75,000	872.94	890.40	908.21	926.37	944.90
80,000	931.14	949.76	968.76	988.13	1,007.90
85,000	989.34	1,009.12	1,029.30	1,049.89	1,070.89
90,000	1,047.53	1,068.48	1,089.85	1,111.65	1,133.88
95,000	1,105.73	1,127.84	1,150.40	1,173.41	1,196.88
100,000	1,163.92	1,187.20	1,210.95	1,235.17	1,259.87
110,000	1,280.32	1,305.92	1,332.04	1,358.68	1,385.86
120,000	1,396.71	1,424.64	1,453.14	1,482.20	1,511.84
130,000	1,513.10	1,543.36	1,574.23	1,605.72	1,637.83
140,000	1,629.49	1,662.08	1,695.33	1,729.23	1,763.82
150,000	1,745.89	1,780.80	1,816.42	1,852.75	1,889.80
160,000	1,862.28	1,899.52	1,937.52	1,976.27	2,015.79
170,000	1,978.67	2,018.24	2,058.61	2,099.78	2,141.78
180,000	2,095.06	2,136.97	2,179.70	2,223.30	2,267.76
190,000	2,211.46	2,255.69	2,300.80	2,346.82	2,393.75
200,000	2,327.85	2,374.41	2,421.89	2,470.33	2,519.74

TABLE IV-59. Graduated Payment Mortgage, FHA Plan IV at 14.0% Interest, Graduated at 2.0%

FHA GRADUATED PAYMENT PLAN IV
TERM: 30 YEARS INTEREST: 14.00% GRADUATED AT 2.00%

PAYMENT AMCUNT	YEAR 1	YEAR 2	YEAR 3	YEAR 4	YEAR 5	YEAR 6
50	0.54	0.55	0.56	0.57	0.58	0.59
100	1.07	1.09	1.11	1.14	1.16	1.18
200	2.14	2.19	2.23	2.27	2.32	2.37
300	3.21	3.28	3.34	3.41	3.48	3.55
400	4.29	4.37	4.46	4.55	4.64	4.73
500	5.36	5.46	5.57	5.68	5.80	5.91
600	6.43	6.56	6.69	6.82	6.96	7.10
700	7.50	7.65	7.80	7.96	8.12	8.28
800	8.57	8.74	8.92	9.09	9.28	9.46
900	9.64	9.83	10.03	10.23	10.44	10.65
1,000	10.71	10.93	11.15	11.37	11.60	11.83
2,000	21.43	21.85	22.29	22.74	23.19	23.66
3,000	32.14	32.78	33.44	34.11	34.79	35.48
4,000	42.85	43.71	44.58	45.47	46.38	47.31
5,000	53.56	54.64	55.73	56.84	57.98	59.14
6,000	64.28	65.56	66.87	68.21	69.58	70.97
7,000	74.99	76.49	78.02	79.58	81.17	82.79
8,000	85.70	87.42	89.16	90.95	92.77	94.62
9,000	96.42	98.34	100.31	102.32	104.36	106.45
10,000	107.13	109.27	111.46	113.69	115.96	118.28
15,000	160.69	163.91	167.18	170.53	173.94	177.42
20,000	214.26	218.54	222.91	227.37	231.92	236.56
25,000	267.82	273.18	278.64	284.21	289.90	295.69
30,000	321.38	327.81	334.37	341.06	347.88	354.83
35,000	374.95	382.45	390.10	397.90	405.86	413.97
40,000	428.51	437.08	445.82	454.74	463.84	473.11
45,000	482.08	491.72	501.55	511.58	521.81	532.25
50,000	535.64	546.35	557.28	568.43	579.79	591.39
55,000	589.20	600.99	613.01	625.27	637.77	650.53
60,000	642.77	655.62	668.74	682.11	695.75	709.67
65,000	696.33	710.26	724.46	738.95	753.73	768.81
70,000	749.90	764.89	780.19	795.80	811.71	827.95
75,000	803.46	819.53	835.92	852.64	869.69	887.08
80,000	857.02	874.16	891.65	909.48	927.67	946.22
85,000	910.59	928.80	947.38	966.32	985.65	1,005.36
90,000	964.15	983.44	1,003.10	1,023.17	1,043.63	1,064.50
95,000	1,017.72	1,038.07	1,058.83	1,080.01	1,101.61	1,123.64
100,000	1,071.28	1,092.71	1,114.56	1,136.85	1,159.59	1,182.78
110,000	1,178.41	1,201.98	1,226.02	1,250.54	1,275.55	1,301.06
120,000	1,285.54	1,311.25	1,337.47	1,364.22	1,391.51	1,419.34
130,000	1,392.66	1,420.52	1,448.93	1,477.91	1,507.46	1,537.61
140,000	1,499.79	1,529.79	1,560.38	1,591.59	1,623.42	1,655.89
150,000	1,606.92	1,639.06	1,671.84	1,705.28	1,739.38	1,774.17
160,000	1,714.05	1,748.33	1,783.30	1,818.96	1,855.34	1,892.45
170,000	1,821.18	1,857.60	1,894.75	1,932.65	1,971.30	2,010.73
180,000	1,928.30	1,966.87	2,006.21	2,046.33	2,087.26	2,129.00
190,000	2,035.43	2,076.14	2,117.66	2,160.02	2,203.22	2,247.28
200,000	2,142.56	2,185.41	2,229.12	2,273.70	2,319.18	2,365.56

TABLE IV-59. (*Continued*)

FHA GRADUATED PAYMENT PLAN IV
TERM:30 YEARS INTEREST:14.00% GRADUATED AT 2.00%

PAYMENT AMOUNT	YEAR 7	YEAR 8	YEAR 9	YEAR 10	YEARS 11-30
50	0.60	0.62	0.63	0.64	0.65
100	1.21	1.23	1.26	1.28	1.31
200	2.41	2.46	2.51	2.56	2.61
300	3.62	3.69	3.77	3.84	3.92
400	4.83	4.92	5.02	5.12	5.22
500	6.03	6.15	6.28	6.40	6.53
600	7.24	7.38	7.53	7.68	7.84
700	8.45	8.61	8.79	8.96	9.14
800	9.65	9.84	10.04	10.24	10.45
900	10.86	11.08	11.30	11.52	11.75
1,000	12.06	12.31	12.55	12.80	13.06
2,000	24.13	24.61	25.10	25.61	26.12
3,000	36.19	36.92	37.66	38.41	39.18
4,000	48.26	49.22	50.21	51.21	52.24
5,000	60.32	61.53	62.76	64.01	65.29
6,000	72.39	73.83	75.31	76.82	78.35
7,000	84.45	86.14	87.86	89.62	91.41
8,000	96.51	98.45	100.41	102.42	104.47
9,000	108.58	110.75	112.97	115.23	117.53
10,000	120.64	123.06	125.52	128.03	130.59
15,000	180.97	184.58	188.28	192.04	195.88
20,000	241.29	246.11	251.04	256.06	261.18
25,000	301.61	307.64	313.79	320.07	326.47
30,000	361.93	369.17	376.55	384.08	391.77
35,000	422.25	430.70	439.31	448.10	457.06
40,000	482.57	492.23	502.07	512.11	522.35
45,000	542.90	553.75	564.83	576.13	587.65
50,000	603.22	615.28	627.59	640.14	652.94
55,000	663.54	676.81	690.35	704.15	718.24
60,000	723.86	738.34	753.11	768.17	783.53
65,000	784.18	799.87	815.86	832.18	848.82
70,000	844.50	861.39	878.62	896.20	914.12
75,000	904.83	922.92	941.38	960.21	979.41
80,000	965.15	984.45	1,004.14	1,024.22	1,044.71
85,000	1,025.47	1,045.98	1,066.90	1,088.24	1,110.00
90,000	1,085.79	1,107.51	1,129.66	1,152.25	1,175.30
95,000	1,146.11	1,169.04	1,192.42	1,216.26	1,240.59
100,000	1,206.44	1,230.56	1,255.18	1,280.28	1,305.88
110,000	1,327.08	1,353.62	1,380.69	1,408.31	1,436.47
120,000	1,447.72	1,476.68	1,506.21	1,536.33	1,567.06
130,000	1,568.37	1,599.73	1,631.73	1,664.36	1,697.65
140,000	1,689.01	1,722.79	1,757.25	1,792.39	1,828.24
150,000	1,809.65	1,845.85	1,882.76	1,920.42	1,958.83
160,000	1,930.30	1,968.90	2,008.28	2,048.45	2,089.42
170,000	2,050.94	2,091.96	2,133.80	2,176.47	2,220.00
180,000	2,171.58	2,215.02	2,259.32	2,304.50	2,350.59
190,000	2,292.23	2,338.07	2,384.83	2,432.53	2,481.18
200,000	2,412.87	2,461.13	2,510.35	2,560.56	2,611.77

TABLE IV-60. Graduated Payment Mortgage, FHA Plan IV at 14.5% Interest, Graduated at 2.0%

FHA GRADUATED PAYMENT PLAN IV
TERM: 30 YEARS INTEREST: 14.50% GRADUATED AT 2.00%

PAYMENT AMOUNT	YEAR 1	YEAR 2	YEAR 3	YEAR 4	YEAR 5	YEAR 6
50	0.55	0.57	0.58	0.59	0.60	0.61
100	1.11	1.13	1.15	1.18	1.20	1.22
200	2.22	2.26	2.31	2.35	2.40	2.45
300	3.33	3.39	3.46	3.53	3.60	3.67
400	4.44	4.53	4.62	4.71	4.80	4.90
500	5.55	5.66	5.77	5.89	6.00	6.12
600	6.66	6.79	6.92	7.06	7.20	7.35
700	7.77	7.92	8.08	8.24	8.41	8.57
800	8.87	9.05	9.23	9.42	9.61	9.80
900	9.98	10.18	10.39	10.60	10.81	11.02
1,000	11.09	11.32	11.54	11.77	12.01	12.25
2,000	22.19	22.63	23.08	23.54	24.02	24.50
3,000	33.28	33.95	34.62	35.32	36.02	36.74
4,000	44.37	45.26	46.17	47.09	48.03	48.99
5,000	55.47	56.58	57.71	58.86	60.04	61.24
6,000	66.56	67.89	69.25	70.63	72.05	73.49
7,000	77.65	79.21	80.79	82.41	84.05	85.74
8,000	88.75	90.52	92.33	94.18	96.06	97.98
9,000	99.84	101.84	103.87	105.95	108.07	110.23
10,000	110.93	113.15	115.42	117.72	120.08	122.48
15,000	166.40	169.73	173.12	176.59	180.12	183.72
20,000	221.87	226.30	230.83	235.45	240.16	244.96
25,000	277.33	282.88	288.54	294.31	300.20	306.20
30,000	332.80	339.46	346.25	353.17	360.23	367.44
35,000	388.27	396.03	403.95	412.03	420.27	428.68
40,000	443.73	452.61	461.66	470.89	480.31	489.92
45,000	499.20	509.19	519.37	529.76	540.35	551.16
50,000	554.67	565.76	577.08	588.62	600.39	612.40
55,000	610.13	622.34	634.78	647.48	660.43	673.64
60,000	665.60	678.91	692.49	706.34	720.47	734.88
65,000	721.07	735.49	750.20	765.20	780.51	796.12
70,000	776.54	792.07	807.91	824.07	840.55	857.36
75,000	832.00	848.64	865.61	882.93	900.59	918.60
80,000	887.47	905.22	923.32	941.79	960.62	979.84
85,000	942.94	961.79	981.03	1,000.65	1,020.66	1,041.08
90,000	998.40	1,018.37	1,038.74	1,059.51	1,080.70	1,102.32
95,000	1,053.87	1,074.95	1,096.45	1,118.37	1,140.74	1,163.56
100,000	1,109.34	1,131.52	1,154.15	1,177.24	1,200.78	1,224.80
110,000	1,220.27	1,244.67	1,269.57	1,294.96	1,320.86	1,347.28
120,000	1,331.20	1,357.83	1,384.98	1,412.68	1,440.94	1,469.76
130,000	1,442.14	1,470.98	1,500.40	1,530.41	1,561.01	1,592.24
140,000	1,553.07	1,584.13	1,615.81	1,648.13	1,681.09	1,714.71
150,000	1,664.00	1,697.28	1,731.23	1,765.85	1,801.17	1,837.19
160,000	1,774.94	1,810.44	1,846.64	1,883.58	1,921.25	1,959.67
170,000	1,885.87	1,923.59	1,962.06	2,001.30	2,041.33	2,082.15
180,000	1,996.80	2,036.74	2,077.48	2,119.02	2,161.41	2,204.63
190,000	2,107.74	2,149.89	2,192.89	2,236.75	2,281.48	2,327.11
200,000	2,218.67	2,263.04	2,308.31	2,354.47	2,401.56	2,449.59

TABLE IV-60. (*Continued*)

FHA GRADUATED PAYMENT PLAN IV
TERM:30 YEARS INTEREST:14.50% GRADUATED AT 2.00%

PAYMENT AMOUNT	YEAR 7	YEAR 8	YEAR 9	YEAR 10	YEARS 11-30
50	0.62	0.64	0.65	0.66	0.68
100	1.25	1.27	1.30	1.33	1.35
200	2.50	2.55	2.60	2.65	2.70
300	3.75	3.82	3.90	3.98	4.06
400	5.00	5.10	5.20	5.30	5.41
500	6.25	6.37	6.50	6.63	6.76
600	7.50	7.65	7.80	7.95	8.11
700	8.75	8.92	9.10	9.28	9.47
800	9.99	10.19	10.40	10.61	10.82
900	11.24	11.47	11.70	11.93	12.17
1,000	12.49	12.74	13.00	13.26	13.52
2,000	24.99	25.49	26.00	26.52	27.05
3,000	37.48	38.23	38.99	39.77	40.57
4,000	49.97	50.97	51.99	53.03	54.09
5,000	62.46	63.71	64.99	66.29	67.61
6,000	74.96	76.46	77.99	79.55	81.14
7,000	87.45	89.20	90.98	92.80	94.66
8,000	99.94	101.94	103.98	106.06	108.18
9,000	112.44	114.69	116.98	119.32	121.70
10,000	124.93	127.43	129.98	132.58	135.23
15,000	187.39	191.14	194.96	198.86	202.84
20,000	249.86	254.86	259.95	265.15	270.45
25,000	312.32	318.57	324.94	331.44	338.07
30,000	374.79	382.28	389.93	397.73	405.68
35,000	437.25	446.00	454.92	464.02	473.30
40,000	499.72	509.71	519.91	530.30	540.91
45,000	562.18	573.43	584.89	596.59	608.52
50,000	624.65	637.14	649.88	662.88	676.14
55,000	687.11	700.85	714.87	729.17	743.75
60,000	749.58	764.57	779.86	795.46	811.36
65,000	812.04	828.28	844.85	861.74	878.98
70,000	874.50	891.99	909.83	928.03	946.59
75,000	936.97	955.71	974.82	994.32	1,014.21
80,000	999.43	1,019.42	1,039.81	1,060.61	1,081.82
85,000	1,061.90	1,083.14	1,104.80	1,126.90	1,149.43
90,000	1,124.36	1,146.85	1,169.79	1,193.18	1,217.05
95,000	1,186.83	1,210.56	1,234.78	1,259.47	1,284.66
100,000	1,249.29	1,274.28	1,299.76	1,325.76	1,352.27
110,000	1,374.22	1,401.71	1,429.74	1,458.33	1,487.50
120,000	1,499.15	1,529.13	1,559.72	1,590.91	1,622.73
130,000	1,624.08	1,656.56	1,689.69	1,723.49	1,757.96
140,000	1,749.01	1,783.99	1,819.67	1,856.06	1,893.18
150,000	1,873.94	1,911.42	1,949.65	1,988.64	2,028.41
160,000	1,998.87	2,038.84	2,079.62	2,121.21	2,163.64
170,000	2,123.80	2,166.27	2,209.60	2,253.79	2,298.87
180,000	2,248.73	2,293.70	2,339.57	2,386.37	2,434.09
190,000	2,373.66	2,421.13	2,469.55	2,518.94	2,569.32
200,000	2,498.58	2,548.56	2,599.53	2,651.52	2,704.55

TABLE IV-61. Graduated Payment Mortgage, FHA Plan IV at 15.0% Interest, Graduated at 2.0%

FHA GRADUATED PAYMENT PLAN IV
TERM:30 YEARS INTEREST:15.00% GRADUATED AT 2.00%

PAYMENT AMCUNT	YEAR 1	YEAR 2	YEAR 3	YEAR 4	YEAR 5	YEAR 6
50	0.57	0.59	0.60	0.61	0.62	0.63
100	1.15	1.17	1.19	1.22	1.24	1.27
200	2.30	2.34	2.39	2.44	2.48	2.53
300	3.44	3.51	3.58	3.65	3.73	3.80
400	4.59	4.68	4.78	4.87	4.97	5.07
500	5.74	5.85	5.97	6.09	6.21	6.34
600	6.89	7.02	7.16	7.31	7.45	7.60
700	8.03	8.19	8.36	8.53	8.70	8.87
800	9.18	9.37	9.55	9.74	9.94	10.14
900	10.33	10.54	10.75	10.96	11.18	11.40
1,000	11.48	11.71	11.94	12.18	12.42	12.67
2,000	22.95	23.41	23.88	24.36	24.85	25.34
3,000	34.43	35.12	35.82	36.54	37.27	38.01
4,000	45.91	46.83	47.76	48.72	49.69	50.69
5,000	57.38	58.53	59.70	60.90	62.11	63.36
6,000	68.86	70.24	71.64	73.08	74.54	76.03
7,000	80.34	81.94	83.58	85.25	86.96	88.70
8,000	91.81	93.65	95.52	97.43	99.38	101.37
9,000	103.29	105.36	107.46	109.61	111.81	114.04
10,000	114.77	117.06	119.40	121.79	124.23	126.71
15,000	172.15	175.59	179.11	182.69	186.34	190.07
20,000	229.54	234.13	238.81	243.58	248.46	253.43
25,000	286.92	292.66	298.51	304.48	310.57	316.78
30,000	344.30	351.19	358.21	365.38	372.68	380.14
35,000	401.69	409.72	417.91	426.27	434.80	443.49
40,000	459.07	468.25	477.62	487.17	496.91	506.85
45,000	516.45	526.78	537.32	548.07	559.03	570.21
50,000	573.84	585.31	597.02	608.96	621.14	633.56
55,000	631.22	643.85	656.72	669.86	683.25	696.92
60,000	688.61	702.38	716.43	730.75	745.37	760.28
65,000	745.99	760.91	776.13	791.65	807.48	823.63
70,000	803.37	819.44	835.83	852.55	869.60	886.99
75,000	860.76	877.97	895.53	913.44	931.71	950.35
80,000	918.14	936.50	955.23	974.34	993.83	1,013.70
85,000	975.52	995.04	1,014.94	1,035.23	1,055.94	1,077.06
90,000	1,032.91	1,053.57	1,074.64	1,096.13	1,118.05	1,140.41
95,000	1,090.29	1,112.10	1,134.34	1,157.03	1,180.17	1,203.77
100,000	1,147.68	1,170.63	1,194.04	1,217.92	1,242.28	1,267.13
110,000	1,262.44	1,287.69	1,313.45	1,339.72	1,366.51	1,393.84
120,000	1,377.21	1,404.76	1,432.85	1,461.51	1,490.74	1,520.55
130,000	1,491.98	1,521.82	1,552.25	1,583.30	1,614.97	1,647.27
140,000	1,606.75	1,638.88	1,671.66	1,705.09	1,739.19	1,773.98
150,000	1,721.51	1,755.94	1,791.06	1,826.88	1,863.42	1,900.69
160,000	1,836.28	1,873.01	1,910.47	1,948.68	1,987.65	2,027.40
170,000	1,951.05	1,990.07	2,029.87	2,070.47	2,111.88	2,154.12
180,000	2,065.82	2,107.13	2,149.28	2,192.26	2,236.11	2,280.83
190,000	2,180.58	2,224.20	2,268.68	2,314.05	2,360.33	2,407.54
200,000	2,295.35	2,341.26	2,388.08	2,435.85	2,484.56	2,534.25

TABLE IV-61. (*Continued*)

FHA GRADUATED PAYMENT PLAN IV
TERM:30 YEARS INTEREST:15.00% GRADUATED AT 2.00%

PAYMENT AMOUNT	YEAR 7	YEAR 8	YEAR 9	YEAR 10	YEARS 11-30
50	0.65	0.66	0.67	0.69	0.70
100	1.29	1.32	1.34	1.37	1.40
200	2.58	2.64	2.69	2.74	2.80
300	3.88	3.95	4.03	4.11	4.20
400	5.17	5.27	5.38	5.49	5.60
500	6.46	6.59	6.72	6.86	7.00
600	7.75	7.91	8.07	8.23	8.39
700	9.05	9.23	9.41	9.60	9.79
800	10.34	10.55	10.76	10.97	11.19
900	11.63	11.86	12.10	12.34	12.59
1,000	12.92	13.18	13.45	13.72	13.99
2,000	25.85	26.37	26.89	27.43	27.98
3,000	38.77	39.55	40.34	41.15	41.97
4,000	51.70	52.73	53.79	54.86	55.96
5,000	64.62	65.92	67.23	68.58	69.95
6,000	77.55	79.10	80.68	82.29	83.94
7,000	90.47	92.28	94.13	96.01	97.93
8,000	103.40	105.47	107.57	109.73	111.92
9,000	116.32	118.65	121.02	123.44	125.91
10,000	129.25	131.83	134.47	137.16	139.90
15,000	193.87	197.75	201.70	205.74	209.85
20,000	258.49	263.66	268.94	274.32	279.80
25,000	323.12	329.58	336.17	342.89	349.75
30,000	387.74	395.50	403.41	411.47	419.70
35,000	452.36	461.41	470.64	480.05	489.65
40,000	516.99	527.33	537.87	548.63	559.60
45,000	581.61	593.24	605.11	617.21	629.55
50,000	646.23	659.16	672.34	685.79	699.51
55,000	710.86	725.08	739.58	754.37	769.46
60,000	775.48	790.99	806.81	822.95	839.41
65,000	840.11	856.91	874.05	891.53	909.36
70,000	904.73	922.82	941.28	960.11	979.31
75,000	969.35	988.74	1,008.51	1,028.68	1,049.26
80,000	1,033.98	1,054.66	1,075.75	1,097.26	1,119.21
85,000	1,098.60	1,120.57	1,142.98	1,165.84	1,189.16
90,000	1,163.22	1,186.49	1,210.22	1,234.42	1,259.11
95,000	1,227.85	1,252.40	1,277.45	1,303.00	1,329.06
100,000	1,292.47	1,318.32	1,344.69	1,371.58	1,399.01
110,000	1,421.72	1,450.15	1,479.15	1,508.74	1,538.91
120,000	1,550.96	1,581.98	1,613.62	1,645.90	1,678.81
130,000	1,680.21	1,713.81	1,748.09	1,783.05	1,818.71
140,000	1,809.46	1,845.65	1,882.56	1,920.21	1,958.62
150,000	1,938.70	1,977.48	2,017.03	2,057.37	2,098.52
160,000	2,067.95	2,109.31	2,151.50	2,194.53	2,238.42
170,000	2,197.20	2,241.14	2,285.97	2,331.60	2,378.32
180,000	2,326.45	2,372.97	2,420.43	2,468.84	2,518.22
190,000	2,455.69	2,504.81	2,554.90	2,606.00	2,658.12
200,000	2,584.94	2,636.64	2,689.37	2,743.16	2,798.02

TABLE IV-62. Graduated Payment Mortgage, FHA Plan IV at 15.5% Interest, Graduated at 2.0%

FHA GRADUATED PAYMENT PLAN IV
TERM:30 YEARS INTEREST:15.50% GRADUATED AT 2.00%

PAYMENT AMOUNT	YEAR 1	YEAR 2	YEAR 3	YEAR 4	YEAR 5	YEAR 6
50	0.59	0.61	0.62	0.63	0.64	0.65
100	1.19	1.21	1.23	1.26	1.28	1.31
200	2.37	2.42	2.47	2.52	2.57	2.62
300	3.56	3.63	3.70	3.78	3.85	3.93
400	4.75	4.84	4.94	5.04	5.14	5.24
500	5.93	6.05	6.17	6.29	6.42	6.55
600	7.12	7.26	7.41	7.55	7.70	7.86
700	8.30	8.47	8.64	8.81	8.99	9.17
800	9.49	9.68	9.87	10.07	10.27	10.48
900	10.68	10.89	11.11	11.33	11.56	11.79
1,000	11.86	12.10	12.34	12.59	12.84	13.10
2,000	23.73	24.20	24.68	25.18	25.68	26.19
3,000	35.59	36.30	37.03	37.77	38.52	39.29
4,000	47.45	48.40	49.37	50.36	51.36	52.39
5,000	59.31	60.50	61.71	62.94	64.20	65.49
6,000	71.18	72.60	74.05	75.53	77.04	78.58
7,000	83.04	84.70	86.39	88.12	89.88	91.68
8,000	94.90	96.80	98.74	100.71	102.73	104.78
9,000	106.77	108.90	111.08	113.30	115.57	117.88
10,000	118.63	121.00	123.42	125.89	128.41	130.97
15,000	177.94	181.50	185.13	188.83	192.61	196.46
20,000	237.26	242.00	246.84	251.78	256.81	261.95
25,000	296.57	302.50	308.55	314.72	321.02	327.44
30,000	355.88	363.00	370.26	377.67	385.22	392.92
35,000	415.20	423.50	431.97	440.61	449.42	458.41
40,000	474.51	484.00	493.68	503.56	513.63	523.90
45,000	533.83	544.50	555.39	566.50	577.83	589.39
50,000	593.14	605.00	617.10	629.45	642.03	654.87
55,000	652.45	665.50	678.81	692.39	706.24	720.36
60,000	711.77	726.00	740.52	755.33	770.44	785.85
65,000	771.08	786.50	802.23	818.28	834.64	851.34
70,000	830.40	847.00	863.94	881.22	898.85	916.82
75,000	889.71	907.50	925.65	944.17	963.05	982.31
80,000	949.02	968.00	987.36	1,007.11	1,027.25	1,047.80
85,000	1,008.34	1,028.51	1,049.08	1,070.06	1,091.46	1,113.29
90,000	1,067.65	1,089.01	1,110.79	1,133.00	1,155.66	1,178.77
95,000	1,126.97	1,149.51	1,172.50	1,195.95	1,219.86	1,244.26
100,000	1,186.28	1,210.01	1,234.21	1,258.89	1,284.07	1,309.75
110,000	1,304.91	1,331.01	1,357.63	1,384.78	1,412.47	1,440.72
120,000	1,423.54	1,452.01	1,481.05	1,510.67	1,540.88	1,571.70
130,000	1,542.16	1,573.01	1,604.47	1,636.56	1,669.29	1,702.67
140,000	1,660.79	1,694.01	1,727.89	1,762.45	1,797.70	1,833.65
150,000	1,779.42	1,815.01	1,851.31	1,888.34	1,926.10	1,964.62
160,000	1,898.05	1,936.01	1,974.73	2,014.22	2,054.51	2,095.60
170,000	2,016.68	2,057.01	2,098.15	2,140.11	2,182.92	2,226.57
180,000	2,135.30	2,178.01	2,221.57	2,266.00	2,311.32	2,357.55
190,000	2,253.93	2,299.01	2,344.99	2,391.89	2,439.73	2,488.52
200,000	2,372.56	2,420.01	2,468.41	2,517.78	2,568.14	2,619.50

TABLE IV-62. (*Continued*)

FHA GRADUATED PAYMENT PLAN IV
TERM:30 YEARS INTEREST:15.50% GRADUATED AT 2.00%

PAYMENT AMOUNT	YEAR 7	YEAR 8	YEAR 9	YEAR 10	YEARS 11-30
50	0.67	0.68	0.69	0.71	0.72
100	1.34	1.36	1.39	1.42	1.45
200	2.67	2.73	2.78	2.84	2.89
300	4.01	4.09	4.17	4.25	4.34
400	5.34	5.45	5.56	5.67	5.78
500	6.68	6.81	6.95	7.09	7.23
600	8.02	8.18	8.34	8.51	8.68
700	9.35	9.54	9.73	9.92	10.12
800	10.69	10.90	11.12	11.34	11.57
900	12.02	12.26	12.51	12.76	13.01
1,000	13.36	13.63	13.90	14.18	14.46
2,000	26.72	27.25	27.80	28.35	28.92
3,000	40.08	40.88	41.70	42.53	43.38
4,000	53.44	54.51	55.60	56.71	57.84
5,000	66.80	68.13	69.50	70.89	72.30
6,000	80.16	81.76	83.39	85.06	86.76
7,000	93.52	95.39	97.29	99.24	101.22
8,000	106.88	109.01	111.19	113.42	115.69
9,000	120.24	122.64	125.09	127.59	130.15
10,000	133.59	136.27	138.99	141.77	144.61
15,000	200.39	204.40	208.49	212.66	216.91
20,000	267.19	272.53	277.98	283.54	289.21
25,000	333.99	340.67	347.48	354.43	361.52
30,000	400.78	408.80	416.97	425.31	433.82
35,000	467.58	476.93	486.47	496.20	506.12
40,000	534.38	545.07	555.97	567.09	578.43
45,000	601.18	613.20	625.46	637.97	650.73
50,000	667.97	681.33	694.96	708.86	723.03
55,000	734.77	749.46	764.45	779.74	795.34
60,000	801.57	817.60	833.95	850.63	867.64
65,000	868.36	885.73	903.45	921.51	939.95
70,000	935.16	953.86	972.94	992.40	1,012.25
75,000	1,001.96	1,022.00	1,042.44	1,063.29	1,084.55
80,000	1,068.76	1,090.13	1,111.93	1,134.17	1,156.86
85,000	1,135.55	1,158.26	1,181.43	1,205.06	1,229.16
90,000	1,202.35	1,226.40	1,250.92	1,275.94	1,301.46
95,000	1,269.15	1,294.53	1,320.42	1,346.83	1,373.77
100,000	1,335.94	1,362.66	1,389.92	1,417.71	1,446.07
110,000	1,469.54	1,498.93	1,528.91	1,559.49	1,590.68
120,000	1,603.13	1,635.20	1,667.90	1,701.26	1,735.28
130,000	1,736.73	1,771.46	1,806.89	1,843.03	1,879.89
140,000	1,870.32	1,907.73	1,945.88	1,984.80	2,024.50
150,000	2,003.92	2,044.00	2,084.87	2,126.57	2,169.10
160,000	2,137.51	2,180.26	2,223.87	2,268.34	2,313.71
170,000	2,271.11	2,316.53	2,362.86	2,410.12	2,458.32
180,000	2,404.70	2,452.79	2,501.85	2,551.89	2,602.92
190,000	2,538.29	2,589.06	2,640.84	2,693.66	2,747.53
200,000	2,671.89	2,725.33	2,779.83	2,835.43	2,892.14

TABLE IV-63. Graduated Payment Mortgage, FHA Plan IV at 16.0% Interest, Graduated at 2.0%

FHA GRADUATED PAYMENT PLAN IV
TERM:30 YEARS INTEREST:16.00% GRADUATED AT 2.00%

PAYMENT AMOUNT	YEAR 1	YEAR 2	YEAR 3	YEAR 4	YEAR 5	YEAR 6
50	0.61	0.62	0.64	0.65	0.66	0.68
100	1.23	1.25	1.27	1.30	1.33	1.35
200	2.45	2.50	2.55	2.60	2.65	2.71
300	3.68	3.75	3.82	3.90	3.98	4.06
400	4.90	5.00	5.10	5.20	5.30	5.41
500	6.13	6.25	6.37	6.50	6.63	6.76
600	7.35	7.50	7.65	7.80	7.96	8.12
700	8.58	8.75	8.92	9.10	9.28	9.47
800	9.80	10.00	10.20	10.40	10.61	10.82
900	11.03	11.25	11.47	11.70	11.94	12.17
1,000	12.25	12.50	12.75	13.00	13.26	13.53
2,000	24.50	24.99	25.49	26.00	26.52	27.05
3,000	36.75	37.49	38.24	39.00	39.78	40.58
4,000	49.01	49.99	50.98	52.00	53.04	54.11
5,000	61.26	62.48	63.73	65.01	66.31	67.63
6,000	73.51	74.98	76.48	78.01	79.57	81.16
7,000	85.76	87.47	89.22	91.01	92.83	94.68
8,000	98.01	99.97	101.97	104.01	106.09	108.21
9,000	110.26	112.47	114.72	117.01	119.35	121.74
10,000	122.51	124.96	127.46	130.01	132.61	135.26
15,000	183.77	187.44	191.19	195.02	198.92	202.90
20,000	245.03	249.93	254.92	260.02	265.22	270.53
25,000	306.28	312.41	318.66	325.03	331.53	338.16
30,000	367.54	374.89	382.39	390.04	397.84	405.79
35,000	428.80	437.37	446.12	455.04	464.14	473.42
40,000	490.05	499.85	509.85	520.05	530.45	541.06
45,000	551.31	562.33	573.58	585.05	596.75	608.69
50,000	612.56	624.82	637.31	650.06	663.06	676.32
55,000	673.82	687.30	701.04	715.06	729.37	743.95
60,000	735.08	749.78	764.77	780.07	795.67	811.58
65,000	796.33	812.26	828.51	845.08	861.98	879.22
70,000	857.59	874.74	892.24	910.08	928.28	946.85
75,000	918.85	937.22	955.97	975.09	994.59	1,014.48
80,000	980.10	999.71	1,019.70	1,040.09	1,060.90	1,082.11
85,000	1,041.36	1,062.19	1,083.43	1,105.10	1,127.20	1,149.75
90,000	1,102.62	1,124.67	1,147.16	1,170.11	1,193.51	1,217.38
95,000	1,163.87	1,187.15	1,210.89	1,235.11	1,259.81	1,285.01
100,000	1,225.13	1,249.63	1,274.62	1,300.12	1,326.12	1,352.64
110,000	1,347.64	1,374.59	1,402.09	1,430.13	1,458.73	1,487.91
120,000	1,470.15	1,499.56	1,529.55	1,560.14	1,591.34	1,623.17
130,000	1,592.67	1,624.52	1,657.01	1,690.15	1,723.95	1,758.43
140,000	1,715.18	1,749.48	1,784.47	1,820.16	1,856.57	1,893.70
150,000	1,837.69	1,874.45	1,911.94	1,950.18	1,989.18	2,028.96
160,000	1,960.21	1,999.41	2,039.40	2,080.19	2,121.79	2,164.23
170,000	2,082.72	2,124.37	2,166.86	2,210.20	2,254.40	2,299.49
180,000	2,205.23	2,249.34	2,294.32	2,340.21	2,387.01	2,434.75
190,000	2,327.75	2,374.30	2,421.79	2,470.22	2,519.63	2,570.02
200,000	2,450.26	2,499.26	2,549.25	2,600.23	2,652.24	2,705.28

TABLE IV-63. (Continued)

FHA GRADUATED PAYMENT PLAN IV
TERM:30 YEARS INTEREST:16.00% GRADUATED AT 2.00%

PAYMENT AMOUNT	YEAR 7	YEAR 8	YEAR 9	YEAR 10	YEARS 11-30
50	0.69	0.70	0.72	0.73	0.75
100	1.38	1.41	1.44	1.46	1.49
200	2.76	2.81	2.87	2.93	2.99
300	4.14	4.22	4.31	4.39	4.48
400	5.52	5.63	5.74	5.86	5.97
500	6.90	7.04	7.18	7.32	7.47
600	8.28	8.44	8.61	8.78	8.96
700	9.66	9.85	10.05	10.25	10.45
800	11.04	11.26	11.48	11.71	11.95
900	12.42	12.67	12.92	13.18	13.44
1,000	13.80	14.07	14.35	14.64	14.93
2,000	27.59	28.15	28.71	29.28	29.87
3,000	41.39	42.22	43.06	43.92	44.80
4,000	55.19	56.29	57.42	58.57	59.74
5,000	68.98	70.36	71.77	73.21	74.67
6,000	82.78	84.44	86.13	87.85	89.61
7,000	96.58	98.51	100.48	102.49	104.54
8,000	110.38	112.58	114.83	117.13	119.47
9,000	124.17	126.66	129.19	131.77	134.41
10,000	137.97	140.73	143.54	146.41	149.34
15,000	206.95	211.09	215.32	219.62	224.01
20,000	275.94	281.46	287.09	292.83	298.69
25,000	344.92	351.82	358.86	366.04	373.36
30,000	413.91	422.19	430.63	439.24	448.03
35,000	482.89	492.55	502.40	512.45	522.70
40,000	551.88	562.92	574.17	585.66	597.37
45,000	620.86	633.28	645.95	658.86	672.04
50,000	689.85	703.64	717.72	732.07	746.71
55,000	758.83	774.01	789.49	805.28	821.38
60,000	827.82	844.37	861.26	878.49	896.06
65,000	896.80	914.74	933.03	951.69	970.73
70,000	965.79	985.10	1,004.80	1,024.90	1,045.40
75,000	1,034.77	1,055.47	1,076.58	1,098.11	1,120.07
80,000	1,103.76	1,125.83	1,148.35	1,171.31	1,194.74
85,000	1,172.74	1,196.20	1,220.12	1,244.52	1,269.41
90,000	1,241.72	1,266.56	1,291.89	1,317.73	1,344.08
95,000	1,310.71	1,336.92	1,363.66	1,390.94	1,418.75
100,000	1,379.69	1,407.29	1,435.43	1,464.14	1,493.43
110,000	1,517.66	1,548.02	1,578.98	1,610.56	1,642.77
120,000	1,655.63	1,688.75	1,722.52	1,756.97	1,792.11
130,000	1,793.60	1,829.47	1,866.06	1,903.39	1,941.45
140,000	1,931.57	1,970.20	2,009.61	2,049.80	2,090.80
150,000	2,069.54	2,110.93	2,153.15	2,196.21	2,240.14
160,000	2,207.51	2,251.66	2,296.69	2,342.63	2,389.48
170,000	2,345.48	2,392.39	2,440.24	2,489.04	2,538.82
180,000	2,483.45	2,533.12	2,583.78	2,635.46	2,688.17
190,000	2,621.42	2,673.85	2,727.32	2,781.87	2,837.51
200,000	2,759.39	2,814.58	2,870.87	2,928.29	2,986.85

TABLE IV-64. Graduated Payment Mortgage, FHA Plan IV at 16.5% Interest, Graduated at 2.0%

FHA GRADUATED PAYMENT PLAN IV
TERM:30 YEARS INTEREST:16.50% GRADUATED AT 2.00%

PAYMENT AMCUNT	YEAR 1	YEAR 2	YEAR 3	YEAR 4	YEAR 5	YEAR 6
50	0.63	0.64	0.66	0.67	0.68	0.70
100	1.26	1.29	1.32	1.34	1.37	1.40
200	2.53	2.58	2.63	2.68	2.74	2.79
300	3.79	3.87	3.95	4.02	4.11	4.19
400	5.06	5.16	5.26	5.37	5.47	5.58
500	6.32	6.45	6.58	6.71	6.84	6.98
600	7.59	7.74	7.89	8.05	8.21	8.37
700	8.85	9.03	9.21	9.39	9.58	9.77
800	10.11	10.32	10.52	10.73	10.95	11.17
900	11.38	11.61	11.84	12.07	12.32	12.56
1,000	12.64	12.89	13.15	13.42	13.68	13.96
2,000	25.28	25.79	26.31	26.83	27.37	27.92
3,000	37.93	38.68	39.46	40.25	41.05	41.87
4,000	50.57	51.58	52.61	53.66	54.74	55.83
5,000	63.21	64.47	65.76	67.08	68.42	69.79
6,000	75.85	77.37	78.92	80.49	82.10	83.75
7,000	88.49	90.26	92.07	93.91	95.79	97.70
8,000	101.14	103.16	105.22	107.33	109.47	111.66
9,000	113.78	116.05	118.37	120.74	123.16	125.62
10,000	126.42	128.95	131.53	134.16	136.84	139.58
15,000	189.63	193.42	197.29	201.24	205.26	209.37
20,000	252.84	257.90	263.06	268.32	273.68	279.16
25,000	316.05	322.37	328.82	335.40	342.10	348.95
30,000	379.26	386.85	394.58	402.47	410.52	418.73
35,000	442.47	451.32	460.35	469.55	478.95	488.52
40,000	505.68	515.80	526.11	536.63	547.37	558.31
45,000	568.89	580.27	591.87	603.71	615.79	628.10
50,000	632.10	644.74	657.64	670.79	684.21	697.89
55,000	695.31	709.22	723.40	737.87	752.63	767.68
60,000	758.52	773.69	789.17	804.95	821.05	837.47
65,000	821.73	838.17	854.93	872.03	889.47	907.26
70,000	884.94	902.64	920.69	939.11	957.89	977.05
75,000	948.15	967.12	986.46	1,006.19	1,026.31	1,046.84
80,000	1,011.36	1,031.59	1,052.22	1,073.27	1,094.73	1,116.63
85,000	1,074.57	1,096.06	1,117.99	1,140.35	1,163.15	1,186.42
90,000	1,137.78	1,160.54	1,183.75	1,207.42	1,231.57	1,256.20
95,000	1,200.99	1,225.01	1,249.51	1,274.50	1,299.99	1,325.99
100,000	1,264.20	1,289.49	1,315.28	1,341.58	1,368.41	1,395.78
110,000	1,390.62	1,418.44	1,446.81	1,475.74	1,505.26	1,535.36
120,000	1,517.04	1,547.39	1,578.33	1,609.90	1,642.10	1,674.94
130,000	1,643.47	1,676.33	1,709.86	1,744.06	1,778.94	1,814.52
140,000	1,769.89	1,805.28	1,841.39	1,878.22	1,915.78	1,954.10
150,000	1,896.31	1,934.23	1,972.92	2,012.37	2,052.62	2,093.67
160,000	2,022.73	2,063.18	2,104.44	2,146.53	2,189.46	2,233.25
170,000	2,149.15	2,192.13	2,235.97	2,280.69	2,326.31	2,372.83
180,000	2,275.57	2,321.08	2,367.50	2,414.85	2,463.15	2,512.41
190,000	2,401.99	2,450.03	2,499.03	2,549.01	2,599.99	2,651.99
200,000	2,528.41	2,578.98	2,630.56	2,683.17	2,736.83	2,791.57

TABLE IV-64. (*Continued*)

FHA GRADUATED PAYMENT PLAN IV
TERM:30 YEARS INTEREST:16.50% GRADUATED AT 2.00%

PAYMENT AMCUNT	YEAR 7	YEAR 8	YEAR 9	YEAR 10	YEARS 11-30
50	0.71	0.73	0.74	0.76	0.77
100	1.42	1.45	1.48	1.51	1.54
200	2.85	2.90	2.96	3.02	3.08
300	4.27	4.36	4.44	4.53	4.62
400	5.69	5.81	5.92	6.04	6.16
500	7.12	7.26	7.41	7.55	7.71
600	8.54	8.71	8.89	9.07	9.25
700	9.97	10.17	10.37	10.58	10.79
800	11.39	11.62	11.85	12.09	12.33
900	12.81	13.07	13.33	13.60	13.87
1,000	14.24	14.52	14.81	15.11	15.41
2,000	28.47	29.04	29.62	30.22	30.82
3,000	42.71	43.57	44.44	45.33	46.23
4,000	56.95	58.09	59.25	60.43	61.64
5,000	71.18	72.61	74.06	75.54	77.05
6,000	85.42	87.13	88.87	90.65	92.46
7,000	99.66	101.65	103.69	105.76	107.87
8,000	113.90	116.17	118.50	120.87	123.28
9,000	128.13	130.70	133.31	135.98	138.70
10,000	142.37	145.22	148.12	151.08	154.11
15,000	213.55	217.83	222.18	226.63	231.16
20,000	284.74	290.43	296.24	302.17	308.21
25,000	355.92	363.04	370.30	377.71	385.26
30,000	427.11	435.65	444.36	453.25	462.32
35,000	498.29	508.26	518.43	528.79	539.37
40,000	569.48	580.87	592.49	604.34	616.42
45,000	640.66	653.48	666.55	679.88	693.48
50,000	711.85	726.09	740.61	755.42	770.53
55,000	783.03	798.70	814.67	830.96	847.58
60,000	854.22	871.30	888.73	906.50	924.63
65,000	925.40	943.91	962.79	982.05	1,001.69
70,000	996.59	1,016.52	1,036.85	1,057.59	1,078.74
75,000	1,067.77	1,089.13	1,110.91	1,133.13	1,155.79
80,000	1,138.96	1,161.74	1,184.97	1,208.67	1,232.85
85,000	1,210.14	1,234.35	1,259.03	1,284.21	1,309.90
90,000	1,281.33	1,306.96	1,333.09	1,359.76	1,386.95
95,000	1,352.51	1,379.56	1,407.16	1,435.30	1,464.00
100,000	1,423.70	1,452.17	1,481.22	1,510.84	1,541.06
110,000	1,566.07	1,597.39	1,629.34	1,661.92	1,695.16
120,000	1,708.44	1,742.61	1,777.46	1,813.01	1,849.27
130,000	1,850.81	1,887.82	1,925.58	1,964.09	2,003.37
140,000	1,993.18	2,033.04	2,073.70	2,115.18	2,157.48
150,000	2,135.55	2,178.26	2,221.82	2,266.26	2,311.59
160,000	2,277.92	2,323.48	2,369.95	2,417.35	2,465.69
170,000	2,420.29	2,468.69	2,518.07	2,568.43	2,619.80
180,000	2,562.66	2,613.91	2,666.19	2,719.51	2,773.90
190,000	2,705.03	2,759.13	2,814.31	2,870.60	2,928.01
200,000	2,847.40	2,904.35	2,962.43	3,021.68	3,082.12

TABLE IV-65. Graduated Payment Mortgage, FHA Plan IV at 17.0% Interest, Graduated at 2.0%

FHA GRADUATED PAYMENT PLAN IV
TERM:30 YEARS INTEREST:17.00% GRADUATED AT 2.00%

PAYMENT AMOUNT	YEAR 1	YEAR 2	YEAR 3	YEAR 4	YEAR 5	YEAR 6
50	0.65	0.66	0.68	0.69	0.71	0.72
100	1.30	1.33	1.36	1.38	1.41	1.44
200	2.61	2.66	2.71	2.77	2.82	2.88
300	3.91	3.99	4.07	4.15	4.23	4.32
400	5.21	5.32	5.42	5.53	5.64	5.76
500	6.52	6.65	6.78	6.92	7.05	7.20
600	7.82	7.98	8.14	8.30	8.47	8.63
700	9.12	9.31	9.49	9.68	9.88	10.07
800	10.43	10.64	10.85	11.07	11.29	11.51
900	11.73	11.97	12.21	12.45	12.70	12.95
1,000	13.03	13.30	13.56	13.83	14.11	14.39
2,000	26.07	26.59	27.12	27.67	28.22	28.78
3,000	39.10	39.89	40.68	41.50	42.33	43.17
4,000	52.14	53.18	54.25	55.33	56.44	57.57
5,000	65.17	66.48	67.81	69.16	70.55	71.96
6,000	78.21	79.77	81.37	83.00	84.66	86.35
7,000	91.24	93.07	94.93	96.83	98.77	100.74
8,000	104.28	106.36	108.49	110.66	112.87	115.13
9,000	117.31	119.66	122.05	124.49	126.98	129.52
10,000	130.35	132.96	135.61	138.33	141.09	143.92
15,000	195.52	199.43	203.42	207.49	211.64	215.87
20,000	260.70	265.91	271.23	276.65	282.19	287.83
25,000	325.87	332.39	339.04	345.82	352.73	359.79
30,000	391.05	398.87	406.84	414.98	423.28	431.75
35,000	456.22	465.35	474.65	484.15	493.83	503.70
40,000	521.40	531.82	542.46	553.31	564.37	575.66
45,000	586.57	598.30	610.27	622.47	634.92	647.62
50,000	651.74	664.78	678.07	691.64	705.47	719.58
55,000	716.92	731.26	745.88	760.80	776.02	791.54
60,000	782.09	797.73	813.69	829.96	846.56	863.49
65,000	847.27	864.21	881.50	899.13	917.11	935.45
70,000	912.44	930.69	949.30	968.29	987.66	1,007.41
75,000	977.62	997.17	1,017.11	1,037.45	1,058.20	1,079.37
80,000	1,042.79	1,063.65	1,084.92	1,106.62	1,128.75	1,151.32
85,000	1,107.96	1,130.12	1,152.73	1,175.78	1,199.30	1,223.28
90,000	1,173.14	1,196.60	1,220.53	1,244.94	1,269.84	1,295.24
95,000	1,238.31	1,263.08	1,288.34	1,314.11	1,340.39	1,367.20
100,000	1,303.49	1,329.56	1,356.15	1,383.27	1,410.94	1,439.16
110,000	1,433.84	1,462.51	1,491.76	1,521.60	1,552.03	1,583.07
120,000	1,564.19	1,595.47	1,627.38	1,659.93	1,693.12	1,726.99
130,000	1,694.53	1,728.42	1,762.99	1,798.25	1,834.22	1,870.90
140,000	1,824.88	1,861.38	1,898.61	1,936.58	1,975.31	2,014.82
150,000	1,955.23	1,994.34	2,034.22	2,074.91	2,116.41	2,158.73
160,000	2,085.58	2,127.29	2,169.84	2,213.23	2,257.50	2,302.65
170,000	2,215.93	2,260.25	2,305.45	2,351.56	2,398.59	2,446.56
180,000	2,346.28	2,393.20	2,441.07	2,489.89	2,539.69	2,590.48
190,000	2,476.63	2,526.16	2,576.68	2,628.22	2,680.78	2,734.40
200,000	2,606.98	2,659.12	2,712.30	2,766.54	2,821.87	2,878.31

TABLE IV-65. (*Continued*)

FHA GRADUATED PAYMENT PLAN IV
TERM:30 YEARS INTEREST:17.00% GRADUATED AT 2.00%

PAYMENT AMOUNT	YEAR 7	YEAR 8	YEAR 9	YEAR 10	YEARS 11-30
50	0.73	0.75	0.76	0.78	0.79
100	1.47	1.50	1.53	1.56	1.59
200	2.94	2.99	3.05	3.12	3.18
300	4.40	4.49	4.58	4.67	4.77
400	5.87	5.99	6.11	6.23	6.36
500	7.34	7.49	7.64	7.79	7.94
600	8.81	8.98	9.16	9.35	9.53
700	10.28	10.48	10.69	10.90	11.12
800	11.74	11.98	12.22	12.46	12.71
900	13.21	13.48	13.75	14.02	14.30
1,000	14.68	14.97	15.27	15.58	15.89
2,000	29.36	29.95	30.54	31.16	31.78
3,000	44.04	44.92	45.82	46.73	47.67
4,000	58.72	59.89	61.09	62.31	63.56
5,000	73.40	74.86	76.36	77.89	79.45
6,000	88.08	89.84	91.63	93.47	95.34
7,000	102.76	104.81	106.91	109.05	111.23
8,000	117.44	119.78	122.18	124.62	127.12
9,000	132.11	134.76	137.45	140.20	143.00
10,000	146.79	149.73	152.72	155.78	158.89
15,000	220.19	224.59	229.09	233.67	238.34
20,000	293.59	299.46	305.45	311.56	317.79
25,000	366.98	374.32	381.81	389.45	397.24
30,000	440.38	449.19	458.17	467.34	476.68
35,000	513.78	524.05	534.54	545.23	556.13
40,000	587.18	598.92	610.90	623.12	635.58
45,000	660.57	673.78	687.26	701.00	715.02
50,000	733.97	748.65	763.62	778.89	794.47
55,000	807.37	823.51	839.98	856.78	873.92
60,000	880.76	898.38	916.35	934.67	953.37
65,000	954.16	973.24	992.71	1,012.56	1,032.81
70,000	1,027.56	1,048.11	1,069.07	1,090.45	1,112.26
75,000	1,100.95	1,122.97	1,145.43	1,168.34	1,191.71
80,000	1,174.35	1,197.84	1,221.79	1,246.23	1,271.16
85,000	1,247.75	1,272.70	1,298.16	1,324.12	1,350.60
90,000	1,321.15	1,347.57	1,374.52	1,402.01	1,430.05
95,000	1,394.54	1,422.43	1,450.88	1,479.90	1,509.50
100,000	1,467.94	1,497.30	1,527.24	1,557.79	1,588.94
110,000	1,614.73	1,647.03	1,679.97	1,713.57	1,747.84
120,000	1,761.53	1,796.76	1,832.69	1,869.35	1,906.73
130,000	1,908.32	1,946.49	1,985.42	2,025.13	2,065.63
140,000	2,055.11	2,096.22	2,138.14	2,180.90	2,224.52
150,000	2,201.91	2,245.95	2,290.87	2,336.68	2,383.42
160,000	2,348.70	2,395.68	2,443.59	2,492.46	2,542.31
170,000	2,495.50	2,545.41	2,596.31	2,648.24	2,701.21
180,000	2,642.29	2,695.14	2,749.04	2,804.02	2,860.10
190,000	2,789.08	2,844.87	2,901.76	2,959.80	3,018.99
200,000	2,935.88	2,994.60	3,054.49	3,115.58	3,177.89

TABLE IV-66. Graduated Payment Mortgage, FHA Plan IV at 17.5% Interest, Graduated at 2.0%

FHA GRADUATED PAYMENT PLAN IV
TERM:30 YEARS INTEREST:17.50% GRADUATED AT 2.00%

PAYMENT AMOUNT	YEAR 1	YEAR 2	YEAR 3	YEAR 4	YEAR 5	YEAR 6
50	0.67	0.68	0.70	0.71	0.73	0.74
100	1.34	1.37	1.40	1.43	1.45	1.48
200	2.69	2.74	2.79	2.85	2.91	2.97
300	4.03	4.11	4.19	4.28	4.36	4.45
400	5.37	5.48	5.59	5.70	5.81	5.93
500	6.71	6.85	6.99	7.13	7.27	7.41
600	8.06	8.22	8.38	8.55	8.72	8.90
700	9.40	9.59	9.78	9.98	10.18	10.38
800	10.74	10.96	11.18	11.40	11.63	11.86
900	12.09	12.33	12.57	12.83	13.08	13.34
1,000	13.43	13.70	13.97	14.25	14.54	14.83
2,000	26.86	27.40	27.94	28.50	29.07	29.65
3,000	40.29	41.09	41.92	42.75	43.61	44.48
4,000	53.72	54.79	55.89	57.01	58.15	59.31
5,000	67.15	68.49	69.86	71.26	72.68	74.14
6,000	80.58	82.19	83.83	85.51	87.22	88.96
7,000	94.01	95.89	97.81	99.76	101.76	103.79
8,000	107.44	109.59	111.78	114.01	116.29	118.62
9,000	120.87	123.28	125.75	128.26	130.83	133.45
10,000	134.30	136.98	139.72	142.52	145.37	148.27
15,000	201.44	205.47	209.58	213.77	218.05	222.41
20,000	268.59	273.96	279.44	285.03	290.73	296.55
25,000	335.74	342.46	349.31	356.29	363.42	370.69
30,000	402.89	410.95	419.17	427.55	436.10	444.82
35,000	470.04	479.44	489.03	498.81	508.78	518.96
40,000	537.19	547.93	558.89	570.07	581.47	593.10
45,000	604.33	616.42	628.75	641.32	654.15	667.23
50,000	671.48	684.91	698.61	712.58	726.83	741.37
55,000	738.63	753.40	768.47	783.84	799.52	815.51
60,000	805.78	821.89	838.33	855.10	872.20	889.65
65,000	872.93	890.39	908.19	926.36	944.88	963.78
70,000	940.08	958.88	978.05	997.62	1,017.57	1,037.92
75,000	1,007.22	1,027.37	1,047.92	1,068.87	1,090.25	1,112.06
80,000	1,074.37	1,095.86	1,117.78	1,140.13	1,162.93	1,186.19
85,000	1,141.52	1,164.35	1,187.64	1,211.39	1,235.62	1,260.33
90,000	1,208.67	1,232.84	1,257.50	1,282.65	1,308.30	1,334.47
95,000	1,275.82	1,301.33	1,327.36	1,353.91	1,380.99	1,408.60
100,000	1,342.96	1,369.82	1,397.22	1,425.17	1,453.67	1,482.74
110,000	1,477.26	1,506.81	1,536.94	1,567.68	1,599.04	1,631.02
120,000	1,611.56	1,643.79	1,676.66	1,710.20	1,744.40	1,779.29
130,000	1,745.85	1,780.77	1,816.39	1,852.71	1,889.77	1,927.56
140,000	1,880.15	1,917.75	1,956.11	1,995.23	2,035.14	2,075.84
150,000	2,014.45	2,054.74	2,095.83	2,137.75	2,180.50	2,224.11
160,000	2,148.74	2,191.72	2,235.55	2,280.26	2,325.87	2,372.39
170,000	2,283.04	2,328.70	2,375.28	2,422.78	2,471.24	2,520.66
180,000	2,417.34	2,465.68	2,515.00	2,565.30	2,616.60	2,668.94
190,000	2,551.63	2,602.67	2,654.72	2,707.81	2,761.97	2,817.21
200,000	2,685.93	2,739.65	2,794.44	2,850.33	2,907.34	2,965.48

TABLE IV-66. (*Continued*)

FHA GRADUATED PAYMENT PLAN IV
TERM:30 YEARS INTEREST:17.50% GRADUATED AT 2.00%

PAYMENT AMOUNT	YEAR 7	YEAR 8	YEAR 9	YEAR 10	YEARS 11-30
50	0.76	0.77	0.79	0.80	0.82
100	1.51	1.54	1.57	1.60	1.64
200	3.02	3.09	3.15	3.21	3.27
300	4.54	4.63	4.72	4.81	4.91
400	6.05	6.17	6.29	6.42	6.55
500	7.56	7.71	7.87	8.02	8.19
600	9.07	9.26	9.44	9.63	9.82
700	10.59	10.80	11.01	11.23	11.46
800	12.10	12.34	12.59	12.84	13.10
900	13.61	13.88	14.16	14.44	14.73
1,000	15.12	15.43	15.73	16.05	16.37
2,000	30.25	30.85	31.47	32.10	32.74
3,000	45.37	46.28	47.20	48.15	49.11
4,000	60.50	61.71	62.94	64.20	65.48
5,000	75.62	77.13	78.67	80.25	81.85
6,000	90.74	92.56	94.41	96.30	98.22
7,000	105.87	107.99	110.14	112.35	114.59
8,000	120.99	123.41	125.88	128.40	130.97
9,000	136.12	138.84	141.61	144.45	147.34
10,000	151.24	154.26	157.35	160.50	163.71
15,000	226.86	231.40	236.02	240.75	245.56
20,000	302.48	308.53	314.70	320.99	327.41
25,000	378.10	385.66	393.37	401.24	409.27
30,000	453.72	462.79	472.05	481.49	491.12
35,000	529.34	539.93	550.72	561.74	572.97
40,000	604.96	617.06	629.40	641.99	654.83
45,000	680.58	694.19	708.07	722.24	736.68
50,000	756.20	771.32	786.75	802.48	818.53
55,000	831.82	848.45	865.42	882.73	900.39
60,000	907.44	925.59	944.10	962.98	982.24
65,000	983.06	1,002.72	1,022.77	1,043.23	1,064.09
70,000	1,058.68	1,079.85	1,101.45	1,123.48	1,145.95
75,000	1,134.30	1,156.98	1,180.12	1,203.73	1,227.80
80,000	1,209.92	1,234.12	1,258.80	1,283.97	1,309.65
85,000	1,285.54	1,311.25	1,337.47	1,364.22	1,391.51
90,000	1,361.16	1,388.38	1,416.15	1,444.47	1,473.36
95,000	1,436.78	1,465.51	1,494.82	1,524.72	1,555.21
100,000	1,512.40	1,542.64	1,573.50	1,604.97	1,637.07
110,000	1,663.64	1,696.91	1,730.85	1,765.46	1,800.77
120,000	1,814.88	1,851.17	1,888.20	1,925.96	1,964.48
130,000	1,966.12	2,005.44	2,045.55	2,086.46	2,128.19
140,000	2,117.36	2,159.70	2,202.90	2,246.95	2,291.89
150,000	2,268.59	2,313.97	2,360.25	2,407.45	2,455.60
160,000	2,419.83	2,468.23	2,517.60	2,567.95	2,619.31
170,000	2,571.07	2,622.50	2,674.95	2,728.44	2,783.01
180,000	2,722.31	2,776.76	2,832.30	2,888.94	2,946.72
190,000	2,873.55	2,931.02	2,989.65	3,049.44	3,110.43
200,000	3,024.79	3,085.29	3,146.99	3,209.93	3,274.13

TABLE IV-67. Graduated Payment Mortgage, FHA Plan IV at 18.0% Interest, Graduated at 2.0%

FHA GRADUATED PAYMENT PLAN IV
TERM:30 YEARS INTEREST:18.00% GRADUATED AT 2.00%

PAYMENT AMOUNT	YEAR 1	YEAR 2	YEAR 3	YEAR 4	YEAR 5	YEAR 6
50	0.69	0.71	0.72	0.73	0.75	0.76
100	1.38	1.41	1.44	1.47	1.50	1.53
200	2.77	2.82	2.88	2.93	2.99	3.05
300	4.15	4.23	4.32	4.40	4.49	4.58
400	5.53	5.64	5.75	5.87	5.99	6.11
500	6.91	7.05	7.19	7.34	7.48	7.63
600	8.30	8.46	8.63	8.80	8.98	9.16
700	9.68	9.87	10.07	10.27	10.48	10.69
800	11.06	11.28	11.51	11.74	11.97	12.21
900	12.44	12.69	12.95	13.21	13.47	13.74
1,000	13.83	14.10	14.38	14.67	14.97	15.27
2,000	27.65	28.21	28.77	29.34	29.93	30.53
3,000	41.48	42.31	43.15	44.02	44.90	45.80
4,000	55.30	56.41	57.54	58.69	59.86	61.06
5,000	69.13	70.51	71.92	73.36	74.83	76.33
6,000	82.96	84.62	86.31	88.03	89.80	91.59
7,000	96.78	98.72	100.69	102.71	104.76	106.86
8,000	110.61	112.82	115.08	117.38	119.73	122.12
9,000	124.44	126.92	129.46	132.05	134.69	137.39
10,000	138.26	141.03	143.85	146.72	149.66	152.65
15,000	207.39	211.54	215.77	220.09	224.49	228.98
20,000	276.52	282.05	287.70	293.45	299.32	305.30
25,000	345.66	352.57	359.62	366.81	374.15	381.63
30,000	414.79	423.08	431.54	440.17	448.98	457.96
35,000	483.92	493.60	503.47	513.54	523.81	534.28
40,000	553.05	564.11	575.39	586.90	598.64	610.61
45,000	622.18	634.62	647.32	660.26	673.47	686.94
50,000	691.31	705.14	719.24	733.62	748.30	763.26
55,000	760.44	775.65	791.16	806.99	823.13	839.59
60,000	829.57	846.16	863.09	880.35	897.96	915.91
65,000	898.70	916.68	935.01	953.71	972.79	992.24
70,000	967.83	987.19	1,006.93	1,027.07	1,047.62	1,068.57
75,000	1,036.97	1,057.70	1,078.86	1,100.44	1,122.44	1,144.89
80,000	1,106.10	1,128.22	1,150.78	1,173.80	1,197.27	1,221.22
85,000	1,175.23	1,198.73	1,222.71	1,247.16	1,272.10	1,297.55
90,000	1,244.36	1,269.25	1,294.63	1,320.52	1,346.93	1,373.87
95,000	1,313.49	1,339.76	1,366.55	1,393.89	1,421.76	1,450.20
100,000	1,382.62	1,410.27	1,438.48	1,467.25	1,496.59	1,526.52
110,000	1,520.88	1,551.30	1,582.33	1,613.97	1,646.25	1,679.18
120,000	1,659.14	1,692.33	1,726.17	1,760.70	1,795.91	1,831.83
130,000	1,797.41	1,833.35	1,870.02	1,907.42	1,945.57	1,984.48
140,000	1,935.67	1,974.38	2,013.87	2,054.15	2,095.23	2,137.13
150,000	2,073.93	2,115.41	2,157.72	2,200.87	2,244.89	2,289.79
160,000	2,212.19	2,256.44	2,301.57	2,347.60	2,394.55	2,442.44
170,000	2,350.45	2,397.46	2,445.41	2,494.32	2,544.21	2,595.09
180,000	2,488.72	2,538.49	2,589.26	2,641.05	2,693.87	2,747.74
190,000	2,626.98	2,679.52	2,733.11	2,787.77	2,843.53	2,900.40
200,000	2,765.24	2,820.55	2,876.96	2,934.50	2,993.19	3,053.05

TABLE IV-67. (*Continued*)

FHA GRADUATED PAYMENT PLAN IV
TERM:30 YEARS INTEREST:18.00% GRADUATED AT 2.00%

PAYMENT AMOUNT	YEAR 7	YEAR 8	YEAR 9	YEAR 10	YEARS 11-30
50	0.78	0.79	0.81	0.83	0.84
100	1.56	1.59	1.62	1.65	1.69
200	3.11	3.18	3.24	3.30	3.37
300	4.67	4.76	4.86	4.96	5.06
400	6.23	6.35	6.48	6.61	6.74
500	7.79	7.94	8.10	8.26	8.43
600	9.34	9.53	9.72	9.91	10.11
700	10.90	11.12	11.34	11.57	11.80
800	12.46	12.71	12.96	13.22	13.48
900	14.01	14.29	14.58	14.87	15.17
1,000	15.57	15.88	16.20	16.52	16.85
2,000	31.14	31.76	32.40	33.05	33.71
3,000	46.71	47.65	48.60	49.57	50.56
4,000	62.28	63.53	64.80	66.09	67.42
5,000	77.85	79.41	81.00	82.62	84.27
6,000	93.42	95.29	97.20	99.14	101.12
7,000	108.99	111.17	113.40	115.67	117.98
8,000	124.56	127.06	129.60	132.19	134.83
9,000	140.13	142.94	145.80	148.71	151.69
10,000	155.71	158.82	162.00	165.24	168.54
15,000	233.56	238.23	242.99	247.85	252.81
20,000	311.41	317.64	323.99	330.47	337.08
25,000	389.26	397.05	404.99	413.09	421.35
30,000	467.12	476.46	485.99	495.71	505.62
35,000	544.97	555.87	566.99	578.33	589.89
40,000	622.82	635.28	647.98	660.94	674.16
45,000	700.67	714.69	728.98	743.56	758.43
50,000	778.53	794.10	809.98	826.18	842.70
55,000	856.38	873.51	890.98	908.80	926.97
60,000	934.23	952.92	971.98	991.42	1,011.24
65,000	1,012.09	1,032.33	1,052.97	1,074.03	1,095.51
70,000	1,089.94	1,111.74	1,133.97	1,156.65	1,179.78
75,000	1,167.79	1,191.15	1,214.97	1,239.27	1,264.06
80,000	1,245.64	1,270.56	1,295.97	1,321.89	1,348.33
85,000	1,323.50	1,349.97	1,376.97	1,404.51	1,432.60
90,000	1,401.35	1,429.38	1,457.96	1,487.12	1,516.87
95,000	1,479.20	1,508.79	1,538.96	1,569.74	1,601.14
100,000	1,557.06	1,588.20	1,619.96	1,652.36	1,685.41
110,000	1,712.76	1,747.02	1,781.96	1,817.60	1,853.95
120,000	1,868.47	1,905.84	1,943.95	1,982.83	2,022.49
130,000	2,024.17	2,064.66	2,105.95	2,148.07	2,191.03
140,000	2,179.88	2,223.47	2,267.94	2,313.30	2,359.57
150,000	2,335.58	2,382.29	2,429.94	2,478.54	2,528.11
160,000	2,491.29	2,541.11	2,591.94	2,643.78	2,696.65
170,000	2,646.99	2,699.93	2,753.93	2,809.01	2,865.19
180,000	2,802.70	2,858.75	2,915.93	2,974.25	3,033.73
190,000	2,958.41	3,017.57	3,077.92	3,139.48	3,202.27
200,000	3,114.11	3,176.39	3,239.92	3,304.72	3,370.81

TABLE IV-68. Graduated Payment Mortgage, FHA Plan IV at 18.5% Interest, Graduated at 2.0%

FHA GRADUATED PAYMENT PLAN IV
TERM:30 YEARS INTEREST:18.50% GRADUATED AT 2.00%

PAYMENT AMOUNT	YEAR 1	YEAR 2	YEAR 3	YEAR 4	YEAR 5	YEAR 6
50	0.71	0.73	0.74	0.75	0.77	0.79
100	1.42	1.45	1.48	1.51	1.54	1.57
200	2.84	2.90	2.96	3.02	3.08	3.14
300	4.27	4.35	4.44	4.53	4.62	4.71
400	5.69	5.80	5.92	6.04	6.16	6.28
500	7.11	7.25	7.40	7.55	7.70	7.85
600	8.53	8.71	8.88	9.06	9.24	9.42
700	9.96	10.16	10.36	10.57	10.78	10.99
800	11.38	11.61	11.84	12.08	12.32	12.56
900	12.80	13.06	13.32	13.59	13.86	14.13
1,000	14.22	14.51	14.80	15.10	15.40	15.70
2,000	28.45	29.02	29.60	30.19	30.79	31.41
3,000	42.67	43.53	44.40	45.29	46.19	47.11
4,000	56.90	58.04	59.20	60.38	61.59	62.82
5,000	71.12	72.54	74.00	75.48	76.98	78.52
6,000	85.35	87.05	88.79	90.57	92.38	94.23
7,000	99.57	101.56	103.59	105.67	107.78	109.93
8,000	113.80	116.07	118.39	120.76	123.18	125.64
9,000	128.02	130.58	133.19	135.86	138.57	141.34
10,000	142.24	145.09	147.99	150.95	153.97	157.05
15,000	213.37	217.63	221.99	226.43	230.95	235.57
20,000	284.49	290.18	295.98	301.90	307.94	314.10
25,000	355.61	362.72	369.98	377.38	384.92	392.62
30,000	426.73	435.27	443.97	452.85	461.91	471.15
35,000	497.85	507.81	517.97	528.33	538.89	549.67
40,000	568.98	580.36	591.96	603.80	615.88	628.20
45,000	640.10	652.90	665.96	679.28	692.86	706.72
50,000	711.22	725.44	739.95	754.75	769.85	785.24
55,000	782.34	797.99	813.95	830.23	846.83	863.77
60,000	853.46	870.53	887.94	905.70	923.82	942.29
65,000	924.59	943.08	961.94	981.18	1,000.80	1,020.82
70,000	995.71	1,015.62	1,035.94	1,056.65	1,077.79	1,099.34
75,000	1,066.83	1,088.17	1,109.93	1,132.13	1,154.77	1,177.87
80,000	1,137.95	1,160.71	1,183.93	1,207.60	1,231.76	1,256.39
85,000	1,209.07	1,233.26	1,257.92	1,283.08	1,308.74	1,334.92
90,000	1,280.20	1,305.80	1,331.92	1,358.56	1,385.73	1,413.44
95,000	1,351.32	1,378.35	1,405.91	1,434.03	1,462.71	1,491.97
100,000	1,422.44	1,450.89	1,479.91	1,509.51	1,539.70	1,570.49
110,000	1,564.69	1,595.98	1,627.90	1,660.46	1,693.67	1,727.54
120,000	1,706.93	1,741.07	1,775.89	1,811.41	1,847.64	1,884.59
130,000	1,849.17	1,886.16	1,923.88	1,962.36	2,001.60	2,041.64
140,000	1,991.42	2,031.25	2,071.87	2,113.31	2,155.57	2,198.69
150,000	2,133.66	2,176.33	2,219.86	2,264.26	2,309.54	2,355.73
160,000	2,275.91	2,321.42	2,367.85	2,415.21	2,463.51	2,512.78
170,000	2,418.15	2,466.51	2,515.84	2,566.16	2,617.48	2,669.83
180,000	2,560.39	2,611.60	2,663.83	2,717.11	2,771.45	2,826.88
190,000	2,702.64	2,756.69	2,811.82	2,868.06	2,925.42	2,983.93
200,000	2,844.88	2,901.78	2,959.82	3,019.01	3,079.39	3,140.98

TABLE IV-68. (*Continued*)

FHA GRADUATED PAYMENT PLAN IV
TERM:30 YEARS INTEREST:18.50% GRADUATED AT 2.00%

PAYMENT AMOUNT	YEAR 7	YEAR 8	YEAR 9	YEAR 10	YEARS 11-30
50	0.80	0.82	0.83	0.85	0.87
100	1.60	1.63	1.67	1.70	1.73
200	3.20	3.27	3.33	3.40	3.47
300	4.81	4.90	5.00	5.10	5.20
400	6.41	6.54	6.67	6.80	6.94
500	8.01	8.17	8.33	8.50	8.67
600	9.61	9.80	10.00	10.20	10.40
700	11.21	11.44	11.67	11.90	12.14
800	12.82	13.07	13.33	13.60	13.87
900	14.42	14.71	15.00	15.30	15.61
1,000	16.02	16.34	16.67	17.00	17.34
2,000	32.04	32.68	33.33	34.00	34.68
3,000	48.06	49.02	50.00	51.00	52.02
4,000	64.08	65.36	66.66	68.00	69.36
5,000	80.09	81.70	83.33	85.00	86.70
6,000	96.11	98.04	100.00	102.00	104.04
7,000	112.13	114.38	116.66	119.00	121.38
8,000	128.15	130.72	133.33	136.00	138.72
9,000	144.17	147.05	150.00	153.00	156.06
10,000	160.19	163.39	166.66	169.99	173.39
15,000	240.28	245.09	249.99	254.99	260.09
20,000	320.38	326.79	333.32	339.99	346.79
25,000	400.47	408.48	416.65	424.99	433.49
30,000	480.57	490.18	499.98	509.98	520.18
35,000	560.66	571.88	583.32	594.98	606.88
40,000	640.76	653.58	666.65	679.98	693.58
45,000	720.85	735.27	749.98	764.98	780.28
50,000	800.95	816.97	833.31	849.97	866.97
55,000	881.04	898.67	916.64	934.97	953.67
60,000	961.14	980.36	999.97	1,019.97	1,040.37
65,000	1,041.23	1,062.06	1,083.30	1,104.97	1,127.07
70,000	1,121.33	1,143.76	1,166.63	1,189.96	1,213.76
75,000	1,201.42	1,225.45	1,249.96	1,274.96	1,300.46
80,000	1,281.52	1,307.15	1,333.29	1,359.96	1,387.16
85,000	1,361.61	1,388.85	1,416.62	1,444.96	1,473.86
90,000	1,441.71	1,470.54	1,499.95	1,529.95	1,560.55
95,000	1,521.80	1,552.24	1,583.29	1,614.95	1,647.25
100,000	1,601.90	1,633.94	1,666.62	1,699.95	1,733.95
110,000	1,762.09	1,797.33	1,833.28	1,869.94	1,907.34
120,000	1,922.28	1,960.73	1,999.94	2,039.94	2,080.74
130,000	2,082.47	2,124.12	2,166.60	2,209.93	2,254.13
140,000	2,242.66	2,287.51	2,333.26	2,379.93	2,427.53
150,000	2,402.85	2,450.91	2,499.92	2,549.92	2,600.92
160,000	2,563.04	2,614.30	2,666.59	2,719.92	2,774.32
170,000	2,723.23	2,777.69	2,833.25	2,889.91	2,947.71
180,000	2,883.42	2,941.09	2,999.91	3,059.91	3,121.11
190,000	3,043.61	3,104.48	3,166.57	3,229.90	3,294.50
200,000	3,203.80	3,267.88	3,333.23	3,399.90	3,467.90

TABLE IV-69. Graduated Payment Mortgage, FHA Plan IV at 19.0% Interest, Graduated at 2.0%

FHA GRADUATED PAYMENT PLAN IV
TERM:30 YEARS INTEREST:19.00% GRADUATED AT 2.00%

PAYMENT AMOUNT	YEAR 1	YEAR 2	YEAR 3	YEAR 4	YEAR 5	YEAR 6
50	0.73	0.75	0.76	0.78	0.79	0.81
100	1.46	1.49	1.52	1.55	1.58	1.61
200	2.92	2.98	3.04	3.10	3.17	3.23
300	4.39	4.47	4.56	4.66	4.75	4.84
400	5.85	5.97	6.09	6.21	6.33	6.46
500	7.31	7.46	7.61	7.76	7.91	8.07
600	8.77	8.95	9.13	9.31	9.50	9.69
700	10.24	10.44	10.65	10.86	11.08	11.30
800	11.70	11.93	12.17	12.42	12.66	12.92
900	13.16	13.42	13.69	13.97	14.25	14.53
1,000	14.62	14.92	15.21	15.52	15.83	16.15
2,000	29.25	29.83	30.43	31.04	31.66	32.29
3,000	43.87	44.75	45.64	46.56	47.49	48.44
4,000	58.50	59.67	60.86	62.08	63.32	64.58
5,000	73.12	74.58	76.07	77.60	79.15	80.73
6,000	87.74	89.50	91.29	93.12	94.98	96.88
7,000	102.37	104.42	106.50	108.63	110.81	113.02
8,000	116.99	119.33	121.72	124.15	126.64	129.17
9,000	131.62	134.25	136.93	139.67	142.47	145.32
10,000	146.24	149.17	152.15	155.19	158.30	161.46
15,000	219.36	223.75	228.22	232.79	237.44	242.19
20,000	292.48	298.33	304.30	310.39	316.59	322.92
25,000	365.60	372.92	380.37	387.98	395.74	403.66
30,000	438.72	447.50	456.45	465.58	474.89	484.39
35,000	511.84	522.08	532.52	543.17	554.04	565.12
40,000	584.97	596.66	608.60	620.77	633.19	645.85
45,000	658.09	671.25	684.67	698.37	712.33	726.58
50,000	731.21	745.83	760.75	775.96	791.48	807.31
55,000	804.33	820.41	836.82	853.56	870.63	888.04
60,000	877.45	895.00	912.90	931.16	949.78	968.77
65,000	950.57	969.58	988.97	1,008.75	1,028.93	1,049.50
70,000	1,023.69	1,044.16	1,065.05	1,086.35	1,108.07	1,130.24
75,000	1,096.81	1,118.75	1,141.12	1,163.94	1,187.22	1,210.97
80,000	1,169.93	1,193.33	1,217.20	1,241.54	1,266.37	1,291.70
85,000	1,243.05	1,267.91	1,293.27	1,319.14	1,345.52	1,372.43
90,000	1,316.17	1,342.50	1,369.35	1,396.73	1,424.67	1,453.16
95,000	1,389.29	1,417.08	1,445.42	1,474.33	1,503.82	1,533.89
100,000	1,462.41	1,491.66	1,521.50	1,551.93	1,582.96	1,614.62
110,000	1,608.66	1,640.83	1,673.64	1,707.12	1,741.26	1,776.09
120,000	1,754.90	1,789.99	1,825.79	1,862.31	1,899.56	1,937.55
130,000	1,901.14	1,939.16	1,977.94	2,017.50	2,057.85	2,099.01
140,000	2,047.38	2,088.33	2,130.09	2,172.70	2,216.15	2,260.47
150,000	2,193.62	2,237.49	2,282.24	2,327.89	2,374.45	2,421.93
160,000	2,339.86	2,386.66	2,434.39	2,483.08	2,532.74	2,583.40
170,000	2,486.10	2,535.83	2,586.54	2,638.27	2,691.04	2,744.86
180,000	2,632.34	2,684.99	2,738.69	2,793.47	2,849.33	2,906.32
190,000	2,778.59	2,834.16	2,890.84	2,948.66	3,007.63	3,067.78
200,000	2,924.83	2,983.32	3,042.99	3,103.85	3,165.93	3,229.25

TABLE IV-69. (*Continued*)

FHA GRADUATED PAYMENT PLAN IV
TERM:30 YEARS INTEREST:19.00% GRADUATED AT 2.00%

PAYMENT AMCUNT	YEAR 7	YEAR 8	YEAR 9	YEAR 10	YEARS 11-30
50	0.82	0.84	0.86	0.87	0.89
100	1.65	1.68	1.71	1.75	1.78
200	3.29	3.36	3.43	3.50	3.57
300	4.94	5.04	5.14	5.24	5.35
400	6.59	6.72	6.85	6.99	7.13
500	8.23	8.40	8.57	8.74	8.91
600	9.88	10.08	10.28	10.49	10.70
700	11.53	11.76	11.99	12.23	12.48
800	13.18	13.44	13.71	13.98	14.26
900	14.82	15.12	15.42	15.73	16.04
1,000	16.47	16.80	17.13	17.48	17.83
2,000	32.94	33.60	34.27	34.95	35.65
3,000	49.41	50.40	51.40	52.43	53.48
4,000	65.88	67.19	68.54	69.91	71.31
5,000	82.35	83.99	85.67	87.39	89.13
6,000	98.81	100.79	102.81	104.86	106.96
7,000	115.28	117.59	119.94	122.34	124.79
8,000	131.75	134.39	137.08	139.82	142.61
9,000	148.22	151.19	154.21	157.29	160.44
10,000	164.69	167.99	171.35	174.77	178.27
15,000	247.04	251.98	257.02	262.16	267.40
20,000	329.38	335.97	342.69	349.54	356.53
25,000	411.73	419.96	428.36	436.93	445.67
30,000	494.07	503.96	514.04	524.32	534.80
35,000	576.42	587.95	599.71	611.70	623.94
40,000	658.77	671.94	685.38	699.09	713.07
45,000	741.11	755.93	771.05	786.47	802.20
50,000	823.46	839.93	856.73	873.86	891.34
55,000	905.80	923.92	942.40	961.25	980.47
60,000	988.15	1,C07.91	1,028.07	1,048.63	1,069.60
65,000	1,070.49	1,C91.90	1,113.74	1,136.02	1,158.74
70,000	1,152.84	1,175.90	1,199.42	1,223.40	1,247.87
75,000	1,235.19	1,259.89	1,285.09	1,310.79	1,337.01
80,000	1,317.53	1,343.88	1,370.76	1,398.18	1,426.14
85,000	1,399.88	1,427.88	1,456.43	1,485.56	1,515.27
90,000	1,482.22	1,511.87	1,542.11	1,572.95	1,604.41
95,000	1,564.57	1,595.86	1,627.78	1,660.33	1,693.54
100,000	1,646.92	1,679.85	1,713.45	1,747.72	1,782.67
110,000	1,811.61	1,847.84	1,884.80	1,922.49	1,960.94
120,000	1,976.30	2,015.82	2,056.14	2,097.26	2,139.21
130,000	2,140.99	2,183.81	2,227.49	2,272.04	2,317.48
140,000	2,305.68	2,351.80	2,398.83	2,446.81	2,495.74
150,000	2,470.37	2,519.78	2,570.18	2,621.58	2,674.01
160,000	2,635.06	2,687.77	2,741.52	2,796.35	2,852.28
170,000	2,799.76	2,855.75	2,912.07	2,971.12	3,030.55
100,000	2,964.45	3,023.74	3,084.21	3,145.90	3,208.81
190,000	3,129.14	3,191.72	3,255.56	3,320.67	3,387.08
200,000	3,293.83	3,359.71	3,426.90	3,495.44	3,565.35

TABLE IV-70. Graduated Payment Mortgage, FHA Plan IV at 19.5% Interest, Graduated at 2.0%

FHA GRADUATED PAYMENT PLAN IV
TERM:30 YEARS INTEREST:19.50% GRADUATED AT 2.00%

PAYMENT AMOUNT	YEAR 1	YEAR 2	YEAR 3	YEAR 4	YEAR 5	YEAR 6
50	0.75	0.77	0.78	0.80	0.81	0.83
100	1.50	1.53	1.56	1.59	1.63	1.66
200	3.01	3.07	3.13	3.19	3.25	3.32
300	4.51	4.60	4.69	4.78	4.88	4.98
400	6.01	6.13	6.25	6.38	6.51	6.64
500	7.51	7.66	7.82	7.97	8.13	8.29
600	9.02	9.20	9.38	9.57	9.76	9.95
700	10.52	10.73	10.94	11.16	11.38	11.61
800	12.02	12.26	12.51	12.76	13.01	13.27
900	13.52	13.79	14.07	14.35	14.64	14.93
1,000	15.03	15.33	15.63	15.94	16.26	16.59
2,000	30.05	30.65	31.26	31.89	32.53	33.18
3,000	45.08	45.98	46.90	47.83	48.79	49.77
4,000	60.10	61.30	62.53	63.78	65.06	66.36
5,000	75.13	76.63	78.16	79.72	81.32	82.95
6,000	90.15	91.95	93.79	95.67	97.58	99.53
7,000	105.18	107.28	109.43	111.61	113.85	116.12
8,000	120.20	122.61	125.06	127.56	130.11	132.71
9,000	135.23	137.93	140.69	143.50	146.37	149.30
10,000	150.25	153.26	156.32	159.45	162.64	165.89
15,000	225.38	229.89	234.48	239.17	243.96	248.84
20,000	300.51	306.52	312.65	318.90	325.28	331.78
25,000	375.63	383.14	390.81	398.62	406.60	414.73
30,000	450.76	459.77	468.97	478.35	487.92	497.67
35,000	525.88	536.40	547.13	558.07	569.23	580.62
40,000	601.01	613.03	625.29	637.80	650.55	663.56
45,000	676.14	689.66	703.45	717.52	731.87	746.51
50,000	751.26	766.29	781.61	797.25	813.19	829.46
55,000	826.39	842.92	859.78	876.97	894.51	912.40
60,000	901.52	919.55	937.94	956.70	975.83	995.35
65,000	976.64	996.18	1,016.10	1,036.42	1,057.15	1,078.29
70,000	1,051.77	1,072.80	1,094.26	1,116.15	1,138.47	1,161.24
75,000	1,126.90	1,149.43	1,172.42	1,195.87	1,219.79	1,244.18
80,000	1,202.02	1,226.06	1,250.58	1,275.59	1,301.11	1,327.13
85,000	1,277.15	1,302.69	1,328.74	1,355.32	1,382.43	1,410.07
90,000	1,352.27	1,379.32	1,406.91	1,435.04	1,463.75	1,493.02
95,000	1,427.40	1,455.95	1,485.07	1,514.77	1,545.06	1,575.97
100,000	1,502.53	1,532.58	1,563.23	1,594.49	1,626.38	1,658.91
110,000	1,652.78	1,685.84	1,719.55	1,753.94	1,789.02	1,824.80
120,000	1,803.03	1,839.09	1,875.87	1,913.39	1,951.66	1,990.69
130,000	1,953.29	1,992.35	2,032.20	2,072.84	2,114.30	2,156.58
140,000	2,103.54	2,145.61	2,188.52	2,232.29	2,276.94	2,322.48
150,000	2,253.79	2,298.87	2,344.84	2,391.74	2,439.58	2,488.37
160,000	2,404.04	2,452.12	2,501.17	2,551.19	2,602.21	2,654.26
170,000	2,554.30	2,605.38	2,657.49	2,710.64	2,764.85	2,820.15
180,000	2,704.55	2,758.64	2,813.81	2,870.09	2,927.49	2,986.04
190,000	2,854.80	2,911.90	2,970.14	3,029.54	3,090.13	3,151.93
200,000	3,005.05	3,065.16	3,126.46	3,188.99	3,252.77	3,317.82

TABLE IV-70. (*Continued*)

FHA GRADUATED PAYMENT PLAN IV
TERM:30 YEARS INTEREST:19.50% GRADUATED AT 2.00%

PAYMENT AMOUNT	YEAR 7	YEAR 8	YEAR 9	YEAR 10	YEARS 11-30
50	0.85	0.86	0.88	0.90	0.92
100	1.69	1.73	1.76	1.80	1.83
200	3.38	3.45	3.52	3.59	3.66
300	5.08	5.18	5.28	5.39	5.49
400	6.77	6.90	7.04	7.18	7.33
500	8.46	8.63	8.80	8.98	9.16
600	10.15	10.36	10.56	10.77	10.99
700	11.84	12.08	12.32	12.57	12.82
800	13.54	13.81	14.08	14.37	14.65
900	15.23	15.53	15.84	16.16	16.48
1,000	16.92	17.26	17.60	17.96	18.32
2,000	33.84	34.52	35.21	35.91	36.63
3,000	50.76	51.78	52.81	53.87	54.95
4,000	67.68	69.04	70.42	71.83	73.26
5,000	84.60	86.30	88.02	89.78	91.58
6,000	101.53	103.56	105.63	107.74	109.89
7,000	118.45	120.82	123.23	125.70	128.21
8,000	135.37	138.07	140.84	143.65	146.53
9,000	152.29	155.33	158.44	161.61	164.84
10,000	169.21	172.59	176.04	179.57	183.16
15,000	253.81	258.89	264.07	269.35	274.74
20,000	338.42	345.19	352.09	359.13	366.31
25,000	423.02	431.48	440.11	448.91	457.89
30,000	507.63	517.78	528.13	538.70	549.47
35,000	592.23	604.08	616.16	628.48	641.05
40,000	676.84	690.37	704.18	718.26	732.63
45,000	761.44	776.67	792.20	808.05	824.21
50,000	846.04	862.97	880.22	897.83	915.79
55,000	930.65	949.26	968.25	987.61	1,007.36
60,000	1,015.25	1,035.56	1,056.27	1,077.40	1,098.94
65,000	1,099.86	1,121.86	1,144.29	1,167.18	1,190.52
70,000	1,184.46	1,208.15	1,232.31	1,256.96	1,282.10
75,000	1,269.07	1,294.45	1,320.34	1,346.74	1,373.68
80,000	1,353.67	1,380.74	1,408.36	1,436.53	1,465.26
85,000	1,438.28	1,467.04	1,496.38	1,526.31	1,556.84
90,000	1,522.88	1,553.34	1,584.40	1,616.09	1,648.41
95,000	1,607.48	1,639.63	1,672.43	1,705.88	1,739.99
100,000	1,692.09	1,725.93	1,760.45	1,795.66	1,831.57
110,000	1,861.30	1,898.52	1,936.49	1,975.22	2,014.73
120,000	2,030.51	2,071.12	2,112.54	2,154.79	2,197.89
130,000	2,199.72	2,243.71	2,288.58	2,334.36	2,381.04
140,000	2,368.93	2,416.30	2,464.63	2,513.92	2,564.20
150,000	2,538.13	2,588.90	2,640.67	2,693.49	2,747.36
160,000	2,707.34	2,761.49	2,816.72	2,873.05	2,930.52
170,000	2,876.55	2,934.08	2,992.76	3,052.62	3,113.67
180,000	3,045.76	3,106.68	3,168.81	3,232.19	3,296.83
190,000	3,214.97	3,279.27	3,344.85	3,411.75	3,479.99
200,000	3,384.18	3,451.86	3,520.90	3,591.32	3,663.14

TABLE IV-71. Graduated Payment Mortgage, FHA Plan IV at 20.0% Interest, Graduated at 2.0%

FHA GRADUATED PAYMENT PLAN IV
TERM:30 YEARS INTEREST:20.00% GRADUATED AT 2.00%

PAYMENT AMOUNT	YEAR 1	YEAR 2	YEAR 3	YEAR 4	YEAR 5	YEAR 6
50	0.77	0.79	0.80	0.82	0.83	0.85
100	1.54	1.57	1.61	1.64	1.67	1.70
200	3.09	3.15	3.21	3.27	3.34	3.41
300	4.63	4.72	4.82	4.91	5.01	5.11
400	6.17	6.29	6.42	6.55	6.68	6.81
500	7.71	7.87	8.03	8.19	8.35	8.52
600	9.26	9.44	9.63	9.82	10.02	10.22
700	10.80	11.02	11.24	11.46	11.69	11.92
800	12.34	12.59	12.84	13.10	13.36	13.63
900	13.88	14.16	14.45	14.73	15.03	15.33
1,000	15.43	15.74	16.05	16.37	16.70	17.03
2,000	30.86	31.47	32.10	32.74	33.40	34.07
3,000	46.28	47.21	48.15	49.12	50.10	51.10
4,000	61.71	62.95	64.20	65.49	66.80	68.13
5,000	77.14	78.68	80.25	81.86	83.50	85.17
6,000	92.57	94.42	96.31	98.23	100.20	102.20
7,000	107.99	110.15	112.36	114.60	116.90	119.23
8,000	123.42	125.89	128.41	130.98	133.60	136.27
9,000	138.85	141.63	144.46	147.35	150.29	153.30
10,000	154.28	157.36	160.51	163.72	166.99	170.33
15,000	231.42	236.04	240.76	245.58	250.49	255.50
20,000	308.55	314.73	321.02	327.44	333.99	340.67
25,000	385.69	393.41	401.27	409.30	417.49	425.84
30,000	462.83	472.09	481.53	491.16	500.98	511.00
35,000	539.97	550.77	561.78	573.02	584.48	596.17
40,000	617.11	629.45	642.04	654.88	667.98	681.34
45,000	694.25	708.13	722.29	736.74	751.47	766.50
50,000	771.39	786.81	802.55	818.60	834.97	851.67
55,000	848.52	865.49	882.80	900.46	918.47	936.84
60,000	925.66	944.18	963.06	982.32	1,001.97	1,022.01
65,000	1,002.80	1,022.86	1,043.31	1,064.18	1,085.46	1,107.17
70,000	1,079.94	1,101.54	1,123.57	1,146.04	1,168.96	1,192.34
75,000	1,157.08	1,180.22	1,203.82	1,227.90	1,252.46	1,277.51
80,000	1,234.22	1,258.90	1,284.08	1,309.76	1,335.96	1,362.67
85,000	1,311.35	1,337.58	1,364.33	1,391.62	1,419.45	1,447.84
90,000	1,388.49	1,416.26	1,444.59	1,473.48	1,502.95	1,533.01
95,000	1,465.63	1,494.94	1,524.84	1,555.34	1,586.45	1,618.18
100,000	1,542.77	1,573.63	1,605.10	1,637.20	1,669.94	1,703.34
110,000	1,697.05	1,730.99	1,765.61	1,800.92	1,836.94	1,873.68
120,000	1,851.32	1,888.35	1,926.12	1,964.64	2,003.93	2,044.01
130,000	2,005.60	2,045.71	2,086.63	2,128.36	2,170.93	2,214.35
140,000	2,159.88	2,203.08	2,247.14	2,292.08	2,337.92	2,384.68
150,000	2,314.16	2,360.44	2,407.65	2,455.80	2,504.92	2,555.01
160,000	2,468.43	2,517.80	2,568.16	2,619.52	2,671.91	2,725.35
170,000	2,622.71	2,675.16	2,728.67	2,783.24	2,838.90	2,895.68
180,000	2,776.99	2,832.53	2,889.18	2,946.96	3,005.90	3,066.02
190,000	2,931.26	2,989.89	3,049.69	3,110.68	3,172.89	3,236.35
200,000	3,085.54	3,147.25	3,210.20	3,274.40	3,339.89	3,406.69

TABLE IV-71. (Continued)

FHA GRADUATED PAYMENT PLAN IV
TERM:30 YEARS INTEREST:20.00% GRADUATED AT 2.00%

PAYMENT AMOUNT	YEAR 7	YEAR 8	YEAR 9	YEAR 10	YEARS 11-30
50	0.87	0.89	0.90	0.92	0.94
100	1.74	1.77	1.81	1.84	1.88
200	3.47	3.54	3.62	3.69	3.76
300	5.21	5.32	5.42	5.53	5.64
400	6.95	7.09	7.23	7.38	7.52
500	8.69	8.86	9.04	9.22	9.40
600	10.42	10.63	10.85	11.06	11.28
700	12.16	12.41	12.65	12.91	13.16
800	13.90	14.18	14.46	14.75	15.05
900	15.64	15.95	16.27	16.59	16.93
1,000	17.37	17.72	18.08	18.44	18.81
2,000	34.75	35.44	36.15	36.88	37.61
3,000	52.12	53.16	54.23	55.31	56.42
4,000	69.50	70.89	72.30	73.75	75.23
5,000	86.87	88.61	90.38	92.19	94.03
6,000	104.24	106.33	108.46	110.63	112.84
7,000	121.62	124.05	126.53	129.06	131.64
8,000	138.99	141.77	144.61	147.50	150.45
9,000	156.37	159.49	162.68	165.94	169.26
10,000	173.74	177.22	180.76	184.38	188.06
15,000	260.61	265.82	271.14	276.56	282.09
20,000	347.48	354.43	361.52	368.75	376.13
25,000	434.35	443.04	451.90	460.94	470.16
30,000	521.22	531.65	542.28	553.13	564.19
35,000	608.09	620.26	632.66	645.31	658.22
40,000	694.96	708.86	723.04	737.50	752.25
45,000	781.83	797.47	813.42	829.69	846.28
50,000	868.70	886.08	903.80	921.88	940.31
55,000	955.58	974.69	994.18	1,014.06	1,034.35
60,000	1,042.45	1,063.29	1,084.56	1,106.25	1,128.38
65,000	1,129.32	1,151.90	1,174.94	1,198.44	1,222.41
70,000	1,216.19	1,240.51	1,265.32	1,290.63	1,316.44
75,000	1,303.06	1,329.12	1,355.70	1,382.81	1,410.47
80,000	1,389.93	1,417.73	1,446.08	1,475.00	1,504.50
85,000	1,476.80	1,506.33	1,536.46	1,567.19	1,598.53
90,000	1,563.67	1,594.94	1,626.84	1,659.38	1,692.57
95,000	1,650.54	1,683.55	1,717.22	1,751.57	1,786.60
100,000	1,737.41	1,772.16	1,807.60	1,843.75	1,880.63
110,000	1,911.15	1,949.37	1,988.36	2,028.13	2,068.69
120,000	2,084.89	2,126.59	2,169.12	2,212.50	2,256.75
130,000	2,258.63	2,303.81	2,349.88	2,396.88	2,444.82
140,000	2,432.37	2,481.02	2,530.64	2,581.25	2,632.88
150,000	2,606.11	2,658.24	2,711.40	2,765.63	2,820.94
160,000	2,779.86	2,835.45	2,892.16	2,950.00	3,009.00
170,000	2,953.60	3,012.67	3,072.92	3,134.38	3,197.07
180,000	3,127.34	3,189.88	3,253.68	3,318.76	3,385.13
190,000	3,301.08	3,367.10	3,434.44	3,503.13	3,573.19
200,000	3,474.82	3,544.32	3,615.20	3,687.51	3,761.26

TABLE IV-72. Graduated Payment Mortgage, FHA Plan IV at 20.5% Interest, Graduated at 2.0%

FHA GRADUATED PAYMENT PLAN IV
TERM: 30 YEARS INTEREST: 20.50% GRADUATED AT 2.00%

PAYMENT AMOUNT	YEAR 1	YEAR 2	YEAR 3	YEAR 4	YEAR 5	YEAR 6
50	0.79	0.81	0.82	0.84	0.86	0.87
100	1.58	1.61	1.65	1.68	1.71	1.75
200	3.17	3.23	3.29	3.36	3.43	3.50
300	4.75	4.84	4.94	5.04	5.14	5.24
400	6.33	6.46	6.59	6.72	6.85	6.99
500	7.92	8.07	8.24	8.40	8.57	8.74
600	9.50	9.69	9.88	10.08	10.28	10.49
700	11.08	11.30	11.53	11.76	12.00	12.24
800	12.67	12.92	13.18	13.44	13.71	13.98
900	14.25	14.53	14.82	15.12	15.42	15.73
1,000	15.83	16.15	16.47	16.80	17.14	17.48
2,000	31.66	32.30	32.94	33.60	34.27	34.96
3,000	47.49	48.44	49.41	50.40	51.41	52.44
4,000	63.33	64.59	65.88	67.20	68.55	69.92
5,000	79.16	80.74	82.35	84.00	85.68	87.40
6,000	94.99	96.89	98.83	100.80	102.82	104.87
7,000	110.82	113.04	115.30	117.60	119.95	122.35
8,000	126.65	129.18	131.77	134.40	137.09	139.83
9,000	142.48	145.33	148.24	151.20	154.23	157.31
10,000	158.31	161.48	164.71	168.00	171.36	174.79
15,000	237.47	242.22	247.06	252.00	257.05	262.19
20,000	316.63	322.96	329.42	336.01	342.73	349.58
25,000	395.78	403.70	411.77	420.01	428.41	436.98
30,000	474.94	484.44	494.13	504.01	514.09	524.37
35,000	554.10	565.18	576.48	588.01	599.77	611.77
40,000	633.25	645.92	658.84	672.01	685.45	699.16
45,000	712.41	726.66	741.19	756.01	771.14	786.56
50,000	791.57	807.40	823.55	840.02	856.82	873.95
55,000	870.72	888.14	905.90	924.02	942.50	961.35
60,000	949.88	968.88	988.25	1,008.02	1,028.18	1,048.74
65,000	1,029.04	1,049.62	1,070.61	1,092.02	1,113.86	1,136.14
70,000	1,108.19	1,130.36	1,152.96	1,176.02	1,199.54	1,223.53
75,000	1,187.35	1,211.10	1,235.32	1,260.02	1,285.23	1,310.93
80,000	1,266.51	1,291.84	1,317.67	1,344.03	1,370.91	1,398.33
85,000	1,345.66	1,372.58	1,400.03	1,428.03	1,456.59	1,485.72
90,000	1,424.82	1,453.32	1,482.38	1,512.03	1,542.27	1,573.12
95,000	1,503.98	1,534.06	1,564.74	1,596.03	1,627.95	1,660.51
100,000	1,583.13	1,614.80	1,647.09	1,680.03	1,713.63	1,747.91
110,000	1,741.45	1,776.28	1,811.80	1,848.04	1,885.00	1,922.70
120,000	1,899.76	1,937.75	1,976.51	2,016.04	2,056.36	2,097.49
130,000	2,058.07	2,099.23	2,141.22	2,184.04	2,227.72	2,272.28
140,000	2,216.39	2,260.71	2,305.93	2,352.05	2,399.09	2,447.07
150,000	2,374.70	2,422.19	2,470.64	2,520.05	2,570.45	2,621.86
160,000	2,533.01	2,583.67	2,635.35	2,688.05	2,741.81	2,796.65
170,000	2,691.33	2,745.15	2,800.06	2,856.06	2,913.18	2,971.44
180,000	2,849.64	2,906.63	2,964.76	3,024.06	3,084.54	3,146.23
190,000	3,007.95	3,068.11	3,129.47	3,192.06	3,255.90	3,321.02
200,000	3,166.27	3,229.59	3,294.18	3,360.07	3,427.27	3,495.81

TABLE IV-72. (*Continued*)

FHA GRADUATED PAYMENT PLAN IV
TERM:30 YEARS INTEREST:20.50% GRADUATED AT 2.00%

PAYMENT AMCUNT	YEAR 7	YEAR 8	YEAR 9	YEAR 10	YEARS 11-30
50	0.89	0.91	0.93	0.95	0.96
100	1.78	1.82	1.85	1.89	1.93
200	3.57	3.64	3.71	3.78	3.86
300	5.35	5.46	5.56	5.68	5.79
400	7.13	7.27	7.42	7.57	7.72
500	8.91	9.09	9.27	9.46	9.65
600	10.70	10.91	11.13	11.35	11.58
700	12.48	12.73	12.98	13.24	13.51
800	14.26	14.55	14.84	15.14	15.44
900	16.05	16.37	16.69	17.03	17.37
1,000	17.83	18.19	18.55	18.92	19.30
2,000	35.66	36.37	37.10	37.84	38.60
3,000	53.49	54.56	55.65	56.76	57.89
4,000	71.31	72.74	74.20	75.68	77.19
5,000	89.14	90.93	92.74	94.60	96.49
6,000	106.97	109.11	111.29	113.52	115.79
7,000	124.80	127.30	129.84	132.44	135.09
8,000	142.63	145.48	148.39	151.36	154.39
9,000	160.46	163.67	166.94	170.28	173.68
10,000	178.29	181.85	185.49	189.20	192.98
15,000	267.43	272.78	278.23	283.80	289.47
20,000	356.57	363.70	370.98	378.40	385.97
25,000	445.72	454.63	463.72	473.00	482.46
30,000	534.86	545.56	556.47	567.60	578.95
35,000	624.00	636.48	649.21	662.20	675.44
40,000	713.15	727.41	741.96	756.80	771.93
45,000	802.29	818.33	834.70	851.40	868.42
50,000	891.43	909.26	927.45	946.00	964.92
55,000	980.58	1,000.19	1,020.19	1,040.59	1,061.41
60,000	1,069.72	1,091.11	1,112.94	1,135.19	1,157.90
65,000	1,158.86	1,182.04	1,205.68	1,229.79	1,254.39
70,000	1,248.01	1,272.97	1,298.42	1,324.39	1,350.88
75,000	1,337.15	1,363.89	1,391.17	1,418.99	1,447.37
80,000	1,426.29	1,454.82	1,483.91	1,513.59	1,543.86
85,000	1,515.44	1,545.74	1,576.66	1,608.19	1,640.36
90,000	1,604.58	1,636.67	1,669.40	1,702.79	1,736.85
95,000	1,693.72	1,727.60	1,762.15	1,797.39	1,833.34
100,000	1,782.86	1,818.52	1,854.89	1,891.99	1,929.83
110,000	1,961.15	2,000.37	2,040.38	2,081.19	2,122.81
120,000	2,139.44	2,182.23	2,225.87	2,270.39	2,315.80
130,000	2,317.72	2,364.08	2,411.36	2,459.59	2,508.78
140,000	2,496.01	2,545.93	2,596.85	2,648.79	2,701.76
150,000	2,674.30	2,727.78	2,782.34	2,837.99	2,894.75
160,000	2,852.58	2,909.64	2,967.83	3,027.18	3,087.73
170,000	3,030.87	3,091.49	3,153.32	3,216.38	3,280.71
180,000	3,209.16	3,273.34	3,338.81	3,405.58	3,473.69
190,000	3,387.44	3,455.19	3,524.30	3,594.78	3,666.68
200,000	3,565.73	3,637.04	3,709.79	3,783.98	3,859.66

TABLE IV-73. Graduated Payment Mortgage, FHA Plan V at 12.0% Interest, Graduated at 3.0%

FHA GRADUATED PAYMENT PLAN V
TERM:30 YEARS INTEREST:12.00% GRADUATED AT 3.00%

PAYMENT AMCUNT	YEAR 1	YEAR 2	YEAR 3	YEAR 4	YEAR 5	YEAR 6
50	0.44	0.45	0.46	0.48	0.49	0.51
100	0.87	0.90	0.93	0.95	0.98	1.01
200	1.74	1.80	1.85	1.91	1.96	2.02
300	2.62	2.70	2.78	2.86	2.95	3.03
400	3.49	3.59	3.70	3.81	3.93	4.05
500	4.36	4.49	4.63	4.77	4.91	5.06
600	5.23	5.39	5.55	5.72	5.89	6.07
700	6.11	6.29	6.48	6.67	6.87	7.08
800	6.98	7.19	7.40	7.63	7.85	8.09
900	7.85	8.09	8.33	8.58	8.84	9.10
1,000	8.72	8.99	9.26	9.53	9.82	10.11
2,000	17.45	17.97	18.51	19.07	19.64	20.23
3,000	26.17	26.96	27.77	28.60	29.46	30.34
4,000	34.90	35.94	37.02	38.13	39.27	40.45
5,000	43.62	44.93	46.28	47.66	49.09	50.57
6,000	52.34	53.91	55.53	57.20	58.91	60.68
7,000	61.07	62.90	64.79	66.73	68.73	70.79
8,000	69.79	71.88	74.04	76.26	78.55	80.91
9,000	78.51	80.87	83.30	85.79	88.37	91.02
10,000	87.24	89.86	92.55	95.33	98.19	101.13
15,000	130.86	134.78	138.83	142.99	147.28	151.70
20,000	174.48	179.71	185.10	190.65	196.37	202.27
25,000	218.10	224.64	231.38	238.32	245.47	252.83
30,000	261.71	269.57	277.65	285.98	294.56	303.40
35,000	305.33	314.49	323.93	333.65	343.66	353.96
40,000	348.95	359.42	370.20	381.31	392.75	404.53
45,000	392.57	404.35	416.48	428.97	441.84	455.10
50,000	436.19	449.28	462.75	476.64	490.94	505.66
55,000	479.81	494.20	509.03	524.30	540.03	556.23
60,000	523.43	539.13	555.31	571.96	589.12	606.80
65,000	567.05	584.06	601.58	619.63	638.22	657.36
70,000	610.67	628.99	647.86	667.29	687.31	707.93
75,000	654.29	673.91	694.13	714.96	736.40	758.50
80,000	697.90	718.84	740.41	762.62	785.50	809.06
85,000	741.52	763.77	786.68	810.28	834.59	859.63
90,000	785.14	808.70	832.96	857.95	883.69	910.20
95,000	828.76	853.62	879.23	905.61	932.78	960.76
100,000	872.38	898.55	925.51	953.27	981.87	1,011.33
110,000	959.62	988.41	1,018.06	1,048.60	1,080.06	1,112.46
120,000	1,046.86	1,078.26	1,110.61	1,143.93	1,178.25	1,213.59
130,000	1,134.10	1,168.12	1,203.16	1,239.26	1,276.43	1,314.73
140,000	1,221.33	1,257.97	1,295.71	1,334.58	1,374.62	1,415.86
150,000	1,308.57	1,347.83	1,388.26	1,429.91	1,472.81	1,516.99
160,000	1,395.81	1,437.68	1,480.81	1,525.24	1,571.00	1,618.13
170,000	1,483.05	1,527.54	1,573.37	1,620.57	1,669.18	1,719.26
180,000	1,570.29	1,617.39	1,665.92	1,715.89	1,767.37	1,820.39
190,000	1,657.52	1,707.25	1,758.47	1,811.22	1,865.56	1,921.52
200,000	1,744.76	1,797.10	1,851.02	1,906.55	1,963.74	2,022.66

TABLE IV-73. *(Continued)*

FHA GRADUATED PAYMENT PLAN V
TERM:30 YEARS INTEREST:12.00% GRADUATED AT 3.00%

PAYMENT AMOUNT	YEAR 7	YEAR 8	YEAR 9	YEAR 10	YEARS 11-30
50	0.52	0.54	0.55	0.57	0.59
100	1.04	1.07	1.11	1.14	1.17
200	2.08	2.15	2.21	2.28	2.34
300	3.13	3.22	3.32	3.41	3.52
400	4.17	4.29	4.42	4.55	4.69
500	5.21	5.36	5.53	5.69	5.86
600	6.25	6.44	6.63	6.83	7.03
700	7.29	7.51	7.74	7.97	8.21
800	8.33	8.58	8.84	9.11	9.38
900	9.38	9.66	9.95	10.24	10.55
1,000	10.42	10.73	11.05	11.38	11.72
2,000	20.83	21.46	22.10	22.77	23.45
3,000	31.25	32.19	33.15	34.15	35.17
4,000	41.67	42.92	44.20	45.53	46.90
5,000	52.08	53.65	55.26	56.91	58.62
6,000	62.50	64.38	66.31	68.30	70.34
7,000	72.92	75.10	77.36	79.68	82.07
8,000	83.33	85.83	88.41	91.06	93.79
9,000	93.75	96.56	99.46	102.44	105.52
10,000	104.17	107.29	110.51	113.83	117.24
15,000	156.25	160.94	165.77	170.74	175.86
20,000	208.33	214.58	221.02	227.65	234.48
25,000	260.42	268.23	276.28	284.56	293.10
30,000	312.50	321.88	331.53	341.48	351.72
35,000	364.58	375.52	386.79	398.39	410.34
40,000	416.67	429.17	442.04	455.30	468.96
45,000	468.75	482.81	497.30	512.22	527.58
50,000	520.83	536.46	552.55	569.13	586.20
55,000	572.92	590.11	607.81	626.04	644.82
60,000	625.00	643.75	663.06	682.96	703.44
65,000	677.08	697.40	718.32	739.87	762.06
70,000	729.17	751.04	773.57	796.78	820.68
75,000	781.25	804.69	828.83	853.69	879.31
80,000	833.33	858.33	884.08	910.61	937.93
85,000	885.42	911.98	939.34	967.52	996.55
90,000	937.50	965.63	994.60	1,024.43	1,055.17
95,000	989.58	1,019.27	1,049.85	1,081.35	1,113.79
100,000	1,041.67	1,072.92	1,105.11	1,138.26	1,172.41
110,000	1,145.84	1,180.21	1,215.62	1,252.09	1,289.65
120,000	1,250.00	1,287.50	1,326.13	1,365.91	1,406.89
130,000	1,354.17	1,394.79	1,436.64	1,479.74	1,524.13
140,000	1,458.34	1,502.09	1,547.15	1,593.56	1,641.37
150,000	1,562.50	1,609.38	1,657.66	1,707.39	1,758.61
160,000	1,666.67	1,716.67	1,768.17	1,821.21	1,875.85
170,000	1,770.84	1,823.96	1,870.68	1,935.04	1,993.09
180,000	1,875.00	1,931.25	1,989.19	2,048.87	2,110.33
190,000	1,979.17	2,038.55	2,099.70	2,162.69	2,227.57
200,000	2,083.34	2,145.84	2,210.21	2,276.52	2,344.81

TABLE IV-74. Graduated Payment Mortgage, FHA Plan V at 12.5% Interest, Graduated at 3.0%

FHA GRADUATED PAYMENT PLAN V
TERM: 30 YEARS INTEREST: 12.50% GRADUATED AT 3.00%

PAYMENT AMOUNT	YEAR 1	YEAR 2	YEAR 3	YEAR 4	YEAR 5	YEAR 6
50	0.45	0.47	0.48	0.50	0.51	0.53
100	0.91	0.94	0.96	0.99	1.02	1.05
200	1.82	1.87	1.93	1.98	2.04	2.11
300	2.72	2.81	2.89	2.98	3.07	3.16
400	3.63	3.74	3.85	3.97	4.09	4.21
500	4.54	4.68	4.82	4.96	5.11	5.26
600	5.45	5.61	5.78	5.95	6.13	6.32
700	6.36	6.55	6.74	6.95	7.15	7.37
800	7.26	7.48	7.71	7.94	8.18	8.42
900	8.17	8.42	8.67	8.93	9.20	9.47
1,000	9.08	9.35	9.63	9.92	10.22	10.53
2,000	18.16	18.71	19.27	19.84	20.44	21.05
3,000	27.24	28.06	28.90	29.77	30.66	31.58
4,000	36.32	37.41	38.53	39.69	40.88	42.11
5,000	45.40	46.76	48.17	49.61	51.10	52.63
6,000	54.48	56.12	57.80	59.53	61.32	63.16
7,000	63.56	65.47	67.43	69.46	71.54	73.69
8,000	72.64	74.82	77.07	79.38	81.76	84.21
9,000	81.72	84.17	86.70	89.30	91.98	94.74
10,000	90.80	93.53	96.33	99.22	102.20	105.26
15,000	136.20	140.29	144.50	148.83	153.30	157.90
20,000	181.60	187.05	192.66	198.44	204.40	210.53
25,000	227.01	233.82	240.83	248.06	255.50	263.16
30,000	272.41	280.58	289.00	297.67	306.60	315.79
35,000	317.81	327.34	337.16	347.28	357.70	368.43
40,000	363.21	374.11	385.33	396.89	408.80	421.06
45,000	408.61	420.87	433.50	446.50	459.90	473.69
50,000	454.01	467.63	481.66	496.11	510.99	526.32
55,000	499.41	514.40	529.83	545.72	562.09	578.96
60,000	544.81	561.16	577.99	595.33	613.19	631.59
65,000	590.22	607.92	626.16	644.94	664.29	684.22
70,000	635.62	654.69	674.33	694.56	715.39	736.85
75,000	681.02	701.45	722.49	744.17	766.49	789.49
80,000	726.42	748.21	770.66	793.78	817.59	842.12
85,000	771.82	794.97	818.82	843.39	868.69	894.75
90,000	817.22	841.74	866.99	893.00	919.79	947.38
95,000	862.62	888.50	915.16	942.61	970.89	1,000.02
100,000	908.02	935.26	963.32	992.22	1,021.99	1,052.65
110,000	998.83	1,028.79	1,059.65	1,091.44	1,124.19	1,157.91
120,000	1,089.63	1,122.32	1,155.99	1,190.67	1,226.39	1,263.18
130,000	1,180.43	1,215.84	1,252.32	1,289.89	1,328.59	1,368.44
140,000	1,271.23	1,309.37	1,348.65	1,389.11	1,430.78	1,473.71
150,000	1,362.04	1,402.90	1,444.98	1,488.33	1,532.98	1,578.97
160,000	1,452.84	1,496.42	1,541.32	1,587.56	1,635.18	1,684.24
170,000	1,543.64	1,589.95	1,637.65	1,686.78	1,737.38	1,789.50
180,000	1,634.44	1,683.48	1,733.98	1,786.00	1,839.58	1,894.77
190,000	1,725.25	1,777.00	1,830.31	1,885.22	1,941.78	2,000.03
200,000	1,816.05	1,870.53	1,926.65	1,984.44	2,043.98	2,105.30

TABLE IV-74. (*Continued*)

FHA GRADUATED PAYMENT PLAN V
TERM:30 YEARS INTEREST:12.50% GRADUATED AT 3.00%

PAYMENT AMOUNT	YEAR 7	YEAR 8	YEAR 9	YEAR 10	YEARS 11-30
50	0.54	0.56	0.58	0.59	0.61
100	1.08	1.12	1.15	1.18	1.22
200	2.17	2.23	2.30	2.37	2.44
300	3.25	3.35	3.45	3.55	3.66
400	4.34	4.47	4.60	4.74	4.88
500	5.42	5.58	5.75	5.92	6.10
600	6.51	6.70	6.90	7.11	7.32
700	7.59	7.82	8.05	8.29	8.54
800	8.67	8.93	9.20	9.48	9.76
900	9.76	10.05	10.35	10.66	10.98
1,000	10.84	11.17	11.50	11.85	12.20
2,000	21.68	22.34	23.01	23.70	24.41
3,000	32.53	33.50	34.51	35.54	36.61
4,000	43.37	44.67	46.01	47.39	48.81
5,000	54.21	55.84	57.51	59.24	61.02
6,000	65.05	67.01	69.02	71.09	73.22
7,000	75.90	78.17	80.52	82.93	85.42
8,000	86.74	89.34	92.02	94.78	97.62
9,000	97.58	100.51	103.52	106.63	109.83
10,000	108.42	111.68	115.03	118.48	122.03
15,000	162.63	167.51	172.54	177.71	183.05
20,000	216.85	223.35	230.05	236.95	244.06
25,000	271.06	279.19	287.56	296.19	305.08
30,000	325.27	335.03	345.08	355.43	366.09
35,000	379.48	390.86	402.59	414.67	427.11
40,000	433.69	446.70	460.10	473.91	488.12
45,000	487.90	502.54	517.62	533.14	549.14
50,000	542.11	558.38	575.13	592.38	610.15
55,000	596.33	614.22	632.64	651.62	671.17
60,000	650.54	670.05	690.15	710.86	732.18
65,000	704.75	725.89	747.67	770.10	793.20
70,000	758.96	781.73	805.18	829.34	854.22
75,000	813.17	837.57	862.69	888.57	915.23
80,000	867.38	893.40	920.21	947.81	976.25
85,000	921.59	949.24	977.72	1,007.05	1,037.26
90,000	975.81	1,005.08	1,035.23	1,066.29	1,098.28
95,000	1,030.02	1,060.92	1,092.74	1,125.53	1,159.29
100,000	1,084.23	1,116.75	1,150.26	1,184.77	1,220.31
110,000	1,192.65	1,228.43	1,265.28	1,303.24	1,342.34
120,000	1,301.07	1,340.11	1,380.31	1,421.72	1,464.37
130,000	1,409.50	1,451.78	1,495.33	1,540.19	1,586.40
140,000	1,517.92	1,563.46	1,610.36	1,658.67	1,708.43
150,000	1,626.34	1,675.13	1,725.39	1,777.15	1,830.46
160,000	1,734.76	1,786.81	1,840.41	1,895.62	1,952.49
170,000	1,843.19	1,098.48	1,955.44	2,014.10	2,074.52
180,000	1,951.61	2,010.16	2,070.46	2,132.58	2,196.55
190,000	2,060.03	2,121.83	2,185.49	2,251.05	2,318.59
200,000	2,168.46	2,233.51	2,300.52	2,369.53	2,440.62

TABLE IV-75. Graduated Payment Mortgage, FHA Plan V at 13.0% Interest, Graduated at 3.0%

FHA GRADUATED PAYMENT PLAN V
TERM:30 YEARS INTEREST:13.00% GRADUATED AT 3.00%

PAYMENT AMCUNT	YEAR 1	YEAR 2	YEAR 3	YEAR 4	YEAR 5	YEAR 6
50	0.47	0.49	0.50	0.52	0.53	0.55
100	0.94	0.97	1.00	1.03	1.06	1.09
200	1.89	1.94	2.00	2.06	2.13	2.19
300	2.83	2.92	3.00	3.09	3.19	3.28
400	3.78	3.89	4.01	4.13	4.25	4.38
500	4.72	4.86	5.01	5.16	5.31	5.47
600	5.66	5.83	6.01	6.19	6.38	6.57
700	6.61	6.81	7.01	7.22	7.44	7.66
800	7.55	7.78	8.01	8.25	8.50	8.76
900	8.50	8.75	9.01	9.28	9.56	9.85
1,000	9.44	9.72	10.02	10.32	10.63	10.94
2,000	18.88	19.45	20.03	20.63	21.25	21.89
3,000	28.32	29.17	30.05	30.95	31.88	32.83
4,000	37.76	38.90	40.06	41.27	42.50	43.78
5,000	47.20	48.62	50.08	51.58	53.13	54.72
6,000	56.65	58.34	60.09	61.90	63.75	65.67
7,000	66.09	68.07	70.11	72.21	74.38	76.61
8,000	75.53	77.79	80.13	82.53	85.01	87.56
9,000	84.97	87.52	90.14	92.85	95.63	98.50
10,000	94.41	97.24	100.16	103.16	106.26	109.45
15,000	141.61	145.86	150.24	154.74	159.39	164.17
20,000	188.82	194.48	200.32	206.33	212.52	218.89
25,000	236.02	243.10	250.40	257.91	265.64	273.61
30,000	283.23	291.72	300.47	309.49	318.77	328.34
35,000	330.43	340.34	350.55	361.07	371.90	383.06
40,000	377.64	388.96	400.63	412.65	425.03	437.78
45,000	424.84	437.58	450.71	464.23	478.16	492.51
50,000	472.04	486.21	500.79	515.81	531.29	547.23
55,000	519.25	534.83	550.87	567.40	584.42	601.95
60,000	566.45	583.45	600.95	618.98	637.55	656.67
65,000	613.66	632.07	651.03	670.56	690.68	711.40
70,000	660.86	680.69	701.11	722.14	743.81	766.12
75,000	708.07	729.31	751.19	773.72	796.93	820.84
80,000	755.27	777.93	801.27	825.30	850.06	875.57
85,000	802.47	826.55	851.35	876.89	903.19	930.29
90,000	849.68	875.17	901.42	928.47	956.32	985.01
95,000	896.88	923.79	951.50	980.05	1,009.45	1,039.73
100,000	944.09	972.41	1,001.58	1,031.63	1,062.58	1,094.46
110,000	1,038.50	1,069.65	1,101.74	1,134.79	1,168.84	1,203.90
120,000	1,132.91	1,166.89	1,201.90	1,237.96	1,275.09	1,313.35
130,000	1,227.31	1,264.13	1,302.06	1,341.12	1,381.35	1,422.79
140,000	1,321.72	1,361.37	1,402.22	1,444.28	1,487.61	1,532.24
150,000	1,416.13	1,458.62	1,502.37	1,547.44	1,593.87	1,641.68
160,000	1,510.54	1,555.86	1,602.53	1,650.61	1,700.13	1,751.13
170,000	1,604.95	1,653.10	1,702.69	1,753.77	1,806.38	1,860.58
180,000	1,699.36	1,750.34	1,802.85	1,856.93	1,912.64	1,970.02
190,000	1,793.77	1,847.58	1,903.01	1,960.10	2,018.90	2,079.47
200,000	1,888.18	1,944.82	2,003.17	2,063.26	2,125.16	2,188.91

TABLE IV-75. (*Continued*)

FHA GRADUATED PAYMENT PLAN V
TERM:30 YEARS INTEREST:13.00% GRADUATED AT 3.00%

PAYMENT AMOUNT	YEAR 7	YEAR 8	YEAR 9	YEAR 10	YEARS 11-30
50	0.56	0.58	0.60	0.62	0.63
100	1.13	1.16	1.20	1.23	1.27
200	2.25	2.32	2.39	2.46	2.54
300	3.38	3.48	3.59	3.70	3.81
400	4.51	4.64	4.78	4.93	5.08
500	5.64	5.81	5.98	6.16	6.34
600	6.76	6.97	7.18	7.39	7.61
700	7.89	8.13	8.37	8.62	8.88
800	9.02	9.29	9.57	9.85	10.15
900	10.15	10.45	10.76	11.09	11.42
1,000	11.27	11.61	11.96	12.32	12.69
2,000	22.55	23.22	23.92	24.64	25.38
3,000	33.82	34.83	35.88	36.95	38.06
4,000	45.09	46.44	47.84	49.27	50.75
5,000	56.36	58.06	59.80	61.59	63.44
6,000	67.64	69.67	71.76	73.91	76.13
7,000	78.91	81.28	83.72	86.23	88.81
8,000	90.18	92.89	95.68	98.55	101.50
9,000	101.46	104.50	107.63	110.86	114.19
10,000	112.73	116.11	119.59	123.18	126.88
15,000	169.09	174.17	179.39	184.77	190.32
20,000	225.46	232.22	239.19	246.36	253.75
25,000	281.82	290.28	298.99	307.96	317.19
30,000	338.19	348.33	358.78	369.55	380.63
35,000	394.55	406.39	418.58	431.14	444.07
40,000	450.92	464.44	478.38	492.73	507.51
45,000	507.28	522.50	538.17	554.32	570.95
50,000	563.64	580.55	597.97	615.91	634.39
55,000	620.01	638.61	657.77	677.50	697.83
60,000	676.37	696.67	717.57	739.09	761.26
65,000	732.74	754.72	777.36	800.68	824.70
70,000	789.10	812.78	837.16	862.27	888.14
75,000	845.47	870.83	896.96	923.87	951.58
80,000	901.83	928.89	956.75	985.46	1,015.02
85,000	958.20	986.94	1,016.55	1,047.05	1,078.46
90,000	1,014.56	1,045.00	1,076.35	1,108.64	1,141.90
95,000	1,070.93	1,103.05	1,136.14	1,170.23	1,205.34
100,000	1,127.29	1,161.11	1,195.94	1,231.82	1,268.77
110,000	1,240.02	1,277.22	1,315.54	1,355.00	1,395.65
120,000	1,352.75	1,393.33	1,435.13	1,478.18	1,522.53
130,000	1,465.48	1,509.44	1,554.72	1,601.37	1,649.41
140,000	1,578.21	1,625.55	1,674.32	1,724.55	1,776.28
150,000	1,690.93	1,741.66	1,793.91	1,847.73	1,903.16
160,000	1,803.66	1,857.77	1,913.51	1,970.91	2,030.04
170,000	1,916.39	1,973.88	2,033.10	2,094.09	2,156.92
180,000	2,029.12	2,090.00	2,152.70	2,217.28	2,283.79
190,000	2,141.85	2,206.11	2,272.29	2,340.46	2,410.67
200,000	2,254.58	2,322.22	2,391.88	2,463.64	2,537.55

TABLE IV-76. Graduated Payment Mortgage, FHA Plan V at 13.5% Interest, Graduated at 3.0%

FHA GRADUATED PAYMENT PLAN V
TERM: 30 YEARS INTEREST: 13.50% GRADUATED AT 3.00%

PAYMENT AMOUNT	YEAR 1	YEAR 2	YEAR 3	YEAR 4	YEAR 5	YEAR 6
50	0.49	0.50	0.52	0.54	0.55	0.57
100	0.98	1.01	1.04	1.07	1.10	1.14
200	1.96	2.02	2.08	2.14	2.21	2.27
300	2.94	3.03	3.12	3.21	3.31	3.41
400	3.92	4.04	4.16	4.29	4.41	4.55
500	4.90	5.05	5.20	5.36	5.52	5.68
600	5.88	6.06	6.24	6.43	6.62	6.82
700	6.86	7.07	7.28	7.50	7.73	7.96
800	7.84	8.08	8.32	8.57	8.83	9.09
900	8.82	9.09	9.36	9.64	9.93	10.23
1,000	9.81	10.10	10.40	10.71	11.04	11.37
2,000	19.61	20.20	20.81	21.43	22.07	22.73
3,000	29.42	30.30	31.21	32.14	33.11	34.10
4,000	39.22	40.40	41.61	42.86	44.14	45.47
5,000	49.03	50.50	52.01	53.57	55.18	56.84
6,000	58.83	60.60	62.42	64.29	66.22	68.20
7,000	68.64	70.70	72.82	75.00	77.25	79.57
8,000	78.44	80.80	83.22	85.72	88.29	90.94
9,000	88.25	90.90	93.62	96.43	99.33	102.30
10,000	98.05	101.00	104.03	107.15	110.36	113.67
15,000	147.08	151.49	156.04	160.72	165.54	170.51
20,000	196.11	201.99	208.05	214.29	220.72	227.34
25,000	245.14	252.49	260.07	267.87	275.90	284.18
30,000	294.16	302.99	312.08	321.44	331.08	341.02
35,000	343.19	353.49	364.09	375.01	386.26	397.85
40,000	392.22	403.98	416.10	428.59	441.45	454.69
45,000	441.25	454.48	468.12	482.16	496.63	511.52
50,000	490.27	504.98	520.13	535.73	551.81	568.36
55,000	539.30	555.48	572.14	589.31	606.99	625.20
60,000	588.33	605.98	624.16	642.88	662.17	682.03
65,000	637.35	656.48	676.17	696.45	717.35	738.87
70,000	686.38	706.97	728.18	750.03	772.53	795.70
75,000	735.41	757.47	780.20	803.60	827.71	852.54
80,000	784.44	807.97	832.21	857.18	882.89	909.38
85,000	833.46	858.47	884.22	910.75	938.07	966.21
90,000	882.49	908.97	936.23	964.32	993.25	1,023.05
95,000	931.52	959.46	988.25	1,017.90	1,048.43	1,079.89
100,000	980.55	1,009.96	1,040.26	1,071.47	1,103.61	1,136.72
110,000	1,078.60	1,110.96	1,144.29	1,178.62	1,213.97	1,250.39
120,000	1,176.65	1,211.95	1,248.31	1,285.76	1,324.34	1,364.07
130,000	1,274.71	1,312.95	1,352.34	1,392.91	1,434.70	1,477.74
140,000	1,372.76	1,413.95	1,456.37	1,500.06	1,545.06	1,591.41
150,000	1,470.82	1,514.94	1,560.39	1,607.20	1,655.42	1,705.08
160,000	1,568.87	1,615.94	1,664.42	1,714.35	1,765.78	1,818.75
170,000	1,666.93	1,716.94	1,768.44	1,821.50	1,876.14	1,932.43
180,000	1,764.98	1,817.93	1,872.47	1,928.64	1,986.50	2,046.10
190,000	1,863.04	1,918.93	1,976.50	2,035.79	2,096.86	2,159.77
200,000	1,961.09	2,019.92	2,080.52	2,142.94	2,207.23	2,273.44

TABLE IV-76. (Continued)

FHA GRADUATED PAYMENT PLAN V
TERM:30 YEARS INTEREST:13.50% GRADUATED AT 3.00%

PAYMENT AMCUNT	YEAR 7	YEAR 8	YEAR 9	YEAR 10	YEARS 11-30
50	0.59	0.60	0.62	0.64	0.66
100	1.17	1.21	1.24	1.28	1.32
200	2.34	2.41	2.48	2.56	2.64
300	3.51	3.62	3.73	3.84	3.95
400	4.68	4.82	4.97	5.12	5.27
500	5.85	6.03	6.21	6.40	6.59
600	7.02	7.24	7.45	7.68	7.91
700	8.20	8.44	8.69	8.96	9.22
800	9.37	9.65	9.94	10.24	10.54
900	10.54	10.85	11.18	11.51	11.86
1,000	11.71	12.06	12.42	12.79	13.18
2,000	23.42	24.12	24.84	25.59	26.36
3,000	35.12	36.18	37.26	38.38	39.53
4,000	46.83	48.24	49.69	51.18	52.71
5,000	58.54	60.30	62.11	63.97	65.89
6,000	70.25	72.36	74.53	76.76	79.07
7,000	81.96	84.42	86.95	89.56	92.24
8,000	93.67	96.48	99.37	102.35	105.42
9,000	105.37	108.54	111.79	115.15	118.60
10,000	117.08	120.59	124.21	127.94	131.78
15,000	175.62	180.89	186.32	191.91	197.67
20,000	234.16	241.19	248.43	255.88	263.55
25,000	292.71	301.49	310.53	319.85	329.44
30,000	351.25	361.78	372.64	383.82	395.33
35,000	409.79	422.08	434.74	447.79	461.22
40,000	468.33	482.38	496.85	511.76	527.11
45,000	526.87	542.68	558.96	575.73	593.00
50,000	585.41	602.97	621.06	639.69	658.89
55,000	643.95	663.27	683.17	703.66	724.77
60,000	702.49	723.57	745.28	767.63	790.66
65,000	761.03	783.87	807.38	831.60	856.55
70,000	819.58	844.16	869.49	895.57	922.44
75,000	878.12	904.46	931.59	959.54	988.33
80,000	936.66	964.76	993.70	1,023.51	1,054.22
85,000	995.20	1,025.06	1,055.81	1,087.48	1,120.11
90,000	1,053.74	1,085.35	1,117.91	1,151.45	1,185.99
95,000	1,112.28	1,145.65	1,180.02	1,215.42	1,251.88
100,000	1,170.82	1,205.95	1,242.13	1,279.39	1,317.77
110,000	1,287.91	1,326.54	1,366.34	1,407.33	1,449.55
120,000	1,404.99	1,447.14	1,490.55	1,535.27	1,581.33
130,000	1,522.07	1,567.73	1,614.76	1,663.21	1,713.10
140,000	1,639.15	1,688.33	1,738.98	1,791.15	1,844.88
150,000	1,756.23	1,808.92	1,863.19	1,919.08	1,976.66
160,000	1,873.32	1,929.52	1,987.40	2,047.02	2,108.43
170,000	1,990.40	2,050.11	2,111.61	2,174.96	2,240.21
180,000	2,107.48	2,170.71	2,235.83	2,302.90	2,371.99
190,000	2,224.56	2,291.30	2,360.04	2,430.84	2,503.77
200,000	2,341.65	2,411.90	2,484.25	2,558.78	2,635.54

TABLE IV-77. Graduated Payment Mortgage, FHA Plan V at 14.0% Interest, Graduated at 3.0%

FHA GRADUATED PAYMENT PLAN V
TERM:30 YEARS INTEREST:14.00% GRADUATED AT 3.00%

PAYMENT AMOUNT	YEAR 1	YEAR 2	YEAR 3	YEAR 4	YEAR 5	YEAR 6
50	0.51	0.52	0.54	0.56	0.57	0.59
100	1.02	1.05	1.08	1.11	1.15	1.18
200	2.03	2.10	2.16	2.22	2.29	2.36
300	3.05	3.14	3.24	3.34	3.44	3.54
400	4.07	4.19	4.32	4.45	4.58	4.72
500	5.09	5.24	5.40	5.56	5.73	5.90
600	6.10	6.29	6.48	6.67	6.87	7.08
700	7.12	7.34	7.56	7.78	8.02	8.26
800	8.14	8.38	8.63	8.89	9.16	9.44
900	9.16	9.43	9.71	10.01	10.31	10.61
1,000	10.17	10.48	10.79	11.12	11.45	11.79
2,000	20.35	20.96	21.59	22.23	22.90	23.59
3,000	30.52	31.44	32.38	33.35	34.35	35.38
4,000	40.69	41.92	43.17	44.47	45.80	47.18
5,000	50.87	52.39	53.97	55.59	57.25	58.97
6,000	61.04	62.87	64.76	66.70	68.70	70.76
7,000	71.22	73.35	75.55	77.82	80.15	82.56
8,000	81.39	83.83	86.35	88.94	91.61	94.35
9,000	91.56	94.31	97.14	100.05	103.06	106.15
10,000	101.74	104.79	107.93	111.17	114.51	117.94
15,000	152.61	157.18	161.90	166.76	171.76	176.91
20,000	203.47	209.58	215.87	222.34	229.01	235.88
25,000	254.34	261.97	269.83	277.93	286.27	294.85
30,000	305.21	314.37	323.80	333.51	343.52	353.82
35,000	356.08	366.76	377.77	389.10	400.77	412.80
40,000	406.95	419.16	431.73	444.68	458.03	471.77
45,000	457.82	471.55	485.70	500.27	515.28	530.74
50,000	508.69	523.95	539.67	555.86	572.53	589.71
55,000	559.56	576.34	593.63	611.44	629.78	648.68
60,000	610.42	628.74	647.60	667.03	687.04	707.65
65,000	661.29	681.13	701.57	722.61	744.29	766.62
70,000	712.16	733.53	755.53	778.20	801.54	825.59
75,000	763.03	785.92	809.50	833.78	858.80	884.56
80,000	813.90	838.32	863.47	889.37	916.05	943.53
85,000	864.77	890.71	917.43	944.95	973.30	1,002.50
90,000	915.64	943.11	971.40	1,000.54	1,030.56	1,061.47
95,000	966.50	995.50	1,025.37	1,056.13	1,087.81	1,120.44
100,000	1,017.37	1,047.89	1,079.33	1,111.71	1,145.06	1,179.41
110,000	1,119.11	1,152.68	1,187.26	1,222.88	1,259.57	1,297.36
120,000	1,220.85	1,257.47	1,295.20	1,334.05	1,374.08	1,415.30
130,000	1,322.59	1,362.26	1,403.13	1,445.23	1,488.58	1,533.24
140,000	1,424.32	1,467.05	1,511.06	1,556.40	1,603.09	1,651.18
150,000	1,526.06	1,571.84	1,619.00	1,667.57	1,717.59	1,769.12
160,000	1,627.80	1,676.63	1,726.93	1,778.74	1,832.10	1,887.06
170,000	1,729.54	1,781.42	1,834.86	1,889.91	1,946.61	2,005.01
180,000	1,831.27	1,886.21	1,942.80	2,001.08	2,061.11	2,122.95
190,000	1,933.01	1,991.00	2,050.73	2,112.25	2,175.62	2,240.89
200,000	2,034.75	2,095.79	2,158.66	2,223.42	2,290.13	2,358.83

TABLE IV-77. (*Continued*)

FHA GRADUATED PAYMENT PLAN V
TERM:30 YEARS INTEREST:14.00% GRADUATED AT 3.00%

PAYMENT AMOUNT	YEAR 7	YEAR 8	YEAR 9	YEAR 10	YEARS 11-30
50	0.61	0.63	0.64	0.66	0.68
100	1.21	1.25	1.29	1.33	1.37
200	2.43	2.50	2.58	2.65	2.73
300	3.64	3.75	3.87	3.98	4.10
400	4.86	5.00	5.16	5.31	5.47
500	6.07	6.26	6.44	6.64	6.84
600	7.29	7.51	7.73	7.96	8.20
700	8.50	8.76	9.02	9.29	9.57
800	9.72	10.01	10.31	10.62	10.94
900	10.93	11.26	11.60	11.95	12.31
1,000	12.15	12.51	12.89	13.27	13.67
2,000	24.30	25.02	25.78	26.55	27.35
3,000	36.44	37.54	38.66	39.82	41.02
4,000	48.59	50.05	51.55	53.10	54.69
5,000	60.74	62.56	64.44	66.37	68.36
6,000	72.89	75.07	77.33	79.65	82.04
7,000	85.04	87.59	90.21	92.92	95.71
8,000	97.18	100.10	103.10	106.20	109.38
9,000	109.33	112.61	115.99	119.47	123.05
10,000	121.48	125.12	128.88	132.74	136.73
15,000	182.22	187.69	193.32	199.12	205.09
20,000	242.96	250.25	257.76	265.49	273.45
25,000	303.70	312.81	322.19	331.86	341.82
30,000	364.44	375.37	386.63	398.23	410.18
35,000	425.18	437.93	451.07	464.60	478.54
40,000	485.92	500.50	515.51	530.98	546.91
45,000	546.66	563.06	579.95	597.35	615.27
50,000	607.40	625.62	644.39	663.72	683.63
55,000	668.14	688.18	708.83	730.09	752.00
60,000	728.88	750.74	773.27	796.47	820.36
65,000	789.62	813.31	837.71	862.84	888.72
70,000	850.36	875.87	902.14	929.21	957.09
75,000	911.10	938.43	966.58	995.58	1,025.45
80,000	971.84	1,000.99	1,031.02	1,061.95	1,093.81
85,000	1,032.58	1,063.56	1,095.46	1,128.33	1,162.18
90,000	1,093.32	1,126.12	1,159.90	1,194.70	1,230.54
95,000	1,154.06	1,188.68	1,224.34	1,261.07	1,298.90
100,000	1,214.80	1,251.24	1,288.78	1,327.44	1,367.27
110,000	1,336.28	1,376.37	1,417.66	1,460.19	1,503.99
120,000	1,457.76	1,501.49	1,546.53	1,592.93	1,640.72
130,000	1,579.24	1,626.61	1,675.41	1,725.67	1,777.44
140,000	1,700.72	1,751.74	1,804.29	1,858.42	1,914.17
150,000	1,822.20	1,876.86	1,933.17	1,991.16	2,050.90
160,000	1,943.68	2,001.99	2,062.05	2,123.91	2,187.62
170,000	2,065.16	2,127.11	2,190.92	2,256.65	2,324.35
180,000	2,186.64	2,252.23	2,319.80	2,389.40	2,461.08
190,000	2,308.11	2,377.36	2,448.68	2,522.14	2,597.80
200,000	2,429.59	2,502.48	2,577.56	2,654.88	2,734.53

TABLE IV-78. Graduated Payment Mortgage, FHA Plan V at 14.5% Interest, Graduated at 3.0%

FHA GRADUATED PAYMENT PLAN V
TERM:30 YEARS INTEREST:14.50% GRADUATED AT 3.00%

PAYMENT AMOUNT	YEAR 1	YEAR 2	YEAR 3	YEAR 4	YEAR 5	YEAR 6
50	0.53	0.54	0.56	0.58	0.59	0.61
100	1.05	1.09	1.12	1.15	1.19	1.22
200	2.11	2.17	2.24	2.30	2.37	2.45
300	3.16	3.26	3.36	3.46	3.56	3.67
400	4.22	4.34	4.48	4.61	4.75	4.89
500	5.27	5.43	5.59	5.76	5.93	6.11
600	6.33	6.52	6.71	6.91	7.12	7.34
700	7.38	7.60	7.83	8.07	8.31	8.56
800	8.44	8.69	8.95	9.22	9.50	9.78
900	9.49	9.78	10.07	10.37	10.68	11.00
1,000	10.55	10.86	11.19	11.52	11.87	12.23
2,000	21.09	21.72	22.38	23.05	23.74	24.45
3,000	31.64	32.59	33.56	34.57	35.61	36.68
4,000	42.18	43.45	44.75	46.09	47.48	48.90
5,000	52.73	54.31	55.94	57.62	59.35	61.13
6,000	63.27	65.17	67.13	69.14	71.21	73.35
7,000	73.82	76.03	78.31	80.66	83.08	85.58
8,000	84.36	86.89	89.50	92.19	94.95	97.80
9,000	94.91	97.76	100.69	103.71	106.82	110.03
10,000	105.45	108.62	111.88	115.23	118.69	122.25
15,000	158.18	162.93	167.82	172.85	178.04	183.38
20,000	210.91	217.24	223.75	230.47	237.38	244.50
25,000	263.64	271.55	279.69	288.08	296.73	305.63
30,000	316.36	325.86	335.63	345.70	356.07	366.75
35,000	369.09	380.16	391.57	403.32	415.42	427.88
40,000	421.82	434.47	447.51	460.93	474.76	489.00
45,000	474.55	488.78	503.45	518.55	534.11	550.13
50,000	527.27	543.09	559.38	576.17	593.45	611.25
55,000	580.00	597.40	615.32	633.78	652.80	672.38
60,000	632.73	651.71	671.26	691.40	712.14	733.51
65,000	685.46	706.02	727.20	749.02	771.49	794.63
70,000	738.18	760.33	783.14	806.63	830.83	855.76
75,000	790.91	814.64	839.08	864.25	890.18	916.88
80,000	843.64	868.95	895.02	921.87	949.52	978.01
85,000	896.37	923.26	950.95	979.48	1,008.87	1,039.13
90,000	949.09	977.57	1,006.89	1,037.10	1,068.21	1,100.26
95,000	1,001.82	1,031.87	1,062.83	1,094.72	1,127.56	1,161.38
100,000	1,054.55	1,086.18	1,118.77	1,152.33	1,186.90	1,222.51
110,000	1,160.00	1,194.80	1,230.65	1,267.57	1,305.59	1,344.76
120,000	1,265.46	1,303.42	1,342.52	1,382.80	1,424.28	1,467.01
130,000	1,370.91	1,412.04	1,454.40	1,498.03	1,542.97	1,589.26
140,000	1,476.37	1,520.66	1,566.28	1,613.27	1,661.66	1,711.51
150,000	1,581.82	1,629.28	1,678.15	1,728.50	1,780.35	1,833.76
160,000	1,687.28	1,737.89	1,790.03	1,843.73	1,899.04	1,956.02
170,000	1,792.73	1,846.51	1,901.91	1,958.97	2,017.73	2,078.27
180,000	1,898.19	1,955.13	2,013.78	2,074.20	2,136.42	2,200.52
190,000	2,003.64	2,063.75	2,125.66	2,189.43	2,255.11	2,322.77
200,000	2,109.09	2,172.37	2,237.54	2,304.66	2,373.80	2,445.02

TABLE IV-78. (*Continued*)

FHA GRADUATED PAYMENT PLAN V
TERM:30 YEARS INTEREST:14.50% GRADUATED AT 3.00%

PAYMENT AMOUNT	YEAR 7	YEAR 8	YEAR 9	YEAR 10	YEARS 11-30
50	0.63	0.65	0.67	0.69	0.71
100	1.26	1.30	1.34	1.38	1.42
200	2.52	2.59	2.67	2.75	2.83
300	3.78	3.89	4.01	4.13	4.25
400	5.04	5.19	5.34	5.50	5.67
500	6.30	6.48	6.68	6.88	7.09
600	7.56	7.78	8.02	8.26	8.50
700	8.81	9.08	9.35	9.63	9.92
800	10.07	10.38	10.69	11.01	11.34
900	11.33	11.67	12.02	12.38	12.76
1,000	12.59	12.97	13.36	13.76	14.17
2,000	25.18	25.94	26.72	27.52	28.34
3,000	37.78	38.91	40.08	41.28	42.52
4,000	50.37	51.88	53.43	55.04	56.69
5,000	62.96	64.85	66.79	68.80	70.86
6,000	75.55	77.82	80.15	82.56	85.03
7,000	88.14	90.79	93.51	96.32	99.21
8,000	100.73	103.76	106.87	110.08	113.38
9,000	113.33	116.73	120.23	123.84	127.55
10,000	125.92	129.70	133.59	137.59	141.72
15,000	188.88	194.54	200.38	206.39	212.58
20,000	251.84	259.39	267.17	275.19	283.44
25,000	314.80	324.24	333.97	343.99	354.31
30,000	377.76	389.09	400.76	412.78	425.17
35,000	440.71	453.94	467.55	481.58	496.03
40,000	503.67	518.78	534.35	550.38	566.89
45,000	566.63	583.63	601.14	619.18	637.75
50,000	629.59	648.48	667.93	687.97	708.61
55,000	692.55	713.33	734.73	756.77	779.47
60,000	755.51	778.18	801.52	825.57	850.33
65,000	818.47	843.02	868.31	894.36	921.20
70,000	881.43	907.87	935.11	963.16	992.06
75,000	944.39	972.72	1,001.90	1,031.96	1,062.92
80,000	1,007.35	1,037.57	1,068.70	1,100.76	1,133.78
85,000	1,070.31	1,102.42	1,135.49	1,169.55	1,204.64
90,000	1,133.27	1,167.26	1,202.28	1,238.35	1,275.50
95,000	1,196.23	1,232.11	1,269.08	1,307.15	1,346.36
100,000	1,259.18	1,296.96	1,335.87	1,375.95	1,417.22
110,000	1,385.10	1,426.66	1,469.46	1,513.54	1,558.95
120,000	1,511.02	1,556.35	1,603.04	1,651.13	1,700.67
130,000	1,636.94	1,686.05	1,736.63	1,788.73	1,842.39
140,000	1,762.86	1,815.74	1,870.22	1,926.32	1,984.11
150,000	1,888.78	1,945.44	2,003.80	2,063.92	2,125.84
160,000	2,014.70	2,075.14	2,137.39	2,201.51	2,267.56
170,000	2,140.61	2,204.83	2,270.98	2,339.11	2,409.28
180,000	2,266.53	2,334.53	2,404.56	2,476.70	2,551.00
190,000	2,392.45	2,464.22	2,538.15	2,614.30	2,692.72
200,000	2,518.37	2,593.92	2,671.74	2,751.89	2,834.45

TABLE IV-79. Graduated Payment Mortgage, FHA Plan V at 15.0% Interest, Graduated at 3.0%

FHA GRADUATED PAYMENT PLAN V
TERM:30 YEARS INTEREST:15.00% GRADUATED AT 3.00%

PAYMENT AMOUNT	YEAR 1	YEAR 2	YEAR 3	YEAR 4	YEAR 5	YEAR 6
50	0.55	0.56	0.58	0.60	0.61	0.63
100	1.09	1.12	1.16	1.19	1.23	1.27
200	2.18	2.25	2.32	2.39	2.46	2.53
300	3.28	3.37	3.48	3.58	3.69	3.80
400	4.37	4.50	4.63	4.77	4.92	5.06
500	5.46	5.62	5.79	5.97	6.15	6.33
600	6.55	6.75	6.95	7.16	7.37	7.60
700	7.64	7.87	8.11	8.35	8.60	8.86
800	8.74	9.00	9.27	9.55	9.83	10.13
900	9.83	10.12	10.43	10.74	11.06	11.39
1,000	10.92	11.25	11.59	11.93	12.29	12.66
2,000	21.84	22.50	23.17	23.87	24.58	25.32
3,000	32.76	33.74	34.76	35.80	36.87	37.98
4,000	43.68	44.99	46.34	47.73	49.16	50.64
5,000	54.60	56.24	57.93	59.67	61.46	63.30
6,000	65.52	67.49	69.51	71.60	73.75	75.96
7,000	76.44	78.74	81.10	83.53	86.04	88.62
8,000	87.36	89.98	92.68	95.46	98.33	101.28
9,000	98.28	101.23	104.27	107.40	110.62	113.94
10,000	109.20	112.48	115.86	119.33	122.91	126.60
15,000	163.81	168.72	173.78	179.00	184.37	189.90
20,000	218.41	224.96	231.71	238.66	245.82	253.20
25,000	273.01	281.20	289.64	298.33	307.28	316.49
30,000	327.61	337.44	347.57	357.99	368.73	379.79
35,000	382.22	393.68	405.49	417.66	430.19	443.09
40,000	436.82	449.92	463.42	477.32	491.64	506.39
45,000	491.42	506.16	521.35	536.99	553.10	569.69
50,000	546.02	562.40	579.28	596.65	614.55	632.99
55,000	600.62	618.64	637.20	656.32	676.01	696.29
60,000	655.23	674.88	695.13	715.98	737.46	759.59
65,000	709.83	731.12	753.06	775.65	798.92	822.89
70,000	764.43	787.36	810.99	835.31	860.37	886.19
75,000	819.03	843.60	868.91	894.98	921.83	949.48
80,000	873.64	899.84	926.84	954.65	983.28	1,012.78
85,000	928.24	956.08	984.77	1,014.31	1,044.74	1,076.08
90,000	982.84	1,012.33	1,042.70	1,073.98	1,106.20	1,139.38
95,000	1,037.44	1,068.57	1,100.62	1,133.64	1,167.65	1,202.68
100,000	1,092.04	1,124.81	1,158.55	1,193.31	1,229.11	1,265.98
110,000	1,201.25	1,237.29	1,274.41	1,312.64	1,352.02	1,392.58
120,000	1,310.45	1,349.77	1,390.26	1,431.97	1,474.93	1,519.17
130,000	1,419.66	1,462.25	1,506.12	1,551.30	1,597.84	1,645.77
140,000	1,528.86	1,574.73	1,621.97	1,670.63	1,720.75	1,772.37
150,000	1,638.07	1,687.21	1,737.83	1,789.96	1,843.66	1,898.97
160,000	1,747.27	1,799.69	1,853.68	1,909.29	1,966.57	2,025.57
170,000	1,856.48	1,912.17	1,969.54	2,028.62	2,089.48	2,152.16
180,000	1,965.68	2,024.65	2,085.39	2,147.95	2,212.39	2,278.76
190,000	2,074.88	2,137.13	2,201.25	2,267.28	2,335.30	2,405.36
200,000	2,184.09	2,249.61	2,317.10	2,386.61	2,458.21	2,531.96

TABLE IV-79. (Continued)

FHA GRADUATED PAYMENT PLAN V
TERM:30 YEARS INTEREST:15.00% GRADUATED AT 3.00%

PAYMENT AMCUNT	YEAR 7	YEAR 8	YEAR 9	YEAR 10	YEARS 11-30
50	0.65	0.67	0.69	0.71	0.73
100	1.30	1.34	1.38	1.42	1.47
200	2.61	2.69	2.77	2.85	2.94
300	3.91	4.03	4.15	4.27	4.40
400	5.22	5.37	5.53	5.70	5.87
500	6.52	6.72	6.92	7.12	7.34
600	7.82	8.06	8.30	8.55	8.81
700	9.13	9.40	9.68	9.97	10.27
800	10.43	10.74	11.07	11.40	11.74
900	11.74	12.09	12.45	12.82	13.21
1,000	13.04	13.43	13.83	14.25	14.68
2,000	26.08	26.86	27.67	28.50	29.35
3,000	39.12	40.29	41.50	42.75	44.03
4,000	52.16	53.72	55.33	56.99	58.70
5,000	65.20	67.15	69.17	71.24	73.38
6,000	78.24	80.58	83.00	85.49	88.06
7,000	91.28	94.02	96.84	99.74	102.73
8,000	104.32	107.45	110.67	113.99	117.41
9,000	117.36	120.88	124.50	128.24	132.09
10,000	130.40	134.31	138.34	142.49	146.76
15,000	195.59	201.46	207.51	213.73	220.14
20,000	260.79	268.62	276.67	284.97	293.52
25,000	325.99	335.77	345.84	356.22	366.90
30,000	391.19	402.92	415.01	427.46	440.28
35,000	456.39	470.08	484.18	498.70	513.67
40,000	521.58	537.23	553.35	569.95	587.05
45,000	586.78	604.38	622.52	641.19	660.43
50,000	651.98	671.54	691.68	712.44	733.81
55,000	717.18	738.69	760.85	783.68	807.19
60,000	782.37	805.85	830.02	854.92	880.57
65,000	847.57	873.00	899.19	926.17	953.95
70,000	912.77	940.15	968.36	997.41	1,027.33
75,000	977.97	1,007.31	1,037.53	1,068.65	1,100.71
80,000	1,043.17	1,074.46	1,106.70	1,139.90	1,174.09
85,000	1,108.36	1,141.62	1,175.86	1,211.14	1,247.47
90,000	1,173.56	1,208.77	1,245.03	1,282.38	1,320.85
95,000	1,238.76	1,275.92	1,314.20	1,353.63	1,394.24
100,000	1,303.96	1,343.08	1,383.37	1,424.87	1,467.62
110,000	1,434.35	1,477.38	1,521.71	1,567.36	1,614.38
120,000	1,564.75	1,611.69	1,660.04	1,709.84	1,761.14
130,000	1,695.15	1,746.00	1,798.38	1,852.33	1,907.90
140,000	1,825.54	1,880.31	1,936.72	1,994.82	2,054.66
150,000	1,955.94	2,014.62	2,075.05	2,137.31	2,201.42
160,000	2,086.33	2,148.92	2,213.39	2,279.79	2,348.19
170,000	2,216.73	2,283.23	2,351.73	2,422.28	2,494.95
180,000	2,347.12	2,417.54	2,490.06	2,564.77	2,641.71
190,000	2,477.52	2,551.85	2,628.40	2,707.25	2,788.47
200,000	2,607.92	2,686.15	2,766.74	2,849.74	2,935.23

TABLE IV-80. Graduated Payment Mortgage, FHA Plan V at 15.5% Interest, Graduated at 3.0%

FHA GRADUATED PAYMENT PLAN V
TERM:30 YEARS INTEREST:15.50% GRADUATED AT 3.00%

PAYMENT AMCUNT	YEAR 1	YEAR 2	YEAR 3	YEAR 4	YEAR 5	YEAR 6
50	0.56	0.58	0.60	0.62	0.64	0.65
100	1.13	1.16	1.20	1.23	1.27	1.31
200	2.26	2.33	2.40	2.47	2.54	2.62
300	3.39	3.49	3.60	3.70	3.81	3.93
400	4.52	4.65	4.79	4.94	5.09	5.24
500	5.65	5.82	5.99	6.17	6.36	6.55
600	6.78	6.98	7.19	7.41	7.63	7.86
700	7.91	8.15	8.39	8.64	8.90	9.17
800	9.04	9.31	9.59	9.88	10.17	10.48
900	10.17	10.47	10.79	11.11	11.44	11.79
1,000	11.30	11.64	11.99	12.35	12.72	13.10
2,000	22.60	23.27	23.97	24.69	25.43	26.20
3,000	33.90	34.91	35.96	37.04	38.15	39.29
4,000	45.19	46.55	47.95	49.38	50.87	52.39
5,000	56.49	58.19	59.93	61.73	63.58	65.49
6,000	67.79	69.82	71.92	74.08	76.30	78.59
7,000	79.09	81.46	83.91	86.42	89.02	91.69
8,000	90.39	93.10	95.89	98.77	101.73	104.78
9,000	101.69	104.74	107.88	111.11	114.45	117.88
10,000	112.98	116.37	119.87	123.46	127.16	130.98
15,000	169.48	174.56	179.80	185.19	190.75	196.47
20,000	225.97	232.75	239.73	246.92	254.33	261.96
25,000	282.46	290.93	299.66	308.65	317.91	327.45
30,000	338.95	349.12	359.60	370.38	381.49	392.94
35,000	395.45	407.31	419.53	432.11	445.08	458.43
40,000	451.94	465.50	479.46	493.84	508.66	523.92
45,000	508.43	523.68	539.39	555.57	572.24	589.41
50,000	564.92	581.87	599.33	617.31	635.82	654.90
55,000	621.41	640.06	659.26	679.04	699.41	720.39
60,000	677.91	698.24	719.19	740.77	762.99	785.88
65,000	734.40	756.43	779.12	802.50	826.57	851.37
70,000	790.89	814.62	839.06	864.23	890.15	916.86
75,000	847.38	872.80	898.99	925.96	953.74	982.35
80,000	903.87	930.99	958.92	987.69	1,017.32	1,047.84
85,000	960.37	989.18	1,018.85	1,049.42	1,080.90	1,113.33
90,000	1,016.86	1,047.37	1,078.79	1,111.15	1,144.48	1,178.82
95,000	1,073.35	1,105.55	1,138.72	1,172.88	1,208.07	1,244.31
100,000	1,129.84	1,163.74	1,198.65	1,234.61	1,271.65	1,309.80
110,000	1,242.83	1,280.11	1,318.52	1,358.07	1,398.81	1,440.78
120,000	1,355.81	1,396.49	1,438.38	1,481.53	1,525.98	1,571.76
130,000	1,468.80	1,512.86	1,558.25	1,604.99	1,653.14	1,702.74
140,000	1,581.78	1,629.23	1,678.11	1,728.45	1,780.31	1,833.72
150,000	1,694.77	1,745.61	1,797.98	1,851.92	1,907.47	1,964.70
160,000	1,807.75	1,861.98	1,917.84	1,975.38	2,034.64	2,095.68
170,000	1,920.73	1,978.36	2,037.71	2,098.84	2,161.80	2,226.66
180,000	2,033.72	2,094.73	2,157.57	2,222.30	2,288.97	2,357.64
190,000	2,146.70	2,211.10	2,277.44	2,345.76	2,416.13	2,488.62
200,000	2,259.69	2,327.48	2,397.30	2,469.22	2,543.30	2,619.60

TABLE IV-80. (*Continued*)

FHA GRADUATED PAYMENT PLAN V
TERM:30 YEARS INTEREST:15.50% GRADUATED AT 3.00%

PAYMENT AMOUNT	YEAR 7	YEAR 8	YEAR 9	YEAR 10	YEARS 11-30
50	0.67	0.69	0.72	0.74	0.76
100	1.35	1.39	1.43	1.47	1.52
200	2.70	2.78	2.86	2.95	3.04
300	4.05	4.17	4.29	4.42	4.56
400	5.40	5.56	5.73	5.90	6.07
500	6.75	6.95	7.16	7.37	7.59
600	8.09	8.34	8.59	8.85	9.11
700	9.44	9.73	10.02	10.32	10.63
800	10.79	11.12	11.45	11.79	12.15
900	12.14	12.51	12.88	13.27	13.67
1,000	13.49	13.90	14.31	14.74	15.18
2,000	26.98	27.79	28.63	29.48	30.37
3,000	40.47	41.69	42.94	44.23	45.55
4,000	53.96	55.58	57.25	58.97	60.74
5,000	67.45	69.48	71.56	73.71	75.92
6,000	80.95	83.37	85.88	88.45	91.10
7,000	94.44	97.27	100.19	103.19	106.29
8,000	107.93	111.17	114.50	117.94	121.47
9,000	121.42	125.06	128.81	132.68	136.66
10,000	134.91	138.96	143.13	147.42	151.84
15,000	202.36	208.43	214.69	221.13	227.76
20,000	269.82	277.91	286.25	294.84	303.68
25,000	337.27	347.39	357.81	368.55	379.60
30,000	404.73	416.87	429.38	442.26	455.52
35,000	472.18	486.35	500.94	515.97	531.45
40,000	539.64	555.83	572.50	589.68	607.37
45,000	607.09	625.30	644.06	663.39	683.29
50,000	674.55	694.78	715.63	737.09	759.21
55,000	742.00	764.26	787.19	810.80	835.13
60,000	809.46	833.74	858.75	884.51	911.05
65,000	876.91	903.22	930.31	958.22	986.97
70,000	944.36	972.70	1,001.88	1,031.93	1,062.89
75,000	1,011.82	1,042.17	1,073.44	1,105.64	1,138.81
80,000	1,079.27	1,111.65	1,145.00	1,179.35	1,214.73
85,000	1,146.73	1,181.13	1,216.56	1,253.06	1,290.65
90,000	1,214.18	1,250.61	1,288.13	1,326.77	1,366.57
95,000	1,281.64	1,320.09	1,359.69	1,400.48	1,442.49
100,000	1,349.09	1,389.57	1,431.25	1,474.19	1,518.42
110,000	1,484.00	1,528.52	1,574.38	1,621.61	1,670.26
120,000	1,618.91	1,667.48	1,717.50	1,769.03	1,822.10
130,000	1,753.82	1,806.43	1,860.63	1,916.45	1,973.94
140,000	1,888.73	1,945.39	2,003.75	2,063.87	2,125.78
150,000	2,023.64	2,084.35	2,146.88	2,211.28	2,277.62
160,000	2,158.55	2,223.30	2,290.00	2,358.70	2,429.46
170,000	2,293.46	2,362.26	2,433.13	2,506.12	2,581.31
180,000	2,428.37	2,501.22	2,576.25	2,653.54	2,733.15
190,000	2,563.28	2,640.17	2,719.38	2,800.96	2,884.99
200,000	2,698.18	2,779.13	2,862.50	2,948.38	3,036.83

TABLE IV-81. **Graduated Payment Mortgage, FHA Plan V at 16.0% Interest, Graduated at 3.0%**

FHA GRADUATED PAYMENT PLAN V
TERM:30 YEARS INTEREST:16.00% GRADUATED AT 3.00%

PAYMENT AMOUNT	YEAR 1	YEAR 2	YEAR 3	YEAR 4	YEAR 5	YEAR 6
50	0.58	0.60	0.62	0.64	0.66	0.68
100	1.17	1.20	1.24	1.28	1.31	1.35
200	2.34	2.41	2.48	2.55	2.63	2.71
300	3.50	3.61	3.72	3.83	3.94	4.06
400	4.67	4.81	4.96	5.10	5.26	5.42
500	5.84	6.01	6.20	6.38	6.57	6.77
600	7.01	7.22	7.43	7.66	7.89	8.12
700	8.18	8.42	8.67	8.93	9.20	9.48
800	9.34	9.62	9.91	10.21	10.52	10.83
900	10.51	10.83	11.15	11.49	11.83	12.19
1,000	11.68	12.03	12.39	12.76	13.15	13.54
2,000	23.36	24.06	24.78	25.52	26.29	27.08
3,000	35.04	36.09	37.17	38.29	39.44	40.62
4,000	46.72	48.12	49.56	51.05	52.58	54.16
5,000	58.40	60.15	61.95	63.81	65.73	67.70
6,000	70.08	72.18	74.34	76.57	78.87	81.24
7,000	81.75	84.21	86.73	89.34	92.02	94.78
8,000	93.43	96.24	99.12	102.10	105.16	108.32
9,000	105.11	108.27	111.51	114.86	118.31	121.86
10,000	116.79	120.30	123.91	127.62	131.45	135.39
15,000	175.19	180.44	185.86	191.43	197.18	203.09
20,000	233.58	240.59	247.81	255.24	262.90	270.79
25,000	291.98	300.74	309.76	319.06	328.63	338.49
30,000	350.38	360.89	371.72	382.87	394.35	406.18
35,000	408.77	421.04	433.67	446.68	460.08	473.88
40,000	467.17	481.18	495.62	510.49	525.80	541.58
45,000	525.57	541.33	557.57	574.30	591.53	609.28
50,000	583.96	601.48	619.53	638.11	657.25	676.97
55,000	642.36	661.63	681.48	701.92	722.98	744.67
60,000	700.75	721.78	743.43	765.73	788.71	812.37
65,000	759.15	781.93	805.38	829.54	854.43	880.06
70,000	817.55	842.07	867.34	893.36	920.16	947.76
75,000	875.94	902.22	929.29	957.17	985.88	1,015.46
80,000	934.34	962.37	991.24	1,020.98	1,051.61	1,083.16
85,000	992.74	1,022.52	1,053.19	1,084.79	1,117.33	1,150.85
90,000	1,051.13	1,082.67	1,115.15	1,148.60	1,183.06	1,218.55
95,000	1,109.53	1,142.81	1,177.10	1,212.41	1,248.78	1,286.25
100,000	1,167.92	1,202.96	1,239.05	1,276.22	1,314.51	1,353.94
110,000	1,284.72	1,323.26	1,362.96	1,403.84	1,445.96	1,489.34
120,000	1,401.51	1,443.55	1,486.86	1,531.47	1,577.41	1,624.73
130,000	1,518.30	1,563.85	1,610.77	1,659.09	1,708.86	1,760.13
140,000	1,635.09	1,684.15	1,734.67	1,786.71	1,840.31	1,895.52
150,000	1,751.89	1,804.44	1,858.58	1,914.33	1,971.76	2,030.92
160,000	1,868.68	1,924.74	1,982.48	2,041.96	2,103.21	2,166.31
170,000	1,985.47	2,045.04	2,106.39	2,169.58	2,234.67	2,301.71
180,000	2,102.26	2,165.33	2,230.29	2,297.20	2,366.12	2,437.10
190,000	2,219.06	2,285.63	2,354.20	2,424.82	2,497.57	2,572.49
200,000	2,335.85	2,405.92	2,478.10	2,552.45	2,629.02	2,707.89

TABLE IV-81. (*Continued*)

FHA GRADUATED PAYMENT PLAN V
TERM:30 YEARS INTEREST:16.00% GRADUATED AT 3.00%

PAYMENT AMCUNT	YEAR 7	YEAR 8	YEAR 9	YEAR 10	YEARS 11-30
50	0.70	0.72	0.74	0.76	0.78
100	1.39	1.44	1.48	1.52	1.57
200	2.79	2.87	2.96	3.05	3.14
300	4.18	4.31	4.44	4.57	4.71
400	5.58	5.75	5.92	6.10	6.28
500	6.97	7.18	7.40	7.62	7.85
600	8.37	8.62	8.88	9.14	9.42
700	9.76	10.05	10.36	10.67	10.99
800	11.16	11.49	11.84	12.19	12.56
900	12.55	12.93	13.32	13.71	14.13
1,000	13.95	14.36	14.79	15.24	15.70
2,000	27.89	28.73	29.59	30.48	31.39
3,000	41.84	43.09	44.38	45.72	47.09
4,000	55.78	57.46	59.18	60.96	62.78
5,000	69.73	71.82	73.97	76.19	78.48
6,000	83.67	86.18	88.77	91.43	94.18
7,000	97.62	100.55	103.56	106.67	109.87
8,000	111.57	114.91	118.36	121.91	125.57
9,000	125.51	129.28	133.15	137.15	141.26
10,000	139.46	143.64	147.95	152.39	156.96
15,000	209.18	215.46	221.92	228.58	235.44
20,000	278.91	287.28	295.90	304.78	313.92
25,000	348.64	359.10	369.87	380.97	392.40
30,000	418.37	430.92	443.85	457.16	470.88
35,000	488.10	502.74	517.82	533.36	549.36
40,000	557.83	574.56	591.80	609.55	627.84
45,000	627.55	646.38	665.77	685.74	706.32
50,000	697.28	718.20	739.75	761.94	784.80
55,000	767.01	790.02	813.72	838.13	863.28
60,000	836.74	861.84	887.70	914.33	941.76
65,000	906.47	933.66	961.67	990.52	1,020.24
70,000	976.19	1,005.48	1,035.64	1,066.71	1,098.72
75,000	1,045.92	1,077.30	1,109.62	1,142.91	1,177.19
80,000	1,115.65	1,149.12	1,183.59	1,219.10	1,255.67
85,000	1,185.38	1,220.94	1,257.57	1,295.30	1,334.15
90,000	1,255.11	1,292.76	1,331.54	1,371.49	1,412.63
95,000	1,324.83	1,364.58	1,405.52	1,447.68	1,491.11
100,000	1,394.56	1,436.40	1,479.49	1,523.88	1,569.59
110,000	1,534.02	1,580.04	1,627.44	1,676.26	1,726.55
120,000	1,673.48	1,723.68	1,775.39	1,828.65	1,883.51
130,000	1,812.93	1,867.32	1,923.34	1,981.04	2,040.47
140,000	1,952.39	2,010.96	2,071.29	2,133.43	2,197.43
150,000	2,091.84	2,154.60	2,219.24	2,285.81	2,354.39
160,000	2,231.30	2,298.24	2,367.19	2,438.20	2,511.35
170,000	2,370.76	2,441.88	2,515.14	2,590.59	2,668.31
180,000	2,510.21	2,585.52	2,663.09	2,742.98	2,825.27
190,000	2,649.67	2,729.16	2,811.03	2,895.37	2,982.23
200,000	2,789.13	2,872.80	2,958.98	3,047.75	3,139.19

TABLE IV-82. Graduated Payment Mortgage, FHA Plan V at 16.5% Interest, Graduated at 3.0%

FHA GRADUATED PAYMENT PLAN V
TERM:30 YEARS INTEREST:16.50% GRADUATED AT 3.00%

PAYMENT AMOUNT	YEAR 1	YEAR 2	YEAR 3	YEAR 4	YEAR 5	YEAR 6
50	0.60	0.62	0.64	0.66	0.68	0.70
100	1.21	1.24	1.28	1.32	1.36	1.40
200	2.41	2.48	2.56	2.64	2.72	2.80
300	3.62	3.73	3.84	3.95	4.07	4.20
400	4.83	4.97	5.12	5.27	5.43	5.59
500	6.03	6.21	6.40	6.59	6.79	6.99
600	7.24	7.45	7.68	7.91	8.15	8.39
700	8.44	8.70	8.96	9.23	9.50	9.79
800	9.65	9.94	10.24	10.54	10.86	11.19
900	10.86	11.18	11.52	11.86	12.22	12.59
1,000	12.06	12.42	12.80	13.18	13.58	13.98
2,000	24.13	24.85	25.59	26.36	27.15	27.97
3,000	36.19	37.27	38.39	39.54	40.73	41.95
4,000	48.25	49.70	51.19	52.72	54.31	55.94
5,000	60.31	62.12	63.99	65.91	67.88	69.92
6,000	72.38	74.55	76.78	79.09	81.46	83.90
7,000	84.44	86.97	89.58	92.27	95.04	97.89
8,000	96.50	99.40	102.38	105.45	108.61	111.87
9,000	108.56	111.82	115.18	118.63	122.19	125.86
10,000	120.63	124.25	127.97	131.81	135.77	139.84
15,000	180.94	186.37	191.96	197.72	203.65	209.76
20,000	241.25	248.49	255.95	263.62	271.53	279.68
25,000	301.57	310.61	319.93	329.53	339.42	349.60
30,000	361.88	372.74	383.92	395.44	407.30	419.52
35,000	422.19	434.86	447.91	461.34	475.18	489.44
40,000	482.51	496.98	511.89	527.25	543.07	559.36
45,000	542.82	559.11	575.88	593.15	610.95	629.28
50,000	603.13	621.23	639.87	659.06	678.83	699.20
55,000	663.45	683.35	703.85	724.97	746.72	769.12
60,000	723.76	745.47	767.84	790.87	814.60	839.04
65,000	784.07	807.60	831.82	856.78	882.48	908.96
70,000	844.39	869.72	895.81	922.69	950.37	978.88
75,000	904.70	931.84	959.80	988.59	1,018.25	1,048.80
80,000	965.01	993.97	1,023.78	1,054.50	1,086.13	1,118.72
85,000	1,025.33	1,056.09	1,087.77	1,120.40	1,154.02	1,188.64
90,000	1,085.64	1,118.21	1,151.76	1,186.31	1,221.90	1,258.56
95,000	1,145.95	1,180.33	1,215.74	1,252.22	1,289.78	1,328.48
100,000	1,206.27	1,242.46	1,279.73	1,318.12	1,357.67	1,398.40
110,000	1,326.90	1,366.70	1,407.70	1,449.93	1,493.43	1,538.24
120,000	1,447.52	1,490.95	1,535.68	1,581.75	1,629.20	1,678.07
130,000	1,568.15	1,615.19	1,663.65	1,713.56	1,764.97	1,817.91
140,000	1,688.78	1,739.44	1,791.62	1,845.37	1,900.73	1,957.75
150,000	1,809.40	1,863.68	1,919.60	1,977.18	2,036.50	2,097.59
160,000	1,930.03	1,987.93	2,047.57	2,109.00	2,172.27	2,237.43
170,000	2,050.66	2,112.18	2,175.54	2,240.81	2,308.03	2,377.27
180,000	2,171.28	2,236.42	2,303.51	2,372.62	2,443.80	2,517.11
190,000	2,291.91	2,360.67	2,431.49	2,504.43	2,579.56	2,656.95
200,000	2,412.54	2,484.91	2,559.46	2,636.24	2,715.33	2,796.79

TABLE IV-82. (Continued)

FHA GRADUATED PAYMENT PLAN V
TERM:30 YEARS INTEREST:16.50% GRADUATED AT 3.00%

PAYMENT AMOUNT	YEAR 7	YEAR 8	YEAR 9	YEAR 10	YEARS 11-30
50	0.72	0.74	0.76	0.79	0.81
100	1.44	1.48	1.53	1.57	1.62
200	2.88	2.97	3.06	3.15	3.24
300	4.32	4.45	4.58	4.72	4.86
400	5.76	5.93	6.11	6.30	6.48
500	7.20	7.42	7.64	7.87	8.11
600	8.64	8.90	9.17	9.44	9.73
700	10.08	10.38	10.70	11.02	11.35
800	11.52	11.87	12.22	12.59	12.97
900	12.96	13.35	13.75	14.17	14.59
1,000	14.40	14.84	15.28	15.74	16.21
2,000	28.81	29.67	30.56	31.48	32.42
3,000	43.21	44.51	45.84	47.22	48.63
4,000	57.61	59.34	61.12	62.96	64.84
5,000	72.02	74.18	76.40	78.70	81.06
6,000	86.42	89.01	91.68	94.43	97.27
7,000	100.82	103.85	106.96	110.17	113.48
8,000	115.23	118.68	122.25	125.91	129.69
9,000	129.63	133.52	137.53	141.65	145.90
10,000	144.03	148.36	152.81	157.39	162.11
15,000	216.05	222.53	229.21	236.09	243.17
20,000	288.07	296.71	305.61	314.78	324.22
25,000	360.09	370.89	382.02	393.48	405.28
30,000	432.10	445.07	458.42	472.17	486.34
35,000	504.12	519.25	534.82	550.87	567.39
40,000	576.14	593.42	611.23	629.56	648.45
45,000	648.16	667.60	687.63	708.26	729.51
50,000	720.17	741.78	764.03	786.95	810.56
55,000	792.19	815.96	840.44	865.65	891.62
60,000	864.21	890.13	916.84	944.34	972.67
65,000	936.23	964.31	993.24	1,023.04	1,053.73
70,000	1,008.24	1,038.49	1,069.65	1,101.73	1,134.79
75,000	1,080.26	1,112.67	1,146.05	1,180.43	1,215.84
80,000	1,152.28	1,186.85	1,222.45	1,259.13	1,296.90
85,000	1,224.30	1,261.02	1,298.85	1,337.82	1,377.96
90,000	1,296.31	1,335.20	1,375.26	1,416.52	1,459.01
95,000	1,368.33	1,409.38	1,451.66	1,495.21	1,540.07
100,000	1,440.35	1,483.56	1,528.06	1,573.91	1,621.12
110,000	1,584.38	1,631.91	1,680.87	1,731.30	1,783.24
120,000	1,728.42	1,780.27	1,833.68	1,888.69	1,945.35
130,000	1,872.45	1,928.63	1,986.48	2,046.08	2,107.46
140,000	2,016.49	2,076.98	2,139.29	2,203.47	2,269.57
150,000	2,160.52	2,225.34	2,292.10	2,360.86	2,431.69
160,000	2,304.56	2,373.69	2,444.90	2,518.25	2,593.80
170,000	2,448.59	2,522.05	2,597.71	2,675.64	2,755.91
180,000	2,592.63	2,670.40	2,750.52	2,833.03	2,918.02
190,000	2,736.66	2,818.76	2,903.32	2,990.42	3,080.14
200,000	2,880.70	2,967.12	3,056.13	3,147.81	3,242.25

TABLE IV-83. Graduated Payment Mortgage, FHA Plan V at 17.0% Interest, Graduated at 3.0%

FHA GRADUATED PAYMENT PLAN V
TERM: 30 YEARS INTEREST: 17.00% GRADUATED AT 3.00%

PAYMENT AMOUNT	YEAR 1	YEAR 2	YEAR 3	YEAR 4	YEAR 5	YEAR 6
50	0.62	0.64	0.66	0.68	0.70	0.72
100	1.24	1.28	1.32	1.36	1.40	1.44
200	2.49	2.56	2.64	2.72	2.80	2.89
300	3.73	3.85	3.96	4.08	4.20	4.33
400	4.98	5.13	5.28	5.44	5.60	5.77
500	6.22	6.41	6.60	6.80	7.01	7.22
600	7.47	7.69	7.92	8.16	8.41	8.66
700	8.71	8.98	9.24	9.52	9.81	10.10
800	9.96	10.26	10.57	10.88	11.21	11.55
900	11.20	11.54	11.89	12.24	12.61	12.99
1,000	12.45	12.82	13.21	13.60	14.01	14.43
2,000	24.90	25.64	26.41	27.21	28.02	28.86
3,000	37.35	38.47	39.62	40.81	42.03	43.29
4,000	49.79	51.29	52.83	54.41	56.04	57.73
5,000	62.24	64.11	66.03	68.01	70.05	72.16
6,000	74.69	76.93	79.24	81.62	84.07	86.59
7,000	87.14	89.75	92.45	95.22	98.08	101.02
8,000	99.59	102.58	105.65	108.82	112.09	115.45
9,000	112.04	115.40	118.86	122.43	126.10	129.88
10,000	124.49	128.22	132.07	136.03	140.11	144.31
15,000	186.73	192.33	198.10	204.04	210.16	216.47
20,000	248.97	256.44	264.13	272.06	280.22	288.63
25,000	311.21	320.55	330.17	340.07	350.27	360.78
30,000	373.46	384.66	396.20	408.09	420.33	432.94
35,000	435.70	448.77	462.23	476.10	490.38	505.10
40,000	497.94	512.88	528.27	544.12	560.44	577.25
45,000	560.19	576.99	594.30	612.13	630.49	649.41
50,000	622.43	641.10	660.33	680.14	700.55	721.57
55,000	684.67	705.21	726.37	748.16	770.60	793.72
60,000	746.91	769.32	792.40	816.17	840.66	865.88
65,000	809.16	833.43	858.43	884.19	910.71	938.04
70,000	871.40	897.54	924.47	952.20	980.77	1,010.19
75,000	933.64	961.65	990.50	1,020.22	1,050.82	1,082.35
80,000	995.89	1,025.76	1,056.54	1,088.23	1,120.88	1,154.50
85,000	1,058.13	1,089.87	1,122.57	1,156.25	1,190.93	1,226.66
90,000	1,120.37	1,153.98	1,188.60	1,224.26	1,260.99	1,298.82
95,000	1,182.61	1,218.09	1,254.64	1,292.27	1,331.04	1,370.97
100,000	1,244.86	1,282.20	1,320.67	1,360.29	1,401.10	1,443.13
110,000	1,369.34	1,410.42	1,452.74	1,496.32	1,541.21	1,587.44
120,000	1,493.83	1,538.64	1,584.80	1,632.35	1,681.32	1,731.76
130,000	1,618.31	1,666.86	1,716.87	1,768.38	1,821.43	1,876.07
140,000	1,742.80	1,795.08	1,848.94	1,904.40	1,961.54	2,020.38
150,000	1,867.29	1,923.30	1,981.00	2,040.43	2,101.65	2,164.70
160,000	1,991.77	2,051.52	2,113.07	2,176.46	2,241.76	2,309.01
170,000	2,116.26	2,179.75	2,245.14	2,312.49	2,381.87	2,453.32
180,000	2,240.74	2,307.97	2,377.20	2,448.52	2,521.98	2,597.64
190,000	2,365.23	2,436.19	2,509.27	2,584.55	2,662.09	2,741.95
200,000	2,489.71	2,564.41	2,641.34	2,720.58	2,802.20	2,886.26

TABLE IV-83. (*Continued*)

FHA GRADUATED PAYMENT PLAN V
TERM:30 YEARS INTEREST:17.00% GRADUATED AT 3.00%

PAYMENT AMOUNT	YEAR 7	YEAR 8	YEAR 9	YEAR 10	YEARS 11-30
50	0.74	0.77	0.79	0.81	0.84
100	1.49	1.53	1.58	1.62	1.67
200	2.97	3.06	3.15	3.25	3.35
300	4.46	4.59	4.73	4.87	5.02
400	5.95	6.12	6.31	6.50	6.69
500	7.43	7.66	7.88	8.12	8.36
600	8.92	9.19	9.46	9.75	10.04
700	10.40	10.72	11.04	11.37	11.71
800	11.89	12.25	12.62	12.99	13.38
900	13.38	13.78	14.19	14.62	15.06
1,000	14.86	15.31	15.77	16.24	16.73
2,000	29.73	30.62	31.54	32.49	33.46
3,000	44.59	45.93	47.31	48.73	50.19
4,000	59.46	61.24	63.08	64.97	66.92
5,000	74.32	76.55	78.85	81.21	83.65
6,000	89.19	91.86	94.62	97.46	100.38
7,000	104.05	107.17	110.39	113.70	117.11
8,000	118.91	122.48	126.16	129.94	133.84
9,000	133.78	137.79	141.93	146.18	150.57
10,000	148.64	153.10	157.69	162.43	167.30
15,000	222.96	229.65	236.54	243.64	250.95
20,000	297.28	306.20	315.39	324.85	334.60
25,000	371.61	382.75	394.24	406.06	418.25
30,000	445.93	459.31	473.08	487.28	501.90
35,000	520.25	535.86	551.93	568.49	585.54
40,000	594.57	612.41	630.78	649.70	669.19
45,000	668.89	688.96	709.63	730.92	752.84
50,000	743.21	765.51	788.47	812.13	836.49
55,000	817.53	842.06	867.32	893.34	920.14
60,000	891.85	918.61	946.17	974.55	1,003.79
65,000	966.18	995.16	1,025.02	1,055.77	1,087.44
70,000	1,040.50	1,071.71	1,103.86	1,136.98	1,171.09
75,000	1,114.82	1,148.26	1,182.71	1,218.19	1,254.74
80,000	1,189.14	1,224.81	1,261.56	1,299.41	1,338.39
85,000	1,263.46	1,301.36	1,340.41	1,380.62	1,422.04
90,000	1,337.78	1,377.92	1,419.25	1,461.83	1,505.69
95,000	1,412.10	1,454.47	1,498.10	1,543.04	1,589.33
100,000	1,486.42	1,531.02	1,576.95	1,624.26	1,672.98
110,000	1,635.07	1,684.12	1,734.64	1,786.68	1,840.28
120,000	1,783.71	1,837.22	1,892.34	1,949.11	2,007.58
130,000	1,932.35	1,990.32	2,050.03	2,111.53	2,174.88
140,000	2,080.99	2,143.42	2,207.73	2,273.96	2,342.18
150,000	2,229.64	2,296.53	2,365.42	2,436.38	2,509.48
160,000	2,378.28	2,449.63	2,523.12	2,598.81	2,676.77
170,000	2,526.92	2,602.73	2,680.81	2,761.24	2,844.07
180,000	2,675.56	2,755.83	2,838.51	2,923.66	3,011.37
190,000	2,824.21	2,908.93	2,996.20	3,086.09	3,178.67
200,000	2,972.85	3,062.03	3,153.90	3,248.51	3,345.97

TABLE IV-84. Graduated Payment Mortgage, FHA Plan V at 17.5% Interest, Graduated at 3.0%

FHA GRADUATED PAYMENT PLAN V
TERM:30 YEARS INTEREST:17.50% GRADUATED AT 3.00%

PAYMENT AMOUNT	YEAR 1	YEAR 2	YEAR 3	YEAR 4	YEAR 5	YEAR 6
50	0.64	0.66	0.68	0.70	0.72	0.74
100	1.28	1.32	1.36	1.40	1.44	1.49
200	2.57	2.64	2.72	2.81	2.89	2.98
300	3.85	3.97	4.09	4.21	4.33	4.46
400	5.13	5.29	5.45	5.61	5.78	5.95
500	6.42	6.61	6.81	7.01	7.22	7.44
600	7.70	7.93	8.17	8.42	8.67	8.93
700	8.99	9.26	9.53	9.82	10.11	10.42
800	10.27	10.58	10.89	11.22	11.56	11.91
900	11.55	11.90	12.26	12.62	13.00	13.39
1,000	12.84	13.22	13.62	14.03	14.45	14.88
2,000	25.67	26.44	27.24	28.05	28.90	29.76
3,000	38.51	39.67	40.86	42.08	43.34	44.64
4,000	51.35	52.89	54.47	56.11	57.79	59.53
5,000	64.18	66.11	68.09	70.14	72.24	74.41
6,000	77.02	79.33	81.71	84.16	86.69	89.29
7,000	89.86	92.55	95.33	98.19	101.14	104.17
8,000	102.69	105.77	108.95	112.22	115.58	119.05
9,000	115.53	119.00	122.57	126.24	130.03	133.93
10,000	128.37	132.22	136.19	140.27	144.48	148.81
15,000	192.55	198.33	204.28	210.41	216.72	223.22
20,000	256.73	264.44	272.37	280.54	288.96	297.63
25,000	320.92	330.55	340.46	350.68	361.20	372.03
30,000	385.10	396.66	408.56	420.81	433.44	446.44
35,000	449.29	462.76	476.65	490.95	505.68	520.85
40,000	513.47	528.87	544.74	561.08	577.91	595.25
45,000	577.65	594.98	612.83	631.22	650.15	669.66
50,000	641.84	661.09	680.93	701.35	722.39	744.07
55,000	706.02	727.20	749.02	771.49	794.63	818.47
60,000	770.20	793.31	817.11	841.62	866.87	892.88
65,000	834.39	859.42	885.20	911.76	939.11	967.28
70,000	898.57	925.53	953.30	981.89	1,011.35	1,041.69
75,000	962.76	991.64	1,021.39	1,052.03	1,083.59	1,116.10
80,000	1,026.94	1,057.75	1,089.48	1,122.16	1,155.83	1,190.50
85,000	1,091.12	1,123.86	1,157.57	1,192.30	1,228.07	1,264.91
90,000	1,155.31	1,189.97	1,225.67	1,262.44	1,300.31	1,339.32
95,000	1,219.49	1,256.08	1,293.76	1,332.57	1,372.55	1,413.72
100,000	1,283.67	1,322.18	1,361.85	1,402.71	1,444.79	1,488.13
110,000	1,412.04	1,454.40	1,498.04	1,542.98	1,589.27	1,636.94
120,000	1,540.41	1,586.62	1,634.22	1,683.25	1,733.74	1,785.76
130,000	1,668.78	1,718.84	1,770.41	1,823.52	1,878.22	1,934.57
140,000	1,797.14	1,851.06	1,906.59	1,963.79	2,022.70	2,083.38
150,000	1,925.51	1,983.28	2,042.78	2,104.06	2,167.18	2,232.20
160,000	2,053.88	2,115.50	2,178.96	2,244.33	2,311.66	2,381.01
170,000	2,182.25	2,247.71	2,315.15	2,384.60	2,456.14	2,529.82
180,000	2,310.61	2,379.93	2,451.33	2,524.87	2,600.62	2,678.64
190,000	2,438.98	2,512.15	2,587.52	2,665.14	2,745.10	2,827.45
200,000	2,567.35	2,644.37	2,723.70	2,805.41	2,889.57	2,976.26

TABLE IV-84. (Continued)

FHA GRADUATED PAYMENT PLAN V
TERM:30 YEARS INTEREST:17.50% GRADUATED AT 3.00%

PAYMENT AMCUNT	YEAR 7	YEAR 8	YEAR 9	YEAR 10	YEARS 11-30
50	0.77	0.79	0.81	0.84	0.86
100	1.53	1.58	1.63	1.67	1.73
200	3.07	3.16	3.25	3.35	3.45
300	4.60	4.74	4.88	5.02	5.18
400	6.13	6.32	6.50	6.70	6.90
500	7.66	7.89	8.13	8.37	8.63
600	9.20	9.47	9.76	10.05	10.35
700	10.73	11.05	11.38	11.72	12.08
800	12.26	12.63	13.01	13.40	13.80
900	13.79	14.21	14.64	15.07	15.53
1,000	15.33	15.79	16.26	16.75	17.25
2,000	30.66	31.58	32.52	33.50	34.50
3,000	45.98	47.36	48.78	50.25	51.75
4,000	61.31	63.15	65.04	67.00	69.01
5,000	76.64	78.94	81.31	83.75	86.26
6,000	91.97	94.73	97.57	100.49	103.51
7,000	107.29	110.51	113.83	117.24	120.76
8,000	122.62	126.30	130.09	133.99	138.01
9,000	137.95	142.09	146.35	150.74	155.26
10,000	153.28	157.88	162.61	167.49	172.52
15,000	229.92	236.81	243.92	251.24	258.77
20,000	306.55	315.75	325.22	334.98	345.03
25,000	383.19	394.69	406.53	418.73	431.29
30,000	459.83	473.63	487.84	502.47	517.55
35,000	536.47	552.57	569.14	586.22	603.80
40,000	613.11	631.50	650.45	669.96	690.06
45,000	689.75	710.44	731.75	753.71	776.32
50,000	766.39	789.38	813.06	837.45	862.58
55,000	843.03	868.32	894.37	921.20	948.83
60,000	919.66	947.25	975.67	1,004.94	1,035.09
65,000	996.30	1,026.19	1,056.98	1,088.69	1,121.35
70,000	1,072.94	1,105.13	1,138.28	1,172.43	1,207.61
75,000	1,149.58	1,184.07	1,219.59	1,256.18	1,293.86
80,000	1,226.22	1,263.01	1,300.90	1,339.92	1,380.12
85,000	1,302.86	1,341.94	1,382.20	1,423.67	1,466.38
90,000	1,379.50	1,420.88	1,463.51	1,507.41	1,552.64
95,000	1,456.14	1,499.82	1,544.81	1,591.16	1,638.89
100,000	1,532.77	1,578.76	1,626.12	1,674.90	1,725.15
110,000	1,686.05	1,736.63	1,788.73	1,842.39	1,897.67
120,000	1,839.33	1,894.51	1,951.34	2,009.89	2,070.18
130,000	1,992.61	2,052.39	2,113.96	2,177.38	2,242.70
140,000	2,145.88	2,210.26	2,276.57	2,344.87	2,415.21
150,000	2,299.16	2,368.14	2,439.18	2,512.36	2,587.73
160,000	2,452.44	2,526.01	2,601.79	2,679.85	2,760.24
170,000	2,605.72	2,683.89	2,764.40	2,847.34	2,932.76
180,000	2,758.99	2,841.76	2,927.02	3,014.83	3,105.27
190,000	2,912.27	2,999.64	3,089.63	3,182.32	3,277.79
200,000	3,065.55	3,157.52	3,252.24	3,349.81	3,450.30

TABLE IV-85. Graduated Payment Mortgage, FHA Plan V at 18.0% Interest, Graduated at 3.0%

FHA GRADUATED PAYMENT PLAN V
TERM:30 YEARS INTEREST:18.00% GRADUATED AT 3.00%

PAYMENT AMCUNT	YEAR 1	YEAR 2	YEAR 3	YEAR 4	YEAR 5	YEAR 6
50	0.66	0.68	0.70	0.72	0.74	0.77
100	1.32	1.36	1.40	1.45	1.49	1.53
200	2.65	2.72	2.81	2.89	2.98	3.07
300	3.97	4.09	4.21	4.34	4.47	4.6C
400	5.29	5.45	5.61	5.78	5.95	6.13
500	6.61	6.81	7.02	7.23	7.44	7.67
600	7.94	8.17	8.42	8.67	8.93	9.20
700	9.26	9.54	9.82	10.12	10.42	10.73
800	10.58	10.90	11.23	11.56	11.91	12.27
900	11.90	12.26	12.63	13.01	13.40	13.80
1,000	13.23	13.62	14.03	14.45	14.89	15.33
2,000	26.45	27.25	28.07	28.91	29.77	30.67
3,000	39.68	40.87	42.10	43.36	44.66	46.00
4,000	52.91	54.50	56.13	57.81	59.55	61.34
5,000	66.14	68.12	70.16	72.27	74.44	76.67
6,000	79.36	81.74	84.20	86.72	89.32	92.00
7,000	92.59	95.37	98.23	101.17	104.21	107.34
8,000	105.82	108.99	112.26	115.63	119.10	122.67
9,000	119.04	122.61	126.29	130.08	133.98	138.CC
10,000	132.27	136.24	140.33	144.54	148.87	153.34
15,000	198.41	204.36	210.49	216.80	223.31	230.01
20,000	264.54	272.48	280.65	289.07	297.74	306.68
25,000	330.68	340.60	350.81	361.34	372.18	383.34
30,000	396.81	4C8.72	420.98	433.61	446.61	460.01
35,000	462.95	476.84	491.14	505.87	521.05	536.68
40,000	529.C8	544.95	561.30	578.14	595.49	613.35
45,000	595.22	613.07	631.47	650.41	669.92	690.02
50,000	661.35	681.19	701.63	722.68	744.36	766.69
55,000	727.49	749.31	771.79	794.95	818.79	843.36
60,000	793.62	817.43	841.95	867.21	893.23	920.03
65,000	859.76	885.55	912.12	939.48	967.67	996.70
70,000	925.89	953.67	982.28	1,011.75	1,042.10	1,073.36
75,000	992.03	1,021.79	1,052.44	1,084.02	1,116.54	1,150.C3
80,000	1,058.16	1,089.91	1,122.61	1,156.28	1,190.97	1,226.7C
85,000	1,124.30	1,158.03	1,192.77	1,228.55	1,265.41	1,303.37
90,000	1,190.43	1,226.15	1,262.93	1,300.82	1,339.84	1,380.04
95,000	1,256.57	1,294.27	1,333.09	1,373.09	1,414.28	1,456.71
100,000	1,322.70	1,362.39	1,403.26	1,445.36	1,488.72	1,533.38
110,000	1,454.98	1,498.62	1,543.58	1,589.89	1,637.59	1,686.71
120,000	1,587.25	1,634.86	1,683.91	1,734.43	1,786.46	1,840.05
130,000	1,719.52	1,771.10	1,824.23	1,878.96	1,935.33	1,993.39
140,000	1,851.79	1,907.34	1,964.56	2,023.50	2,084.20	2,146.73
150,000	1,984.06	2,043.58	2,104.89	2,168.03	2,233.07	2,300.07
160,000	2,116.33	2,179.82	2,245.21	2,312.57	2,381.95	2,453.4C
170,000	2,248.60	2,316.06	2,385.54	2,457.10	2,530.82	2,606.74
180,000	2,380.87	2,452.29	2,525.86	2,601.64	2,679.69	2,760.08
190,000	2,513.14	2,588.53	2,666.19	2,746.17	2,828.56	2,913.42
200,000	2,645.41	2,724.77	2,806.51	2,890.71	2,977.43	3,066.75

TABLE IV-85. (*Continued*)

FHA GRADUATED PAYMENT PLAN V
TERM:30 YEARS INTEREST:18.00% GRADUATED AT 3.00%

PAYMENT AMCUNT	YEAR 7	YEAR 8	YEAR 9	YEAR 10	YEARS 11-30
50	0.79	0.81	0.84	0.86	0.89
100	1.58	1.63	1.68	1.73	1.78
200	3.16	3.25	3.35	3.45	3.56
300	4.74	4.88	5.03	5.18	5.33
400	6.32	6.51	6.70	6.90	7.11
500	7.90	8.13	8.38	8.63	8.89
600	9.48	9.76	10.05	10.35	10.67
700	11.06	11.39	11.73	12.08	12.44
800	12.64	13.01	13.40	13.81	14.22
900	14.21	14.64	15.08	15.53	16.00
1,000	15.79	16.27	16.76	17.26	17.78
2,000	31.59	32.54	33.51	34.52	35.55
3,000	47.38	48.80	50.27	51.77	53.33
4,000	63.18	65.07	67.02	69.03	71.10
5,000	78.97	81.34	83.78	86.29	88.88
6,000	94.76	97.61	100.53	103.55	106.66
7,000	110.56	113.87	117.29	120.81	124.43
8,000	126.35	130.14	134.05	138.07	142.21
9,000	142.14	146.41	150.80	155.32	159.98
10,000	157.94	162.68	167.56	172.58	177.76
15,000	236.91	244.01	251.33	258.87	266.64
20,000	315.88	325.35	335.11	345.17	355.52
25,000	394.84	406.69	418.89	431.46	444.40
30,000	473.81	488.03	502.67	517.75	533.28
35,000	552.78	569.37	586.45	604.04	622.16
40,000	631.75	650.70	670.23	690.33	711.04
45,000	710.72	732.04	754.00	776.62	799.92
50,000	789.69	813.38	837.78	862.91	888.80
55,000	868.66	894.72	921.56	949.21	977.68
60,000	947.63	976.06	1,005.34	1,035.50	1,066.56
65,000	1,026.60	1,057.39	1,089.12	1,121.79	1,155.44
70,000	1,105.56	1,138.73	1,172.89	1,208.08	1,244.32
75,000	1,184.53	1,220.07	1,256.67	1,294.37	1,333.20
80,000	1,263.50	1,301.41	1,340.45	1,380.66	1,422.08
85,000	1,342.47	1,382.75	1,424.23	1,466.96	1,510.96
90,000	1,421.44	1,464.08	1,508.01	1,553.25	1,599.84
95,000	1,500.41	1,545.42	1,591.78	1,639.54	1,688.72
100,000	1,579.38	1,626.76	1,675.56	1,725.83	1,777.60
110,000	1,737.32	1,789.44	1,843.12	1,898.41	1,955.36
120,000	1,895.25	1,952.11	2,010.68	2,071.00	2,133.13
130,000	2,053.19	2,114.79	2,178.23	2,243.58	2,310.89
140,000	2,211.13	2,277.46	2,345.79	2,416.16	2,488.65
150,000	2,369.07	2,440.14	2,513.34	2,588.74	2,666.41
160,000	2,527.01	2,602.82	2,680.90	2,761.33	2,844.17
170,000	2,684.94	2,765.49	2,848.46	2,933.91	3,021.93
180,000	2,842.88	2,928.17	3,016.01	3,106.49	3,199.69
190,000	3,000.82	3,090.84	3,183.57	3,279.08	3,377.45
200,000	3,158.76	3,253.52	3,351.13	3,451.66	3,555.21

TABLE IV-86. Graduated Payment Mortgage, FHA Plan V at 18.5% Interest, Graduated at 3.0%

FHA GRADUATED PAYMENT PLAN V
TERM:30 YEARS INTEREST:18.50% GRADUATED AT 3.00%

PAYMENT AMOUNT	YEAR 1	YEAR 2	YEAR 3	YEAR 4	YEAR 5	YEAR 6
50	0.68	0.70	0.72	0.74	0.77	0.79
100	1.36	1.40	1.44	1.49	1.53	1.58
200	2.72	2.81	2.89	2.98	3.07	3.16
300	4.09	4.21	4.33	4.46	4.60	4.74
400	5.45	5.61	5.78	5.95	6.13	6.32
500	6.81	7.01	7.22	7.44	7.66	7.89
600	8.17	8.42	8.67	8.93	9.20	9.47
700	9.53	9.82	10.11	10.42	10.73	11.05
800	10.90	11.22	11.56	11.91	12.26	12.63
900	12.26	12.63	13.00	13.39	13.80	14.21
1,000	13.62	14.03	14.45	14.88	15.33	15.79
2,000	27.24	28.06	28.90	29.76	30.66	31.58
3,000	40.86	42.08	43.35	44.65	45.99	47.37
4,000	54.48	56.11	57.79	59.53	61.31	63.15
5,000	68.10	70.14	72.24	74.41	76.64	78.94
6,000	81.72	84.17	86.69	89.29	91.97	94.73
7,000	95.34	98.20	101.14	104.18	107.30	110.52
8,000	108.95	112.22	115.59	119.06	122.63	126.31
9,000	122.57	126.25	130.04	133.94	137.96	142.10
10,000	136.19	140.28	144.49	148.82	153.29	157.89
15,000	204.29	210.42	216.73	223.23	229.93	236.83
20,000	272.39	280.56	288.97	297.64	306.57	315.77
25,000	340.48	350.70	361.22	372.06	383.22	394.71
30,000	408.58	420.84	433.46	446.47	459.86	473.66
35,000	476.68	490.98	505.71	520.88	536.50	552.60
40,000	544.77	561.12	577.95	595.29	613.15	631.54
45,000	612.87	631.26	650.19	669.70	689.79	710.48
50,000	680.97	701.40	722.44	744.11	766.43	789.43
55,000	749.06	771.53	794.68	818.52	843.08	868.37
60,000	817.16	841.67	866.92	892.93	919.72	947.31
65,000	885.26	911.81	939.17	967.34	996.36	1,026.25
70,000	953.35	981.95	1,011.41	1,041.75	1,073.01	1,105.20
75,000	1,021.45	1,052.09	1,083.66	1,116.17	1,149.65	1,184.14
80,000	1,089.55	1,122.23	1,155.90	1,190.58	1,226.29	1,263.08
85,000	1,157.64	1,192.37	1,228.14	1,264.99	1,302.94	1,342.03
90,000	1,225.74	1,262.51	1,300.39	1,339.40	1,379.58	1,420.97
95,000	1,293.84	1,332.65	1,372.63	1,413.81	1,456.22	1,499.91
100,000	1,361.93	1,402.79	1,444.87	1,488.22	1,532.87	1,578.85
110,000	1,498.13	1,543.07	1,589.36	1,637.04	1,686.15	1,736.74
120,000	1,634.32	1,683.35	1,733.85	1,785.86	1,839.44	1,894.62
130,000	1,770.51	1,823.63	1,878.34	1,934.69	1,992.73	2,052.51
140,000	1,906.71	1,963.91	2,022.82	2,083.51	2,146.01	2,210.39
150,000	2,042.90	2,104.19	2,167.31	2,232.33	2,299.30	2,368.28
160,000	2,179.09	2,244.47	2,311.80	2,381.15	2,452.59	2,526.17
170,000	2,315.29	2,384.74	2,456.29	2,529.98	2,605.87	2,684.05
180,000	2,451.48	2,525.02	2,600.77	2,678.80	2,759.16	2,841.94
190,000	2,587.67	2,665.30	2,745.26	2,827.62	2,912.45	2,999.82
200,000	2,723.87	2,805.58	2,889.75	2,976.44	3,065.73	3,157.71

TABLE IV-86. (*Continued*)

FHA GRADUATED PAYMENT PLAN V
TERM:30 YEARS INTEREST:18.50% GRADUATED AT 3.00%

PAYMENT AMOUNT	YEAR 7	YEAR 8	YEAR 9	YEAR 10	YEARS 11-30
50	0.81	0.84	0.86	0.89	0.92
100	1.63	1.68	1.73	1.78	1.83
200	3.25	3.35	3.45	3.55	3.66
300	4.88	5.03	5.18	5.33	5.49
400	6.50	6.70	6.90	7.11	7.32
500	8.13	8.38	8.63	8.89	9.15
600	9.76	10.05	10.35	10.66	10.98
700	11.38	11.73	12.08	12.44	12.81
800	13.01	13.40	13.80	14.22	14.64
900	14.64	15.08	15.53	15.99	16.47
1,000	16.26	16.75	17.25	17.77	18.30
2,000	32.52	33.50	34.51	35.54	36.61
3,000	48.79	50.25	51.76	53.31	54.91
4,000	65.05	67.00	69.01	71.08	73.21
5,000	81.31	83.75	86.26	88.85	91.52
6,000	97.57	100.50	103.52	106.62	109.82
7,000	113.84	117.25	120.77	124.39	128.12
8,000	130.10	134.00	138.02	142.16	146.43
9,000	146.36	150.75	155.27	159.93	164.73
10,000	162.62	167.50	172.53	177.70	183.03
15,000	243.93	251.25	258.79	266.55	274.55
20,000	325.24	335.00	345.05	355.40	366.06
25,000	406.55	418.75	431.31	444.25	457.58
30,000	487.87	502.50	517.58	533.10	549.10
35,000	569.18	586.25	603.84	621.95	640.61
40,000	650.49	670.00	690.10	710.81	732.13
45,000	731.80	753.75	776.37	799.66	823.65
50,000	813.11	837.50	862.63	888.51	915.16
55,000	894.42	921.25	948.89	977.36	1,006.68
60,000	975.73	1,005.00	1,035.15	1,066.21	1,098.19
65,000	1,057.04	1,088.75	1,121.42	1,155.06	1,189.71
70,000	1,138.35	1,172.50	1,207.68	1,243.91	1,281.23
75,000	1,219.66	1,256.25	1,293.94	1,332.76	1,372.74
80,000	1,300.98	1,340.00	1,380.20	1,421.61	1,464.26
85,000	1,382.29	1,423.75	1,466.47	1,510.46	1,555.78
90,000	1,463.60	1,507.50	1,552.73	1,599.31	1,647.29
95,000	1,544.91	1,591.26	1,638.99	1,688.16	1,738.81
100,000	1,626.22	1,675.01	1,725.26	1,777.01	1,830.32
110,000	1,788.84	1,842.51	1,897.78	1,954.71	2,013.36
120,000	1,951.46	2,010.01	2,070.31	2,132.42	2,196.39
130,000	2,114.08	2,177.51	2,242.83	2,310.12	2,379.42
140,000	2,276.71	2,345.01	2,415.36	2,487.82	2,562.45
150,000	2,439.33	2,512.51	2,587.88	2,665.52	2,745.49
160,000	2,601.95	2,680.01	2,760.41	2,843.22	2,928.52
170,000	2,764.57	2,847.51	2,932.93	3,020.92	3,111.55
180,000	2,927.19	3,015.01	3,105.46	3,198.62	3,294.58
190,000	3,089.82	3,182.51	3,277.99	3,376.33	3,477.62
200,000	3,252.44	3,350.01	3,450.51	3,554.03	3,660.65

TABLE IV-87. Graduated Payment Mortgage, FHA Plan V at 19.0% Interest, Graduated at 3.0%

FHA GRADUATED PAYMENT PLAN V
TERM: 30 YEARS INTEREST: 19.00% GRADUATED AT 3.00%

PAYMENT AMCUNT	YEAR 1	YEAR 2	YEAR 3	YEAR 4	YEAR 5	YEAR 6
50	0.70	0.72	0.74	0.77	0.79	0.81
100	1.40	1.44	1.49	1.53	1.58	1.62
200	2.80	2.89	2.97	3.06	3.15	3.25
300	4.20	4.33	4.46	4.59	4.73	4.87
400	5.61	5.77	5.95	6.13	6.31	6.50
500	7.01	7.22	7.43	7.66	7.89	8.12
600	8.41	8.66	8.92	9.19	9.46	9.75
700	9.81	10.10	10.41	10.72	11.04	11.37
800	11.21	11.55	11.89	12.25	12.62	13.00
900	12.61	12.99	13.38	13.78	14.20	14.62
1,000	14.01	14.43	14.87	15.31	15.77	16.25
2,000	28.03	28.87	29.73	30.63	31.54	32.49
3,000	42.04	43.30	44.60	45.94	47.32	48.74
4,000	56.05	57.74	59.47	61.25	63.09	64.98
5,000	70.07	72.17	74.33	76.56	78.86	81.23
6,000	84.08	86.60	89.20	91.88	94.63	97.47
7,000	98.09	101.04	104.07	107.19	110.41	113.72
8,000	112.11	115.47	118.93	122.50	126.18	129.96
9,000	126.12	129.90	133.80	137.82	141.95	146.21
10,000	140.13	144.34	148.67	153.13	157.72	162.45
15,000	210.20	216.51	223.00	229.69	236.58	243.68
20,000	280.27	288.68	297.34	306.26	315.45	324.91
25,000	350.34	360.85	371.67	382.82	394.31	406.14
30,000	420.40	433.02	446.01	459.39	473.17	487.36
35,000	490.47	505.19	520.34	535.95	552.03	568.59
40,000	560.54	577.35	594.67	612.52	630.89	649.82
45,000	630.61	649.52	669.01	689.08	709.75	731.04
50,000	700.67	721.69	743.34	765.64	788.61	812.27
55,000	770.74	793.86	817.68	842.21	867.47	893.50
60,000	840.81	866.03	892.01	918.77	946.34	974.73
65,000	910.87	938.20	966.35	995.34	1,025.20	1,055.95
70,000	980.94	1,010.37	1,040.68	1,071.90	1,104.06	1,137.18
75,000	1,051.01	1,082.54	1,115.02	1,148.47	1,182.92	1,218.41
80,000	1,121.08	1,154.71	1,189.35	1,225.03	1,261.78	1,299.63
85,000	1,191.14	1,226.88	1,263.68	1,301.59	1,340.64	1,380.86
90,000	1,261.21	1,299.05	1,338.02	1,378.16	1,419.50	1,462.09
95,000	1,331.28	1,371.22	1,412.35	1,454.72	1,498.37	1,543.32
100,000	1,401.35	1,443.39	1,486.69	1,531.29	1,577.23	1,624.54
110,000	1,541.48	1,587.72	1,635.36	1,684.42	1,734.95	1,787.00
120,000	1,681.61	1,732.06	1,784.02	1,837.55	1,892.67	1,949.45
130,000	1,821.75	1,876.40	1,932.69	1,990.67	2,050.39	2,111.91
140,000	1,961.88	2,020.74	2,081.36	2,143.80	2,208.12	2,274.36
150,000	2,102.02	2,165.08	2,230.03	2,296.93	2,365.84	2,436.82
160,000	2,242.15	2,309.42	2,378.70	2,450.06	2,523.56	2,599.27
170,000	2,382.29	2,453.76	2,527.37	2,603.19	2,681.29	2,761.72
180,000	2,522.42	2,598.09	2,676.04	2,756.32	2,839.01	2,924.18
190,000	2,662.56	2,742.43	2,824.71	2,909.45	2,996.73	3,086.63
200,000	2,802.69	2,886.77	2,973.37	3,062.58	3,154.45	3,249.09

TABLE IV-87. (*Continued*)

FHA GRADUATED PAYMENT PLAN V
TERM:30 YEARS INTEREST:19.00% GRADUATED AT 3.00%

PAYMENT AMOUNT	YEAR 7	YEAR 8	YEAR 9	YEAR 10	YEARS 11-30
50	0.84	0.86	0.89	0.91	0.94
100	1.67	1.72	1.78	1.83	1.88
200	3.35	3.45	3.55	3.66	3.77
300	5.02	5.17	5.33	5.49	5.65
400	6.69	6.89	7.10	7.31	7.53
500	8.37	8.62	8.88	9.14	9.42
600	10.04	10.34	10.65	10.97	11.30
700	11.71	12.06	12.43	12.80	13.18
800	13.39	13.79	14.20	14.63	15.07
900	15.06	15.51	15.98	16.46	16.95
1,000	16.73	17.23	17.75	18.28	18.83
2,000	33.47	34.47	35.50	36.57	37.67
3,000	50.20	51.70	53.26	54.85	56.50
4,000	66.93	68.94	71.01	73.14	75.33
5,000	83.66	86.17	88.76	91.42	94.16
6,000	100.40	103.41	106.51	109.71	113.00
7,000	117.13	120.64	124.26	127.99	131.83
8,000	133.86	137.88	142.01	146.28	150.66
9,000	150.60	155.11	159.77	164.56	169.50
10,000	167.33	172.35	177.52	182.84	188.33
15,000	250.99	258.52	266.28	274.27	282.49
20,000	334.66	344.70	355.04	365.69	376.66
25,000	418.32	430.87	443.80	457.11	470.82
30,000	501.98	517.04	532.55	548.53	564.99
35,000	585.65	603.22	621.31	639.95	659.15
40,000	669.31	689.39	710.07	731.38	753.32
45,000	752.98	775.57	798.83	822.80	847.48
50,000	836.64	861.74	887.59	914.22	941.65
55,000	920.30	947.91	976.35	1,005.64	1,035.81
60,000	1,003.97	1,034.09	1,065.11	1,097.06	1,129.97
65,000	1,087.63	1,120.26	1,153.87	1,188.48	1,224.14
70,000	1,171.30	1,206.43	1,242.63	1,279.91	1,318.30
75,000	1,254.96	1,292.61	1,331.39	1,371.33	1,412.47
80,000	1,338.62	1,378.78	1,420.15	1,462.75	1,506.63
85,000	1,422.29	1,464.96	1,508.91	1,554.17	1,600.80
90,000	1,505.95	1,551.13	1,597.66	1,645.59	1,694.96
95,000	1,589.62	1,637.30	1,686.42	1,737.02	1,789.13
100,000	1,673.28	1,723.48	1,775.18	1,828.44	1,883.29
110,000	1,840.61	1,895.83	1,952.70	2,011.28	2,071.62
120,000	2,007.94	2,068.17	2,130.22	2,194.13	2,259.95
130,000	2,175.26	2,240.52	2,307.74	2,376.97	2,448.28
140,000	2,342.59	2,412.87	2,485.26	2,559.81	2,636.61
150,000	2,509.92	2,585.22	2,662.77	2,742.66	2,824.94
160,000	2,677.25	2,757.56	2,840.29	2,925.50	3,013.27
170,000	2,844.58	2,929.91	3,017.81	3,108.34	3,201.59
180,000	3,011.90	3,102.26	3,195.33	3,291.19	3,389.92
190,000	3,179.23	3,274.61	3,372.85	3,474.03	3,578.25
200,000	3,346.56	3,446.96	3,550.36	3,656.88	3,766.58

TABLE IV-88. Graduated Payment Mortgage, FHA Plan V at 19.5% Interest, Graduated at 3.0%

FHA GRADUATED PAYMENT PLAN V
TERM:30 YEARS INTEREST:19.50% GRADUATED AT 3.00%

PAYMENT AMOUNT	YEAR 1	YEAR 2	YEAR 3	YEAR 4	YEAR 5	YEAR 6
50	0.72	0.74	0.76	0.79	0.81	0.84
100	1.44	1.48	1.53	1.57	1.62	1.67
200	2.88	2.97	3.06	3.15	3.24	3.34
300	4.32	4.45	4.59	4.72	4.87	5.01
400	5.76	5.94	6.11	6.30	6.49	6.68
500	7.20	7.42	7.64	7.87	8.11	8.35
600	8.65	8.90	9.17	9.45	9.73	10.02
700	10.09	10.39	10.70	11.02	11.35	11.69
800	11.53	11.87	12.23	12.60	12.97	13.36
900	12.97	13.36	13.76	14.17	14.60	15.03
1,000	14.41	14.84	15.29	15.75	16.22	16.70
2,000	28.82	29.68	30.57	31.49	32.44	33.41
3,000	43.23	44.52	45.86	47.24	48.65	50.11
4,000	57.64	59.37	61.15	62.98	64.87	66.82
5,000	72.05	74.21	76.43	78.73	81.09	83.52
6,000	86.46	89.05	91.72	94.47	97.31	100.23
7,000	100.87	103.89	107.01	110.22	113.52	116.93
8,000	115.27	118.73	122.29	125.96	129.74	133.63
9,000	129.68	133.57	137.58	141.71	145.96	150.34
10,000	144.09	148.42	152.87	157.45	162.18	167.04
15,000	216.14	222.62	229.30	236.18	243.27	250.56
20,000	288.19	296.83	305.74	314.91	324.36	334.09
25,000	360.23	371.04	382.17	393.64	405.44	417.61
30,000	432.28	445.25	458.60	472.36	486.53	501.13
35,000	504.33	519.46	535.04	551.09	567.62	584.65
40,000	576.37	593.66	611.47	629.82	648.71	668.17
45,000	648.42	667.87	687.91	708.54	729.80	751.69
50,000	720.46	742.08	764.34	787.27	810.89	835.22
55,000	792.51	816.29	840.78	866.00	891.98	918.74
60,000	864.56	890.49	917.21	944.73	973.07	1,002.26
65,000	936.60	964.70	993.64	1,023.45	1,054.16	1,085.78
70,000	1,008.65	1,038.91	1,070.08	1,102.18	1,135.25	1,169.30
75,000	1,080.70	1,113.12	1,146.51	1,180.91	1,216.33	1,252.82
80,000	1,152.74	1,187.33	1,222.95	1,259.63	1,297.42	1,336.35
85,000	1,224.79	1,261.53	1,299.38	1,338.36	1,378.51	1,419.87
90,000	1,296.84	1,335.74	1,375.81	1,417.09	1,459.60	1,503.39
95,000	1,368.88	1,409.95	1,452.25	1,495.82	1,540.69	1,586.91
100,000	1,440.93	1,484.16	1,528.68	1,574.54	1,621.78	1,670.43
110,000	1,585.02	1,632.57	1,681.55	1,732.00	1,783.96	1,837.48
120,000	1,729.12	1,780.99	1,834.42	1,889.45	1,946.14	2,004.52
130,000	1,873.21	1,929.41	1,987.29	2,046.91	2,108.31	2,171.56
140,000	2,017.30	2,077.82	2,140.16	2,204.36	2,270.49	2,338.61
150,000	2,161.39	2,226.24	2,293.02	2,361.81	2,432.67	2,505.65
160,000	2,305.49	2,374.65	2,445.89	2,519.27	2,594.85	2,672.69
170,000	2,449.58	2,523.07	2,598.76	2,676.72	2,757.02	2,839.74
180,000	2,593.67	2,671.48	2,751.63	2,834.18	2,919.20	3,006.78
190,000	2,737.77	2,819.90	2,904.50	2,991.63	3,081.38	3,173.82
200,000	2,881.86	2,968.32	3,057.36	3,149.09	3,243.56	3,340.87

TABLE IV-88. (*Continued*)

FHA GRADUATED PAYMENT PLAN V
TERM:30 YEARS INTEREST:19.50% GRADUATED AT 3.00%

PAYMENT AMOUNT	YEAR 7	YEAR 8	YEAR 9	YEAR 10	YEARS 11-30
50	0.86	0.89	0.91	0.94	0.97
100	1.72	1.77	1.83	1.88	1.94
200	3.44	3.54	3.65	3.76	3.87
300	5.16	5.32	5.48	5.64	5.81
400	6.88	7.09	7.30	7.52	7.75
500	8.60	8.86	9.13	9.40	9.68
600	10.32	10.63	10.95	11.28	11.62
700	12.04	12.41	12.78	13.16	13.56
800	13.76	14.18	14.60	15.04	15.49
900	15.48	15.95	16.43	16.92	17.43
1,000	17.21	17.72	18.25	18.80	19.36
2,000	34.41	35.44	36.51	37.60	38.73
3,000	51.62	53.16	54.76	56.40	58.09
4,000	68.82	70.89	73.01	75.20	77.46
5,000	86.03	88.61	91.27	94.00	96.82
6,000	103.23	106.33	109.52	112.81	116.19
7,000	120.44	124.05	127.77	131.61	135.55
8,000	137.64	141.77	146.03	150.41	154.92
9,000	154.85	159.49	164.28	169.21	174.28
10,000	172.05	177.22	182.53	188.01	193.65
15,000	258.08	265.82	273.80	282.01	290.47
20,000	344.11	354.43	365.07	376.02	387.30
25,000	430.14	443.04	456.33	470.02	484.12
30,000	516.16	531.65	547.60	564.03	580.95
35,000	602.19	620.26	638.86	658.03	677.77
40,000	688.22	708.86	730.13	752.03	774.60
45,000	774.25	797.47	821.40	846.04	871.42
50,000	860.27	886.08	912.66	940.04	968.24
55,000	946.30	974.69	1,003.93	1,034.05	1,065.07
60,000	1,032.33	1,063.30	1,095.20	1,128.05	1,161.89
65,000	1,118.35	1,151.91	1,186.46	1,222.06	1,258.72
70,000	1,204.38	1,240.51	1,277.73	1,316.06	1,355.54
75,000	1,290.41	1,329.12	1,369.00	1,410.06	1,452.37
80,000	1,376.44	1,417.73	1,460.26	1,504.07	1,549.19
85,000	1,462.46	1,506.34	1,551.53	1,598.07	1,646.02
90,000	1,548.49	1,594.95	1,642.79	1,692.08	1,742.84
95,000	1,634.52	1,683.55	1,734.06	1,786.08	1,839.66
100,000	1,720.55	1,772.16	1,825.33	1,880.09	1,936.49
110,000	1,892.60	1,949.38	2,007.86	2,068.10	2,130.14
120,000	2,064.65	2,126.59	2,190.39	2,256.10	2,323.79
130,000	2,236.71	2,303.81	2,372.92	2,444.11	2,517.44
140,000	2,408.76	2,481.03	2,555.46	2,632.12	2,711.08
150,000	2,580.82	2,658.24	2,737.99	2,820.13	2,904.73
160,000	2,752.87	2,835.46	2,920.52	3,008.14	3,098.38
170,000	2,924.93	3,012.68	3,103.06	3,196.15	3,292.03
180,000	3,096.98	3,189.89	3,285.59	3,384.16	3,485.68
190,000	3,269.04	3,367.11	3,468.12	3,572.16	3,679.33
200,000	3,441.09	3,544.32	3,650.65	3,760.17	3,872.98

TABLE IV-89. Graduated Payment Mortgage, FHA Plan V at 20.0% Interest, Graduated at 3.0%

FHA GRADUATED PAYMENT PLAN V
TERM: 30 YEARS INTEREST: 20.00% GRADUATED AT 3.00%

PAYMENT AMOUNT	YEAR 1	YEAR 2	YEAR 3	YEAR 4	YEAR 5	YEAR 6
50	0.74	0.76	0.79	0.81	0.83	0.86
100	1.48	1.53	1.57	1.62	1.67	1.72
200	2.96	3.05	3.14	3.24	3.33	3.43
300	4.44	4.58	4.71	4.85	5.00	5.15
400	5.92	6.10	6.28	6.47	6.67	6.87
500	7.40	7.63	7.85	8.09	8.33	8.58
600	8.88	9.15	9.43	9.71	10.00	10.30
700	10.36	10.68	11.00	11.33	11.67	12.02
800	11.85	12.20	12.57	12.94	13.33	13.73
900	13.33	13.73	14.14	14.56	15.00	15.45
1,000	14.81	15.25	15.71	16.18	16.67	17.17
2,000	29.61	30.50	31.42	32.36	33.33	34.33
3,000	44.42	45.75	47.13	48.54	50.00	51.50
4,000	59.23	61.00	62.83	64.72	66.66	68.66
5,000	74.03	76.25	78.54	80.90	83.33	85.83
6,000	88.84	91.51	94.25	97.08	99.99	102.99
7,000	103.65	106.76	109.96	113.26	116.66	120.16
8,000	118.45	122.01	125.67	129.44	133.32	137.32
9,000	133.26	137.26	141.38	145.62	149.99	154.49
10,000	148.07	152.51	157.08	161.80	166.65	171.65
15,000	222.10	228.76	235.63	242.70	249.98	257.48
20,000	296.13	305.02	314.17	323.59	333.30	343.30
25,000	370.17	381.27	392.71	404.49	416.63	429.13
30,000	444.20	457.53	471.25	485.39	499.95	514.95
35,000	518.24	533.78	549.80	566.29	583.28	600.78
40,000	592.27	610.04	628.34	647.19	666.60	686.60
45,000	666.30	686.29	706.88	728.09	749.93	772.43
50,000	740.34	762.55	785.42	808.99	833.26	858.25
55,000	814.37	838.80	863.97	889.89	916.58	944.08
60,000	888.40	915.06	942.51	970.78	999.91	1,029.90
65,000	962.44	991.31	1,021.05	1,051.68	1,083.23	1,115.73
70,000	1,036.47	1,067.57	1,099.59	1,132.58	1,166.56	1,201.56
75,000	1,110.51	1,143.82	1,178.14	1,213.48	1,249.88	1,287.38
80,000	1,184.54	1,220.08	1,256.68	1,294.38	1,333.21	1,373.21
85,000	1,258.57	1,296.33	1,335.22	1,375.28	1,416.54	1,459.03
90,000	1,332.61	1,372.59	1,413.76	1,456.18	1,499.86	1,544.86
95,000	1,406.64	1,448.84	1,492.30	1,537.07	1,583.19	1,630.68
100,000	1,480.67	1,525.09	1,570.85	1,617.97	1,666.51	1,716.51
110,000	1,628.74	1,677.60	1,727.93	1,779.77	1,833.16	1,888.16
120,000	1,776.81	1,830.11	1,885.02	1,941.57	1,999.81	2,059.81
130,000	1,924.88	1,982.62	2,042.10	2,103.36	2,166.47	2,231.46
140,000	2,072.94	2,135.13	2,199.19	2,265.16	2,333.12	2,403.11
150,000	2,221.01	2,287.64	2,356.27	2,426.96	2,499.77	2,574.76
160,000	2,369.08	2,440.15	2,513.36	2,588.76	2,666.42	2,746.41
170,000	2,517.15	2,592.66	2,670.44	2,750.55	2,833.07	2,918.06
180,000	2,665.21	2,745.17	2,827.53	2,912.35	2,999.72	3,089.71
190,000	2,813.28	2,897.68	2,984.61	3,074.15	3,166.37	3,261.36
200,000	2,961.35	3,050.19	3,141.69	3,235.95	3,333.02	3,433.01

TABLE IV-89. (*Continued*)

FHA GRADUATED PAYMENT PLAN V
TERM:30 YEARS INTEREST:20.00% GRADUATED AT 3.00%

PAYMENT AMOUNT	YEAR 7	YEAR 8	YEAR 9	YEAR 10	YEARS 11-30
50	0.88	0.91	0.94	0.97	0.99
100	1.77	1.82	1.88	1.93	1.99
200	3.54	3.64	3.75	3.86	3.98
300	5.30	5.46	5.63	5.80	5.97
400	7.07	7.28	7.50	7.73	7.96
500	8.84	9.11	9.38	9.66	9.95
600	10.61	10.93	11.25	11.59	11.94
700	12.38	12.75	13.13	13.52	13.93
800	14.14	14.57	15.01	15.46	15.92
900	15.91	16.39	16.88	17.39	17.91
1,000	17.68	18.21	18.76	19.32	19.90
2,000	35.36	36.42	37.51	38.64	39.80
3,000	53.04	54.63	56.27	57.96	59.70
4,000	70.72	72.84	75.03	77.28	79.60
5,000	88.40	91.05	93.78	96.60	99.50
6,000	106.08	109.26	112.54	115.92	119.39
7,000	123.76	127.47	131.30	135.24	139.29
8,000	141.44	145.68	150.05	154.56	159.19
9,000	159.12	163.89	168.81	173.87	179.09
10,000	176.80	182.10	187.57	193.19	198.99
15,000	265.20	273.16	281.35	289.79	298.49
20,000	353.60	364.21	375.13	386.39	397.98
25,000	442.00	455.26	468.92	482.99	497.48
30,000	530.40	546.31	562.70	579.58	596.97
35,000	618.80	637.36	656.49	676.18	696.47
40,000	707.20	728.42	750.27	772.78	795.96
45,000	795.60	819.47	844.05	869.37	895.46
50,000	884.00	910.52	937.84	965.97	994.95
55,000	972.40	1,001.57	1,031.62	1,062.57	1,094.45
60,000	1,060.80	1,092.63	1,125.40	1,159.17	1,193.94
65,000	1,149.20	1,183.68	1,219.19	1,255.76	1,293.44
70,000	1,237.60	1,274.73	1,312.97	1,352.36	1,392.93
75,000	1,326.00	1,365.78	1,406.76	1,448.96	1,492.43
80,000	1,414.40	1,456.83	1,500.54	1,545.56	1,591.92
85,000	1,502.80	1,547.89	1,594.32	1,642.15	1,691.42
90,000	1,591.20	1,638.94	1,688.11	1,738.75	1,790.91
95,000	1,679.60	1,729.99	1,781.89	1,835.35	1,890.41
100,000	1,768.00	1,821.04	1,875.67	1,931.94	1,989.90
110,000	1,944.80	2,003.15	2,063.24	2,125.14	2,188.89
120,000	2,121.60	2,185.25	2,250.81	2,318.33	2,387.88
130,000	2,298.40	2,367.36	2,438.38	2,511.53	2,586.87
140,000	2,475.20	2,549.46	2,625.94	2,704.72	2,785.86
150,000	2,652.00	2,731.56	2,813.51	2,897.92	2,984.85
160,000	2,828.80	2,913.67	3,001.08	3,091.11	3,183.84
170,000	3,005.60	3,095.77	3,188.65	3,284.30	3,382.83
180,000	3,182.40	3,277.88	3,376.21	3,477.50	3,581.82
190,000	3,359.20	3,459.98	3,563.78	3,670.69	3,780.81
200,000	3,536.00	3,642.09	3,751.35	3,863.89	3,979.80

TABLE IV-90. Graduated Payment Mortgage, FHA Plan V at 20.5% Interest, Graduated at 3.0%

FHA GRADUATED PAYMENT PLAN V
TERM:30 YEARS INTEREST:20.50% GRADUATED AT 3.00%

PAYMENT AMOUNT	YEAR 1	YEAR 2	YEAR 3	YEAR 4	YEAR 5	YEAR 6
50	0.76	0.78	0.81	0.83	0.86	0.88
100	1.52	1.57	1.61	1.66	1.71	1.76
200	3.04	3.13	3.23	3.32	3.42	3.53
300	4.56	4.70	4.84	4.98	5.13	5.29
400	6.08	6.26	6.45	6.65	6.85	7.05
500	7.60	7.83	8.07	8.31	8.56	8.81
600	9.12	9.40	9.68	9.97	10.27	10.58
700	10.64	10.96	11.29	11.63	11.98	12.34
800	12.16	12.53	12.91	13.29	13.69	14.10
900	13.69	14.10	14.52	14.95	15.40	15.86
1,000	15.21	15.66	16.13	16.62	17.11	17.63
2,000	30.41	31.32	32.26	33.23	34.23	35.26
3,000	45.62	46.99	48.40	49.85	51.34	52.88
4,000	60.82	62.65	64.53	66.46	68.46	70.51
5,000	76.03	78.31	80.66	83.08	85.57	88.14
6,000	91.23	93.97	96.79	99.69	102.68	105.77
7,000	106.44	109.63	112.92	116.31	119.80	123.39
8,000	121.65	125.29	129.05	132.93	136.91	141.02
9,000	136.85	140.96	145.19	149.54	154.03	158.65
10,000	152.06	156.62	161.32	166.16	171.14	176.28
15,000	228.09	234.93	241.98	249.23	256.71	264.41
20,000	304.11	313.24	322.63	332.31	342.28	352.55
25,000	380.14	391.55	403.29	415.39	427.85	440.69
30,000	456.17	469.86	483.95	498.47	513.42	528.83
35,000	532.20	548.16	564.61	581.55	598.99	616.96
40,000	608.23	626.47	645.27	664.63	684.56	705.10
45,000	684.26	704.78	725.93	747.70	770.14	793.24
50,000	760.28	783.09	806.59	830.78	855.71	881.38
55,000	836.31	861.40	887.24	913.86	941.28	969.52
60,000	912.34	939.71	967.90	996.94	1,026.85	1,057.65
65,000	988.37	1,018.02	1,048.56	1,080.02	1,112.42	1,145.79
70,000	1,064.40	1,096.33	1,129.22	1,163.10	1,197.99	1,233.93
75,000	1,140.43	1,174.64	1,209.88	1,246.17	1,283.56	1,322.07
80,000	1,216.45	1,252.95	1,290.54	1,329.25	1,369.13	1,410.20
85,000	1,292.48	1,331.26	1,371.19	1,412.33	1,454.70	1,498.34
90,000	1,368.51	1,409.57	1,451.85	1,495.41	1,540.27	1,586.48
95,000	1,444.54	1,487.88	1,532.51	1,578.49	1,625.84	1,674.62
100,000	1,520.57	1,566.18	1,613.17	1,661.57	1,711.41	1,762.75
110,000	1,672.62	1,722.80	1,774.49	1,827.72	1,882.55	1,939.03
120,000	1,824.68	1,879.42	1,935.80	1,993.88	2,053.69	2,115.31
130,000	1,976.74	2,036.04	2,097.12	2,160.03	2,224.84	2,291.58
140,000	2,128.79	2,192.66	2,258.44	2,326.19	2,395.98	2,467.86
150,000	2,280.85	2,349.28	2,419.76	2,492.35	2,567.12	2,644.13
160,000	2,432.91	2,505.90	2,581.07	2,658.50	2,738.26	2,820.41
170,000	2,584.97	2,662.51	2,742.39	2,824.66	2,909.40	2,996.68
180,000	2,737.02	2,819.13	2,903.71	2,990.82	3,080.54	3,172.96
190,000	2,889.08	2,975.75	3,065.02	3,156.97	3,251.68	3,349.23
200,000	3,041.14	3,132.37	3,226.34	3,323.13	3,422.82	3,525.51

TABLE IV-90. (*Continued*)

FHA GRADUATED PAYMENT PLAN V
TERM:30 YEARS INTEREST:20.50% GRADUATED AT 3.00%

PAYMENT AMCUNT	YEAR 7	YEAR 8	YEAR 9	YEAR 10	YEARS 11-30
50	0.91	0.94	0.96	0.99	1.02
100	1.82	1.87	1.93	1.98	2.04
200	3.63	3.74	3.85	3.97	4.09
300	5.45	5.61	5.78	5.95	6.13
400	7.26	7.48	7.70	7.94	8.17
500	9.08	9.35	9.63	9.92	10.22
600	10.89	11.22	11.56	11.90	12.26
700	12.71	13.09	13.48	13.89	14.30
800	14.53	14.96	15.41	15.87	16.35
900	16.34	16.83	17.34	17.86	18.39
1,000	18.16	18.70	19.26	19.84	20.44
2,000	36.31	37.40	38.52	39.68	40.87
3,000	54.47	56.10	57.79	59.52	61.31
4,000	72.63	74.80	77.05	79.36	81.74
5,000	90.78	93.51	96.31	99.20	102.18
6,000	108.94	112.21	115.57	119.04	122.61
7,000	127.09	130.91	134.83	138.88	143.05
8,000	145.25	149.61	154.10	158.72	163.48
9,000	163.41	168.31	173.36	178.56	183.92
10,000	181.56	187.01	192.62	198.40	204.35
15,000	272.35	280.52	288.93	297.60	306.53
20,000	363.13	374.02	385.24	396.80	408.70
25,000	453.91	467.53	481.55	496.00	510.88
30,000	544.69	561.03	577.86	595.20	613.05
35,000	635.47	654.54	674.17	694.40	715.23
40,000	726.25	748.04	770.48	793.60	817.41
45,000	817.04	841.55	866.79	892.80	919.58
50,000	907.82	935.05	963.10	992.00	1,021.76
55,000	998.60	1,028.56	1,059.42	1,091.20	1,123.93
60,000	1,089.38	1,122.06	1,155.73	1,190.40	1,226.11
65,000	1,180.16	1,215.57	1,252.04	1,289.60	1,328.29
70,000	1,270.95	1,309.07	1,348.35	1,388.80	1,430.46
75,000	1,361.73	1,402.58	1,444.66	1,488.00	1,532.64
80,000	1,452.51	1,496.09	1,540.97	1,587.20	1,634.81
85,000	1,543.29	1,589.59	1,637.28	1,686.40	1,736.99
90,000	1,634.07	1,683.10	1,733.59	1,785.60	1,839.16
95,000	1,724.86	1,776.60	1,829.90	1,884.80	1,941.34
100,000	1,815.64	1,870.11	1,926.21	1,984.00	2,043.52
110,000	1,997.20	2,057.12	2,118.83	2,182.40	2,247.87
120,000	2,178.76	2,244.13	2,311.45	2,380.80	2,452.22
130,000	2,360.33	2,431.14	2,504.07	2,579.19	2,656.57
140,000	2,541.89	2,618.15	2,696.69	2,777.59	2,860.92
150,000	2,723.46	2,805.16	2,889.31	2,975.99	3,065.27
160,000	2,905.02	2,992.17	3,081.94	3,174.39	3,269.63
170,000	3,086.58	3,179.18	3,274.56	3,372.79	3,473.98
180,000	3,268.15	3,366.19	3,467.18	3,571.19	3,678.33
190,000	3,449.71	3,553.20	3,659.80	3,769.59	3,882.68
200,000	3,631.27	3,740.21	3,852.42	3,967.99	4,087.03